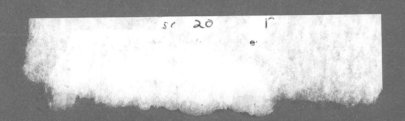

MANUAL
OF
CULTIVATED
CONIFERS

MANUAL OF
CULTIVATED CONIFERS

GERD KRÜSSMANN

Editor: HANS-DIETER WARDA
Translator: MICHAEL E. EPP
Technical Editor: GILBERT S. DANIELS

B.T. Batsford Ltd · London

Uncredited photos on the following plates are by Hans-Dieter Warda: 18, 19, 20, 21, 43, 44, 45, 62, 63, 64, 65, 82, 83, 84, 85, 86, 108, 109, 110, 111, 128, 129, 130, 131, 148, 149, 150.
Other uncredited photos are by Gerd Krüssmann.

During the preparation of the second edition, Dr. h. c. Gerd Krüssmann passed away on the 5th of June, 1980. The publisher, Paul Parey of Berlin, commissioned the Scientific Director of the Hamburg Botanic Gardens, Hans-Dieter Warda, to complete the technical editing of the book. Mr. Warda undertook this task readily and admirably; he will henceforth continue editing and revising the many horticultural works of Gerd Krüssmann.

The first edition was published in 1972, ISBN 3-489-71422-9.

2nd, revised edition
© Verlag Paul Parey, Berlin and Hamburg, 1983
Translation © Timber Press 1985

First published 1985

ISBN 0 7134 5039 8

Printed in Hong Kong
for the Publisher

B.T. Batsford Ltd
4 Fitzhardinge Street
London W1H 0AH

Contents

Foreword to the Second Edition

Although nearly finished, Dr. h.c. Gerd Krüssman was unfortunately not able to bring this second edition to completion. At the request of the publisher, I was only too happy to finish the task. I have made a special effort, when considering new publications, cultivar additions, reclassifications and nomenclatural changes, to be consistent with the interpretation of G. Krüssmann.

I would like to thank the publisher, Paul Parey, for their cooperation, especially in light of the fact that the work was already well into production.

In this edition over 300 new plants are described, mostly cultivars from nurseries and arboreta in the USA, England and Holland. Many interesting and garden worthy introductions, especially dwarf conifers, are included which stem from the German nurseries of J.D. Zu Jeddeloh of Jeddeloh and G. Horstmann, of Schneverdingen. Both firms have contributed greatly to the introduction and preservation of conifer cultivars.

The European Winter Hardiness Zone Map, developed in 1981 by W. Heinze and D. Schreiber based on the USDA Hardiness Zone Map, has been utilized in this edition. Various illustrations, about 1000 references to illustrations and other plates have been added. It is my wish that these plates will surpass a purely dendrological/botanical statement and illuminate the special beauty and diversity of the conifers. The conifers have traditionally been used as screens and barriers in garden design, consequently they are generally found in the background of today's public parks and gardens. A well distributed selection of fully developed specimens would be much preferable.

I would like to extend a very hearty thanks to all those who have unstintingly supported my work. Special credit should go to both a number of nurseries and institutions as well as my colleagues at the Institute for General Botany and Botanic Garden of the University of Hamburg. Particular mention must be made of my good friends Karl Fuchs and Uwe Horstmann, who put many excellent photos at my disposal. A very special thanks is due Mrs. Krüssmann for her generous courtesy and assistance in providing the use of her husband's archives. Moreover I must note that Mrs. Krüssmann proofread many parts of this book. In addition, I'd like to thank my wife for her understanding and untiring support.

The completion of Dr. Krüssmann's nearly finished revision has brought me much enjoyment. I hope that the *Manual of Conifers* in its new edition is not only a useful tool in the daily work of professionals, but also is a trustworthy reference work for gardeners and plant collectors. As always, I am open to any suggestions and encourage constructive criticism.

Hamburg, Summer 1983   HANS-DIETER WARDA

Foreword to the First Edition

Soon after the publication of my three volume *Manual of Cultivated Broad-Leaved Trees and Shrubs,* I was repeatedly asked to publish a similar work on the conifers. I have responded to this request with great pleasure, since I had already spent many years collecting appropriate material, taking photos and visiting conifer collections (see the list at the end of the book).

Naturally the scope of such a book goes far beyond the common conifers; hence the term "conifers" cannot be taken literally since the Taxales, the genera *Gingko* and *Ephedra* are also covered. As one might presume, there is a vast interest in the tropical and subtropical conifers. What with travel and a growing interest in our environment, more people want to know exactly what can be observed in the vast and varied flora of this planet.

Compared to the broad-leaved woody plants, the number of species, varieties and forms of conifers is much smaller; this book contains descriptions of 569 species and 1807 cultivars, including varieties and hybrids. Included are nearly all the existing species and most of the cultivars. Cultivars not generally cultivated are included if they are occasionally mentioned in the modern literature so that the reader will at least be acquainted with them.

To all the gentlemen and institutes throughout Australia, Tasmania, New Zealand, Papua and New Guinea, South America, South Africa, Japan, and North America I wish to extend a hearty thanks for helping me bring this Manual to completion. If I had to choose 2 men whose assistance was exceptionally valuable, one would be my dear friend Harold G. Hillier in Winchester, England. His arboretum is a treasure of plant species and varieties unmatched anywhere in the world. I have spent many days studying and photographing in this garden; much of the material for the pressed images was taken there. The second would be my friend Dr. Donald Wyman of the Arnold Arboretum, one of the greatest arboreta in the world. He provided me with many excellent photos, including enlargements of original shots taken by Ernest H. Wilson in China.

My dear wife, as yet the only person to have read this book from beginning to end, is due many thanks for her proofreading; her constant understanding and her willing concession of our free time together during the preparation of this manuscript.

The publisher Paul Parey should also be acknowledged and is deserving of thanks for bringing my plan to reality.

Dortmund, October 1971   G. KRÜSSMANN

Hardiness Zones and the British Isles

Very few of the trees, shrubs and other garden plants cultivated in Britain are native to the British Isles. Over the centuries they have been introduced from all over the world, though especially from cool and warm temperate climates. How well they thrive in the British Isles largely depends on the climate they evolved in.

Although all plants are closely adapted to the climate of the region in which they occur wild, few have rigid requirements of heat and cold. There are other factors that decide whether a plant will thrive, e.g. soil type and amount of rainfall, but these will be mentioned later; temperature is of primary importance.

The British Isles has an equable oceanic climate which is seldom very cold, hot or dry. As a result, a wide range of the world's plants can be grown outside providing they are sited intelligently. Undoubtedly, some of these plants would prefer more summer sun or a more definite cold winter rest, but their innate adaptability is catered for in the vagaries of our climate. There is, however, a point at which a plant's tolerance ceases. Low temperature is the most important of these tolerances. If a plant cannot survive an average winter outside it is said to be tender. If a plant survives average winters but not the exceptionally hard one it is said to be half-hardy. These terms are, of course, relevant only to the area in which one lives.

Large continental land masses, e.g. North America and Central Europe, have climates that get progressively colder winters as one proceeds northwards and further inland from the sea. North America provides a familiar example, the extreme south being almost tropical, the far north arctic. In the 1930s, the United States Department of Agriculture divided the USA into 7 hardiness zones based upon an average of the absolute minimum temperatures over a period of 20 years. Later, the system was revised and refined and 10 zones recognized (zone 1 is arctic, zone 10 tropical). More recently this Hardiness Zone system has been extended to Europe, including the British Isles. Gardeners in the United States and Canada soon took advantage of the hardiness zone concept and over the years, largely by trial and error, most trees and shrubs and many other plants have been assessed and given zone ratings. Nevertheless, this system, though useful, can only be considered to give approximate hardiness ratings, especially when applied to the British Isles.

Sitting as it does on the eastern edge of the North Atlantic Ocean, the British Isles occupies a unique position. Although its total length, about 650 miles (Cornwall to Orkney), lies within latitudes 50° to 60° N, it falls into zone 8! Moved into the same latitudes in North America, it would lie entirely north of the Canadian border with the tip of Cornwall level with Winnipeg (zone 2–3). Even the eastern coastal region of Canada at these latitudes is no warmer than zones 3–4. Because of the influence of the Gulf Stream the British Isles enjoys a remarkably uniform climate. Such temperature gradients as these are run east to west rather than south to north.

It is a characteristic of temperate oceanic climates to have milder winters and cooler summers than equivalent continental ones and because of their northerly position this is even more marked in the British Isles. For this reason, a number of trees and shrubs which thrive in zone 8 in USA fail to do so well in Britain e.g., *Albizia julibrissin, Lagerstroemia indica,* etc. Such plants may live but fail to bloom, or get cut back severely by the British winters. The factor is primarily lack of summer sun rather than absolute cold.

This lack of summer warmth brings us to the several important ancillary factors which affect a plant's hardiness. Apart from lack of damaging low temperatures a plant needs the right kind of soil, adequate rainfall and humidity, plus sufficient light intensity and warmth. As with low temperature most plants have fairly wide tolerances, though there are noteworthy exceptions. Most members of the *Ericaceae,* especially *Rhododendron* and allied genera, must have an acid soil or they will die however perfect the climate. For plants near the limits of their cold tolerance, shelter is essential. Protection from freezing winds is particularly important. This can be provided by planting in the lee of hedges, fences and walls or among trees with a fairly high canopy. Individual plants can also be protected by matting or plastic sheeting or the bases can be earthed up or mounded around with peat, coarse sand or weathered boiler ash. A thick layer of snow also provides insulation against wind and radiation frost! Plenty of sunshine promotes firm, ripened growth with good food reserves, notably a high sugar content in the cell sap which then takes longer to freeze. If the summer is poor a partial remedy is to apply sulphate of potash (at 10g/per square metre) in late summer. This will boost the amount of sugars and starches in the plant. Half-hardy plants will stand having their tissues moderately frozen providing the thawing-out is gradual. For this reason it is best to grow them in a sheltered site which does not get the first rays of the morning sun. This is especially relevant for species with tender young leaves or early flowers, e.g. *Cercidiphyllum, Camellia* and *Magnolia.*

Zone 9 in the USA is warm-temperate to sub-tropical with hot summers. In the British Isles it tends to have even cooler summers than zone 8, and as a result very few truly sub-tropical plants can be grown in Britain. Most of the plants in the famous so-called, sub-tropical gardens, e.g. Tresco, Logan, Inverewe, etc., are of warm-temperate origin. For the reasons set down above, in Britain, if in doubt, it is best to consider zone 8 as zone 7 and zone 9 as zone 8 for plants of unreliable hardiness.

by Kenneth Beckett

Hardiness Zones

With the extensive introduction of foreign plant material, the question of hardiness and the classification of material in climatic zones has been much discussed among dendrologists. The difficulty lies in the fact that the hardiness of a particular plant or species is variable and not absolute. In most cases, the critical factor in a plant's ability to survive is the minimum average winter temperature. But the influence of many other factors affecting the plant cannot be under-estimated; i.e. summer heat, temperature range, annual rainfall and its distribution, snowfall, winter sun intensity, wind and various soil factors.

It should be noted that the winter hardiness ratings can serve only as rough guidelines. The local climate within a particular zone may vary considerably due to altitude, slopes, valleys, cities, bodies of water, windbreaks, etc. It should also be noted that the absolute minimum temperature recorded for a particular period might lie as much as 11°C lower than the average minimum. For the most successful results, one should use plants with the best tolerance of late frosts and the best adaptation to the growing season of the microclimate.

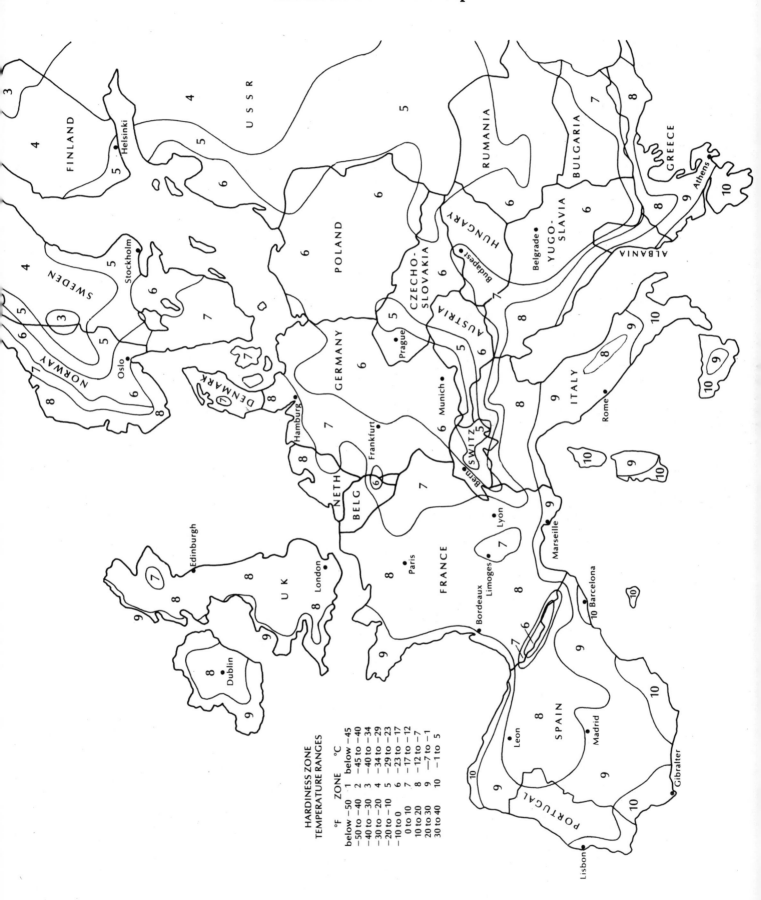

HARDINESS ZONE
TEMPERATURE RANGES

°F	ZONE	°C
below −50	1	below −45
−50 to −40	2	−45 to −40
−40 to −30	3	−40 to −34
−30 to −20	4	−34 to −29
−20 to −10	5	−29 to −23
−10 to 0	6	−23 to −17
0 to 10	7	−17 to −12
10 to 20	8	−12 to −7
20 to 30	9	−7 to −1
30 to 40	10	−1 to 5

Hardiness Zones of North America

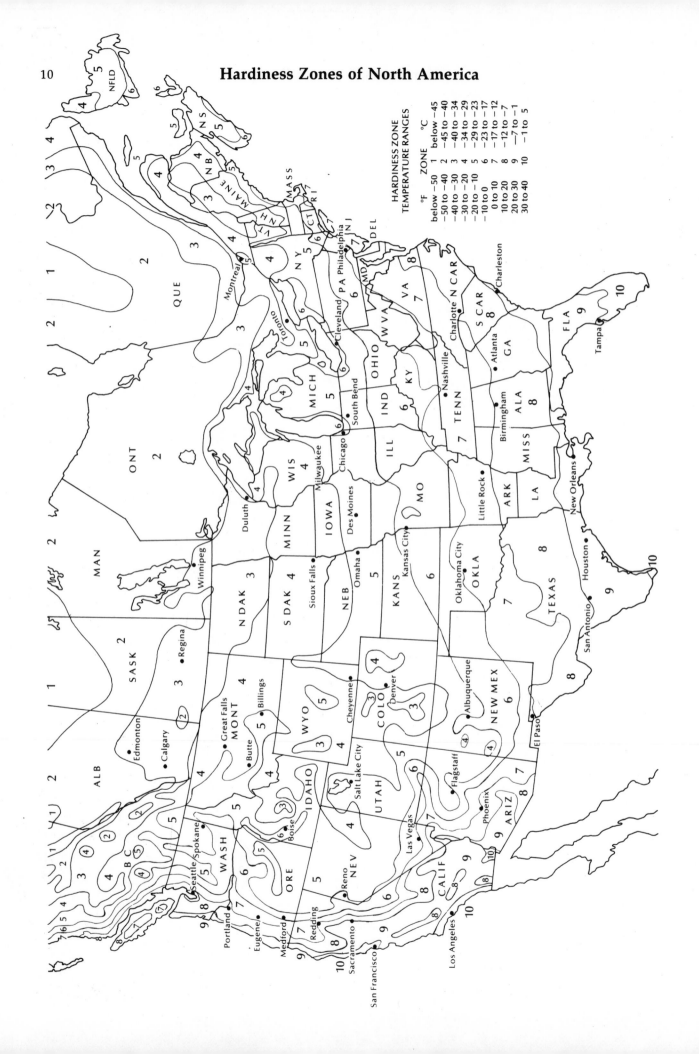

HARDINESS ZONE TEMPERATURE RANGES		
°F	ZONE	°C
below −50	1	below −45
−50 to −40	2	−45 to −40
−40 to −30	3	−40 to −34
−30 to −20	4	−34 to −29
−20 to −10	5	−29 to −23
−10 to 0	6	−23 to −17
0 to 10	7	−17 to −12
10 to 20	8	−12 to −7
20 to 30	9	−7 to −1
30 to 40	10	−1 to 5

Hardiness Zones of China

SOVIET UNION

Mongolia

Heilongjiang

Jilin

Xinjiang

Liaoning

Gansu

Inner Mongolia

KOREA

PEOPLE'S REPUBLIC OF CHINA

Hebei

−4° C

Ningxia

Shanxi

Qinghai

Shandong

Shaanxi

0° C

JAPAN

Henan

Jiangsu

Tibet

Anhui

Hubei

4° C

Sichuan

Zhejiang

8° C

NEPAL

SIKKIM

Hunan

Jiangxi

BHUTAN

INDIA

ASSAM

Guizhou

Fujian

12° C

BANGLADESH

Yunnan

Guangxi

TAIWAN

Tropic of Cancer

Guangdong

BURMA

VIETNAM

LAOS

HAINAN

PHILIPPINES

THAILAND

CAMBODIA

N. BORNEO

HARDINESS ZONE
TEMPERATURE RANGES

°F	ZONE	°C
below −50	1	below −45
−50 to −40	2	−45 to −40
−40 to −30	3	−40 to −34
−30 to −20	4	−34 to −29
−20 to −10	5	−29 to −23
−10 to 0	6	−23 to −17
0 to 10	7	−17 to −12
10 to 20	8	−12 to −7
20 to 30	9	−7 to −1
30 to 40	10	−1 to 5

INDONESIA

MALAYSIA

MALAYSIA

Explanation of Symbols and Abbreviations

Botanical symbols and abbreviations

×   hybrid
cv.   cultivar (the names of the cultivars will be spelled out in single quotes, i.e. 'Rheingold', 'Pumila')
f.   forma—form
var.   varietas—variety
x   haploid chromosome number, half that of a normal genetic cell

Other abbreviations

N = North, S = South, E = East, W = West, C = Central. Date given in plant descriptions designates the year of introduction into garden cultivation. Following the description of cultivars the name of the garden or nursery in which the plant may be (or was) found is given.

(R) = rare, (VR) = very rare, refers to the occurrence of the plant in garden culture.

(EX) = extinct or (EX?) presumably extinct.

z followed by number denotes hardiness zone

Synonyms

Names in italics at the end of a description are invalid names or synonyms.

Illustration references (the following list)-LTThe abbreviation 'Fig.' at the end of a description refers to an illustration in this book. Reference to illustrations in other works is made before the synonyms in the text of the descriptions and is composed of letters and numbers. The letters are literature abbreviations, the numbers are either page, illustration or plate numbers.

example: CCE 84 = Callen, Les Coniféres cultivés en Europe, Pl. 84 (or in case the illustrations are not numbered, then the illustration on p. 84).

In addition to the illustration, reference is occasionally made to: (Br) = Branch, (C) = Cone, (H) = Habitat and (St) = Stem.

List of Abbreviations for the Illustration References

Bai   Baileya (periodical). Ithaca, New York 1953→

BAu   Baker & Smith: A research on the Pines of Australia; 458 pp., many plates. Sydney 1910

BB   Britton, N., & A. Brown: An illustrated Flora of the Northern United States, Canada and the British Possessions from Newfoundland to Virginia; 3 vols., 4081 pp. New York 1898 (New edition see NBB)

BC   Bailey, L. H.: The Standard Cyclopedia of Horticulture; 3 vols., 3639 pp. New York 1950

BCC   Bailey, L. C.: The cultivated Conifers in North America, comprising the Pine family and the Taxads; 404 pp. New York 1933

BFN   Beissner-Fitschen: Handbuch der Nadelholzkunde; 3rd ed., 765 pp. Berlin 1930

BM   Botanical Magazine (Curtis' Botanical Magazine). London 1787–1847 (ns = new series, 1948→)

BR   Botanical Register. London 1815–1847: plate numbers.

BS   Bean, W. J.: Trees and Shrubs hardy in the British Isles; 8th ed. (only Vols. 1–4 of the new edition). London 1971–1980

CB   Clinton-Baker: Illustrations of Conifers; 3 vols. Hertford 1909–1919

CBJ   Clinton-Baker & Jackson: New Illustrations of Conifers. Hertford 1935

CC   Chittenden, F. J.: Conifers in Cultivation; The Report of the Conifer Conference held by the Royal Horticultural Society 1931; 634 pp. London 1932

CCE   Callen, G.: Les Conifères cultivés en Europe; 2 vols., 903 pp., 504 plates. Paris 1976–1977

CFTa   Curtis: The Endemic Flora of Tasmania; Vols. 1–6. London 1967–1978

CIS   Hu-Chun: Icones Plantarum Sinicarum; 250 plates, Reprint. Tokyo 1970

CLP   Critchfield-Little: Geographic Distribution of the Pines of the World; USDA Misc. Publ. 991; 98 pp. & maps. Washington, D.C. 1966

CTa   Curtis W., Student's Flora of Tasmania; 3 parts 1956–1967

DB   Deutsche Baumschule (periodical). Aachen 1949 →

DH   Dallimore, W., Holly, Yew and Box; 283 pp. London 1908

DJ   Dallimore & Jackson, Harrison: A Handbook of Coniferae; 4th ed. London 1966

EH   Elwes & Henry: The Trees of Great Britain and Ireland; 7 vols. Edinburgh 1906–1913

ENP   Engler & Prantl: Die Natürlichen Pflanzenfamilien; 2nd ed. Leipzig 1924 →

FAA   Franco, J., do Amaral: Abetos. An. Inst. Sup. Agron. 17, 1–240. Lisbon, 1950

FK   Flous, F.: Révision du genre *Keteleeria*. Bull. Soc. Hist. Nat. Toulouse 70, 273 to 348. Toulouse 1936

FS   Flore des Serres et des Jardins de l'Europe; 23 vols. Gent 1845–1880: plate numbers.

FSA   Codd/De Winter/Rycroft: Flora of Southern Africa, vol. I; Leistner, O. A.: Podocarpaceae; Marsh, J. A.: Cupressaceae (Widdringtonia). Pretoria 1966

FTs   Flous, F.: Révision du genre *Tsuga*. Extr. Bull. Soc. Hist. Nat. Toulouse 71, 315–450. Toulouse 1936

GGy   Gaussen, H. Les Gymnospermes actuelles et fossiles; 16 parts. Other parts not yet published. Toulouse 1933–1979

Gs   Gartenschönheit (periodical); all Berlin 1920–1942

Gw   Gartenwelt (periodical). Berlin 1897 →; now Hamburg

(H)   Illustration of habit

HAl   Hara, H.: Photo-Album of Plants of Eastern Himalaya. Tokyo 1968

HD   Hornibrook, M.: Dwarf and slow-growing Conifers; 2nd ed., 286 pp., London 1938

HiD   Hillier, H. G.: Dwarf Conifers; 84 pp. Edinburgh 1964

HIF   Hayata, B.: Icones Plantarum Formosanarum; 10 vols. 1911–1921

HW   Hempel & Wilhelm: Die Bäume und Sträucher des deutschen Waldes; 3 vols. Vienna 1889–1899

JA   Journal of the Arnold Arboretum (periodical). Cambridge, Mass., USA 1919 →

JRHS   Journal of the Royal Horticultural Society. London 1846 →

KEv   Kumlien, L. L.: The friendly Evergreens; 2nd ed. Dundee, Ill., USA 1946

KF   Kirk, T.: The Forest Flora of New Zealand; 345 pp. Wellington 1889

KIF   Kurata: Illustrated important Forest Trees of Japan; 5 vols. Tokyo 1964–1976

KN   Krüssmann, G.: Die Nadelgehölze; 3rd ed. 264 pp., 296 illus. Berlin 1979

KO   Kitamura & Okamoto: Coloured Illustrations of Trees and Shrubs of Japan; 306 pp. Osaka 1958

LA   Liu, Tang-Shiu: A Monograph of the genus *Abies*, 608 pp., 78 plates, 42 aerial maps. Taipeh, China 1971

LF   Lee, Sh.-Ch.: Forest of China. Shanghai 1935; Supplement Taipeh 1973

LG   Laubenfels, D. J. de: Flore de la Nouvelle-Calédonie et Dépendances; 4. Gymnospermes; 169 pp., 43 plates & range maps. Paris 1972

LT   Liu, Tang-Shiu: Illustrations of native and introduced Plants of Taiwan; 2 vols. Taipeh 1960–1962

LWT   Li, Hui-Lin: Woody Flora of Taiwan; 974 pp. Narberth, Pa. 1963

LWTP   Little & Wadsworth: Common Trees of Puerto Rico and the Virgin Islands; 548 pp. Washington, D.C. 1964

MC   Magrini, G., Le Conifere; 216 pp. Milano 1967

MD   Mitteilungen der Deutschen Dendrologischen Gesellschaft. 1892 →

MG   Moellers Deutsche Gärtnerzeitung (periodical) 1896–1936

MJu   van Melle: Review of *Juniperus chinensis* et al.; 108 pp. New York 1947

MP   Mirow, N. T.: The Genus *Pinus*; 602 pp. New York 1967

MPi   Mártinez, M.: Los Pinos Mexicanos; 2nd ed., 352 pp. Mexico 1948

NBB   Gleason, H. A.: The New Britton and Brown Illustrated Flora of the Northern United States and adjacent Canada; 3 vols., New York 1958

NF   The New Flora and Silva (periodical). London 1928–1940 (all)

NK   Nakai, T.: Flora Sylvatica Koreana; 21 vols. 1915–1936

NT   Nakai: Trees and Shrubs of Japan proper; 2nd ed. Tokyo 1927

NTC   Native Trees of Canada. Ottawa 1950

OCC   den Ouden & Boom: Manual of Cultivated Conifers hardy in the cold- and warm-temperate Zone; 526 pp. Den Haag 1965

OSL   Ostenfeld & Syrach Larsen: The species of the genus *Larix* and their geographical distribution. Biol. Meddel. 9, 1 to 106. Copenhagen 1930

PFC   Pizarro, C. M.: Sinopsis de la Flora Chilena; 840 pp. Valparaiso 1959

PPF   Parham, J. W.: Plants of the Fiji Islands. Suva, Fiji 1964

RH   Revue Horticole (periodical): plate numbers

SDK   Sokolov (author): Trees and shrubs of the Soviet Union; 7 vols. (in Russian). Moscow 1948–1965

SN   Silva Tarouca & Schneider: Unsere Freiland-Nadelgehölze; 2nd ed. 315 pp. Leipzig 1923

SPa   Sudworth, G. B.: Forest Trees of the Pacific Slope; 441 pp. Washington, D.C. 1908

SPi   Shaw, G. R.: The genus *Pinus*, 96 pp. Jamaica Plain 1914

SS   Sargent, C. S.: The Silva of North America; 14 vols. Boston 1891–1902

TAP   Takeda: Illustr. Manual of Alpine Plants of Japan. Tokyo 1935

TC   Testu, C.: Conifères de nos Jardins; 175 pp. Paris 1970

TFI   Townsend, C. C., & E. Guest: Flora of Iraq; Vol. 2. Bagdad 1966

TM   Tolmatschev: Trees and shrubs of Sachalin (in Russian). Moscow 1956

UJD   Uehara, K.: Jyumoko Daitsusetsu (Japanese Dendrology) 4 vols. (in Japanese). Tokyo 1969

WDw   Welch, H. J.: Dwarf Conifers; a complete Guide; 334 pp. London 1966

WM   Welch, H. J.: Manual of dwarf Conifers; 493 pp., 400 photos and plates. New York 1979

WWC   Wolf & Wagner: The New World Cypresses; 444 pp. Anaheim, Calif. 1948

Range maps.

For the range maps of the conifers the following work was used: Tralau: Index Holmiensis, Vol. 1, 264 pp. Zurich 1970

Systematic Outline of the Modern Gymnosperms
excluding the Cycadales

In this outline, as in the first edition, the classification of the Gymnosperms follows Florin (for the Cupres-saceae) and Li. Many plants in this group have been but briefly described as they are only known from fossil remains. However, these fossil remains had a substantial influence on the interpretation of the Gymno-sperms. As a result of recent studies, the Ginkgoales are now considered closer to the Coniferopsida and not, as classified here, in the Cycadopsida. Fortunately, the names of higher orders are relatively stable, but has little consequence for practical purposes.

Only the genera *Ginkgo* and *Ephedra* (orders 7 and 11), the cultivated conifers and Taxales (orders 9 and 10) and the more extensive tropical species will be dealt with in this work as follows:

from the 7th Order	the genus *Ginkgo;*
from the 9th and 10th Order	the conifers present in cultivation and their cultivars including the extensive tropical species;
from the 11th Order	the genus *Ephedra.*

XVI. Divisions	**GYMNOSPERMAE**	
1. Class	CYCADOPSIDA	
1. Order	Pteridospermae	only known from fossils
2. Order	Caytoniales	only known from fossils
3. Order	Cycadales	genus originating in the Tertiary Period which thrive today
4. Order	Nilssoniales	only known from fossils
5. Order	Bennettitales	only known from fossils
6. Order	Pentoxylales	only known from fossils
7. Order	Ginkgoales	
Family	**Ginkgoaceae**	*Ginkgo*
2. Class	CONIFEROPSIDA	
8. Order	Cordaitales	only known as fossils
9. Order	Coniferae	
Family	Lebachiaceae, Volt-ziaceae, Cheiro-lepidaceae and Protopinaceae	only known as fossils
Family	**Pinaceae**	
Subfamily	Abietoideae	*Abies, Keteleeria, Cathaya, Pseudotsuga, Tsuga, Picea*
Subfamily	Laricoideae	*Psuedolarix, Larix, Cedrus*
Subfamily	Pinoideae	*Pinus*
Family	**Taxodiaceae**	a) *Sequoia, Sequoiadendron*
		b) *Metasequoia*
		c) *Taxodium, Glyptostrobus*
		d) *Cryptomeria*
		e) *Cunninghamia*
		f) *Sciadopitys*
		g) *Athrotaxis, Taiwania*
Family	**Cupressaceae**	
Subfamily	Callitroideae	
Tribe	Actinostrobeae	*Actinostrobus, Callitris, Fitzroya*
Tribe	Libocedreae	*Neocallitropsis, Widdringtonia, Diselma, Papuacedrus, Libocedrus, Calocedrus*
Tribe	Tetraclineae	*Tetraclinis*
Subfamily	Cupressoideae	

Tribe	Cupresseae	*Cupressus, Chamaecyparis,* × *Cupressocyparis, Fokienia*
Tribe	Thujopsideae	*Thujopsis, Thuja*
Tribe	Junipereae	*Juniperus, Microbiota*
Family	**Podocarpaceae**	
Subfamily	Pherosphaeroideae	*Microstrobos*
Subfamily	Phyllocladoideae ·	*Phyllocladus*
Subfamily	Podocarpoideae	*Saxegothaea, Microcachrys, Dacrydium, Podocarpus, Acmopyle*
Family	**Cephalotaxaceae**	*Cephalotaxus*
Family	**Araucariaceae**	*Agathis, Araucaria*
3. **Class**	TAXOPSIDA	
10. **Order**	Taxales	
Family	**Taxaceae**	*Amentotaxus, Torreya, Austrotaxus, Pseudotaxus, Taxus*
4. **Class**	CHLAMYDOSPERMAE	
11. **Order**	Gnetales	
Family	**Welwitschiaceae**	*Welwitschia*
Family	**Ephedraceae**	*Ephedra*
Family	**Gnetaceae**	*Gnetum*

The individual Orders, Families and Genera are more narrowly described in the following summary.

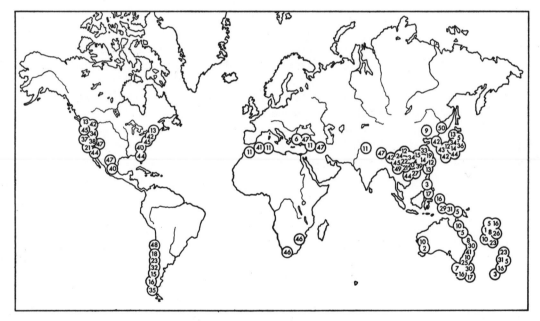

Fig. 2. Systematic view of the range of the Coniferales and Taxales genera (from Hui-Lin Li 1953, enlarged). Not included are the ranges of the genera *Abies, Picea, Larix, Pinus, Juniperus, Podocarpus* and *Taxus*.

The numbers represent:

1	*Acmopyle*	11	*Cedrus*	21	*Calocedrus*	31	*Phyllocladus*	41	*Tetraclinis*
2	*Actinostrobus*	12	*Cephalotaxus*	22	*Keteleeria*	32	*Pilgerodendron*	42	*Thuja*
3	*Agathis*	13	*Chamaecyparis*	23	*Libocedrus*	33	*Pseudolarix*	43	*Thujopsis*
4	*Araucaria*	14	*Cryptomeria*	24	*Metasequoia*	34	*Pseudotsuga*	44	*Torreya*
5	*Amentotaxus*	15	*Cunninghamia*	25	*Microcachrys*	35	*Saxegothaea*	45	*Tsuga*
6	*Arceuthos*	16	*Dacrydium*	26	*Neocallitropsis*	36	*Sciadopitys*	46	*Widdringtonia*
7	*Athrotaxis*	17	*Diselma*	27	*Pseudotaxus*	37	*Sequoia*	47	*Cupressus*
8	*Austrotaxus*	18	*Fitzroya*	28	(= 10)	38	*Sequoiadendron*	48	*Austrocedrus*
9	*Biota*	19	*Fokienia*	29	*Papuacedrus*	39	*Taiwania*	49	*Cathaya*
10	*Callitris*	20	*Glyptostrobus*	30	*Microstrobos*	40	*Taxodium*	50	*Microbiota*

Summary of Characteristics of the Gymnosperms
dealt with in this book
(Orders, Families, Genera)

(from Beissner, revised and enlarged)

Order Ginkgoales and Family **Ginkgoaceae**

Only one genus with the characteristics of the family and order

Ginkgo L.—Ginkgo—Mantissa II (1771) 313, 314; Thunb Fl. Japon. (1784) 358—Many branched tree with long and short shoots and leaf-like, wedge to fan-shaped, incised foliage. Plants dioecious; male flowers (microsporophyll) terminal, singular on an elongated axis, each with 2–7 pendulous pollen sacks; female flowers (macrosporophyll) singular, axillary, with a branched or simple stalk and 1–2 erect seed chambers; these at the end of the stalk and surrounding the base of a collar-like rim (cupule). Fertilized by means of spermatozoids composed of a head spiraled 2.5 times, numerous cilia and a pointed, tail-like appendage. Seeds large, rounded, with a fleshy covering and hard inner shell; ripening in the first year; seedlings large, with 2 cotyledons and very nutritious tissue. (Fig. 3).—Only 1 species; China.

Fertilization begins with the separation of the seed chamber; followed by the development of a branched pollen tube from the pollen chamber, 2 months prior to actual pollination. Before fertilization the upper part of the embryo sac wall becomes slimy and the ciliate portion of the spermatozoid sloughs off, as with the Cycadales.

Order Coniferae

Mostly evergreen trees with branched stems, rarely shrubs, often with long and short shoots; stem with fine pith; wood of durable consistency, with annual rings, without vascular tissues, composed of long, stretched cells (tracheids) with large, single file (occasionally multiple lines) of pits on the radial walls and narrow pith rays, frequently exhibiting resin ducts; bark rather thin, often tough; needles usually persist several years, occasionally abscising in the fall (*Larix, Pseudolarix, Metasequoia, Taxodium*), simple, spiral, opposite, occasionally verticillate, needle form with a middle vein, often decurrent, singular or on short shoots grouped 2 to several, often also scale-like, seldom wide and multiveined. Flowers unisexual; male flowers naked, often with bud scales at the base; stamens numerous, scale-like, with 2–6(–20) pollen sacs; female

Fig. 3. Twig of *Ginkgo biloba* with fruit
(left is cut)

flowers grouped in a cone-like inflorescence, with many or few, densely arranged carpels, either immediately supporting the ovule or as a "bract scale" with an enlarged outgrowth (fruit scale) on the ventral side, inside of which is the ovule, usually in 2's, seldom singular. Ripening as individual seed scales or fused into a woody, occasionally fleshy seed cone composed of bract and seed scales (cone scales), fully ripening in 1, 2 or 3 years; seeds usually nutlets in leathery or hard shells, oval or oblong, often compressed, commonly winged; cotyledons 2–16.—Most species found in the temperate and colder regions of the Northern Hemisphere, forming large forests; 6–8 families with about 50 genera and about 500 species.

The fossil families Lebachiaceae, Voltziaceae, Cheirolepidaceae and Protopinaceae are included here.

Family **Pinaceae**

Trees, occasionally shrubs, branches with spirally arranged, usually evergreen needle foliage; plants usually monoecious; male flowers with numerous, spirally arranged stamens, pollen sacs 2 each, fused on the underside, pollen grains usually with air sacs (except *Larix* and *Pseudotsuga*); female cones with numerous spirally arranged bract scales, the smaller, flat seed scales on the upper side and fused at the base, with 2 ovules, fused along the entire upper side and inverted, micropyle directed inward. Seed cones woody, composed of the woody seed scales and the larger, smaller, absent or quite stunted bract scales; seeds winged on one side or without wings; cotyledons 3–18. —10 genera over the entire Northern Hemisphere.

1. Subfamily: Abietoideae

Trees with only long shoots (except *Cathaya*), seed cones ripen the 1st year.

Abies Miller—Fir—Gard. Dict. (1754)—Large, pyramidal, evergreen trees. Needles have a more or less wide base, sessile on the twig, leaving a circular, flat leaf scar after abscising. Male flowers solitary in the axils of the upper needles, pollen grains with 2 wings; female flowers solitary, terminal, erect, bract scales often enlarged after flowering and surpassing the seed scales in length; cones erect, disintegrating when ripe; seeds with resin blisters, winged; cotyledons 4–8. —About 40 species in the cooler temperate regions of the Northern Hemisphere.

Keteleeria Carrière—Rev. Hort. (1866) 449—Large trees with needle-like leaves, ribbed on both sides, like *Abies,* leaving a round leaf scar when abscising. Male flowers in groups of 5–10 on a common stalk; pollen grains with wings; female flowers terminal on foliate side branches; cones with persistent seed scales, abscising all together when ripe; bract scales hidden between the seed scales. Seeds large, with resin pits, winged; cotyledons 2. —4–8 species in China.

Cathaya Chun & Kuang—Bot. Jour. (Mosk.) 43 (1958): 461–470, with 10 plates—Tall, evergreen tree; branches dimorphic, sterile side branches shortened as in *Larix* and *Cedrus;* needles linear, nearly whorled on short shoots; young needles with ciliate margin at first. Monoecious; male flowers short stalked to nearly sessile; seed scales spiraled, in several rows or imbricate, bract scales caudate tipped; female flowers in erect catkins; cones persisting for 1 year; seeds obovoid, winged. —1 species in China.

Pseudotsuga Carrière—Douglas fir—Traité gén. d. Conif. éd. 2 (1867) 256—Very tall, *Abies*-like tree, buds large; needle base sitting on a narrowed slightly raised, oblique hump, with 2 axillary resin ducts. Male flowers solitary in the axils of the previous year's needles; pollen without wings; female flowers with numerous imbricate scales at the base; cones oblong, ripening the first year, not disintegrating, bract scales 3 pointed, longer than the nearly circular seed scales; seeds without resin blisters, winged; cotyledons 5–8.—5 species in western North America and East Asia.

Tsuga Carrière—Hemlock—Traité gén d. Conif. (1855) 185—Medium-size to tall trees; needles with a knee-like bent petiole sitting on a raised leaf cushion, usually flat and channeled above, with a resin duct. Male flowers solitary, axillary, the female terminal on the previous year's branches; cones small, ripening the first year, but remaining on the tree and not disintegrating, bract scales on the ripe cones ½ to ⅓ as long as the seed scales; seeds with resin blisters, winged; cotyledons 3–6.—18 species from the Himalayas to Japan and in temperate North America.

Picea Dietrich—Spruce—Fl. d. Geg. um Berlin (1824) 974—Evergreen, often tall tree. Needles sitting on a short, decurrent petiole, decurrent on the stem, persisting after leaf fall (the branch therefore raspy-rough, differing among species). Male flowers in the axils of needles on the previous year's branches, pollen grains with wings; female flowers solitary at the end of the previous year's branches; cones pendulous or directed outward, not disintegrating when ripe; bract scales enlarging only slightly after flowering, on ripe cones shorter than the numerous, coarse seed scales; seeds without resin blisters, winged; cotyledons 4–15.— About 50 species in the temperate and cooler regions of the Northern Hemisphere, especially East Asia.

2. Subfamily: Laricoideae

Long shoots and short shoots (which elongate for several years) with needle-leaves, these clustered on the short shoots.

Pseudolarix Gordon—Golden Larch—Pinetum (1858) 292—Tall tree with soft, deciduous, needle-like foliage. Male flowers several, clustered at the end of leafless short shoots; pollen grains with wings; female flowers globose, solitary on short, foliate branches; bract scales shorter than the seed scales; cones erect, ripening the first year, ovate, with large, acute, seed scales abscising when the seed is ripe; seeds winged; cotyledons 4.—1 species in Northeast China.

Larix Link—Larch—Gard. Dict. 4th éd. (1754)—Tall trees with deciduous, soft needles, branches developing as long and short shoots, the latter dying out after a few years leaving a dry stub. Male flowers on thick, leafless short shoots, terminal; pollen grains without wings; female flowers on foliate short shoots, nearly globose; bract scales far surpassing the seed scales at flowering time, later either shorter or longer than the seed scales; cones usually small, ovate or nearly globose, ripening at the end of the 1st year, not disintegrating, persisting for 2–3 years on the tree, with leathery-woody seed scales, rounded on the upper edge; seeds without resin pits, winged; cotyledons usually 6.—10–12 species in the colder regions of the Northern Hemisphere.

Cedrus Trew—Cedar—Cedorum Libani Hist. 4 (1757)—Evergreen, tall trees with needle-form, persistent foliage. Male flowers solitary on the ends of short shoots; pollen grains with wings; female flowers solitary, terminal, surrounded by a cluster of needles; bract scales much shorter than the seed scales; cones erect, ripening in the 2nd or 3rd year, with large, woody, seed scales abscising when the seed is ripe; seeds with resin pits, winged; cotyledons 8–10.—4 species in the Mediterranean region and in the western Himalayas.

3. Subfamily: Pinoideae

Plants with only membranous scale leaves and axillary short shoots, the latter with a few scale leaves and usually 2–5 (occasionally 1–8) persistent needle-leaves, fully developed in the first year. Male flowers at the base of young long shoots, in spike-like clusters; seed scales usually with scale shield (apophysis).

Pinus L.—Pine—Spec. Pl. (1753) 1000 (in a broad sense)—Evergreen trees, rarely shrubs. Long shoots normally composed of a single internode, eventually developing several levels of branches, the cones sub-terminal at first, later axillary. Leaves either scale or needle-form. Male flowers many, clustered at the base of the current year's long shoots; pollen grains with wings; female flowers at the branch tips immediately under the terminal bud or axillary on multiple jointed branches; bract scales very small, later stunted; cones ripening in the 2nd, rarely the 3rd year, usually opening when ripe, sometimes remaining closed for many years on the tree; seed scales usually with a thick apical surface (scale shield or apophysis), this often with a prickly tip; seeds usually winged; cotyledons 4–15.—Over 100 species in the Northern Hemisphere and the Sunda Islands, on high mountains in the tropics.

Family **Taxodiaceae**

Tall trees; leaves awl-shaped (subulate), scale-form, needle-form or sickle-shaped, nearly always (except *Metasequoia*) spirally arranged, evergreen or (on *Metasequoia, Taxodium* and *Glyptostrobus*) deciduous. Plants monoecious, male flowers solitary, terminal or axillary in capitate or panicle-form inflorescences, stamens with a short filament and broad terminal scale, pollen sacs 2–9, distinct, connate at the base, pollen grains without wings; female inflorescences solitary, terminal, seed scales more or less adnate to the bract scales, bulging at first, later enlarged and surpassing the bract scales (missing on *Taiwania*); ovules 2–9, erect or inverted; cone scales usually woody when ripe, originating from the seed bulge and the corresponding bract scale; cones opening when ripe; seeds narrow winged; cotyledons 2–9.—10 genera (a widely disseminated group, fossil remains of the Tertiary period heavily investigated) of unique development and without close family ties; in southeastern North America, northern California and Mexico to East Asia and on Tasmania.

Sequoia Endl.—California Redwood—Syn. Conif. (1847) 197—Tall, evergreen tree; bark furrowed, with fibrous scales; needles dimorphic, alternate; scale-like and spiraled on long shoots, appressed or somewhat outspread, with banded stomata on the underside; 2 ranked on side branches, linear, with 2 white stomatal bands on the underside. Monoecious; male flowers terminal and axillary, with numerous, spirally arranged stamens; female flowers terminal, with 15–20 scales, each with 3 to 7 ovules; cones ovoid, pendulous, ripening the first year; seeds 2 winged; cotyledons 2.—1 species on the west coast of North America.

Sequoiadendron Buchholz—Giant Sequoia—Amer. Jour. Bot. 26 (1939) 536—Tall, evergreen tree; bark deeply grooved, spongy, very thick; needles spirally appressed or outspread, scale-like, sharp acuminate; with 2 stomatal bands on the upper side. Monoecious; male flowers sessile, terminal on short shoots; female flowers terminal, with 25 to 40 scales, each with 3–12 ovules; cones ellipsoid, ripening the 2nd year and persisting for many years on the branch, woody; seeds 2 winged; cotyledons usually 4(3–5).—1 species in California.

Metasequoia Miki—Jap. Jour. Bot. 11 (1941) 261—Deciduous tree with opposite branches and twigs; needles opposite, sessile or nearly so, linear, with 2 stomatal bands on the upper side with 4–6 rows to each band. Monoecious; male flowers axillary and terminal in branched inflorescences, stamens about 20, pollen grains without wings; female flowers with 22–26 carpels, decussate, the lowest and uppermost pair sterile; cones pendulous, long stalked; cone scales shieldlike woody; seeds 5–9, compressed, with encircling wing.—1 species in Central China, first discovered from fossil remains.

Taxodium Rich.—Swamp—Bald Cypress—Ann. Mus. XVI (1810) 298—Tall trees with foliate side shoots, totally abscising in the fall; with "knee-like" growths on the roots. Male flowers in long, often panicle-like spikes, each flower covered by a scale; female flowers few, small at flowering time; carpels acuminate, with a later enlarging scale bulge; ovules 2; cones rounded or ovate, woody, ripening in the first year; persisting after the seeds fall out; cone scales lying shield-like beside one another, tapering to a thin stalk, apex abruptly widened to an irregular, 4 sided plate, the smaller basal portion of the bract scale is separated from the enlarged scale bulge by a furrow; seeds 3 sided, slightly 3 winged; cotyledons 4–9.—3 species in southeastern N. America (typical tree of southern swamps) to Mexico.

Glyptostrobus Endl.—Syn Conif. (1847) 69—Small tree with leaves of 3 different forms, deciduous. Male flowers numerous at the ends of short shoots; female flowers similar to *Taxodium*, the bract scales surpassed by the scale bulge; ovules 2, erect; cones pear-shaped or oblong; cone scales elongated, crenate on the upper margin, forming a roof-like cover; seeds 2, winged; cotyledons 4–5.—1 species in SE. China.

Cryptomeria D. Don—Trans. Linn. Soc. XVIII (1829) 166, Pl. 13, Fig. 1—Tall evergreen tree with scaled buds and decurrent, 3–4 sided, sickle-shaped, incurved, awl-like leaves. Male flowers solitary, terminal, clustered spike-like on young branches; bract scales fused with the seed scale on the basal portion, the distinct apical portion acute; seed scales at first develop as a small bulge, later much enlarged; ovules 2–5, erect; cones ripening the first year, splitting open, with 20–30 cone scales, the distinct portion of the seed scales 4–6 toothed, surpassing the bract scales; seeds with 2–3 wing-ridges; cotyledons 3, seldom 4.—1 species in Japan.

Cunninghamia R. Brown ex Richard—China fir—Mém. Conif. (1826) 149,9.18—Medium-tall or tall tree with linear-sickle shaped leathery leaves, 2 ranked. Male flowers many in heads on the branch tips; female flowers 1–3, terminal, rounded, with many scales; seed scales adnate to the bract scales, with a distinct, 3 lobed margin; ovules 3; cones with, slightly hardened, loosely imbricate, sparsely outspread tips; seeds narrow winged; cotyledons 2.—3 species in South China and on Taiwan.

Sciadopitys Sieb. & Zucc.—Umbrella pine—Flora Jap. II (1842) 1, Pl. 101, 102—Tall evergreen tree. Branches in 2 forms; long shoots covered with small, dry, membranous scale-leaves, clustered at the branch tips, with whorled, leaf-like sprouts (cladodes) in the axils. The cladodes also occur on short shoots with 2 connate needles (double needles). Male flowers clustered in heads at the ends of the branches; female flowers with adnate bract and seed scales, the distinct, membranous apical margin later visible on the dorsal side of the scale; ovules 7–9, inverted; cones with woody, persistent scales, ripening the 2nd year; seeds with encircling wing, cotyledons 2.—1 species in Japan.

Athrotaxis D.Don—Tasmanian cedar—Trans. Linn. Soc. XVIII (1839) 171, Pl. 13, Fig. 2—Evergreen trees with scale-like or short needle-like leaves. Male flowers solitary, terminal on short shoots; female with 12–25 ovate bract scales, these later with a more or less enlarged scale bulge; ovules 3–6, inverted; similar to the cones of *Cryptomeria*, with woody scales, the basal stalk-like portion perpendicular to to central axis.—3 species in Australia, Tasmania.

Taiwania Hayata—Jour. Lin. Soc. XXXVII (1906) 330—Tall, evergreen trees with densely arranged, scale- or needle-like leaves, male flowers 5–7 at the end of short branchlets; scales of the female flowers not readily differentiated between seed and bract scales; ovules 2, inverted; cones leathery, persistent; seeds with wide encircling wings.—2 species on Taiwan.

Family **Cupressaceae**

Erect or procumbent, abundantly branched shrubs or trees; leaves decussate or in whorls of 3, occasionally 4; young leaves needle-like, abscising; the mature leaves occasionally short needle-form, usually small scale-like, densely arranged, often with the lateral leaves on the flattened branches differing from the facial leaves. Plants mono- or dioecious; male flower cones small, usually solitary on the ends of short branchlets, stamens opposite or irregularly arranged, with short filaments and a wide terminal scale, pollen sacs beneath distinct; female flower cones with few opposing pairs or whorls of fertile or partly infertile bract scales; seed bulge one-sided with many ovules, these attached at the base and erect; cones either woody with roof-like, valvate or peltate scales or berry- or drupe-like with persistently fused scales (only on *Juniperus* and *Arceuthos*); seeds distinct or united into a seed pit, winged or not winged; cotyledons 2(–6).—19 genera, in the Northern Hemisphere (especially in North America and East Asia to the Mediterranean region) and in the Southern Hemisphere.

Subfamily Callitroideae
Tribe Actinostrobeae (*Actinostrobus, Callitris, Fitzroya*)

Actinostrobus Miq.—Lehm. Pl. Preissian. I (1845) 644—Stout branched, pyramidal shrubs, branchlets 3-sided or rounded, jointed, leaves scale-like, stiff, sharp acuminate, the distinct portion triangular, often needle-like on sterile twigs. Cone surrounded by numerous infertile scales on the basal portion, cone scales 6, each distinguished by an appendaged infertile scale appressed to the dorsal side; seeds triangular, 2–3 winged.—3 species in Southwest Australia.

Callitris Ventenat—Decad. Gen. Nov. (1808) 10—Trees or shrubs with numerous, forked branches; branchlets jointed; leaves in 3's, whorled, decurrent, with very small, distinct, 3-sided tips, needle-like on young plants. Cones not enveloped in sterile scales (as in the previous genus); cone scales usually 6(rarely 8), in 2 whorls; cones opening valvate when ripe, with a central axis.—About 16 species in Australia, Tasmania, New Caledonia.

Fitzroya Hook. fil. ex W. J. Hooker—Bot. Mag. (1851) Pl. 4616—Evergreen tree with reddish bark exfoliating in narrow strips, and green, thin branchlets; leaves scale-like, in whorls of 3. Cone scales somewhat roof-like, to 9 in 3 whorls, the lower 3 scales small and infertile, the middle ones empty or with a 2 winged seed, the uppermost larger and each with 2–6, 2–3 winged seeds; cones woody, ripening the first year.—1 species in southern Chile and in North Patagonia.

Tribe Libocedreae (*Neocallitropsis, Widdringtonia, Diselma, Papuacedrus, Pilgerodendron, Austrocedrus, Libocedrus, Calocedrus*)

Neocallitropsis Florin—Paleontographica I (1944) 35; Sec. B 590—Medium tall, evergreen tree with unsegmented, cylindrical, densely foliate branchlets, leaves in whorls of 4, scale-like, not decurrent, exterior keeled with inward curving tips. Cone scales 8, in 2 whorls, not woody, narrow, thick, variable when ripe, with a small central axis.—1 species in New Caledonia (= *Callitropis* Compton).

Widdringtonia Endl.—Gen. Pl. Suppl. II (1842) 25—Evergreen, small to tall trees or shrubs of cypress-like appearance; branchlets not segmented; leaves scale-like, not imbricate, often needle-like on young plants, opposite or more or less alternate on strong branchlets, often with a dorsal gland. Cone scales 4, thick, woody, prickled below the apex, tightly closed at first, opening wide-valvate when ripe; cones clustered.— 3 species in South Africa and tropical Africa.

Diselma J. D. Hooker—Flor. Tasman. I (1860) Pl. 98.—Erect, abundantly branched shrub or small tree with 4-sided branchlets, leaves opposite, small, scale-like, densely arranged. Plants dioecious, female flowers very small, somewhat covered with 4 paired-opposite scales, of these only the uppermost are fertile; cones very small.—1 species in Tasmania.

Papuacedrus Li—Jour. Arnold Arboretum 34 (1953) 17–36—Evergreen trees; leaves decussate, stomatal bands on the angular leaves, intermittent beneath.—3 species in New Guinea and the Moluccas. Rarely found in cultivation.

Pilgerodendron Florin—Svensk Bot. Tidskr. 1930—Evergreen tree with 4-sided branches, leaves opposite, quite regular in form, 2 sided, with stomata only on the upper side, erect to appressed and imbricate; cone scales 4, in 2 opposite pairs, the uppermost fertile, each with 2 ovules, all scales with a stiff centrally located, inward curving thorn on the dorsal side.—1 species in southern Chile to Patagonia (= *Libocedrus uvifera* Pilg.).

Austrocedrus Florin & Boutelje—Acta Hort. Bergian. 17 (1953) 28—Evergreen tree, leaves dimorphic, decussate lateral leaves much longer than the facial leaves, with white markings beneath; cones small, with 4 scales, with a small papilla on the dorsal side.—1 species in South America.

Libocedrus Endl. (*sensu stricto*)—Syn. Conif. (1847) 42—Branchlets on a single plane; evergreen trees with flattened branches; leaves scale-form, opposite, appressed or erect, the side scales usually high keeled, keeled leaves and flat leaves quite different, facial leaves only slightly visible between the lateral leaves; cone scales not fused, plate-like over the carpels, best distinguished by a small continuation of the axis; seeds with 2 wings, but the smaller wing only a narrow, membranous margin.—5 species in New Zealand and New Caledonia.

Calocedrus Kurz.—Jour. Bot. (London) II (1873) 196—Evergreen trees, branchlets flattened, leaves to 4 in false whorls, scale-like, leathery, distinctly dimorphic; lateral leaves not touching the facial leaves; with stomata on the upper and lower side; cones ovate, with 6 scales, with a thorn beneath the apex; cone with 2 scale pairs fused into a flat plate over the carpels. Seed with 2 uneven wings.—3 species in North America and SE. Asia.

Tribe Tetraclineae (*Tetraclinis*)

Tetraclinis Masters—Jour. Roy. Hort. Soc. (London) XIV (1892) 250—Small tree with segmented branchlets; leaves in whorls of 4, long decurrent, the distinct apical portion very small, scale-like. Cone scales 4, in 2 pairs, cones nearly cubical, opening 4 valved, without a central axis.—1 species in South Spain, Morocco, Algieria and Tunis.

Subfamily Cupressoideae

Tribe Cupressaceae (*Cupressus, Cupressocyparis, Chamaecyparis, Fokienia*)

Cupressus L.—Cypress—Spec. Pl. (1753) 1002—Evergreen trees or shrubs with somewhat angular, seldom flattened branchlets, leaves needle-like on young plants, later scale-like, opposite, all alike or on the flattened branchlets the lateral leaves somewhat differing from the neighboring facial leaves. Stamens with 3 to 5 pollen sacs each; carpels with more or less numerous ovules at the base; cones ripening in the 2nd year; seeds broad or narrow winged; cotyledons 2.—About 15–20 species in western N. America, East Asia to the eastern Mediterranean region and in the Sahara.

× **Cupressocyparis** (*Cupressus* × *Chamaecyparis*)—Dallimore, in Hand-List Conif. Roy. Bot. Gard. Kew, 4th ed. (1938) 37; without a latin description.

Chamaecyparis Spach—False cypress—Hist. Nat. Vég. Phanér. XI (1942) 329—Evergreen, medium to tall trees with more or less flat branchlets; primordial leaves linear, juvenile forms with short needle-like leaves (earlier referred to as "retinospora"), later leaves scale-like, variable, opposite, stamens with 2–3 pollen sacs each; carpels with few (usually 2–4) ovules; cones ripening the first year; seed broad winged; cotyledons 2.—7 species in North America, Japan and Taiwan.

Fokienia A. Henry & H. H. Thomas—Gard. Chron. XLIX (1911) 66—Trees with opposite, scale-like leaves. Female flowers with 6–8 pairs of opposite carpels; cones ripening the 2nd year, nearly globose, with shield form, eventually diverging scales; seeds with 2 unequal sized wings.—1 species in China.

Tribe Thujopsideae (*Thujopsis, Thuja, Microbiota*)

Thujopsis Sieb. & Zucc.—Fl. Japon. II (1842) 32, Pl. 119, 120—Evergreen tree, usually only shrubby in cultivation, branches and branchlets compressed, flat, rather wide; leaves scale-like, dark green, leathery, opposite, silvery-gray beneath. Female flowers with 6–10 paired scales, only the middle ones fertile; ripe cones globose, nearly erect, with thick, leathery-woody, widely gaping scales.—1 species in Japan.

Thuja L.—Arborvitae—Spec. Pl. (1753) 1002—Evergreen trees or shrubs with flat branches, leaves opposite, scale-like, appressed, imbricate, all nearly alike or the lateral leaves on the axillary branchlets high keeled, flat on the broad side. Female flowers with 6–8(–12) scales, of these 2–6 (or sometimes 1–3) are fertile; cones small, with more or less gaping, leathery or woody scales.—5 species in China, Japan and North America, but widely disseminated in cultivation.

    1. Subgenus: *Euthuja*   Seeds winged; carpels slightly thickened.
    2. Subgenus: *Biota*   Seeds not winged; scales on young cones somewhat fleshy.

Microbiota Komar.—Not. Syst. Herb. Hort. Petrop. IV: 180 (1923)—Dwarf evergreen shrub, usually dioecious; leaves all scale-like, opposite. Female flower cones small, terminal on the branchlets, globose or ovate, with 2–4 leathery scales, these united forming an upward opening cup; ripe cones with nearly woody scales.—1 species in far eastern Russia, near Vladivostok.

Tribe Junipereae (*Juniperus* including *Arceuthos*)

Juniperus L.—Spec. Pl. II (1753) 1038—Evergreen, mono- or dioecious trees or shrubs, leaves opposite or in whorls of 3, needle-form on young plants, later needle- or scale-form. Cones globose, composed of 3–6 connate, fleshy scales, not dehiscing, ripening the 1st or 2nd year; seeds 1–10, hard shelled; cotyledons 2, rarely to 5.—About 60 species in the Northern Hemisphere, south to the West Indies and E. Africa.

Family **Podocarpaceae**

Evergreen trees or shrubs with spirally arranged (decussate on *Microcachrys*) scale- or needle-like or flat lanceolate to ovate leaves, sometimes with leaf-like short shoots (phylloclades). Male flowers on foliate branches, terminal or axillary, usually with numerous stamens having 2 pollen sacs each; pollen grains with wings; female cones or inflorescences with many (or only 1) spiral or decussate or whorled bract scales, with 1 erect or inverted ovule in each axil, with one-sided or complete seed bulge, this occasionally absent and developing into a one sided receptacle when ripe; not a woody cone; cotyledons 2.—6 genera with about 125 species in the tropical and subtropical regions, most in the Southern Hemisphere, especially in the mountains.

Subfamily Pherosphaeroideae

Procumbent or tall shrubs with scale-like leaves; male flowers terminal, nearly globose or broad ellipsoid, the female terminal, reflexed; carpels few, reflexed; receptacle absent; ovules erect at the base of the carpels.

Microstrobos Garden & Johnson—Contr. N. S. Wales Nat. Herb. 1: 316 (1950)—This is the only genus with the characteristics of the subfamily.—2 species in the alpine regions of Tasmania and New South Wales.

Subfamily Phyllocladoideae

Evergreen trees and shrubs with long shoots and leaf-like, leathery short shoots; leaves on the long shoots small, scale-like, sometimes totally absent. Plants monoecious or dioecious, the male flowers in clusters at the end of short branches, the female flowers solitary in the axils of scale-leaves at the base of the secondary growth, or sessile on leaf-like short shoots, or replacing such shoots; ovules erect, borne on a basal disc, seeds with lobed aril (= Phyllocladaceae [Pilger] Core).

Phyllocladus Rich.—Comment. Bot. Conif. (1826) 129—Only genus with the characteristics of the subfamily.—7 species in New Zealand, Tasmania, New Guinea, Borneo, Phillipines.

Subfamily Podocarpoideae

Shrubs or trees with quite variably formed leaves. Plants mono- or dioecious; male flowers terminal or axillary; 1 bract scale with a one-sided and distinctly developed seed bulge and receptacle, the seeds often fully enclosed; ovules erect or inverted.

Saxegothaea Lindl.— Jour. Hort. Soc. London 6 (1851) 258—Evergreen tree with linear, nearly 2-ranked erect leaves. Plants monoecious, the male flowers in axillary spikes, the female terminal on short foliate branchlets; carpels rather numerous, imbricate; ovules in a depression at the base of the many large carpels, inverted; receptacle surrounding the ovules, opening to the interior; seed cones globose, thick, fleshy, with thick, nearly connate scales.—1 species in the forests of southern Chile and the Andes of Patagonia.

Microcachrys Hook. f.—Lond. Jour. Bot. 4 (1845) 149—Monoecious, evergreen, creeping, branched shrub with small, opposite, densely imbricate leaves. Female flowers terminal, small, ovate-globose; carpels numerous, thick, obtuse; receptacle hardly enlarged; ovule at the base of the carpel, inverted; seeds distinct, covered by the receptacle only at the base; cones small, nearly globose, scarlet-red when ripe, fleshy-juicy, mulberry-like.—1 species from the mountains of Tasmania.

Dacydium Sol.—Forster, De plant. esc. Ins. Ocean. Austr. comm. bot. (1786) 80—Evergreen trees or shrubs, leaves small, usually scale-like or linear on young plants, generally changing to the scale-form. Plants dioecious, rarely monoecious, carpels 1–6, distinct; ovules inverted at first and totally enclosed within the well developed receptacle, later more or less erect, the receptacle usually exserted and not adnate to the seed coat; seed oval, in a thin, nearly fleshy hull, ripening the second year.—About 20–25 species in Australia, the South Pacific Islands and Chile.

Podocarpus L'Herit. ex Pers.—Pers. Syn. II (1807) 580—Evergreen, small to very tall trees, occasionally shrubs; leaves usually large, linear or lanceolate to ovate, seldom scale-like. Plants dioecious, very rarely monoecious, the female flowers usually solitary, axillary, usually brightly colored, with a fleshy "foot" (developed from the adnate, fleshy basal part of the scale); carpels 1–2, each with 1 inverted ovule; receptacle large, bowed, tightly adnate to and completely surrounding ovule; seed enclosed within a fleshy outer shell and a more or less hard seed coat; cotyledons 2.—About 100 species in the tropical and subtropical regions of Asia, Africa and the mountainous areas of South America.*-LT

Acmopyle Pilger—in Engler, Pflanzenr. IV. 5 (1903) 117, Fig. 24—Trees from 15–20m high; leaves variably formed scale-like and linear-lanceolate with transition forms. Male flowers 1–3, terminal, the female flowers on a densely scaly, long stalk, with a fleshy, warty base developed from several scale-leaves; carpels usually solitary; receptacle fully adnate to the seed coat; seeds more or less erect, surrounded by the receptacle only at the base.—3 species in the mountains of New Caledonia and the Fiji Islands.

Family **Cephalotaxaceae**

Evergreen trees or shrubs with 2-ranked, erect, narrow-linear leaves, very similar to those of *Taxus*. Plants dioecious, the male flowers several in rounded inflorescences, axillary; female flowers few in the axils of small scale-leaves at the base of quite short, later elongating branches; carpels decussate, each with 2 ovules at the base; seeds large, drupe-like, surpassed by the long scale, ripening the first year; cotyledons 2.—1 genus, *Cephalotaxus*.

Cephalotaxus Sieb. & Zucc. ex Endl.—Gen. Suppl. II (1842) 27—Small trees or shrubs with green branches at first. Male flowers 6–11 in globose inflorescences in the leaf axils of the younger branches, each with 7–12 stamens; female flowers 1–3 in the leaf axils; ovules sunk into the base of the carpels and erect.—8 species, from Himalaya to Japan.

Family **Araucariaceae**

Evergreen trees of the Southern Hemisphere with broad or needle-like, compressed leaves. Plants dioecious, rarely monoecious, the male flower large, cone-like, with numerous stamens; female flowers terminal on short branches; carpels very numerous, with thick, eventually woody apexes, with or without ligulate scales; ovules inverted, solitary; fruit cones large, rounded, disintegrating; seeds not winged or with side wings; cotyledons 2, seldom 4.—2 genera: *Agathis*, *Araucaria*.

Agathis Salisbury—Trans. Linn. Soc. VIII (1807) 311, Pl. 15; Dammara Rumph. Herb. II (1741) 174, Pl. 57—Tall, very resinous trees with ovate-oblong or lanceolate, thick leathery leaves. Male flowers usually axillary, to 6 cm long; stamens with 5–15 pollen sacs; female flower cones on short, terminal, scaly shoots; carpels leathery-woody, broad triangular; ligulate scales absent; ovules solitary, not adnate to the carpel; seeds with one sided wings, ripening in the second year.—About 20 species, from Indonesia to eastern Australia and New Zealand.

Araucaria Jussieu—Gen. Pl. Sec. Ord. Nat. Disp. (1789) 413—Tall trees; leaves leathery, attached in many spiral rows, soon becoming scale-like, loosely imbricate, covering the branches on all sides, soon becoming lanceolate, oblong, dagger-like acute, erect. Male flowers terminal on short branches, large, with many stamens, each with 6–19 pollen sacs; female flowers cone-like; carpels numerous, thick, with a sharp, nearly leaf-like tip; developing ligulate scales, adnate to the seed scales to the apex; ovules solitary, totally adnate to the ligulate scale; seeds very thick.—About 18 species in the Southern Hemisphere.

---

*For the new genera *Falcatifolium, Dacrycarpus* and *Decussocarpus* (D. J. de Laubenfels, in Jour. Arnold Arboretum 5, 274–369, 1969) see *Podocarpus* in the text.

Order TAXALES

Abundantly branched shrubs or small trees, with spiraled, occasionally decussate leaf arrangement; without resin ducts in the wood and leaves. Male flowers solitary or in small spikes in the leaf axils, with scale-like involucral leaves, stamens scale- or shield-form, with 2–8 pollen sacs; female flowers solitary, directly in the leaf axils or (on *Torreya* and *Taxus*) grouped 1–2, rarely more, on secondary side sprouts at the ends of short axillary branches and on scaly primary flower shoots; each flower with normally paired, sterile scale-leaves and a terminal, erect ovule surrounded at the base by a bulging ring; seeds hard shelled, with a thick-fleshy covering (aril) on all sides, developed from the bulging ring; disseminated by birds; cotyledons 2.—Modern classification schemes treat the *Taxales* as an individual race.

Family **Taxaceae**

Trees or shrubs with needle-form or linear-lanceolate (*Austrotaxus*) leaves. Male flowers axillary, solitary or in spikes (*Austrotaxus*); stamens with 2–8 pollen sacs; female flowers on small axillary sprouts, with imbricate scales at the base; with 1 ovule at the apex; seeds partially or totally enclosed by a fleshy hull (aril); cotyledons 2.—5 genera: *Amentotaxus, Torreya, Austrotaxus, Pseudotaxus, Taxus.*

Amentotaxus Pilger—Bot. Jahrb. Syst. LIV (1916) 41—Woody plants with opposite branches and leaves. Male flowers sessile, in catkin-like, pendulous spikes, surrounded by bud scales at the base; stamens clustered on the very short floral axis, usually with 3 pollen sacs; female flowers with 5 pairs of decussate scale-leaves.—1–4 species in western China, Assam.

Torreya Arnott—Ann. Nat. Hist. I (1838) 130—Evergreen, dioecious trees; leaves needle-like, prickly, 2-ranked erect on side branches. Male flowers solitary; female flowers solitary; ovules, paired axillary, each with 2 scale-leaf pairs; aril at first a bulge at the base of the bottle-shaped ovule later enlarging and totally enveloping the seed, adnate nearly to the tip; seeds ripening the 2nd year.—6 species in east Asia and in southern N. America.

Austrotaxus Compton—Jour. Linn. Soc. XLV (1922) 427, Pl. 26—Large tree with dense, bushy crown. Male flowers in axillary spikes; stamens 1–5, with 2–4 pollen sacs each; female flowers on axillary branchlets, these densely covered with wide, thick, imbricate scale-leaves; ovule solitary, terminal, erect; seeds totally enclosed by a fleshy aril.—1 species in northern New Caledonia.

Psuedotaxus Cheng—Res. Note I For. Nat. Cent. Univ. Nanking. Dendr. Ser. 1947)—Shrub, 2–4 m high, evergreen, branches whorled. Plants dioecious. Male flowers solitary in the leaf axils, numerous; female flowers in the leaf axils of the youngest branches, often very numerous, 2–7 mm long; seeds 5 mm long, 4 mm wide, surrounded by a white, campanulate aril.—Only 1 species in western China; not known to be in cultivation.

Taxus L.—Yew—Gen. Pl. ed. I (1737) 312, Nr. 765, ed. V (1754) 462, Nr. 1006; Spec. Pl. (1753) 1040—Evergreen, dioecious, occasionally monoecious trees, occasionally shrubs, usually with 2-ranked, erect, needle-form leaves. Male flowers solitary; female flowers a single ovule, paired on tiny axillary sprouts (one flower usually stunted), each with 3 pairs of scale-leaves; aril at first a cupule surrounding the ovule, later becoming fleshy, totally enveloping the seed, adnate only at the base; seeds ripening the first year.—10 species in the Northern Hemisphere.

Order GNETALES

Twiggy shrubs with widely spaced, whorled scale-leaves (Ephedraceae) or plants with woody, short stems, 30 cm high at most and 2 opposite, persistent, strap-like leaves (Welwitschiaceae), or climbers, occasionally trees or shrub-like plants with reticulately veined leaves, which are very similar to the dicotyledons (Gnetaceae); wood with true vessels in the secondary wood, without resin ducts. Plants dioecious, seldom monoecious, the male flower with at least 2 connate involucral leaves; anthers 1–3 chambered, without filaments, but raised above the perianthon the stalk-like floral axis; female flowers with 1–2 petals and an erect ovule, whose tube-form micropyle protrudes out of the perianth; cotyledons 2.—3 families: Welwitschiaceae, Ephedraceae, Gnetaceae.

Family **Welwitschiaceae** (not covered in the text)

Plants with a woody, short stem, rising only slightly above the ground, thick, carrot-shaped, flattened above, 1 mm wide on older specimens, with a tangle of individual vascular bundles and a deep, strong, taproot; leaves 2, replacing quickly abscising cotyledons, long strap-like, leathery, persistent, growing continually for the life of the plant and split into numerous small strips. Male flowers with 6 stamens fused at the base of a tube and a stunted ovule; anthers 3 chambered; female flowers with broad winged perianth and long, tube-form micropyle.—1 species, *Welwitschia mirabilis,* in the coastal deserts of Southwest Africa (Plate 18).

Family **Ephedraceae**

Twiggy shrubs with relatively negligible secondary wood, branches grooved, like Horsetail (*Equisetum*); leaves sparse, whorled, scale-like. Plants usually dioecious, male flowers solitary or grouped in short to globose spikes, each with 2 involucral leaves and 1 stalk-like column with 2–8 anthers; female flowers 1–3 formed by a plate-like perianth and single ovule with a tube-form micropyle protruding from the perianth; fruits (fruit cones) often berry-like.—Only 1 genus.

Ephedra L.—Sp. Pl. ed. I (1753) 1040—With the characteristics of the family.—About 40 species, xerophytes, from the Asian interior to the Mediterranean region, some in central Europe, western N. America to Mexico, southern Andes (Fig. 4).

Family **Gnetaceae**

Climbing or erect woody plants with opposite leaves and reticulate venation. Male flowers numerous in the axils of connate bract pairs, composed of a plate-like perianth and a stalk and 1–2 anthers; female flowers whorled, with 2 involucral leaves and 1 tube-form micropyle.

Gnetum L. (not covered in the text)—Mant. ed. I (1767) 18—Only genus with the characteristics of the family.—About 30 species in the tropics.

Fig. 4. *Ephedra intermedia.*
Lower left, fruit with involucral scales, above left smaller part of same;
style-like "tubullus" at right; center, male inflorescence

PLANT DESCRIPTIONS

ABIES Mill.—Fir—PINACEAE

Large, evergreen, conical trees with erect, more or less whorled branches; bark on older trees usually thick and grooved, usually smooth on younger trees, often with resin blisters; branches smooth, seldom furrowed; buds resinous or not, globose or ovate to spindle-form; needles usually parted, often completely encircling the branch or bottlebrush-like and directed forward, usually flat with dark green upper side, underside keeled and with bluish or silver-white stomatal bands, resin ducts 2, seldom 4; leaves tapered petiole-like at the base, base flared at the point of attachment to the stem, leaving a flat, circular leaf scar when abscising; plants monoecious; male flowers solitary in the axils of the uppermost needles, pendulous, pollen grains with 2 wings; female flowers erect, terminal, ovate to cylindrical, composed of numerous seed scales each with 2 ovules; bract scales often enlarged after flowering and then protruding past the seed scales; cones erect, oval-oblong to cylindrical, disintegrating when ripe except for the persistent central axis (rachis); seeds with adnate wings; cotyledons 4–10. x = 12.—About 40 species in the northern temperate zone as well as North Africa and the Himalayas, mostly in humid regions.

Outline of the genus *Abies*
(from Franco, modified)

Subgen. I: **Pseudotorreya** (Hickel) Franco
Buds long, ovate-conical, apices long, drawn-out, resin free, bud scales loose, abscising; needles similar on all twigs; needles wide; cones ovate; bract scales 3 lobed at the apex, both side lobes much shorter than the drawn out, awn-like middle lobe; seed scales glabrous, thick, hard.
1 species: *A. bracteata*

Subgen. II: **Sapinus** (Endl.) Franco
Buds small, ovate or globose, obtuse or (rarely) acute, often resinous, bud scales persistent; needles differing on old and young trees; cones cylindrical, oblong or ovate; bract scales with a long or short prominent tip or without; seed scales pubescent on the dorsal side or velvety (but glabrous on *A. firma*), thin (but thick on *A. delavayi* and var. *georgei*).

Sect. 1: **Nobilis** Engelm.
Needles monochromatic, narrow, resin ducts marginal; cones long and thick, cylindrical, violet-purple before ripening; bract scales cuspidate or mucronate, green when young, if exserted; rachis cylindrical-conical, thick; seeds 11–19 mm long.
2 species: *A. magnifica, procera*

Sect. 2: **Oiamel** Franco
Needles bicolored (rarely monochromatic), narrow, resin ducts marginal; cones long or short, thick, oblong or spindle-form, dark violet before ripening; bract scales exserted, blue-violet when young, blade widened to rectangular-cuspidate or spathulate-cuspidate; rachis cylindrical-conical; seeds 6–13 mm long.
4 species: *A. hickeli, oaxacana, religiosa, vejari*

Sect 3: **Balsameae** Engelm.
Needles bicolored (rarely monochromatic), often narrow; cones small, rarely large, violet-purple when young (rarely green); bract scales enclosed (seldom exserted and then green when young), widened to a cuspidate blade; rachis conical, ornamental.

Series 1: **Grandes** (Engelm.) Franco
Needles with narrow marginal resin ducts; cones spindle shaped or cylindrical, often thick; seeds 8–12 mm long.
6 species: *A. amabilis, concolor, durangensis, grandis, guatemalensis, mexicana*

Series 2: **Lasiocarpae** Franco
Needles with wide resin ducts usually in the parenchyma; cones oblong to ovate; seeds 5–9 mm long.
3 species: *A. balsamea, fraseri, lasiocarpa*

Sect. 4: **Pichta** Mayr
Needles bicolored, often narrow, resin ducts usually in the parenchyma (rarely marginal), often wide; cones rather small and cylindrical, violet-purple or nearly blue (rarely green) before ripening; bract scales green when young and exserted (rarely enclosed), widening to a 4 sided blade with a claw; seed scales much wider than high (except on *A. sibirica*); rachis conical, ornamental; seeds 4–8 mm long.
6 species: *A. kawakamii, koreana, sachalinensis, sibirica, veitchii*

Sect. 5: **Momi** Mayr
Needles bicolored, wide or relatively wide; cones rather large or small, often thick, ovate, spindle-form or cylindrical; seeds 7–13 mm long.

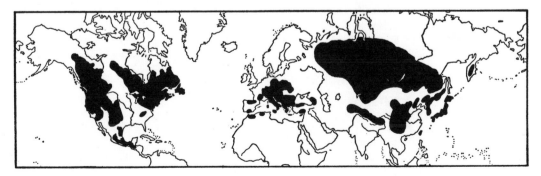

Fig. 5. Range of the genus *Abies* (from Liu 1971)

Outline of the characteristics of the shoots, buds and needles of the more prominent *Abies* species

Abies Species	Young shoots						buds				needles		Stomata	
	Furrowed	Not furrowed	Glabrous	Pubescent	Very pubescent	Color	Not resinous	Slightly resinous	Very resinous	Form	Length in mm	Apex	Over	Under
firma	X—X				X	gray-brown		X		small	35	deep crenate	(X)	X
holophylla	X—X		X			gray-yellow		X		ovate, small	20–40	round-acute		X
delavayi	X		X			red-brown		X		thick, ovate	15–25	crenate-2 pointed		X
fargesii	X		X			reddish		X	X	round	20–30	crenate		X
homolepsis	X		X			yellow		X		ovate	20–30	crenate		X
kawakamii	X			X		yellowish	X			ovate, small	15–25	acute-crenate		X
religiosa	X			X		red-brown, reddish		X		ovate	15–35	acute (crenate)		X
sachalinensis	X			X		gray			X	ovate	40	round-crenate		X
spectabilis	X			X		red-brown		X		globose, large	30–60	round-crenate		X
farg. faxon.	X				X	reddish			X	ovate	15–25	round-crenate		X
koreana	X				X	yellowish-red		X		round	10–20	round-crenate		X
bracteata		X	X			greenish	X			spindle-form	30–60	thorn tipped		X
numidica		X	X			yellow-green	X			ovate, large	15–20	round-crenate		X
concolor		X	X			yellow-green		X		round	40–60	acute-crenate	X	X
chensiensis		X	X			gray-yellow		X		ovate	15–30	acute-2 pointed		X
pinsapo		X	X			brown		X		ovate	15–20	acute	X	X
pindrow		X	X			gray-yellow		X		conical	30–60	crenate		X
× insignis		X	X			rust-brown		X		conical, large	20–30	obtuse-round		X
× vilmorinii		X	X			rust-brown		X		thick, obtuse	20–30	acute-prickly		X
recurvata		X	X			gray-yellow			X	ovate	15–35	acute		X
equi-trojani		X	X			yellowish			X	ovate	15–25	acute-crenate	X	X
cephalonica		X	X			brown-red			X	ovate	15–28	acute-round	(X)	X
nordmanniana		X	X—X			green-yellow	X			acute-ovate	20–35	round-crenate		X
sutchuenensis		X	X—X			dark-brown		X		ovate	15–25	acute-obtuse		X
delavayi forrestii		X	X—X			dark-brown			X	inverted	40	round		X
alba		X		X		gray-brown	X			inverted, ovate	15–30	round-crenate		X
cilicica		X		X		gray-brown	X			ovate, small	20–30	round-crenate		X
sibirica		X		X		gray			X	globose	30	round-2 pointed		X
mariesii		X		X		rust-brown		X		round, small	'8–20	crenate-round		X
grandis		X		X		olive-green		X		ovate	30–60	round-crenate		X
lasiocarpa		X		X		ash-gray		X		ovate, small	25–40	crenate-acute	X	X
—arizonica		X		X		yellow-brown		X		ovate, small	20–30	2 pointed-crenate	X	X
magnifica		X		X		brownish		X		round, small	40	round	X	X
veitchii		X		X		brown			X	round, small	10–25	round-crenate		X
procera		X			X	brown-red		X		round, small	20–35	round	X	X
nephrolepsis		X			X	gray-yellow		X		ovate	10–25	round-crenate		X
borisii-regis		X			X	yellowish		X		ovate	30	acute-round		X
nebrodensis		X			X	brown		X		ovate	12–20	round-crenate		X
balsamea		X			X	gray-yellow			X	ovate, small	15–25	round-crenate		X
fraseri		X			X	gray-yellow			X	round, small	15–25	round-crenate		X
squamata		X			X	brown			X	globose	15–25	round-crenate		X
amabilis		X			X	gray brown			X	round, small	20–30	round-crenate		X
bornmuelleriana		X			X	brown			X	acute, ovate	20–35	crenate-acute	X	X

(X) = Stomata only above at the apex

Series 1: Homolepides Franco
Young cones violet-purple or green; outer scales enclosed, blade round and always clawed; rachis conical, ornamental.
3 species: *A. holophylla, homolepis, mariesii*

Series 2: Firmae Franco
Young cones green; bract scales exserted, green when young, widened to an ovate-triangular, clawed blade; fruit scales glabrous, finely toothed on the upper limb; rachis conical, thick.
1 species: *A. firma*

Series 3: Sinenses Franco
Young cones dark violet or blackish (occasionally green); bract scales exserted (blue-violet when young) or enclosed; rachis oblong and tapered (conical on *A. chensiensis*), thick.
6 species: *A. chensiensis, delavayi, fargesii, recurvata, squamata, sutchuenensis*

Sect. 6: Peuce (D. Don) Spach
Buds resinous or not so; needles bicolored (rarely monochromatic), wide or narrow; cones long, more or less ornamental, cylindrical, green when young; bract scales rounded or nearly rectangular at the apex; rachis conical, ornamental; seeds 10–15 mm long.

Series 1: Albae (Franco) Franco
Bract scales exserted, clawed, green when young.
7 species: *A. alba, borisii-regis, bornmuelleriana, cephalonica, equi-trojani, nebrodensis, nordmanniana*

Series 2: Pinsapones Franco
Bract scales enclosed, clawed.
4 species: *A. cilicica, marocana, numidica, pinsapo*

Sect. 7: Pindrau Mayr
Needles bicolored, narrow or wide; cones large and thick, cylindrical, dark violet before ripening; bract scales enclosed, widening to a round, clawed blade; rachis cylindrical-conical, thick; seeds 12 to 15 mm long.
2 species: *A. pindrow, spectabilis*

Abies alba Mill. European Silver Fir. Tree, 30–50(–65) m high, stem quite straight, bark gray, scaly on older stems, branches whorled, horizontal, bark smooth, twigs gray-brown, rough pubescent, buds ovate, resin free or slightly resinous; needle arrangement pectinate, upper ones shorter, apex rounded to notched or 2 pointed, 20–35 mm long, dark green above, glossy, furrowed, with occasional stomatal lines on the apex, with 2 white stomatal bands beneath; cones erect, 10–14 cm long, to 5 cm thick, greenish when young, dark brown when ripe, scales 25–30 mm wide, tomentose exterior, bract scales exserted, reflexed. FAA 59 to 61 (Br), 66–67 (C); LA 19 (= *A. pectinata* DC.). Mountains of central and southern Europe, in the Black Forest of Germany. Plate 2: Fig. 7 (Br). z5

'Aurea'. Needles partly very gold-yellow, otherwise green (= *A. pectinata auricoma* Carr.). Before 1861. Not consistent. (VR)

'Brevifolia'. Dwarf form with short, wide needles. Originated in the Sénéclauze Nursery in Bourg-Argental, France, 1861 (also from other sources near Chretien in Versailles). (EX)

'Columnaris'. Tall, slender column, branches numerous, very short, of equal length; needles somewhat shorter than those of the species. Found in the forest on Mt. Pila in France, 1855.

'Compacta'. Dwarf form, globose, wider than tall, densely branched; needles very glossy. Originated by Parsons & Sons,

in Flushing, New York, USA about 1885. (VR)

'Elegans'. Bushy dwarf form; needles short, split at the apex. Before 1867. (EX)

'Fastigiata'. Broad columnar habit, like *Populus nigra* 'Italica', not over 3 m wide, branches all ascending at acute angles; needles much shorter and thinner, 10–20 mm long, frequently curved upward. Brought into cultivation by Sénéclauze, 1846.

f. flabellata Beissn. Tree, branches only arising from 2 sides (fan shaped). Illustrated in Prakt. Ratgeber 1910: 192. Found by Insp. Funke in a forest near Erlangen, W. Germany. (EX)

'Green Spiral'. Weeping form, stem vertical, but twisted in a wide spiral, branches short, directed downward in short curves; needles shorter and more densely arranged than those of *A. alba*. Origin unknown. The plant shown in KN 8 from the Secrest Arboretum, Wooster, Ohio, USA (photographed in 1973), was planted out as a 30 cm high grafted plant in 1916, delivered from the Biltmore Nursery as *A. alba* "Tortuosa".

'Irramosa'. Stem practically unbranched; needles very densely arranged. Found in the forest near Chaumont, Switzerland before 1896 by Dr. Coulton. (EX)

'Massonii'. Differing by the radial arrangement of the needles like that of *A. pinsapo*. Before 1884. (EX)

f. microcarpa Nels. Cones especially small. Before 1866. (EX)

'Microphylla'. Dwarf form with short, clustered, thin twigs, winter buds small, red and resinous; needles very thin, narrow, 8–15 mm long, obtuse at the apex. Before 1867. (R)

'Pendula'. 10–15 m high, stem nearly straight upright, later more or less leaning, branches hanging loosely vertical. OCC 3. Found about 1835 in the Godefroy Nursery in Ville d'Avray, France. A large specimen stands in the Botanic Garden of St. Gallen, Switzerland and in Edewecht (Oldenburg), on the main street. Plate 2.

'Pendula Gracilis'. Differs from 'Pendula' in the much longer, mane-like branching. Originated before 1868 by M. Masse, France. (EX)

'Pyramidalis'. Strictly columnar habit when young, later becoming compact conical, 7–10 m high, branches ascending, twigs densely packed and short; needles short, deep green, glossy. In cultivation about 1850 in England. (EX) Plate 2.

f. recurva Sénécl. Branches reflexed and more or less pendulous. Found before 1868 in the forest on Mt. Pila in France. (EX)

'Tenuifolia'. Slow grower; needles quite thin, nearly membranous. Originated in 1862 by Van Geert (today the Kalmthout Arboretum) in Belgium. (EX)

'Tenuiorifolia'. Normal habit; needles longer and thinner; cones to 30 cm long. Present by 1790 in Worlitz Park near Dessau, E. Germany.

'Tortuosa'. Bushy, dwarf form with irregular habit, branches twisted, compact, ascending; needles irregularly arranged, short, 11–19 mm long, bright green (= *A. pectinata nana* Hort.; *A. pectinata prostrata* Hort.). Cultivated since about 1835. (R)

'Umbraculifera'. Crown spreading umbrella-like, branches short and thick, densely arranged, erect and later nodding. Found in a forest on the Loire, France before 1868. (EX)

'Variegata'. Slow growing; needles unequal, somewhat yellowish and white variegated. Before 1839. (EX?)

'Virgata'. Broad columnar with limp, pendulous, 4–5 m long branches, growing downward from the tips. Found in the

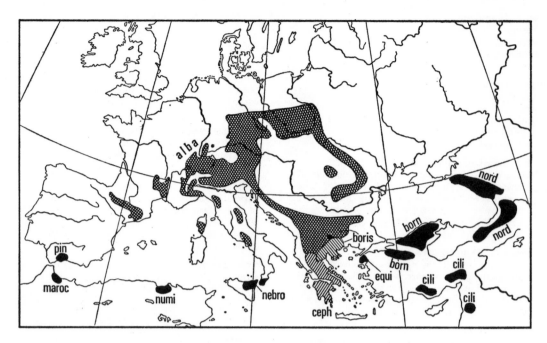

Fig. 6. Range of the European and West Asian **Abies** species. *A. borisii-regis* (boris), *A. bornmuelleriana* (born), *A. cilicica* (cili), *A. cephalonica* (ceph), *A. marocana* (maroc), *A. nebrodensis* (nebro), *A. numidica* (numi), *A. nordmannia* (nord), *A. equi-trojani* (equi), *A. pinsapo* (pin)

Bohemian Forest of W. Germany and in the Alsace region of France, 1879.

A. amabilis Dougl. ex J. Forbes. Red Silver Fir. Tree, 50–80 m high, stem straight, bark smooth, furrowed only at the base, branched down to the base (in open areas!), crown conical, buds globose, dark red, resinous, branches tiered, young branches gray or yellowish-brown; needles very densely arranged, bristle-like above, side rows erect, parted beneath (especially on the lower branches), 20–30 mm long, 2 mm wide, often widest over the middle, apex truncate or 2-pointed, dark green and furrowed above, with 2 white stomatal bands beneath, each with 5–6 lines, with fragrance of oranges when crushed, needles of the uppermost branches often thicker, shorter and also with stomatal lines above; cones erect, ovate-conical, 10–14 cm long, dark purple before ripening, scales 25–28 mm wide, bract scales not visible. BFN 156 (H); JDN 3; LA 34; CCE 15–16. S. Alaska to W. Oregon. Very attractive & especially winter hardy. Plate 2; Fig. 8 (C), (Br). z6

'Compacta'. Dwarf form, very dense habit, grafted from a side branch, only about 90 cm high after 20 years. 1903. (EX?)

'Spreading Star'. Low growing, with a short stem, to only 1 m high, branches spreading horizontally. OCC 5; WDw 27; WM 1E (Br) (= *A. amabilis procumbens* Hort.). Originated in the Blijdenstein Pinetum, Hilversum, Holland, presumably grafted from a side branch. Before 1960. Plate 4.

A. × arnoldiana Nitzelius (*A. koreana* × *A. veitchii*). Tree with branches in regular whorls arising at obtuse angles, crown form similar to that of *A. veitchii*, buds oval, more or less resinous, young branches gray, more or less pubescent; needles not directed forward and clustered like those of *A. veitchii*, 20–30 mm long, but 2.5 mm wide

(like *A. koreana*) toward the tips, and with chalk-white stomatal bands beneath; cones cylindrical, 5.5–6 cm long and 2.3–2.5 cm thick, violet-brown to gray-yellow-brown when ripe, bract scales slightly to distinctly exserted and reflexed. CCE 40. Germinated in 1953 in the Göteborg Botanic Garden, Sweden from seed sent by the Arnold Arboretum. Plate 3. z5

From this hybrid, 2 clones have been chosen and named:

'Violet'. Cones brown-violet (HCC 59A), bract scales only slightly exserted between the seed scales. DB 1970: 79.

'Graciosa'. Cones gray/yellow-brown (HCC 161a), bract scales exserted and reflexed. DB 1970: 80. Plate 3.

Similar hybrids were developed under controlled conditions by D. T. Poulsen in 1959; the seedlings grow faster than *A. koreana*, the needles are larger, the cones blue to violet and develop very early. Difficult to graft.

A. balsamea (L.) Mill. Balsam Fir. Medium tall tree, 15–25 m high, stem slender, crown conical at the apex, bark ash gray, with numerous resin blisters, eventually scaly, young branches yellow-gray, scattered pubescent, buds ovate, small, glossy resinous; needles bristle-form on the upper side (especially on young trees), with a distinct V-shaped furrow, directed forward and upward, parted beneath and on smaller branches, 15–25 mm long, apex round to lightly 2-pointed, deep green above with a few short stomatac lines on the apex, with 2 white, stomatal bands beneath, each with 5–6 lines, strong balsam fragrance when crushed, needles on cone bearing branches shorter, stiffer and more acute, curving more upward; cones erect, small, ovate-cylindrical, 5–9 cm long, dark violet before ripening, gray-brown when ripe, eventually very resinous, scales 15 mm wide, bract scales hidden to somewhat exserted. CB 2, 6; OCC 6 (H). N.

Plate 1

Cedrus deodara in Kew Gardens, London, England
Photo: Krüssmann

Plate 2

Abies alba 'Pendula
in the St. Gallen Botanic Garden, Switzerland

Abies alba 'Pyramidalis'
in the Oeschberg-Koppigen Arboretum, Switzerland
Photo: Jenny

Abies alba
Photo: G. Varga

Abies amabilis
in the Mt. Baker National Forest, Washington, USA
Photo: US Forest Service

Plate 3

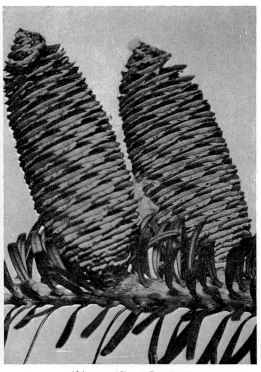

Abies arnoldiana
in the Göteborg Botanic Garden, Sweden

Abies arnoldiana 'Graciosa'
Photo: Nitzelius

Abies cephalonica

Abies cephalonica
in its native habitat in Greece
Photo: Kragh

Plate 4

Abies amabilis 'Spreading Star' in the Blijdenstein Pinetum, Hilversum, Holland

Abies cilicica and *Cedrus libani* in a mixed stand near Alseki, Taurus Mts., Turkey
Photo: Nitzelius

Plate 5

Abies concolor
in the Berlin-Dahlem Botanic Garden, Germany

Abies chensiensis
in the Kámoni Arboretum, Hungary

Abies fargesii var. *faxoniana*
in the Hoersholm Arboretum, Denmark

Abies fargessi var. *faxoniana*
in the Royal Botanic Garden, Edinburgh, Scotland

Plate 6

Abies delavayi var. *forrestii*
in Werrington Park, Cornwall, England

Abies lasiocarpa 'Compacta'
in Aurich (Learning Institute), W. Germany

Abies lasiocarpa in the Mt. Rainier National Park, Washington, USA
By courtesy of National Park Service

Plate 7

Abies equi-trojani
Photo: Nitzelius

Abies fargesii
in the Hillier Arboretum, England

Abies kawakamii
in the Hillier Arboretum

Abies pindrow var. *intermedia*
Hillier Arboretum

Plate 8

Abies homolepis
in the Tannenhoeft Arboretum, Holstein, W. Germany

Abies homolepis

Abies homolepis on Hondo,
in the mountains at 1500 m, Japan
By courtesy of Arnold Arboretum   Photo: E. H. Wilson

Abies holophylla
in the Younger Botanic Garden, Benmore, Scotland

Plate 9

Abies koreana
a wild plant in Korea
By courtesy of Arnold Arboretum. Photo: E. H. Wilson

Abies mariesii in Dawyck, Scotland

Abies mariesii, 5–8 m high; *Rhododendron brachycarpum* in foreground. Hondo Island, Japan at 2000 m
By courtesy of Arnold Arboretum   Photo: E. H. Wilson

Plate 10

Abies nebrodensis
Photo: Nitzelius

Abies nebrodensis
Photo: Nitzelius

Abies nebrodensis in N. Sicily, Monte Scallone de Madonie
Photo: Nitzelius

Plate 11

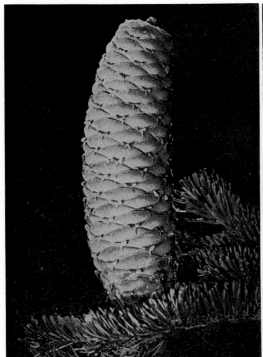

Abies nordmanniana
Photo: G. Varga

Abies nordmanniana, new growth;
Rienbek Arboretum near Hamburg, West Germany

Abies numidica
Photo: G. Varga

Abies numidica
Dortmund Botanic Garden, West Germany

Plate 12

Abies marocana
Photo: Nitzelius

Abies marocana
in the Amance Arboretum near Nancy, France

Abies pardei
in the National Arboretum, Les Barres, France

Abies pinsapo
Photo: G. Varga

Plate 13

Abies spectabilis
in Castlewellan, N. Ireland

Abies recurvata
in the Hillier Arboretum, Winchester, England

Abies procera
Photo: British Features

Abies procera
in the Willamette National Forest, Oregon, USA
Photo: U.S. Forest Service

Plate 14

Abies sachalinensis
in the Göteborg Botanic Garden, Sweden

Abies sachalinensis var. *mayriana* in Japan
Photo: Forest Agency Tokyo

Abies squamata in the Hillier Arboretum, England

Abies veitchii
Photo: Nitzelius

Plate 15

Agathis australis in its native habitat in Kauri Grove, Omahuta State Forest, Northland, New Zealand
Photo: N.Z. Forest Service

Plate 16

Agathis lanceolata
in its native habitat in New Caledonia
Photo: Centre Forestier Tropical (F)

Agathis australis
in the Giessen Botanic Garden, W. Germany

Agathis robusta
(from Baker & Smith)

Agathis palmerstonii in its native habitat,
30 m high, 2.2 m diameter breast high
Photo: Queensland Forest Service

America; Canada to Virginia. The most widely disseminated North American fir species, usually on mountains and in swampy areas. An elegant tree when young, but losing its appeal with age, short-lived. Fig. 8 (C), 11 (Br). z3

'Andover'. Low, without a stem, branches spreading, to 5 m, wide, slow growing; needle arrangement like the type. Found in 1957 in Andover, N.Y., USA by W. A. Smith.

'Albicans'. Young needles white. Found by A. Sénéclauze in France before 1886. (EX)

'Angustata'. Habit narrow-conical, branches and twigs very short, clustered; needles very densely arranged, 6–14 mm long (= A. balsamea f. angustata Rehd.). 1928. Not in cultivation.

'Argentea'. Needles bluish white toned, similar in color to A. procera, densely foliate. (EX)

'Coerulea'. Habit conical, branches very short; needles parted, in 2 rows, deep green above, silvery-white beneath. In cultivation since 1867. (VR)

'Coerulescens'. Vigorous grower; needles very densely arranged, only 6–10 mm long, 2 mm wide, both sides with bluish stomatal lines. Originated by A. Sénéclauze around 1865.

'Columnaris'. Columnar, strong growing, branches short, directed upward at the tips; needles densely arranged, only 5 mm long (= A. balsamea pyramidalis Hort.). Originated in the Frahm Nursery, Elmshorn, W. Germany before 1903.

'Denudata'. Contorted form, main leader without side branches. Originated by Cochet in Suynes, France before 1860. (EX?)

'Elegans'. Branches very dense and short; needles radially arranged around the twig, 8–10 mm long. Originated before 1868 by Sénéclauze. (EX)

f. hudsonia (Jacques) Fern. & Weatherby. Dwarf form, broad, branches very dense, numerous twigs, short; needles half-radially arranged, short, broad, flat, black-green above, blue-green beneath. WDw 31; CCE 18. Natural form from the White Mountains of New Hampshire, USA; introduced before 1810. Similar to 'Nana' and 'Prostrata'.

'Longifolia'. Vigorous grower, branches more steeply ascending than the species; needles longer, narrower, somewhat resembling A. fraseri (occasionally confused with same). Disseminated by J. Booth & Soehne, Hamburg before 1836. (EX)

'Lutescens'. Needles straw-yellow at first, then greening, like Picea abies 'Finedonensis'. Originated before 1903 in the trial garden of Diedorf, Bavaria, W. Germany.

var. macrocarpa Sarg. With larger cones than those of the species, no longer separated from the species.

'Marginata'. Needles of younger branches regularly yellow bordered. Originated in the garden of the Petrowskaja Academy, Moscow. Before 1894. (EX)

'Nana'. Dwarf form with globose habit, branches outspread, very densely arranged; all needles radially arranged or nearly so, 4–10 mm long, 1 mm wide, dark green above, with 2 white stomatal bands beneath, these indented, center and leaf margin light yellow-green. WDw 30; WM 1B (Br) and 103 (H); CCE 18 (= A. balsamea nana globosa Hort.). Known before 1866.

'Nudicaulis'. Another form of the species like 'Denudata', totally without side branches; needles very densely arranged, appressed, long acuminate. Originated before 1867 by A. Leroy

in Angers, France. (EX?)

var. phanerolepis Fern. Growth habit and needle arrangement like the type, but differing in the somewhat smaller cones, the bract scales surpassing the seed scales and with reflexed tips. FAA 31 (Br), 32 (C); Loudon, Arb. et Frut. Brit. 2241 (as "A. balsamea"). Canada.

'Prostrata'. Dwarf form, similar to var. hudsonia, but easily distinguished by the flat, outspread branching and needles arranged "comb-like" (pectinate). WDw 29; WM 1D (Br). Before 1838.(R-VR)

'Variegata'. Needles white variegated (= A. balsamea argenteo-variegata Schelle). Before 1855. (VR)

A. borisii-regis Mattf. Intermediate between A. alba and A. cephalonica, characteristics somewhat variable. Tall tree, to 30 m, not branched on the basal portion, young branches light yellow, dense and soft yellow or black pubescent, but quickly becoming glabrous, buds slightly resinous; needles densely arranged, not parted above, oriented upward and to the side, to 30 mm long, acute to nearly prickly, occasionally somewhat emarginate, furrowed above and usually without stomata, 2 white stomatal bands beneath, each with 6–10 lines; cones cylindrical to conical, to 15 cm long, seed scales short tomentose, bract scales exserted, reflexed. MD 1925: Pl. 1, 4, 5; LA 39; CCE 17. Mountains in Bulgaria, on Mt. Olympus in Thessaly, Greece and on Thasos Island. 1883. Fig. 7 (Br). z6

A. bornmuelleriana Mattf. Intermediate between A. cephalonica and A. nordmanniana. Tall tree, resembling A. nordmanniana in appearance, branched to the ground, stem remains smooth for a long time, branches ascending at first, later horizontal, branches green at first, then brown, quite glabrous, buds acute-ovate, very resinous; needles very densely arranged, tough, not parted above, 25–35 mm long, round to emarginate, also acute on fruiting branches, 2 mm wide, often with stomatal bands above, these running to the middle of the needle, with 2 distinct white bands beneath, cones cylindrical, to 15 cm long and 5 cm thick, scales 25–40 mm wide, bract scales exserted and reflexed, to 10 mm long, drawn out to a long tip. LA 40; CCE 19. South coast of the Black Sea and Asiatic Turkey. Fig. 7 (Br.) z6

A. bracteata (D. Don) D. Don ex Poit. Bristlecone Fir. Tree, 20–30(–60) m high, in its native habitat usually broadly conical with an abruptly spindle-form tapering tip, bark smooth, reddish brown, furrowed at the base on old stems, branches densely arranged, the lower ones pendulous, young branches greenish, glabrous, buds spindle-form, to 2 cm long (!!), resin free; needles loosely arranged, pectinate, very stiff, 30–60 mm long, 2.5–3.5 mm wide, sharp acuminate, prickly, glossy green above, scarcely furrowed, with 2 silver-white stomatal bands beneath each with 8–10 lines; cones ovate, 7–10 cm long, reddish-brown and resinous, bract scales terminating with 3–5 cm long, stiff awns. BM 4740; DJH 4 (= A. venusta [Dougl.] K. Koch). Central California, coastal region, in the Santa Lucia Mts., in cool moist mountain valleys. 1853. Plate 20; Fig. 11 (Br), 13 (C). z7

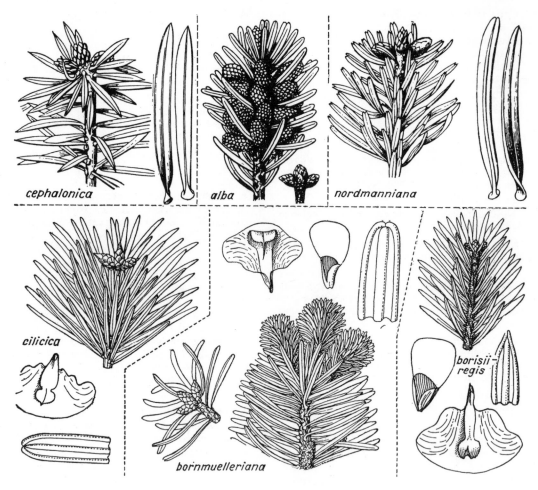

Fig. 7. European *Abies* species

A. cephalonica Loud. Grecian Fir. Tree, 15–30 m high, bark gray, smooth, splitting on older stems, crown conical, branches horizontal, very densely arranged, young branches glabrous, glossy light brown, buds ovate, reddish, very resinous; needles partly radial, partly also more or less parted, directed somewhat forward, the upper middle needles somewhat shorter, 20–30 mm long, 2 mm wide, stiff, generally tapering to a sharp, occasionally prickly tip, especially on young trees, glossy dark green above, with stomatal lines on the apex, 2 white stomatal bands beneath each with 5–6 lines, young needles more or less yellow-brown; cones cylindrical, 12–20 cm long, 4–5 cm thick, brown, very resinous, scales 25–35 mm wide, brown tomentose exterior, bract scales exserted and reflexed. FAA 71–75 (Br), 76 (C); BM 8691; DJH 19; OCC 10 (C); LA 23a (= *A. reginae-amaliae* Heldr.; *A. panachaica* Heldr.; *A. cephalonica* var. *apollinis* [Link] Beissn.). Mountains throughout Greece including the islands of Euboea and Cephalonia, subalpine. 1824. Plate 3; Fig. 7 (Br). z6

var. **apollinis** (Link) Beissn. No longer considered to differ from the species; according to Mattfeld, not like the type, differing in the branches of older trees.

'Acicularis'. Needles very fine, only 5–10 mm long and 0.5–1 mm thick (= *A. cephalonica acicularis* Sénéclauze). 1868. (EX)

'Aurea'. Young branches attractively gold-yellow. Introduced to the trade before 1867 by Sénéclauze. (VR)

'Latifolia'. Needles especially large, wider than the type and loosely arranged. Before 1867. (EX)

'Meyer's Dwarf'. Growth broad and low; without an apical shoot, branches and twigs shorter than those of the type; needles only 8–15 mm long. WM 104 (H) (= *A. cephalonica* 'Nana'). Before 1963. Origin unknown, but disseminated by Hillier, Winchester, England and Konijn, Reeuwijk, Holland. (VR)

'Robusta'. Very vigorous grower, compact, branches strong, long, ascending, the lower ones drooping, wide and distinctly spirally arranged, branches thick and stiff; needles very densely arranged, stiff, blue-white beneath; cones larger than those of the species, bract scales somewhat wider and longer. Originated in France around 1864. Frequently observed in seed beds. (VR)

'Rubiginosa'. New growth rust-brown (usually light green on the species), but very soon greening. Before 1867. Not unusual as chance seedling.

'Submutica'. Differing in cone development, only 10–12 cm long, bract scales in the apical and basal third exserted (normal), but completely hidden in the middle. Observed in France before 1888.

A. chensiensis Tiegh. Shensi Fir. Tree, 15 to 40(–60) m high, stem smooth, gray, young branches usually glabrous, rarely somewhat pubescent, yellow to gray-yellow, thick, buds ovate, somewhat resinous; needles usually curving upward, but with a distinct V-form groove between the 2 rows, 15–35 mm long, acute, obtuse or incised, widest above the middle, dark green and glossy above, with whitish or bluish stomatal bands beneath, cones oval-oblong, 7–10 cm long, green at first, cinnamon-brown when ripe, scales 2–3 cm wide, exterior tomentose, bract scales shorter than the seed scales and therefore hidden. CBJ 26; LA 7; CCE 23 (= *A. ernestii* [Rehd. & Wils.] Rehd.; *A. beissneriana* Rehd. & Wils. non Mott.). W. China, Shensi to the border with Burma. 1907. Plate 5. z6

A. cilicica (Ant. & Kotschy) Carr. Cilician Fir. Tree, 20–30 m high, branched from the ground up, crown narrowly conical, bark ash-gray, eventually deeply grooved, branches whorled and very densely arranged, lower branches horizontal to nodding, young branches at first short, thinly pubescent, but soon becoming glabrous, smooth and yellow-brown, buds acute-ovate, 3–4 mm long, somewhat to not resinous, scales somewhat protruding; needles rather loosely arranged, pointing upward on the upper branch surface with a V-form part, 20–35 mm long, only 1.5 mm wide, base twisted, "foot" broad shield-form, apex emarginate, light green above, with 2 white stomatal bands beneath, each having 7 lines; cones sessile or stalked, 20–30 cm long, 4–6 cm wide, cylindrical, red-brown, scales 4–5 cm wide, bract scales totally hidden, seeds obovoid, 13–14 mm long, brown-red, wings yellow-red. FAA 95 (H), 96, 98 (Br), 99 (C); DJH 5; LA 24; CCE 24 + 25. Asia Minor, Cilician Taurus Mts., 1300–2000 m, forming forests. 1853. Very attractive species. Not easy to identify. Plate 4; Fig. 13 (C). z6

A. coahuilensis see: **A. durangensis** var. **coahuilensis.**

A. concolor (Gord. et Glend.) Lindl. ex Hildebr. White Fir. Tree 25–40 m high, branches very low, whorled, spreading horizontally, bark light gray, rough, young branches gray-green to olive-green, nearly glabrous, buds globose, resinous; needles irregularly arranged, usually sickle shape upward curving, the middle row upward and forward pointing, linear, 40–60 mm long, 2–2.5 mm wide, acute to rounded, both sides more or less silvery bluish-green, somewhat convex in cross section to nearly flat, with 2 pale stomatal bands beneath; cones cylindrical, narrower on the apex, 7–12 cm long, greenish or purple at first, later brown, scales fan shaped, to 25 mm wide, bract scales hidden, seeds obovoid, wings oblique. DJH 6; BFN 159 (H); LA 35a. SW. USA to N. Mexico. 1872. One of the most popular, fast growing, hardy firs; tolerates drought. Plate 5; Fig. 11 (Br), 13 (C). z5

'Albospica'. Needles whitish on the new growth, later fully green. Before 1920.

'Argentea'. Habit as regular as the species; needles quite silver-white, like the silvery forms of *Picea pungens*. KN 19 (= *A. concolor* 'Candicans' Détriché). Before 1903. Occurs occasionally as a chance seedling.

'Aurea'. Vigorous habit, new growth gold-yellow in May, but later becoming silver-gray. Before 1906, by Ansorge.

'Brevifolia'. Vigorous grower; needles short, tough, obtuse, twice as wide as those of the type, apex obtuse. Originated by Ansorge before 1906.

'Butzii'. Needles directed forward, especially on the branch tips, totally different than the type. Found in a park in Kaliningrad, Russia by Butz around 1900. (EX)

'Compacta'. Dwarf form, habit irregularly shrubby, compact, branches and buds like the type, however the branches much more densely arranged, annual growth only 3–5 cm long; needles tougher, erect or sickle form, 25–40 mm long, blue pruinose. WM 105 (H) (= *A. concolor* f. *violaceae compacta* Beissn.; *A. concolor* var. *glauca* 'Compacta' Hillier). Known by 1891. (R)

var. concolor. The type of the species. Crown tighter, branches yellow to yellow-green, buds globose; needles parted, often sickle shaped; cones pale green or purple pruinose before ripening.

'Conica'. Dwarf form, broadly conical habit, branches and twigs very dense, horizontal; needles like the type, but only 20–40 mm long. Found by Slavin in the Durand Eastman Park in Rochester, N.Y. before 1930. (R)

'Fagerhult'. (Horstmann). Very slow grower, branches gracefully nodding; needles very long, light blue. 1977.

'Falcata'. All needles sickle shaped and curved upward. Found by Niemetz before 1905. (EX?)

'Fastigiata'. Columnar habit, branches very short and ascending. Found before 1889 in the nursery of Thibault & Keteleer in Sceaux, near Paris.

'Globosa'. Dwarf form, globose, slow growing, to 70 cm wide, branches short and regular; similar to 'Compacta', but the needles less blue. Found by Niemetz before 1905. (EX?)

'Green Globe'. Globose, dwarf habit, short needles, very densely branched. WM 107 (H). Found and introduced by Verkades Nursery, Wayne, N.Y., USA.

var. lowiana (Gord.) Lemm. Sierra Fir. Tree, always very straight, to 75 m high in its habitat, crown conical, bark very thick on older trees, grooved, in irregular scales on younger plants, branches stiffer and regularly whorled, young branches tending to gray-green, finely pubescent to glabrous, buds small, obtuse, very resinous; needles usually rather regular, 2 ranked, erect, parted in a V-form, upper row somewhat shorter than the others, 45–60 mm long, 2–2.5 mm wide, flat, apex round, occasionally also somewhat emarginate, furrowed above except for the apical third, dull green, with stomatal lines, with 2 blue-white stomatal bands beneath; cones like those of the type, but green before ripening. SN 98 (H); BFN 162 (H); LA 35b; CCE 26 (= *A. lowiana* Murray; *A. concolor* var. *lasiocarpa* Beissn.). SW. USA; Siskiyou Mts. (S. Oregon) and Sierra Nevada (California). z7

'Pendens'. The pendulous form of var. *lowiana* (= *A. lasiocarpa pendula* Carr.). Found in 1890 by Carrière in the Bois de Boulogne, Paris.

'Pendula'. Weeping form, stem usually columnar upright, branches and twigs hanging loosely. Lustgarden 1947: 174 h; JRHS 27: 418. Originated before 1896 by Simon Louis Frères; still present at Les Barres.

'Piggelmee' (Draijer 1972). Dwarf form, scarcely over 30 cm high; needles very densely arranged, 2–3 cm long, blue-gray. WM 108 (H). Developed from a witches'-broom.

'Pyramidalis'. Strong upright habit, but the branches and twigs

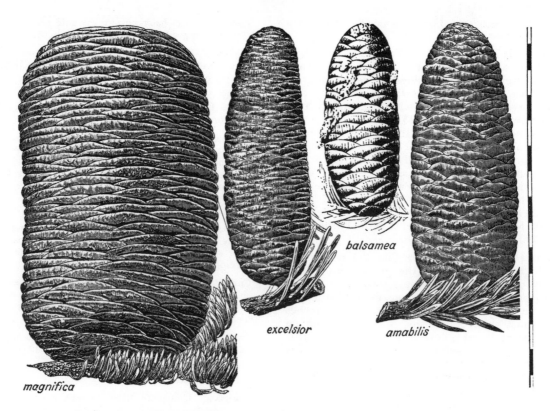

magnifica

excelsior   balsamea   amabilis

Fig. 8. **Abies** cones. *A. balsamea, A. amabilis, A. grandis* (= *A. excelsior*), *A. magnifica*

all ascending at an angle. Whitnal Park, Chicago, USA.

'Recurva'. Needles on the young twigs all bent backward to the branch, 35 mm long, 30 mm long on young twigs, but becoming smaller toward the branch tips, eventually only 5–10 cm long, sharply acuminate. Originated before 1904 by F. G. Grootendorst. (EX)

'Schrammii'. Like 'Violaceae', but the needles not bowed sickle form, otherwise quite straight and 2 ranked, needle rows at an acute angle to each other. Found by Schramm before 1913.

'Variegata'. White variegated form of var. *lowiana* (= *A. lowiana* var. *variegata* [Beissn.] Fitsch.). Originated in the Lobkowitz Nursery, Czechoslovakia, before 1891. (EX)

'Violaceae'. Needles a beautiful blue-white. FAA 22 (Br), 23 (C). 1879. Occurs frequently among the species in its native habitat. Usually grafted in the nursery.

'Wattezii'. Slow grower; needles pale yellow on new growth, generally turning silver-white. 1900. Developed from a mutation on *A. concolor* by D. Wattez in Bussum, Holland.

'Wattezee Prostrata'. Like the above form, but grafted from a side branch and therefore low and wide growing. A very promising cultivar (Welch).

'Wintergold'. Rather normal growth rate; needles yellow on new growth. Selected by G. Horstmann, Schneverdingen, W. Germany 1959.

A. delavayi Franch. Tall tree, regularly conical, crown eventually wide, cedar-like, young branches glossy red-brown, usually glabrous or pubescent in the furrows, buds thick ovate, red-brown, resinous; needles clustered above, but nearly radially arranged, 15–30 mm long, 2 mm wide, margin distinctly revolute (typical!),

midrib distinctly raised beneath, with 2 white stomatal bands, but usually covered by the revolute needle margins; cones black-violet, scales cuneate, bract scales somewhat exserted. Yunnan, West China, in the mountains. Introduction unclear but the true species is in cultivation (contested by Rehder, questioned by Craib; usually confused with the similar var. *forrestii*). z7

Key to *A. delavayi*
its varieties and some closely related species
(from Liu, expanded)

● Resin ducts in the margin;
    + Annual growth glabrous to nearly so; bract scales spathulate, rounded at the apex or notched;
        * Buds reddish-brown, resinous, branches glabrous to finely pubescent, cinnamon-brown; needles distinctly revolute on both margins; bract scales somewhat notched on the apex:
            A. delavayi
      ** Buds whitish resinous, branches glabrous to somewhat pubescent, red-brown; needles not revolute on the margin; bract scales rounded at the apex:
            A. delavayi var. *forrestii*
    ++ Annual growth densely pubescent, rust-red to purple-brown; bract scales oblong, triangular at the apex; buds yellowish resinous:
            A. delavayi var. *georgei*
●● ᐧ Resin ducts centrally located or lying near the margin;
    + Annual growth glabrous; leaf base yellowish;
        * Needles parted, usually emarginate at the

apex, usually 2 pointed at the apex on young trees:

> *A. fargesii*

** Needles densely packed, thick, often acute or somewhat obtuse:

> *A. sutchuenensis*

++ Annual growth densely pubescent; leaf petiole or base not yellowish;

* Bark not thin or exfoliating; needles emarginate or obtuse, without stomatal bands above:

> *A. fargesii* var. *faxoniana*

** Bark paper thin, exfoliating; needles acute to obtuse, with stomatal bands above:

> *A. squamata*

var. **delavayi**. Yunnan Fir. Tree, to 40 m, young branches finely pubescent at first, soon becoming glabrous, yellowish to brown, buds slightly resinous; needles densely packed, 15–25 mm long, apex round or truncate, occasionally slightly emarginate, margin sharply revolute, slightly parted above, the middle needles shorter and nearly parted; cones oblong 6–8 cm long, 3–4.5 cm wide, blue-black, scales 20–25 mm wide, bract scales spathulate, appendage prominent and reflexed (like *A. fargesii* Franch.). BM 9201; CCE 29; LA 8a; OCC 15 (= *A. fabri* [Mast.] D. R. Hunt). West China, Yunnan. 1901. Probably very hardy, but existence in cultivation unknown. z8

var. *faxoniana* see **A. fargesii** var. **faxoniana**

var. **forrestii** (C. C. Rogers) A. B. Jacks. Tree, 20–40 m high, similar to the type and var. *faxoniana*, conical as a young plant, young branches glossy rust-red, conspicuously rugose-warty, not furrowed, glabrous or with scattered pubescence, buds large, globose-ovate, thick, white pubescent; needle arrangement pectinate, with a V-form furrow, shorter and nearly vertically arranged on the upper side, occasionally distinctly backward curving, curved forward and upward on the underside, 15–20(–30) mm long, glossy dark green above, furrowed, with 2 wide, white stomatal bands beneath, each with 10 lines; cones cylindrical, 8–9 cm long, dark purple before ripening, bract scale tips straight, exserted. BM 9201; CC 76; CCE 29–31; OCC 15 (C) (= *A. delavayi* var. *smithii* [Vig. & Gauss.] Liu; *A. forrestii* C. Coltm.-Rogers). West China. 1910. Hardy and attractive, much valued in England. Plate 6. z7

var. **georgei** (Orr) Melville. Very close to var. *forrestii*, but mainly and distinctly differing in the cones with long, exserted bract scales, with the tips elongate caudate; the rust-brown pubescence on the young twigs is not as important a distinction. CBJ 10–12; LA 8a; CCE 24, 30, 31 (= *A. georgii* Orr; *A. ferreana* Bord. & Gauss.). W. China. 1923. z8

A. durangensis Martinez. Durango Fir. Tree 30–40 m high, bark reddish-brown, channeled, young branches opposite, reddish-brown, glabrous or finely pubescent in the furrows; needles 12–30 mm long, about 1 mm wide, obtuse, light green, furrowed above, with somewhat bluish stomatal bands beneath, 2 marginal resin ducts; cones cylindrical-oblong, to 10 cm long, light brown, about 3 cm thick, scales wider than high, bract scales about 16 mm long, oblanceolate, with mucronate tip, hidden by the seed scales. LA 8. Mexico. z9

var. **coahuilensis** (I. M. Johnst.) Mart. Coahuila Fir. Large tree, to 30 new growth allegedly resembling *Pseudotsuga*, young branches brown and short pubescent (like *A. religiosa*); needles more or less 2-ranked, linear, 15–25 mm long and 1–1.5 mm wide, acute or rounded, green above, only slightly bluish beneath, midrib indented on both sides, margin somewhat involute, resin ducts marginal; cones nearly cylindrical, about 10 cm long and 3 cm thick, similar to those of *A. religiosa*, but the bract scales hidden behind the relatively short, tomentose seed scales, somewhat eroded at the tips, the seed likewise smaller. LA 7 (= *A. coahuilensis* I. M. Johnst.). Mexico, Coahuila Province, in dense coniferous forests with *Pinus ayacahuite* and others. z9

A. equi-trojani Aschers. & Sint. Resembles *A. bornmuelleriana*, intermediate between *A. cephalonica* and *A. nordmanniana*. Tall tree, branches quite glabrous, distinctly yellow-brown, buds more or less resinous, with brown scales; needles very densely arranged, 15–25 mm long, distinctly tapered toward the apex, acute to obtuse, seldom emarginate, often with stomatal lines on the upper side, 2 white stomatal bands beneath; cones cylindrical-oblong, scales about 20 mm long and 30 mm wide, rounded above, bract scales markedly exserted and reflexed, with a wide 4 sided terminal blade, seed ovate, 10 mm long, broad winged (= *A. nordmanniana* ssp. *equi-trojani* [Aschers. & Sint.] Coode & Cullen). Only in the Ida Mts. (today the Kaz-Dagh), western Asia Minor, at 1300–1800 m. Few in cultivation (Göteborg Botanic Garden, Sweden). Plate 7, 20. z6

A. fargesii Franch. Farges Fir. Tree, 40 m high with 1.5 m diameter trunk, crown regularly conical, wide branched, later flat-crowned like *Cedrus libani*, young shoots glabrous or dark pubescent on short shoots, red-brown to purple, branches short and thick; needles 20–40 mm long, erect in 2 or more horizontal rows, the needles above only half as long as the needles beneath, apex emarginate to 2-pointed, dark green and furrowed above, with 2 white stomatal bands beneath, each with 9–10 lines; cones 5–8 cm long, purple when young, later red-brown to gray, scarcely resinous, scales 15–20 mm wide, bract scales somewhat exserted and reflexed, seeds 5 mm long, with 7 mm long wings. CBJ 26; SN 142 (H); LA 9a. Central and West China; NW. Hupeh and E. Szechwan Provinces. 1901. One of the most attractive, hardy and easily cultivated Chinese Firs. Plate 7; Fig. 12 (C). z6

var. **faxoniana** (Rehd. & Wils.) Liu. Tree, 20–40 m high, crown conical, bark eventually dark gray, channeled, branches pubescent, spreading horizontally, short, gray, channeled, thinly pubescent, young branches gray-brown, dense rust-red shaggy pubescent, buds ovate, dark red, very resinous; needles in 2 irregular rows, dense, short above, 10–30 mm long, usually sharply notched, seldom obtuse, margin slightly or not involute, glossy dark green above, furrowed, with 2 narrow, chalk-white stomatal bands beneath; cones sessile, oval-oblong, 5–8 cm long, truncate above, violet when young, very resinous, scales 15–20 mm wide, bract scales somewhat exserted, straight or reflexed. CCE 29; LA 9b; FAA 46 (Br); LF 15 (= *A. faxoniana* Rehd. & Wils.). China, Szechwan, Kansu, and Yunnan Provinces in the mountains at 3500 m. 1910. Hardy. Plate 5. z6

A. firma S. & Z. Japanese Fir. Tree, to 40–50 m high in its habitat (the highest and most stately fir in Japan), in cultivation, however, seldom over 20 m, crown regularly conical, bark dark gray, eventually rough, scaly, branches spreading horizontally, young branches light gray-yellow, furrowed, lightly pubescent in the furrows, buds small, only slightly resinous or not so; needle arrangement comb-like (pectinate), tough and stiff, to 35 mm long, widest in the middle, sharply 2-pointed on young plants, on older plants obtuse or emarginate, dark green above and furrowed, with a few stomatal lines on the apex, light green beneath, with 2 indistinct, gray-green stomatal bands; cones cylindrical; 10–12 cm long, yellowish before ripening, scales to 25 mm wide, bract scales exserted, but not reflexed. FAA 38 to 39 (Br), 43, 45 (C); DHJ 8; OCC 17 (C); LA 2; CCE 32–34; KIF 1: 10 (= *A. momi* Sieb.; *A. bifida* S. & Z.). Japan. 1861. Suited only for large parks. Needs plenty of moisture in summer; damaged in spring frost. Fig. 9 (Br), 10 (C) z6

A. fraseri (Pursh) Poir. Fraser's Fir. Small tree, usually 9–12 m high, occasionally to 20 m, crown slender conical to columnar, young bark smooth and with resin blisters, eventually scaly, young branches gray to yellow-brown, densely short haired (hairs longer than on the similar *A. balsamea* but twisted, not straight), buds small, globose to ovate, very resinous; needles parted above, only 12–20 mm long (very short!), 1 mm wide, apex emarginate or round, flat, furrowed above, dark green, often with stomatal lines on the apex, with 2 wide, chalk-white stomatal bands beneath, each with 8–12 lines (the similar *A. balsamea* has only 4–8 lines in each stomatal band!); cones small, ovate, only 3–6 cm long, 2.5–3 cm wide, purple, scales like those of *A. balsamea,* but the bract scales gold-brown, markedly exserted and reflexed (!). FAA 35 (C); OCC 18 (C); CB 2, 13; LA 9. Mountains of SE. USA. 1811. Attractive as a young tree; however short-lived. z5

'**Prostrata**'. Dwarf form, appressed to the ground, branches spreading widely, can reach a height of 1.5 m with a width of 4 m; needles like the type. DB 1969: 196 (= *A. fraseri* 'Horizontalis' Hort.). 1916. Found in the Kelsey-Highlands Nursery, East Boxford, Mass., USA.

A. grandis (Dougl. ex D. Don) Lindl. Giant Fir. Fast growing tree, 30–70 (occasionally 90–100) m high, largest of all the *Abies* species, crown an attractive conical form, branches bowed outward, ascending at the tips, bark smooth, but with many resin blisters, eventually deep brown and grooved, young branches thin, olive-green to brownish, quite finely pubescent, buds small, globose, glossy resinous; needles always with pectinate arrangement, often much shorter on the upper side, 20–35 mm long, 2 mm wide, notched at the apex, flat, always furrowed above, bright glossy green, without stomata, underside with 2 white stomatal bands, each with 7–10 lines; cones cylindrical, 5–10 cm long, greenish-brown when young, to 4 cm thick, scales 25–30 mm wide, entire, bract scales hidden and very small, seeds angular, about 10 mm long, wings keeled, nearly 10 mm wide and 7 mm long. FAA 27 and 28 (Br); DJH 9; SN 38 (H) (= *A. excelsior* Franco). N. America; northern Pacific coast, inland to N. Montana and East Oregon. Likes moist soil. Fig. 8 (C), 11 (Br). z6

> The Monograph of the Genus *Abies,* T.-S. Liu, recommends retaining the name *A. grandis.*

'**Aurea**'. Needles gold-yellow. Originated in 1891 by Hesse-Weener. (EX)

'**Compacta**'. Dwarf form, needles like the type, but only 10–15 mm long. Originated before 1891 by Hesse. (EX)

'**Pendula**'. Weeping form, branches distinctly pendulous. Originated by Späth-Berlin before 1896. (EX)

A. guatemalensis Rehd. Guatemalan Fir. Tree, to 35 m, young branches reddish-brown, pubescent; needles more or less parted, 15–30 mm long, to 2 mm wide, with 2 distinct stomatal bands beneath, obtuse and emarginate, 2 marginal resin ducts; cones oblong-cylindrical, to 10 cm long and 5 cm wide, bract scales cuneate-obovate, hidden behind the seed scales, pubescent on the margin, seeds light brown. LA 33. W. Guatemala, in the mountains. z9

A. hickeli Flous & Gaussen. Tree, 25–35 m high, young branches reddish-brown, glabrous or becoming so, strong side shoots with pubescent furrows; needles spreading widely, more or less 2 ranked, 12–30 mm long, 1.5 mm wide, with distinct stomatal bands beneath, obtuse and emarginate at the apex, usually with 4–8 (seldom 10) resin ducts, some marginal, some in the center; cones oblong-cylindrical, brown, 7 cm long, 3 cm thick, bract scales oblong-lanceolate, drawn out to an obtuse apex and protruding past the seed scales. LA 30. Mexico, in the mountains of Oaxaca, located between *A. religiosa* and *A. guatemalensis.* z9

A. holophylla Maxim. Manchurian Fir. Tree, to 30 m, occasionally to 50 m in its habitat, similar to *A. alba* and *A. firma* in habit, buds small, thin, slightly pubescent, young branches light yellow, slightly furrowed, glabrous; needles dense, comblike arrangement (pectinate) beneath, 25–40 mm long, shorter on the branch tips, 2 mm wide, with V-form furrow on the upper side, stiff, strong, leathery, apex sharp and prickly on young plants, flat above, glossy green, lightly channeled, with 2 dull green stomatal bands beneath, each with 6–8 lines; cones cylindrical, 12–15 cm long and to 4 cm wide, green when young, brown and very resinous when ripe, scales 30–50 mm wide, half-moon shaped, bract scales hidden, very small, seeds cuneate, about 10 mm long, wings 13 mm long. CBI 13, 14; NF 1: 4; LA 3; CCE 37–39. Manchuria, Korea. 1905. Plate 8. z6

A. homolepis S. & Z. Nikko Fir. Tree, about 30(–40) m high, bark gray, scaly, crown regular conical, branches stout, regular and stiff spreading, frequently developing a wide, cedar-like crown in the open, young branches deeply furrowed, light yellow-brown, glossy, glabrous, buds oval-conical, obtuse, resinous; upper needles directed forward and sideways, with a broad V-furrow, parted on the branch underside and forming a right angle, outer needles 20–30 mm long and 1.5–2 mm wide, the middle needles shorter and stiff, dark green above, glossy, with 2 white stomatal bands beneath, usually short 2 pointed or obtuse on the apex; cones cylindrical, 7–10 cm long and 2.5–4 cm wide, purple when young (occasionally green), brown when ripe, scales fan shaped, very thin, about 20 mm wide, bract scales enclosed, half as long as the scales, seeds cuneate, 7–8 mm long, wings rectangular. FAA 37 (Br); DJH 10; OCC 20; LA 4; CCE 37–39; KIF 1: 12 (= *A. brachyphylla* Maxim.). Japan. 1870. Tolerates and thrives in shade as a young plant. Plate 8; Fig. 9 (Br), 12 (C). z5

'**Scottiae**'. Dwarf form, probably propagated from a witches'-broom. Originated by Mrs. A. H. Scott in Media, Penn., USA. Before 1932.

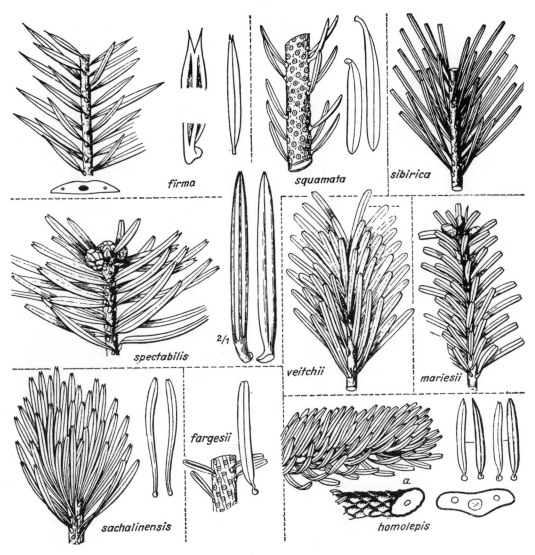

firma   *squamata*   *sibirica*

spectabilis   2/1   *veitchii*   *mariesii*

fargesii

sachalinensis   *a.*   *homolepis*

Fig. 9. Asiatic *Abies* species

f. **tomomi** Rehd. Crown more slender than the type, sparsely branched; needles shorter, only 8–15 mm long, by exception to 20 mm. JRHS 76: 1. Originated in the USA before 1909. (R)

var. **umbellata** (Mayr) Wils. Branches, buds and needles hardly different from those of the type, cones however, greenish-yellow before ripening, flat on the apex with a more acute middle, bract scales exserted on the base. OCC 20 (C); LA 44 (= *A. umbilicata* Mayr; *A. umbellata* Mayr): Occurs with the type in Japan.

A. × **insignis** Carr. ex Bailly (*A. nordmanniana* × *A. pinsapo*). Tree, to 30 m high, regular conical habit, straight, very vigorous, bark ash-gray or whitish, young branches glossy rust-brown, pubescent at first, later glabrous, branches whorled, bowed slightly upward, densely needled, buds oval-conical, thick, short, resinous; needles especially dense on the upper side, spreading sideways beneath, linear, straight or sickle shaped, thick, leathery, 20–30 mm long, 2–3 mm thick, drawn out in a short, twisted petiole, with obtuse or

rounded, seldom incised apexes on the lower branches, bright green above, glossy, only very slightly furrowed, with a few stomatal lines on the apex, 2 whitish stomatal bands beneath, very cuneate and with a thick margin; cones nearly like those of *A. pinsapo*, scales swollen, irregular in form, bract scales hidden. FAA 78 (H), 79–84 (Br), 85–86 (C); OCC 21; LA 41. Developed as a hybrid around 1850 in the Renault nursery in Bulguéville, France. z6

Including several other hybrid forms:

'Andreana'. Intermediate hybrid, needles loosely arranged, in several rows, all erect, the middle ones just as long as the side needles, about 20 mm, ascending, green above, with 2 white stomatal bands beneath (= *A. andreana* Mottet). Developed by Mottet. 1878.

'Beissneriana'. More akin to *A. nordmanniana*, needles of uneven length, in few rows, less stiff, erect, seldom directed upward, those in the middle on the upper side shorter than the others (= *A. beissneriana* Mottet). Developed by Mottet in 1878.

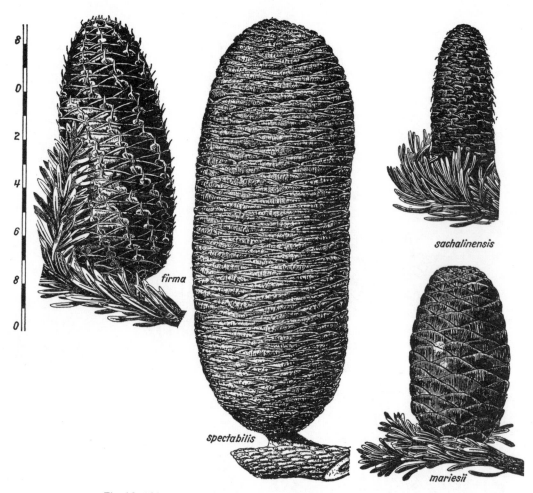

Fig. 10. **Abies** cones. *A. firma, A. spectabilis, A. mariesii, A. sachalinensis*

'Kentiana'. Intermediate form, young branches green to brown, with few brown hairs; needles more or less like those of *A. pinsapo*, very dense and arranged in many rows, all directed upward and of rather equal length, 20–25 mm, rather flat and green above, with distinct midrib beneath and 2 whitish stomatal bands (= *A. kentiana* Mottet). Developed by Mottet in 1878.

'Mastersiana'. Resembling *A. pinsapo*, needles in many rows, the side needles erect, the middle needles only slightly oriented upward and directed forward at the branch tips, 10–15 mm long (= *A. mastersiana* Mottet). Developed by Mottet in 1878.

'Pendula'. Branches very pendulous and nearly appressed to the stem. Found by J. do Amaral Franco in the Sierra de Sintra, Portugal before 1950.

'Speciosa'. Intermediate hybrid, like *A. nordmanniana* in habit; needles dense and radially arranged like *A. pinsapo*, short, only 10–15 mm long (= *A. nordmanniana speciosa* Bailly). Developed by Croux in Sceaux, France in 1871.

A. kawakamii (Hayata) Ito. Formosan Fir. Tree, 15–35 m high in its habitat, crown conical, buds not resinous, young branches usually very pubescent, yellowish, deeply furrowed; needles 15–25 mm long, directed forward, except for the upper row which is curved upward, narrowly acuminate or 2-pointed, green on both sides, the stomatal bands on the underside only faintly visible; cones cylindrical-ovate, 6–12 cm long, about 4 cm wide, round at the apex, purple-violet, scales triangular-ovate, bract scales spathulate, totally enclosed, seeds blackish, 7 mm long. CBJ 15; LA 6; CCE 40 (= *A. mariesii* var. *kawakamii* Hayata). In the mountains of Taiwan. 1916. Plate 7. z6

A. koreana Wils. Korean Fir. Tree, to about 15 m high, bark rough on older trees, branches only thinly pubescent, yellowish, later glabrous and reddish, buds thin resinous, nearly globose, red-brown; needles clustered, 10–20 mm long, usually becoming somewhat wider toward the branch tips, round or emarginate apex, but acute on young plants, glossy above, white except for the green midrib beneath; cones cylindrical except for the short tapered tip, 4–7 cm long, about 2.5 cm thick, violet-purple before ripening, but also green, seed scales about 20 mm wide, bract scales as long as the seed scales, but usually somewhat exserted and reflexed, seeds obovoid, 10 mm long, violet, wings purple. DJH 11; BMns 40; CBJ 16, 17; LA 12. Korea; in the mountains in the southern part of the country. Fruits abundantly, even as young plants. Plate 9. z6

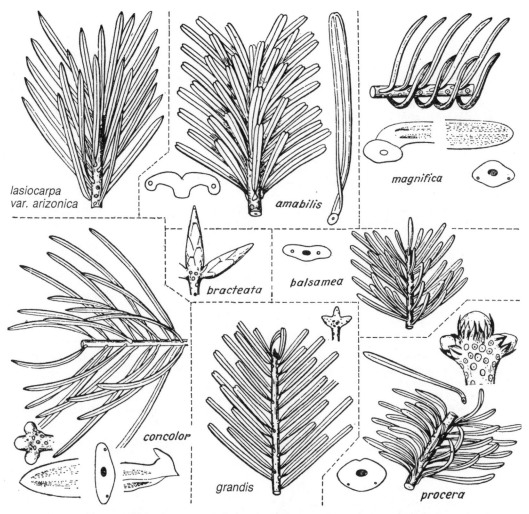

Fig. 11. North American *Abies* species (*Lasiocarpa* var. *arizonica, grandis*)

'Blauer Pfiff'. Needles blue-green rather than green. Developed through cobalt treatments of the seed, by K. Wittboldt-Müller, 309 Verden-Eitze. (*A. koreana* 'Glauca', from Kromhout & Zonen, Hazerswoude, Holland, is likewise blue-green.)

'Blue Standard'. Habit normal, like the type, but selected for its deep violet cones, darker than on the other cultivars. Introduced in 1962 by J. D. Zu Jeddeloh, 2905 Jeddeloh, Oldenburg. Plate 20.

'Brevifolia'. A rather slow grower, annual growth 5–7 cm, conical, dense; needles much more loosely arranged than those of the type, stiffer, 6–10 mm long, 2 mm wide, dull green above, gray-white beneath; cones much smaller than those of the type, violet. Originated by Jeddeloh about 1965.

'Compact Dwarf'. Dwarf form, flat growing, branches spreading horizontally, without a dominant leader, growth slow, only 5–8 cm per year, does not produce cones. OCC 23; WM 110 (H) (= *A. koreana compacta; A. koreana nana* Hort.). A beautiful plant grows in the Blijdenstein Pinetum, Holland. Plants sold as dwarf don't necessarily always remain so since a dominant leader is often developed which then grows normally.

'Flava'. Fully ripe cones green, eventually yellowish-brown, 5–6 cm long, seed wings dark brown (= *A. koreana* var. *flava*

Browicz). Originated from imported seed in the Kornik Arboretum, Poland in 1933.

'Horstmanns Silberlocke' (G. Horstmann). Habit normal, like the type, needles however, along the entire branch length hemispherical, upward curving and loosely twisted, so that the silver-white underside shows, general impression a beautful silver. KN Plate 1. The oldest plant is 1.5 m high (G. Horstmann, Schneverdingen, W. Germany). A very promising form.

'Piccolo'. Broad, flat habit, oldest plant 1.5 m wide, but only 30 cm high; needles more widely spaced than those of the type. WM 2E (Br). Selection of Konijn.

f. sikokiana Nakai ex Vig. & Gams. Cones only 4 to 4.5 cm long, 2 cm wide, apex of the bract scales smaller; seeds only 4 mm long. Not in cultivation.

'Silver Show' (Willboldt-Müller, Verden 1969). Needles very twisted, showing the silvery-white underside, remains whitish the entire year, and on older plants.

A. lasiocarpa (Hook.) Nutt. Alpine Fir. Tree, to 30 m, occasionally to 40 m, crown narrowly conical to nearly columnar, young bark smooth, silver-gray, eventually gray or gray-brown, furrowed, young branches ash-gray, short haired, seldom glabrous, buds small, ovate, very resinous, needles brush-like upward pointing or irregularly parted, loosely arranged, often widely spaced, 25–40 mm long and 1.5 mm wide, round or acute, occasionally emarginate, upper surface pale blue-green, furrowed, with 2 stomatal bands, 2 silver-gray stomatal bands beneath, each with 5–6 lines (one of the few species with stomatal bands the total length of the upper needle surface!!); cones cylindrical, erect, in groups of several together, 6–10 cm long, flattened or concave, dark purple when young, scales 20–25 mm wide, bract scales hidden. SPa 38–39; BM 9600; RWF 1; OCC 24; LA 38a; CCE 43 (= *A. subalpina* Engelm.). N. America; Alaska to Oregon, Utah and New Mexico, only in the mountains near the tree line together with *Picea engelmannii*. 1863. An excellent, fragrant park tree, but only in cool, moist climates. Very tolerant of a heavy snow load. Plate 6; Fig. 13 (C). z2

'Argentea'. The silver needled form of var. *arizonica* (= *A. lasiocarpa arizonica argentea* André). Introduced by Purpus about 1900.

var. arizonica (Merr.) Lemm. Cork Fir. Medium tall or small tree, differing from the type in the thick, cream-white, corky elastic bark, branches glabrous or pubescent, yellowish-brown; needle arrangement more pectinate, frequently notched on the apex, more bluish-green above, bluish-white beneath with 2 white stomal bands, to 45 mm long; cones about 5 cm long and 2 cm thick, scales much wider than long, bract scales exserted to about the midpoint on the scale. OCC 26 (C); LA 38b; CCE 42 + 43 (= *A. arizonica* Merriam). Arizona, in the mountains from 1200–2600 m. Very attractive fir for its needle color. Fig. 11 (Br), 13 (C).

'Beissneri'. Dwarf form with sickle-shaped needles, partly twisted, with the blue-white underside showing (= *A. subalpina* var. *beissneri* Hesse). Originated by H. A. Hesse, Weener, W. Germany before 1901. (EX?)

'Coerulescens'. Needles intensely bluish, 20–35 mm long (= *A. subalpina* var. *coerulescens* Froebel ex Beissn.). Found in a nursery seedbed by Froebel in Zurich, Switzerland before 1891. (EX?)

'Compacta'. Broadly conical dwarf form, branches very dense and ascending, buds grouped in 3's, yellow-brown, attractive; needles a very attractive silver-blue, densely arranged, erect and directed somewhat forward, curved, 15–25 mm long, 1–1.5 mm wide, with distinct white stomatal bands beneath. WDw 28; WM 2A (Br) + 113 (H) (= *A. arizonica compacta* Grootend.; *A. arizonica glauca compacta* Hort.). Originated about 1927 by J. Boer in Boskoop, Holland; one of the most common cultivars in cultivation today. Plate 6.

'Conica'. Dwarf form, compact habit, broadly conical, annual growth about 5–6 cm, branches ascending, glabrous or also finely pubescent, buds 3 mm long, light brown; needles very densely arranged, very thin and fine, about 25 mm long and 1 mm wide, curved, directed forward, gray-green, stomatal bands not so distinctly visible as 'Compacta' (= *A. lasiocarpa* var. *conica* Hornibr.). Originated in the Arnold Arboretum from seed collected in Colorado about 1873.

var. lasiocarpa. The type of the species. Tree, to 30 m high, bark rather thin, silver-gray on young trees, later more ash-gray, branches ash-gray to gray-brown, short pubescent; needles acute or slightly incised, pale blue-green, with 2 white stomatal bands beneath; cones about 9 cm long and 3.5 cm wide, scales nearly circular, bract scales hidden. Alaska to Oregon and New Mexico. 1963.

'Pendula'. Like the type, but with branches pendulous (= *A. subalpina pendula* Ordnung). Developed before 1909 by Von Ordnung in Eisenberg, Bohemia, W. Germany.

A. magnifica Murr. Californian Red Fir. Tree, to 60 m high in its habitat, crown narrowly conical, branches densely arranged in regular, horizontal whorls, stiff, short, young branches brownish, short pubescent, buds small, ovate, resinous on the apex, usually surrounded by needles; needles not parted on the upper branch, erect or somewhat reflexed, needles on the underside with a sharp sideways bend and directed downward, 20–40 mm long, 1 mm wide, obtuse on the apex, cuneate on both sides, therefore rectangular in cross section (the similar *A. procera* has furrowed needles!), gray-green, with stomata on all 4 sides, but more distinct on the underside and with 4–5 stomatal lines on each side; cones cylindrical, 15–22 cm long, 7–9 cm thick, violet when young, brown when ripe, scales fan-shaped, 30–35 mm wide, entire, bract scales enclosed. BM 8552; OCC 27 (C); DJH 12, Pl. 4; SPa. 52–53; LA 28; CCE 45 + 49 (= *A. nobilis magnifica* Mast.). Oregon to California, in the mountains from 1500–3500 m. Slow growing; winter hardy in protected areas. Fig. 8 (C), 11 (Br) z6

'Argentea'. Needles blue-white. Before 1909. (EX)

'Glauca'. Needles conspicuously blue-green. Before 1891.

'Nana'. Dwarf form, habit low and very wide. Origin unknown (USA?).

'Prostrata'. Shrubby habit, without a stem, branches spreading along the ground; needles blue-green. Originated by Jurissen, Naarden, Holland in 1904. (EX)

var. shastensis Lemm. Tree, not as tall as the type, cones shorter, bract scales exserted and more or less reflexed. OCC 28 (H) (= *A. nobilis robusta* Mast.). N. America; mountain cliffs on the Pacific coast. (R)

var. xanthocarpa Lemm. Small tree, cones 10–12 cm long, golden-yellow while developing. Subalpine region of Mount Shasta and Mount Whitney, southern Sierra Nevada.

A. mariesii Mast. Marie's Fir. Tree, to about 25 m high, stem to 60 cm thick, bark smooth, light gray, rough on the base of older trunks, branches erect, stiff, the basal ones inclined downward, the uppermost ascending, branches rust-brown, densely pubescent, buds globose, small, resinous; needles clustered on the upper side, the center row nearly appressed and directed forward, the outermost longer and more erect, linear, somewhat wider on the apical half, rounded to 2 pointed on the apex, 15–22 mm long, to 2 mm wide, glossy dark green above, furrowed and without stomatal lines, 2 white stomatal bands beneath; cones elliptic-cylindrical, 6–10 cm long, 4–5 cm wide, purple-violet when young, seed scales nearly 25 mm wide, entire, bract scales hidden, seeds obovate, 10 mm long. CB 2, 18; BM 8089 and n.s. 45; LA 5; KIF 1: 14. Central Japan, in the mountains; Taiwan. 1879. Plate 9, Fig. 9 (Br), 10 (C). z6

A. marocana Trabut. Moroccan Fir. Small tree, crown conical, young branches gray-yellow, glabrous, slightly furrowed, buds ovate, resinous; needles similar to those of *A. pinsapo*, but wider, longer (10–15 mm), but not so thick, acute, not twisted at the base, green, with 1–2 stomatal lines on the upper side, whitish stomatal bands beneath, resin ducts on the epidermis of the needle underside (definite distinction from *A. Pinsapo*, in which the resin ducts lie in the interior); cones cylindrical, tapering to both ends, irregular in form, about 15 cm

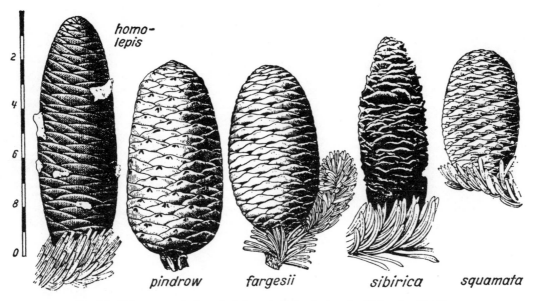

homo-
lepis

pindrow   fargesii   sibirica   squamata

Fig. 12. **Abies** cones. *A. fargesii, A. homolepis, A. pinsapo, A. sibirica, A. squamata*

long, to 6 cm thick, light brown in the middle, scales 28–35 mm wide, bract scales linear-spathulate, only half as long as the seed scales, seeds 12 mm long, brown. OCC 29 (H), 30 (C); LA 25b; CCE 46 (= *A. pinsapo* ssp. *marocana* [Trabut] Cetallos & Bolanos). Found in Morocco in the mountains south of Tetuan by Joly in 1906. (VR) Plate 12. z6

A. nebrodensis (Lojac.) Mattei. Sicilian Fir. Tree, scarcely over 15 m high, crown broadly conical, later flat and spreading, trunk unbranched on the basal portion, young branches glabrous, buds resinous; needles very densely arranged, erect, pointing upward and outward, 10–12 mm long, obtuse, with 2 white stomatal bands beneath, each with 6–10 lines; cones short stalked, small, 2.5–3.5 cm long and nearly as wide, cylindrical-elliptic, scales ovate-rhombic, 17 mm long, bract scales exserted, linear-spathulate with a long apex. LA 20; CCE 47 (= *A. pectinata* var. *nebrodensis* Lojac.). N. Sicily; native stands nearly completely eradicated. The rarest European *Abies* species; thriving well and fruiting in the Hillier Arboretum. Plate 10. 26

A. nephrolepis (Trautv.) Maxim. Manchurian Fir. Tree, 15–18 m high, crown densely branched, trunk 30–40 cm thick, bark smooth, gray, young branches yellowish, brown pubescent, buds ovate, red-brown, slightly resinous; needles not parted on the upper side, 10–22(–35) mm long, about 2 mm wide, obtuse or distinctly 2-pointed, flat, furrowed above, occasionally with 2 stomatal bands beneath; cones 6–7 cm long, 2 cm thick, with prominent apexes, reddish at first, then violet-black, eventually brown, scales half-moon shaped, 18–20 mm wide, bract scales totally enclosed, seeds with 7 mm long, purple wings. LA 13 (= *A. sibirica* var. *nephrolepis* Trautv.; *A. gracilis* Komar.). E. Siberia, Korea, N. China. 1908.

f. **chlorocarpa** Wils. Differing only in the green color of the young cones. Korea. 1918.

A. nordmanniana (Stev.) Spach. Nordman Fir. Tree, 25–30(–50) m, densely branched from the ground up, branches whorled, regularly arranged, lower branches widely spaced to drooping, trunk straight, bark black-gray, young branches green-yellow, glossy, pubescent or glabrous, buds ovate, resin free; needles dense, arranged brush-like, not parted or only parted on the underside of short branches, 20–30 mm long and 2–2.5 mm wide, base distinctly widened shield-like and twisted, apex round and emarginate, furrowed above, very glossy, only the underside with 2 silver-white stomatal bands; cones 15(–20) cm long, 5 cm thick, greenish when young, dark brown when ripe, scales broadly conical, entire, bract scales exserted and reflexed. FAA 48 (Br), 53 (C); DJH 13; SN 10(H); BFN 117(H); LA 21; CCE 48 + 49. Caucasus Mountains; developing forests with *Picea orientalis*. 1840. Plate 11, Fig. 7(Br). z5

'**Albospicata**'. Young branches with white tips. Originated before 1898 by Gebbers, Wiesenburg-Mark, Germany. (EX?)

'**Aurea**'. Needles gold-yellow. In cultivation before 1891. (EX)

'**Aureospica**'. Needles always gold-yellow on the apical third. Originated by Hesse, Weener, Germany before 1891. (EX)

'**Aureovariegata**'. Needles of some branches partly or totally golden-yellow. Found in the Diedorf Forstgarten near Augsburg, W. Germany by Ganchofer before 1903.

'**Brevifolia**'. Dwarf form, compact conical habit, branches contorted; needles distinctly shorter, wider, more 2 ranked. Before 1867 in France. (EX)

'**Compacta**'. Remaining low, compact conical habit, branches upright, very short and thick; needles quite variable, usually 4–5 mm long and 1 mm wide, but also 20–30 mm long and 2 mm wide (= *A. nordmanniana nana compacta* Sénécl.) Originated as a seedling by Sénéclauze, 1867.

'**Erecta**'. Branches narrowly ascending. Originated before 1907 by F. Pittet in Lausanne, Switzerland. (EX)

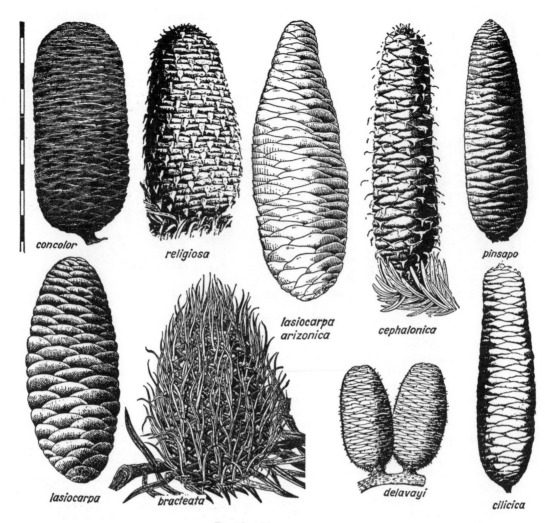

Fig. 13. **Abies** cones.
A. concolor, A. religiosa, A. lasiocarpa with var. arizonica, A. bracteata, A. delavayi, A. cilicica, A. pinsapo

'Glauca'. Needles very luxurious, blue-green. Occurs occasionally as a chance seedling.

'Golden Spreader'. Dwarf form, branches outspread, light brown, annual growth 4–5 cm; needles slightly curved, 12–25 mm long, 1.8–2 mm wide, light yellow above, yellowish-white beneath, with 2 indistinct stomatal bands. Originated in the nursery of S. N. Schoots in Culemborg, Holland before 1961.

'Horizontalis'. Dwarf form, broad habit, without a central leader, all branches and twigs horizontal. Originated in the nursery of Voudrey-Evrard in Misacours, Vosges, France before 1887.

'Jensen'. Strong growing, weeping form with short, 10–18 mm long needles (= A. nordmanniana pendula Jensen). Originated by Asger M. Jensen before 1944 in Holmstrup, Denmark.

f. macrolepis Vig. & Gauss. Needles often 30–35 mm long; seed scales triangular-ovate, 4 cm long and wide, seeds 15 mm long, wings 20 mm long and 15 mm wide. Not in cultivation.

'Pendula'. Weeping form, vigorous upright habit, branches hanging nearly vertically along the stem. Has occurred in cultivation several times, 1847 by Maurice Young in Milford, Surrey, England; and before 1869 in the Courtois Nursery in Clamart, France.

'Procumbens'. Very slow growing, without a stem, the few branches growing along the ground. Originated in the Kornik Arboretum, Poland in 1834, presumably grafted from a side branch.

'Refracta'. Compact conical habit, vigorous; needles oriented upward, white underside very visible (= A. nordmanniana speciosa Hort.). 1867 in France. Occurs occasionally as a chance seedling.

'Robusta'. Strong grower, branches compact, thick; needles very densely arranged, blue-green, thickish, occasionally twisted and radially arranged. Found in the Sénéclauze Nursery, France, in 1866.

'Tortifolia'. Needles 25–30 mm long, not evenly directed forward, very sickle-shaped and bowed inward, irregular and open. Found in the garden of W. B. Cuttery in Oaksdale, Long Island, N.Y., 1920.

A. numidica De Lannoy ex Carr. Algerian Fir. Tree, 15–20 mm high, crown densely branched, regularly conical, branches in whorls, heavily branched, horizontally arranged, young branches yellowish green or brown, glabrous, glossy, buds large, ovate, not resinous or only somewhat when young, scales fit loosely, light brown;

needles very densely arranged, directed upward, brush-like, but also in 2 rows on older trees, 15–20 mm long, thick, stiff, flat, twisted at the base, furrowed above, deep green, few stomatal lines at the apex, with 2 white stomatal bands beneath, each with 7–10 lines; cones erect, cylindrical, 15–20 cm long, 4–6 cm thick, brown, seed scales with wide, reflexed margin, bract scales enclosed, seeds 12 mm long, wings 18 mm long. CB 2, 21; DJH 14; LA 26; CCE 50 + 51 (= *A. baborensis* Coss.). E. Algeria, in the Babor Mts., and west to Constantine. 1862. Plate 11. z6

'Glauca'. Needles shorter, wider, distinctly blue-green, with few stomatal lines above. Found before 1909 in the Les Barres Arboretum, France.

'Lawrenceville'. Dwarf form, needles especially light green. Developed from a witches'-broom in the USA.

'Pendula'. Slow growing form, but 3–4 m high with age, stem curved in a bow and compressed, branches and twigs stiff, outspread-nodding, very densely branched; needles like those of the species. CCE 51.

A. oaxacana Martinez. See the description of the other Mexican species *A. hickeli*, from which this differs in the glabrous branches, somewhat wider needles with truncate or 2-pointed apex and the 8–10, occasionally 11–12 resin ducts; cones 10–12 cm long, 5 cm wide, bract scales exserted. CCe 51. Mexico; Oaxaca and Guerrero Provinces, in the mountains. z9

A. pardei Gaussen. Pardé Fir. Very similar to *A. numidica*, but with young branches distinctly black pubescent, buds very resinous; needles 15–28 mm long, apex rounded or slightly acuminate, not very densely arranged; cones 18–20 cm long, bract scales somewhat exserted, but not reflexed. BMns 242 (as *A. pinsapo* var. *vel hybrida*); LA 22; CCE 52. Native habitat unknown, presumably N. Africa. Plate 12. z6

A. pindrow Royle. West Himalayan Fir. Tall tree, to 60 m in its habitat, trunk 1.8–2.4 m thick, crown narrowly conical in cultivation, young bark smooth and gray, later becoming gray-brown and furrowed, young branches not furrowed, yellowish-gray, glossy, soon becoming glabrous, buds globose, very resinous, bluish at the base; needles narrow linear, 30–60 mm long, 1.5–2 mm wide, acute or unevenly 2 pointed (young plants only acute), bright green above, gray-green beneath with 2 dull stomatal bands, each with 5–6 lines, thin and loosely arranged on the upper side of the twig, erect in all directions, side needles horizontal, parted on the underside; cones cylindrical, 12–17 cm long, 6–7 cm thick, dark purple at first, eventually brown, bract scales short and totally hidden. CB2, 23; FAA 108 (Br); LA 18; CCE 56. W. Himalayas. 1837. Very sensitive, only for the mildest regions. Fig. 12 (C) z8–9.

var. **brevifolia** Dallim. & Jacks. Young branches red-brown (not gray) like *A. spectabilis*; needles shorter, only 25–35 mm long, stiffer than those of the type, acute, but not 2 pointed. DJH 15 (= *A. gamblei* Hickel). Himalaya. 1923. z8–9

var. **intermedia** Henry. Actually more a transition form between *A. pindrow* and *A. spectabilis*, bark, branches and buds like those of *A. pindrow*, but the needles with pectinate arrangement, to 55 mm long, convex beneath. Origin unknown, first described from a tree in Eastnor Castle, Herefordshire,

England. Another larger tree grows in Londonderry (Brooke Hall), Ireland. Plate 7. z8–9

A. pinsapo Boiss. Spanish Fir. Tree, 20 m or more, trunk to 1 m thick, crown broadly conical, branches in regular whorls, bark smooth at first, later rough, young branches red-brown, glabrous, buds oval, obtuse, very resinous; needles radially erect, stiff, thick, 8–15 mm long, base expanded shield-like, not twisted, apex seldom prickly, upper side convex and not furrowed, with stomatal lines, 2 distinct whitish stomatal bands beneath; male flowers dark red; cones erect, sessile, cylindrical, 10–15 cm long, 4–5 cm thick, light brown, scales triangular-cuneate, bract scales totally hidden, seeds obovate, 7 mm long, dark brown, with 1.5 cm long wings. CB 2, 24; DJH 16; FAA 90 (Br), 93 (C); LA 25a. S. Spain. 1839. Cannot be confused with any other species because of its stiff, radially arranged needles. Plate 12; Fig. 13 (C). z7

> For a very exact map depicting all 6 ranges of the species in Spain, please refer to the 1969 Year Book of the Intern. Dendrology Society, London: 104.

'Argentea'. Needles blue-gray to silver-white. Known before 1866.

'Aurea'. Needles an attractive yellow on the new growth, later generally greening. Found in 1868 in the Sénéclauze Nursery, France. Not rare.

'Clarke'. Dwarf form, a 20 year old plant in 1948 was only 1 m high. Found in the nursery of W. B. Clarke in San Jose, California, USA.

'Fastigiata'. Columnar form, branches ascending at acute angles, rather short. Originated before 1868 by Sénéclauze. Not unusual.

'Glauca'. Needles a conspicuous blue-green, with a wax-like coating, more tolerant of adverse situations than the species. Originated before 1867 by Desfosse & Thuillier in Orléans, France. Widely grown.

'Hammondii'. Dwarf form, trunk short and prostrate, branches wide spreading, twigs and needles shorter than the species. Brought into cultivation by Veitch in 1881. (EX?)

'Horstmann'. Dwarf form, upright growth, very densely branched, short needled, an intense blue-gray. Originated by G. Horstmann, Schneverdingen, W. Germany. Good frost hardiness.

'Kelleriis'. Especially vigorous selection with regular branch arrangement, branch tips somewhat ascending; needles blue. CCE 53. Selected by D. T. Poulsen, Kelleriis, Denmark. Very good winter hardiness.

'Pendula'. Weeping form, trunk nearly upright, but the tip nodding, branches partly horizontal, partly weeping. 1891. (R)

'Pyramidata'. Dwarf form, conical, branches dense, erect; needles like the species. Before 1868 in France. (EX)

A. procera Rehd. Noble Fir. Tall tree, 60(–90) m in its habitat, branched from the ground up, crown slender conical, bark often with resin blisters on young trees, bark on older trees dark brown and deeply furrowed, young branches with fine rust-brown pubescence, buds small, globose, resinous; needles with pectinate arrangement on the underside, dense above, the bottom rows erect, needles in the middle rows much shorter, those at the base of the branch appressed, then bent upward, linear, 25–35 mm long, distinctly furrowed on the apical portion (!), 1.5 mm wide, round or very slightly emarginate on the apex, blue-green with stomatal lines above, underside with 2 narrow stomatal bands; cones cylindrical-oblong, becoming somewhat thinner toward the tip, 14–25 cm long, 7–8 cm thick, green when young, purple-brown when ripe, scales 30–35 mm wide, bract scales markedly exserted and reflexed. SP 50–51; DJH 17; OCC 38 (H); FAA 13 (Br); LA 27; CCE 55 + 56 (= *A. nobilis* [Dougl. & Lamb.] Lindl.). Cascade Mts., Oregon, Siskiyou Mts., California, USA. 1825. Differing from the very similar *A. magnifica* in the distinctly furrowed apex of the needles and in not having a rectangular cross section of the needle. Plate 13; Fig. 11 (Br). z6

'Argentea'. Needles bluish-white, silvery glossy, but only slightly differing from 'Glauca'. Before 1886. (VR)

'Blaue Hexe'. Broad and flat globose habit, about like *A. balsamea* 'Nana', short branched, very dense; needles short and wide. Originated from a witches'-broom by G. D. Boehlje, Westerstede, Holland around 1965. One of the most beautiful dwarf *Abies*. Promising cultivar!

'Glauca'. Needles a beautiful blue-white, otherwise only as attractive and regular growing as the type. SN 150 (H). Known before 1863. Occurs occasionally as a seedling but normally grafted. The best plants come from grafts of the top branches.

'Glauca Prostrata'. Grows broad and densely flat; foliage is a constant blue.

'Jeddeloh'. Similar to 'Blaue Hexe', likewise flat globose and dwarf, but the foliage is more greenish-blue. Originated as a witches'-broom from Jeddeloh about 1960.

'Nobel'. Habit when young flat and wide, later developing upright branches; needles bowed brush-like upward, very densely arranged, becoming smaller to the base and the branch tips, 5–15 mm long, both sides equally blue. From the Nobel Collection in Golden Gate Park, San Francisco.

'Prostrata'. Irregular, bushy habit, flat, blue-green. WDw 32; WM 114 (H) (= *A. nobilis compacta* Hort.). Before 1932. Possibly also taken from a side branch.

'Robusta'. Strong grower; needles larger, tougher, more loosely arranged. Before 1867. (EX)

'Sherwoodii'. Needles always golden-yellow. Found in 1933, in the Sherwood Nursery in Portland, Oregon, USA.

A. recurvata Mast. Tree, 20–30(–40) m high, crown conical, spreading and becoming flattened with age, trunk to 3.5 m thick, bark rough, gray to brown, young branches glabrous, glossy, light gray-yellow, buds ovate, very resinous; needles very reflexed (important characteristic!!), 12–35 mm long, acute to sharply acuminate, glossy green on both sides, but lighter beneath and with 2 faint stomatal bands, each with 8–9 lines; cones clustered, short stalked, oval-oblong, 5–9 cm long, 3–4 cm wide, purple-violet at first, gray-brown when ripe, slightly resinous, scales crosswise elliptic, bract scales totally enclosed. CBJ 21, 22; LA 10; CCE 57. China, W. Szechwan. 1910. Easily recognized by its recurved needles. Plate 13. z6

A. religiosa (H. B. K.) Schlecht. Sacred Fir. Tree, 30–35 m high, trunk to 2 m thick, bark smooth and gray-brown, but rough and plated with age, young branches red-brown to purple, pubescent and furrowed especially when young, buds very resinous and fragrant; needles densely arranged, directed upward and forward on the upper side and not parted, horizontally outspread on the underside and parted, 25–35 mm long, about 1.5 mm wide, acute, but occasionally also rounded or obtuse, dark green and glossy above, with 2 white stomatal bands beneath; cones cylindrical, but becoming thinner toward the apex, 10–15 cm long, blue when young, scales fan-shaped, 30 mm wide, bract scales markedly exserted and reflexed. FAA 16 (H), 17(Br), 19(C); BM 6753; CB 2, 25; LA 29 (= *A. hirtella* Lindl.). Mexico, Guatemala; in the mountains. 1838. Hardy only in mild climates. The name *religiosa* refers to the use of its branches in Mexico for decorating churches and cemeteries. Fig. 13. z9

var. **glaucescens** (Gord.) Carr. Needles much longer, silvery-blue on both sides; cones wider, bract scales large, reflexed, much larger than the seed scales, except at the tip of the cone, where they are usually absent, limb fringed, with a long, caudate-like appendage (= *A. glaucescens* Gord.). Mexico; Monte de las Cruces.

A. rolii Bordères-Rey & Gaussen. Tree, to 15 m high, in the opinion of some similar to *A. delavayi* var. *georgei*, but the young branches are lighter pubescent; needles of the fruiting branches have centrally located resin ducts, needles clustered, the variable needle length and angle of attachment is probably a result of observation at varying stages of growth. China; mountains in Yuhnan. z6

A. sachalinensis (Schmidt) Mast. Sachalin Fir. Tree, to 40 m high, bark smooth, gray-white, young branches somewhat furrowed, gray, pubescent in the furrows, buds small, nearly globose, bluish, resinous; needles similar to *A. veitchii*, but only about 1.5 mm wide, to 4 mm long, glossy bright green above, with 2 rather narrow stomatal bands beneath, each with 7–8 lines, round to emarginate on the apex; cones cylindrical, 7–8 cm long, about 3 cm wide, olive-green when young, black-brown to blue-black when ripe, seed scales entire, densely pubescent on the dorsal side, bract scales exserted and reflexed. CB 2, 26; LA 14a; CCE 58, 59, 61; KIF 1: 16(= *A. veitchii* var. *sachalinensis* Schmidt). N. Japan, Sachalin, Kurilen. 1878. Needs a moist climate. Plate 14; Fig. 9 (Br), 10 (C). z6

var. **mayriana** Miy. & Kudo. Young branches pubescent in the furrows; needles shorter, 12–25 mm long, deep green above, light green beneath with 2 stomatal bands, each with 4–5 lines; seed scales kidney-shaped and distinctly "eared". LA 14b; CCE 59, 63 (= *A. mayriana* Miy. & Kudo). Japan. 1929. Plate 14.

var. **nemorensis** Mayr. Needles similar to *A. veitchii*, but longer, less silvery beneath; cones to 6 cm long, bract scales totally enclosed. CCE 59 (= *A. wilsonii* Miy. & Kudo). 1914.

A. sibirica Ledeb. Siberian Fir. Tree, to 30 m, crown conical, bark gray, smooth, but with numerous resin blisters, buds small, globose, resinous; needles clustered above and directed forward, linear, thin, standing horizontally beneath and longer than the needles on the upper side, the former 30–40 mm long, the latter only 10–15 mm long, all very aromatic, about 1 mm wide, very flat, furrowed above, rounded apex or 2 pointed and with 2–3 short stomatic lines, with 2 gray stomatal bands beneath; cones cylindrical, sessile, 5–8 cm long, bluish before ripening, eventually brown, scales broad cuneate, bract scales totally enclosed. CB 2, 27; LA 16a (= *A. pichta* Forbes; *A. semenovii* Fedtsch.). Northern Soviet Union to Kamchatka, south to Manchuria and Turkestan. 1820. Prefers a moist, cool climate, suffers in a late frost. Fig. 9 (Br), 12(C). z2

'Alba'. Needles light green, distinctly white on the underside. Found in northern Russia. 1853. (EX?)

'Pendula'. Weeping form with short, thick branches, twigs pendulous, partly lying on the ground. Found in 1881 in the nursery of Regel & Kesselring. (EX)

A. spectabilis (D. Don) G. Don. Himalayan Fir. Tree, to 50 m in its habitat, crown broadly conical, branches spreading widely, bark rough scaly, young branches red-brown, deeply furrowed, furrows pubescent, buds globose, large, resinous; needles leathery, stiff, parted in 2–4 rows, with a V-shaped furrow, much shorter on the upper side, 2.5–5 cm long, 2–3 mm wide, linear, distinctly 2 pointed on the apex, dark green and glossy above, deeply furrowed, with 2 wide white stomatal bands beneath; cones cylindrical, 12–15 cm long, 7 cm thick, violet-purple when young, brown when ripe, scales about 20 mm wide, bract scales totally hidden. DJH 18; H.AL 1, 156, 181; CB 2, 29 (as *webbiana*; LA 17 (= *A. webbiana* Lindl.). Himalaya; Sikkim, Bhutan, in the mountains at 2500–4000 m. Easily damaged by late frost. Plate 13; Fig. 9 (Br), 10 (C). z8–9

var. **brevifolia** (Henry) Rehd. Very different in that the gray twigs are less furrowed; needles much shorter, only about 30 mm long, stomatal bands on the underside more gray. CB 3, 70. NW. Himalaya.

A. squamata Mast. Flaky Barked Fir. Tree, 15–40 m high, trunk 70–150 cm wide, bark brown, paper thin, exfoliating (like a *Betula*; important characteristic!), young branches blackish-brown pubescent, buds globose, very resinous; needles densely arranged, not parted, only 12–25 mm long, abruptly acuminate or also obtuse, curved, furrowed above, bluish-green, with 2 whitish stomatal bands beneath, each with 8–9 lines; cones oval-oblong, 5–6 cm long, violet when young, the narrow tips of bract scales protruding past the seed scales, reflexed, disintegrating quickly. CBJ 24; LA 11; CCE 60. China; W. Szechwan. 1910. Easily recognized by the exfoliating bark on 6 year old trunk and branches. Plate 14; Fig. 9 (Br), 9 (C). z6

A. sutchuenensis (Franch.) Rehd. & Wils. Szechwan Fir. Tree, 20–15 m high, but reaching to 60 m in its habitat, bark whitish-brown, young branches reddish-brown, in general glabrous and glossy, short branches densely pubescent, buds distinctive in form, resinous; needles on older trees 12–25 mm long, obtuse or round or indistinctly emarginate on the apex, glossy green above, flat, furrowed, with 2 white stomatal bands beneath, oriented upward on the branch upper side, not parted, densely arranged, otherwise directed forward and sideways and densely overlapping, with distinct yellow petioles; cones ovate-oblong, rounded on the apex, 5–7 cm long, 3 cm thick, purple or violet-black when young, only slightly resinous, scales broad kidney-shaped, only

the awn-shaped tips protruding past the bract scales. LA 9c; CCE 61 (= *A. fargesii* var. *sutchuensis* Franch.). W. China. 1925. z6 One of the world's most beautiful fir species; crushed needles unpleasant smelling, the similar *A. fargesii* needles, however, smell like oranges, the latter also has much larger needles.

A. tacanensis C. L. Lundell. Resembling *A. guatemalensis*, but the needles more densely arranged, narrower; bract scales nearly as long as the seed scales or exserted at the tips. Mexico. z9

A. × vasconcellosiana Franco (*A. pindrow* × *A. pinsapo*). Tree, 18 m high, presumably becoming taller, young branches gray like *A. pindrow*, needles resemble those of *A. pindrow* but shorter, only 20–30 mm long, 2–2.5 mm wide, obtuse, with a few stomatal lines above, 2 gray-white stomatal bands beneath, each with 6–8 lines, shorter on fruiting branches, wider and acute, resin ducts medial, arrangement of the needles somewhat parted, partly radial; cones cylindrical, 12–15 cm long, 4–5 cm thick, dark purple when young, brown when ripe, scales 30–40 mm wide, tomentose exterior, bract scales not visible. FAA 101 (H), 102–105(Br), 107(C); LA 45. Found in 1945 by Franco in Pena Park in Sintra, near Lisbon, Portugal; tree came from seed of an *A. pindrow* which grows near *A. pinsapo*. z6?

'Amaral Franco'. A type selected for its conical crown and especially dense branching habit. Bai 9: 41. (1961).

A. veitchii Lindl. Veitch Fir. Tree, 15–25 m high, crown narrowly conical, branched to the ground, bark gray and smooth, whitish-gray toward the apex, branches short, spreading horizontally with ringed folds near the base (typical!!), young branches usually reddish-brown, more or less dense and short pubescent, buds small, rather globose, reddish, translucent resinous; needles clustered, upper ones directed forward and mostly upward, parted beneath, linear, 10–25 mm long, truncate on the apex and 2 pointed, glossy deep green and furrowed above, with 2 chalk-white stomatal bands beneath, cones cylindrical, 6–7 cm long, 3 cm wide, bluish-purple when young, occasionally green, scales very densely arranged, only 15 mm wide, bract scales somewhat exserted and recurved, seeds 7 mm long, yellow, wings blackish. DJH 19; OCC 44(C); CCE 62 + 63; KIF 1:18 (= *A. sikokiana* Nakai; *A. veitchii* var. *reflexa* Koidz.). Central and South Japan, in the mountains. 1861. Plate 14; Fig. 9 (Br). z3

var. **nikkoensis** Mayr. Cones 5 cm long, the tips of the bract scales somewhat exserted between the seed scales.

var. **olivaceae** Shiras. Cones about 7 cm long, olive-green when young, gray-brown when ripe, otherwise like and occurring with the type.

A. vejari Martinez. Tree, 30–40 m high, closely related to *A. religiosa*, but young branches becoming glabrous or with persistent pubescence in the furrows; needles irregularly arranged, 15–20 mm long, 1.5 mm wide, straight or curved and somewhat appressed to the stem at the base, obtuse or short acuminate, both sides with stomatal lines; cones shorter and thicker, to about 8 cm long and 5 cm thick, purple when young, greenish-brown when ripe, scales nearly triangular, 2 cm wide, bract scales oblong, the narrow, triangular tip exserted. LA 31a; CCE 64. Mexico; Tamaulipa Province, growing over a 500 hectare area (from Martinez). A rare species outside its habitat. z7–8.

var. **mexicana** (Mart.) Liv. Mexican Fir. Tree, 30–40 m high; needles radially arranged, straight or slightly curved, directed obliquely forward and overlapping, 15–20 mm long, 1.5 mm wide, obtuse acuminate, with 2 marginate resin ducts, green above, blue-green beneath; cones ovate, 5–8 cm long, 3.5–5 cm wide, enclosed within the seed scales. LA 31b, CCE 51 (= *A. mexicana* Martinez). Mexico. 1942.

A. × vilmorinii Mast. (*A. cephalonica* × *A. pinsapo*). Tree, crown broadly conical, branches ash-gray, young branches rust-brown, smooth; needles similar to those of *A. pinsapo*, but longer, not so stiff, less radial, partly more 2 ranked, 20–30 mm long, 2 mm wide, dark green above, the underside with 2 silvery stomatal bands, otherwise blue-green and very keeled; bears cones abundantly, these spindle-shaped, 14–20 cm long, 4 to 5 cm wide, base tapered, conical at the apex, scales rounded on the tip, bract scales somewhat exserted and reflexed, seeds triangular, glossy brown. OCC 45 (C); CBJ 25, 26; LA 11; CCE 64. Developed in cultivation by M. De Vilmorin in Verrières near Paris in 1868, but also occurs naturally among the parents. z6

A. yuana Bordères-Rey & Gaussen. Probably not an independent species, rather only a variety of *A. delavayi*; in many respects similar to *A. delavayi* var. *georgei*, but differing in the medial resin ducts and cones with much shorter bract scales. China; Yunnan. Included by T.-S. Liu with *A. fargesii* var. *faxoniana*.

Lit. Franco J. Do A.: Abetos, 260 pp. (Figs. 1 to 109). Ann. Inst. Sup. Agron. Lisbon 1950 ● Fulling, E. H.: Identification by leaf structure, of the species of *Abies* cultivated in the United States. Bull. Torrey Bot. Club LXI (9), 497–524, 1934 (with ills. 1–43). ● Fulling. E. H.: *Abies intermedia*, the Blue Ridge Fir, a new species. Castanea I, 91–94, 1936 (with 3 ills.) ● Hillier, E. L.: The newer Asiatic Silver Firs and their characteristics described from British-grown specimens. Jour. RHS 1941, 400–411 and 431–434 (with 5 ills.). ● Lie, T.-S.: A monograph of the genus *Abies*, 608 pp. Taipeh 1971 (about 400 plates, 42 range maps). ● M'Nab, W. R.: A revision of the species of *Abies*. Proc. Roy. Irish Acad., ser. 2 (Science) **2**, 673–704, 1877. ● Martinez, M.: Los *Abies* Mexicanos. Ann. Inst. Biol. Méx. 1948, 11–104 (Fig. 1–82). ● Mattei, G. E.: L'Abetele dele Nebrodi. Bol. R. Orto Bot. Giard. Colon. Palermo 1908, 59–69. ● Mattfeld, J.: Die in Europa und dem Mittelmeergebiet wildwachsenden Tannen. Mitt. Deutsch. Dendr. Ges. 1925, 1–37 (Plates 1–10). ● Mattfeld, J.: Über hybridogene Sippen der Tannen. Bibl. Bot. C. 1930, 1–84 (Pls. 1–2, Figs. 1 to 41). ● Matzenko, A.: Conspectus generis *Abies*. Not. Syst. (Leningrad) **22**, 33–42, 1963. ● Nitzelius, T.: A review of the firs in the Mediterranean. Lustgarden 1969, 146–189 (Figs. 1–16). ● Nitzelius, T.: Über *Abies koreana*—die Korea-Tanne, und *A. × arnoldiana*, eine neue Hybride. Dtsch. Baumsch. **22**, 98–105, 1970 (with ills.). ● Rehder, A.: The firs of Mexico and Guatemala. Jour. Arnold Arb. 1939, 282–287. ● Vigue, M. T., & H. Gaussen: Révision du genre *Abies*. Bull. Soc. Hist. Nat. Toulouse; **57**, 369–434, 1929; **58**, 245–564, 1939.

Fig. 14. *Acmopyle pancheri*. Left, 2 branches from the shady side; right, a branch from the sunny side (from De Laubenfels, altered)

ACMOPYLE Pilger—PODOCARPACEAE

Evergreen trees, closely related to *Dacrydium* and *Podocarpus*, but the receptacle is shorter than the seed and only surrounds the base (totally encloses seed on *Podocarpus*); leaves variously arranged. — 3 species in New Caledonia and on the Fiji Islands.

Acmopyle alba Buchholz. From New Caledonia, distinguished from *A. pancheri* only in the larger staminate cones; these 18–20 mm long and 3 mm wide, as opposed to only 10–13 mm long and 2 mm wide on *A. pancheri*. De Laubenfels suggested both be placed in the same species with *A. alba*; later classed as a variety when better known.

A. pancheri (Brongn. & Gris.) Pilg. Evergreen tree, 12–15 m high, branches upright; leaves variously formed, thick, scaly on the elongated branches, linear-lanceolate on the shorter branches (similar to *Taxus*), sessile, 8–20 mm long, curved at the apex, green, with 2 indistinct stomatal bands above, 2 wide, bluish stomatal bands beneath and a green midrib; male flowers 1–3, terminal, 2.5–3 cm long, female flowers on a densely scaly long stalk, terminal, with a fleshy, resinous, humped "foot" composed of several scale-leaves; carpels usually solitary, receptacle absent, only a single ovule present, fused to a conical seed with a stony seed coat, micropyle near the apical end of the ovule. BM 7854 (as *Podocarpus pectinata*); LG 9. New Caledonia, common in the coniferous forest at the top of Mont Mou. Introduced to England in 1891. Plate 23; Fig. 14. z9

A. sahniana Buchh. & Gray. Small evergreen tree, similar to *A. pancheri*, but leaves somewhat wider, midrib not lying exactly in the middle, apex acutely sickle-shaped. Fiji Islands; known only from one specimen, found in 1927 on Mt. Vakorogasiu, Namosi by J. W. Gillepsie. z9

Lit. De Laubenfels, D. J.: A Revision of the Malesian and Pacific Rainforest Conifers (I); Podocarpaceae; *Acmopyle*. Jour. Arnold Arboretum **50**, 337 to 340, 1969.

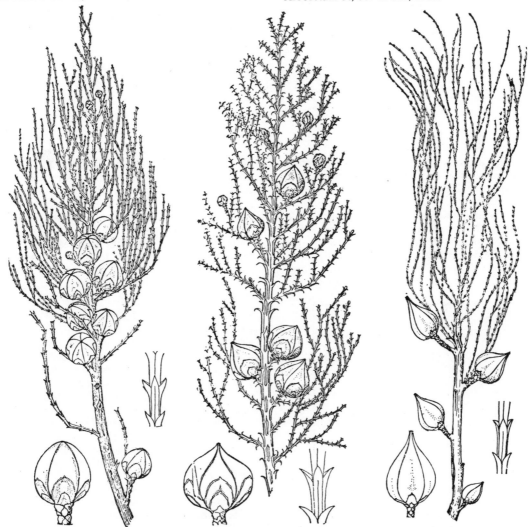

Fig. 15. **Actinostrobus.** Left, *A. pyramidalis*; middle *A. arenarius*; right, *A. acuminatus*, with fruits and enlarged branch (from Blombery)

ACTINOSTROBUS Miq.— CUPRESSACEAE

Evergreen, pyramidal shrubs, abundantly branched, resembling *Callitris*, but differing in the form of the cones and the numerous, 3 whorled sterile scales at the base; branchlets 3 sided or rounded, jointed, leaves alternate, in 3 rows, often needle-like on young plants and sterile branches, 8–15 mm long, scale-like on older plants and fruiting branches, then 3–4 mm long, stiff, sharp acuminate, the distinct portion triangular; plants monoecious; male flowers oblong, anthers in whorls of 3, with wide anther scales and 2–3 sporangia at the base of the scale; female flowers solitary, with short, scaly stalks, globose, with 6 evenly formed scales arranged around an axis, each with 1–2, triangular, 3 winged seeds at the base.—3 species in W. Australia. Greenhouse plants in cooler climates.

Actinostrobus acuminatus Parl. Smaller than *A. pyramidalis*, branches finer; leaves smaller, needle-leaves however, somewhat longer; male flowers terminal, somewhat longer, anther scales acuminate, cone scales ending in a short, outspread tip. W. Australia; between the Moore and Murchison rivers. In cultivation not noticeably different from *A. pyramidalis*. Fig. 15. z9

A. arenarius C. A. Gardn. Shrub, 2–5 m high, branches more or less spreading, branchlets 3 sided; needles in 3's, scale-like, usually 2 mm long, the distinct portion not quite 1 mm long, green, triangular-ovate (ovate on *A. pyramidalis* and more erect!); cones 1.5–1.6 cm long and about as wide, fertile fruit scales larger than the others, blue-green, with erect, somewhat acute, not incurved tips. W. Australia. Earlier included with *A. pyramidalis*, but later recognized as distinctly different and separated in 1964. Fig. 15. z9

A. pyramidalis Miq. Shrub, 1–3 m high, abundantly branched, branches upright, densely arranged, branches quite fine, glabrous; leaves scale-like, tightly appressed at the base, to 2 mm long, prickly, 3–4 mm long on young main shoots, primary leaves narrow needle-like, 7–8 mm long; cones about 15 mm long and wide, with 6 sided, acute scales, opening valvate. CBJ 3, 74; HI 1272; BAU 292. W. Australia; often found on salty sand plains. Fig. 15. z9

Lit. Gardner, C. A.: 9. Contributiones Florae Australiae Occidentalis XIII. Jour. Roy. Soc. West Austral. 1964, 54.

AGATHIS Salib.—Dammar Pine—ARAUCARIACEAE

Tall, evergreen, very resinous trees, trunk columnar; bark thick, very resinous, scaly, a milky sap flows from wounds and hardens in the air; branches horizontal, often whorled on young trees, more irregular on older specimens, partly abscising leaving a circular scar; buds short, globose, with few scales; leaves large, lanceolate to elliptic or ovate, short petioled, leathery, more or less arranged in a row on the side branches, alternate to often nearly opposite, often lasting 15–20 years, new growth reddish, later dark green, parallel venation, exceptionally variable in size and form, often varying greatly on the same branch, leaving a leaf cushion after abscising; plants dioecious or monoecious; male flowers usually axillary, to 6 cm long, stamens with 5–15 pollen sacs; female flower cones globose, wider than high, terminal, on short scale covered stalks; cones ripening the 2nd year, globose to broad rounded, seed scales fan-shaped, with thickened margin, abscising when ripe; with a seed chamber under each scale, seeds ringed on one side. x = 13.—About 16 species in Australia, New Zealand, New Caledonia, Fiji Islands and the Phillipines. Occasionally found in botanic gardens or conservatories. z9

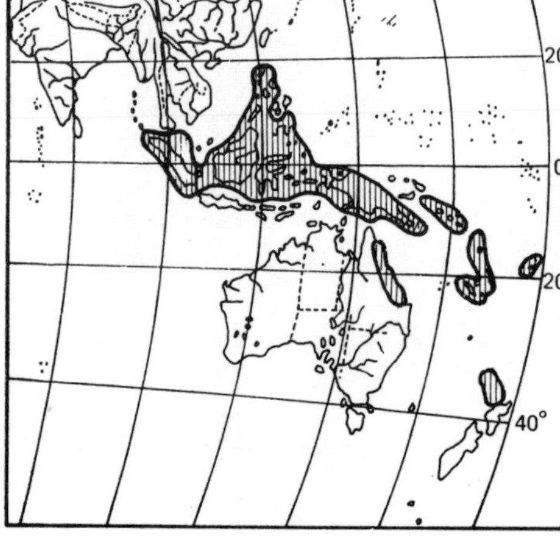

Agathis australis (D. Don) Salisb. Kauri Pine. Evergreen tree, 25–40 m high, trunk 2 to 3 m in diameter, occasionally taller and wider, bark bluish-gray, very thick and resinous, branches in whorls or irregularly spreading horizontally; leaves variable in form; erect on young plants, at wide angles apart, 5–10 cm long, about 1 cm wide, lanceolate, tough, short stalked, blue-green, opposite or nearly opposite on side shoots, shorter on old plants, more oblong, 2–3.5 cm long, densely arranged, occasionally petioled, otherwise usually sessile; plants frequently monoecious; seed cones woody, ovate or globose, 8–10 cm thick. CC 152(H), 45; KF 80 to 81; DJ 20; SFP 54. New Zealand, North Island; developing complete stands. Brought to Europe in 1823. Leaves smaller and narrower than the other species. Plate 15 and 16; Fig. 17. z9

A. dammara (Lamb.) L. C. Rich. Tree, to 50 m high, trunk to 5 m thick, crown conical, branches somewhat

Fig. 16. Range of the genus *Agathis* (from Florin)

pendulous, bark reddish-gray, thick and resinous, young branches dull, light green, buds globose, with few appressed scales; leaves deep green, oblong-lanceolate, 6–12 cm long, 1.5–5 cm wide, often smaller on fruiting branches, leathery, lasting several years, obtuse and rounded on the apex, but also occasionally acuminate, margin occasionally also thick and reflexed, petiole indistinct, flattened, 3–5 mm long; male inflorescences solitary, axillary, 2 to 7 cm long, 2–2.5 cm wide; cones globose to obtuse ovate, to 10 cm long, scales to 25 mm wide; thickened and reflexed at the tip. LT 19; BM 5359 (= *A. alba* [Bl.] Foxworthy; *A. loranthifolia* Salisb.; *A. orientalis* [D. Don] Hook.). Malaysia, Polynesia. Manila-copal, a type of resin from which lacquer and varnish is made, is obtained from this plant. Dammar resin, on the other hand, is obtained from a *Shorea* species rather than from this plant. z9

Included in *A. dammara* are a number of subspecies (treated as species by Meijer Drees) which will be omitted here.

A. flavescens Ridley. Tree, to 12 m high, trunk to about 1 m thick at the base, young branches yellowish; leaves alternate, elliptic-obovate, obtuse, thick and leathery, yellowish-green, 35–65 mm long and 12 to 25 mm wide; male inflorescences cylindrical, 25–35 mm long, 12 mm wide; cones globose, about 6 cm long and 4.5 cm wide, scales 30 mm long and 25 mm wide, seeds ellipsoid. Malaysia; Pandang Mts., Gunong, Tahan. 1700. z9

A. labillardieri Warb. Tree, to 60 m high; leaves oblong-lanceolate or elliptic, 6 to 10 cm long and 18–30 mm wide, generally tapering to an obtuse or nearly acute tip, base abruptly narrowing to a wide petiole; male inflorescences axillary, broad cylindrical, 20–30 mm long, 10–15 mm wide; cones globose, 7.5–8 cm thick. New Guinea. z9

A. lanceolata (Pancher) Warb. Tall tree, lowest branch often 15 m off the ground, crown irregular, dense, branches ascending, bark reddish-brown, smooth, peeling in thin scales, young branches compressed or 4 sided, buds 3–6 mm thick, with numerous scales; leaves large, opposite, ascending and overlapping or also erect, lanceolate to narrow oblong with short tips, base generally tapered, 4.5–12 cm long, 8–16 mm wide, leathery, venation very dense, glossy dark green above, lighter and less glossy beneath, margin thick and reflexed; male inflorescences paired opposite in the leaf axils. LG 35. New Caledonia; in large forests. Plate 16. z9

A. macrophylla (Lindl.) Mast. Tree, to 30 m high, branches spreading widely, young branches stiff, often 4 sided near the tips, buds globose; leaves ovate to lanceolate, 10–20 cm long, 2–5 cm wide, leathery, tapering to an obtuse apex, base with a flat petiole, margin recurved, deep green above, lighter beneath, densely veined; cones erect, globose, about 10 cm high and 8–10 cm thick. Polynesia; Solomon Islands and La Perouse. Very similar to *A. dammara*, but with larger leaves. z9

A. microstachys J. F. Bailey & C. T. White. Black Kauri Pine. Tree, to over 50 m high; leaves 35–60 mm long, 12–15 mm wide, with a short, indistinct petiole; male inflorescences nearly globose or short ovate, 6 mm long;

cones similar to those of *A. robusta*. Australia; tropical Queensland, along the coast. z9

A. moorei (Lindl.) Mast. Tree, 15–20 m high, erect, ornamental habit, branches slender, with pendulous tips, young shoots greenish; leaves opposite or nearly so, lanceolate to elliptic, to 10 cm long and 2.5 cm wide, glossy dark green above, with an obtuse apex, lighter beneath, with many parallel veins; male inflorescences solitary, cylindrical, erect, 15 mm long and 7 mm wide, axillary; cones globose to pear shaped, symmetrical, to 12 cm long and 10 cm thick. LG 34. New Caledonia, 300–600 m, in the mountains. z9

A. obtusa (Lindl.) Morrison. Similar to *A. australis*, but leaves larger, variable in form and size, usually oblong, to 10 cm long and 3 cm wide, thick, leathery, dark green and glossy above, rounded at the apex or obtuse; cones more cylindrical, rounded at both ends, 7–8 cm long and 4 cm thick, scales convex on the end, 4 times as long as wide. New Hebrides. z9

A. ovata Warburg. Tree, scarcely over 10 m high, bark rough, gray, deeply furrowed, young branches either alternate or opposite or whorled 3–4, yellowish-brown, buds globose, with 4 large, tightly appressed scales; leaves erect, opposite or nearly so, 7.5–11 cm long, 2–3 cm wide (occasionally only 3.5 cm long and 1.5 cm wide), broad lanceolate or oblong-elliptic, thick, leathery, margin thickened and somewhat curved, apex rounded, base narrowed to a flat petiole, deep green above, lighter or more bluish beneath, parallel veined on both sides; cones ellipsoid, to 11 cm long and nearly 10 cm wide, scales flat, about 3.5 cm high and wide, brown, outer margin somewhat thickened. LG 37. New Caledonia. z9

Fig. 17. *Agathis australis*. Branch with cones; male and female flowers and seed (from Poole/Adams)

A. palmerstonii F. v. Muell. Tall tree, stem columnar and largely unbranched, bark 2 cm thick and resinous; leaves very similar to those of *A. robusta*, but smaller and narrower, usually lanceolate, 5–10 cm long, 1 to 2 cm wide, dark green, apex obtuse, base tapering to a small, 3 mm long petiole; male inflorescences solitary, cylindrical, 2.5 cm long; cones ovate, to 13 cm long and 10 cm wide. Australia; Queensland. Plate 16. z9

A. rhomboidalis Warburg. Tall tree, to over 50 m high; leaves opposite or nearly so, lanceolate to elliptic, 5–8 cm long, 2–4 cm wide, with rather distinct petiole; male inflorescences cylindrical to oblong-ovate, to 8 cm long and 3 cm wide; cones globose, about 6 cm thick; seeds oblong. Malaysia, N. Sumatra. z9

A. robusta (C. Moore) F. M. Bailey. Tall tree, 40–45 m high, stem columnar, straight, lowest branch some distance from the ground, bark brown, thick, scaly, buds globose, scales densely appressed; leaves opposite or nearly so, leathery, ovate to elliptic, 5 to 12 cm long, 2–5 cm wide, glossy dark green above, lighter beneath, parallel veined, margin thickened and somewhat recurved, tapering to a wide, flat petiole; male inflorescences axillary, cylindrical, dense, 5–10 cm long to 1 cm wide; cones nearly globose or ovate, 10–12 cm

long and 7–10 cm thick, scales densely overlapping, 2.5–3 cm wide. Australia; Queensland and Fraser Islands, from the plains to about 1000 m. Plate 16. z9

A. vitiensis (Seem.) Drake. Tree, 15–18 m high, occasionally to 30 m, first branch very high, bark whitish outside, inside reddish, young branches greenish, buds small, globose, brown, scales densely appressed; leaves broad lanceolate, 5–6 cm long, 2–2.5 cm wide, leathery, dark glossy green above, lighter and more obtuse beneath, densely parallel veined, tapering to both ends, rounded to obtuse at the apex, base with about a 6 mm long petiole; male inflorescences 2.5–3 cm long, cylindrical; cones blue-green, ovate to globose, 8–10 cm long, 6–8 cm thick, scales fan-shaped, 2.5–3 cm wide. Parham, Pl. Fiji Isl. fig. 20. Fiji Islands; widely disseminated. z9

Lit. Meijer Drees, E.: The genus *Agathis* in Malaysia. Bull. Jard. Bot. Buitenzorg 3, ser. 16, 455 to 477, 1938–1940. ● Franco, J. Do Amaral: Espécies do género *Agathis* Salisb. cultivadas em Portugal. An. Inst. Sup. Agronomia 18, 99–115, 1951 (with 17 ills.). ● De Laubenfels, D. J.: Diagnoses de nouvelles espèces d'Araucariacées de Nouvelle-Calédonie (*A. nemorosa, A. scopulorum, A. schmidii*). Trav. Lab. Forest. Toulouse 8, V, 1–2, 1969.

AMENTOTAXUS Pilger—TAXACEAE

Evergreen shrubs or small trees, similar to *Cephalotaxus*, but differing in the slender, pendulous, branched male inflorescences (not erect on the branch) and the solitary ovules in the axils of the branchlets, the latter opposite; needles opposite, persisting on the apical portion of the branch, sessile to short petioled, linear-lanceolate, leathery, acuminate, deep green with raised midrib above, with 2 bluish stomatal bands beneath, margin and midrib green; plants dioecious, flowering on the current year's wood, male flowers in spike-like racemes in pendulous groups of 1–4, female flowers solitary, petioled, fruits drupe-like, the reddish-yellow aril open at the apex, scales persisting on the base.—4 species known to date, all in China.

Amentotaxus argotaenia (Hance) Pilg. Shrub, 2–4 m high, wide habit, (like *Cephalotaxus*); needles 3.5–7 cm long, 6 mm wide, thick, leathery, straight or somewhat curved, apex acute or obtuse, margin slightly involuted, stomatal bands white, as wide as the green margin stripes; male inflorescences solitary and 2–3 together, 5–7 cm long. CCE 68. China; Kwangtung, Lantoa Island; Hong Kong. Plate 24; Fig. 18. z6?

A. cathayensis Li. Shrub or small tree, 2–5 m high; needles 6–10 cm long, 6 mm wide, usually sickle-shaped, occasionally straight, long acuminate, margin slightly involuted, stomatal bands white, only as wide as the green margin stripe. China; W. Hupeh. Not well known.

A. formosana Li. Shrub or small tree, to 9 m high, only sparsely branched; only a few needles, distinctly sickle-shaped, bowed, 5–8 cm long, 6–8 mm wide, acute to obtuse at the base, margin involuted, stomatal bands white, twice as wide as the green margin stripe; male catkins usually grouped 3–4, 3 cm long, fruits oblong-ellipsoid, 2–2.5 cm long, on a 2 cm long, thin petiole. CCE 68. China and Taiwan. Fig. 18. z6?

A. yunnanensis Li. Small tree, branches thin, erect; needles mostly straight, 3–7 cm long, base broad cuneate to rounded, margin slightly involuted, stomatal bands cuneate to rounded, margin slightly involuted, stomatal bands brownish to yellowish-white, to nearly 3 times as wide as the green margin stripes; fruits ovate, about 2 cm long, short petioled. China; Yunnan. z6

Lit. Li, H.-L.: The genus *Amentotaxus*. Jour. Arnold Arboretum 33, 192–198, 1955.

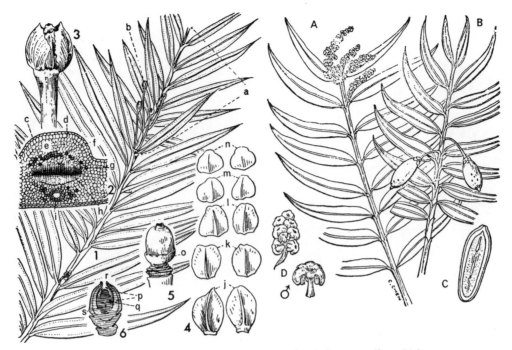

Fig. 18. **Amentotaxus.** Left. *A. argotaenia;* right, *A. formosana* (from Liu)

ARAUCARIA Juss.—ARAUCARIACEAE

Tall evergreen trees, branches arranged in regular whorls, the lower ones often pendulous; young branches green, without distinct buds; leaves alternate, occasionally somewhat 2 ranked, awl-shaped to oval-lanceolate, stiff, densely arranged; flowers on short side shoots, cone-like and terminal, cylindrical, to 15 cm long, stamens densely spirally arranged, female flowers in a large, nearly globose, to 20 cm wide, terminal cone; carpels very numerous, densely imbricate, thickened at the apex and with a nearly ball-like sharp tip; cones ripening in 2 to 3 years, then disintegrating; ovules solitary, inverted, adnate to the scales; cotyledons usually 2, seldom 4. x = 13.—About 18 species in New Guinea, E. Australia, New Zealand, Norfolk Island, New Caledonia and S. Brazil to Chile.

Sect. **Colymbea** Endl.
Leaves flat, multiveined; carpels thick and scale-like, not winged, cones very large; cotyledons 2, germinating underground:
 A. araucaria, angustifolia, bidwillii

Sect. **Intermedia** C. T. White
Young leaves awl-shaped, mature leaves flat, wide, 5–10 cm long; carpels winged, cones relatively small, cotyledons 2–4, germinating above ground:
 A. klinkii

Sect. **Eutacta** Endl.
Leaves all awl-shaped and bowed, carpels thin membranous winged, cones rather small, cotyledons 2–4, germinating above ground:
 A. balansae, beccarii, biramulata, bernieri, columnaris, cunninghamii, heterophylla, humboldtensis, luxurians, montana, muelleri, rulei

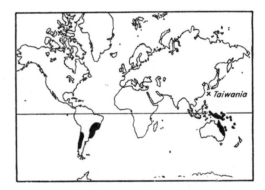

Fig. 19. Range of the Genera
Araucaria and *Taiwania* (✕)

Araucaria angustifolia (Bertol.) Kuntze. Brazilian Araucaria. Tree, to 35 m high, crown eventually flat, sparsely branched, branches spreading horizontally in whorls of 4 to 8, somewhat pendulous with ascending tips, lower branches generally abscising; leaves on sterile branches appear to be opposite, lanceolate, 3–6 cm long, 6 mm wide, green or blue-green, thicker on fruiting branches, shorter and dense, spirally arranged, stomatal bands well developed beneath; cones wider than high, about 16 cm wide and 12 cm high, tapered on the apical half, carpels with a curled thorn on the tip, seeds light brown, 5 cm long, 2 cm wide. BCC Pl. 33; CCE 69 + 71 (= *A. brasiliana* A. Rich.). In the mountains of S. Brazil and Argentina. Fig. 21 (Br). z9

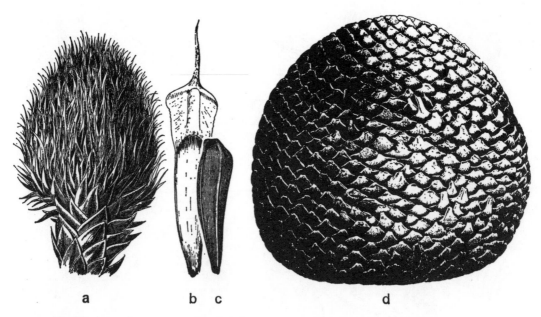

Fig. 20. *Araucaria araucana.* a. female inflorescence, b. seed scale, c. seed, d. whole cone

'Elegans'. Leaves narrower, not so stiff, less acute, dense, covering the branches and stem on younger plants (= *A. brasiliensis* var. *elegans* Laws.; *A. brasiliensis* var. *gracilis* Carr.). Known since 1852.

'Ridofiana'. More vigorous grower; leaves longer and wider. Known since 1858.

'Saviana'. Leaves narrower, but blue-green. 1868.

A. araucana (Molina) K. Koch. Monkey Puzzle Tree, Chile Pine. Tree, 30–50 m high in its habitat (female trees 30–50 m, male only 15–18 m high), seldom over 10 m in cultivation, stem straight, crown conical, branched to the ground in open areas, branches in whorls, spreading horizontally, uppermost branches ascending, lower ones pendulous; leaves dense, spirally arranged, ovate-lanceolate, base much widened and sessile, 25–35 mm long, with sharp, prickly tip, concave above, convex beneath, both sides with split openings, dark green, persisting about 10–15 years; cones erect, globose, to 15 cm thick, brown, seed scales densely spiraled, oblong-cuneate with long, linear appendages, seeds 3–4.5 cm long, reversed oval-oblong, red-brown, edible ("Piñones"), germinating underground. BCC 33 (= *A. imbricata* Pav.). Chile, SW. Argentina, on the west slopes of the Andes. 1795. Only (somewhat) winter hardy species; thrives best in a fertile, well drained, evenly moist soil and moist air; in marginal situations provide winter protection especially for young plants. Tolerates coastal winds and salt well. Plate 17, 18, 19 and 22; Fig. 20. z8

'Andenzwerg'. Slow growing dwarf form, annual growth only about 10 cm; needles smaller than those of the species. Raised by G. Horstmann of Schneverdingen, W. Germany, from seed collected in the Parque Nacional Tolhuaca, in the Andes of Chile, Malleco Province. The original plant was grown by H. Neulen, Helgoland, W. Germany. (R)

'Angustifolia'. Branches longer and more slender. Not unusual in cultivation.

'Aurea'. Leaves gold-yellow. Originated around 1855 by Taylor, Castle Kennedy, and disseminated by W. Barron & Sons, Barrowash, England.

'Densa'. Branches loosely arranged, often solitary; leaves very short, densely packed on the branches. 1867. (EX)

'Denudata'. Sparsely branched, branches few and very thin; leaves somewhat shorter. Developed by A. Leroy in Angiers, France before 1867. (EX)

'Distans'. Strong grower, branch whorls at least 1 m apart. Before 1867. (EX)

'Kurt Sachs'. Has grown in Hamburg, W. Germany for 24 years without winter damage! z7–8

'Platyfolia'. Leaves very short and wide. 1901.

'Striata'. Bark and leaves green with yellow stripes. Originated in Angiers, France by A. Leroy. Before 1858.

'Variegata'. Leaves straw-yellow, occasionally with green leaves intermixed on young branches, with totally green branches among them. Originated before 1858 in Glendining's Nursery in Turnham Green (near London), England.

A. balansae Brongn. & Gris. Tree, 12–18 m high, branches long and thin, pendulous; needles small and evenly formed, awl-shaped, densely appressed, only 3 mm long, persisting for many years, curved inward, stomata only on the inside; cones ovate, terminal on short shoots, 6–7.5 cm long and 5–6 cm wide, seed scales within stiff, lanceolate tips. New Caledonia. 1875. Similar to *A. columnaris*, but more slender in habit and smaller. Plate 22; Fig. 21 (Br). z9

A. beccarii Warburg. Tree, 20–25 m high, very similar to *A. cunninghamii*, but not as symmetrically branched and without the candelabra-type growth; needles of mature trees awl-shaped, about 1 cm long, sharp acuminate and bowed on the apex; cones not yet clearly known, presumably much larger than *A. cunninghamii*, seed scales longer, base narrower, more acuminate at the apex. New Guinea, Arfak Mts. z9

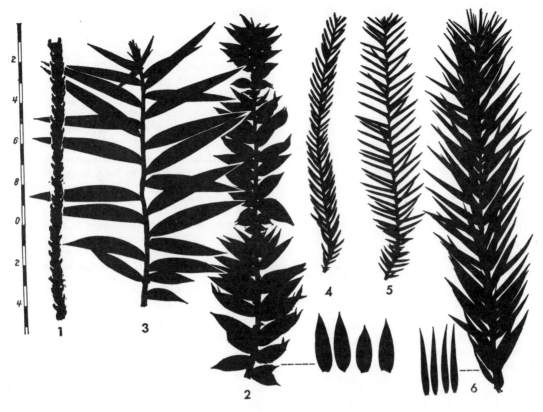

Fig. 21. **Araucaria** species. 1. *A. balansae*; 2, *A. bidwillii*; 3. the same but from a younger plant; 4. *A. cunninghamii*; 5. *A. cunninghamii* 'Glauca'; 6. *A. angustifolia* (Original)

A. bernieri Buchholz. A not yet well known species, closely related to *A. balansae*, but differing in the form of the needles and the distinct blue-green cones, young leaves smaller and with raised keel, not dorsiventrally flattened, leaves of older trees, however, triangular, with wide base, not as curved as on *A. balansae*; male inflorescences 7–10 cm long, 8 mm wide, bluish-white; cones cylindrical-ovate, to 10 cm long and 7.5 cm wide, blue-white pruinose. LG 30. New Caledonia; Rivière de Pirogues, Plaine des Lacs. z9

A. bidwillii Hook. "Bunya-Bunya". Tree, to 50 m, conical when young, bark thick, peeling in thin layers, branches in whorls of 10–15, dense and symmetrical, branches on older trees sparse and drooping, young branches green; leaves spirally arranged, lanceolate on sterile branches, to· 5 cm long, 5–10 mm wide, stiff, very dark green, terminating in a long, stiff pointed tip, leaves more densely arranged on the uppermost and fruiting branches, also shorter, often only 2 cm long and bowed inward, with irregular stomatal lines above, regular lines beneath; cones very large, elliptic-ovate, to 30 cm high and 23 cm thick, seed scales to 10 cm long and 7 cm wide, markedly tapered at the apex, seeds nearly pear-shaped, to 6 cm long and 2.5 cm wide, edible (a cone can contain up to 150 seeds and weigh nearly 5 kilograms). CCE 72. Australia; along the coast of Queensland. 1843. Frequently planted in the subtropics and Mediterranean region. Plate 17 and 19; Fig. 21 (Br). z9

A. biramulata Buchholz. Tree, to 15 m high, the outermost twigs branching, twisted and pendulous; needles broad awl-shaped to ovate-lanceolate, dorsiventrally flattened and more or less keeled, 8–10 mm long, to 6 mm wide at the base, both sides with stomata; male inflorescences to 7 cm long and 2 cm wide; cones to 10 cm long and nearly as wide. LG 23. New Caledonia. z9

A. columnaris (Forster) Hook. Tree, to 60 m high, the lower branches usually abscising, short shoots arise from the adventitious buds at the base, this portion of the stem is then densely covered to make a "green column", branches horizontal, side branches long, slender, whip-like in appearance, bark exfoliating, paper thin; needles of the younger shoots triangular to lanceolate, to 12 mm long, acute, broadly ovate on older branches, about 6 mm long and 3 mm thick, stiff, densely overlapping, bowed forward and inward (like a twisted rope in appearance); male inflorescences 2.5–6 cm long, 12–20 mm thick, surrounded at the base by cupule forming needles; cones ellipsoid, to 15 cm long, 11 cm thick, scales about 3 cm wide, seeds with about 12 mm wide wings on either side, with a terminal, 8 mm long thorny tip. BM 4635; CCE 73; LG 26 (= *A. cookii* R. Br. ex Endl.; *A. excelsa* [Lamb.] R. Br.). New Caledonia, Polynesia. Differing from the similar *A. heterophylla* in the compact, less "feathery" habit and the columnar, "green stem". Plate 17. z9

A. cunninghamii D. Don. Tree, 45–60 m high, stem to 3 m wide, bark rough, peeling horizontally in thin layers, branches in whorls of 4–7, the uppermost ascending, young branches on the branch tips frequently grouped in clusters; needles in 2 forms: spirally arranged on young trees and side shoots, lanceolate, 8–15 mm long, straight, sharply pointed, on older trees and fruiting branches more densely packed, shorter, more imbricate, short acuminate and curved inward, midrib decurrent, green to blue-green, both sides with stomatal lines; cones ovate-globose, about 10 cm long, 7.5 cm wide, seed scales terminating in a lanceolate, reflexed tip, seed with a narrow, membranous wing on either side. BAU 322; LT 20; CCE 71, 73, 74. Australia; northern New South Wales; New Guinea. Plate 17; Fig. 21 (Br). z9

'Glauca'. Needles more silver-gray or blue-gray. Imported into Europe from Moreton Bay by Loddiges about 1840. Fig. 21 (Br). z9

'Longifolia'. Needles longer and straighter. About 1840. z9

'Pendula'. Branches pendulous. 1867. z9

'Taxifolia'. Needles nearly 2 ranked, branches not clustered, more distinct, very densely arranged. Before 1867.

A. heterophylla (Salisb.) Franco. The well known "Norfolk Island Pine" of greenhouse culture. Tree, to 70 m high, branches in whorls of 4–7, bark exfoliating in thin layers; needles in 2 forms, on young plants and side branches soft, awl-shaped, bowed inward and not overlapping (mature needles hardly ever seen on plants in cultivation!); cones usually wider than high, to 12 cm wide and 10 cm high, seeds 2.5–3 cm long and 12 mm wide (without the well developed wing). LT 21; CCE 74–75 (= *A. excelsa* auct.). Norfolk Island. 1793. Very frequently found in cultivation in warmer regions or as a house plant. Plate 19. z9

Includes a number of cultivars with varying needle colors or shapes.

'Albospica'. Needles and branches silvery variegated but often becoming green (= *A. excelsior* 'Silver Star'; *A. excelsior variegata alba* Carr.). 1867.

'Aurea Variegata'. Needles blue-green with a wide, light yellow stripe. 1867

'Compacta'. Habit densely compact. 1891.

'Glauca'. Needles more blue-green.

'Gracilis'. Habit compact and ornamental, popular as a potted plant. 1923.

'Leopoldii'. Compact habit; needles blue-green. 1923.

'Monstrosa'. Branches often in clusters and with white tips. 1867.

'Muelleri'. Especially strong growing form. 1923.

'Robusta'. Strong grower; needles deep green (= *A. goldieana* Hort.; *A. sanderiana* Hort.). 1881.

'Speciosissima'. Very similar to *A. cunninghamii* in appearance, but coarser and more compact; needles to 4 cm long, curved. Originated before 1847 by Rougier in Chauvière near Paris.

'Virgata'. Similar to *Picea abies* 'Virgata' in appearance, with or without short side branches. Found in a Palermo, Sicily garden before 1906.

A. humboldtensis Buchholz. Tree, 12–15 m high, bark light gray; leaves broadly ovate, acute, about 6 mm long and 4 mm wide; male inflorescences as yet unknown; cones nearly globose or broadly ovate, to 8 cm long, on about a 2.5 cm long stalk. LG 28. New Caledonia, Mount Humboldt. Not well known. z9

A. klinkii Lauterbach. Tree, to 50 m high in its habitat, bark dark reddish-brown, rough, secretes a great deal of resin, branches in whorls; leaves clustered on both ends of the branch. NE. New Guinea. Not well known. z9

A. luxurians (Brongn. & Griseb.) Laubf. Tree, with columnar habit, to 30 m high in its habitat, but often much smaller, with round, dense crown apex, bark gray, peeling in narrow, horizontal bands, branches with mature foliage 10–18 mm in diameter (including the needles); juvenile needles erect, 6–12 mm long, much larger on older branches and more widely spaced, usually more or less straight, to 13 mm long and 5 mm wide; male cones 12–17 cm long and 25–28 mm wide, seed cones 10–12 cm long and 8–10 cm wide, seed scales to 35 mm long with about a 10 mm long tip. LG 22 (= *A. cookii* var. *luxurians* Brongn. & Griseb.). New Caledonia. Fig. 22. z9

A. montana Brongn. & Griseb. Tree, with columnar habit, 10–40 m high in its habitat, branches in the upper part of the crown outspread, abscising on the lower trunk and replaced by many adventitious sprouts, branches with mature foliage 15–22 mm wide (including the needles); leaves lanceolate on young trees and adventitious shoots, also imbricate, 10 × 4–5 mm, generally larger, mature needles erect, curved forward in an attractive manner and imbricate; male cones 8–13 cm long and 2–3 cm wide, seed cones about 8 to 9 cm long, seed scales to 32 mm long with a 5–10 mm long apex. LG 25. New Caledonia, common in the mountains. Fig. 22. z9

A. muelleri (Carrière) Brongn. & Griseb. Tall tree, similar to *A. rulei*, but leaves larger and coarser, thick, leathery, 25–30 mm long and 12–15 mm wide, ovate, densely overlapping like *A. araucaria*, sharply acuminate, with stomatal lines on both sides; male inflorescences terminal, to 25 cm long and 3 cm wide; cones ovate, 11–15 cm long, 8–10 cm wide, like small cones of *A. auraucaria* in appearance. LG 20. New Caledonia. z9

A. rulei F. Muell. ex Lindl. Tree, to 15 m high, stem densely covered with erect branches arising on all sides, branches up to 5 m high tail-like, to 3 cm thick; leaves dark green, bowed inward, glossy, overlapping densely and totally encircling the twig, stiff, leathery to hard, quite variable in size and differing from plant to plant, 12–25 mm long and 6–8 mm wide at the base, apex short acuminate, stomata tiny, only on the upper side; male inflorescences terminal, 5 cm long, 2.5 cm wide; cones similar to those of *A. columnaris*, tips of the scales with a thorn-like, 2 cm long appendage, seed about 8 mm long and 4 mm wide, narrow winged. LG 24; CCE 74. New Caledonia. z9

'Goldieana'. More graceful habit; leaves smaller. Plate 22.

'Elegans'. Branch whorls more closely spaced, branches thinner; leaves smaller. Before 1884.

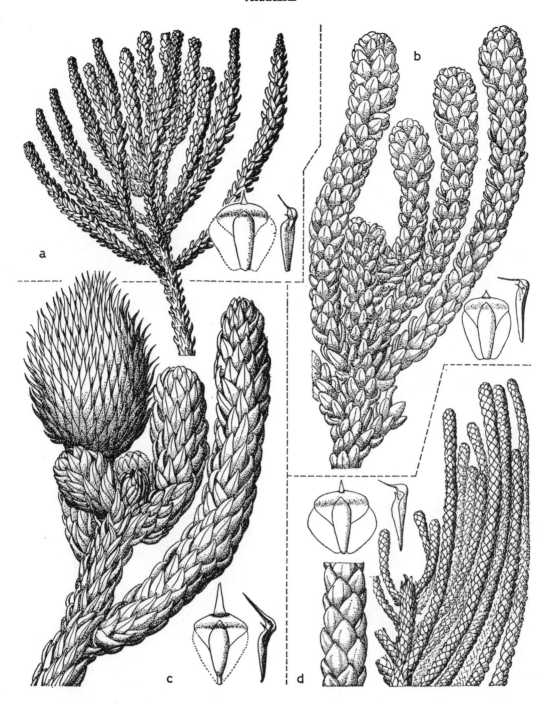

Fig. 22. **Araucaria.** a. *A. luxurians;* b. *A. montana;* c. *A. rulei;* d. *A. columnaris*
(from De Laubenfels, modified)

'Intermedia'. Needles intermediate between *A. rulei* and *A. columnaris.*

'Polymorpha'. Young shoots often pendulous; leaves compressed, obtuse 4 sided, more or less awl-shaped on the tip.

Lit. Mattos, J. R.: O Pinheiro Brasileiro; 620 pp., 370 ills. Sao Paulo 1972.

ATHROTAXIS D. Don—Tasmanian Cedars— TAXODIACEAE

Evergreen, small or medium sized trees, some resembling *Cryptomeria;* bark lightly furrowed, exfoliating in long strips; branches small, rather dense and irregularly arranged, branchlets erect; leaves small, spirally arranged, either scale-like and appressed or more lanceolate and somewhat loosely outspread; plants monoecious; male flowers solitary, terminal, catkin-like at the branch tips, with spirally arranged, compact anthers; female flowers solitary, terminal, with 15–25 spiral, ovate bract scales, each with 3–6 inverted ovules; cones ripening in the first year, similar to *Cryptomeria,* scales woody, with the basal woody portion vertically erect from the cone axis; seeds small, oblong, thin, with 2 narrow wings, similar to those of *Sequoiadendron;* cotyledons 2. x = 11.—3 species in the mountains of Tasmania; over winter in the greenhouse in cooler climates.

Athrotaxis cupressoides D. Don. Tree, 6–12 m high; leaves all scale-like, scarcely 3 mm long, obtuse, densely appressed to the branch, thick, margin translucent, finely toothed; cones globose, 8–12 mm wide, scales woody, short pointed. NF 3: 9 (native habitat); HI 559. Western Tasmania; Lake St. Clair District. Plate 23; Fig. 23. z8–9

A. laxifolia Hook. Tree, to 9 m high; leaves betweeen *A. cupressoides* and *A. selaginoides* in form, 4–6 mm long, awl-shaped to lanceolate, thick, slightly diverging from the branch, apex curved inward, margin translucent, not toothed, with 2 blue stomatal bands above, whitish depressions beneath; cones about 18 mm thick. HI 573. Western Tasmania; in the mountainous regions. Plate 21; Fig. 23. z8–9

A. selaginoides D. Don. Tree, to 35 m high, bark fibrous and somewhat furrowed, abundantly branched; leaves 8–12 mm long, ovate-lanceolate, sharply acuminate, very similar to those of *Cryptomeria,* spreading widely, sickle-shaped, inclined inward, with stomatal bands on both sides, margin not translucent; cones globose, 12–18 mm thick, scales numerous, with thorn-like, upward pointing tips. CTa 4; BM 9639. Western Tasmania; in the mountains over 1000 m. Plate 23; Fig. 23. z9

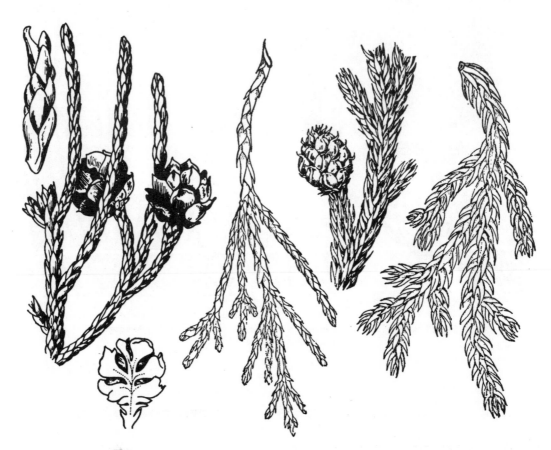

Fig. 23. **Athrotaxis.** From left to right: *A. cupressoides* with cones, cone in cross section, twig, enlarged; *A. laxifolia,* branch; *A. selaginoides,* 2 branches, on left with cone (from Gray, Bailey and Gard. Chron.)

AUSTROCEDRUS Florin & Boutelje — CUPRESSACEAE

A monotypic genus, closely related to *Libocedrus*. Evergreen trees or shrubs, broad conical habit when young, eventually flat crowned; branches short, divaricate, alternate or opposite, densely branched; leaves dimorphic, opposite, somewhat spreading outspread or appressed, 4 rowed imbricate, with stomata on the underside, stomatal bands of the folded leaves not subdivided, outer walls of the stomatal guard cells at least as strongly cutinized as the epidermal cells surrounding the stomatal bands, only 1 protuberance (papilla) on the stomatal guard cells; male flowers terminal on short shoots, solitary, tiny, globose to oblong; female flowers terminal on short side branches, oblong; cones small, with 4 scales, with a small "wart" (not thorn!) on the dorsal side under the apex; seeds usually 4, with 2 uneven wings, of which the smaller is only a narrow limb; cotyledons 2. x = 11. — 1 Species in S. America. See range map under Libocedrus.

Austrocedrus chilensis (D. Don) Florin & Boutelje. Chilean Cedar. Small tree, rarely to 20 m high, stem straight, crown narrow, but wider with age, branchlets densely packed, 2 ranked, like *Thuja;* lateral leaves much longer than the facial leaves, thick, furrowed on both sides, with a sharp inward curving tip, facial leaves much smaller, nearly totally covered, with obtuse tips and indistinct dorsal glands on the dorsal side, with white markings on the underside; cones solitary, terminal, with 4 scales, the lowest pair small and reflexed, seeds small, narrow, winged (= *Libocedrus chilensis* [D. Don] Endl.). Mountain slopes in the Andes of Chile, from northern Valparaiso to Valdivia. 1847. Plate 24; Fig. 24. z8–9

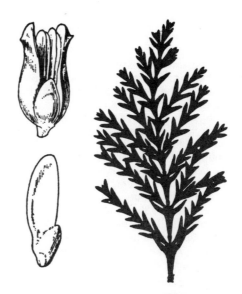

Fig. 24. *Austrocedrus chilensis.* Twig, actual size (Original); left, cones, seed beneath, enlarged

AUSTROTAXUS Compton—TAXACEAE

Monotypic genus, similar to *Podocarpus* in appearance, especially in habit and foliage, but the fruits are very similar to those of *Taxus;* male inflorescences in the leaf axils, in small spikes, at the base of younger shoots. See the following description.

Austrotaxus spicata Compt. Large evergreen tree, crown dense and bushy; leaves resembling those of *Podocarpus,* spirally arranged, linear, 8–12 cm long, 4 mm wide, short acuminate, margin somewhat involuted, dark green above, midrib distinctly indented above, raised on the underside; male flowers in axillary spikes, about 15 mm long, stamens 1–5, with 2–4 pollen sacs each, female flowers on axillary branchlets, these densely covered with wide, thick, imbricate scales; seed chambers solitary, terminal, erect, fruit about 3 cm long, enclosed nearly to the apex with an aril, like *Taxus,* seed drupelike, 12–15 mm long. LG 2. New Caledonia; in moist forests. Fig. 25. z9

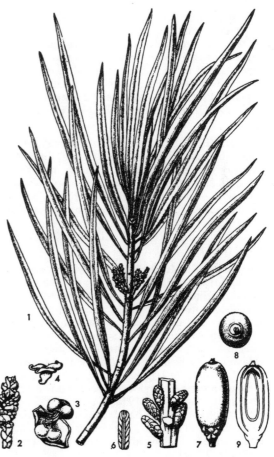

Fig. 25. *Austrotaxus spicata.* 1. Branch with male flower cones; 2–4. flowers; 5–6. female flowers; 7–9. fruit (from Compton)

CALLITRIS Vent.—Cypress Pines—CUPRESSACEAE

Evergreen trees and shrubs with hard, split or shredding bark, branches short, erect, jointed; leaves in whorls of 3, totally covering the branch to the small, triangular, somewhat thickened, erect and inward curving tips, juvenile foliage narrow, 8–13 mm long; plants monoecious; male flowers solitary or 2–3 terminal, cylindrical or oblong, anthers in whorls of 3–4; female flowers solitary or in clusters of 6–8 scales, each with numerous seed chambers; cones globose, ovate or conical, persisting for several years after releasing the seed, with 6–8 scales grouped in a whorl; seeds oblong, 2–9 per scale, with 2 or 3 wide wings. x = 11. — Some 16 species in Australia, Tasmania and New Caledonia; not winter hardy but found in the conservatories of many botanic gardens. A valuable forest tree in its habitat, very tolerant of drought. All z9

Sect. I. **Octoclinis** Benth.
Cones large, ovate, conically tapered, cone scales and stamens in 2 whorls of 4:
C. macleayana

Sect. II. **Hexaclinis** Benth.
Cones with 6 scales, nearly globose to broad ovate:
all the other species

Callitris baileyi C. T. White. Tree with slender habit; leaves green, 5 mm long, but only 2 mm long on the outer branch tips, dorsally keeled; cones solitary on thin fruiting branches, ovate or oblong, often also twisted, 12 mm wide, scales 6, thick, the dorsal side with a raised spot and a furrow, the larger scales usually oriented toward the tip, seeds few, with 2 uneven wings. Australia; SE. Queensland and NE. New South Wales. z9

C. canescens (Parl.) S. T. Blake. Shrub or small tree, 6–9 m high, branches divided into fine branchlets, internodes short; leaves scale-like, usually most shorter than 4 mm, blue-green, obtuse; cones solitary or in clusters, globose, 8–20 mm thick, smooth, gray on short, thick stalks, scales, the alternate ones much smaller and more regularly triangular than the others, seed with 2 wings, blackish. BAU 260–261; CCE 79. W. Australia; gravelly areas. z9

C. columellaris F. J. Muell. Shrub or small, slow growing tree, exceptionally to 25 m high, bark gray-brown, hard, fissured, branches densely foliate, distributed in dense branch clusters; needles about 2.5 mm long, blue-green, rounded on the dorsal side giving the branch a cylindrical appearance; cones solitary or in clusters, globose, to 15 mm thick, on 8 mm long stalks, scales 6, variable in size on the same cone, the smaller scales only about ⅓ the size of the largest, woody, but thin, opening to the base when ripe, never warty, seed reddish-brown, with 2–3 light wings. BAU 119 (as *C. glauca*) (= *C. arenosa* A. Cunn.; *C. glauca* R. Br. ex Bak. & Smith; *C. hugilii* Auct. [non *Frenela hugelii* Carr.]; *C. intratropica* Bak. & Smith). Australia; widely disseminated, especially in the East. Plate 23; Fig. 26. z9

C. drummondii (Parl.) Benth. & Hook. Shrub or tree, to 15 m high, bark fissured, hard, branches angular, longer

and coarser than most of the other species; needles larger than most of the other species, the branches totally appressed except for the obtuse tips; cones solitary or clustered, on striped stalks, globose, somewhat blue-green, 12 mm thick, scales thick, woody, brown, rough exterior, the raised spot found near the tip or absent, the alternate scales only slightly smaller than the others. BAU 252. W. Australia. z9

C. endlicheri (Parl.) F. M. Bailey. Tree, 18–25 m high, upright, conical crown, bark deep brown to black, deeply furrowed, branches compact, subdivided into many small branchlets; needles scale-like, keeled, the distinct tips sharp or obtuse; cones solitary or in clusters, oval-oblong, 12 mm long and 8 mm thick, on a 6–12 mm long stalk, scales 6, smooth or somewhat rough and with a wart near the tip, seeds small, dark brown, wings much larger than the seeds. BAU 195 (= *C. calcarata* R. Br.). Australia, eastern states, in the hills. Fig. 26. z9

C. macleayana (Muell.) Muell. Tall tree, to 50 m high, trunk 1–1.5 m in diameter, but usually much smaller, crown conical, bark red, striated-fibrous, branches distinctly triangular resulting from the arrangement of the needles; needles in 2 forms; juvenile leaves needle-like, light green, often in whorls of 4, 6–8 mm long, often persistent on the lower branches, mature foliage scale-like, sharply keeled toward the branch tips; male inflorescences oblong, 8 mm long; cones solitary, large, oval or conical, 25 mm high and wide (at the base), tapering to the acute tip, stalk 25 mm long, scales 8, thick, woody, acuminate, rather equal in size, furrowed on the dorsal side, with a recurved point at the apex, seeds winged. BAU 279 (= *C. parlatorei* Muell.). Australia; on the coast between Newcastle and Queensland. Fig. 26. z9

C. monticola Garden. Shrub, bushy, erect, about 2.5 m high; needles blue-green, 2–4 mm long, with a raised keel; cones solitary or clustered, on thick fruiting branches, broadly ovate to flat-globose, to 25 mm wide, scales 6, thick, with a rugose exterior before ripening and a point near the apex, the larger scales directed toward the apex, seeds numerous, dark brown, 2 winged. Australia; SE. Queensland and NE. New South Wales. z9

C. muelleri (Parl.) F. J. Muell. Shrub or also a small tree, columnar habit, to 15 m high, crown very dense, bark black, tight, hard, branches ascending at acute angles to the stem, branches dense and with long internodes, appearing angular from the stem clasping bases; mature foliage somewhat erect, olive-green, 6–10 mm long, longer than most of the other species, the distinct tips rather obtuse, juvenile foliage occasionally present on fruiting branches; cones solitary or grouped, rather globose with a flattened tip, 18–30 mm wide, scales 6, the largest oblong and obtuse, the smallest triangular and acute, seeds 2, dark brown, usually 2 winged. BAU 264. Australia; New South Wales. Fig. 26. z9

C. neo-caledonica Duemmer. Small, wide crowned tree, to 8 m high, the 3rd year branches thick, round, coarse, gray-brown, covered with the leaf scars of the abscised scale-leaves, current year's shoots short, jointed, triangular, foliate, 2.5–7 cm long and 2.5 mm thick, densely packed; needles in groups of 3, imbricate, scale-like, 3–5 mm long, distinctly keeled, margin tiny toothed, apexes acute. LG 42 (= *C. sulcata* var. *alpina* Compton). New Caledonia; in the mountains at 1000 m. z9

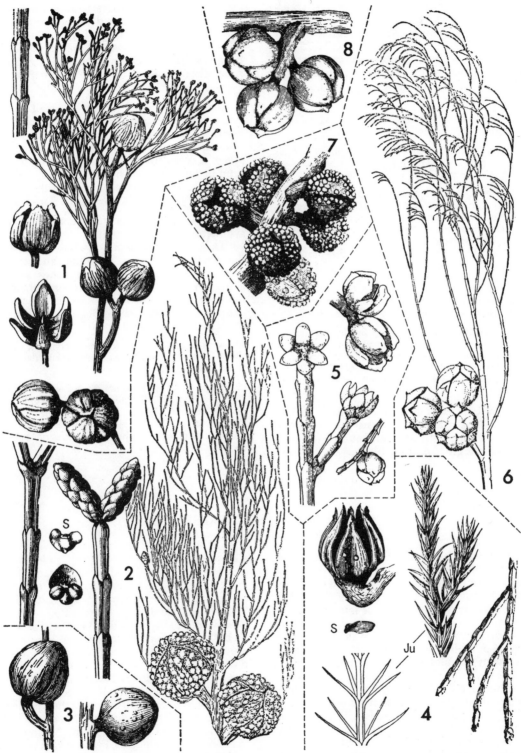

Fig. 26. 1. *C. columellaris*; 2. *C. preissii* ssp. *preissii*; 3. *C. preissii* ssp. *murrayensis*; 4. *C. macleayana* with mature and juvenile foliage; 5. *C. endlicheri*; 6. *C. rhomboidea*; 7. *C. preissii* ssp. *verrucosa*; 8. *C. muelleri* (from Maiden; Poole/Adams) (S = Seed; Ju = juvenile branches)

C. oblonga Rich. Smaller, erect shrub or a small, symmetrical tree, to 8 m high, very strongly branched with many fine twigs; needles 4–5 mm long, keeled, the upper portion distinctly acutely triangular, the basal portion tightly appressed forming angular internodes; cones solitary or in clusters, ovate, much tapered toward the apex, short stalked or sessile, scales 6, but also 8 on young shoots, woody, the largest obtuse and 20–25 mm long, the others half as long, the spot on the apex distinct, seeds broadly ellipsoid, deep brown, wings variable in size and form. BAU 272; DJ 25; CCE 79 (= *C. gunnii* Hook. f.). Tasmania. z9

C. preissii Miq. This species is composed of the following 3 subspecies:

ssp. **murrayensis** Garden. Like ssp. *preissii*, but differing in the longer than wide cones (when ripe), and fewer or totally absent warts. S. Australia, but not in the West. Fig. 26. z9

ssp. **preissii.** Tree with erect or outspread branches, only shrubby in coastal areas; needles very small, 2–4 mm long, not keeled on the dorsal side; male inflorescences cylindrical, 5 mm long; cones solitary or in clusters, sessile to nearly so, ovate to flat-globose, often shorter than wide, to 25 cm wide or more when ripe, often with large oil or resin warts, these to 2 mm wide, scales 6, thick, woody, the larger ones obtuse, the smaller tapering to the apex, seeds dark brown, 2 winged. BAU 88 (as *C. robusta*) (= *C. gracilis* R. T. Baker; *C. robusta* [A. Cunn. ex Parl.] F. M. Bailey; *C. propinqua* R. Brown ex Endl.). S. Australia; widely disseminated. Very valuable forestry tree. Fig. 26. z9

ssp. **verrucosa** (A. Cunn ex Endl.) Garden. Smaller, frequently multistemmed tree, differing from the type in the broadly ovate or flat-globose cones, generally less than 25 mm wide, scales densely covered with small papillae. BAU 100; CRV 54 (= *C. verrucosa* [A. Cunn. ex Endl.] F. J. Muell.). S. Australia. Fig. 26. z9

C. rhomboidea R. Br. ex L. C. Rich. Small tree, 9–15 m high, trunk 30–40 cm thick, crown narrow and very dense, branches much divided into numerous, thin twigs; needles light green or more blue-green, 2–3 mm

long, the branches densely appressed along their entire length, keeled, terminating in a short point; cones globose, 8–12 mm thick, gray-brown, on short, stout stalks, scales 6, thick, rhombic, with a thick, raised, centrally located point, the smaller scales only half as large as the larger, seeds dark brown, rounded, small, with 2 very narrow wings. BAU 223; CRV 44 (= *C. cupressiformis* F. J. Muell.; *C. tasmanica* [Benth.] R. T. Baker & H. G. Smith). Australia, except western Australia; naturalized in New Zealand. Plate 21; Fig. 16. z9

C. roei (Endl.) Muell. Shrub or small tree, branches stout, erect, smaller branches flexible, outspread; needles 3–5 mm long, sharply keeled on the dorsal side; cones globose, 12–18 mm thick, on short, thick stalks, scales 6, very thick, the smaller ones triangular and acuminate, the largest obtuse, smooth, with prominent ridges (when closed), each scale with a large, conical point near the apex. W. Australia. Rare tree. z9

C. sulcata (Parl.) Schlecht. Tree, to 12 m high, crown symmetrical, stem straight and conical; young branches with needles in whorls of 3 or 4, these narrow, encircling the branches, about 6 mm long and 1.2 mm wide, generally shorter on older branches but eventually elongating again, obtuse keeled on the dorsal side; cones to about 18 mm thick, ovate or flat-globose, scales 6, nearly alike, all with raised point on the dorsal side. LG 41. New Caledonia. z9

All species only suitable for warm climates, especially well suited for dry climates. Resistance to termite damage makes the wood quite valuable.

Lit. Baker, R. T., & H. G. Smith: A Research of the Pines of Australia. Sydney 1907 (pp. 13–289: The Genus *Callitris*, with many plates). ● Garden, J.: A Revision of the genus *Callitris* Vent. Contr. N.S.W. Nat. Herb. **2**, 363–392, 1957. ● Moore, H. E. : Further notes on Conifer nomenclature. Baileya 1967, 26 (only *Callitris*).

CALOCEDRUS Kurz—CUPRESSACEAE

Evergreen trees with flat branchlets; leaves decussate in mock whorls of 4, scale-like, leathery, distinctly dimorphic, at least in the transition stage, lateral leaves not touching the facial leaves, facial leaves easily visible between the laterals, stomata more or less distinct on both sides, plants monoecious, the male flowers solitary, terminal, with 12–16 stamens; female flowers nearly globose, ovate or oblong, with 1 pair of seed producing scales, each with 2 ovules and a pair of infertile scales beneath; cones ovate or oblong, ripening in the first year, scales 6, with a long or short thorn on the dorsal side under the tip, the upper pair of scales united in a flat plate between the outer scales; seeds with 2 unequal wings, the smaller distinctly developed; cotyledons 2. x = 11.—3 species in Pacific N. America and subtropical East Asia, usually in mixed or coniferous forests, seldom in a pure stand, in ravines or mountain slopes, 300–2500 m. See range map under *Libocedrus*.

Calocedrus decurrens (Torrey) Florin. California Incense Cedar. Tree, to 45 m high, branches very short, erect, developing a very narrow, columnar crown, becoming more irregular with age (see Plate 25), bark light brown, exfoliating, older trunks with red-brown, deeply split bark, branchlets very flattened, dark green on both sides, about 1.5–2 mm wide, leaves oval-oblong, acuminate, densely appressed to the branch, apex distinct, lateral leaves about the same length as the facial leaves, their margins not touching, about 3 mm long; cones oblong, 2–2.5 cm long, pendulous, light red-brown, with 6 scales, all thorny at the tip, the upper pair connate to form a flat plate (= *Libocedrus decurrens* Torr.; *Heyderia decurrens* [Torr.] K. Koch). N. America; Oregon to Nevada and California, in moist valleys on fertile soil with *Abies concolor*, and others. 1853. Plate 21 and 25; Fig. 27. z7

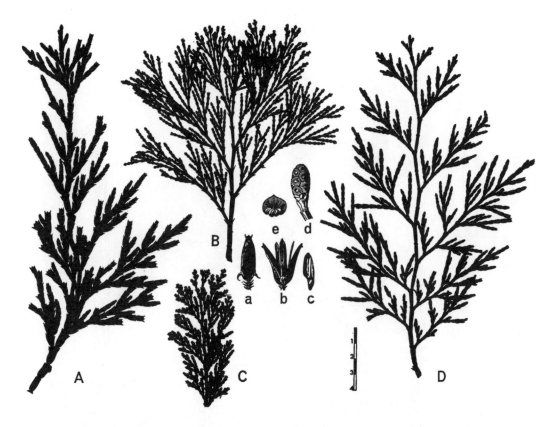

Fig 27. **Calocedrus.** A. *C. macrolepis*; B. *C. decurrens* (a–b. cones, c. seed, d. female flower, e. stamen interior); C. *C. decurrens* 'Intricata'; D. *C. formosana*

'Aureovariegata'. Gold-yellow branchlets scattered over the entire plant. Observed in 1896. Plate 25.

'Columnaris'. Very narrow columnar form with especially short, compactly arranged branches. Occurs often from seed.

'Compacta'. Habit more compact, globose, densely branched (= 'Nana'?). Known since 1891. Westonbirt Arboretum, England.

'Glauca'. Like the species, but with distinctly blue-green needles. 1884.

'Horizontalis'. Branches conspicuously horizontal. Brought into the trade by Spaeth in 1891, but no longer in cultivation.

'Intricata'. Dwarf form, compact upright habit, very densely branched, branch tips with a brownish tinge in winter. Originated from seed by James R. Noble in San Francisco, California, USA about 1938. A 12 year old plant is about 60 cm high and 35–45 cm wide. Plate 25; Fig. 27.

C. formosana (Florin) Florin. Large tree, to 23 m high, and 3 m diameter at the base, stem often very curved, bark smooth, purple-brownish, branchlets 2-ranked, alternate; leaves scale-like, obtuse, about 1.5–2.5 mm wide, dark green above, lighter green beneath; cones oblong, 1–1.5 cm long, somewhat curved, with 4 scales, each scale with 1 to 2 seeds, these 8–12 mm long, including the 10 mm long and 3 mm wide wing. LWT 15; LT 51 (= *Libocedrus formosana* Florin; *Heyderia formosana* [Florin] Li). Taiwan; in the northern and central part of the island, at 300–1900 m. Fig. 27. z9

C. macrolepis S. Kurz. Tree, to 30 m high, crown broadly conical, bark gray-white, scaly; leaves larger, thinner and flatter than those of *C. decurrens*, to 12 mm long on the terminal leader, side branches 6–8 mm long, about 2.5 mm wide, bluish-white beneath, keel of the lateral leaves straight or curved outward near the sharp apex, facial leaves inverted triangular, midrib with a distinct depression in the middle of the upper side, midrib indistinct on the underside, abruptly terminating in a sharp point; cones ellipsoid, 6–12 mm long, on thin, 4 sided, to 3 cm long branches, scales 6, similar to those of *C. decurrens*, usually 1 seed per fertile scale. LF 38; JRHS 68: 4; CBJ 56 (Br) (= *Libocedrus macrolepis* [Kurz] Benth. & Hook.; *Heyderia macrolepis* [Kurz] Li). China; S. Yunnan, Hainan and the Burmese border, in ravines and along mountain streams at 1200–1500 m. 1900. Fig. 27. z9

CATHAYA Chun & Kuang—PINACEAE

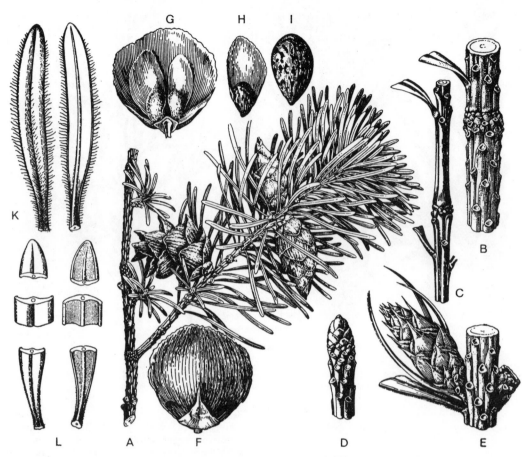

Fig. 28. *Cathaya argyrophylla*. A. Branch with cones; B. and C. branches; D. terminal buds; E. young cones; F. seed scales, outside; G. seed scales, inside with 2 seeds; H. seed with wings; I. seed; K. juvenile leaves; L. mature leaves, from above and beneath (from Chun and Kuang, modified)

Tall, evergreen trees branching horizontally; branches dimorphic, the sterile side branches shortened (like *Larix*) and with elongated leaf bases, but with narrow, sharply delineated furrows with a nearly rectangular-rounded leaf scar, like *Larix* in the cushion-like leaf bases on the branch tips, like *Picea* in the more basal leaf bases; buds not resinous, terminal buds conspicuous, nearly ovate, with membranous, abscising bud scales; needles linear, often a slightly curved sickle-shape at the tips, short petioled base, spirally arranged, close together, nearly in whorls on short shoots, young needles ciliate on the margin at first, with more or less persistent, tiny bristly hairs above; mature needles deep green above and smooth except for the middle furrow, bright green beneath, with 2 silver-white stomatal bands adjacent to the raised midrib; 2nd year needles with 2 resin ducts, in cross section positioned marginally under the epidermis; plants monoecious; male catkins erect, ovate-oblong at first, later spike-like; female catkins nearly ovate, short stalked or nearly sessile; seed scales in several rows spirally or imbricately arranged, often absent on the basal portion of the cone; ripe cones

persisting for many years among the small side branches, erect at first, later more or less directed outward; bract scales caudate tipped and very long; seeds obovate, winged.—Only 1 species in China in the Kwangsi and Szechwan Provinces; 1 further fossil species has been found in W. Germany.

Some botanists, including P. Gregus, Szeged, Hungary, have determined by xylotomic examination that this genus is very closely related to *Pseudotsuga* and can perhaps be considered a subgenus of the latter.

Cathaya argyrophylla Chun & Kuang. Tree, to 20 m high, stem to 40 cm thick or more, bark gray and irregularly narrowly fissured, branches arranged horizontally, young shoots brown striped, densely short pubescent, glabrous in the 2nd year, buds oval conical, yellow-brown, 6–8 mm long; needles on long shoots arising radially around the branch, 4–5 cm long and 2.5–3 mm wide, but nearly whorled on short shoots and only 2.5 cm long, juvenile foliage densely ciliate on the margin, needles all coarse, margin narrow, revolute, underside with bluish-white stomatal bands on either

Plate 17

Araucaria columnaris
in its native habitat in New Caledonia
Photo: Centre Forestier Tropical (F)

Araucaria cunninghamii
in La Mortola, Italy

Araucaria araucana, 13 m high,
in Balestrand, Norway
Photo: Reisaeter, Vollebekk

Araucaria bidwillii, male inflorescences,
half natural size (from Baker & Smith)

Plate 18

Welwitschia mirabilis with pistillate inflorescences in its native habitat in the Namib Desert, South Africa

Araucaria araucana in its native habitat in the Andes, Chile
Photo: Desmond Clark

Plate 19

Araucaria araucana
in Benmore, Scotland

Araucaria araucana
with pistillate and staminate flowers(!)
on the Vierwaldstättersee, Switzerland

Araucaria bidwillii
in the Villa Thuret Garden in Cap d'Antibes,
southern France

Araucaria heterophylla
in the Sea Aquarium park in Miami, Florida; the
"Norfolk Island Pine" is, next to *Pinus halepensis,* the
most salt and wind tolerant conifer.

Plate 20

Abies bracteata,
in Mount Usher, County Wicklow, Southern Ireland

Abies bracteata,
young cones, Santa Lucia Mts., California
Photo: Uwe Horstmann

Abies equi-trojani
in the Landesarboretum Stuttgart-Hohenheim,
W. Germany

Abies koreana 'Blue Standard'
selected for its deep violet cones by J. D. Zu
Jeddeloh Nursery, W. Germany

Plate 21

Athrotaxis laxifolia
in Benmore, Scotland

Callitris rhomboidea with cones
in the Hamburg Botanic Garden, W. Germany

Calocedrus decurrens,
the cones ripen in early fall
and persist on the tree until spring

Calocedrus decurrens
in the Römischen Garden, Hamburg-Blankenese, W.
Germany

Plate 22

Araucaria balansae
in the Dortmund Botanic Garden, W. Germany

Araucaria rulei 'Goldieana'
in the Hamburg Botanic Garden, W. Germany

Araucaria araucana in its native habitat in Parque Nacional Los Paraguas, Chile
Photo: Bianchi, Minist. de Tierras y Colonisacion, Chile

Plate 23

Athrotaxis cupressoides
in the Royal Botanic Garden, Edinburgh, Scotland

Athrotaxis selaginoides in its native habitat in
Tasmania (from Baker & Smith)

Acmopyle pancheri, actual size,
from Kew Gardens, London, England

Callitris columellaris in the Suchumi Botanic Garden,
Black Sea coast, USSR

Plate 24

Austrocedrus chilensis
Photo: R. Florin

Austrocedrus chilensis in its habitat
Photo: Prof. Dr. Krieger

Amenotaxus argotaenia in the Canton Botanic Garden, China
Photo: F. Bencat

Plate 25

Calocedrus decurrens in the Lassen National Park,
California, USA; *Abies concolor* in the background
Photo: U.S. Forest Service

Calocedrus decurrens 'Intricata'
in the Hillier Arboretum, England

Calocedrus decurrens 'Aureovariegata' in Les Barres Arboretum, France

Plate 32

Chamaecyparis lawsoniana, cultivars. Left: 'Golden King'; middle: 'Masonii';
right: 'Gracilis Pendula'; all in the Hillier Arboretum, England

Chamaecyparis lawsoniana 'Pottenii', 6 m high,
in the Gimborn Pinetum, Doorn, Holland

Chamaecyparis lawsoniana 'Fletcheri', 8 m high,
in the Taranto Gardens, Pallanza, Italy

side of the midrib, each with 11–17 lines; ripe cones oblong-ovate, 3–5 cm long, 1.5–2 cm wide, with 13–16 seed scales, these rounded to broad round or oval-rounded, 15–25 mm long and 10–25 mm wide, chestnut-brown when ripe, later becoming darker brown, seeds somewhat oblique-obovate, 5–6 mm long, 3–4 mm thick, olive-black with irregular, lighter spots, wings 10–15 mm long and 4–6 mm wide, asymmetrical. CCE 84. China; Kwangsi Province; found in May 1955, by members of the Kwangfu Lingchu expedition. Fig. 28. z6?

C. nanchuensis Chun & Kuang, was originally described as a separate species, found by Y. C. Yang in Yunnan Province at Nanchuan Hsien. In China today considered an ecotype of *C. argyrophylla*.

Lit. Chun, W. Y., & K. Kuang: A new Pinaceae species, *Cathaya*, from the south and west of China. Bot. Jour. Moscow **43**, 461–470. 1958 (10 plates; in Latin and Russian)

CEDRUS Trew—Cedar—PINACEAE

Tall evergreen trees, broad, irregular crown, bark dark gray, smooth on young trees, on older trees fissured and scaly, branches with long and short shoots, buds small, ovate, persisting for 3–6 years, spirally arranged and widely spaced on long shoots, in dense clusters on short branches, stiff, acuminate, usually triangular in cross section, with 2 resin ducts near the epidermis; plants monoecious, inflorescences solitary, terminal on short branches; male inflorescences cylindrical, 5 cm long, erect; female flowers 1 to 1.5 cm long, reddish, ovate, composed of numerous rounded scales; cones erect, ovate to oval-oblong or cylindrical, ripening in the 2nd to 3rd year, disintegrating when ripe, seed scales very tightly appressed, wider than long, woody; seeds irregularly triangular, with a thin shell and large wing; cotyledons 9–10. x = 12.—4 species in the mountains of the southern and southeastern Mediterranean region and in the western Himalayas.

Cedrus atlantica (Endl.) Manetti ex Carr. Atlas Cedar. Tree, to 40 m high, crown always pyramidal, loose and open, branches always steeply ascending, central leader erect or leaning slightly sideways; needles bluish-green, under 25 mm long; cones 5–7 cm long, 4 cm wide, glossy light brown, seed scales to 3.5 cm wide, seeds 12 mm long, with 15 mm long wings. N. Africa; Atlas Mts. in Algeria and Morocco. Introduced into Europe in 1839. z7

'Albospica'. Young branches nearly white. Before 1868.

'Argentea Fastigiata'. Like 'Glauca', but crown narrowly conical. Introduced to the trade in 1961 by Hillier.

'Aurea'. Slow growing, conical, branches spreading more horizontally; needles golden-yellow in the first year, often with a grayish glow, greening in the second year. Originated in Boskoop before 1900. Damaged by bright sun. Plate 26.

'Aurea Robusta'. Conical habit, stronger than 'Aurea'; needles somewhat longer, lighter yellow, occasionally with bluish undertones (especially after transplanting or in the shade). Originated by H. den Ouden & Zoon in Boskoop, Holland, 1932.

'Columnaris'. Slender pyramidal habit, branches ascending; needles green. Originated in France before 1889. (EX)

'Fastigiata'. Columnar habit, tall growing, limbs short, ascending, densely branched; needles light green, blue-green beneath. Originated in Nantes, France by Lalande before 1890.

'Glauca'. Blue Atlas Cedar. Grows like the species, but much more densely branched; needles a gorgeous gray-blue, color especially intense on new growth. One of the most beautiful ornamentals, frequently found in cultivation. Found in the wild in the Atlas Mts. but there the blue color is more variable. Plate 26, 43.

'Glauca Horizontalis'. Branches more or less bowed downward, but the branches not touching the ground; needles an attractive blue. Only one plant known, in the Jardin Botanique, Nantes, France (in 1977 it was 3 m wide, 1 m high).

'Glauca Pendula'. Stem erect-drooping, branches densely arranged, hanging "mane-like" from the limbs; needles lighter or darker gray-blue. Originated before 1900 by Paillet in Chatenay, France.

'Pendula.' Habit nearly columnar, erect at first, then the tip becomes nodding and the branches hang more or less vertically; needles green. First observed in 1875 by Moreau in Fontenay-aux-Roses, near Paris. Plate 42.

'Pyramidalis'. Slender conical habit, branches horizontal, short, irregularly arranged. Originated by Paillet in Chatenay near Paris, 1889. Plate 26.

'Rustic'. Selection with especially impressive blue needle color. Introduced to the trade in 1962 by Monrovia Nursery, California, USA.

'Variegata'. Young branches yellowish, white variegated, likewise the needles, but not consistent. Originated by Sénéclauze, France, before 1867.

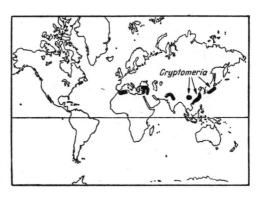

Fig. 29. Range of the genus *Cedrus* and *Cryptomeria*

More Prominent Characteristics of the *Cedrus* Species

	Habit	Central Leader	Needles	Cones
atlantica	crown light and open, branches steeply upright	straight, erect, pubescent	cross section about as high as wide	cylindrical, apex flat or concave
brevifolia	usually a stunted tree or shrub	usually curved	very short, only 12 mm long	cylindrical, apex concave with a blunt projection from the surface
deodara	conical when young, irregular when older, branch tips pendulous	whip-like, nodding	to 5 cm long, acuminate	barrel-shaped, apex round (not flat)
libani	crown flat, umbrella shaped, branches upright at least at the base	spreading sideways, glabrous or pubescent	wider than high in cross section	barrel-shaped, apex flat or concave

C. brevifolia (Hook. f.) Henry. Cypress Cedar. Slow grower, usually a stunted tree or tall shrub, to 12 m high with age, crown broad umbrella-form, limbs short, stiff, irregular, usually horizontal; needles 5–8 (–12) mm long, thick, slightly curved, with a short apex, blue-green; cones cylindrical, concave at the apex and with a large projection in the center. WM 3 A (Br) (= *C. libani* var. *brevifolia* Hook. f.). Cypress, in the mountains. Plate 26. z7

'Compacta'. Dwarf form, habit very dense; needles a conspicuous gray-blue. The parent plant was found in the garden of Mr. Archer in 1964 when it was 20 years old and measured 70 cm wide and 30 cm high. Introduced by Hillier, England.

'Horizontalis'. Quite flat habit. Also introduced by Hillier in 1964. Another flat growing dwarf form probably originating as a grafted lateral branch.

C. deodara (D. Don) G. Don. Himalayan Cedar. To 50 m high in its habitat, with 3 m diameter trunk, crown conical when young, branches horizontally arranged, nearly tiered, branch tips usually nodding, young branches densely pubescent; needles blue-green, grouped to 30 in clusters, 3–5 cm long, as long as wide in cross section; cones 1 or 2 together, on short shoots, ovate or more barrel-shaped, 7–10 cm long, 5–6 cm wide, rounded at the apex, bluish glaucous when young, reddish-brown when ripe, scales numerous, cuneate, 5–6 cm wide, usually not pubescent on the dorsal side, seeds 1.6–1.7 cm long, whitish, with large, light brown wings. The Himalayas, at 1200 m and more; introduced to Europe in 1822. Plate 1 and 27. z8

'Albospica'. Pyramidal habit, medium height, tips of the young shoots whitish, later yellowish, eventually totally green. CCE 93. Observed by Annesley in Castlewellan, N. Ireland before 1899.

'Argentea.' Fast growing cultivar; needles longer, silver-gray to bluish-gray. Cultivated by Minier, in Angers, France.

'Aurea'. Habit like the species, but scarcely taller than 3 to 5 m; needles gold-yellow on the new growth, generally greening in fall, greenish-yellow and pruinose in winter. 1966. Les Barres, France.

'Compacta'. Compact habit, globose-conical, becoming only a few meters high, branches densely arranged, tips nodding. Cultivated in France before 1867; also before 1917 by Gebr. Ellerbroek in Boskoop, Holland.

'Crassifolia'. Weak grower (probably an alpine form), branches few, short, wide spreading and somewat ascending, thick; needles not numerous, much shorter than on the species, sparsely arranged, straight, thick. Before 1855.

'Eisregen'. Branch tips much branched, not so conspicuously pendulous as the type; needles light blue-gray. Selected from the Paktia group and propagated by G. Horstmann, Schneverdingen, W. Germany. The only cedar, other than *C. libani* var. *stenocoma* to withstand –26.6°C in the winter of 1978/79 in the conifer collection of G. Horstmann. The hardiest clone of *C. deodara* and quite a valuable cultivar! z6–7.

'Eiswinter' (G. Horstmann). Frost hardy selection from the 'Paktia' group with light gray-green needles. 1983.

'Erecta'. Growth narrowly upright; foliage an outstanding silver-blue. Originated by Cripps in Tunbridge Wells, England, 1875.

'Fastigiata'. Columnar habit, limbs thick, ascending, not very well branched, widely spaced, young branches short, rather thick, smooth, reddish-gray; needles very uneven in length, straight, widely spaced, thickish, the long needles widely angled, the shorter ones more erect or directed forward. Found in a garden near Toulouse before 1867 by Dr. Turrel. (EX?)

'Flava'. Needles yellowish to whitish. Originated before 1867 by A. Leroy in Angers, France. (EX?)

'Fontinalis'. Especially regular conical habit. Before 1884. (EX)

'Glauca'. Foliage blue-green to silver-gray. Before 1909, and still in cultivation. (Jeddeloh).

'Golden Horizon'. (Van Vliet). Broad, flat habit, but strong growing; needles an intensive yellow to greenish-yellow in full sun, otherwise more blue-green, 15–28 mm long, to 4 cm long on young shoots. Selected as a seedling by Gebr. Van Vliet, Boskoop, Holland. 1975.

'Hesse'. Dwarf form, very dense growing, 40 cm high. Originated in the Nursery of Herm. A. Hesse, Weener, near Hanover, W. Germany before 1963.

'Karl Fuchs'. Clone of seedlings from Pakistan, the bluest of the Paktia forms. KN (Plate 1)

'Kashmir'. Normal growth habit but with silver-gray needles, supposedly hardy to –31°C. (Ill. in American Nurseryman, 4/15/1970: cover). Found in the J. F. Styler Nursery in Concordville, Pennsylvania, USA (1934). z7

'Mutabilis'. Regular conical habit. Before 1884. (EX)

'Nana'. Low, bushy habit, rather flattened on the apex, otherwise compact globose, very slow growing. WM 116. In the rock garden at Kew, London.

'Nivea'. Broad bushy habit, branches nodding; needles on the new growth nearly snow-white. Found by Annesley in Castle-wellan, N. Ireland, 1899.

"Paktia". Provisional name for plants descended from trees in the Paktia Province in Afghanistan. Very fast growing, fine needled, bluish-green to whitish-blue foliage. KN 45. Propagated by G. Horstmann, 3043 Schneverdingen, W. Germany. The most beautiful clone is 'Karl Fuchs'. More valuable than 'Kashmir'.

'Pendula'. Weeping form, often tied to a standard, branches loosely pendulous. BFN 94. Cultivated before 1900.

'Polarwinter'. (G. Horstmann). Winter hardy Paktia seedling with stout, pendulous branches and green needles. 1983.

'Prostrata'. Habit broad and flat. Hillier described a 20-year old plant as 30 cm high and and 75 cm wide.

'Pygmy'. An exceptionally small form with nearly globose habit, annual growth 6 mm; foliage blue-green. WDw 35; WM 117 (= C. deodara 'Pygmaea' Hillier). Found by Wm. T. Gotelli (a U.S. conifer collector) in a nursery around 1943; the plant at 17 years was only 30 cm high and 40 cm wide.

'Repandens'. Very pendulous habit or branches nearly procumbent. CCE 94. Originated in the Clarke nursery in San Jose, California, USA about 1930.

'Robusta'. Strong growing, conical, branches stout, thick, nodding, foliage very dense; needles 5–6 (–8) cm long, thick, straight, bluish-green. CCE 93 (= C. deodara gigantea Hort.). Found in France before 1850, still in cultivation. The heavy limbs must be supported to prevent breakage.

'Tristis'. Branches widely spaced, short, erect at first, then distinctly nodding, twigs more densely arranged and short (= C. deodara gracilis Sénécl.). Before 1855.

'Uncinata'. Variable in habit; needles somewhat hook-like. Before 1907. (EX?)

'Variegata'. Foliage white varieted, but not consistent (= C. deodara argenteovariegata de Vos.). Before 1887. (EX)

'Verticillata'. Branches nearly whorled; needles green. In La Maulévrie Arboretum, Angers, France.

'Verticillata Glauca'. Narrow upright habit, 3–5 m high, limbs spreading horizontally, sparsely branched, with wide internodes, limbs regularly spaced; needles whorled on young long .shoots, distinctly blue-green. CCE 94. Found in France before 1891, still in cultivation.

'Viridis'. Branches less pendulous; needles conspicuously bright green, glossy, much thinner than those of the species (= C. deodara tenuifolia Hort.). Cultivated in France before 1853.

'Wiesemannii'. Upright habit, much more compact than the species, limbs more densely compact, ascending-nodding, foliage very dense; needles blue-green. Originated before 1933 by P. Moll in Heisterbacherrott, Siegkreis, W. Germany.

C. libani A. Rich. Cedar of Lebanon. Tree, 20–40 m high, slow growing, crown conical when young, umbrella-shaped when older, limbs very strong, obliquely ascending when young, later horizontal, bark black-gray, fissured, branches short, forming plate-like tiers; needles usually dark green, stiff, 1.5–3.5 cm long, 30–40 in clusters, 4 sided, wider than high in cross section, acuminate; cones stalked, solitary, erect, barrel-shaped, 8–10 cm long and 4–6 cm wide, with protuberant tips, brown, seed scales to 5 cm wide with short pubescence on the exterior, very densely arranged, ripe cones open first in the middle, then toward the base, seed 15–18 mm long, with 25 mm long wings (= C. libanotica Link; C. libanensis Juss. ex Mirb.). Taurus Mts., Antitaurus and Lebanon, developing forests. 1638. Plate 43. z7

'Aurea'. Slow growing, conical; needles gold-yellow with green undertone, especially during the winter (C. atlantica 'Aurea' has a gray undertone!).

'Aurea prostrata'. Low growing form with yellow foliage. Origin: perhaps a grafted side branch from 'Aurea'.

'Comte de Dijon' (Barbier). A clone of 'Nana'. Broad oval-conical habit, very densely branched, limbs spreading horizontally; needles, in part, radially arranged, 20–25 mm long, fine, straight or slightly bowed, widest in the middle, becoming thinner at both ends, drawn out to a sharp apex. WDw 38; HD 32. Introduced to the trade in 1908 by Barbier, Orléans, France. The original plant (proven by Hornibrook in 1938) grows in the National Botanic Garden Glasnevin, Dublin (Ireland) and is about 5 m high and 4 m wide (considered the "type"). Another of the 4 original plants stands in the park of Myddleton House (earlier Bowle's Garden) and was illustrated in Gardeners Chronicle, 9/27/1967. z8

'Decidua'. Slow growing, bushy, branches numerous, dense, short; most of the needles abscising in winter. Originated by Sénéclauze in 1851, but also often seen in the habitat of the species.

'Denudata'. Stem straight upright, irregularly branched; needles dull green. Found in the nursery of Jaquemont-Bonnefond in Annonay, France around 1840.

f. fusiformis Carr. Cones distinctly spindle-shaped, with nearly acute tips. 1859.

'Glauca'. Branches usually shorter; needles blue-green to silver-gray (= C. libani argentea Lodd. ex Gord.). Before 1855. Occurs together with the species, especially in the Silesian Taurus Mts.

'Golden Dwarf'. Weak growing, remaining low, branches spreading, without a central leader; needles golden-yellow. KN 79 (= C. libani 'Prostrata' Krüssmn.; C. libani 'Aurea Prostrata' Hillier). A beautiful specimen stands in Kew Gardens, London.

f. microcarpa Carr. Cones very small, nearly globose. Found in a park in Roissy (Seinne et Oies), France before 1859.

'Multicaulis'. Low, nearly conical, then flat crowned, limbs ascending, numerous, branches erect, short; needles dark green. Originated at the Audibert Nursery in Tonelle, France before 1868.

'Nana'. Dwarf form, limbs very densely arranged, developing a globose bush, widely spaced, regularly arranged; needles 15–18 mm long on the long shoots, 1 mm wide, slightly sickle-shaped, acute, gray-green beneath, 30–40 in a bundle on short shoots. CCE 96; WM 3B (Br), 118 (H) (= C. libanotica var. nana Bail.). Common in cultivation; first observed in England in 1838. Plate 27.

'Nana Pyramidata'. Dwarf form, slow growing, conical, about 1 m high, branches numerous, spreading irregularly, twigs upright, thin; needles short, green. Observed by Sénéclauze before 1827. Occasionally cultivated under the name 'Nana'.

'Pendula'. This form is generally grafted on a high standard (OCC 65) and then becomes tree-like; if grafted low the branches grow horizontally along the ground. Known in cultivation since 1850. Occurs occasionally in the seed bed. Plate 28.

'Sargentii'. Dwarf form, slow growing, 1–1.5 m high, short stemmed, branches numerous, spreading horizontally at first, later nodding in all directions; needles long, thick, bluish pruinose. CCE 95; WM 3C (Br), 119 (H) (= *C. libani* var. *pendula sargentii* Hornibr.). Originated in the Arnold Arboretum, USA in 1919. Plate 28.

var. **stenocoma** (Schwarz) Davis. Slender conical habit at first, then more columnar, nearly spruce-like, branches spread horizontally, tips nodding slightly, crown never umbrella-form; needles silver-gray, needles and cones intermediate between those of *C. libani* and *C. atlantica*. The clone was brought into the trade by Fa. H. A. Hesse. Is more frost hardy than *C. libani*! JRHS 1949: 39–40 (= *C. libani* ssp. *stenocoma* Schwarz). SW. Anatolia, Turkey in the mountains at 1000–1800 m, developing forests.

'Stricta'. Narrow conical habit, very densely branched (stem not visible), branches short, ascending; needles glossy gray-green to silver-gray. Found before 1859 in the garden of an M. David in House near Auck, France.

'Tortuosa'. Branches and twigs twisted spirally. Found in 1903 in a private garden in Dulwich, England.

'Viridis'. Vigorous grower, branches ascending; like the species, but the needles are bright green, glossy. Before 1867 in a French nursery.

Lit. Franco, J. do Amaral: *Cedrus libanensis* et *Pseudotsuga menziesii.* Bol. Soc. Broteriana **24**, 73 to 77, 1950. ● Nitzelius, T.: Preliminaert om Cedar och deras odling i Sverige. Lustgarden 1966/6, 11 to 24, 1968. ● Sevim, M.: Die natuerliche Verbreitung und Standortbedingungen der Libanonzeder in der Turkei (in Turkish with German summary). Istanbul Univ. Orman fákult. dergisi, Istanbul 1952.

CEPHALOTAXUS S. & Z.—Plum Yew—— CEPHALOTAXACEAE

Evergreen trees and shrubs; branches opposite, young branches green; buds ovate, with numerous persistent scales; leaves needle-like, spirally arranged, but nearly 2-ranked, on an even plane, with distinct midrib above, 2 wide stomatal bands beneath; plants dioecious, rarely monoecious, axillary; male flowers in globose heads in the leaf axils of younger shoots; female flowers 1–3 in the basal scales of very young shoots; fruits large, drupe-like, shell fleshy on the outside, green to reddish, with 1–2 seeds in each fruit, about 2.5 cm long, stalked, resinous, interior hard and woody, ripening the 2nd year. x = 12.—8 species from the Himalayas to East Asia, only 2 generally hardy in temperate climates.

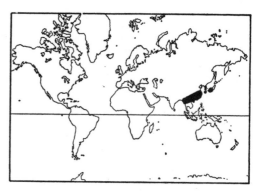

Fig. 30. Range of the genus *Cephalotaxus*

Most Important Leaf Characteristics of the *Cephalotaxus* Species

Species	Length	Arrangement	Apex	Underside
oliveri	21–25	flat, quite narrow	short acuminate	bluish
harringtonia var. *drupacea*	25–35	V-formed	short acuminate	gray
hainanensis	24–40	horizontal	short acuminate	
wilsoniana	30–40	horizontal	short acuminate	gray-white
sinensis	40–50	horizontal	short acuminate	bluish
harringtonia	40–60	irregular	short acuminate	gray
griffithii	ca. 50	horizontal	short acuminate	white
mannii	ca. 50	horizontal	short acuminate	nearly green!
fortunei	50–90	horizontal	short acuminate	white

Cephalotaxus fortunei Hook. A tree to 12 m high in its habitat, only a shrub in temperate zone cultivation, occasionally to 5–6 m high, often multistemmed, bark red-brown, fissured, branches whorled, outspread and somewhat nodding, buds small, with apical tips, glossy, red-brown scales, these persisting on the base of the young shoots until the next year; needles distinctly and nearly horizontally 2-ranked, widely spaced, linear, curved somewhat sickle-shape, 5–9 cm long, 3–4 mm wide, although also longer on younger plants, apex

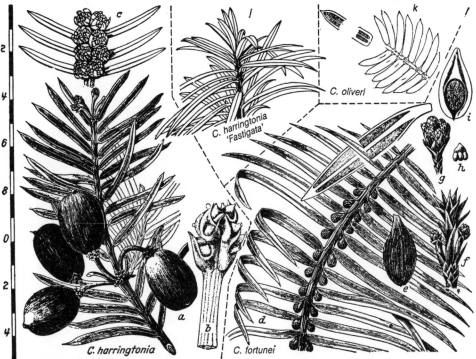

Fig. 31. **Cephalotaxus.** a. *C. harringtonia,* branch with fruits, b. female inflorescence, c. male inflorescence, d. *C. fortunei,* branch with male flowers, e. fruit, f. female flowers, g. male flowers, h. stamen, i. fruit, longitudinal section, j. *C. harringtonia* 'Fastigiata', branch, k. *C. oliveri* branch (from Beissner, Shirasawa and Gard. Chron.)

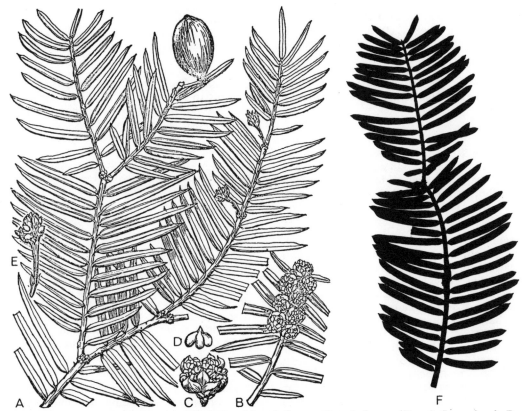

Fig. 32. **Cephalotaxus.** A. *C. wilsoniana,* branch with fruit and female flowers, B. male flowers, C. male flower heads, D. stamens, E. female flower; F. *C. harringtonia* var. *drupacea* (A–E. from Liu; F. Original)

generally drawn out to a sharp tip, base with a short petiole, with a distinctly raised midrib above and glossy green, 2 distinct white stomatal bands beneath, each with 18–22 lines; seeds ellipsoid-ovate, 2–3 cm long and 1–1.5 cm thick, bluish-green at first, olive-brown when ripe. FS 555; F10 188; BM 4499; CCE 98. Central and SW. China, in mountain forests. 1848. Fig. 31; Plate 63. z7–8

var. **alpina** L. Shrub or small tree, 2–12 m high; needles 4–7 cm long; male inflorescences nearly sessile. Mountains of NW. Yunnan and Sikiang.

'**Brevifolia**'. Like the type, but with shorter needles. (VR)

var. **concolor** Franch. Needles about 5 cm long, 4 mm wide, light green above, stomatal bands bluish and indistinct beneath, otherwise like the species. China; Szechwan; generally in thickets at 1200 m.

'**Grandis**'. Female form with especially long needles. Selected by Hillier. 1928.

'**Longifolia**'. Needles longer than those of the type.

'**Prostrata**'. Cultivar propagated from the lateral branches of the type, habit quite flat and broad (= *C. fortunei* 'Prostrate Spreader' Boom). Introduced to the trade by Hillier. 1964. Considered quite meritorious.

'**Pendula**'. Branch conspicuously nodding. 1866.

'**Robusta**'. Habit more vigorous and regular than the type; needles flatter and longer. In cultivation in France since 1867.

C. griffithii Hook. Small tree, needles about 5 cm long, 3–4 mm wide, glossy green above, white beneath; seeds about 4 cm long, usually grouped 3–4, oblong, short acuminate above, tapering at the base. CCE 102. Assam; Mishmi Hills, in the mountains at 2000 m. Very similar to *C. mannii*, but easily distinguished by the white stomatal bands. (The plant illustrated in Hookers Icones Plantarum on Plate 1933, from the year 1891 is the same as that illustrated as *C. oliceri* Mast., illustrated in Fang, W. P., Icones Plantarum Omeiesium. Plate 189 [1946].) z9

C. hainanensis Li. Closely related to *C. sinensis*, but becoming tree-like, 10–18 m high; needles shorter and wider, rather thin and flat, margin not involuted when dry, 2.5–4 cm long, 2–4 mm wide, linear, abruptly narrowed to a short prickly tip at the apex (not generally drawn out). China; Hainan, in mixed forests. z6?

C. harringtonia (Forbes) K. Koch. Small tree, scarcely over 10 m high, often only a shrub in cultivation, bark gray and exfoliating in strips, branches outspread to somewhat nodding; needles somewhat irregular 2-ranked, linear, often somewhat sickle-shape, pointing more or less upward on long shoots, 4–6 cm long, 3 to 4 mm wide, sharply acuminate, light green and very glossy above, with 2 gray stomatal bands beneath, each with about 15 lines, base short petioled; male flowers on a 1–2.5 cm long stalk; seeds olive-green, 2–2.5 cm long, with a small, prickly tip (mucro) in a rounded indention at the apex (= *C. pedunculata* S. & Z.: *C. drupacea* var. *pedunculata* [S. & Z.] Miq.; *Taxus harringtonia* Knight ex Forbes). Korea, N. China, Japan (Hondo; Shikoku, Kyushu). 1829. Fig. 31. z7

var. **drupacea** (S. & Z.) Koidz. A small tree in its habitat, 5–10 m high, branches spreading widely, developing a wide, rounded crown, often only shrubby in cultivation, limbs arranged in whorls, bark gray, narrow furrowed, in slightly exfoliating strips, twigs green at first, later red-brown, not nodding; needles 2-ranked, ascending at an angle, nearly V-shaped in cross section, rather densely arranged, linear, 2.5–3.5 cm long, abruptly acuminate, 2–3 mm wide, very short petioled, with 2 gray stomatal bands beneath, each with 15 lines; seeds obovate, about 3 cm long, stalk 6–12 mm long. DJ 30; MI 2723; BM 8285; WM 122 (H) (= *C. drupacea* S. & Z.). Japan, mountain forests; Central and W. China. 1829. Fig. 32. z6

'**Fastigiata**'. Nearly columnar habit. Branching steeply upright, long, rod-like, scarcely branched; all needles spirally arranged (not 2-ranked!), bowed, 3–5 cm long, 3 mm wide, apices short and sharp, glossy dark green above. MI 2724; KN 84; WM 3D (Br), 120 (H) (= *C. buergeri* Miq.; *Podocarpus koraiana* Endl.; *C. pedunculata* var. *fastigiata* Carr.). Japan, but only known in cultivation. 1830. (See the notes at *Podocarpus macrophyllus* var. *maki*!) Plate 63; Fig. 31.

var. **koreana** (Nakai) Rehd. Low, dense bush, very slow growing, only 1–1.5 m high; needles not bowed sickle-shape; fruits nearly globose, pale purple, edible. DB 14; 213 (= *C. nana* Nak.; *C. drupacea* var. *nana compacta* Froeb.). North and Central Japan, in the mountains. 1916. (VR)

'**Prostrata**'. Differing from the type only in the low spreading habit, a 30-year old plant at Hillier's about 2.5 m wide and 70 cm high; needles exactly like the type. WDw Pl. 6, G (Br); WM 3E (Br), 121 (H) (= *C. drupacea* var. *pedunculata* 'Prostrata' Hillier). Presumably originating from a lateral branch of the type.

'**Sphaeralis**'. Shrub, to 3 m high, branches green, older branches chestnut brown; needles linear, curving sickle-shape, 3.5–5 cm long; seeds in clusters near the branch base, globose, brownish. GC 21: 113 (1887) (= *C. pedunculata* var. *sphaeralis* Mast.). It is not certain whether or not this plant is identical to the much smaller leaved *C. sinensis* f. *globosa* of W. Hupeh; see the latter. (VR)

C. mannii Hook. Small tree; needles linear, gradually tapering to the apex, straight or bowed slightly sickle-shape, about 5 cm long, 3–4 mm wide, glossy green above, paler with scarcely visible stomatal bands beneath (!!); male inflorescence globose, on about a 6 mm long stalk; seeds about 4 cm long, nearly pear-shaped, with a short, protruding apical tip, becoming narrower at the base, often 3–4 seeds on a common stalk. HI 1523; CCE 102. India; Khasia Mts. 1500 m. z7

C. oliveri Mast. Shrub, 2–3 m high, branches in whorls or opposite, green at first, yellow-green in the 2nd year; needles conspicuously 2-ranked, feathery, so closely spaced that the margins nearly touch, rather stiff, linear, curving slightly upward, 21–25 mm long, rarely to 35 mm long, 3 mm wide, truncate at the base, quite short petioled, short compressed at the apex, dark green and glossy above, yellow-green beneath with 2 bluish stomatal bands, with over 15 lines; seeds ovate, widest at the middle, about 2.5–3 cm long and 1.5 cm wide, with protruding tips, stalk 1–1.2 cm long. FIO Pl. 189 (= *C. griffithii* Oliv. non Hook. F. in HI Pl. 1933). China; W. Hupeh, Szechwan Provinces; Mt. Omei. Fig. 31. z7

C. sinensis (Rehd. & Wils.) Li. Small tree, 3–10 m high, bark brownish, shredding, branches smooth, light brown; needles linear-lanceolate, 4–5 cm long, 3–5 mm wide, sharp acuminate, dark green and glossy above, bluish-green beneath, limb revolute; seeds ovate, 15 mm long, 8 mm thick, bluish pruinose. CCE 102 (= *C. drupacea* var. *sinensis* Rehd. & Wils.; *C. harringtonia* var. *sinensis* [Rehd & Wils.] Rehd.). Central and W. China. z7

f. **globosa** (Rehd. & Wils.) Li. Shrub, to 2.5 m high, young branches green; needles smaller, 22 mm long, 3 mm wide, sharply acuminate, light green above, bluish beneath with 2 stomatal bands, all needles more or less 2-ranked and flat spreading; male flowers brownish; fruits globose to obovoid, to 16 mm long and 12 mm wide, fleshy, brownish. China; W. Hupeh Province, in the mountains at 1000 m.

C. wilsoniana Hayata. Medium sized tree, to about 10 m high, trunk to 40 cm thick, bark smooth, fibrous, branches pendulous; needles linear, distinctly 2-ranked and horizontal, curved to slightly sickle-shape, 3–4 cm long, 2.5–3 mm wide, acute, tapering to the base, midrib above distinctly conspicuous, limb slightly involuted, with 2 gray-white stomatal bands beneath; seeds ovate to obovoid, 18–25 mm long, 10 mm thick, stalk about 10 mm long. LWT 4; LT Pl. 22. China; Taiwan. Fig. 32. z9

CHAMAECYPARIS Spach.—False Cypress—CUPRESSACEAE

Evergreen, usually conical, tall trees with nodding branch tips; branches spreading, branchlets more or less flattened; leaves scale-like, awl-like only when young; plants monoecious; male flowers terminal on the side branches, oval-oblong, usually yellow; female flowers on side branchlets, solitary, terminal, nearly globose, with 6–8 (seldom 4 or 10–12) decussate scales; cones small, globose, hard, ripening the first year (*C. nootkatensis*, however, in the 2nd year); fruit scales peltate, angular or circular, margins overlapping, gaping open when ripe; seeds 2, occasionally 5, 2 winged, elliptic to circular; cotyledons 2; x = 11.—7 species in N. America, Japan, China and Taiwan.

Chamaecyparis formosensis Matsum. Formosan Falsecypress. A very tall tree in its habitat, to 65 m with the trunk to 6.5 m diameter, bark more or less reddish-brown, branchlets flattened; leaves scale-like, short tips, triangular, imbricate, green above, whitish beneath; ripe cones ellipsoid (very important distinction!), 10–12 mm long, 8–9 mm wide, with 10–13 peltate scales, seeds slightly winged, 3 mm wide. LT 48; LWT 14; OCC 71. Taiwan, mountains in the north and central parts of the island at 1000–2900 m; develops large stands together with *C. obtusa* var. *formosana* with trees up to 1500 years old (!). 1910. Very similar to *C. obtusa* in appearance but distinctly differing in the ellipsoid fruits. Fig. 35 C. z8–9

C. funebris (Endl.) Franco. Tree, to 20 m high, stem straight upright, bark smooth, brown, branches spreading more or less horizontally or ascending, twigs, however, all weeping vertically (!), thin, secondary branches all on an even plane and in 2 opposing rows, flat in cross section; leaves all densely appressed, with apex distinct, light green monochrome or also somewhat more gray-green, 2–3 mm long; cones globose, 8 to 12 mm thick, dark brown, on short stalks, scales 8, with small, ovate continuation of the rachis, seeds 3–5 in each scale. SN 113 (H) (= *Cupressus funebris* Endl.). Widely planted in China. 1849. No longer included in *Cupressus* beacuse of the small cones and few seeds. Plate 35; Fig. 34. z9

'Gracilis'. Branches loosely arranged, outspread-nodding, branchlets in 2 quite regular rows (= *Cupressus funebris* var. *gracilis* Carr.). Before 1867.

'Viridis'. Ornamental branching pattern, bright green, branches thin (= *Cupressus funebris* var. *viridis* Sénécl.). 1868.

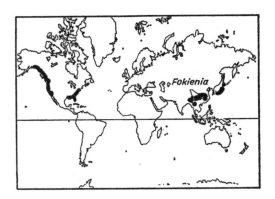

Fig. 33. Range of the genus *Chamaecyparis* and *Fokienia*

Fig. 34. *Chamaecyparis funebris*. Left, juvenile form, center and right, branches from mature plants

Outline of the most Important Characteristics of the *Chamaecyparis* Species

	formosensis (Fig. 35C)	*funebris* (Fig. 34)	*lawsoniana* (Fig. 36B)	*nootkatensis* (Fig. 35A)	*obtusa* (Fig. 35B)	*pisifera* (Fig. 36D)	*thyoides* (Fig. 36A)
branching arrangement	always horizontal	weeping vertically	always ± horizontal	vertical at the tip	always ± horizontal	always ± horizontal	irregular
leaf arrangement	always loosely appressed	always thickly appressed	always tightly appressed	tightly appressed on short shoots, more loosely appressed on long shoots	always tightly appressed	always loosely appressed	on short shoots tightly appressed, more loosely appressed on long shoots
pattern on the leaf underside	very white markings	without any markings	often with faded lines	without markings, occasional white border	raised silver-white lines	oblong white spots	2 blue bands
proportion of lateral leaves to facial leaves	lateral leaves much larger	nearly alike	lateral leaves much larger	nearly alike	lateral leaves much larger	nearly alike	nearly alike
oil glands on the leaves	channeled	very small but distinct	often with glands	channeled	absent	indistinct	very large
scale number in the cones	10	8	8	4–6	8 (–10)	8–10 (–12)	4–5 (6)

C. lawsoniana (Murr.) Parl. Lawson False cypress. Tree, 20–50 m high, trunk 0.9–1.7 m diameter, crown acutely conical, branches short, spreading horizontally, branch tips usually nodding, bark reddish-brown, with rounded scaly plates, branchlets flat, in an even plane; needles appressed, more or less acute, lateral leaves keeled with a distinct tip, facial leaves much smaller, rhombic, often with a gland, underside with indistinct white lines; cones numerous, small, globose, 8 mm thick, blue-green at first, ripening in the first fall, then brown, 8 scales, with compressed papillae. SPa 67. N. America; SW. Oregon to NW. California. Countless cultivars in existence today, all developed within the last 100 years. See the outline which follows. Plate 44; Fig. 36 B.

Outline of the Mentioned Forms of *C. lawsoniana*

( ) = probably extinct cultivars

1. Habit upright, conical to columnar, normal vigor, tall to medium height

● green
'Atrovirens'
'Drummondii'
'Erecta'
'Erecta Viridis'
'Green Hedger'
'Green Pillar'
'Green Spire'
'Green Wall'
'Hollandia'
'Masonii'
'Melfard'
'Pottenii'
'Pyramidalis'
'Robusta'
'Rosenthalii'
'Schongariana'
('Souvenir de Leide')
'Stricta'
'Stricta Excelsa'
'Witzeliana'

● blue-green and silvery
'Alumii'
'Alumii Magnifica'
'Argentea'
'Argentea Waterer'
'Beissneriana'
'Blom'
'Blue Gown'
'Blue Jacket'
'Booth'
'Bruinii'
'Coerulea'
'Coerulea Erecta'
'Columnaris'
'Darleyensis'
'Erecta Glaucescens'
'Falcata'
'Felix'
'Fraseri'
'Friesia'
'Glauca'
'Glauca Argentea'
'Glauca Elegans'
'Kelleriis'
'Kilmacurragh'
'Kloosterhuis'
'Kooy'
'Lombartsii'
'Monumentalis'
'Monumentalis Glauca'
'Monumentalis Nova'
'Olbrichii'
'Pembury Blue'
'Plumosa Glauca'
'Pyramidalis Glauca'
'Robusta Argentea'
'Robusta Glauca'
'Silver Queen'
'Spek'
'Stricta Glauca'
'Triomf van Boskoop'
'Veitch'
'Worleei'

● yellow
'Alumigold'
'Ashton Gold'
'Aurea'
'Aurea Nova'
'Aureospica'
'Aureovariegata'
'Boeri'
'Broomhill Gold'
'Delorme'
'Depkenii'
'Doré de Croux'
'Elegantissima'
'Erecta Aurea'
'Erecta Aureospica'
'Luteocompacta'
'Luteogracilis'
'Lutescens'
'Maas'
'Magnifica Aurea'
'Moerheimii'
'Monumentalis Aurea'
'Moonlight'
'Naberi'
'New Golden'
'President Roosevelt'
'Pulverulenta'
('Pyramidalis Gracilis Lutea')
'Pyramidalis Lutea'

'Flavescens'
'Golden King'
'Golden Prince'
'Golden Spire'
'Golden Triumph'
'Golden Wonder'
'Harkin'
'Hillieri'
'Killiney Gold'
'Lane'
'Lombartsii'
'Lutea'
'Lutea Smith'

'Robusta Aurea'
'Smithii'
'Southern Gold'
'Stewartii'
'Stricta Aurea'
'Triomf van Lombarts'
'Van Eck'
'Van Tol'
'Versicolor'
'Viner's Gold'
'Westermannii'
'Westermannii
  Aureovariegata'
'Winston Churchill'

● white variegated
'Albospica'
'Argenteovariegata'
'Argenteovariegata Nova'
'Croftway'
'Erecta Alba'
'Erecta Argenteovariegata'

'Nivea'
'Overeynderi'
'Pyramidalis Alba'
'Silver Gem'
'Silver Queen'
'White Spot'

2. Compact habit, broadly conical, dwarf

● green
'Compacta Nova'
'Derbyshire Dwarf'
'Globosa'

'Krameri'
'Minima'
'Nana'

● blue-green
'Compacta'
'Delorme'
('Filicifolia Pendula Nana')
'Forsteckensis'
'Gimbornii'
'Minima Glauca'

'Nana Argentea'
'Nana Compacta'
'Nana Glauca'
'Pygmaea Argentea'
'Shawii'

● yellowish green to
   yellow
'Aurea Densa'
'Forsteckensis Variegata'
'Juniperina'

'Lutea Nana'
'Minima Aurea'
'Stardust'

● white variegated
'Albovariegata'
'Minima Argenteo-
  variegata'
'Nana Albospica'
'Nana Albovariegata'

'Nana Argentea'
'Nana Argenteovariegata'
('Pyramidalis Alba Nana')

3. Habit broad dwarf, half globe, without a terminal

● blue-green and silvery
'Alumii Nana Compacta'
'Coerulescens'
'Fragrans Argentea'
'Glauca Globus'
'Gnome'

'Nana'
'Nana Glauca'
'Pixie'
'Rogersii'

● green
'Compacta Nova'

● yellow
'Duncanii'

4. Other growth habits (not in 1.–3.)

● Branches pendulous or nodding
'Billwoodiana'
'Bowleri'
'Filiformis'
'Filiformis Compacta'
('Fragrans')
('Fragrans Argentea')
'Gracilis'
'Gracilis Aurea'
'Gracilis Glauca'
'Gracilis Nana'
'Gracilis Nova'
'Gracilis Pendula'
'Gracilis Pygmaea'

'Gracillima'
'Intertexta'
'Intertexta Atrovirens'
'Intertexta Pendula'
'Patula'
'Pendula'
'Pendula Alba'
'Pendula Aurea'
'Pendula Nova'
'Pendula Vera'
'Raievskyana'
'Youngii'

● Branches filamentous
'Casuarinifolia'
'Casuarinifolia
  Aureovariegata'
'Caudata'
'Erecta Filiformis'

'Filifera'
'Filiformis'
'Filiformis Compacta'
'Filiformis Glauca'

● Branchlets crispate
'Crispa'
'Cristata'
'Laxa'
'Lycopodioides'
'Lycopodioides Aurea'
'Milfordensis'

'Plumosa'
'Tharandtensis'
'Tharandtensis Caesia'
'Tilgate'
'Wisselii'
'Wisselii Nana'

● Habit wide and flat
'Dow's Gem'
'Grandi'
'Knowefieldensis'
'Nestoides'
'Nidiformis'
'Parsons'

'Pena Park'
'Procumbens'
'Prostrata Glauca'
'Tabuliformis'
'Tamariscifolia'
'Weisseana'

● Stem and branches twisted
'Spiralis'
'Tortuosa'

● Leaves all needle form
'Bleu Nantais'
'Blue Surprise'
'Chilworth Silver'
'Ellwoodii'
'Ellwoodii Glauca'
'Ellwoodii Pygmy'
'Ellwood's Gold'
'Ellwood's Silver'
'Ellwood's White'
'Epacroides'

'Ericoides'
'Fletcheri'
'Fletcheri Nana'
'Fletcher's Compact'
'Fletcher's Pillar'
'Fletcher's White'
'Kestonensis'
'Squarrosa'
'Yellow Transparent'

The exceptional variability of seedling plants stirred growers very early into selecting and propagating interesting plants. The majority being from British nurseries (James Smith, Waterer, Rogers, Hogger), others from Holland (P. Lombarts, Wezelenburg, the Tottenham Nurseries), Germany (P. Smith) and in former Austria (Hungary) the nursery of Prince Lobkowitz in Eisenberg. These nurseries accounted for about 5–6 cultivars each; the others have come from various nurseries throughout Europe, the USA and New Zealand.

'Albospica' (Young). Habit narrow conical-upright, medium height, branch tips cream-white. Originated in Young's Nursery before 1875 in Milford, England.

'**Albovariegata'** (Veitch). Dwarf form, ovate to conical habit, 2–3 m high, crown peak eventually rounded; needles dark green with many white spots, also with partially white branch tips, these however dying back in winter. WDw Pl. 3F (Br) (= *C. lawsoniana* f. *albomaculata* Schnd.; *C. lawsoniana* f. *albopicta* Schnd.). Originated before 1881 in the Coombe Wood Nursery of James Veitch & Sons, England.

'**Alumigold'** (J. Maks). Habit like 'Alumii', but more compact; foliage pure yellow, becoming more bluish yellow-green inside the plant. Originated as a mutation on 'Alumii' from J. Maks, Dedemsvaart, Holland. Introduced to the trade in 1966.

'**Alumii'** (R. Smith & Co., Worcester, England; around 1870). Narrow conical-upright, to 15 m high, branches ascending on young plants, spreading more widely on older plants, twigs very numerous and dense, flat, soft to the touch; needles attractively blue pruinose, later more gray-blue. Easily propagated. Widely disseminated and popular. Fig. 37D.

'**Alumii Magnifica'.** Habit narrower than on the typical form; foliage more intensely blue and loosely arranged.

'**Alumii Nana Compacta'.** Habit flat-globose, rather open, branchlets radiating from all sides, good blue-green like 'Alumii'. Disseminated by Minier, Angers, France. 1975.

'**Argentea Smith'** (J. Smith). Conical-upright habit, lightly and gracefully branched, finely nodding twigs; needles turning silver-gray on both sides. Originated between 1866 and 1874 by James Smith & Sons, Darley Dale, near Matlock, England.

'**Argentea Waterer'** (A. Waterer). Upright habit, branches erect, twigs short and outspread; leaves silvery-green above, light green beneath. Introduced to the trade in 1864 by Anth. Waterer, Knap Hill, England.

'**Argenteovariegata'** (Lawson). Strong grower, branches with white, variegated needles, appearing spotty. SN 110 (H). Developed before 1862, by Lawson in Edinburgh, Scotland.

'**Argenteovariegata Nova'** (Overeynder). Branches and twigs white variegated, not harmed by full sun. Developed before 1887 by C. G. Overeynder in Boskoop, Holland. (EX)

'**Ashton Gold'.** Similar to 'Lutea', but a better grower with a better crown apex, habit upright, branches ascending; foliage an attractive gold-yellow. From Ireland, before 1968. Introduced by Jan Spek, Boskoop, Holland.

'**Atrovirens'.** Regular, conical-upright habit, 20 m high or more, main branches stout, spreading, branchlets flat on both sides, one sided at the branch base; needles glossy dark green. 1891.

'**Aurea'** (J. Waterer). Compact conical habit, slow growing; foliage golden-yellow. Introduced to the trade before 1862 by J. Waterer, Bagshot, Surrey, England. Not identical to 'Lutea', which see.

'**Aurea Densa'** (Rogers). Very slow growing, dwarf form, 60–80 cm high, more shrubby at first, later obtuse conical, branchlets rather stiff, very densely arranged, somewhat shell-like in form and outspread; needles very short and wide, densely appressed, evenly golden-yellow for the entire year. WH 123 (H). Developed before 1939 at W. H. Rogers & Sons in England. Very beautiful form. Plate 29.

'**Aurea Nova'** (van der Elst). Upright, broadly conical, to 10 m high, branches and twigs like the species, branchlets flat, branch tips on the new growth greenish-yellow, later golden-yellow, eventually greening; needles very small. Originated as a mutation by Van Der Elst, Tottenham Nurseries, Holland, before 1893. Good winter hardiness.

'**Aureospica'.** Conical, medium strong grower, branches brownish-yellow, twigs and needles on the new growth golden-yellow, later green (= *C. lawsoniana* var. *aureospicata* Jurissen). Developed by Jac. Jurissen & Zonen, Naarden, Holland before 1887. (EX)

'**Aureovariegata'** (J. Waterer). Conical habit, branches partly yellow variegated; needles often only yellowish-white. Developed before 1861 by J. Waterer, Bagshot, England. z7

'**Beissneriana'** (P. Smith). Vigorous habit, ascending; foliage bright gray-blue. Introduced to the trade before 1891 by P. Smith, Bergedorf, W. Germany. (EX)

'**Billwoodiana'.** English form with pendulous branches. Apparently no longer in cultivation.

'**Bleu Nantais'** (Renault, Gorron, France, 1967). Mutation of 'Ellwoodii'. Dwarf form, upright habit, similar to 'Fletcheri', branches yellow-green; foliage silver-blue.

'**Blom'** (A. Blom). Dwarf form, columnar, dense, only 2–3 m high, branches and twigs erect, smallest shoots erect to outspread, very densely arranged; leaves small, outermost more blue pruinose, inner foliage blue-green. OCC 74; TC 79; CCE 109 (= *C. lawsoniana erecta* 'Blom' den Ouden). Originated as a mutation of 'Alumii' by Adr. Blom, Boskoop, Holland about 1930, but first introduced to the trade in 1942. Easily propagated by cuttings.

'**Blue Gown'** (Hogger). Conical habit, 5–10 m high, branches and twigs outspread, regularly arranged, smallest shoots blue pruinose (= *C. lawsoniana* 'Hogger' den Ouden). Developed about 1935 by J. Hogger, Felbridge, East Grinstead, England. Not especially outstanding, but often used in England for hedges.

'**Blue Jacket'** (M. Young). Broad conical habit, branches outspread, twigs densely packed, very fine, blue-green; needles small, with bluish-white markings on the underside. CCE 108 (= *C. lawsoniana* 'Milford Blue Jacket' Dall. & Jacks.). Developed by M. Young in Milford, England before 1932.

'**Blue Plume'.** Refer to 'Plumose Glauca'.

'**Blue Surprise'** (de Beer). Dense conical habit, upright, branchlets erect, very well branched; leaves all needle-form, 3–6(–9) mm long and 0.75–1.5 mm wide, conspicuously blue-green, thin and sharp. Developed from seed by Anth. P. J. de Beer in Tilburg, Holland. Similar to 'Ellwoodii', but fast growing and more compact.

'**Boeri'** (J. Boer). Slow growing, columnar form, branches and twigs narrowly upright, rather thick, branchlets short, tips light greenish-yellow, totally green at the base; needles small, tightly appressed, yellowish-green at first, eventually green. Developed before 1937 by Jan Boer Wz. & Zoon; Boskoop, Holland.

'**Booth'.** Upright habit, somewhat coarser than the type, somewhat rounded at the apex, gray-green with bluish-green tones (= *C. lawsoniana* 'Glauca Booth' F. G. Meyer). Origin unknown; disseminated by M. Koster & Zonen, Boskoop, Holland, before 1963.

'**Bowleri'** (J. Smith). Dwarf form, globose habit, dense, 1–1.2 m high, branches outspread, limply nodding, likewise the graceful twigs, branchlets widely spaced, thin, both sides equally green; needles small, narrow, glossy dark green. Developed before 1883 by James Smith & Sons of Darley Dale Nurseries, England.

'**Broomhill Gold'.** Habit like that of 'Erecta Viridis', but somewhat more open; foliage gold-yellow at first, later greenish-yellow. Introduced around 1975 by Stewart's Ferndown Nurseries, Broomhill, Winborne, Dorset, England. Attractive form.

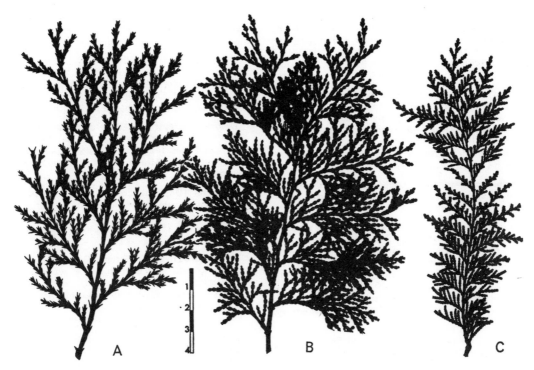

Fig. 35. **Chamaecyparis** species. A. *C. nootkatensis*; B. *C. obtusa*;
C. *C. formosensis*

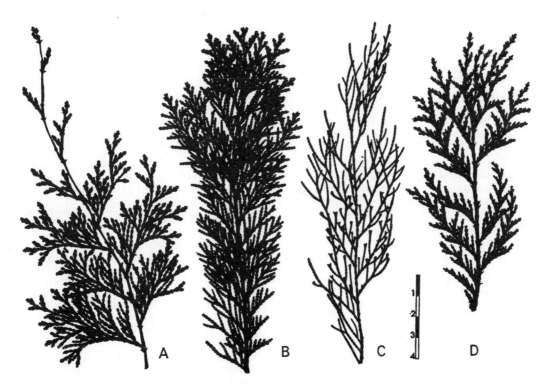

Fig. 36. **Chamaecyparis** species. A. *C. nootkatensis*; B. *C. obtusa*;
C. *C. formosensis*

'Bruinii' (W. de Bruin). Conical upright habit, to 10 m high, branches regularly spreading, likewise the twigs, branch tips somewhat nodding, branchlets less regular, rather long and fine; leaves glossy dark green, blue pruinose, sharp to the touch. Originated around 1928 by W. De Bruin Gz., Boskoop, Holland.

'Casuarinifolia' (Lobkowitz). Habit more or less globose and densely branched, somewhat resembling a *Casuarina*, branchlets partly filamentous, partly twisted, wavy or contorted, dull blue-green, with white markings beneath. Developed before 1891, in the nursery of Prince Lobkowitz in Eisenburg, Bohemia. Still growing in the garden of Dr. O. Mayr in Tullnerbach-Lawies, near Vienna, Austria.

'Casuarinifolia Aureovariegata' (Lobkowitz). Like the above, but with yellow variegated leaves. Likewise originated in the Lobkowitz Nursery, before 1904. (VR)

'Caudata' (Gebr. Goudkade). Dwarf form, irregularly shrubby conical habit, dense, slow growing, 2–3 m high, rather rigid, branches red-brown, twigs numerous, branch tips with nearly clustered needles; leaves partly scale-like and appressed with distinct tips, occasionally with exserted, conspicuous shoots, these pendulous, tail-like thin, 10–20 cm long, on these branches all the needles appressed the entire length. OCC 75; CCE 108 (H). Originated by Gebr. Gouklade in Boskoop, Holland, before 1934.

'Chilworth Silver'. Dwarf form, very similar to 'Blue Surprise', but slow growing, rather dense and upright; foliage needle-like, blue-gray. England. About 1970. Allegedly a mutation from 'Blue Surprise', but perhaps also a seedling (?).

'Coerulea' (van Leeuwen). Upright habit, conical, dense, branches and twigs ascending, densely covered with small branchlets; needles green with a trace of light blue. Developed in 1860 by A. Van Leeuwen Sr., head gardener of G. J. Alberts, Boskoop, Holland.

'Coerulea Erecta'. Similar to 'Coerulea', but more strictly upright. Cultivated in Germany before 1909. (EX?)

'Coerulescens'. Dwarf habit, more or less globose; foliage blue-green. Introduced to the trade before 1873 by Thibault & Keteleer, Sceaux, near Paris. (EX)

'Columnaris' (J. Spek). Narrow columnar habit, 5–10 m high or more, densely branched, branches narrowly upright, rather thin, twigs upright, regular, branchlets flat, dark green above, somewhat bluish toward the branch tips, distinctly blue-green beneath. CCE 110. Developed about 1940 by Jan Spek in Boskoop, Holland. Plate 31.

'Compacta'. Dwarf form, very similar to 'Minima', but stronger grower, broadly conical, grows densely and slowly, reaching 2–3(–4) m high with age, branchlets fan-shaped (= *C. lawsoniana compacta nana* de Vos). Known before 1867; from Holland.

'Compacta Nova'. Dwarf form, compact conical habit, branchlets fan-shaped, spreading, light green. 1891. (EX?)

'Conica', please see 'Wisselii'.

'Cooperi'. Conical habit, branches outspread, twigs long and thin, branchlets arranged in nearly vertical planes, likewise long and thin; leaves small, blue-green. Origin unknown; disseminated by P. Lombarts, Zundert, Holland. 1906. (EX)

'Crispa' (Jongkindt Coninck). Conical habit, contorted, branches with crispate tips. CCE 108 (H). Originated by A. M. J. Jongkindt Coninck, Tottenham, Dedemsvaart, Holland, before 1891. (EX)

'Cristata'. Ascending habit, dense, slow growing, branches contorted, cockscomb-like fasciated on the apex, blue-green. Developed before 1888. (EX)

'Crostway'. Medium vigorous grower, conical, branch tips whitish, older foliage, however, deep green. Before 1972. No particular ornamental merit.

'Darleyensis'. (J. Smith). Conical, slow growing, silvery pruinose (= *Cupressus lawsoniana darleyensis* 'Smith's New Silver'). Developed before 1880 by James Smith & Son, Darley Dale, England. Occasionally a yellow form is found with the above name, but this should be 'Smithii'; which see.

'Delorme' (Delorme). Slow growing, broad, low, conical, narrowly upright, like the 'Erecta' forms, very densely branched, branchlets fine, blue-green. In the trade before 1965; disseminated by Minier, Angers, France. No particular garden merit.

'Depkenii' (Depken). Conical, slender, to 10 m high or more, branches outspread, twigs thin and nodding, branchlets fine; needles small, dull, white-yellow, gradually greening in fall. Developed in 1901 by S. W. Depken, Bremen-Oberneuland, W. Germany.

'Derbyshire Dwarf'. (J. Smith). Dwarf form, flat globose habit, strong grower, to 1 m high and as wide or wider, branches spreading widely and nodding, twigs green, branchlets regularly arranged on both sides; needles small, light green, thin pruinose. Developed by James Smith & Son, Darley Dale, England, around 1938. Difficult to transplant.

'Doré de Croux'. Narrow conical habit, the side branches spreading more or less widely; foliage yellow, bronze-yellow in winter. Introduced by Croux, Versailles, France, before 1970. No particular garden merit.

'Dow's Gem' (Dow). Dwarf form, similar to 'Knowefieldensis', growth broad, rather vigorous and open, branching very coarse, nearly *Thuja*-like; leaves rather long, gray-blue, very white pruinose beneath. WDw 44 (H), Pl. 3C (Br), WM 5D (Br), 125 (H); CCE 107 (= 'Dow's Variety', 'Noble's Variety'). Originated from seed in Dow's Nursery in Oakdean, California USA.

'Drummondii'. Broadly conical, 3–5 m high, branches outspread, twigs numerous, of even length, branchlets very thin; needles small, glossy, dark green. CCE 110. Origin unknown. 1937.

'Duncanii' (Duncan & Davis). Dwarf form, irregularly flat-globose, to 2 m high with age and 5 m wide, branching open and nodding, branchlets nearly filamentous, fine, blue-green. WDw 45 (H), Pl. 2G (Br); WM 126 (H). Introduced by Duncan Davis, New Plymouth, New Zealand in 1953.

'Elegantissima' (Barron). Conical-upright habit; foliage always light yellow. KN Pl. 2. Introduced to the trade in 1875 by Wm. Barron & Son, Barrowash, England.

'Ellwoodii'. Conical habit, scarcely higher than 2 to 3 m, densely branched, branches ascending and densely arranged, likewise the secondary branches, branch tips erect, slightly drooping, likewise the short, thin blue green branchlets; leaves needle-awl-form, very similar to those of 'Fletcheri', but thinner and more blue, also the leaves inside the plant are light gray (these dark green on 'Fletcheri'!), leaves more steel-blue in fall. HD 38; Wdw 50 (H), Pl. 2J (Br); CCE 110; WM 6B (Br), 127 (H). Originated as a seedling before 1929 in Swanmore Park, Bishop's Waltham, Great Britain. Very easily propagated from cuttings. Named for the gardener, Ellwood, in Swanmore Park. Plate 31; Fig. 39A.

'Ellwoodii Glauca'. More intensely light blue than the normal 'Ellwoodii' and somewhat coarser, but less winter hardy. Attractive.

'Ellwoodii Pygmy'. Like 'Ellwoodii', but especially slow growing and without a dominant leader. WDw 46 (H); WM 128

(H); CCE 108 (H) (= *C. lawsoniana* 'Ellwoodii Nana' Hort.). Origin unknown.

'Ellwood's Gold'. Mutation with golden-yellow branch tips in spring and summer, although fading in fall.

'Ellwood's Pillar'. Like 'Ellwoodii', but narrower in habit and yet wider branched, remaining lower, blue-green.

'Ellwood's White'. Taken from the white variegated branches which occasionally occur on 'Ellwoodii' (= *C. lawsoniana ellwoodii variegata* Hort.).

'Epacroides' (Lobkowitz). Slender conical habit and rather open, branches ascending; leaves partly needle-form ("Epacris-like"). Developed before 1904 in the nursery of Prince Lobkowitz of Eisenberg, Bohemia. (EX)

'Erecta' (R. Smith). Columnar habit, dense. In the trade about 1874 but no longer cultivated.

'Erecta Alba' (Keessen). Slender conical, to 5–10 m high, branches strong and outspread, twigs normal, branch tips silver-white, becoming greener toward the base. Developed around 1891 by W. Keesen Jz. & Zonen, Terra Nova, Aalsmeer, Holland. Beautiful, meritorious form.

'Erecta Argenteovariegata' (A. Koster). Dwarf form, resembling a dwarf 'Erecta Viridis', very distinctly white variegated especially on the crown apex. Originated as a mutation of 'Erecta Viridis' by A. Koster Mz. and known since 1874. Very attractive, although often bare at the base.

'Erecta Aurea'. Low conical form, to 3 m high, branches erect, likewise the branchlets, delicate; needles gold-yellow. CCE 110 + 116. Developed in Holland before 1876 and still in cultivation. Often damaged by late frost. z7

'Erecta Aureospica' (Overeynder). Upright habit, similar to 'Erecta Aurea', but more densely branched and with only the tips of the branchlets yellow. Originated by C. G. Overeynder in Boskoop, Holland, 1874. (EX)

'Erecta Filiformis' (Neumann). Conical habit, delicate, densely branched, branches steeply ascending, but the secondary branches more filamentous, thin, slightly drooping; needles very small, dark green. CCE 108. Developed from seed by R. Neumann in Waldorf, Saxony, in 1896. Occasionally mistakenly labeled 'Filiformis Compacta' in cultivation, which cultivar is, however, globose.

'Erecta Glaucescens'. Slender columnar habit, 5–10 m high, branches ascending, secondary branches steeply upright, 10–25 cm long, regularly flat; leaves appressed, blue-green and pruinose (= *Cupressus lawsoniana erecta glauca* de Vos). Known since 1868. Similar to 'Erecta Viridis' in habit, but blue-green; not identical to 'Monumentalix Nova', as mentioned by Beissner.

'Erecta Viridis' (A. Waterer). Slender conical, 5–10 m high, branches distinctly spirally arranged on older plants, twigs very densely arranged and, like the branchlets, all erect and on an even plane; needles bright green, also in winter. CCE 112; KN Pl. 2. Developed in 1850 by Anth. Waterer from seed obtained in California, then introduced to the trade as *Cupressus lawsoniana erecta* (not to be confused with the 'Erecta' from R. Smith!), but renamed by the firm in 1870 to the current name. Plate 44.

'Ericoides'. Dwarf form of nearly *Erica*-like appearance, branches red-brown and stiff, major branches very densely packed and upright, green to brown, branchlets to 10 cm long and 2.5 cm wide; needles mostly scale-form and 1.5–3 mm long, but not appressed, otherwise totally distinct and (like an *Erica*) erect spreading, straight or bowed, drawn out to a sharp apex, concave above and with narrow, bluish stomatal bands, convex and keeled beneath. Known since 1884. (VR)

'Falcata' (Lobkowitz). Upright habit, branches bowed, sickle-shape, with small, clustered branchlets at the tip. Developed in the nursery of Prince Lobkowitz in Eisenburg before 1904 by Insp. Ordnung. (EX)

'Felix' (Felix & Dijkhuis). Conical, vigorous, 10–20 m high, similar to 'Triomf de Boskoop' in habit, but branches and branchlets finer; softer to the touch, branches and twigs outspread, branchlets dense, directed forward, fine; leaves appressed, evenly blue pruinose, blue-green beneath (= *C. lawsoniana glauca* 'Felix'). Originated in Boskoop, Holland, by Felix & Dijkhuis in 1937.

'Filicifolia Pendula Nana'. Slow growing, irregular conical with nodding branch tips, these with dark green, densely packed branchlets, somewhat resembling *C. obtusa* 'Filicoides'. In the trade before 1930 in Orléans, France. Plate 29.

'Filifera'. Not to be confused with 'Filiformis'! Upright habit, very sparse and open branched, branchlets not numerous, pendulous, dark green, very short needled. CCE 115. Fig. 37B. (VR)

'Filiformis'. Delicate textured, broadly conical, 10 m high or more, very open branched, branches outspread, nodding, branch tips filamentous, green. CCE 114. Several introductions before 1877, first in Belgium. Plate 33. z7

'Filiformis Compacta'. Dwarf form, flat globose habit, about 1 m high, but much wider, branches clustered, outspread, branch tips nearly filamentous and nodding; leaves tightly appressed, small, dark blue-green. WDw 48 (H); WM 4D (Br); 129 (H); CCE 111 (= *C. lawsoniana* 'Globosa Filiformis' (Hort.). 1891. Very similar to 'Filiformis', but a dwarf form and blue-green. Plate 34; Fig. 37A.

'Filiformis Glauca' (C. de Vos). Broadly conical, 3–5 m high, branches nodding, secondary branches pendulous, thin, filamentous, very densely branched; leaves dark blue-green. CCE 115. Developed about 1886 by C. De Vos, then introduced by K. Wezelenburg, Hazerswoude, near Boskoop, Holland.

'Flavescens' (Cripps). Branches and foliage pale yellow-green (= *Cupressus lawsoniana lutea flavescens* Cripps). Developed by the Cripps Nurseries in Tunbridge Wells, England before 1867. (EX)

'Fletcheri' (Fletcher). Columnar to conical habit, 5–8 m high, branches and twigs ascending, very densely arranged, branch tips occasionally somewhat reddish-blue, branchlets evenly blue-green, turning purple in fall; leaves partly needle-, partly more scale-like, decussate, spreading obliquely, upper third curving somewhat inward, blue-green, similar to 'Ellwoodii', but always lighter in color, more gray, but branchlets inside the plant always dark green!!, (on 'Ellwoodii' gray-blue!). HD 39; WDw 49: Pl. 2K (Br); WM 6A (Br); CCE 110. Originated in 1911 as a mutation on a normal *C. lawsoniana* in the Fletcher Bros. Nursery near Chertsey, England. In England—and perhaps elsewhere—old plants of this type produce cones with viable seed, from which are produced especially slow growing progeny. Plate 32; Fig. 39C. z7

'Fletcheri Nana'. Dwarf form, broadly conical or nearly cushion-like habit, only to about 1(–1.5) m high; needles somewhat thinner and finer, more outspread, otherwise the same as 'Fletcheri'. Known since 1939. Perhaps originated as a cutting from a stunted lateral branch.

'Fletcher's Compact' is a collective named coined by Welch for especially slow or compact growing plants which otherwise appear like 'Fletcheri' (= 'Kestonensis'?).

'Fletcher's White'. Originated as a white variegated mutation on 'Fletcheri'. Fast growing, therefore hardly a dwarf conifer.

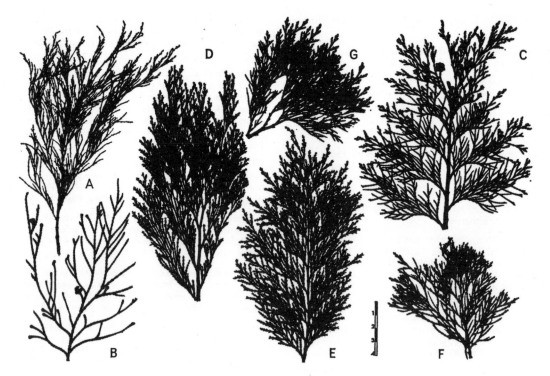

Fig. 37. *Chamaecyparis lawsoniana* cultivars. A. 'Filiformis Compacta'; B. 'Filifera';
C. 'Triomf van Boskoop'; D. 'Alumii'; E. 'Tamariscifolia'; F. 'Globosa'; G. 'Gimbornii'

'Forsteckensis'. Dwarf form, broadly globose, eventually to 1.5 m high and 2 m wide with age (such a specimen exists in the Grueningen Arboretum, Switzerland), very densely branched, branches short, crispate, some so thick they appear moss-like on the tips, vigorous; needles very small, appressed, gray-blue. WDw 47 (H), Pl. 2C and D (Br); WM 4E (Br), 130 (H); CCE 115 (= *C. lawsoniana forsteckeana* Beissn.). Developed before 1891 in the Forstecker Nursery in Forsteck, near Kiel, N. Germany and widely grown today.

'Forsteckensis Variegata'. Like the above, but somewhat more open in habit and the needles yellowish variegated, not consistent. 1909.

'Fragrans' (Standish). Strong upright habit, branches slender and nodding, twigs blue-green, pleasantly aromatic when crushed. Developed by Standish before 1875. (EX)

'Fragrans Argentea'. Differing from 'Fragrans' in the more silver-gray foliage. CCE 111. Presumably developed before 1891 in Kew Gardens, London; at least cultivated there at that time. (EX)

'Fraseri'. Slender conical habit, to 10 m high or more, similar to 'Alumii', but the branchlets thicker, coarser, bluer, also grows wider (= *C. lawsoniana fraseri glauca* Lomb.). Known by 1891; origin unknown. Good winter hardiness.

'Friesia'. Originated as a mutation on 'Triomf van Boskoop' before 1911 in a NW. German nursery. Supposedly more narrow growing than the mother plant. (EX?)

'Gimbornii' (v. Gimborn). Dwarf form, rather like 'Nana Glauca' in habit and form, densely compact, globose, but acuminate at the crown apex, slow growing, scarcely over 2 m high, branches erect, thick and stiff, purple-blue on the new growth; leaves blue pruinose. WDw 51; OCC 82; WM 131 (H); CCE 112. Originated from seed in the Von Gimborn park in

Doorn, Holland, and introduced in 1937 by H. den Ouden & Zonen, Boskoop, Holland. Plate 34; Fig. 37G.

'Glauca' (Lawson). Like the typical species, but needles bluish. Selected by Lawson before 1882 in Edinburgh, Scotland. No longer in the trade as many other and better blue forms are available.

'Glauca Argentea' (Hesse). Conical, 5–10 m high, branches outspread; needles blue-green, conspicuously white pruinose. Introduced to the trade in 1913 by Herm. A. Hesse, Weener, near Hanover, W. Germany. Good form.

'Glauca Elegans'. Slender conical, 5–10 m high or more, branches and twigs ascending, conspicuously blue-white in summer, more blue in winter; needles rather large and coarse (giving rise to the often used "robusta"), blue pruinose (= *C. lawsoniana robusta glauca* Hort. non Beissn.; *C. lawsoniana robusta elegans* Hort.). In the trade before 1909 but origin unknown.

'Glauca Globus' (Barabits). Globose, to about 1.5 m high and wide, branchlets an attractive blue-green, the uppermost nearly vertically arranged, the others horizontal or slightly drooping. KN Pl. 2. Selected in 1952 in the Sopron Botanic Garden, Hungary, by E. Barabits. Very attractive form.

'Glauca Lombartsii' (Lombarts). Conical, elegant habit, 5–10 m high, branches irregular, not numerous, branchlets short and thin; needles very small and appressed, blue pruinose above, lighter and indistinctly marked beneath. CCE 125. Originated about 1910 by Pierre Lombarts, Zundert, Holland, but not introduced into the trade until 1926.

'Glauca Veitch' (Veitch). Conical, 5–10 m high, branches and twigs outspread-nodding, branchlets regular, flat, directed sideways and forward; needles appressed, green, blue pruinose, light green and pruinose beneath. Known since 1937. Presumably originated as "*C. lawsoniana glauca*" in the Veitch Nursery.

'**Globosa**'. Dwarf form, broadly conical, scarcely over 1 m high, slow growing, branches and twigs stout, upright, branchlets short and thickish, light green, some with needle-like leaves. Known since 1876 in Holland. Fig. 37F.

'**Gnome**' (Hart). Dwarf form, somewhat similar to 'Forsteckensis', but slower growing, habit nearly flat-globose, very dense, then gradually becoming densely conical; needles in juvenile form with distinct, spreading tips, later like those of the normal *C. lawsoniana*. GC 1970 (5th June; 3 ills.); WM 4F (Br), 132 (H). Developed before 1950 in Warnham Court, Horsham, Surrey, (Mr. W. Hart), England. Then purchased by the Heath End Nurseries (Mr. D. Hatch) by whom it was named and offered in the trade.

'**Golden King**' (Wezelenburg). Vigorous grower, 10–15 m high, branches erect-nodding, secondary branches broad, fan-shaped, oriented outward; needles above golden-yellow, more brownish-yellow in winter, yellowish-green beneath. CCE 117 + 120. Originated from seed of 'Triomf van Boskoop' by K. Wezelenburg & Zoon Nursery in Hazerswoude, near Boskoop, Holland before 1931. Difficult to transplant. Plate 32.

'**Golden Prince**' (W. J. Hooftman, 1978). Improved 'Golden King', strong grower, branches brown-yellow, somewhat nodding; foliage yellow.

'**Golden Spire**' (Bolwijn). Very similar (or identical?) to 'Kelleriis Gold', habit rather narrowly upright, greenish-yellow, more green in winter (young plants usually green-yellow) to somewhat brownish-yellow. From G. E. F. Bolwijn, Putten, Holland; introduced by Darthuizer Boomkwekerijen in 1972 (first disseminated as 'Columnaris Aurea').

'**Golden Triumph**' (Mauritz). Conical upright habit, with many erect branches; foliage a good yellow, orange-brown in winter. Introduced in 1972 by Mauritz, of Bussum, Holland. Much used in culture.

'**Golden Wonder**' (Bosman). Strong upright grower, conical, similar to 'Lane', but the needle color is deeper golden-yellow, also in winter. CCE 117. Found as a seedling around 1955 by N. Th. Bosman in Boskoop, Holland; introduced in 1963 by J. Spek, Boskoop.

'**Gracilis**'. (Waterer). Ascending, usually conical in the nursery, tall growing, branches outspread, tips nodding, the longer branch tips gracefully arching; needles very small, dark green and glossy, bluish pruinose. CCE 111. Developed about 1870 by Waterer, Knap Hill, England.

'**Gracilis Aurea**' (Davis). Broad upright habit, branches wide-spreading and nodding, secondary branches pendulous; foliage yellow in summer, greenish-yellow in fall. Found about 1894 by Davis, Hillsborough Nursery, County Down, Ireland.

'**Gracilis Aurea Pygmaea**'. Developed in 1948 by Dallimore & Jackson as a delicate dwarf form with gold-yellow foliage. No longer in cultivation.

'**Gracilis Glauca**' (Wezelenburg). Globose form, slender, slow growing, branches nodding, twigs rather coarse; needles green, blue-pruinose. Developed in the nursery of W. Wezelenburg & Zoon in Hazerswoude, Holland around 1925.

'**Gracilis Nana**'. Low, erect form, very densely branched, very finely textured. 1891. Similar to 'Gracilis', but remaining low.

'**Gracilis Nova**'. Habit open conical-upright, branches and twigs outspread, branchlets spreading irregularly; leaves blue-green. Origin unknown; cultivated for many years in Boskoop, Holland but still rare. (R)

'**Gracilis Pendula**'. (Barron). Like 'Gracilis', but the branches are longer and weep. Developed before 1881 by Wm. Barron & Son in Barrowash, Great Britain. Plate 32.

'**Gracillima**'. Upright habit, very similar to 'Gracilis', but more finely textured, likewise bright green. 1884. (EX?)

'**Grandi**' (Clark & Co.). Dwarf form, similar to 'Tamariscifolia', flat-globose habit, branches spreading more or less horizontally, secondary branches spreading widely, branchlets partly twisted and showing the blue undersides; needles dark blue-green. Introduced into the trade in 1950 by W. B. Clarke & Co., San Jose, California.

'**Green Hedger**' (Jackman). Strong upright grower, conical, dense; foliage a good bright green. Found as a seedling before 1949 by Jackman in Woking, Surrey, England and for a long period cultivated under the erroneous name 'Westermannii'.

'**Green Pillar**' (Hogger). Upright, conical, medium height, branches and twigs narrowly upright; leaves bright green with a distinct golden tone in early spring. CCE 114. Developed shortly before 1940 by J. Hogger's Nurseries, Felbridge, East Grinstead, England. Alleged to hold up well under a snow load.

'**Green Spire**' (Hogger). Regular conical habit, branches short and stout; foliage bright green. About 1947. This form arose simultaneously in the Hogger Nursery (who named it 'Green Spire') and the Jackman Nursery in Woking, England (who gave it the name *C. lawsoniana erecta* 'Jackman's Variety', but soon changed it to the former).

'**Green Wall**' (Tromp, Boskoop, 1978). Similar to 'Green Pillar', foliage fine, green.

'**Harkin**' (Branksome Nursery). Foliage a good orange-yellow (= *Cupressus lawsoniana* 'Harkin's Variety'). Developed before 1896 in the Branksome Nursery, Bournemouth, Great Britian. Not well known.

'**Hillieri**' (Hillier). Upright habit, branching open and feathery; leaves yellow. CCE 120. Introduced to the trade by Hillier, Winchester, England in 1928. Considered the best yellow cultivar.

'**Hollandia**' (Koster & Co.). Conical, slender, vigorous, to 10 m high or more, branches spreading horizontally, twigs fan-shaped with nodding tips, these shoots at the bowed portion directed upward; needles dark green. Introduced around 1895 by Koster & Co., Boskoop. Quite winter hardy.

'**Howarth's Gold**'. Compact conical-upright habit, branches on an even plane; foliage light yellow, light green inside the plant. An English form.

'**Intertexta**' (Lawson). Upright habit, to 10 m high or more, main branches widely spaced, limp, tips nodding, branches likewise, branchlets 5–10 cm long; leaves appressed on the young shoots, more loosely arranged on the older shoots, thick, blue-green pruinose. OCC 85; Gs 1925: 231; CCE 123. Developed about 1869 by Lawson in Edinburgh, Scotland. Quite meritorious; young plants will benefit from extra winter protection. Plate 31.

'**Intertexta Atrovirens**'. Distinguished from the normal 'Intertexta' by the dark green needle color. Before 1909. (EX?)

'**Intertexta Pendula**'. Quite flat, bowed habit, older plants about 1.5 m high and 5 m wide; foliage like 'Intertexta', but somewhat coarser. Original plant grows in the Mount Usher Gardens in Ireland.

'**Juniperina**'. Wide, compact, conical, to 2 m high, branches spreading, numerous, branchlets 12–15 cm long, flat, about 6 cm wide, much finer and flatter than those of 'Nana' and 'Minima', main shoot distinctly yellowish-green; needles very small, tightly appressed, but with spreading tips (therefore somewhat resembling *Juniperus sabina*) (= *Cupressus lawsoniana* var. *juniperina* Kent.; *C. lawsoniana* var. *juniperoides* Hornibr.). Known before 1900.

'Kelleriis' (D. F. Poulsen). Conical habit, of medium vigor, very similar to 'Triomf van Boskoop', but foliage bluer. Introduced to the trade by D. F. Poulsen, Kelleriis, Denmark in 1944. No longer propagated because of the improved 'Spek' and 'Triomf van Boskoop'.

'Kelleriis Gold' (D. F. Poulsen). Slender columnar habit; needle color dull yellow. CCE 116. Introduced as *C. lawsoniana aurea* 'Kelleriis' in 1944. Considered in Denmark to be the most winter hardy of the yellow cultivars. In propagating one should avoid scion wood of green color and all the lower part of the plant.

"Kestonensis" is actually nothing more than a slow growing 'Ellwoodii'; and therefore should not be specifically named. CCE 112. Presumably found by Reuthe in Keston, Kent, England.

'Killiney Gold'. Columnar habit, branches somewhat nodding; foliage a good golden-yellow, also in winter. From Ireland. Before 1976.

'Kilmacurragh' (Hillier). Medium grower, very narrowly conical-columnar, gradually tapering from the base to the tip, branches and twigs ascending at a 30–40° angle, very short, densely arranged, branchlets somewhat irregularly arranged, flat and rounded; leaves dark gray-green. CCE 115. Found in Kilmacurragh, County Wicklow, Ireland; introduced by Hillier in 1951.

'Kloosterhuis' (Kloosterhuis). Conical habit, open, to 10 m high or more, branches outspread-nodding, secondary branches angular, green, branchlets flat, outspread, directed forward, to 20 cm long, very thin; needles small, appressed, blue-green, pruinose. Developed in 1910 by Egb. Kloosterhuis Nursery, Veendam, Holland, but little known in cultivation. (VR)

'Knowefieldensis' (Little & Ballantine). Dwarf form, habit very broad and flat, to 1 m high, branches outspread, distinctly nodding, secondary branches thin and nodding, dark brown, branchlets regularly arranged, 5–6 cm long; leaves loosely appressed, very thin and fine, dark blue-green above, only slightly bluish beneath. WDw Pl. 3G (Br); WM 5E (Br); CCE 114 (= *Cupressus lawsoniana knowefieldensis* Hort.). Developed before 1911 in Little & Ballantine's Nursery, Carlisle, England.

'Kooy' (G. Kooy & Zonen). Conical, densely branched, to 10 m high, main branches outspread, thin, branch tips slightly nodding, branchlets alternately arranged, very thin; leaves small, blue pruinose, with waxy stripes on both sides, lighter beneath (= *C. lawsoniana glauca* 'Kooy' Valk. Suring.). Developed about 1925 by G. Kooy & Zonen, Boskoop, Holland.

'Krameri'. Dwarf form, globose-shrubby habit, about 1 m high, main branches outspread and nodding, branches long, branchlets however, short and filamentous, sparsely arranged on the branch tips, leaves glossy dark green, densely appressed except for the spreading tips. CCE 119. Known since 1909.

'Lane' (Lane). Rather columnar habit, medium strong grower, 5 m high or taller, main branches outspread, twigs thin, numerous, tips yellow, branchlets thin, penniform, golden-yellow; leaves golden-yellow above, more yellow-green beneath, yellow-green inside the plant. CCE 120 (= *C. lawsoniana* 'Lane's Aurea'; *C. lawsoniana lanei* Hort.). Developed

before 1945 in Lanes Nurseries, Great Beckhamsted, England. Meritorious yellow form. Plate 45.

'Laxa'. Vigorous but sparse grower, branches stout with thick internodes. Before 1891. (EX)

'Lombartsii' (P. Lombarts). Conical, 10 m high, strong grower, coarsely branched, branches outspread, tips nodding, branchlets spreading widely, directed forward; needles golden-yellow above, slightly blue pruinose, darker in winter, yellow-green beneath, pruinose. Developed in 1904 by P. Lombarts, Zundert, Holland; introduced to the trade in 1915.

'Lutea' (Rollison). Slender upright habit, to 10 m high, rather slow growing, main branches short and outspread, branches pendulous, often also twisted, penniform, branchlets golden-yellow, more yellowish-white in the middle; needles appressed, rather short, dull. SN Pl. 5 (H); TC 90; CCE 122. Found around 1870 in the nursery of G. & W. Rollison in Tooting (London), England. Especially valued in England for its beautiful yellow color even on older plants and its ability to go without pruning. Young plants are however, somewhat sensitive to an early frost. z7

'Lutea Nana' (Rogers). Dwarf form, broad conical habit, but a rather strong grower, more open; foliage yellow. Introduced to the trade about 1930 by W. H. Rogers & Son, Eastleigh, Hampshire, England. Not especially meritorious and therefore not often cultivated today. (EX?)

'Luteocampacta' (Gimborn). Densely conical habit, to 5 m high or taller, main branches regularly outspread, twiggy branches likewise, but also nodding, branchlets light yellow on the tips, lighter to yellow-green at the base; needles appressed, small, acute, golden-yellow, yellow-green beneath and inside the plant. Developed in the Von Gimborn Arboretum, Koorn, Holland and introduced in 1938 by H. den Ouden, Boskoop.

'Luteogracilis'. Graceful, open habit, branches somewhat nodding; needles golden-yellow, more yellowish-green in winter, light green beneath. Origin unknown. 1949.

'Lutescens'. (van Houtte). Strong upright habit, conical. Developed before 1875 by L. Van Houtte in Ghent, Belgium, but practically identical to 'Lutea'.

'Lycopodioides' (van der Elst). Conical habit, 5–6 m meters high, densely branched, twigs long, drawn out, twisted corkscrew-like and contorted; needles densely appressed, somewhat resembling *C. obtusa* 'Coralliformis', but with the needle tips always distinct (!!), otherwise scale-like imbricate, blue-green. OCC 88; WDw 52: Pl. 2F (Br); Gs 1925: 231; WM 6C (Br), 133 (H). Originated from seed around 1890 by Van Der Elst, Kwekerij Tottenham, Dedemsvaart, Holland. Fig. 39D. z7

'Maas' (P. Lombarts). Conical habit, branches ascending and outspread, resembling 'Triomf van Lombarts' in habit, but differing in the finer branching and yellowish needles. CCE 118. Developed by P. Lombarts, Zundert, Holland and introduced to the trade in 1957.

'Magnifica Aurea'. Vigorous grower, luxuriant blue-green foliage with branchlet tips conspicuously gold-yellow. CCE 118. Before 1891. (EX?)

'Masonii'. Conical habit, dense, slow growing; foliage green. CCE 117. Cultivated in England since 1932. Alleged to be very winter hardy. Plate 32.

'Melfard' (Melfard). Strong upright grower, branches however, bowed downward, not very attractive since the central leader is only branched to one side (like 'Golden King'). Selected by Melfard, Denmark, before 1937; cultivated in Boskoop by Gebr. Boer. Winter hardy, but not particularly attractive.

'Milfordensis'. Dwarf form, narrow conical habit, branches ascending and very densely arranged, regularly branched, nearly fern-like, very fine, blue-green, about 12 cm long and 6 cm wide. The best blue of the dwarf forms.

'Minima'. Globose dwarf form with a quite short or mostly absent stem (typical of all 'Minima' forms!) and, therefore, consisting of a large number of erect branches of nearly equal length, branchlets somewhat twisted, light green; needles densely arranged, appressed, distinctly bluish pruinose, especially on the underside. SN 170 (H); WDw 54 (H), Pl. 2A (Br); WM 4A (Br). ln cultivation since 1874. Plate 30; Fig. 38.

'Minima Argenteovariegata'. Like the above in habit, but the branchlets cream-white variegated. Very rare and sensitive in culture. z7–8

'Minima Aurea' (Rogers). Dwarf form, acute-ovate habit, to about 80 cm high, branches outspread and not so stiff as those of 'Aurea Densa', branchlets golden-yellow, also yellow inside the plant. WDw 42; WM 124 (H); CCE 118 (= *Cupressus lawsoniana minima aurea rogersii* Rogers). Developed by H. W. Rogers & Son before 1929. Plate 29.

'Minima Glauca'. Dwarf form, compact habit, more or less flat globose, branches erect and partly outspread, branchlets always erect, slightly shell-like, cupped, short; needles blue-green with white markings. This form is seldom found in cultivation; that nearly always found by this name is the broad crowned 'Nana Glauca'; this situation is probably a result of an erroneous illustration in Hornibrook (2nd ed., p. 33). A correct illustration may be found in Gs 1926: 39 (H); WM 134 (H); CCE 115. Plate 30.

'Moerheimii' (Ruys). Conical, tall growing, to 10 m high or more, branches and twigs erect and outspread, branchlets light yellow above, more yellow-green at the base; needles yellow, yellowish-green inside the plant. CCE 122. Developed before 1934 by B. Ruys, Kwekerij Moerheim, Dedemsvaart, Holland. Good winter hardiness, good yellow color, easily transplanted.

'Monumentalis' (de Vos). Densely columnar, to 10 m high, branches ascending, strong, densely covered with upright twigs and branchlets; needles appressed, blue pruinose, the small distinct tips curved inward. TC 163; CCE 127. Developed in 1873 by C. De Vos in Hazerswoude, near Boskoop, Holland.

'Monumentalis Glauca'. Densely conical, 5–10 m high, branchlets outspread, flat, bluish pruinose, outermost branch tips distinctly yellowish; needles small, dull dark blue-green, pruinose. Well-known form in the trade as early as 1891, frequently mistaken for 'Fraseri', but differing in the dull green leaves.

'Monumentalis Nova'. Columnar habit, loosely branched, 5 m high or more, main branches outspread, thin, limp, sparsely arranged, nearly horizontal on older plants or somewhat ascending, branchlets widely spaced, somewhat nodding, very short on the branch tips; needles small, fine, blue pruinose, light green beneath (not = 'Erecta Glauca', as given by Beissner). CCE 124. Known before 1891.

'Moonlight'. (Watson & Sons, Dublin). Upright habit, branching habit somewhat *obtusa*-like, crispate, yellowish gray-green, lighter in summer than in winter. Disseminated by J. F. B. Schupper, Hazerswoude, Holland, 1975.

'Naberi' (Naber). Conical, to 10 m high, branches and twigs outspread; needles on the growing branch tips sulfur-yellow, bluish pruinose on the base, bluish and yellowish-white in winter. Developed around 1929 by Naber & Co. in Gouda, Holland. Often referred to in the trade as "yellow Triomf van Boskoop".

Fig. 38. These 2 forms are often confused in cultivation! All *Chamaecyparis lawsoniana* 'Nana' forms have a central stem, the 'Minima' forms have only a short or totally absent central stem (Original)

'Nana' (Dauvesse). Dwarf form, short and broadly conical habit, always with a dominant leader and central stem (!!), this holds true for all the 'Nana' forms, to 2 m high, branches ascending, secondary branches more or less outspread; needles very small, glossy light green. WDw 53 (H), Pl. 2B (Br); WM 4B (Br), 135 (H). Developed by Dauvesse in Orléans, France, 1861. Plate 30; Fig. 38. z7

'Nana Albospica'. Like 'Nana', but the branch tips white. WDw 55 (H), Pl. 3E (Br) (= *Cupressus lawsoniana alba spica nana* Barron; *C. lawsoniana alba nana* [R. Sm.] Nich.). Known since 1874.

'Nana Albovariegata'. Dwarf form, conical, with a central leader, branches and twigs outspread, with nodding tips; foliage pale yellowish-green with whitish spots. Before 1891. (EX)

'Nana Argentea'. Dwarf form, broad ovate, with a dominant leader, densely branched, branches very compact, with more or less nodding tips; needles greenish-white when young, later gray-green (= *C. lawsoniana minima argentea* Hornibr.). Known since 1884.

'Nana Argenteovariegata'. Conical, slow growing, but not dwarf, densely branched, branchlets finer than those of 'Nana', with white tips ("as if covered with snow", as described by den Ouden). Before 1887.

'Nana Compacta'. A somewhat obscure form; said to be a synonym for 'Nana Glauca' by Beissner, and described by den Ouden as an individual form with blue-green foliage; in any case, no longer found in cultivation. 1891.

'Nana Glauca'. This is grown in many nurseries as 'Minima Glauca', it always has a central stem, which is absent from the true (rare) 'Minima Glauca'; otherwise like 'Nana', but the foliage is coarser and blue-green. Probably introduced by Veitch before 1881.

'Nana Rogersii' see **'Rogersii'**

'Nestoides' (J. Manten, Vancouver, B.C.). Hardly more than the type for 'Tamariscifolia', very slow growing, all branches flat spreading, blue-green, more silvery-blue on the new growth. Plate 34.

'New Golden' (Lombarts). Upright growing, conical, open branched; foliage yellow. CCE 119. Origin unknown; introduced in 1957 by P. Lombarts.

'Nidiformis' (Rovelli). Dwarf form, more open and "nest-like", always multistemmed, branches horizontally spreading-ascending, secondary branches nodding, branchlets rather coarse, nodding; needles short, loosely appressed, very flat, about 1.5 mm wide, blue-green, more blue beneath. DB 1970: 9; WDw 58: Pl. 3B (Br); WM 9B (Br); 137 (H) (= *C. nidifera* [Nich.] Hornibr.). Originated from seed around 1890 by Rovelli Frat. in Pallanza, on Lake Maggiore, Italy. A specimen 8 m high and 2 m wide stands in the Giardino Botanico Brissago (Lake Maggiore).

'Nivea' (van Geert). Conical habit; needles blue-white pruinose and white speckled. Introduced in 1862 by Van Geert, of Antwerp, Belgium.

'Olbrichii' (Froebel). Columnar, densely branched, branchlets delicate, fern-like; needles loosely appressed, acute, blue-green. TC 167. Developed in Zurich Switzerland by Froebel Nursery. Before 1904. z7

'Overeynderi' (Overeynder?). Slow growing but regular, branch tips bright white. Originated before 1891. Cultivated today in the Kalmthout Arboretum, Belgium.

'Parsons' (Hillier). Dwarf form, flat and dense habit, mounded, the branches and twigs layered. CCE 121 (= *C. lawsoniana* 'Parsonii' Hillier). Introduced to the trade by Hillier in 1964. Plate 34.

'Patula'. Conical, open, rather broad, to 5 m high or taller, branches outspread, branchlets partly oriented upward; needles tightly appressed, fine, sharply acuminate, nearly black-green in winter. Common in collections.

'Pembury Blue' (Baggesen, Pembury). Medium tall conical form (maximum height not yet known), branches on the lower portion of the plant spreading more or less horizontally or nodding, very thin branches, a beautiful silver-blue in the 1st year, becoming more greenish in the 2nd. KN Plate 2. Developed before 1965 by Baggesen in Kent, England, but introduced by Jackman. Until now, the best blue cultivar, but sensitive in cultivation. z7

'Pena Park'. Dwarf form, foliage deep green. As yet not available in the trade. The only known plant is about 80 years old, about 2.5 m high and nearly 10 m wide. Discovered by Fred G. Meyer in Pena Park, Sintra, Portugal.

'Pendula'. Narrow upright weeping form, to 10 m high, sparsely branched, major branches bowed upward, secondary branches widely spaced, pendulous, branchlets outspread, flat; needles small, glossy, dark green. Before 1891.

'Pendula Alba' (W. Paul). Upright, branches hanging gracefully, branch tips white, especially conspicuous on young plants (= *C. lawsoniana alba pendula* Beissn.). Developed around 1869 by Wm. Paul & Son. (EX)

'Pendula Aurea'. Weeping form, to 10 m high, branches and twigs hanging limp, lowest branches growing upward again from the ground; needles green-yellow at first, later a good golden-yellow. 1909. (EX?)

'Pendula Nova'. Columnar habit, branches elongated and drooping. 1909. (EX)

'Pendula Vera' (Hesse). Differing from 'Pendula' in the prostrate habit, must be tied to a standard as young plants, otherwise similar to 'Pendula' in the branching character, but even more pendulous. GFl 1890: 449. Developed by Herm. A. Hesse, Weener, near Hanover, W. Germany before 1890.

'Pixie' (seedling selection of Th. Streng, Boskoop, 1975). Globose to broadly ellipsoid habit, crown apex somewhat acute, densely branched; foliage fine blue-green. Dfl 11–12: 59 (H). Similar to 'Minima Glauca', but more finely textured.

'Plumosa' (Lieb). Broad columnar, branches ascending at acute angles, branches nodding gracefully, dark green, branchlets feather-form crispate, deep green. Developed before 1901 by E. Lieb in Partenit, Crimea, USSR.

'Plumosa Glauca'. Broad columnar habit, branchlets flat, very wide, intensively blue-green (= *C. lawsoniana* 'Blue Plume' den Ouden/Boom 1965). Very attractive, but also very sensitive

form, disseminated before 1914 (according to Raymond Chenault) from Orléans, France. One specimen grows on Isola Madre, Lake Maggiore, Italy. Fig. 39B. z7

'Pottenii' (Potten). Very narrow columnar form, to 10 m high, densely branched, major branches erect, long, thin, glossy brown, secondary branches likewise erect, but with the tips somewhat bowed downward, branchlets numerous, thin, soft to the touch; needles narrow, loosely appressed, somewhat gray-green pruinose (= *Cupressus lawsoniana* var. *pottenii* Dall. & Jacks.; *Cupressus lawsoniana pottenii* Hillier). Developed in the Potten Nursery in Cranbrook, England before 1910. Somewhat touchy in culture. Plate 32. z7

'President Roosevelt' (Hogger). Conical habit, open branched, major branches outspread, twigs and branchlets nodding, the latter light green on both sides, speckled yellow. CCE 125. Developed by J. Hogger, England and disseminated by him since 1945.

'Procumbens' (Backhouse). Dwarf form, broad procumbent habit; foliage green. Developed by James Backhouse & Son, York, England before 1939.

'Prostrata Glauca' (Lobkowitz). Creeping form with gray-green branches. Developed in 1891 in the nursery of Prince Lobkowitz, Eisenberg, Bohemia. Very frost sensitive and short-lived. (EX)

'Pulverulenta' (Lieb). Conical habit, luxuriant; foliage coarse, bluish, yellow pulverulent, very tolerant of hot sun. Developed before 1903 by E. Lieb in Partenit near Alupka, Crimea, USSR. (VR or EX).

'Pygmaea Argentea' (Backhouse). Dwarf form, very slow growing, flat-globose, erect branched, twigs dark green, but with greenish-white foliage near the tips; leaves densely packed. HD 60; WDw 56 (H), Pl. 3D (Br); WM 138 (H) (= *C. lawsoniana* 'Backhouse Silver'). Known before 1891. Suffers from sunscald in summer and very slow growing, therefore best used as a container plant. Plate 30.

'Pyramidalis' (P. Smith). Like the type in branching character and foliage color, habit however, especially narrowly columnar, nearly like a pyramidal poplar. Cultivated before 1867 by P. Smith in Bergedorf near Hamburg, W. Germany.

'Pyramidalis Alba'. Narrowly conical habit, somewhat like 'Pyramidalis', becoming tall; needles small, narrow, yellowish-white and pruinose on the branch tips. CCE 124 (= *C. lawsoniana* f. *pulcherrima* Beissn.). Cultivated before 1887 in Holland. Very conspicuous form.

'Pyramidalis Alba Nana'. Compact conical habit, young shoots white. Rev. Hort. Belge 1878: 281 (color plate). (EX)

'Pyramidalis Glauca'. Slender conical habit; needles blue pruinose. Named in 1909 by Schelle, but not completely described. (EX)

'Pyramidalis Lutea'. Slender ascending; needles golden-yellow. Described by Beissner in 1891, but not completely. (EX)

'Pyramidalis Lutea Gracilis'. Differing from 'Pyramidalis Lutea' primarily in its more elegant branching character. Named by Beissner in 1891, but not completely described. (EX)

'Raievskyana' (Lieb.). Dwarf form, branches wide spreading, branchlets pendulous and finely textured; foliage silvery light green. Developed in 1901 by E. Lieb in Partenit, Crimea from seed of 'Fragrans', obtained from Kew Gardens. (EX?)

'Rijnhof' (K. van Rijn, Hazerswoude 1979). Lawsoniana seedling, habit flat to flat-globose, to 1 m wide and 30 cm high, very densely branched; foliage needle-form (juvenile!), gray-green, blue-green beneath. Completely winter hardy. Good as groundcover or as a specimen.

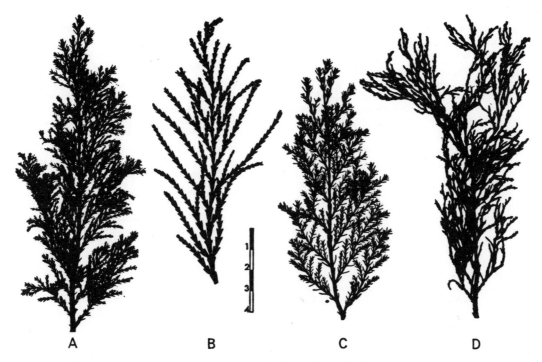

Fig. 39. *Chamaecyparis lawsoniana* cultivars.
A. 'Ellwoodii', B. 'Plumosa Glauca', C. 'Fletcheri', D. 'Lycopodioides'

'**Robusta**' (Jongkindt Coninck). Broadly columnar, strong grower, to 20 m high, branches ascending, stout, likewise the twigs, branchlets stiff; needles rather thick, both sides compressed and 4 sided, coarse, dark green. Developed in 1847 by C. Jongkindt Coninck, Kwekerij Tottenham, Dedemsvaart, Holland.

'**Robusta Argentea**'. Resembling 'Robusta', but more slender, yet stronger growing, branchlets thicker; needles gray blue. 1891.

'**Robusta Aurea**'. Broadly columnar, vigorous grower, luxurious, branch tips pendulous; needles a shimmering golden-yellow. 1891. (VR)

'**Robusta Glauca**'. Broadly upright, to 20 m high, branches ascending, vigorous, tips nodding, branchlets likewise with nodding tips, short, thick, gray-blue and pruinose. CCE 124 (= *C. lawsoniana* f. *robusta glauca* Beissn. non Hort.). Cultivated before 1891. To avoid confusion, take special note of the fact that *C. lawsoniana robusta glauca* hort. non Beissn. may only be a synonym for the white variegated *C. lawsoniana* 'Glauca Elegans'; which see.

'**Rogersii**' (Rogers). Dwarf form, loose globose or as an old plant more conical and to 2 m high, branches irregularly upright, usually however, outspread, likewise the secondary branches and the approx. 5 cm long branchlets; needles appressed, very small, green, but bluish pruinose, attractive. WDw 57 (H); CCE 123 (= *C. lawsoniana nana rogersii* Rogers; since the plant didn't belong in the nana group, its name had to be corrected). Developed about 1930 by W. R. Rogers & Son in England.

'**Rosenthalii**' (P. Smith). Conical, to 10 m high, branches ascending, secondary branches partly so, partly outspread; foliage light green. CCE 118. Introduced to the trade about 1884 by P. Smith of Bergedorf, Germany.

'**Royal Gold**'. Upright habit, but rather broadly conical, branching intensive yellow, more yellow than 'Golden Wonder'. Origin unknown, perhaps from Guernsey Island, Channel Islands. Disseminated through J. F. B. Schupper, Hazerswoude, Holland.

'**Schongariana**' (Pfitzer). Dense and ascending habit, to 10 m high, branches and twigs upright, branchlets outspread, stout; needles dark green, blue pruinose, with narrow markings beneath, apices distinct. Disseminated before 1909 by W. Pfitzer, Stuttgart, W. Germany.

'**Shawii**'. Dwarf form, regular globose habit with a somewhat higher apex, branches wide spreading, open; needles bluish light green. 1891.

'**Silver Gem**'. Conical; foliage fine gray-green, young branch tips with silver-white or yellowish-white needles, resembling 'Albospica', but later becoming more yellowy-green and gray. Similar to 'Silver Queen' but with better white color in spring. Unfortunately, not as winter hardy as the latter. z7

'**Silver Queen**'. Conical, regular and wide, to 10 m high, branches ascending and outspread, twigs cream-white to yellowish-green on the tips, especially attractive on the new growth. CCE 116. Allegedly originating in England; known in Germany before 1891 and often encountered there today.

'**Smithii**' (J. Smith). Conical upright habit, rather open and slow growing, branches ascending and outspread, secondary branches somewhat irregularly arranged; needles gold-yellow. CCE 125 (= *C. lawsoniana* lutea 'Smith' den Ouden; *C. lawsoniana darleyensis* Beissn.). Introduced in 1898 by J. Smith & Son of Darley Dale, England. z7–8

'**Southern Gold**'. Conical habit, lateral branches nodding; foliage a good pure yellow, green speckled inside the plant. From Southern Nurseries, England; disseminated by Darthuizer Boomkwekerijen. Beautiful, but not very winter hardy (?).

'Souvenir de Leide' (de Vos). This form, with somewhat bowed branches and light green foliage, was introduced in 1887 by C. De Vos Nursery in Hazerswoude near Boskoop, Holland. Probably no longer in cultivation.

'Spek' (J. Spek). Conical, 10 m high or more, branches rather thick and strong, twigs light brown; needles gray-blue, somewhat rough to the touch (= *C. lawsoniana glauca* 'Spek' den Ouden). Introduced in 1942 by Jan Spek Nursery of Boskoop and one of the best blue forms.

'Spiralis' (Lobkowitz). Conical habit, stem twisting spirally from left to right; foliage normal. Developed in the nursery of Prince Lobkowitz in Eisenberg, Bohemia, before 1909. (EX?)

'Squarrosa'. Conical habit; needles fine and narrow, awl-shaped, outspread, light green (so called "juvenile form"). Originated from seed by Prof. Dr. Heinrich Mayr in Munich, W. Germany in 1906, but died after transplanting. It is therefore doubtful that the name on the plant growing in the Koeszeg Arboretum in Komitat Vas, Western Hungary is correct.

'Stardust' (L. C. Langenberg). Vigorous grower, broadly conical, branchlets feathery; needles sulfur-yellow, likewise inside the plant. Originated from seed by L. C. Langenberg Nursery in Boskoop, Holland before 1965. Good winter hardiness.

'Stewartii' (D. Stewart). Conical, rather strong growing, to 10 m high, branches and twigs rather upright, branchlets golden-yellow, more yellow-green toward the base, also yellow-green in winter. TC 86; CCE 121 + 122. Developed around 1900 by D. Stewart & Son in Bournemouth, England. Commonly planted, hardy form, but surpassed in color by many newer forms. Plate 31.

'Stricta' (J. Waterer). A form very similar to 'Erecta Viridis' with conical habit, densely branched, bright green foliage. Developed before 1888 by J. Waterer & Son of Bagshot, England.

'Stricta Aurea'. Broadly conical habit, slow growing, 3–4 m high in 30 years, branchlets oriented upward, dark green with numerous yellow tips. In the trade in Orléans, France before 1930. (Possibly identical to 'Erecta Aureospica'?)

'Stricta Excelsa'. An uncertain form, allegedly similar to 'Stricta', but growing more vigorously. Named by Schelle in 1909.

'Stricta Glauca'. Narrowly conical, to 10 m high or more, branches and twigs ascending-outspread, branchlets fine, tips nodding; needles green, blue pruinose. Originated in Belgium before 1937.

"Tabuliformis" is apparently identical to 'Knowefieldensis'.

'Tamariscifolia' (J. Smith). Dwarf form, without a central stem, broad and vigorous habit, nearly umbrella-form, to 3 m high and 4 m wide, main branches stout, bowed upward, growing up and outward, wide spreading and irregular, partly also nodding, branchlets similar to those of 'Nidiformis', but the needles light blue-green, to 2 mm wide and nearly always distinctly glandular ('Nidiformis' only to 1.5 mm wide and almost never with glands). WDw 59 (H), Pl. 3A (Br); CCE 120 + 126; WM 5A (Br), 139 (H). Developed before 1923 by J. Smith & Son in Darley Dale, England. Plate 29; Fig. 37E.

'Tharandtensis' Dwarf form, globose at first, later more broadly conical, to 2 m high and 3 m wide, with only a few, stout branches, branchlets very numerous and densely crowded, crispate, green(!); needles very small, loosely appressed. Developed in 1890 in the Tharandter Forstgarten (near Dresden), E. Germany. Plate 34. (VR)

'Tharandtensis Caesia' Dwarf form, like 'Tharandtensis', but the needles dull blue-gray pruinose. WDw 60 (H), Pl. 2E (Br); TC 89. Likewise developed in the Tharandt Forstgarten and much cultivated today. Grown for years under the erroneous name of 'Forsteckensis Glauca'.

'Tilgate' (Tilgate Pl. Res. Stat.) Dwarf form, flat globose habit, branches more or less twisted, rather loosely arranged; the more open type of 'Forsteckensis' appears to be identical with this plant. CCE 121. Developed in the Plant Research Station in Tilgate, England; disseminated by R. G. Reuthe in Keston, Kent.

'Tortuosa'. Conical habit, branches and twigs conspicuously thick and fattened. 1891 (EX?)

'Triomf Van Boskoop' (Grootendorst). Conical, very strong grower, to 15 m high, branches ascending and outspread, blue-green, evenly silver pruinose, somewhat lighter beneath, rough to the touch. CCE 123. Developed by D. Grootendorst in Boskoop, Holland about 1890. Widely disseminated today. Fig. 37C.

'Triomf van Lombarts' (Lombarts). Conical habit, broad, fast growing, branches outspread; foliage yellow, small. Developed before 1940 by P. Lombarts, Zundert, Holland.

'Van Eck' (G. van Eck). Conical, of medium vigor, densely branched, branches outspread, branch tips yellow, paler inside the plant, from bluish-green to yellowish-green. Originated from seed by the G. van Eck Nursery of Boskoop, Holland in 1934.

'Van Tol' (P. van Tol). Strong grower, conical, similar to 'Alumii' in habit, but leaves golden-yellow, more yellowish-green in winter. Originated from seed of 'Alumii' which had crossed with a (yellow) 'Triomf van Lombarts' growing nearby at the P. van Tol mz. in Boskoop, Holland, 1946.

'Versicolor' (Jongkindt Coninck). Broadly conical, tall, open growing, branches and twigs ascending to outspread; needles green and speckled partly yellowish-white, partly light green, green beneath. SN 169 (H); CCE 125. Originated from seed by C. Jongkindt Coninck, Kwekerijen Tottenham, Dedemsvaart, Holland. z8

'Viner's Gold'. Columnar habit, lateral branches outspread and rather dense; foliage an attractive golden-yellow. Very pretty form from Waterer Sons & Crisp, England; cultivated by Darthuizer Boomkwekerijen.

'Weisseana' (J. Hansen). Flat umbrella-form, branch tips nodding. Illustrated in Moeller's Deutsche Gartnerzeitung 1890: 245. Developed by Julius Hansen in Pinnenberg; introduced about 1890 by W. Weisse Nursery in Kamenz (Saxony).

'Westermannii' (K. Jurissen). Conical, dense, to 5 m high or branches and twigs ascending-outspread, branches more or less nodding; needles lighter or darker yellow on the branch tips, more yellow-green toward the base. TC 88; CCE 119. Developed about 1880 by Jac. Jurrissen & Zoon in Naarden, Holland. z7

'Westermannii Aureovariegata'. Like 'Westermannii', but the branchlets speckled yellow. Before 1909. (EX)

'White Spot' (D. T. Poulsen). Mutation of 'Monumentalis Nova' with the same characteristics, but some of the leaves white or white marbled, new growth cream-white, greening in summer except for a few needles and tips, not conspicuously colored in winter. CCE 125.

'Winston Churchill' (Hogger). Conical habit, upright, branches outspread, branchlets a good gold-yellow on the upper surface, some light green and yellowish-green speckled, gray-green beneath, here likewise somewhat yellow checked. Originated from seed by J. Hogger of East Grinstead, England and introduced about 1945.

'Wisselii' (v. d. Wissel). Narrowly conical habit, to 10 m high or higher, branches and twigs stout, ascending to upright, but also spreading horizontally on very old plants, branchlets dense and arising from all sides of the twig, fern-like to cockscombform; needles very small, densely arranged, blue-green. WDw Pl. 2H; CCE 125 (= *C. lawsoniana fragrans conica* Beissner; *C. lawsoniana conica* Gebbers). Developed around 1885 in the nursery of F. Van der Wissel in Epe, Holland. Plate 31.

'Wisselii Nana' is nothing more than a slow growing 'Wisselii', presumably developed from a side branch on the lower part of the plant. Not always constant, reverts back to the normal form readily.

'Witzeliana'. Columnar habit, 5 m high or more, branches very densely covering the stem, strictly upright, branchlets 5–10 cm long, narrowly upright; leaves appressed, small, dull dark green. CCE 125. Origin unknown, introduced in 1934 as *C. lawsoniana erecta witzeliana*. Appears almost like *Juniperus communis hibernica*. Plate 31.

'Worlei' (P. Smith). Upright habit, branches and twigs dense, branchlets short and thick; foliage gray-green. Introduced by P. Smith of Bergedorf near Hamburg, W. Germany before 1891. (EX)

'Yellow Transparent' ('van 't Hof'). A yellow 'Fletcher', brownish in winter, but somewhat slower growing. CCE 125. Developed about 1955 by H. van 't Hof Nursery of Boskoop, Holland.

'Youngii' (M. Young). Slender conical form, to 10 m high, branches erect and outspread, rather stiff, secondary branches more open, more or less twisted, branchlets rather long, nearly fern-like; needles thick, glossy dark green, remaining so in winter. CCE 121. Developed by Maurice Young of Milford, England and introduced in 1874.

C. nootkatensis (D. Don) Spach. Nootka False Cypress. Tree, 30–40 m high, stem to 2 m thick, slender conical habit, branches densely spreading-nodding, bark brownish-gray, exfoliating in large plates, branchlets usually pendulous, spreading in an even plane, nearly 4 sided; leaves tightly appressed (spreading on vigorous shoots), dark green, without white markings, dorsal side keeled or rounded, usually without glands, unpleasant smelling when crushed; male flowers yellow; cones globose, 1 cm thick, brownish pruinose, ripening the second year, scales 4–6, with hook-like, protruding, erect tips (= *C. nutkaensis* Lindl. & Gord.). Coastal tree of northwestern N. America, Nootka Sound, Alaska, British Columbia. 1850. Likes high humidity. Plate 35 and 45; Fig. 35A.

'Aurea'. Habit like the species, but not growing as tall, branchlets and leaves light yellow, later becoming light green (= *C. nootkatensis* var. *lutea* [Webst.] Rehd.). 1891.

'Aureovariegata' (M. Young). Young branches yellowish variegated, lighter in summer, more brownish-yellow in winter. Introduced in 1875 by Maurice Young, Milford, England.

'Columnaris'. Good columnar form, branches spreading horizontally to 1 m long, thin, branches and branchlets pendulous; leaves dark green; fruits abundantly. Developed in the Tuebingen Botanic Garden, near Stuttgart, W. Germany before 1909. EX

'Compacta'. Dwarf form, compact, densely bushy, developing a gracefully open crown, twigs few, branchlets numerous, 5–10 cm long, erect and rather flat; needles loosely appressed, narrow, small, light green. SN 166 (H); WDw 61 (H), Pl. 6A, (Br); WM 6F (Br), 140 (H) (= *C. nootkatensis compacta viridis* Schelle). 1873.

'Compacta Glauca'. Dwarf globose form, very dense habit, branches erect; needles blue-green. 1909. Plate 35. (R)

'Ericoides' (von Saaghy). Mutation with awl-shaped leaves, compact and bushy habit, branch tips also partly with large, more needle form tips, but also with outspread scale leaves; leaves 5–8 mm, arranged radially around the twig, linear, acuminate, tapering to a long apex, thickish, blue-green, slightly keeled beneath. BFN 532. Originated from seed by Von Saaghy in Kamon, Hungary in 1904. (EX)

'Glauca'. Like the species, but branches stouter, thicker, often heavy, nodding; needles distinctly blue-green, producing an abundance of cones (seeds often not viable). 1858. Frequently found in cultivation.

'Glauca Aureovariegata'. Conical habit, medium strong grower; foliage blue-green with golden variegated markings. 1891. (VR)

'Glauca Vera'. Compact conical habit, needles smaller than those of 'Glauca' and darker blue. 1884.

'Gracilis'. Dwarf form, dense globose habit, densely branched; foliage dark green. (EX?)

'Nana' is no longer a collective name for the dwarf forms of this species (= *C. nootkatensis* var. *nana* Schnd.).

'Nidifera' (Rovelli, Pallanza, Italy before 1889). Seedling of *C. nootkatensis*, dwarf growing, foliage loose, with relatively few branchlets, branch tips nodding; leaves never blue beneath(!!). WM 5F (Br), 141 (H). Totally different from the "nest-like" forms of *C. lawsoniana*, but often confused with these. (Refer to the detailed historical account by Welch in WM 163–165.)

'Nutans' (J. Boer Wz.). Conical habit, of medium vigor, branches outspread, secondary branches nodding; foliage gray-blue. Developed before 1949 by J. Boer Wz., Boskoop, Holland. Presumably a mutation of 'Glauca'.

'Pendula' (A. Van Leeuwen). Pendulous form, upright, to 15 m high, apex nodding, branches widely spaced, declining obliquely downward, the secondary branches hanging limply and vertically, likewise the branchlets; needles green. Developed before 1884 in the nursery of A. van Leeuwen in Naarden, Holland. One of the best weeping conifers for a specimen plant. Plate 35.

'Pendula Variegata'. Like the normal 'Pendula', but distinctly white variegated and attractive. (Jeddeloh).

'Pyramidalis'. Very narrow habit, compact conical, very densely branched. Developed in the nursery in Auteuil, near Paris, 1867. (EX?)

'Tatra' (F. Machala, Czechoslovakia, 1975). Broad conical habit, multistemmed, and therefore very dense; foliage blue-green, especially in summer, a better blue than *C. nootkatensis* 'Glauca', finer, softer to the touch.

'Variegata'. Grows like the species, but branchlets white-speckled; leaves otherwise blue-green (= *C. nootkatensis argenteovariegata* [Veitch] Dall. & Jacks.). Known since 1873. Fig. 45D.

'Viridis'. Narrowly columnar, branch tips slightly nodding; foliage bright green. 1867.

'Viridis Pendula'. Conical habit, branches pendulous, thin and filamentous, conspicuously light green. Found in the garden of the Grand Hotel in Les Avants, Switzerland in 1910. (EX?)

C. obtusa (S. & Z.) Endl. Hinoki False Cypress. Tree, to 40 m high, stem to 2 m thick, crown wide, acutely conical on the apical half, dense, bark red-brown, rather smooth, exfoliating in thin strips, branch tips pendulous, branchlets flattened, in an even plane; needles thickish, nearly appressed, dark green, with distinct white lines beneath, facial needles ovate-rhombic, dorsal side convex with rounded glands, lateral needles coarser, nearly sickle-shape, acute; cones solitary, on short stalks, 8–10 mm thick, orange-brown, cone scales usually 8(– 10), thick, woody, concave on the dorsal side, with a short tip. KIF 1: 44. Japan, Taiwan. 1861. Succeeds best in cool areas with good soil, full sun. Fig. 35B. z3

Outline of the Described Cultivars of *C. obtusa*

1. Tall to medium height, upright, conical, normal vigor

    ● green
var. *breviramea*	'Gracilis'
'Erecta'	'Kamakurahiba'
'Fontana'	'Magnifica'
var. *formosana*	

    ● yellow
'Goldilocks'	'Lutea Nova'
'Keteleeri'	'Magnifica Aurea'

    ● fern-like branches
'Aonokujahuhiba'	'Filicoides'

2. Low growing to dwarf, compact, conical

    ● green
'Compacta'	'Opaal'
'Contorta'	'Nana Gracilis'
'Graciosa'	'Nana Pyramidalis'
'Green Diamond'	'Rigid Dwarf'
'Hage'	'Spiralis'
'Kosteri'	'Tempelhof'
'Laxa'	

    ● yellow
'Aurea'	'Nana Aurea'
'Crippsii'	'Nana Lutea'
'Goldspire'	'Yellowtip'
'Gracilis Aurea'	'Youngii'
'Mariesii'	

    ● white variegated
'Albospica'	'Tonia'
'Argentea'	

    ● filamentous branches
'Coralliformis'	'Suirova-Hiba'

3. Dwarf habit, globose to flat

    ● hemispherical to globose
'Bassett'	'Minima'
'Caespitosa'	'Nana'
'Flabelliformis'	'Nana Argentea'
'Intermedia'	'Nana Compacta'

'Juniperoides'	'Stoneham'
'Juniperoides Compacta'	

● flat and wide
'Prostrata'	'Pygmaea Aurescens'
'Pygmaea'	'Repens'

● Leaves all needle-form
'Ericoides' (= 'Chabo-yadori')

4. Other growth habits

    ● branches filamentous
'Filiformis'	'Filiformis Aurea'

    ● branches pendulous
    'Pendula'

    ● branches cockscomb-like
'Densa'	'Lycopodioides'
'Draht'	'Lycopodioides Aurea'
'Kanaamahiba'	'Tetragona Aurea'
'Kojolkohiba'	'Troubetzkoyana'

    ● branchlets fern-like
'Chilworth'	'Filicoides'
'Compact Fernspray'	

'Albospica'. Dwarf form, conical habit, to 2 m high, densely branched, branches horizontal, secondary branches ascending, branchlets crispate, tips yellowish-white on new growth and in summer, later gradually greening. Before 1874.

'Albovariegata'. White variegated form. 1884. No longer in cultivation. (EX?)

'Aonokujahuhiba'. Habit not known, very similar in appearance to 'Filicoides', but the side branches only 1–3 cm long, fern-like. Japan.

'Argentea'. Branchlets and needles to a partly silvery-white, but with green evenly mixed throughout the plant (= *C. obtusa argenteovariegata* Schelle). Imported from Japan by R. Fortune about 1860; in general cultivation there.

'Aurea'. Conical, to 5 m high, young branches golden-yellow, but often with young twigs entirely green. KN Pl. 3. Introduced from Japan around 1860, but far surpassed today by 'Crippsii'.

'Bassett' (Rogers). Dwarf form, similar to 'Juniperoides', but becoming much taller and with ascending branches; needles dark green.

var. **breviramea** (Maxim.) Regel. Tall tree, crown narrow, branches short, horizontally arranged, twigs thick, drawn out narrower; needles thickish, glossy green on both sides, without white markings on the underside; cones smaller than those of the species (= *C. breviramea* Maxim.). Japan; northern Kyushu.

'Caespitosa' (Rogers). Dwarf form, compact habit, cushion-form, annual growth only 0.5 cm, branches and branchlets shell-like, distinctly bluish-green (!); needles very small. WDw Pl. 4a (Br), 62 (H); HD 67; WM 7A (Br), 142 (H). Developed in 1923.

'Chilworth' (Gardner). Grows like a dwarf tree, the branches outspread, nearly feather-like and bowed downward, light green, with a brownish touch in winter. WDw Pl. 4B (Br), 64 (H); WM 7E (Br). Fig. 41C.

'Compacta'. Broad conical habit, to 5 m high, branches ascending to outspread, secondary branches rather long, branchlets and needles normal green. Before 1875.

'Compact Fernspray'. Very similar to 'Filicoides', but low, broad bushy, the fern-like branchlets much smaller, very slow growing. WDw Pl. 4R (Br); WM 7G (Br) (= 'Filicoides Compacta' Hillier; 'Filicoid Dwarf' Boom). Plate 38.

'Contorta' (den Ouden). Conical, to 2 m high, branches short, twisted, outspread, with long, twisted tips, branchlets with short, thick, filamentous shoots; needles densely arranged, light green. CCE 136. Originated from seed of 'Nana Gracilis'; introduced to the trade in 1945. Plate 46.

'Coralliformis'. Dwarf form, somewhat flat-globose, to 50 cm high, branches thin, growing chaotically throughout each other, secondary branches thin, more or less filamentous, branchlets thickish, coral-like with irregular thickenings; needles bluish-green, somewhat brown speckled, WDw Pl. 4F (Br), 63 (H); WM 8C (Br), 143 (H) (= C. obtusa torulosa Hort.). Developed before 1909. Similar to 'Lycopodioides', but much smaller.

'Crippsii' (Cripps & Sons). Broadly conical, to 5 m high or more, branches and twigs outspread-nodding, branchlets fan-shaped, golden-yellow; needles partly golden-yellow, yellow-green inside the plant and on the leaf undersides. WDw 66 (H); CCE 136. Developed before 1901. z8

'Densa'. Dwarf form, high arching habit, a plant at Hillier's is only 60 cm high and wide after 35 years, very densely branched, branchlets nearly cockscomb-like crispate, deep green. (R)

'Draht' (G. J. Draht, Barmstedt, around 1960?) Habit conical, dense, compact, 4–5 m high (or taller?); leaves all scale-like, very densely arranged, spiraled, in about 6 rows, the bases appressed, apices more thick, awl-shaped, and half distinct, dull green somewhat resembling 'Lycopodioides'.

'Erecta' (Waterer & Sons). Conical form, to 5 m high, branches ascending, tips long, drawn out, nodding, secondary branches short; needles narrow, light green, glossy green beneath. Introduced to the trade about 1870.

'Ericoides'. Small, dense bush with small, light green needle-form leaves, branchlets somewhat crispate, here and there over the entire plant are a few small branch tips with scale leaves like C. obtusa (best distinction). WDw 65 (H); WM 9A (Br), 144 (H) (= 'Chabo Yadori'). Plate 37; Fig. 41E.

'Filicoides'. Upright habit, occasionally a tall, narrow crowned tree, to 16 m (Brissago), or also shrubby and slow growing, branches long, narrow, flat, covered on both sides with short, nearly equally long, fern-like branchlets, these dark green above, more blue-green beneath; needles small, ovate, thick, obtuse, keeled, imbricately arranged in 4 rows. WDw Pl. 4Q (Br), 67 (H); CCE 137; WM 8E (Br), 145 (H). Imported about 1860 by Siebold and in 1861 by Veitch from Japan. Plate 37; Fig. 44C

'Filiformis'. Conical habit, branches with up to 50 cm long, filamentous, nodding tips, slender, bright green (= C. pendula Maxim.). Found in a garden in Tokyo by Maximowicz about 1865, cultivated about 1902 by H. A. Hesse. (EX?)

'Filiformis Aurea'. Like the above but foliage yellow variegated. (EX?)

'Flabelliformis' (Rogers). Dwarf form, globose, eventually more ovate, very slow growing, scarcely over 15 cm high, branchlets very short, fan-shaped, light green, partly blue pruinose. HiD 22. Developed about 1939 by Rogers.

'Fontana' (C. Verboom, Boskoop 1970). Mutation of C. obtusa 'Nana Gracilis'. Broadly conical habit, to 4 × 2 m or perhaps taller, rather dense with the fan-shaped branches and twisted shoots, tips gracefully nodding, young branches brown-red; needles scale-like, bright green.

var. formosana (Hayata) Rehd. Tree, to 40 m high in its habitat, stem to 3 m thick, bark shredding; needles scale-like, tightly appressed, deep green above, with white markings beneath, obtuse apex; ripe cones globose, 10–11 mm thick, with 8–10 umbrella-shaped scales, seeds narrow winged, 4 mm wide, also smaller than those of C. obtusa. LT 50 (= C. taiwanensis Masamune & Suzuki). Taiwan; in the mountains at 1300–2000 m, often intermixed with C. formosensis.

'Goldilocks' (F. J. Grootendorst, Boskoop 1978). Mutation of C. obtusa 'Nana Lutea'. Conical habit, very dense foliage golden-yellow.

'Goldspire' (Blijdenstein). To 5 m high, narrow conical, branchlets irregularly arranged, branch tips always lemon-yellow. CCE 136 (= C. obtusa aureospicata Hort). Found in the Blijdenstein Pinetum. Introduced into the trade in 1963 by L. Konijn. Pretty.

'Gracilis'. Conical, more compact than the species, to 5 m high or higher, branches outspread, branchlets irregularly arranged, shell-form; needles short, dense, light green beneath and somewhat glossy. Imported from Japan around 1862 by Siebold. Fig. 40C.

'Gracilis Aurea' (Veitch). Conical, 2–3 m high, branches outspread, secondary branches broadly fan-shaped with nodding tips; needles yellow-green, yellowish-white on the underside; otherwise like the above. CCE 136. Introduced to the trade before 1875 by J. Veitch.

'Graciosa' (Konijn). Mutation of 'Nana Gracilis', but more open growing, more coarsely branched, to 3 m high; needles lighter green. CCE 138 (= C. obtusa 'Loenik'). Developed by Konijn about 1935. Plate 36.

'Green Diamond' (from USA). Upright habit, rather densely branched with fan-shaped, spreading branches, tips nodding, young shoots red-brown; foliage dull dark green, conspicuously glossy in winter, with blue-white markings beneath. Introduced from the USA to Holland about 1965 under the name 'Columnaris', but this name was changed in 1977 to the present one.

'Hage'. (Hage). Dwarf form, densely compact, broadly conical, very slow growing, becoming about 1 m high, branches tightly crowded, twisted; needles very small, bright green, the tips occasionally somewhat yellow-brown in winter. Introduced about 1928 by Wm. Hage & Co., Boskoop. Plate 38.

'Intermedia' (Rogers). Dwarf form, tall globose, open, only about 30 cm high, very slow growing, branches outspread or also with downward curving tips; needles light green. WDw Pl. 4C (Br), 69 (H); WM 7F (Br), 146 (H). Developed by Rogers & Son about 1930. Plate 38; Fig. 40A.

'Juniperoides' (Rogers). Dwarf form, habit globose and open, to 25 cm high and wide, annual growth only about 1 cm, branchlets sparsely arranged, fan-shaped, tips bowed downward; needles narrow, with distinct tips, but incurved, dark green. WDw Pl. 4D (Br), 68 (H); WM 7C (Br), 147 (H). Developed by Rogers & Son before 1923. Plage 41; Fig. 41A.

'Juniperoides Compacta' (Rogers). Smaller in all respects than the previous form, but lower, and therefore more dense, branch tips curving downward; the foliage somewhat yellowish-green. WDw Pl. 4E (Br), 70 (H); WM 7D (Br), 148 (H). Developed by Rogers & Son before 1923. Fig. 41B.

'Kanaamihiba'. Dwarf form with thickish, contorted at the tips, cockscomb-like clustered branches. Introduced from Japan around 1900, but presumably no longer in cultivation. Now and then reverting back to the original form.

'Kamakurahiba'. Branching very similar to 'Breviramea', fan-shaped, but more similar to the normal *C. obtusa*, intermediate between the two. Cultivated only in Japan.

'Kojolkohiba'. Very similar to 'Tetragona Aurea', but less sensitive to sunscald and growing better, the branches longer, obliquely ascending. Apparently disseminated from New Zealand; in cultivation in England.

'Keteleerii' (Keteleer). Like the species, but the branchlets half yellow. Introduced to the trade about 1860 by Keteleer. Similar to 'Crippsii'. (EX?)

'Kosteri' (Koster & Zoon). Dwarf form, compact, conical, to about 1.2 m high, open, branches ascending, branchlets thickish, somewhat shell-form, brownish, branch tips curving partly upward, partly downward; needles light green. WDw Pl. 4K (Br), 71 (H); WM 8A (Br), 149 (H) (= *C. obtusa nana kosteri* Hornibr.). Brought into the trade by M. Koster & Zoon about 1915. An intermediate form between 'Nana' and 'Pygmaea'. Plate 36; Fig. 40B.

'Laxa' (Rogers). Seedling of 'Nana Gracilis', habit intermediate between 'Nana' and 'Nana Gracilis', more loose and open; needles deep green. Developed before 1939 by Rogers & Son, but only cultivated in RHS Gardens, Wisley, England.

'Lutea Nova' (v. d. Kraats). Mutation, open conical habit, to 5 m high, branches outspread, tips inclined downward, branchlets thin, fine, yellow, more bronze-yellow in winter. CCE 136. Developed before 1904 by J. Van Der Kraats, Boskoop, Holland. Poor wind tolerance.

'Lycopodioides'. Dwarf form, to 2.5 m high and 2 m wide, shrubby or more or less open globose, branches ascending, somewhat irregular, twigs thick, tips with cockscomb-like clustered branchlets; needles variably formed, dense, radially arranged, bluish dark green. WDw Pl. 4N (Br), 72 (H); WM 150 (H) (= *C. obtusa* 'Rashahiba'). Introduced around 1861 by Siebold from Japan. Plate 37; Fig. 41D.

'Lycopodioides Aurea'. Dwarf form like the above, but slower growing, scarcely over 1 m high; needles light yellow. SN 107 (H); CCE 136. Introduced from Japan to Europe about 1890.

'Magnifica' (R. Smith). Broadly conical habit, to 5 m high or taller, strong growing, branches spreading horizontally, branchlets fan-shaped, light green. About 1874.

'Mariesii'. Dwarf form, very slow growing, scarcely over 60 cm high and 80 cm wide in 50 years, conical, branches thin, nodding; needles yellowish-white to nearly milk-white, more yellow-green in winter. WDw Pl. 4M (Br), 73 (H); WM 151 (H); CCE 136 (= *C. obtusa* 'Nana Albo-Variegata'). Plate 37.

'Minima' (Rogers). Dwarf "ball form", similar to 'Caespitosa', but slower growing and with distinct light green foliage, branchlets not shell-form, rather compact and ascending, 4 sided in cross section, 20 year old plants are about 10 cm wide. WDw Pl. 4d (Br), 74 (H); CC 64 (H); WM 155 (H). Developed around 1923 by Rogers & Son. Despite the synonym 'Tetragona Minima', it has nothing to do with 'Tetragona'.

'Nana'. Dwarf form, very slow growing, broadly globose, to 60 cm high and 90 cm wide, horizontal branching, branchlets shell-like, put partly horizontal, partly bowed upward ("saddle-like" according to Welch); needles blackish-green. WDw Pl. 4 (Br), 76 (H); OCC 107 (H); WM 8B (Br), 156 (H). Frequently confused with 'Nana Gracilis', but quite different. Plate 38.

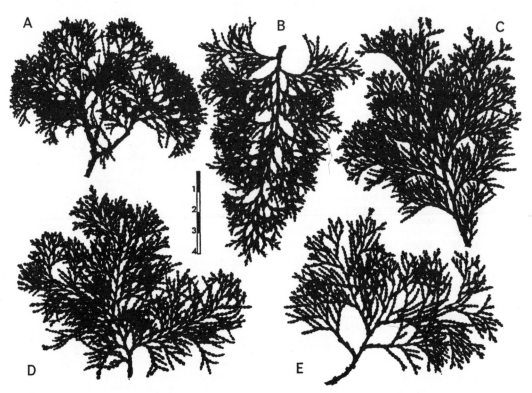

Fig. 40. Cultivars of *Chamaecyparis obtusa*.
A. 'Intermedia'; B. 'Kosteri'; C. 'Gracilis'; D. 'Nana Gracilis'; E. 'Pygmaea'

'Nana Argentea'. Differing from 'Nana' in the more compact habit and somewhat white variegated color. Cultivated since 1909. (Veitch).

'Nana Aurea'. Dwarf form, conical, but to 2 m high, branches spreading horizontally, branchlets golden-yellow and partly whitish-yellow, more yellow-green inside the plant; the needles likewise, undersides light green. WDw Pl. 4P (Br); CCE 140. Imported from Japan before 1867. Plate 36.

'Nana Compacta'. Dwarf form, old plants broadly conical-rounded with a dominant central leader; foliage bright green. WDw 78 (H); WM 157 (H). Not = C. obtusa nana compacta Hort., which is only a synonym of 'Nana Gracilis'.

'Nana Gracilis'. Dwarf form, old plants broadly conical, to 2 m high, young plants irregular, at first partly more or less globose to conical, branches horizontal, twigs irregular, branchlets shell-form to pouch-like twisted, dark green, but glossy. WDw Pl. 40 (Br); WM 8D (Br), 158 (H); CCE 139. One of the most frequently cultivated forms, occasionally under the wrong names, C. obtusa 'Nana' and C. obtusa 'Nana Compacta'. Fig. 40D.

'Nana Lutea' (Spek.) Dwarf form, compact habit, but usually rather open branched, branch tips similar to 'Intermedia', bowed downward, but pure golden-yellow during the entire year. WDw Pl. 4J (Br); WM 159 (H); CCE 139.

'Nana Pyramidalis' (den Ouden). Dwarf form, conical, very dense and compact, very slow growing, scarcely over 1 m high (mother plant in 30 years was 60 cm high and 45 cm wide at the base), horizontal branching, branchlets shell-form cupped; needles very small, deep green. Developed around 1905 from seed of 'Nana Gracilis', but first brought into the trade in 1934.

'Opaal' (Konijn). Very similar to 'Nana Gracilis', but foliage more yellow-green and fruiting abundantly on very young plants. (Jeddeloh).

'Pendula'. Weeping form, branches long nodding, twigs thickish, tips filamentous and weeping. Developed in the nursery of Prince Lobkowitz, Eisenberg, Bohemia. Very beautiful, hardy form, but probably extinct today. (EX?)

'Prostrata'. Procumbent habit, branches outspread, nearly mat-like across the ground. Described in 1923 by Hornibrook, but little cultivated today. (EX?)

'Pygmaea'. Dwarf form, broadly globose, to 1.5 m high and wide as a grafted plant, as a rooted plant presumably scarcely higher than 60 cm, but then much wider, branches spreading, twigs fan-shaped, branchlets conspicuously red-brown, more brown in winter, tips curving somewhat downward; needles bright green, somewhat brownish in fall and winter. WDw Pl. 4L (Br); WM 160 (H); CCE 139. Imported from Japan in 1861 and well disseminated today, although often confused with the following form. Plate 38; Fig. 40E.

'Pygmaea Aurescens' (Wezelenburg). Like the previous form, but growing more strongly both as a cutting grown or grafted plant, strong horizontal shoots occasionally seen on the plant, the others more fan-shaped; foliage always distinctly brownish-green, bronze-brown in winter. Originated as a mutation of 'Nana Hage Nursery, Boskoop, Holland; introduced to the trade in 1949. Plate 38.

'Repens' (Hage). Dwarf, very wide, only about 60 cm high, but 60–120 cm wide or more, resembles 'Pygmaea', but is more coarsely branched; needles a constant fresh green, never bronze-green. WDw 79 (H); WM 161 (H); CCE 176. Appeared as a mutation on 'Nana Gracilis' at the nursery of Wm. Hage, Boskoop, Holland. Introduced into the trade in 1949. Plate 38.

'Rigid Dwarf'. Dwarf form, narrowly upright, about 90 cm high in 25 years, branches stiff, main stem nearly vertically upright, while the branchlets hang finger-like; foliage very dark green. CCE 140 (= C. obtusa 'Nana Rigida' Hillier). Developed in England.

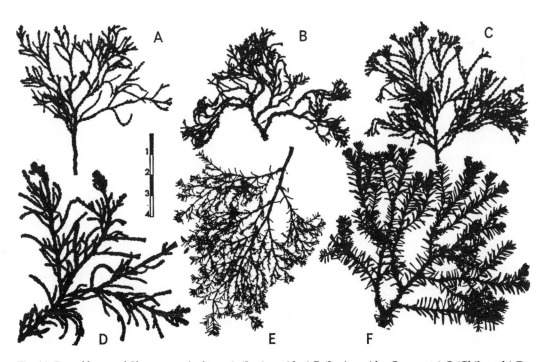

Fig. 41. Dwarf forms of *Chamaecyparis obtusa*. A. 'Juniperoides'; B. 'Juniperoides Compacta'; C. 'Chilworth'; D. 'Lycopodioides'; E. 'Ericoides'; F. *Thuja orientalis* 'Sanderi'

'Sanderi' see *Thuja orientalis* 'Sanderi'

'Spiralis' (Rogers). Dwarf form, upright, conical, very slow growing, about 60 cm high in 30 years, twigs somewhat spirally twisted and shell-like cupped. CCE 141 (= *C. obtusa* 'Nana Spiralis' Hillier; *C. obtusa* 'Nana Contorta' Hort. ex Hillier). Developed about 1930 by Rogers. Distinctive form, but as a young plant hardly distinguishable from 'Nana'.

'Stoneham'. Dwarf form, very slow growing, about 30 cm wide and 20 cm high, the branchlets somewhat layered one over another, resembling a tiny 'Nana' (= *C. obtusa* 'Nana Stoneham' Hillier). 1964.

'Suirova-Hiba'. Shrubby habit, medium tall, similar to 'Coralliformis', loosely branched, branches and branchlets partly filamentous and twisted. Japanese cultivar. (Hillier; Horstmann).

'Tempelhof' (Konijn). Dwarf form, strong growing, broadly ovate to conical, to 2.5 cm high, branchlets fan-shaped, green to yellowish-green, often with a brownish trace like 'Pygmaea Aurescens'. CCE 141. Found in the Konijn Nursery before 1964.

"Tetragona". This plant probably doesn't exist at all! If it does, then it looks like a green-needled 'Tetragona Aurea'. Plants labelled by this name in cultivation have always proven to be the yellow form. Such plant may occasionally become more or less green. See also Welch (1966), p. 141.

'Tetragona Aurea'. Dwarf form, usually shrubby-bushy, upright, branches ascending to outspread, seldom taller than 2 m (occasionally to 6 m high in England!), branches irregularly arranged, short, tips often cockscomb-like (fasciated), the branchlets 4 sided; needles in 4 rows, densely imbricate, glossy golden-yellow to more bronze-yellow, the shady areas more yellow-green to blue-green. WDw 8C (H); HD 43 (H); WM 162 (H); CCE 140 + 141. Introduced from Japan around 1870 by Wm. Barron & Sons of Barrowash, England. Plate 46; Fig. 44B.

'Tonia' (Hage). Dwarf form, resembling 'Nana Gracilis' or 'Nana Compacta', but much slower growing; foliage deep green with white branch tips, these however, occasionally only appearing on plants several years old. WDw 82 (Br). Developed about 1928 by Wm. Hage & Co.

'Troubetzkoyana'. Dwarf form, compact and dense, branches short and wide spreading; needles densely appressed, light green, thickish, awl-shaped, with glands on the dorsal side. Originated in the garden of Prince Troubetzkoy in Pallanza, Lake Maggiore, Italy as a seedling before 1890, and introduced by Rovelli in 1891. (EX?)

'Tsatsumi' is probably identical with 'Coralliformis'.

'Yellowtip' (v. d. Akker). Dwarf form, compact, slow growing, nearly shrubby, later broadly conical, branches outspread, branchlets shell-form cupped, often twisted, branch tips yellow, the other needles dark green. Originated in 1945 as a mutation of 'Nana Gracilis' at the C. A. Van Den Akker Nursery, Boskoop, Holland.

'Youngii' (Young). Tall growing, like the type, but branchlets somewhat nodding; needles yellow, but not so intense as those of 'Aurea', more green-yellow inside the plant and on the leaf undersides (= *C. obtusa* 'Aurea Youngii'). Developed before 1919 in Young's Nursery, Milford, England.

C. pisifera (S. & Z.) Endl. Sawara False Cypress. Tree, to 50 m high, crown narrowly conical, stem to 2 m thick, bark red-brown, smooth, exfoliating in thin strips, branches spreading horizontally, branchlets flat, in a single plane, nodding; needles appressed, glossy green above, usually with oblong, very distinct white markings beneath, facial needles boat-shaped (navicular), sharp, with protruding tips, only slightly aromatic when crushed; cones numerous, clustered, small, globose, to 6 mm thick, dark brown, with 8–12 scales, slightly woody, rugose above, slightly acuminate above the middle, margin crenate, seeds 1–2 in each scale, with a broad winged limb, margin incised at the base and the apex. KIF 1: 44. Japan; Hondo; moist soil and valleys. Brought to Europe by Siebold in 1860. Fig. 36D. z3

> Following are the numerous cultivars, some with scale leaves, some with needle leaves, some intermediate; includes outlines of 'Filifera', 'Nana', 'Plumosa' and 'Squarrosa'.

'Argenteovariegata'. Habit like the species, to about 10 m high, branchlets somewhat white variegated on the tips. CCE 145 (= *C. pisifera argentea* Hort.). Introduced from Japan in 1861 by Fortune. Very attractive in new spring growth.

'Aurea'. Like the species, to 10 m high or more, branchlets and needles golden-yellow, but greening inside the plant. BFN 571 (H). Introduced by Fortune from Japan in 1861. Plate 39.

'Aurea Nana'. Dwarf form, conical to globose-bushy, otherwise somewhat like the species in appearance, but the foliage remaining golden-yellow the entire year. WDw 84 (H); CCE 145 (= *C. pisifera nana fretsii* Hornibr.; *C. pisifera aurea nana* Beissn.). Known since 1891.

'Boulevard' (Kempenaar). Originated as a sport of 'Squarrosa'. Height on a full grown plant as yet unknown, but surely 5 m or more, conical, symmetrical; needles awl-shaped, 5–6 mm long, finely acuminate, curved inward, especially on the branch tips, impressive silver-blue in summer, more gray-blue in winter. WDw Pl. 5E (Br); WM 10A (Br). Introduced to the trade in 1934 by Boulevard Nurseries (Kempenaar) as *Retinospora squarrosa* K. & C. (= *C. pisifera cyanoviridis* Hort.). Widely disseminated in recent years. Plate 46.

'Clouded Sky' (Konijn). 'Squarrosa' mutation. Conical habit, strong growing, branches outspread; leaves all needle-like, also on the basal part of the twig, both sides distinctly blue. CCE 145. Developed by L. Konijn & Co.

'Compacta'. Dwarf form, to 1 m high and wide, flat globose or also wider than high, compact, much coarser than the similar 'Nana', all branches with deep green mature needles, branchlets densely arranged and only slightly curved downward, among them however, also strong upright growing shoots, these with tightly packed foliage first appearing early the next year. WDw Pl. 5C (Br); WLM 10C (Br). *C. pisifera* 'Nana' is often confused with *C. pisifera* 'Compacta', as pointed out by Welch. Fig. 43F.

'Compacta Variegata'. Mutation of 'Compacta' with yellow or yellowish speckles on branch tips, dwarf form, otherwise like the previous form. WDw 85 (H); WM 164 (H). This form is more frequently encountered than the green type.

'Ericoides'. Dwarf form, conical compact habit to more ovate, dense, branches stiffly upright, reddish-brown, shoots compact, erect, tightly crowded, branchlets long and soft; needles usually in 3's, on stunted branches in 2's, flat, sharp acuminate, thin, light green, somewhat brownish in winter, bluish beneath, both sides with narrow, raised midrib. First described by Regel in 1883, but nearly always incorrectly labeled in cultivation! (Usually confused with *C. thyoides* 'Ericoides'.)

'Filifera'. Broadly conical habit, generally to 5 m high and equally wide, occasionally also tree-like (a plant in Bicton, England in 1959 was 18 m high), branches nodding to outspread, branchlets thin, filamentous, pendulous; needles in

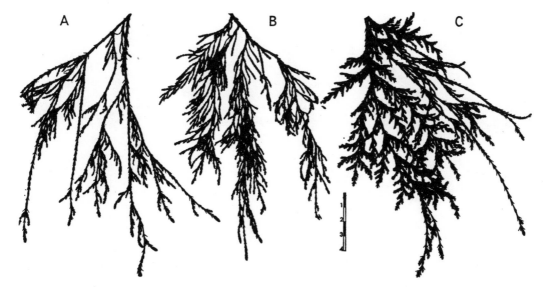

Fig. 42. *Chamaecyparis pisifera* cultivars.
A. 'Filifera'; B. 'Filifera Aurea Nana'; C. 'Gold Spangle'

opposing pairs, sharply acuminate, gray-green, white on the inside; fruits only occasionally. WM 10B (Br); CCE 147. Introduced about 1861 by Fortune from Japan. Fig. 42A.

Since the 'Filifera' forms are occasionally confused, this outline is presented to ease identification.

Normal growth rate and size, 4–5 m high:
   'Filifera', green
   'Filifera Gracilis', light green
   'Filifera Aurea', yellow
   'Filifera Sungold', yellow
   'Gold Spangle', yellow, only in part with filamentous shoots

Lower growing, about 1–1.5 m high:
   'Filifera Argenteovariegata', white-yellow variegated
   'Filifera Aureovariegata', yellow variegated

Dwarf, under 1 m (full grown):
   'Filifera Nana', green
   'Golden Mop', yellow ("Filifera Nana Aurea")

'Filifera Argenteovariegata'. Remaining low, 1 to 1.5 m high, conical to broadly conical, branches yellowish-white variegated over the entire plant. Known since before 1891. Pretty.

'Filifera Aurea'. Broadly conical habit, also grows flat, 4–5 m high, but very slow growing, 2.5 m high and 4.5 m wide in 30 years, branches and twigs like the green 'Filifera', but yellow. Known in cultivation before 1891.

"Filifera Aurea Nana". That cultivated by this name is simply a low, slow growing plant propagated from the side shoots of 'Filifera Aurea' which in time will achieve the size and appearance of the parent plant. CCE 146. The real, constantly dwarf yellow form is 'Golden Mop'; which see. Fig. 42B.

'Filifera Aureovariegata'. Remaining low, 1–1.5 m high, very similar to 'Filifera Argenteovariegata', but yellow variegated, not yellow-white variegated. CCE 146.

'Filifera Crispa' (Neder). Dense, conical habit, branch tips filamentous; needles outspread, blue-green, crispate. BFN 162. Developed before 1897 by Neder, Frankfurt, W. Germany. (EX?)

'Filifera Gracilis'. Similar to the green 'Filifera', but more slender and open growing, the branchlets clustered on the branch tips; foliage yellowish-green. BFN 163. Known before 1875. Plate 41.

'Filifera Nana'. Dwarf form, dense bushy growth habit, only 60 cm high and 90 cm wide in 25 years, branch tips filamentous, nodding on all sides; needles deep green. WDw Pl. 5A (Br), 87 (H); WM 165 (H). Developed before 1897 in the Tharandt Forstgarten, Saxony.

'Filifera Sungold'. Somewhat more coarsely branched than the normal 'Filifera Aurea', only yellow-green, but very sun tolerant while the other yellow forms are easily scorched. From Denmark?

'Golden Mop'. Dwarf form, like 'Filifera Nana', but always golden-yellow (not a young plant of Filifera Aurea!!). Since there was no valid name for this plant, this one was chosen by Welch in 1960.

'Gold Spangle' (Koster). Conical habit, wide, 3 m high or more, originated as a mutation of 'Filifera Aurea', but differing in the branchlets, some short, slightly twisted, lighter yellow and some filamentous, darker yellow. CCE 146. Originated before 1900 at Koster & Zonen Nursery, Boskoop, Holland. Fig. 42C.

'Nana'. Dwarf form, very slow growing, compact globose to cushion form, to 0.60 m high and 1.5 m wide in 40 years, branches spreading, branchlets fan-shaped, very dense, margin revolute, tips somewhat crispate; needles very small, deep green above, more blue-green beneath. WDw Pl. 5B, 86 (H); HiD 26; WM 10D (Br), 166 (H). Known before 1891. Often confused in the nursery with *C. pisifera* 'Compacta'; which see. Plate 41; Fig. 43G.

'Nana Albovariegata'. Like 'Nana', but slightly white variegated (not markedly), occasionally with an entirely white small branch (= *C. pisifera nana variegata* Carr.). Before 1867.

'Nana Aureovariegata'. Like 'Nana', but the entire plant with a golden-yellow glimmer with the occasional branch reverting back to the pure green type. 1874.

'Plumosa'. Conical habit, 10–20 cm high, branches outspread, branchlets feathery crispate; leaves needle-form, acute,

Fig. 43. *Chamaecyparis pisifera* cultivars. A. 'Plumosa Rogersii'; B. 'Plumosa Compressa';
C. 'Plumosa Cristata'; D. 'Squarrosa'; E. 'Plumosa'; F. 'Compacta'; G. 'Nana'

somewhat spreading, 3–4 mm long, green, occasionally somewhat brownish in winter; fruits occasionally. SN 108 (H); CCE 148. Introduced from Japan in 1861 by J. G. Veitch. Much valued form with delicate foliage. Fig. 43F.

'Plumosa' includes a large number of forms, all easily recognizable by the foliage which is intermediate between the scale-needles of *C. pisifera* and those of the 'Squarrosa' group. These forms were earlier mistakenly described as "fixed juvenile forms" (see pp. 91–92).

Outline of the Plumosa Form Group

Normal growth rate, upright:
'Plumosa', green
'Plumosa Vera', green
'Plumosa Argentea', white speckled
'Plumosa Aurea', yellow

Slow growing, 1–2 m high, conical:
'Plumosa Compacta', green
'Plumosa Cristata', green
'Plumosa Pygmaea', green
'Plumosa Albopicta', white variegated
'Plumosa Aurea Compacta', yellow
'Plumosa Rogersii', yellow
'Plumosa Flavescens', light yellow

Dwarf, flat to globose:
'Plumosa Compressa', bluish to yellowish
'Plumosa Nana Aurea', yellow
'Plumosa Juniperoides', yellow and green
'Snow', white variegated

'Plumosa Albopicta'. Low, to 2 m high; needles very small, deep green with many white tips. WDw Pl. 5H (Br), 88 (Br); CCE 149. 1884. Especially attractive as a young plant in spring and summer. Plate 41.

'Plumosa Argentea'. Like 'Plumosa', becoming tall, but somewhat slender; needles dark green with small white branch tips, these greening in the 2nd year when the new growth appears. Introduced by Fortune from Japan in 1861. Plate 41.

'Plumosa Aurea'. Grows like the normal green 'Plumosa', to 10 m tall or more, needles however, gold-yellow (not light yellow!). WDw 84 (H); WM 10E (Br), 167 (H) (= *C. pisifera* 'Gold Dust' Hort. Americ.). Introduced from Japan by Fortune in 1861.

'Plumosa Aurea Compacta'. Usually more or less globose, but eventually more ovate and 1.5–2 m tall; needles golden-yellow, much larger than 'Plumosa', more closely resembling 'Squarrosa', all needles with 2 white stripes on the underside. CCE 147; WM 168 (H). Known since 1891. Often confused with 'Plumosa Rogersii', but the white stripes on the underside of the latter not so distinct, otherwise the latter has a dominant leader even as a young plant ('Plumosa Aurea Compacta' has not).

'Plumosa Compacta'. Presumably a seedling of 'Plumosa', broad conical habit, very compact, slow growing, to 2 m high, branches and twigs short and spreading, tips curving somewhat upward, densely branched, crispate; needles variable, some needle-form transition leaves, soft, blue above, green beneath, others like those of 'Plumosa'. CCE 147. Found in a nursery in Ede, Holland; named by den Ouden in 1949. Plate 40.

Fig. 44. **Chamaecyparis** forms.
A. *C. pisifera* 'Squarrosa Intermedia'; B. *C. obtusa* 'Tetragona Aurea'; C. *C. obtusa* 'Filicoides'

'Plumosa Compressa' (Koster). Originated as a mutation of 'Squarrosa'. Dwarf form, very densely branched, to about 60 cm high, irregular cushion-form, branches and branchlets very dense and crispate; needles partly like 'Plumosa', partly like 'Squarrosa', color varying between yellowish, green, gray and bluish. WDw Pl. 5D (Br), 91 (H); CCE 152; WM 169 (H). Developed by Koster & Zonen, introduced before 1929 by C. B. Van Nes & Zoon, both of Boskoop, Holland. Quite variable and, therefore, often found under various names in the trade. The plants suffer from sunscald, becoming an ugly brown in scalded areas. Plate 41; Fig. 43B.

'Plumosa Cristata'. Low form, branches somewhat cockspur-like crispate at the tips, but not very conspicuous. CCE 148. Exported from Japan in 1900, but only now cultivated in England (Hillier 1970). Fig. 43C.

'Plumosa Flavescens'. Dwarf form, conical or also globose, to about 1 m high, branches and twigs ascending, branchlets yellowish-white, likewise the needles, but always more or less greening in fall. WDw Pl. 5F (Br). Imported from Japan about 1866 by von Siebold. Plate 45.

'Plumosa Juniperoides'. Somewhat similar to 'Plumosa Compressa', but stronger growing, the juvenile leaves broader and directed forward, gold-yellow in early summer, later greening. WM 170 (H) (= *C. pisifera* 'Plumosa Aurea Compacta'). From the USA. 1965.

'Plumosa Nana' (Herre). Globose dwarf form, 30 cm high, green; needles like 'Plumosa' (EX)

'Plumosa Nana Aurea'. Dwarf form, slow growing, flat-globose, to 80 cm high, branchlets and needles resembling those of 'Squarrosa', but golden-yellow, very reflexed, greenish-yellow inside the plant. HiD 27 (H). Known before 1923. Suffers from sunscald.

'Plumosa Pygmaea'. Dwarf form, globose, to 2 m high. A very old plant grows in the Glasnevin Botanic Garden, Dublin, Ireland. Described by Welch as a green 'Plumosa Rogersii' and very attractive.

'Plumosa Rogersii' (Rogers). Dwarf, conical, about 1 m high eventually; foliage similar to 'Squarrosa', golden-yellow, also in winter. WDw Pl. 5G (Br), 90 (H); CCE 148 (= *C. pisifera plumosa aurea rogersii* Hort.). Developed by Rogers about 1930. Plate 41; Fig. 43A.

'Plumosa Vera'. Like 'Plumosa', but needles lighter green and not colored in winter, needles on older wood partly like 'Squarrosa', partly very distinctly crispate. CCE 149. In cultivation before 1904.

'Snow'. Dwarf form of the 'Plumosa' group, flat-globose; foliage moss-like fine and dense, blue-green, but white on the branch tips, therefore very sensitive to sunscald and cold. WM 171 (H); CCE 146. Introduced before 1971 from Japan.

'Squarrosa'. 10–20 cm high, crown broad and open conical, densely twiggy, branches spreading, tips nodding, branchlets a good silver-gray, moss-like crispate, soft to the touch; leaves all needle-form, dense radially arranged, soft, blue-green above, silvery-white beneath. CCE 150. Introduced from Japan by Von Siebold in 1843. By modern interpretation, this is not an artificially fixed juvenile form (never substantiated!), rather it is a mutation with needle-form leaves. Plate 39 and 45; Fig. 43D.

'Squarrosa' contains several other cultivars with the same needle-form foliage, from which identification, with the help of the following outline, should not be difficult.

Tall growing, 10–20 m:
   'Squarrosa', silver-gray
   'Squarrosa Aurea', yellow

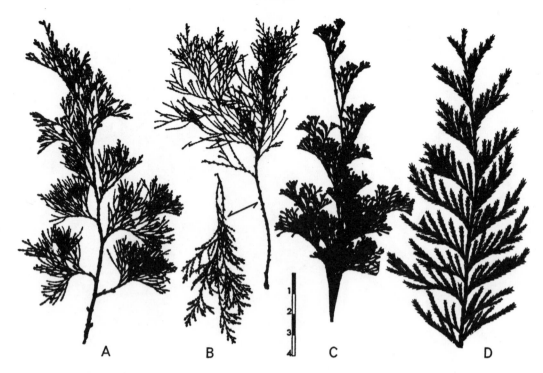

Fig. 45. **Chamaecyparis.** A. *C. thyoides* 'Andelyensis'; B. *C. thyoides* var. *henryae;*
C. *C. thyoides* 'Atrovirens'; D. *C. nootkatensis* 'Variegata'

Medium height, 2–5 m high:
 'Squarrosa Argentea', silver-gray, to 2 m
 'Squarrosa Sulphurea', light yellow, 5 m
 'Squarrosa Intermedia', silver-gray, 3 m

Dwarf, 0.8–1 m:
 'Squarrosa Dumosa', gray-green, 1 m
 'Squarrosa Lutea', yellow, 80 cm
 'Squarrosa Minima', gray-blue, 80 cm

'Squarrosa Argentea'. Medium tall shrub, to 2 m; foliage like
'Squarrosa', but more conspicuously silver-gray. CCE 151 (=
C. pisifera 'Squarrosa Argentea Compacta' Hort.). Introduced
from Japan in 1843 by Siebold. Plate 40.

'Squarrosa Aurea'. Strong grower, like the type, but foliage
more or less golden-yellow. Known since before 1866. Healthy
plant.

'Squarrosa Dumosa'. Habit dense bushy-rounded, to 1 m high,
never conical, branches short, twigs thick; needles rather large,
gray-green in summer, with a trace of bronze in winter. WDw
Pl. 5J (Br), 92 (H); WM 9C (Br), 172 (H). Found in the Berlin
Botanic Garden before 1890. Plate 34.

'Squarrosa Intermedia'. Unique, open bushy, upright form
with needle- and scale-leaves; in culture, young plants are
usually trimmed globose and then have the needle-leaves,
arranged in 3's, blue, later arising from the plant are some thin,
long, erect shoots with widely spaced, small dark green (!)
scale-leaves. WDw Pl. 5L (Br), 93 (H); CCE 151; WM 173 (H).
Rather widely disseminated form of unknown origin; in
cultivation before 1923. The trimmed globes have also been
called 'Dwarf Blue' (Hesse). Plate 39; Fig. 44A.

'Squarrosa Lutea' (Koster). Globose habit, to about 80 cm high;
needles very long, about 7–8 mm long, always golden-yellow.
WDw Pl. 5K (Br). Originated before 1949 at Koster & Zonen
Nursery as a mutation. Sensitive to frost and wind. Very
attractive.

'Squarrosa Minima'. Dwarf form, resembling 'Squarrosa Intermedia' and occasionally reverting back to such, but all needles
thickish, with 2 whitish bands above, margin of the middle line
green, with 2 white stripes beneath. WDw 95 (H). The reverting
branches always evenly spaced.

'Squarrosa Sulphurea' (Koster). Similar to 'Squarrosa', but not
so tall, scarcely over 5 m; needles sulfur-yellow in summer,
more silver-gray in winter. WDw 97 (H); WM 174 (H).
Developed before 1900 by Koster & Zonen, Boskoop,
Holland.

C. thyoides (L.) B. S. P. A tall tree in its habitat, 25–30 m
high, stem to 1 m diameter, crown slender, narrow,
branches upright or outspread, bark reddish-brown,
branchlets thin, to 1.3 mm wide, short, spreading from
all sides (not in an even plane!); needles aromatic when
crushed, tightly appressed, tips outspread on strong
growing shoots, dark bluish to light green, without white
markings, acute, flat keeled, usually with a distinct gland;
cones very numerous, often clustered on small twigs,
globose, 6 mm thick, with 4–5 scales, seldom 6, these
hooked in the middle with reflexed tips (= *C. sphaeroidea*
[Spreng.] Spach). USA, from Maine to Florida,
westward to the Mississippi, especially in swamps.
Introduced to gardens in 1736. Fig. 36A. z3

var. **thyoides.** The type of this species. Found along the Atlantic
coast from Waldo County in S. Maine to Lexington County in
central South Carolina, but it has died out along the Savannah
River near Augusta, Georgia. Plate 47.

var. **henryae** (Li) Little. Tree, to 25 m high, differing from the
type in the flatter furrowed bark, with the furrows spiraling
around the stem, branchlets less flat; needles lighter green and
more appressed, the needle-form juvenile foliage is green
beneath (with 2 blue bands on the type); cones larger, only

slightly bluish, seeds larger, broader winged (= *C. henryae* Li). NW. Florida to S. Alabama and S. Mississippi. In cultivation since about 1955. Fig. 45B.

'Andelyensis' (Cauchois). Dwarf, conical, to 3 m high, but always with several main branches at the peak, rather stiff, branches strictly upright, twigs short, dense, branchlets somewhat fan-shaped; needles partly linear and then in whorls of 3, partly scale-form in opposite, appressed pairs, blue-green, very aromatic when crushed; fertile, cones like the species (seedlings produce the species or transition forms). WDw Pl. 6F (Br), 94 (H); WM 175 (H) (= *C. sphaeroidea andelyensis* Carr.). Developed about 1850 by Cauchois, Les Andelys, Eure, France. Plate 47; Fig. 45A. z7

'Andelyensis Nana'. Very similar to 'Andelyensis', but much lower, wider than high, the erect shoots predominantly with needle-leaves. WDw 96 (H); WM 176 (H); CCE 155. Found in Angers, France before 1939 by Détriché.

'Atrovirens'. Foliage pure dark green, without a trace of blue. Known before 1852. Fig. 45C.

'Aurea' (Gaujard). Conical habit, regular, acute; needles totally golden-yellow, more bronze in winter. Developed before 1974 by N. Gaujard, Ghent, Belgium.

'Conica' (Konijn). Mutation of 'Andelyensis'. Dwarf habit, 25–30 cm high in 10 years, conical, low, very slow growing, very densely branched, annual growth only 2–3 cm long, branches stiffly upright; leaves all needle-form and grouped in 3's, acuminate, somewhat bowed, 6–8 mm long, blue-green, somewhat brownish in winter, with 2 indistinct stomatal bands beneath; young cones carmine. CCE 154. Developed by Konijn about 1940 in Reeuwijk, Holland. z8

'Ericoides' (Bergéot). Regular conical habit, to about 1.5 m high, very compact, densely branched, stiff; leaves all needle-form, soft to the touch, in whorls of 3, outspread, acuminate, flat, 6–7 mm long, with 2 stomatal bands beneath, blue-green in summer, red-brown to reddish-violet in winter. WDw Pl. 6E (Br), 98 (H); BFN 526; CCE 156; WM 9D (Br), 177 (H) (= *C. ericoides* Carr.). Developed in the Bergéot Nursery in Le Mans, France. 1840. Plate 47. z8–9

'Glauca'. Gracefully conical, compact, branches numerous, short, reddish; needles an attractive silvery blue-green. 1852.

'Hoveyi'. Contorted form, slender habit, branch tips cockscomblike crowded. 1881.

'Nana'. Dwarf form, globose, very small; needles all blue-green. KN Pl. 3. 1842. Plate 47. (EX)

'Pygmaea' (Sénéclauze). Dwarf form, flat cushion-form habit, branches spreading along the ground, blue-green; leaves scale-like, tightly imbricate, marked with bluish lines. Developed in 1867 by Sénéclauze. Smallest dwarf form. (EX)

'Pyramidata' (Sénéclauze). Dwarf, small, narrow columnar form, short and densely branched. 1867. (EX)

'Variegata'. Like the species, rather thinly branched, branches irregularly arranged, branchlets about half yellowish variegated. In cultivation before 1831.

Lit. Beissner, L.: Interessantes über Coniferen. Mitt. DDG 1900, 201–213. ● Li, H. L.: A new species of *Chamaecyparis*. Morris Arb. Bull. **13**, 43 to 46, 1962. ● Little, E. L.: Varietal transfers in *Cupressus* and *Chamaecyparis*. Madroño **18**, 161 to 167, 1966. ● Unger, A.: *Juniperus sanderi*. Mitt. DDG 1900, 213–217. ● Bayer, R.: *Shishindenia ericoides* Makino; zur Geschichte der Jugendform einer Conifere. Dtsch. Baumschule **22**, 258–267, 1970.

CHRYSOLARIX H. E. Moore = **PSUEDOLARIX**; which see

Lit. Moore, H. E.: *Chrysolarix*, a new name for the Golden Larch. Baileya **13**, 131–143. 1965.

CRYPTOMERIA D. Don—TAXODIACEAE

I would like to thank Prof. Dr. H. Kruse, Tokyo, Japan for his cooperation on the *Cryptomeria* section; for important supplemental information and especially for sending material to complete the twig illustrations. Author.

Evergreen trees with reddish bark, exfoliating in long strips, conical crown, branches outspread, buds small, unscaled; leaves needle-awl-like, in 5 spirally arranged rows, directed forward and curved inward, laterally compressed, obtuse 4 sided in cross section; male flowers solitary, axillary, clustered spike-like on young shoots; female flowers globose, solitary, terminal on short shoots; bract scales adnate to the seed scale from the base to just over the middle; fruit a globose, brown cone, ripening the first year, but persisting after the seed is released, with 20–30 woody, cuneate scales widening to a "disk"; with 3–5 seeds under each scale, these triangular-oblong, somewhat compressed, narrow winged; cotyledons 3, sometimes only 2. $x = 11$.—Only 1 species in Japan and S. China.

Cryptomeria japonica D. Don. Japanese Cedar or Surgi. Tree, 30–40 m high (tallest tree in Japan however, is 64 m high with a 7 m diameter trunk; according to Kruse 1968), trunk straight, slender, usually not over 1–2 m in diameter in its habitat, branches densely arranged, outspread or ascending, young branches green, glabrous; needles sickle-shaped, curving inward, rather stiff, 6–12 mm long, decurrent on the twig, sharp keeled beneath, obtuse above, dark green, with stomata on both sides; cones solitary, globose, 1–3 cm long, brown, dehiscing when ripe, margin of the seed scales acute toothed, seeds 6–8 mm long, red-brown. KIF 1: 42. Japan. 1842. A very important forestry tree in its habitat. Plate 51 and 62; Fig. 46. z7

In Japan, Ishisaki (see Kruse) listed no less than 337 races and geographical varieties, which upon further examination were reduced to slightly more than 200. There are many Japanese garden forms not grown in the Western world and likewise many cultivars grown here which are

Fig. 46. *Cryptomeria japonica.* a. Branch with male flowers and 1 cone; b. female flowers; c. cones; d–f. seed scales; g. seed scales with ovules; h–i. stamens; k. seed; l. leaf cross section; m. branch from *C. japonica* 'Elegans' (from Beissner and Pardé)

not available in Japan, i.e. 'Vilmoriniana'. Therefore the names will sometimes be Japanese and sometimes Latin. Here follows a short outline of the synonyms.

Japanese Cultivar Names

The name in the left-hand column is synonymous with the valid name in the right-hand column, the latter will be described in the text. If a Japanese cultivar name is generally used in the trade, it will be found listed alphabetically in the text and not in this list of synonyms (* = not described).

'Ashigo-sugi'	= var. *radicans*
'Chabo-sugi'	= 'Nana'
'Dai-sugi'	= var. *radicans*
'Eizan-sugi'*	= 'Uncinata'
'Enko-sugi'	= 'Araucarioides'
'Furi-bandai-sugi'	= 'Albospica'
"Hao-sugi"	= 'Hoo-sugi'
'Hoo-sugi'	= 'Selaginoides'
"Husari-sugi"	= 'Kusari-sugi'
'Okina-sugi'	= 'Nana Albospicata'
'Ikari-sugi'	= 'Lycopodioides'
'Kusari-sugi'	= 'Spiralis'
'Midori-sugi'*	= 'Viridis'
'Mitama-sugi'	= 'Globosa Nana'
'Oogon-sugi'	= 'Aurea'
'Sekka-sugi'	= 'Cristata'
'Sennin-sugi'	= 'Dacrydioides'
'Yenko-sugi'	= 'Enko-sugi'

Outline by Growth Habit

Normal, conical:
    var. *radicans,* var. *sinensis,* 'Compacta', 'Lobbii'

Dwarf form with long shoots, most sparsely, branched:
    'Araucarioides', 'Dacrydioides', "Filifera", 'Ito-sugi', 'Selaginoides', 'Viminalis'

Dwarf form with short shoots:
    'Bandai-sugi', 'Compacta Nana', 'Gracilis', 'Jindai-sugi', 'Lycopodioides', 'Pungens', 'Pyramidata'

Globose forms:
    'Compressa', 'Globosa', 'Globosa Nana', 'Vilmoriniana'

Cockscomb forms: (fasciated)
    'Cristata', 'Fasciata', 'Kilmacurragh'

Branches twisted:
    'Nana', 'Pygmaea', 'Spiralis', 'Torta', 'Yore-sugi'.

Forms with soft foliage:
    'Elegans', 'Elegans Aurea', 'Elegans Compacta', 'Elegans Variegata', 'Elegans Viridis', 'Lobbii Nana'

Forms with large, outspread needles:
    'Mankichi-sugi', 'Monstrosa'

Forms with variegated foliage:
    'Albospica', 'Aurea', 'Aurescens', 'Aureovariegata', 'Knaptonensis', 'Nana Albospica', 'Sekkan-sugi', 'Variegata'

'Albospica' (Hellemann). Normal upright habit, only the branch tips white when young, later greening (= *C. japonica albospica* de Vos; *C. japonica argenteospicata* Beissn.). Developed before 1887 in the nursery of Hellemann, W. Germany.

'Araucarioides'. Habit irregular and wide at first, with 1–3 stems, eventually broadly conical, branched to the ground, branches very long, spreading to nodding, the apex with a cluster of branches of various length; needles shorter, thicker, more bowed than those of the species and also more widely spaced, very dark green (!). OCC 122; WM 13C (Br), 178 (H) (*C. japonica araucarioides* Gord.; 'Enko-sugi'). Imported from Japan in 1859 by Siebold and not unusual today. Plate 46; Fig. 47C.

'Ashio-sugi' see var. *radicans*

'Aurea'. Needles gold-yellow (= 'Oogon-sugi'). Fig. 48D.

Plate 33

Chamaecyparis lawsoniana 'Filiformis' with branch tips over 1 m long(!) in Bicton Park, England

Plate 34

Chamaecyparis lawsoniana 'Tharandtensis'
in the Zurich Botanic Garden, Switzerland

Chamaecyparis lawsoniana 'Filiformis Compacta'
at Konijn in Reeuwijk, Holland

Chamaecyparis lawsoniana 'Parsons'
Hillier Arboretum, England

Chamaecyparis lawsoniana 'Nestoides'
at Welch, Devizes, England

Chamaecyparis pisifera 'Squarrosa Dumosa'
at Welch, Devizes

Chamaecyparis lawsoniana 'Gimbornii'
in RHS Gardens, Wisley, England

Plate 35

Chamaecyparis nootkatensis
in its native habitat in Alaska
Photo: US Forest Service

Chamaecyparis nootkatensis 'Pendula'
in the nursery
Photo: Herm. A. Hesse, Weener

Chamaecyparis nootkatensis 'Compacta Glauca'
in Les Barres Arboretum, France

Chamaecyparis funebris
in the Horticultural Research Station, Pretoria,
S. Africa

Plate 36

Chamaecyparis obtusa 'Kosteri'
in the Gardening Institute, Aurich, W. Germany

Chamaecyparis obtusa 'Graciosa'
in a nursery in Boskoop, Holland

Chamaecyparis obtusa 'Nana Aurea'
in RHS Gardens, Wisley, England

Chamaecyparis pisifera 'Plumosa Rogersii'
in the Blijdenstein Pinetum, Holland

Plate 37

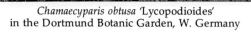

Chamaecyparis obtusa 'Ericoides'
in the Hillier Arboretum, England

Chamaecyparis obtusa 'Filicoides'
in the Hoersholm Arboretum, Denmark

Chamaecyparis obtusa 'Lycopodioides'
in the Dortmund Botanic Garden, W. Germany

Chamaecyparis obtusa 'Mariesii'
in the Boskoop Experiment Station, Holland

Plate 48

Cryptomeria japonica 'Jindai-sugi'
in the Blijdenstein Pinetum, Holland

Cryptomeria japonica 'Compacta Nana', 4 m high,
in the Batumi Botanic Garden on the Black Sea,
USSR

Cryptomeria japonica 'Nana'
in the Pygmy Pinetum, Devizes, England

Cryptomeria japonica 'Monstrosa'
at Konijn in Reeuwijk, Holland

Fig. 47. **Cryptomeria** branches, half the actual size.
A. *C. japonica*; B. 'Gracilis'; C. 'Araucarioides'; D. 'Kilmacurragh'; E. 'Lobbii' (Original)

'Aureovariegata'. Normal, only the young shoots partly yellow variegated. 1868.

'Aurescens' (Blijdenstein Pinetum). Conical and dense, broad, branches clustered; needles 12 to 15 mm long, greenish-yellow in summer, light green in winter (= *C. japonica aurescens* den Ouden). Developed in the Blijdenstein Pinetum, Hilversum, Holland. 1937.

'Bandai-sugi'. Habit more globose at first, later more upright and irregularly shrubby, to 2 m high, with short and long shoots, contorted branchlets at the base of long shoots; needles variable in length, usually 12–15 mm on young shoots, only 3 mm long on others, usually stiff and thick, blue-green, with a reddish tinge in winter. WDw Pl. 8B (Br), 99 (H); WM 11C (BR). Introduced from Japan before 1934. Widely planted today. Fig. 49C.

'Compacta' (Thibault & Keteleer). Tree, 10–15 m high, conical, densely branched, shoots numerous, 10–30 cm long; needles short, coarse, blue-green. WDw 100 (H). Developed by Thibault & Keteleer in 1877. Occasionally the name 'Lobbii Compacta' is used for this form. Plate 62.

'Compacta Nana'. Dwarf form, broadly conical with rounded apex, very old plants growing to 4–5 m high with a width of 3 m, branches short; needles light green and glossy. Selected by Beissner in 1891. Plate 48.

'Compressa'. Dwarf form, conical to widely conical, very similar to 'Vilmoriniana', but differing in the numerous, small, somewhat protruding terminal leaders, these with nearly rosette-form reflexed needles at the tip, 5–10 mm long, glossy dark green, blue-green inside the plant, winter color a distinct red-brown. WDw Pl. 7E (Br); WM 17A (Br). Introduced from Japan by J. Blaauw and Cie., Boskoop, Holland in 1942. Fig. 50B.

'Cristata'. Narrow conical-upright habit, 6–8 m high or higher, branches short, ascending, twigs short, stiff and compact, very frequently with wide, fasciated cockscomb-like tips which after a few years become brown and die off. WDw Pl. 8f (Br), 101 (H); WM 13B (Br) (= 'Sekka-sugi'). Imported from Japan to Germany by L. Unger 1900. Plate 62; Fig. 48C.

'Dacrydioides'. Differs from the somewhat similar 'Araucarioides' in that the branches spread in all directions with few side shoots, not clustered at the branch tips(!); only sparsely foliate (= 'Sennin-sugi'). Plate 49.

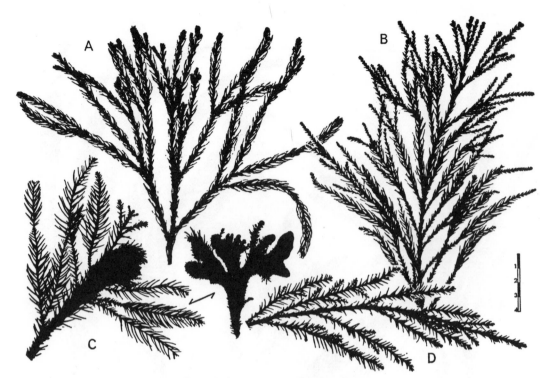

Fig. 48. *Cryptomeria japonica* cultivars.
A. 'Globosa Nana'; B. var. *radicans*; C. 'Cristata'; D. 'Aurea' (Original)

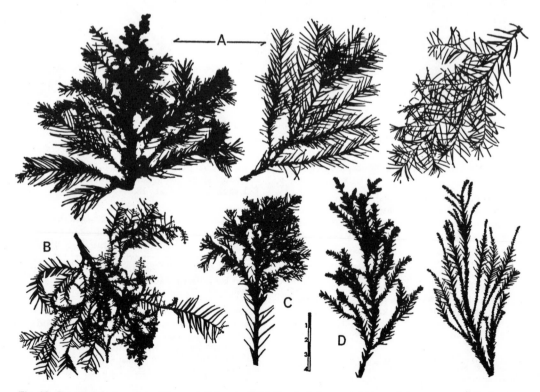

Fig. 49. *Cryptomeria japonica* cultivars. A. 'Monstrosa', left apical shoot, right lateral shoot; 'Elegans Compacta'
(right above); B. 'Shishi-gashira', a form of the 'Mankichi-sugi'; C. 'Bandai-sugi'; D. 'Jindaisugi' from Germany;
to the right from Japan (Original)

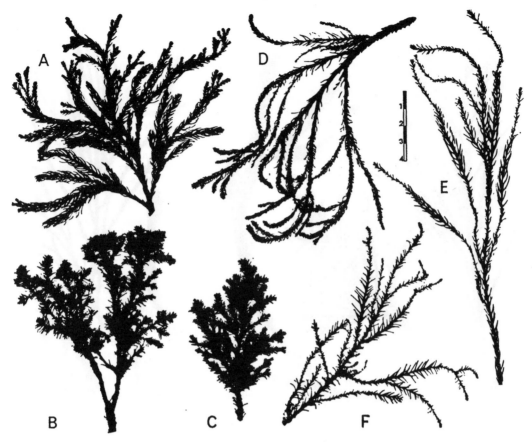

Fig. 50. *Cryptomeria japonica* cultivars. A. 'Spiralis'; B. 'Compressa'; C. Vilmorinana';
D. 'Yore-sugi' (= 'Spiraliter Falcata'); E. 'Torta'; F. 'Pygmaea' (Original)

'Elegans'. Irregular habit, but occasionally also a small tree, to 10 m or occasionally more, usually only 3–5 m, branches spreading, very dense; leaves 1–2.5 cm long, thin, soft, sparsely arranged, bluish-green, red-brown in winter or green with a trace of violet; cones smaller than the species and produced on young plants, seeds however, seldom viable (seedlings are the normal *C. japonica,* some dwarf plants) (= *C. elegans* Makoy; *C. japonica elongata* Regel ex Gord.; *C. gracilis* Hort. non Sieb.; 'Yawara-sugi'). Imported from Japan to England in 1854. Hardiness variable. Fig. 46.

'Elegans Aurea'. Height unknown; foliage like the type, but (according to Welch) yellow-green instead of violet in winter. From New Zealand.

'Elegans Compacta'. Dwarf form, scarcely over 2 m high, flat-globose and very compact, with short and long annual growth, these occasionally delicately curved; needles about 20 mm long, soft, blue-green in summer, with a trace of violet in winter. WDw Pl. 7C (Br), 103 (H) (= *C. japonica elegans nana* [Veitch] Nich.; *C. japonica* var. *elegans compacta* Dall. & Jacks.). Here, as in Welch, the name 'Elegans Compacta' is retained to avoid confusion with 'Lobbii Nana' ("Elegans Nana" is often·used in England). Fig. 49.

'Elegans Variegata'. Slow growing, foliage like that of 'Elegans', but white variegated, often predominantly white. Cultivated by Van Geert, in Kalmthout, Belgium before 1887. (EX?)

'Elegans Viridis'. Like the type, but equally green in summer and winter (= *C. japonica* var. *elegans viridis* Hornib.). 1939.

'Fasciata'. Another dwarf form with fused branches, growth very slow and irregular, shoots thick and very "mossy-crispate" with some short needles, some shoots with short, foliate outgrowths. WDw Pl. 8H (Br); WM 17F (Br). Of the 3 "cristata" forms described, this is the slowest growing and rarest; also called (according to Welch) "Nyewood Form" and "Clark's Mossy" in England.

'Filifera'. This very long branched, low shrub is totally different from all other forms. Perhaps the only example in Europe is in the E. Mosca Park in Biella, N. Italy. (This plant is illustrated in KN 111 as "Dacrydioides" and in Magrini/Peluzzi [Le Conifere; Milano 1967], Pl. 98 as "var. filifera". Apparently unknown in Japan. Fig. 51C.

'Globosa' (Lombarts). Globose habit to flat-globose, wider than high, presumably not over 1.5 m high, branches spreading outward, twigs twisted and with tips directed upward; needles thick, 1–1.5 cm long, blue-green, but rust-brown in winter. WDw Pl. 7F (Br); WM 12D (Br). Developed by P. Lombarts of Zundert, Holland and introduced to the trade in 1942. Quite winter hardy, but only slight ornamental value, especially in winter. This plant stays lower than 'Globosa Nana'!

'Globosa Nana'. Dwarf form, broadly conical and compact habit, although occasionally "lumpy" with several "humps" and possibly to 2–4 m high, branches very dense and regular, ascending, branchlets short, drooping; needles short, thick, unevenly long, appressed, yellow-green, more blue-green in winter. WDw 104 (H), Pl. 8A (Br); OCC 125; WM 12A (Br) (= 'Mitama-sugi'; *C. japonica* f. *clathrata* hort. jap.). Very attractive and winter hardy form. Plate 62; Fig. 48A.

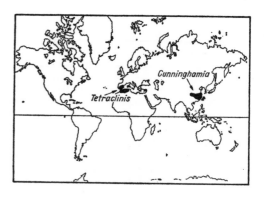

Fig. 53. Range of the genera *Cunninghamia* and *Tetraclinis*

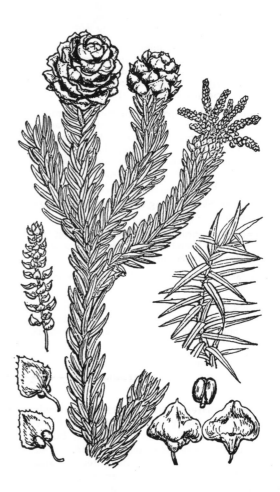

Fig. 52 *Cunninghamia lanceolata.* a. Branch with cones; b. male flowers; c. female flowers; d. needle-less branch section; e. single leaf; f. leaf apex; g. stamens; h. seed scales; i. seed; k. leaf cross section (from Beissner)

Fig. 54. *Cunninghamia knoishii.* Middle, mature branch with 2 cones and male flowers; left, male inflorescence and 2 individual scales; right, juvenile branch, with 2 seed scales and a seed beneath (from T. S. Liu)

C. konishii Hayata. A large tree in its habitat, to 50 m high, stem to 2.5 m in diameter, branches spreading, bark scaly furrowed; needles linear-lanceolate, about 2 cm long, 2.5 mm wide, acute, decurrent at the base, stiff, leathery, stomatal bands on both sides, but more distinct beneath, persisting about 8 years; cone scales rounded, distinctly clawed, seeds 3 under each scale, ovate to elliptic, hard, narrowly winged. LWT 12; LT 42. Formosa 1918. Fig. 54. z9

C. lanceolata (Lamb.) Hook. Tree, 10(–25) m in its habitat, straight stem, bark exfoliates in strips, branches on lower trunk abscise quickly, branches on young plants in whorls, irregularly arranged on older plants, twigs green at first; needles very dense and alternate, 2 ranked spreading, 3–7 cm long, 0.5 cm wide, linear-lanceolate, leathery, stiff, sharply acuminate, margin slightly serrate, bright green above, with 2 wide blue-white stomatal bands beneath; cones 3–4 cm long, usually grouped, appear on very young plants in its habitat. LT 43 (= *C. sinensis* R. Br.). S. and Central China, mountain valleys. 1804. Does best in semishade, in a protected area, frost sensitive. Plate 51 and 52; Fig. 52. z8

'Compacta' (Bano). Dwarf form without a central leader, about 50 cm high in 10 years. DB 18: 139. Selected from seedlings in 1955 by I. Bano in the Forestry Experiment Station Kamoni, Hungary. Much hardier than the type. Easily propagated from cuttings. Plate 55.

'Glauca'. Exactly like the species, but needles an outstanding blue-green (= *C. sinensis* var. *glauca* Knight & Perry). Known since 1855. The blue form is substantially more frost tolerant than the type. z7–8

× CUPRESSOCYPARIS Dall.—CUPRESSACEAE

Natural hybrid between *Chamaecyparis* and *Cupressus*. For characteristics, see the individual hybrids and their respective clones. All were derived from selections in England and meritorious for their rapid growth. All z7–8

× **Cupressocyparis leylandii** (Dall. & Jacks.) Dall. (*Cupressus macrocarpa* × *Chamaecyparis nootkatensis*). Tall tree, 30 m high or higher, crown dense, conical to columnar, like the columnar form of *Cupressus macrocarpa*, leaves however, very similar in form, size and arrangement to those of *Chamaecyparis nootkatensis*, but the branchlets finer, longer and more slender; cones to 2 cm in diameter, most with 8 scales, with 5 seeds under each scale, these with tiny "warts", like *Cupressus macrocarpa* (= *Cupressus leylandii* Dall. & Jacks.). Seed taken from a *Cupressus macrocarpa* growing near a stand of *Chamaecyparis nootkatensis* by J. M. Naylor at Leighton Hall, Welshpool, England in 1911. Plate 50.

In 1888, C. J. Leyland, a brother-in-law of J. M. Naylor grew a similar hybrid from Leighton Hall, but this one came from seed of *Chamaecyparis nootkatensis*. Some of these seedlings were planted at Haggerston Castle, Northumberland where they have developed, unobserved, into large trees. Finally, for a third time about 1940, the same hybrid was raised in the nursery of M. Barthelemy, Stapehill, Dorset from seed of *Cupressus macrocarpa*. Several clones of these 3 hybrids have since been named and propagated, while many more have as yet only numbers.

'Castlewellan Gold'. Very strong grower, but substantially slower than × *C. leylandii*; foliage on young shoots an attractive yellow. Chance seedling of × *C. leylandii* selected in the Castlewellan Forest Park, England by the park director, John Keown, and first named *Cupressus macrocarpa* Keownii, 1963. Widely propagated after 1970. Quite hardy, tolerant of wind, pollution and sea breezes. No particular soil preference. (R)

'Green Spire' (= Clone Nr. 1 from Haggerston Castle, 1888). Tree, narrowly columnar, very dense, central leader frequently poorly developed, branchlets spaced irregularly and with varying angles to the stem, directed forward on an even plane; foliage bright green. Named by Ovens, Blight & Mitchell in 1964.

'Haggerston Grey' (= Clone Nr. 2 from Haggerston Castle, 1888). Tree with rather open branching, branchlets partly opposite and arising at right angles, partly also decussate, therefore arranged in 2 even planes, the smallest shoots often clustered, gray-green. KN 134 (Br); CCE 168. Named by Ovens, Blight & Mitchell. Most resembles *Cupressus macrocarpa*. Fig. 56C.

'Leighton Green' (= Clone Nr. 11 from Leighton Hall, 1911). Tree, narrowly columnar at first, always with a distinct central leader, branches somewhat irregularly arranged and dense, lying flat on an even plane, tips of the youngest shoots flat in cross section; foliage bright green to yellowish-green; develops cones frequently. CCE 168. Named by Ovens, Blight & Mitchell in 1964. Most resembles *Chamaecyparis nootkatensis*. This clone is by far the most extensively cultivated. It is identical to the plant often labeled as × *Cupressocyparis leylandii*. Fig. 56A.

'Naylor's Blue' (= Clone Nr. 10 from Leighton Hall, 1911). Similar to 'Leighton Green', but branching more open, tips of the youngest branches round in cross section; foliage gray-blue; develop cones only rarely. Named in 1964 by Ovens, Blight & Mitchell. Not widely cultivated. Fig. 56B.

'Robinson's Gold' (George Robinson). Chance seedling, growth exceptionally fast and strong, but more compact and conical than the green × *C. leylandii* (original plant about 6 m high and 3 m wide in 20 years), very densely branched; foliage an attractive bronze-yellow in spring, gradually turning lemon-green and gold-yellow. Found by George Robinson about 1962 in Belvoir Park, Belfast, N. Ireland. Introduced to the trade in 1978 by the Green Leaf Nurseries of Belfast, N. Ireland.

× **C. notabilis** Mitchell (*Cupressus glabra* × *Chamaecyparis nootkatensis*). Garden hybrid, intermediate between the parents. Tree, narrowly conical, twigs bowed upward, shoots penniform in arrangement, nodding; needles scale-like, blue-green; male inflorescence yellow, female cones globose, 12 mm in diameter, blue-green, 6–7 scales, with a curved thorn on each scale. Originated from seed of *Cupressus glabra*, growing near a *Chamaecyparis nootkatensis*; the seeds were sown in the nursery of the Forest Research Station in Alice Holt Lodge, Hampshire, England (1970) where the 2 original plants now stand 7.5 m high. Fig. 57A.

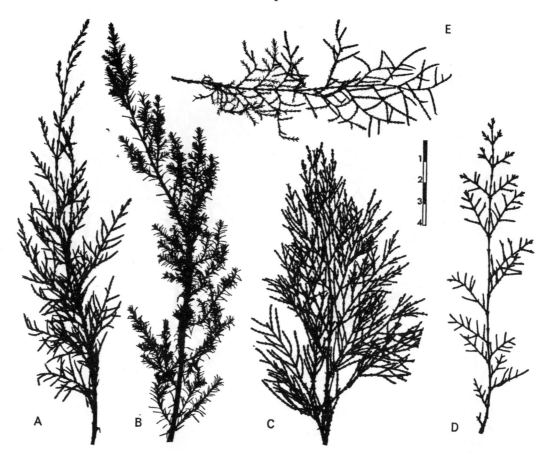

Fig. 62. **Cupressus** twigs. A. *C. lusitanica*; B. and C. *C. sempervirens* (B. juvenile twig);
D. *forbesii*; E. *C. goveniana* (Original)

'Coerulea'. Fewer branches than the type, branches similarly wide spreading, branchlets shorter, very conspicuously blue-green; cones, very blue when young as well as when ripe (= *C. lusitanica coerulea* Carr.; *C. lusitanica argentea* Hillier). Developed in France before 1867, cataloged by Hillier in 1928.

'Flagellifera'. Branches "whip-like", long, drooping, nearly like *Chamaecyparis pisifera* 'Filifera'; needles awl-shaped and spreading at the tips, especially on the younger branch tips. CCE 178. England, before 1927.

'Glauca'. Blue Mexican Cypress. Branches not flattened; leaves more blue-green, with distinct resin glands. Found before 1910 by Henry in Montserrat, Portugal.

'Glauca Pendula'. Branches pendulous, very blue-green. CCE 180. Cultivated by Hillier since 1925.

'Knightiana'. Only slightly different from var. *benthamii*, young shoots, especially the leaves, somewhat more blue, but these variations occur also in the wild (Lt. Clarke, in Bean, 8th. ed.) (= *C. knightiana* Perry & Gord.). Selected before 1840 in England and named by the Joseph Knight nursery.

'Pendula'. Growth upright, branches then very long and drooping, very openly branched; needles dark green, tips outspread. The mother tree stands in a public park in Lisbon, Portugal. It has a crown diameter of 15 m (see Nat. Hort. Magaz. 40: 272). Since I have not observed the other weeping forms of *C. lusitanica*, I cannot be sure which name is correct and thus I have used that which is commonly used in Portugal. Fig. 60C.

'Variegata'. Needles yellowish-green. Known in English gardens since 1864.

C. macnabiana Murr. Bushy, conical shrub, occasionally a small tree, usually multistemmed, 6–12 m high, bark dark red to grayish, fibrous and furrowed, branchlets short, not lying in a single plane, very thin and compressed; leaves tightly appressed, dark or bluish-green, scale-form, rather thick, about 1 mm long, obtuse, arched, with distinct resin glands on the dorsal side; cones globose, short stalked, about 2 cm thick, several grouped together, with 6(–8) scales, these shield-like (peltate), angular, dorsal side arched, with thick, curved thorn, rather blue at first, later brown, seeds brown. WWC 2(Br), 6 (C), 18 and 56 (H); SPa 64; SN 178 (H); CCE 172 (= *C. glandulosa* Hook.). California; dry hills, low slopes. 1854. Fig. 63C. z8–9

'Sulphurea'. Young shoots with yellow tips. Known since 1923.

C. macrocarpa Hartweg ex Gordon. Monterey Cypress. Tree, 12–20 m, narrow or broadly conical when young, broadly spreading crown with age, stem with red-brown bark at first, later gray and channeled-scaly, branches eventually spreading horizontal or somewhat nodding, branchlets round, not on a single plane, outspread or nodding, somewhat thickish (1 to 1.5 mm), with lemon

C. konishii Hayata. A large tree in its habitat, to 50 m high, stem to 2.5 m in diameter, branches spreading, bark scaly furrowed; needles linear-lanceolate, about 2 cm long, 2.5 mm wide, acute, decurrent at the base, stiff, leathery, stomatal bands on both sides, but more distinct beneath, persisting about 8 years; cone scales rounded, distinctly clawed, seeds 3 under each scale, ovate to elliptic, hard, narrowly winged. LWT 12; LT 42. Formosa 1918. Fig. 54. z9

C. lanceolata (Lamb.) Hook. Tree, 10(–25) m in its habitat, straight stem, bark exfoliates in strips, branches on lower trunk abscise quickly, branches on young plants in whorls, irregularly arranged on older plants, twigs green at first; needles very dense and alternate, 2 ranked spreading, 3–7 cm long, 0.5 cm wide, linear-lanceolate, leathery, stiff, sharply acuminate, margin slightly serrate, bright green above, with 2 wide blue-white stomatal bands beneath; cones 3–4 cm long, usually grouped, appear on very young plants in its habitat. LT 43 (= C. sinensis R. Br.). S. and Central China, mountain valleys. 1804. Does best in semishade, in a protected area, frost sensitive. Plate 51 and 52; Fig. 52. z8

'Compacta' (Bano). Dwarf form without a central leader, about 50 cm high in 10 years. DB 18: 139. Selected from seedlings in 1955 by I. Bano in the Forestry Experiment Station Kamoni, Hungary. Much hardier than the type. Easily propagated from cuttings. Plate 55.

'Glauca'. Exactly like the species, but needles an outstanding blue-green (= C. sinensis var. glauca Knight & Perry). Known since 1855. The blue form is substantially more frost tolerant than the type. z7–8

× CUPRESSOCYPARIS Dall.—CUPRESSACEAE

Natural hybrid between *Chamaecyparis* and *Cupressus*. For characteristics, see the individual hybrids and their respective clones. All were derived from selections in England and meritorious for their rapid growth. All z7–8

× **Cupressocyparis leylandii** (Dall. & Jacks.) Dall. (*Cupressus macrocarpa* × *Chamaecyparis nootkatensis*). Tall tree, 30 m high or higher, crown dense, conical to columnar, like the columnar form of *Cupressus macrocarpa*, leaves however, very similar in form, size and arrangement to those of *Chamaecyparis nootkatensis*, but the branchlets finer, longer and more slender; cones to 2 cm in diameter, most with 8 scales, with 5 seeds under each scale, these with tiny "warts", like *Cupressus macrocarpa* (= *Cupressus leylandii* Dall. & Jacks.). Seed taken from a *Cupressus macrocarpa* growing near a stand of *Chamaecyparis nootkatensis* by J. M. Naylor at Leighton Hall, Welshpool, England in 1911. Plate 50.

In 1888, C. J. Leyland, a brother-in-law of J. M. Naylor grew a similar hybrid from Leighton Hall, but this one came from seed of *Chamaecyparis nootkatensis*. Some of these seedlings were planted at Haggerston Castle, Northumberland where they have developed, unobserved, into large trees. Finally, for a third time about 1940, the same hybrid was raised in the nursery of M. Barthelemy, Stapehill, Dorset from seed of *Cupressus macrocarpa*. Several clones of these 3 hybrids have since been named and propagated, while many more have as yet only numbers.

'Castlewellan Gold'. Very strong grower, but substantially slower than × C. leylandii; foliage on young shoots an attractive yellow. Chance seedling of × C. leylandii selected in the Castlewellan Forest Park, England by the park director, John Keown, and first named *Cupressus macrocarpa* Keownii, 1963. Widely propagated after 1970. Quite hardy, tolerant of wind, pollution and sea breezes. No particular soil preference. (R)

'Green Spire' (= Clone Nr. 1 from Haggerston Castle, 1888). Tree, narrowly columnar, very dense, central leader frequently poorly developed, branchlets spaced irregularly and with varying angles to the stem, directed forward on an even plane; foliage bright green. Named by Ovens, Blight & Mitchell in 1964.

'Haggerston Grey' (= Clone Nr. 2 from Haggerston Castle, 1888). Tree with rather open branching, branchlets partly opposite and arising at right angles, partly also decussate, therefore arranged in 2 even planes, the smallest shoots often clustered, gray-green. KN 134 (Br); CCE 168. Named by Ovens, Blight & Mitchell. Most resembles *Cupressus macrocarpa*. Fig. 56C.

'Leighton Green' (= Clone Nr. 11 from Leighton Hall, 1911). Tree, narrowly columnar at first, always with a distinct central leader, branches somewhat irregularly arranged and dense, lying flat on an even plane, tips of the youngest shoots flat in cross section; foliage bright green to yellowish-green; develops cones frequently. CCE 168. Named by Ovens, Blight & Mitchell in 1964. Most resembles *Chamaecyparis nootkatensis*. This clone is by far the most extensively cultivated. It is identical to the plant often labeled as × *Cupressocyparis leylandii*. Fig. 56A.

'Naylor's Blue' (= Clone Nr. 10 from Leighton Hall, 1911). Similar to 'Leighton Green', but branching more open, tips of the youngest branches round in cross section; foliage gray-blue; develop cones only rarely. Named in 1964 by Ovens, Blight & Mitchell. Not widely cultivated. Fig. 56B.

'Robinson's Gold' (George Robinson). Chance seedling, growth exceptionally fast and strong, but more compact and conical than the green × C. leylandii (original plant about 6 m high and 3 m wide in 20 years), very densely branched; foliage an attractive bronze-yellow in spring, gradually turning lemon-green and gold-yellow. Found by George Robinson about 1962 in Belvoir Park, Belfast, N. Ireland. Introduced to the trade in 1978 by the Green Leaf Nurseries of Belfast, N. Ireland.

× **C. notabilis** Mitchell (*Cupressus glabra* × *Chamaecyparis nootkatensis*). Garden hybrid, intermediate between the parents. Tree, narrowly conical, twigs bowed upward, shoots penniform in arrangement, nodding; needles scale-like, blue-green; male inflorescence yellow, female cones globose, 12 mm in diameter, blue-green, 6–7 scales, with a curved thorn on each scale. Originated from seed of *Cupressus glabra*, growing near a *Chamaecyparis nootkatensis*; the seeds were sown in the nursery of the Forest Research Station in Alice Holt Lodge, Hampshire, England (1970) where the 2 original plants now stand 7.5 m high. Fig. 57A.

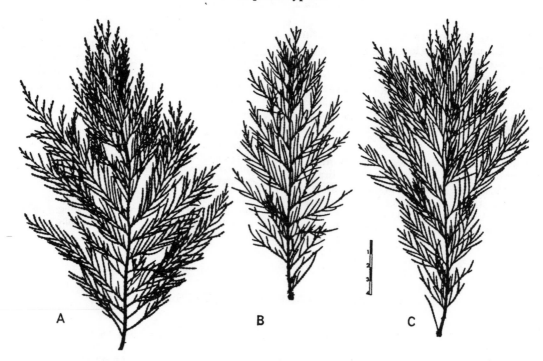

Fig. 56 Clone of × *Cupressocyparis leylandii.*
A. 'Leighton Green'; B. 'Naylor's Blue'; C. 'Haggerston Grey' (Original)

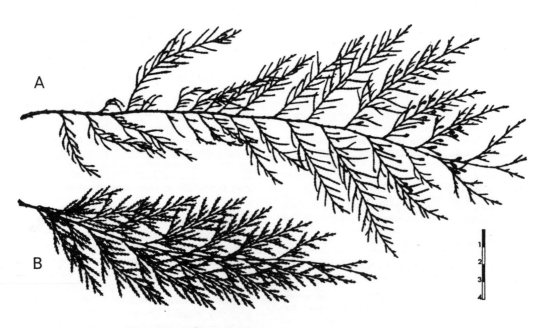

Fig. 57. × **Cupressocyparis.** A. × *C. notabilis; B.* × *C. ovensii*
(from material off the original plant)

× **C. ovensii** Mitchell (*Cupressus lusitanica* × *Chamaecyparis nootkatensis*). Garden hybrid, intermediate between the parents, habit like *Chamaecyparis nootkatensis*, branches green at first, then purple-pink, shoots penniform on an even plane; needles deep blue-green, tips outspread and acute, with white stomatal bands beneath; no cones yet recorded. Developed from seed of *Cupressus lusitanica* growing among *Chamaecyparis nootkatensis* in Silk Wood, Westonbirt Arboretum, Gloucestershire, England. Seeds sown in the Ovens Nursery in Talybont, Cardiganshire. 1961. These plants were about 2 m high in 1970. Fig. 57B.

× **C. 'Stapehill Hybrid'** (*Cupressus macrocarpa* × *Chamaecyparis lawsoniana*). Tall tree, strong grower, similar to 'Leighton Green' in appearance, foliage as thick and heavily textured, but darker blue-green, distinctly blue-gray on the underside; bark of the young shoots yellow-green at first, then orange-brown, eventually purple-brown. Developed in 1940 in the Barthelemy Nursery in Stapehill, Wimborne, Dorset, S. England from seed collected from a *Cupressus macrocarpa* with only a *Chamaecyparis lawsoniana* growing nearby (no *C. nootkatensis*). From these seedlings, 2 were selected, widely propagated and disseminated as 'Stapehill Hybrid'.

Lit. Ovens, Blight & Mitchell: In: Quarterly Jour. Forst. **58**, 8–19, 1964 ● Mitchell, A. F.: A note on two new hybrid Cypresses. Jour. Roy. Hort. Soc. **94**, 453–454, 1970.

CUPRESSUS L.—Cypress—CUPRESSACEAE

Usually tall evergreen trees, occasionally only shrubs; bark usually exfoliating in long strips; branches 4-sided or cylindrical, occasionally somewhat flattened; leaves scale-like, small, very densely arranged, overlapping, juvenile foliage needle-form; plants monoecious, flowers on different branches, male flowers small, oblong or cylindrical, stamens each with 2 pollen sacs, female flowers with several, small decussate bracts, these with numerous seed chambers (ovules) at the base; cones globose, woody, with 6–12 scales, ripening the 2nd year; cone scales very thick, tightly closed before ripening, with an "umbo" or soft prickle; seeds oblong, broadly or narrowly winged; cotyledons 2 or 3–4.—15–20 species from the Mediterranean to the Himalayas, in the Sahara, in No. America in tropical and subtropical regions.

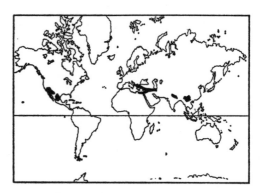

Fig. 58. Range of the genus *Cupressus*

Cupressus abramsiana C. B. Wolf. Santa Cruz Cypress. Small tree, 10–12 m high, broadly conical, bark gray, with deep longitudinal furrows, main branches spreading horizontally, smaller branches ascending at acute angles; needles yellowish-green, 1.5 mm long, obtuse acuminate, with resin glands indistinct or absent; cones globose to somewhat oblong, 20–25 mm long, eventually glossy brown, scales 8(–10), thorns about 2 mm long, seeds dull brown, usually very slightly bluish pruinose. WWC 13 (C), 36 (H and St), 78 (H). California; Santa Cruz Mts. z7

C. arizonica Greene. Arizona Cypress. This collective species (according to the latest interpretation) is composed of 5 geographical varieties, which until recently had been classified as individual species. Collective range in N. America is from Texas to central Arizona and S. California and northern Mexico.

var. **arizonica**. The type of the species. Stem of older trees with rough, furrowed bark, gray to black-brown, branchlets alternate or opposite and outspread; needles usually 2 mm long, sharply acuminate, usually blue-green or gray-green, keeled, limb finely toothed, resin glands usually not active and indistinct, but variable; cones globose, to 2.5 cm wide, with 6–8 scales, with conspicuous thorns, remaining closed for several years, seeds dark brown, occasionally also bluish pruinose,

about 90–120 per cone. WWC 8 (C), 23 (H), 24 (St); CCE 169 (= *C. arizonica* var. *glomerata* Martinez; *C. arizonica* var. *minor* Martinez). Texas (Chisos Mountains) to SE. Arizona and northern Mexico. Plate 52, 53; Fig. 59a. z7–8

'Compacta'. Dwarf, very slow growing, globose to conical, very dense and short branched; foliage an attractive gray-green. WDw 116 (H), Pl. 6B (Br); SM 181 (H); WM 198 (H). Plate 55.

'Conica'. Conical, branches ascending, branchlets very numerous, loosely arranged, short and stiff; leaves tightly appressed, conspicuously blue-gray. TC 73; CCE 169. From France. z8

'Fastigiata' (Gino Bartolini). Growth narrowly upright, but compact, blue-gray. KN 84; CCE 170. Considered an improvement on 'Conica'. Plate 63.

'Fastigiata Aurea'. Conical upright habit, rather open, branchlets sulfur-yellow. Presumably from France. Disseminated by Tromp Export B.V., Boskoop. 1978.

var. **glabra** (Sudw.) Little. Smooth Barked Cypress. Tree, old stems with smooth, cherry red to mahogany-brown bark, peeling in thin plates; needles like var. *arizonica*, but with very active resin glands; seeds 4–5 mm long, blue pruinose. WWC 10 (C), 28 and 67 (St), 67 (H); CCE 171 (= *C. glabra* Sudw.). Central Arizona. z7 Many plants in England labeled as "C. arizonica" are actually this variety.

Outline of the Genus *Cupressus*
(according to Dallimore-Jackson, modified and enlarged)

- **Branchlets all on one plane, like** *Chamaecyparis;*
  - ■ Needles appressed;
    - ✕ The smallest twigs irregular and scattered, shoots often long, rectangular in cross section:
        C. torulosa
    - ✕✕ Smallest twigs alternate, penniform, regular, fern-like; shoots gradually becoming smaller, more or less flattened in cross section:
        C. lusitanica var. *benthamii*
  - ■ ■ Needles outspread;
    - Branchlets long and pendulous, needles blue-green:
        C. cashmeriana
- ● ● **Branchlets partly on an even plane, partly spreading on all sides;**
  - Branch tips short, pale green to blue-green:
        C. macnabiana
- ● ● ● **Branchlets not on an even plane, rather spreading in all directions;**
  - ■ Needles with distinct resin glands on the dorsal side;
    - ✕ Young shoots usually slender, thinner than 1 mm, needles gray-green, sharply acuminate, cones 10–20 mm in diameter:
        C. bakeri
    - ✕✕ Young shoots usually over 1 mm thick;
      - ☆ Needles obtuse or somewhat so;
        - ○ Bark smooth, red-brown, exfoliating in thin plates; needles blue-green:
            C. guadalupensis
        - ○ ○ Bark fibrous, gray to brown, not exfoliating, needles dull green:
            C. sargentii
      - ☆☆ Needles acute;
        - ○ Trunk of older trees rough, fibrous, gray or deep brown, at least on the base;
          - + Cones opening soon after ripening, with 8–12 scales; seeds not bluish:
              C. arizonica var. *montana*
          - ++ Cones remaining closed for several years, scales 6–8; seeds occasionally somewhat bluish;
            - V Bark of the branches and upper stem exfoliating in thin plates, then smooth and red-brown:
                C. arizonica
            - VV Bark on the branches and upper stem not exfoliating, gray to red-brown:
                C. arizonica var. *nevadensis*
        - ○ ○ Stem on older trees usually smooth, red to brown, exfoliating in thin plates;
          - + Needles 1 mm long, rounded on the dorsal side, some resin glands undeveloped:
              C. arizonica var. *stephensonii*
          - ++ Needles 1.5–2 mm long, keeled on the dorsal side:
              C. arizonica var. *glabra*
  - ■ ■ Needles without distinct resin glands on the dorsal side;
    - ✕ Branchlets pendulous;
      - ☆ Branches widely outspread, needles acute, blue-green, young cones blue-white, later brown, 10–15 mm in diameter:
            C. lusitanica
      - ☆☆ Branches short, horizontal, needles obtuse, light-or bluish-green, cones 20–25 mm in diameter:
            C. duclouxiana
    - ✕✕ Branchlets upright or stiff;
      - ☆ Needles obtuse or somewhat so;
        - ○ Stem and larger branches with smooth red to brown bark, exfoliating in thin plates;
          - + Needles bright or dull green, not blue-green, cones to 25 mm long:
              C. forbesii
          - ++ Needles bluish-green, often blue; cones 30–40 mm long:
              C. guadalupensis
        - ○ ○ Stem and larger branches with fibrous bark, which does not peel, brown-gray bark;
          - + Branchlets rather thick and rough;
            - * Needles bright to dark green, swollen toward the apex; seeds red-brown, warty, glossy:
                C. macrocarpa
            - ** Needles dull green; seeds dark brown, bluish pruinose:
                C. sargentii
          - ++ Branchlets thinner, not rough;
            - * Needles deep green, not swollen toward the tip; cones 25–30 mm in diameter, with 8–14 scales:
                C. sempervirens
            - ** Needles bright green;
              - V Needles bright green, cones 20–25 mm long, seeds dull brown, not pruinose:
                  C. abramsiana

VV Needles yellow-green, cones 10–15 mm long, seeds black-brown, not pruinose:
         C. goveniana
☆☆ Needles sharply acuminate;
         O Needles dull dark green, cones 15–20 mm long, with 8–10 scales, seed black-brown, usually glossy:
                  C. goveniana var. *pygmaea*
         O O Needles blue-gray to gray-green, cones 12–30 mm long, with 6–8 scales;
                  + Needles 1 mm long, rounded on the dorsal side:
                           C. arizonica var. *stephensonii*
                  ++ Needles 2 mm long, keeled on the dorsal side:
                           C. arizonica

'Glauca' Juvenile form, conical habit, regular and dense, intensive silver-gray. 1916. z7–8 (R)

var. **montana** (Wiggins) Little. Tree, old stems with rough, furrowed, gray to dark brown bark; needles like var. *arizonica*, but with active resin glands; cones opening when ripe. WWC 8 (C), 60 (H) (= *C. montana* Wiggins). N. California. z6

var. **nevadensis** (Abrams) Little. Piute Cypress. Tree, old stems with rough, furrowed, gray to deep brown bark; needles with distinct, active resin glands; cones usually remaining closed for several years. WWC 9 (C), 25 (St), 63 (H) (= *C. nevadensis* Abrams; *C. macnabiana* var. *nevadensis* [Abrams] Abrams). California. This variety is most similar to the type, var. *arizonica*. z6

'Pyramidalis'. Narrowly conical; foliage an attractive blue-gray. Cultivated by Hillier since 1928 as *C. glabra* 'Pyramidalis'.

var. **stephensonii** (Wolf) Little. Cuyamaca Cypress. Intermediate between var. *arizonica* and var. *glabra*. Tree, old stems with smooth, cherry-red to mahogany-brown bark, exfoliating in thin plates; needles with relatively active resin glands; seeds usually over 5 mm long, not blue pruinose. WWC 8 (C), 26 (St), 65 (H) (= *C. stephensonii* Wolf). Found in the Cuyamaca Mts., San Diego, California. z7

'Sulfurea'. Compact, upright habit; foliage gray-yellow. CCE 170.

'Variegata'. Branch tips an attractive variegated white.

C. bakeri Jeps. Modoc Cypress. Tree, to 10 m, occasionally higher, bark thin, reddish, splitting into thin plates, twigs radiating from all sides of the branch, branchlets thin, 4 sided; leaves dull, bright or dark green, with distinct resin glands, keeled; cones nearly globose, to 2 cm thick, gray, with 6 scales, drawn out abruptly to a short, straight thorn, the apex frequently with 2 pairs of small scales; with about 50 seeds in the cone, light brown. WWC 7A (C), 20 (St), 57 (H) (= *C. macnabiana* var. *bakeri* [Jeps.] Jeps.). Northern California. Very winter hardy. z6

ssp. **matthewsii** C. B. Wolf. Siskiyou Cypress. Tall, to 30 m high, branchlets longer, light gray-green; cones 15–20 mm in diameter, light gray-brown, as distinctly warty as the species, but the thorn not so apparent. WWC 7B (C), 22 (St), 59 (H). California and Oregon; Siskiyou Mts. Fig. 61C. z6

C. cashmeriana Royle ex Carr. Kashmir Cypress. Small, conical tree, usually only columnar in cultivation, branches ascending, but branches long and heavily pendulous, branchlets all flat; leaves distinctly outspread, blue-green; cones globose, 12 mm thick, light green at first and blue pruinose, later dark brown, scales 10, compressed in the middle, with recurved tips, triangular thorn, with about 10 seeds under each scale.

KN 140 (H). Native habitat not certain, presumably Kashmir or Tibet. Plate 82; Fig. 60A. z9

C. duclouxiana Hickel. Tall, slender, densely branched tree, branches outspread, similar to *Cupressus sempervirens* var. *horizontalis*, branchlets arising on all sides, not in a single plane, very thin; leaves very small, 1 mm long, blue-green, indistinctly glandular; cones globose, 2 cm in diameter, scales 8, rather flat, seeds reddish-brown. BM 9049; CIS 52; LF 40, CBJ 43; CCE 173. China; W. Yunnan, Szechwan to Kansu Provinces. Cultivated in the British Isles but very tender. z8–9

C. dupreziana A. Camus. Tree, very closely related to *Cupressus sempervirens* (presumably only a geographical form), differing mainly in the distinctly flattened shoots and small leaves with a small gland-pit at the base; cones much smaller and longer, seeds nearly circular when fully developed (mostly sterile!), wings wider, but thinner. CCE 167. Tassili Mts., in the Sahara between Ghat and Djanet; first discovered in 1864, the stems at that time were up to 2.5 m in diameter, only some of which are alive today. These trees may be over a thousand years old. z9

C. forbesii Jeps. Tecate Cypress. Small tree, scarcely to 9 m high, stem with smooth, red-brown to cherry-red bark, exfoliating in thin plates, numerous ascending branches, needles light green, resin glands indistinct or

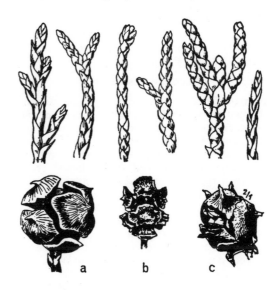

Fig. 59. **Cupressus** branchlets and cones
a. *C. arizonica*; b. *C. torulosa*; c. *C. lusitanica*

Fig. 60. **Cupressus** twigs. A. *C. cashmeriana;* B. *C. arizonica;* C. *C. lusitanica* 'Pendula';
D. *C. macrocarpa* 'Coneybearii' (Original)

totally absent; cones gray to brownish, globose, about 25 mm thick, with rather short thorns on the scales, seeds dark red-brown. WWC 2 (Br), 11 (C), 30 and 69 (H), 31 (St); CCE 176. California, USA, in 2 adjacent areas (San Diego Co. and Orange Co.), also in Mexico, Baja California. Plate 52; Fig. 62D. z9

C. funebris see: **Chamaecyparis funebris**

C. goveniana Gordon. Tree, to 18 m (in cultivation), but in its habitat often only 5–6 m high; bark of older stems gray to dark brown, rough, exfoliating, twigs arising from all sides of the branch, soft, giving the impression of being 3-pinnate, branch tips 4-sided and 1 mm thick, very aromatic when crushed; leaves bright green to yellow-green, tightly appressed in 4 similar rows, acute, with or without resin glands; male flowers numerous, yellow; cones globose to more oblong, 6–18 mm in diameter, glossy dark brown, ripening the 2nd year, but persisting another year after the seeds are released, then gray, with 8–10 scales, these with a short, obtuse or acute thorn; seeds dark brown to black, winged. WWC 13 (C), 35 and 37 (H), 35 (St); CB II 73; SPa 62; CCE 178. California, coast of Monterey Co. 1848. Fig. 62E, 63A. z8–9

'**Bregeonii**'. Shrubby, branches thin, blue-green; cones globose and ash-gray, 1.5 cm thick (= *C. bregeonii* R. Smith; *C. sempervirens* var. *bregeonii* [R. Smith] Camus).

'**Compacta**'. Regular broad conical habit, apex obtuse. Developed from seed before 1896 by Ch. Détriché, Angers, France.

'**Cornuta**'. Shrubby, differing primarily in the irregular, large, thick, nearly black cones, whose apical scales have a horn-like tip. Found in a garden in Hyères, Alpes Maritimes, France before 1876. (EX?)

'**Pendula**'. Shrubby grower, branches long, gracefully nodding; needles partly appressed, partly outspread, sharply acuminate (= *C. californica* Carr.). 1855.

var. **pygmaea** Lemm. Mendocino Cypress. Differing from the type mainly in the vigorous growth on good soil (therefore with a misleading name!), then to 30 m high or more, on poor soil only a few meters high, bark gray-brown, fibrous, branches thin, only about 1 mm thick; leaves dull, dark green, 1–1.5 mm long, acute, round and without resin glands on the dorsal side; cones often in dense clusters, globose, 1.5–2cm in diameter, with 8–10 scales, brown at first, then gray, seeds brown to black, usually glossy. WWC 12 (C), 34 (St), 76 (H); CB III 55; CCE 175 (= *C. pygmaea* [Lemm.] Sarg.). California; Mendocino Co. Fig. 63D. z8–9

Fig. 61. **Cupressus** twigs. A. and B. C. *torulosa;* C. C. *bakeri* var. *matthewsii;*
D. and E. C. *sempervirens;* F. C. *guadalupensis* (Original)

C. guadalupensis S. Wats. Guadalupe Cypress. Broad crowned tree, 12–15m high, bark smooth, cherry-red to dark gray, exfoliating in thin plates, branches thin; needles blue-green or blue, with dark resin glands, 1.5–2 mm long, rather acute, but shorter and more obtuse on weaker shoots, very finely toothed, cones globose, 3–3.5 cm in diameter, usually 8–10 scales, these with distinct thorns; seeds about 100 in a cone, dark brown, often blue pruinose. WWC 11 (C), 32 and 74 (H), 32 (St); CCE 179 (= C. *macrocarpa* var. *guadalupensis* [Wats.] Mast.). Mexico; Guadalupe Island. 1880. Plate 52 and 63; Fig. 61F. z9

C. lusitanica Mill. Mexican Cypress. Large tree, to 30 m high, branches widely outspread and nodding at the tips, stem red-brown, bark longitudinally grooved, branchlets 4 sided, not in a single plane and irregularly arranged; leaves a conspicuous blue-green, in 4 rows, ovate, densely appressed, usually with long, sharp, spreading tips; cones globose, about 12 mm thick, short stalked, 6–8 scales, with a stout, recurved thorn in the center, straight thorns on the apical scales; about 75 seeds per cone, brown, winged and with resin glands. BM 9434; WWC 10 (C), 29 (St), 68 (H); CB III 53;CCE 180, 181 (= C. *lindleyi* Klotsch; G. *glauca* Lam.). Mexico to Honduras; not from Portugal (= Lusitania), despite the name *"lusitanica"*. Plate 53; Fig. 59C, 62A. z9

Martinez (in Los *Cupressus* de Mexico, 1947) suggested that this species is not native to Mexico and identified the native species as C. *lindleyi* Klotsch. A discussion of this work may be found in Wolf (l.c.), p. 437ff.

var. **benthamii** (Endl.) Carr. Growth more narrow, elegant, regularly branched, with feathery (or fern-like) branchlets in opposite rows on an even plane, the smallest branch tips flat and compressed, 1.5 mm wide; leaves uneven, lateral leaves narrow and with distinct tips, facial leaves flat, acute ovate, with distinct gland-pits, needle color like the species; cones like the species. CB III 54; CCE 172 (= C. *benthamii* Endl.; C. *lusitanica* var. *skinneri* Henry). Mexico; in the mountains northwest of Pachuca (according to Martinez). z8?

'Chamaecyparissoides'. Branches "whip-like". Introduced to the trade by Cripps & Son; also by Hillier 1925.

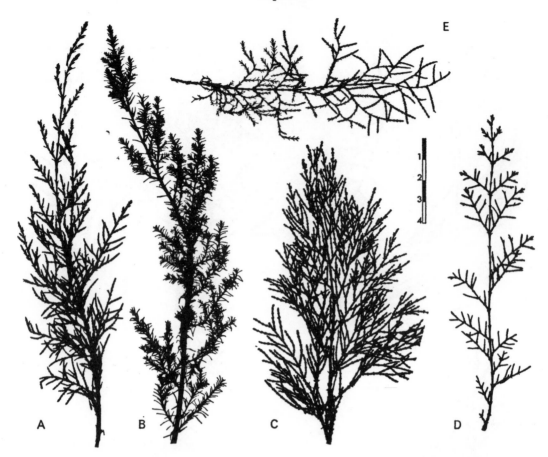

Fig. 62. **Cupressus** twigs: A. *C. lusitanica;* B. and C. *C. sempervirens* (B. juvenile twig);
D. *forbesii;* E. *C. goveniana* (Original)

'Coerulea'. Fewer branches than the type, branches similarly wide spreading, branchlets shorter, very conspicuously blue-green; cones, very blue when young as well as when ripe (= *C. lusitanica coerulea* Carr.; *C. lusitanica argentea* Hillier). Developed in France before 1867, cataloged by Hillier in 1928.

'Flagellifera'. Branches "whip-like", long, drooping, nearly like *Chamaecyparis pisifera* 'Filifera'; needles awl-shaped and spreading at the tips, especially on the younger branch tips. CCE 178. England, before 1927.

'Glauca'. Blue Mexican Cypress. Branches not flattened; leaves more blue-green, with distinct resin glands. Found before 1910 by Henry in Montserrat, Portugal.

'Glauca Pendula'. Branches pendulous, very blue-green. CCE 180. Cultivated by Hillier since 1925.

'Knightiana'. Only slightly different from var. *benthamii,* young shoots, especially the leaves, somewhat more blue, but these variations occur also in the wild (Lt. Clarke, in Bean, 8th. ed.) (= *C. knightiana* Perry & Gord.). Selected before 1840 in England and named by the Joseph Knight nursery.

'Pendula'. Growth upright, branches then very long and drooping, very openly branched; needles dark green, tips outspread. The mother tree stands in a public park in Lisbon, Portugal. It has a crown diameter of 15 m (see Nat. Hort. Magaz. 40: 272). Since I have not observed the other weeping forms of *C. lusitanica,* I cannot be sure which name is correct and thus I have used that which is commonly used in Portugal. Fig. 60C.

'Variegata'. Needles yellowish-green. Known in English gardens since 1864.

C. macnabiana Murr. Bushy, conical shrub, occasionally a small tree, usually multistemmed, 6–12 m high, bark dark red to grayish, fibrous and furrowed, branchlets short, not lying in a single plane, very thin and compressed; leaves tightly appressed, dark or bluish-green, scale-form, rather thick, about 1 mm long, obtuse, arched, with distinct resin glands on the dorsal side; cones globose, short stalked, about 2 cm thick, several grouped together, with 6(–8) scales, these shield-like (peltate), angular, dorsal side arched, with thick, curved thorn, rather blue at first, later brown, seeds brown. WWC 2(Br), 6 (C), 18 and 56 (H); SPa 64; SN 178 (H); CCE 172 (= *C. glandulosa* Hook.). California; dry hills, low slopes. 1854. Fig. 63C. z8–9

'Sulphurea'. Young shoots with yellow tips. Known since 1923.

C. macrocarpa Hartweg ex Gordon. Monterey Cypress. Tree, 12–20 m, narrow or broadly conical when young, broadly spreading crown with age, stem with red-brown bark at first, later gray and channeled-scaly, branches eventually spreading horizontal or somewhat nodding, branchlets round, not on a single plane, outspread or nodding, somewhat thickish (1 to 1.5 mm), with lemon

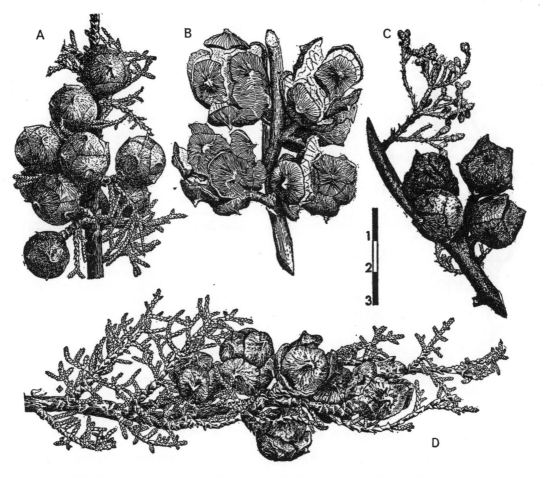

Fig. 63. **Cupressus** cones. A. *C. goveniana;* B. *C. macrocarpa;* C. *C. macnabiana;*
D. *C. goveniana* var. *pygmaea* (from Sudworth)

scent when crushed; leaves scale-like, about 1.5 mm long, regularly formed in 4 rows tightly appressed to the branch, overlapping only at the base, otherwise rhombic, green, somewhat acuminate, with an often indistinct gland, not precisely in the middle; cones globose or also somewhat broad ellipsoid, 25–35 mm in diameter, grouped 1–2 together, on short, thick stalks, scales 8–14, uneven, nearly circular or irregularly angular, convex on the dorsal side or slightly concave with a short thorn in the middle; seeds about 140 per cone, irregularly formed, brown, with many tiny resin blisters on either side, narrowly winged. WWC 12 (C), 33 (St); CB II 73; SPa 61; CCE 182, 183 (= *C. lambertiana* Carr.; *C. hartwegii* Carr.). California, Monterey Bay. 1847. Plate 53; Fig. 63B. z8–9

'Charles Détriché' nom. nov. Very old cultivar, conical habit, like 'Lutea', but narrower, delicately branched, yellow (= *C. macrocarpa* 'Souvenir de Charles Détriché'). Cultivated in France and England.

'Coneybearii'. Weeping form, branches very long and thin, sparsely branched, yellow. Probably originated in Australia; distributed by Kemp's Nurseries Pty. Ltd., Kingswood, **Australia.** Cultivated in England. (Hillier). Fig. 60D.

'Crippsii' (Th. Cripps). Form with awl-shaped (subulate)

needles, branches short and stiff, tips silvery-white. Originated from seed around 1850 by Th. Cripps in Tunbridge Wells, England.

'Donard Gold' (Slieve Donard). Habit like 'Lutea', conical, but the foliage is a better golden-yellow. JRHS 83: 99. Developed in the Slieve Donard Nursery.

'Fastigiata'. Columnar or narrowly conical, branches narrowly upright, not spreading with age. Presumably imported with the type in 1838 by Lambert. Occurs occasionally as a chance seedling.

'Globe'. Dwarf globose form, needles scale-like, appressed (= *C. macrocarpa* 'Globosa' Hillier). Introduced by Hillier in 1964.

'Goldcrest' (Treseder). Columnar, a good gold-yellow. Introduced about 1947 by Treseder in Truro, England.

'Golden Cone' (Barthélemy). Strong grower, but compact; foliage an intense yellow. Selected in the Barthelemy Nurseries, Stapehill, Dorset, England; introduced in 1971.

'Golden Pillar'. Very narrow conical habit, all branches directed upward; foliage a distinct golden-yellow, only the needles on the inside of the plant yellow-green. CCE 182; WM 195 (H).

'Lutea' (Dickson). Broad conical habit; foliage an attractive

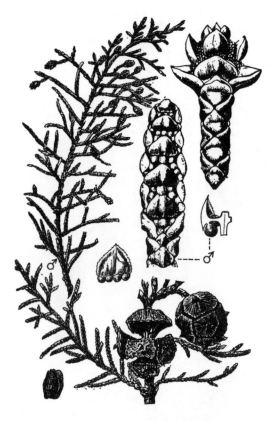

Fig. 64. *Cupressus sempervirens*. Branches with male flowers, these enlarged to the right, in cross section and a single scale, below a branch with 2 cones and a seed (from Beissner and Wettstein)

yellow in the first year, but becoming green in the second year; cones also yellow. CCE 182 (= *C. lambertiana aurea* Hort.). Developed about 1890 by Dickson in Chester, England.

'Minima' (R. Menzies). Dwarf form, globose and very dense at first, branches with awl-shaped needles, later developing larger branches with scale-leaves, which somewhat alters the habit. WDw 117 (H); WM 196 (H) (= *C. macrocarpa* 'Minima' Corley; *C. macrocarpa* 'Nisbet's Gem'). Developed in Golden Gate Park, San Francisco, USA by R. Menzies before 1962.

'Pendula'. The plant in Hillier's Arboretum displays a conical habit, nodding branch tips and needle-form leaves, decussate, wide.

'Pygmaea' (Carshalton Nursery). Dwarf form, very low growing, flat-globose, to about 50 cm high and wide in 30 years, branches spreading, with both leaf forms; leaves on the branch tips scale-like, appressed, bright green, with a resin gland on the dorsal side, needle-form leaves on the basal part of the branch, decussate, broadly awl-shaped, about 1 mm long. WDw 119 (H); WM 197 (H). Developed from seed in 1929 by Marcham of Carlshalton Nurseries, Surrey, England.

'Variegata'. Young shoots white variegated, but not especially attractive; irregular (= *C. macrocarpa lebretonii* Hillier). Known since 1866.

'Woking' (Jackman). Dwarf form, columnar upright, about 60 cm and 30 cm wide in 20 years, annual growth about 2 cm, somewhat irregular, the branches ascending slightly, but the branch tips are reflexed or somewhat pendulous; all needles subulate, bright green, 1 mm long, outspread, arranged in 4 rows and very dense. WDw 118 (H); WM 198 (H). Developed by G. Jackman, Woking, and named "Mrs. Anley's Variety" at first.

C. sargentii Jeps. Tree-like or bushy, usually with a central leader, then 10–25 m high, narrowly conical or also broadly bushy, bark gray to dark brown to nearly black, thick and fibrous, branches rather stiff; foliage distinctly dull green (either gray or green), about 2 mm long and wide, obtusely acuminate, round or slightly keeled on the dorsal side, with darker (usually inactive) resin glands; cones globose to oblong, 1.5–2.5 cm long, glossy brown at first, later brown or gray, with 6–8 scales, these usually with indistinct thorns; seeds about 100 per cone, dark brown and pruinose. WWC 2 (Br), 14 (C), 37 and 80 (H); CCE 175 (= *C. goveniana* var. *sargentii* [Jeps.] Henry). California, in the coastal areas. 1908. z9

C. sempervirens L. Mediterranean Cypress. Tree, 20–30 m high or higher, branches either spreading horizontally or narrowly upright, bark thin, smooth, gray-brown, somewhat fissured, branchlets not in a single plane, the smallest branch tips round or 4 sided in cross section, about 1 mm thick; leaves scale-like, decussate, densely imbricate appressed, ovate, dull dark green, obtuse at the apex, with longitudinal furrows on the dorsal side; cones on short stalks, pendulous, globose to more oblong, 2–3 cm long, with 8–14 scales, arranged in 4 rows, opposite, uneven angled, concave to flat on the dorsal side, with a small umbo in the middle with a prickly tip, glossy brown to gray, seeds 8–20 under each scale, brown, narrowly winged, without resin glands. Mountains of N. Iran, Asia Minor, Crete, Cyprus; introduced into Italy in ancient times. Naturalized today throughout the Mediterranean region. z8

The species is now divided into the following 2 forms:

f. sempervirens. Strict columnar or narrowly conical, but quite variable (= *C. sempervirens fastigiata* Hansen; *C. sempervirens* var. *pyramidalis* Nyman; *C. sempervirens* var. *stricta* Ait.; *C. pyramidalis* Targ.-Tozz.). Plate 54; Fig. 61 D–E. z8

The above form includes the typical columnar plants occurring in the wild or from seed.

f. horizontalis (Mill.) Voss. Wild Mediterranean Cypress. Cedar-like habit, branches spreading more or less horizontally (= *C. horizontalis* Mill.). This is the type, occurring in the eastern part of the Mediterranean region, from Crete to Saudi Arabia. z8

var. indica Royle. Stiff columnar form, peak conspicuously long acuminate; cones globose, with 10 scales, each with a sharp dorsal thorn (= *C. whitleyana* Carr.). Southern Himalayan region. z9

'Swaine's Gold'. Compact columnar form, grows much like *Juniperus* 'Skyrocket'; foliage green, turning yellowish. From Australia. (Hillier). z8–9

C. torulosa D. Don. Himalayan Cypress. Tree, 30–40 m high or more, bark brown, exfoliating in long strips, horizontal branches, crown broadly conical, twigs widely nodding with whip-like tips, branchlets all in an even plane; leaves tightly appressed, obtuse, dark green, all of equal form, curving inward and somewhat thickened on the apex, frequently furrowed on the dorsal side; cones globose or ellipsoid, very short stalked, 10–12 mm thick, purple when young, with 8 scales (rarely 10), concave in the center and with a small, triangular, often reflexed thorn, seeds 6–8 under each scale, red-brown winged. SN 177 (H); CCE 185, 186. W. Himalaya; W. Szechwan Province, China. 1824 Fig. 59b, 61A and B. z9

'**Corneyana**'. Branches more pendulous than the type and irregularly arranged (not in 2 opposing rows). CCE 185 (= *C. corneyana* Knight ex Carr.; *C. gracilis* Gord., *C. torulosa pendula* Sénécl.). Known since 1850 and widely cultivated today. z7–8

'**Ericoides**'. Mutation with needle-form leaves. Shrub, open bushy habit; leaves awl-shaped, coloring light brownish in winter (= *C. torulosa* var. *ericoides* Hornib.). Developed from seed about 1912 by Hornibrook.

'**Majestica**'. Growth stronger and taller than the type, much more winter hardy, branches yellow, somewhat thicker than other cultivars, branchlets thicker, curved; leaves scale-like, somewhat imbricately arranged, in 4 rows, occasionally somewhat recurved on the apex, with longitudinal furrows on the dorsal side (= *C. torulosa* var. *majestica* Knight). Before 1855.

Lit. Camus, A.: Les Cyprès. Encyclopédie Economique de Sylviculture, vol. 2, 1–106. Paris 1914 (425 ills.). ● Camus, A.: Le *Cupressus dupreziana* A. Camus; cyprès nouveau du Tassili. Bull. Soc. Dender. France **58**, 39–44, 1926 (with ills.). ● Corley, R. S.: The dwarf varieties of *Cupressus macrocarpa*. Gard. Chron. 1962 (I), 326–327. ● Little, E. L.: Varietal transfers in *Cupressus* and *Chamaecyparis*. Madrono **18**, 161–167, 1966. Martinez, M.: Los Cupressus de Mexico. Anal. Inst. Biol. Mexico 18, 71–149, 1947. Masters, M.T.: A general view of the genus *Cupressus*. Jour. Linn. Soc. **31**, 312–363, 1895–97. ● Wolf, C. B.: Taxonomic and distributional studies of the New World cypresses. El Aliso **1**, 1–250, 1948.

DACRYDIUM Solander ex Forster—PODOCARPACEAE

Evergreen trees or shrubs, very closely related to *Podocarpus*, but leaves small, usually scale-form or linear on young plants and on the lower branches of mature plants, changing gradually to scale-form leaves; plants dioecious, seldom monoecious, male flowers axillary in the upper leaves, oblong or cylindrical, anthers sessile, 2 celled, pollen with wings; female flowers terminal or nearly so, composed of only a few scales; seed chambers inverted at first and totally surrounded by the always well developed receptacle, later more or less erect, and usually exserted, ovules not adnate to the receptacle; seeds oval, in a thin, nearly fleshy hull, ripening the 2nd year. x = 12.—About 17 species, most in New Zealand, Tasmania, Australia, Borneo, New Caledonia and Chile. Grown only in the mildest climates or in the greenhouse. Range map Fig. 65.

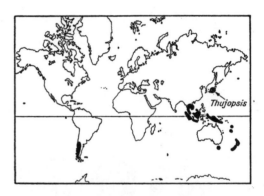

Fig. 65. Range of the genera *Dacrydium* and *Thujopsis*

Dacrydium araucarioides Brongn. & Gris. Small tree, to only 6 m high, branches in candelabra-like, erect layers, branchlets short, cylindrical, branch- tips becoming fleshy and purple at fruiting time; leaves linear and spreading to erect on young plants, scale-like on older plants, 3 mm long, spirally arranged in several rows, overlapping, base clasps the stem, apex truncated and distinct, seeds grouped 1–3 with a fleshy aril. LG 4; CCE 189. New Caledonia; in dry mountainous areas. Fig. 67a. z9

D. balansae Brongn. & Gris. Tree, 4–12 m high or more in its habitat, bark with thick, brown plates; juvenile foliage finely needle-like, to 13 mm long, gradually changing to the mature scale form, these blunt awl-shaped, dense, distinctly keeled on the dorsal side, 3–4.5 mm long, often blue-green, rectangular in cross section; staminate cones cylindrical, to 15 mm long, 2 mm wide, fruits on shoots, 5 × 3.5 mm in size. LG 3; CCE 188. New Caledonia. Fig. 67c. z9

D. bidwillii Hook. f. ex Kirk. Shrub, 0.5–4 m high, densely branched, branches procumbent or erect, leaves linear on young plants, sessile, 6–8 mm long, changing quite suddenly to the scale-form leaves, these triangular, leathery, obtuse on the apex, 1 to 2 mm in size, very thick, branchlets 1.5 mm thick, cylindrical (terete); seeds 1–2.3 mm long, striped, with a white aril. KF 37; SFP 150. New Zealand; in swampy forests or in subalpine regions. Fig. 68D. z9

D. biforme (Hook.) Pilg. Tree, to 10 m high, bark gray to red-brown, branchlets 4 sided, 2 to 2.5 mm thick; juvenile foliage linear, short petioled, acute, 5–20 mm long, changing quickly to the mature leaf form, these scale-like, 1–2 mm long, densely crowded and overlapping, very thick, keeled, obtuse; seeds normally solitary, 1–2.5 mm long, striped, aril white. HI 544 (as *Podocarpus biformis*); PRP 68; CCE 188 (= *D. colensoi* Kirk non Hook.). New Zealand; mountain forests. Fig. 66D. z9

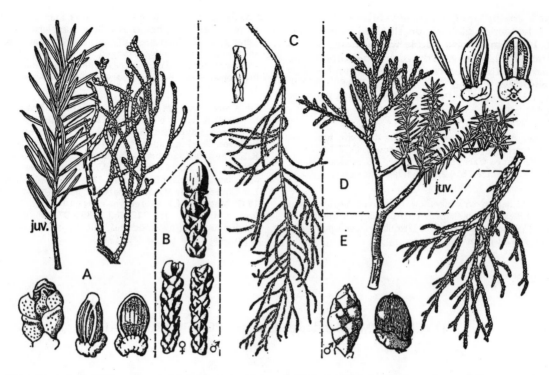

Fig. 66. **Dacrydium.** A. *D. kirkii,* mature and juvenile twigs, flower and 2 fruits; B. *D. fonkii,* 2 branches with flowers and fruit; C. *D. franklinii,* mature twig with small enlargement; D. *D. biforme,* branch with juvenile and mature twigs, a juvenile needle and 2 fruits; E. *D. colensoi,* mature branch, fruit and flower (from Poole-Adams)

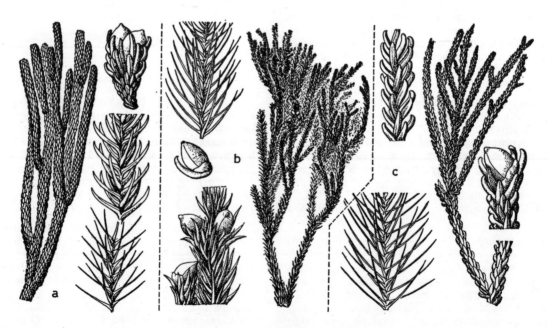

Fig. 67. **Dacrydium.** a. *D. araucarioides;* b. *D. lycopodioides;* c. *D. balansae.* Branch with short needles is mature, that with long needles juvenile, center at (a) is a transition form (from De Laubenfels, modified)

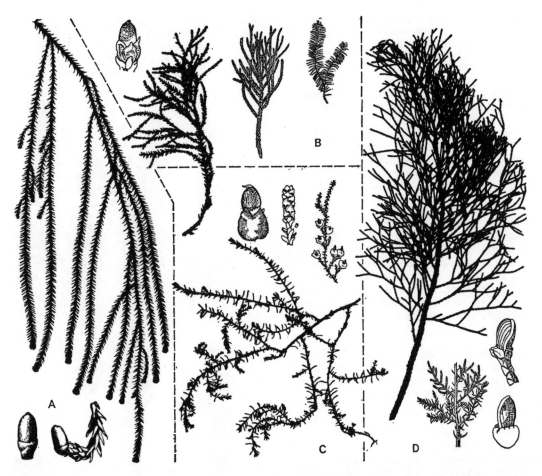

Fig. 68. **Dacrydium**. A. *D. cupressinum*, fruits below; B. *D. intermedium*, left fruit, next intermediate twig, middle a mature twig, right juvenile twig; C. *D. laxifolium*, juvenile twig beneath, mature twig above with fruits, next left male inflorescence and fruit; D. *D. bidwillii*, mature twig above, juvenile twig below with some mature parts, 2 fruits (the branches original, drawings by Poole/Adams)

D. colensoi Hook. Small tree, to 12 m high, conical habit, bark exfoliating in large plates, branchlets thin; juvenile needle-leaves persisting, loosely arranged, linear, cylindrical, 0.6–3 cm (!) long, gradually changing to the 1.5–2 mm long scale-like mature leaves, these obtuse at the apex and not thickened, often curving inward; seeds grouped 1–3 together, 2.5 mm long, smooth, aril occasionally swollen, whitish. KF 96 and 85 (as *D. westlandicum*); HI 548 (not 544!) and 1218; SFP 184 (= *D. westlandicum* Kirk). New Zealand. Fig. 66E. z9

D. cupressinum Sol. ex Lambert. Rimu. Tree, to 50 m high in its habitat, conical when young, later developing a more rounded crown with wide spreading, nodding branches; juvenile foliage needle-form and ascending, 4–6 mm long, deep green, gradually changing to the 2.5–3 mm long mature foliage, these more appressed, triangular; female flowers on reflexed branch tips, seeds 3 mm long, aril red, either fleshy or dry. KF 18 and 19; CBJ 46; SFP 67. New Zealand. Valuable lumber tree. Plate 55, 82; Fig. 68A. z9

D. elatum (Roxb.) Wall ex Hook. Tree, conical crown, outspread branches, pendulous branchlets; leaves awl-shaped subulate in juvenile form, very densely arranged, outspread, deeply furrowed, 8 to 16 mm long, leaves small and scale-like on the fertile branches, densely overlapping, apex obtuse or tiny acuminate; seeds distributed along the fertile shoots, 4 mm long. PPF 21. Malaysia, Borneo, Phillipines, Fiji Islands. z9

D. fonkii Benth. Shrub, densely branched, branches short and upright; leaves scale-like, tightly appressed, densely imbricate, dorsally keeled, apex obtuse and curving inward; seeds on the tips of smaller branches, 6 mm long. PFC 23; CCE 189. S. Chile. While rarely found in cultivation, this species is supposedly the hardiest. Fig. 66B. z9

D. franklinii Hook. f. Tree, 15–30 m high in its habitat, branches spaced widely and spreading gracefully with long drooping tips; leaves small, scale-like, dark green, about 1 mm long, keeled, with scattered white stomata on the dorsal side (important characteristic for distinguishing form the *Cuperssus* weeping forms!); seeds globose, 2 mm thick, but hardly distinguishable from branch tips due to their small size. BAu 397; CTa 1; CBJ 47; CCE 189. Tasmania. Fig. 66C z9

'**Pendulum**'. Upright habit (young plants should be staked?), all branches hang limply downward in a short arch, bright green. A very attractive old plant, about 6 m high (1977), is growing on Garnish Island, Ireland (in KN Plate 4). Extraordinarily beautiful. z9

D. intermedium T. Kirk. Small tree, to 12 m high, dark gray, spreading branches; leaves narrow-linear on young plants, 1 cm long, outspread, cylindrical, for quite some time, persisting for quite some time (!), gradually becoming shorter and more densely crowded, eventually only 1.5–2.5 mm long, 3 sided and densely imbricate, obtuse, keeled; seeds 3–4 mm long, rather smooth, with small tips. KF 86; SFP 185. New Zealand. Fig. 68B. z9

D. kirkii F. Muell. ex Parl. Tree, to 25 m high, bark light brown, the lower branches outspread, while the upper branches are upright; juvenile leaves linear, with a short petiole, quickly changing to the mature form, these scale-like, on cylindrical, 1.5 mm thick branchlets, 2–3 mm long, leathery-thick, with a membranous limb; seeds 1–5, 3.5–4 mm long, striped, aril orange. HI 1219; KF 97; CBJ 48; SFP 183. New Zealand; in mixed forests. Fig. 66A. z9

D. laxifolium Hook. f. (Known as the "smallest conifer in the world".) Procumbent to ascending shrublet, scarcely 10 cm high, but creeping shoots to 1 m long; female plants often only 10 cm high and wide, branches thin and filamentous, nearly *Erica*-like; leaves in the juvenile stage spreading, subulate, 3–8 mm long, gradually becoming shorter, thicker, darker green with age, eventually only 1.5 mm long, plants mono- or dioecious; nuts 3 mm long, always surrounded by a distinct, carmine-red aril. KF 87; HI 815; CC 40–41 (H); SFP 147; CCE 188. New Zealand, in moist areas in the mountains; valued as a ground stabilizer. Fig. 68. z9

D. lycopodioides Brongn. & Gris. Tree, to 25 m or more, crown abundantly branched; juvenile leaves needle-

like, to 10 mm long, gradually changing to the mature form, these lanceolate, with prickly tips, to 4.5 mm long, 0.7 mm wide, bright green; staminate cones terminal, to 7 mm long, 0.7 mm wide; fruits to 3.5 mm long, brown, glossy. LG 5; CCE 188. New Caledonia. Fig. 67b. z9

Fig. 69. *Diselma archeri*. Middle: branch with female flowers; below left, male flower; above left, individual leaf; above right, branch piece (3 × actual size), below right, fruit; above, seed (from Hooker)

DISELMA Hook. f.—CUPRESSACEAE

Monotypic genus, recognized by the tiny, tightly appressed scale leaves, dioecious flowers and small cones with 4 scales, of which only the uppermost pair are fertile.

Diselma archeri Hook. f. Upright or wide spreading shrub, usually 1–1.5 m high, occasionally also to 4 m, compact or irregularly branched depending on the site, the twigs finely divided; leaves scale-form, decussate, very densely imbricate, crowded and appressed, thick, obtuse at the apex, keeled, dark green; plants dioecious, male flowers terminal, oblong, pollen vessels in 3–4 pairs, scarcely differing from normal branches in appearance, female flowers terminal, solitary; cones small, about 5 mm thick and globose, composed of 2 scale pairs, each with 2 seeds, these eventually with 2–3 wings, exserted past the scales, brown. CTa 3; CCE 190 (= *Fitzroya archeri* Benth. & Hook. f.). x = 11. Tasmania; in the mountains along the west coast. Rarely found in cultivation. Fig. 69. z9

EPHEDRA L.—EPHEDRACEAE

Reed-like shrub of "horsetail (*Equisetum*)-like" appearance, occasionally climbing on other trees and shrubs; branches decussate or 3–4 in whorls, gray-green to bright green; leaves usually opposite, very small, nearly always sheath-like connate at the base, on some species with a semi-terete, about 1 mm thick, short and invalid leaf blade; plants dioecious, seldom monoecious, male flowers solitary or grouped in short to globose spikes, each with 2–24 flowers, anthers without filaments, but on a common, stalk-like support; female flowers solitary or 2–3 terminal, ovules solitary, erect, the tube-form throat (micropyle) exserted from the pouch-form perianth; fruit enclosed within a woody or sometimes berry-like fleshy hull. x = 2.—About 40 species in S. Europe, N. Africa, in temperate and tropical Asia and subtropical regions of the Americas, several in desert and prairie regions of the warmer zones. Positive identification of the species is possible only by the flowers and fruit.

No complete modern monograph dealing with this complicated genus is available. A few modern writers (Florin, Cutler) have dealt with some of the species. The oldest monograph (C. A. Meyer 1849) was based on the orientation of the micropyle tube and its opening; the monograph by Stapf (1889) centered on the properties of the mock-fruits.

Ephedra alata Decne. Shrub, to 1 m high, branches yellow-green, finely scabrous, always more than 1 mm thick; leaves grouped 2–3, about 5 mm long, connate to the midpoint or further, the membranous portion of the leaf sheath shorter than 3 mm; male catkins in dense, 10 mm thick clusters, anthers stalked together in groups of 5, female catkins with bracts distinct to the base, 5 pairs of bracts with 2 green longitudinal stripes and a broad membranous margin; seeds 6–7 mm long, flat, margin narrowly winged. TFI 10. N. Africa to Iran; in calcareous desert soils. z6?

E. alte C. A. Mey. Shrub climbing to 2 m, similar to *E. foliata*, but the distinct portion of the leaves is seldom more than 3 mm long, the connate portion only 1 mm long, whitish pith; male catkins borne only at the branch tips, densely clustered, the anther stalks frequently over 1 mm longer than the subtending bracts, the lower bracts of the female cones are connate for half their length or more; seeds 1–2 mm longer than the upper bracts. Iran, Asia Minor westward to Cyrenaica. z9

E. altissima Desf. Shrub climbing to 8 m, branches blue-green to gray-green, similar to *E. foliata*, but the male spikes grouped into panicles with 2–6 pairs of flowers, these light yellow; fruits red, micropyle straight. BM 7670. N. Africa, and southward to the Tuareg Mts. 1823. Fig. 71A. z9

E. americana Humb. & Bonpl. Quite variable shrub depending upon location, procumbent (top of the Andes Mts.) or a 0.5–2 m tall, *Cytisus*-like shrub or a 3–4 m high small tree, branches and twigs bowed downward, branchlets with 3 to 9 internodes; leaves usually sheath-like connate, occasionally also to 1 cm long; anthers sessile, female inflorescences with 1–2 fruits; fruits 5–8 mm long, seeds brown, enclosed or somewhat exserted. Andes; Ecuador to Patagonia. z6?

var. **andina** Stapf. Shrub, more or less procumbent, the green shoots distinctly long, the old shoots blackish-gray and to 5 mm thick, young shoots green, finely striped, the youngest 0.5–1 mm thick, pith red-brown, internodes 7–35 mm long, usually quite smooth to finely scabrous; leaves on the young shoots 4–5 mm long; female inflorescences with 1 (rarely 2) flowers; fruits broadly ovate, about 1.5 cm long, fleshy, bright red. PFC 21B; BMns 142 (= *E. andina* Poepp. ex C. A. Mey.; *E. peruviana* Brot.; *E. chilensis* (Miers). At higher elevations in the Andes mountains. Plate 56.

E. californica Wats. Shrub, procumbent or ascending, branches always grouped 2–3 together, pale green to blue-green; leaf scales in 3's, about 5 mm long or shorter, acute, connate at first, but splitting quickly, then abscising; male flower catkins usually solitary, sessile, female catkins short stalked, flowers solitary, surrounded by about 8 somewhat membranous bracts; fruit cones dry when ripe, bract scales not winged, fruits about 8 mm long, seeds 4 sided, black. AI 163; MS 17. California. z9

E. coryi Reed. Shrub, slender upright, 0.2 to 0.9 m high, branches grouped 2 or 3 together, terete, internodes 2–4 cm long, young shoots green and finely striped, older shoots red-brown, arising from many underground runners; leaves opposite, connate for ⅓ to ¾ of their length, thickened in the middle, abscising early, but the dry base persists; male catkins 2 to several at a node, sessile to short stalked, female catkins as in the male flower, but globose to obovate, bracts opposite, in 3 to 4 whorls; fruits brownish, micropyle straight. VT 41. USA, Texas. z6

E. compacta Rose. Shrub, 30–50 cm high, very densely branched, branches smooth, pale green; leaf scales opposite; fruits sessile or nearly so, fleshy, red. Mexico. z7

E. distachya L. Shrub, to 0.5 m high, occasionally procumbent or (rarely) to 1 m high, with underground runners, branches blue-green or dark green, rather stiff, finely striped, internodes 1.5–5 cm long, straight or bowed, to 2 mm thick; leaves to 2 mm long, green in the center of the dorsal side, limb border dry membranous; male inflorescences sessile to stalked, oval-oblong, with 4–8 flower pairs, female inflorescences 2 flowered, usually with 3 pairs of bracts, micropyle straight, 1.5 mm long; fruits globose, 6–7 mm thick, red. HF 79 (= *E. vulgaris* Rich.). S. Europe, north to NW. France, S. Czechoslovakia, Ukraine and to Siberia. z3

ssp. **distachya**. Branches ascending, pale green or bluish, red-brown pith; female inflorescences stalked, micropyle straight. 2n = 24, 28. In the region of the species, along sandy coastal areas and river banks.

ssp. **helvetica** (C. A. Mey.) Aschers. & Graeb. Low shrub, scarcely 0.5 m high, branches erect, deep green, pith red-brown; female inflorescences sessile, micropyle twisted corkscrew-like. HM 34 (= *E. helvetica* C. A. Mey.). Switzerland. Plate 56; Fig. 71B.

Fig. 70. **Ephedra.** A. *E. foliata;* B. *E. likiangensis;* C. *E. fragilis;* D. *E. minuta;*
E. *E. gerardiana;* F. *E. major* (Original)

var. **monostachya** (L.) Stapf. Quite low, branches only 1 mm thick; male flower spikes and female fruit cones usually solitary, anthers solitary. Caucasus, Crimea, in dry areas.

E. equisetina Bge. Upright shrub, 1–2 m high, similar to *E. major,* but branches thicker and distinctly blue-green or bluish, stiff and hard, internodes 1–2 cm long, 1.5 to 2 mm thick; leaves sheath-like, in 2's, connate for ⅔ of their length; male spikes 1–3 sessile, female spikes nearly sessile, with 2–3 pairs of bracts, the basal ones to ⅓, the uppermost ⅔ connate; fruits nearly globose, fleshy, red, seeds ovate. CIS 55. Turkestan, Altai, Central Asia to NW. China. Plate 56. z7

E. foliata Boiss. ex C. A. Mey. Shrub, climbing to 5 m or procumbent, branches flexible, smooth or finely hirsute pubescent, gray-green, light green to blue-green, striped, about 1 mm thick, however often much thinner, internodes to 8 cm long; leaves usually 1–5 mm long, of which 1 mm is the basal sheath, occasionally 10–30 mm long, green; male catkins clustered, seldom solitary, with 4–12 pairs of flowers, female catkins 6–7 mm long and 5–6 mm wide, usually with 3 pairs of bracts; fruits oblong, 6 mm thick, red. TFI 10; SN 182 (= *E. ciliata* C. A. Mey.; *E.*

kokanica Reg.; *E. polylepis* Boiss. & Hauskn.). Iran, Turkestan, Arabia. 1895. Fig. 70A. z9

E. fragilis Desf. Climbing to 5 m or procumbent, branches flexible; leaves to 2 mm long, green on the dorsal side; male inflorescences nearly sessile, ovate, with 4–8 flower pairs, bracts tight, nearly circular, female inflorescences with 1–2 flowers, 2–3 pairs of bracts, micropyle 3 mm long; fruit 8–9 mm long, red. Mediterranean region, S. Portugal. Fig. 70C. z8

ssp. **fragilis.** More or less upright, branches fragile and easily broken at the nodes, pith yellow to brown; inflorescences very slender. Western Mediterranean region; S. Portugal.

ssp. **campylopoda** (C. A. Mey.) Aschers. & Graebn. Climbing with branches nodding, less easily broken, white pith; wide inflorescence. Eastern Mediterranean region.

E. gerardiana Wall. Very low shrub, normally no higher than 5 cm(!), branches very thin and dark green, finely striped; leaves scale-like, about 2 mm long, connate to half its length; male spikes grouped 1–2, sessile, oval-globose, with 2–3 pairs of flowers, female spikes solitary, sessile to stalked, with 3–4 pairs of bracts, these connate

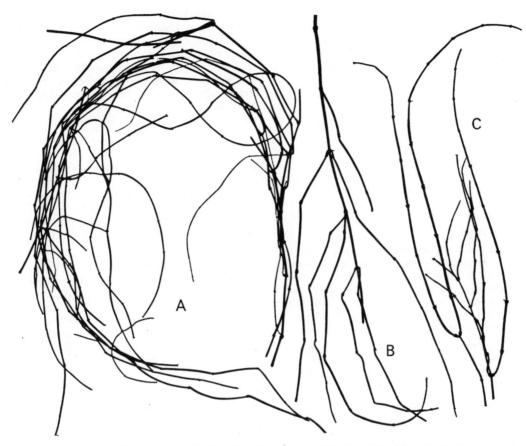

Fig. 71. **Ephedra**. A. *E. altissima*; B. *E. distachya* ssp. *helvetica*; C. *E. sinica* (Original)

on the basal third, micropyle straight; fruits globose, 5–7 mm thick, red, with 1–2 seeds, exserted. SW. China, Himalayas; dry mountain valleys. Fig. 70E. z7

var. **saxatilis** Stapf. Taller, branches more ascending. The Himalayan Mtns.

var. **sikkimensis** Stapf. Taller, branches to 15 cm long, vigorous, narrowly upright; leaves longer than those of the species; male flower spikes larger. HAl 202. Sikkim. Develops abundant fruit.

E. intermedia Schrenk ex C. A. Mey. Shrub, to 1 m high, densely branched and upright or prostrate, branches rigid, twigs 2–3 mm thick, yellow-green or bluish-green, distinctly striped, smooth or rough; leaves in 2's, seldom 3–4, scale-form, usually 2–4 mm long, membranous, connate to ⅔ their length; plants sometimes monoecious, male spikes globose to ovate, with 3 to 4 flower pairs, female spikes solitary, stalked, with 2–3 flowers, these with 2–3 pairs of bracts, which are usually connate to over the midpoint, micropyle twisted corkscrew-like; fruits 6–7 mm long, red. Central Asia, in the steppes and deserts; Turkestan, Iran. 1902. Plate 56; Fig. 4. z6

E. likiangensis Florin. Upright shrub, 1.5–1.8 m high in its habitat, older bark brown and rough, young shoots green; leaves connate, forming a short sheath around the nodes; plants dioecious, male flowers yellow, in clusters along young green shoots; female flowers purple, large, solitary; fruit a red, fleshy berry. China; Likiang, Yunnan, 3300 m. Fig. 70B. z6

E. lomatolepis Schrenk. Low shrub, 30–50 cm high and twice as wide, "porcupine-stiff", branches short, thick, stiff, green, smooth; leaves grouped 2–3, about 3.5 mm long, connate to about half their length. Central Asia; Kazakstan; Priilijska Desert (USSR). Not in cultivation? Plate 56. z6

E. major Host. Shrub, to 2 m high; leaves to 3 mm long, totally membranous, old leaf sheaths dark brown; male inflorescences short stalked, 1 flowered, usually with 2 pairs of bracts, micropyle 3 mm long; fruit 5–7 mm long, red or yellow. SN 131. Mediterranean region to the Himalayas. z6

ssp. **major**. Branches rough, pith red-brown; female inflorescences wide; seeds ovate. $2n = 14$ (= *E. nebrodensis* Tineo; *E. scoparia* Lange). Western and central Mediterranean region. Plate 56; Fig. 70F.

ssp. **procera** (Fisc. & C. A. Mey.) Markgr. Branches completely smooth, pith red-brown; female inflorescences long and slender; seeds ovate-oblong. BM 9204 (= *E. procera* Fisch. & C. A. Mey.; *E. nebrodensis* var. *procera* [Fisch. & Mey.] Stapf). Mountains of S. Greece.

E. minima Hao. To only 3 cm high in its habitat, erect or procumbent, very densely branched, branches knobby and jointed; sheaths 1.5 mm long at the nodes and composed of the 2 opposing leaves, female inflorescences in the sheath axils at the branch tips; fruits 6 mm long, bright red, fleshy exterior. China; Kokonor, in the mountains to 4350 m. z6

E. minuta Florin. Only 7–10 cm high in its habitat, procumbent shrub, however, in cultivation over 20 cm high, branches very numerous, thin, dull green; leaves sheath-like surrounding the nodes, with sharp apexes, male flowers solitary, large, purple, terminal on small shoots. W. China, in the mountains from 3500–4700 m. Cultivated in the Göteborg Botanic Garden, Sweden. Plate 57; Fig. 70D. z6

E. nevadensis Wats. Closely resembles *E. viridis*, 0.5 to 1 m high, but the branches spread widely, blue-green, rough; leaves paired, opposite, 3–6 mm long, sheath-like, connate to about the middle, abscising with age; male cones sessile, with 4–6 pairs of bracts, carpels in 4–5 pairs, sessile, oval; fruits smaller and shorter than those of *E. viridis*. AI 162; MS 19. SW. USA. z6

var. **aspera** (Engelm.) Benson. Branches stiffly upright, yellow-green to dark green when young, rough; leaves sheath-like, connate to half their length; seeds about ⅓ longer than the bracts. VT 38 (= *E. aspera* Engelm.). SW. USA to Mexico.

E. pachyclada Boiss. Shrub, upright, 0.5–1 m high, stem short and thick or branched at the base, branches very stiff, erect, internodes 2–6 cm long, 2–3 mm thick, blue-green, rough, thin striped; leaves in 2's, seldom 3, 2–3 mm long, connate to about ⅔ its length; male spikes grouped 2–5, in dense globules, 6–7 mm long, female spikes short stalked, with 1–2 flowers, bracts deeply divided; fruits 7–8 mm long. S. Iran to Afghanistan. z6

E. przewalskii Stapf. Shrub, to 1.5 m high, branches usually in whorls, yellow-green, stiff, rough; leaves in 3's or 2's; male spikes sessile, with 4–6 pairs of flowers, female spikes with 2–3 flowers and about 5 whorls of bracts, these thickened on the dorsal side and curved inward on the apex, broad winged; fruits 5–6 mm long. Central Asia. 1912. z6

E. sinica Stapf. Similar to *E. distachya*. Shrub, to 30 cm, loosely branched, the uppermost internodes 2 sided; leaf sheath red-brown at the base; male flowers terminal, 4 mm long, with 4–5 pairs of flowers, female spikes 1–3 on the branch tips, with 2 flowers, the upper bracts connate up to ⅔ their length. CIS 56. N. China. Fig. 71C. z5?

E. torreyana Wats. Shrub, 0.3–1 m high, branches usually in whorls of 3, outspread, flexible, about 2 mm thick, internodes 2–5 cm long, bluish to yellowish-green, finely striped, not thorned; leaves in 3's, ⅓ to ⅔ connate, membranous; male catkins sessile, globose-ovate, with 6–8 flower whorls, female spikes grouped 1–3, ovate, bracts membranous, in many whorls of 3; fruits grouped 1–3, as long as the bracts or exserted, micropyle protruding distinctly. VT 40. SW. USA. z9

E. transitoria Riedl. Small shrub, about 0.5 m high, branches gray-green, finely scabrous, the thinnest twigs occasionally less than 1 mm thick; leaves usually 3–4 mm long, of which 1–2 mm is connate; male cones either in the leaf axils or in groups of 1–3 at the end of about 1 cm long shoots, female cones 7 mm long and 4 mm wide, bracts in 2's or whorls of 3, the innermost becoming fleshy when ripe; seeds oblong, 6 mm long, angular. TPI 10. Iran. z6

E. trifurca Torr. Upright shrub, about 1 m high, branches hard, rigid, thorny tips, 3–5 mm thick, pale green to blue-green at first, eventually yellow-green and rather smooth; leaves in 3's, seldom 2, scale-like, 8–10 mm long, connate to the midpoint or further, with an awned tip; male flower spikes with winged bracts; fruits dry, bract scales totally membranous, without a dorsal keel, to 1.5 cm long. AI 164; MS 15; VT 40. SW. USA, in the prairie regions. z9

E. viridis Coville. Upright shrub, 0.5–1 m high, branches thin, bright green, finely striped, finely scabrous, rather stiff, leaf scales opposite, awl-shaped, 3–6 mm long, green, connate only at the base, forming a membranous sheath; male cones sessile, with 4–5 pairs of bracts, stamens 6–8, female spikes short stalked, usually 2 flowered, with 3–5 bract pairs; fruits fleshy, red, standing distinctly above the bracts. AI 161; VT 39; BM 9366; MS 18. California to Colorado and Arizona. z9

Lit. Blakelock, R. A., & J. B. Gillett: in C. C. Townsend & E. Guest: Flora of Iraq, vol. 2, 82–89, 1966. ● Cahen, E.: *Ephedra* through the ages. Jour. Roy. Hort. Soc. London 1944, 292–296 (ill.) ● Cutler, H. C.: Monograph of the North American species of the genus *Ephedra*. Ann. Mo. Bot. Gard. **26**, 373–427, 1939. ● Groff, G. W., & G. W. Clark: The Botany of *Ephedra*. Calif. Univ. Publ. Bot. **14**, 247–282, 1928. ● Markgraf, F.: Ephedraceae. In Engler-Prantl, Die naturlichen Pflanzen-familien, 2nd ed.. **13**, 406–419, 1926. ● Markgraf, F.: *Ephedra*. In Flora Europaea I, 40, 1964. ● Meyer, C. A.: Versuch einer Monographie der Gattung *Ephedra*, durch Abbildungen erlaeutert. Mém. Acad. Petersbourg, St. Petersburg **5**, 35–108, 1846 (8 plates). ● Miers, J.: On *Ephedra*. Ann. Mag. Nat. Hist. III, 421–437, 1862; III, 133–140, 1863. ● Stapf, O.: Die Arten der Gattung *Ephedra*. Denkschr. K. K. Akad. Wiss. math.-naturwiss. Kl. Vienna **56**, 1–112, 1889. ● Widder, F.: Die Markfarbe als Untersheidungsmarkmal von *Ephedra*-Arten. Phyton **1**, 71–75, 1948.

Fig. 72. A. to E. *Fitzroya cupressoides*. A. Branch, nearly actual size; B. fruiting branch; C. cones; D. partial branch, enlarged; E. seed. F. to I. *Glyptostrobus lineatus*. F. young branch with needle-leaves; G. branch with persistent, appressed leaves; H. cross section through a leaf from F; I. cones (A. and F. Original; otherwise from Koehne, Bot. Mag. and Bailey)

FITZROYA Hook.f.—CUPRESSACEAE

Monotypic genus. Evergreen tree; leaves scale-like in whorls of 3; male flowers solitary, axillary, near the ends of the branchlets, with 15–24 stamens in whorls of 3, each with 4 pollen sacs; female flowers singular, globose, with 9 scales in whorls of 3, of those the uppermost and sometimes the middle scales fertile, with 3 awl-shaped or clavate, resin secreting scales reduced to glands on the apex; ovules 3; cones woody, 6–8 mm wide, ripening the first year; cone scales flat, valvate, with a wide triangular tip on the dorsal side, loosening up when ripe; seeds ovate, with 2 half-moon shaped wings; cotyledons 2. x = 11.—1 species in southern Chile, Valdivia.

Fitzroya cupressoides (Molina) Johnson. Alerce. Tree, to 35 m high with a 5 m diameter trunk, only shrubby in high mountainous areas, bark reddish, furrowed, exfoliating in long strips, branches pendulous, flexible, thin, green at first, red with age, buds ovate or globose, green scaly; leaves in 3 parted whorls, more or less spreading, oblong to lanceolate, about 3 mm long, with very small inward curving tips, convex on the underside, with a wide, green midrib, midrib with a white stomatal band on both sides; for flower and cone characteristics see genus description. DJ 15; BM 4616; CB 3: 81; KN Plate 4 (= *F. patagonica* Hook.f.). Southern S. America, from Valdiva southward, W. Patagonia, between 41 and 43° S. latitude. 1849. A 2000-year old tree stands at Lago Mendenez. Plate 82; Fig. 72 A–E. z8–9

FOKIENIA Henry & Thomas—CUPRESSACEAE

Trees with scale-form leaves; branchlets flat and lying on an even plane; male inflorescences in terminal cones, usually solitary, occasionally groups of 2–3, cylindrical, 1.5–2 mm long, 1 to 1.2 mm wide, with 8–10 opposite or decussate scales, these with 3 anthers each; female flowers terminal at the tips of the youngest shoots, with 6–8 opposite scale pairs, petiole about 4 mm long; cones on 4 mm long stalks, pear-shaped, 12–18 mm long, ripening in the second year, with 12–16 woody scales, these obovate, rather thin, with short tips on the dorsal side, 2 seeds under each scale; seeds oval or more oblong, acute, with 2 very uneven wings. x = 11.—3 species in China, which have recently been reclassified as a single species. Range map with *Chamaecyparis*, Fig. 33.

Fokienia hodginsii (Dunn) Henry & Thomas. Tree, about 12 m high in its habitat, resembling *Calocedrus* *macrolepis* in physical characteristics, intermediate between it and *Chamaecyparis* in appearance; leaves scale-like, on older trees in whorls at similar height, 2.5 mm long, with white stomatal lines on the inside, facial leaves oblanceolate, with triangular tips, furrowed above, leaves of young plants about 8 mm long with nearly thorn-like tips; flowers and cones as in genus description. CIS 13; CB 3:85; DJ 46; LF 39. E. China; Fukien Province, also in the provinces of Chekiang, Kwantung, Kweichow and Yunnan as well as in Vietnam; Tongking and Annam. 1909. Fig. 73. z9

F. kawai Hayata, in Tokyo Bot. Mag. 31: 116(ill.) and *F. maclurei* Merr. in Philipp. Jour. Sci. 21: 492 (ill.), were separated on the basis of different seed characteristics. Refuted by S.-Y. Hu and now included in *F. hodginsii*.

Lit. Hu, S.-Y: Notes on the Flora of China. I. *Fokienia hodginsii*. Jour. Arnold Arb. **32**, 390–391, 1951.

Fig. 73. *Fokienia hodginsii*
(Original; material from the plant at Borde Hill, England)

GINKGO L.—GINKGOACEAE

Monotypic genus. Tall, deciduous tree, with long and short shoots; leaves fan-shaped, parallel venation; plants dioecious, male flowers catkin-like, solitary, axillary, numerous stamens, loosely arranged, female flowers long stalked, solitary, axillary, with 2 opposing ovules at the end of the thickened stalk apex; seed drupe-like, outer shell fleshy, nut bone hard; cotyledons 2; fertilization occurs by spermatozoids. x = 8.—This was a widely distributed and species rich genus in prehistoric times (about 180 million years ago!). Only a single species has survived to modern times. China, Japan. Range map Fig. 74.

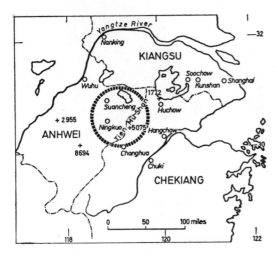

Fig. 74. Range of *Ginkgo biloba* (from H.-L. Li)

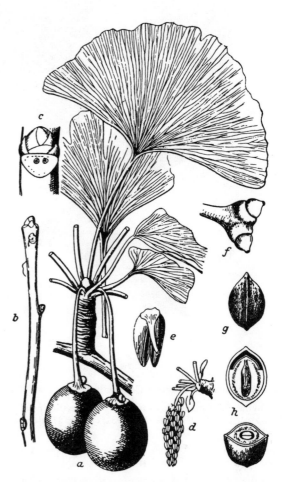

Fig. 75. *Ginkgo biloba.* a. branch with fruits; b. winter twig; c. bud with leaf scar; d. male flower; e. stamen; f. female flower; g. and h. fruit (from Beissner, Schneider, Shirasawa)

The disagreement in the modern botanic literature over the correct spelling of the name—Ginkgo, Ginkyo, Gingkyo or Gingko—will be laid aside, and Linnaeus' first spelling of 1771 retained.

The question frequently arises as to how one can distinguish male and female plants of *Ginkgo* when they are not in flower. It may safely be said that the sex cannot be determined by the tree's habit or its leaf form. In the nursery of L. Späth, Berlin, following decades of observation of a large number of young trees and on older trees (whose sex was known), it was determined that the leaves of the two sexes fall in distinct periods 3–4 weeks apart. The male trees drop their leaves 2 weeks earlier than the females but leaf out 2 weeks earlier in spring. Despite this observation the propagator can only be sure by propagating from known-sex trees. The same conclusion was arrived at by A. Kados in the year 1900 and published in a Hungarian periodical.

Ginkgo biloba L. Maidenhair, Ginkgo Tree (the Japanese word translates to "Silver Apricot"). Tree, to 40 m high, habit variable, narrowly conical or spreading, bark gray, deeply furrowed on older trunks; leaves alternate on long shoots, clustered 3–5 on short shoots, fan-shaped, leathery tough, 5–8 cm wide, long petioled, often incised on the margin or lobed, parallel and forked

venation, bright green, golden-yellow in fall, then abscising quickly; fruits nearly like small plums, yellow-green, 2.5 cm long, fleshy exterior, interior with a 2 sided stone pit, unpleasant smelling, seeds are eaten in E. Asia, sweet. Occurs naturally only in Chekiang Province, China; only known in cultivation in Japan, Korea and Manchuria where it is used primarily around temples. Used as a street tree in Japan. Introduced into Europe from Japan in 1727. First planted at the Botanic Garden in Utrecht, Holland. Plate 58 and 64; Fig. 75 and 76.

A variety of *Ginkgo* cultivars have been developed from seed. They display varying growth habits, the most common being broadly conical. The following cultivars are recognized:

'**Aurea**'. Leaves always yellow.

'**Autumn Gold**' (Saratoga). Male form, broadly conical habit, at selection 12 m high and 6 m wide, very regular; fall color

Fig. 76. *Ginkgo biloba,* leaf form (Original)

especially bright golden-yellow. Amer. Nurseryman, 3/15/1964 (cover photo). Selected at the Saratoga Horticultural Foundation, Saratoga, California, USA about 1958.

'Epiphylla'. Fruit stalks broad and wing-like on the apical portion, adnate to the leaf petiole. MD 1931: P1. 5 and 6 (described by OHWI).

'Fairmont' (Saratoga). Male form, narrowly upright habit. Mother tree is in Fairmont Park, Philadelphia, USA.

'Fastigiata'. Acute conical to columnar habit. Illustrated as the cover photo on American Nurseryman, 6/1/1965.

'Mayfield'. Male form, quite narrowly columnar habit. Illust. in Proc. Plant Prop. Soc. 1951: 28. Selected in Ohio about 1948.

'Laciniata'. Vigorous growing conical habit; leaves very large, 20–30 cm wide, kidney-shaped, with many incisions, venation distinctly raised. FS 10, on Pl. 1013 (= G. *biloba macrophylla* Hort.; *Salisburya adiantifolia macrophylla* Hort.). Originated as a seedling before 1850 in the Reynier Nursery, Avignon, France.

Fig. 77. *Ginkgo biloba* 'Variegata'
(Original; half the actual size)

'Pendula'. Small tree, crown broad umbrella form or hemispherical, branches more or less nodding or spreading horizontally, otherwise like the species. SB 21: 280 & 281 (1969). Beautiful old specimens of this tree stand in the Botanic Gardens of Nancy, France and Prague, Czechoslovakia.

'St. Cloud'. A straight form with a dominant leading stem, main branches widely spreading and covered with very short side branches along their entire length. Bai. 9: 45. Mother plant is in the Albert Kahn garden in St. Cloud-sur-Seine, Paris, France.

'Tit'. Dense, bushy dwarf form, presumably originated from a witches'-broom, develops knots on the stem, from which leaves sprout. Introduced from Japan by K. Kromhout & Zonen of Hazerswoude, Holland. First shown in 1978.

'Tremonia' (Dortmund Bot. Garden). Narrow, columnar form, at the time of this writing about 12 m high and 80 cm wide; good fall foliage color. Introduced to the trade by the Dortmund Botanic Garden, Germany, in 1970. The mother tree originated in the Garden from a seedling in 1930.

'Variegata'. Leaves more or less yellow-green striped to totally yellow. Fig. 77.

Lit. Barcley, J. G.: The name *Ginkgo.* Jour. Roy. Hort. Soc. (London) 1944, 68-69. ● Esser: Ausbildung der "Tschitschi" an einem Ginkgobaum im Schlossgarten Dyck. Mitt. DDG 1928, 121–126 ● Li, H.-L.: *Ginkgo,* the Maidenhair Tree. Ann. Hort. Mag. **40,** 239–249, 1961 ● Miyoshi, M.: Merkwuerdige *Ginkgo biloba* in Japan. Mitt. DDG 1931, 21 to 22 (with 2 plates). ● Moule, A. C.: The name *Ginkgo biloba* and other names of the tree. T'oung Pao **33,** 193–219, 1939. ● Moule, A. C.: The name *Ginkgo.* Jour. Roy. Hort. Soc. **69,** 166, 1944. ● Pulle, A.: Over de *Ginkgo* alia *Ginkyo.* Jaarb. Nederl. Dendr. Ver. 1940–1946, 25–35. ● Thommen, E.: Neues zur Schreibung des Namens *Ginkgo.* Verh. naturf. Ges. Basel **60,** 77–103, 1949. ● Widder, F.: Die Rechtschreibung des Namens *Ginkgo.* Phyton **1,** 47–52, 1948 (with 41 Lit. references).

GLYPTOSTROBUS Endl.—TAXODIACEAE

Monotypic genus, very closely related to *Taxodium,* but differs in the form of the leaves and the fruit.

Glyptostrobus lineatus (Poiret) Druce. Deciduous, small to medium size tree, lower branches outspread, upper branches more upright, branches rigid, in 2 forms: persisting twigs with small scale-like leaves, appressed or slightly spreading, spirally arranged, with buds in the leaf axils, short, or abscising twigs (as on *Taxodium*) with sickle-shaped needles, spreading from the base, more or less rectangular in cross section, on the youngest shoots and especially on very young plants arranged in 2 rows, sea-green, red-brown in fall before leaf drop; plants monoecious; male flowers terminal on short branchlets, numerous, crowded, female flowers terminal on lateral branches, ovules 2, erect; cones narrow, obovate, the scales imbricately arranged, seeds ovate with a well developed wing. CIS 51; GC 66 (1919): 258 (= *G. pensilis* [Staunton] K. Koch; *G. heterophyllus* Endl.; *Taxodium heterophyllum* Brong.). S. China, Canton; probably extinct in the wild, but frequently planted along the canals bordering rice fields where it develops respiratory "knees" like *Taxodium.* Plate 57 and 64; Fig. 72 F–I. z9

Lit. Henry, A., & M. McIntyre: The swamp cypresses, *Glyptostrobus* of China and *Taxodium* of America, with notes on allied genera. Proc. Irish Acad. **37B**, 90–116, 1926 (detailed discussion in Mitt. DDG 1926, 359–360). ● Metcalf, F. P.: Distribution, propagation, and uses of *Glyptostrobus pensilis* in southeastern China (in Chinese and English). Lingnan Agr. Jour. **2** , 397–406, 1936.

JUNIPERUS L.—CUPRESSACEAE

Small or large trees or abundantly branched shrubs with thin, occasionally scaly bark; leaves opposite or in whorls of 3, needle- or scale-like, always needle-like on young plants, on older plants either all needle-like or all scale-like or both types together; plants dioecious or monoecious, male flowers ovate, terminal on short branchlets or axillary, several grouped in heads, rarely solitary, female flowers globose, with short, scaly stalks or (on *J. sabina*) at the end of longer branchlets; berry-cones composed of 3–6 fleshy, enlarged scales, tightly enclosed within the scale bulge, ripening in the first or second year, usually dark blue when ripe and whitish pruinose, fruit flesh dry, fibrous or soft, very resinous; seeds 1–10, distinct or grouped in a seed pit, hard shelled, angular; cotyledons usually 2 or 4–6. $x = 11$, on *J. chinensis* $x = 22$.—About 60 species in the Northern Hemisphere, widely disseminated from the polar region to the mountains of the tropics. Range map, Fig. 78.

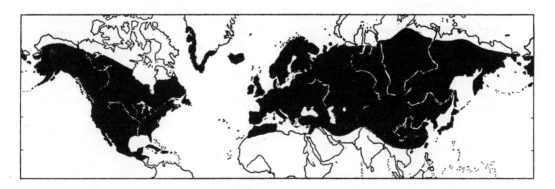

Fig. 78. The range of the genus *Juniperus,* with the exception of *J. procera,* E. Africa
(from Meusel, modified)

Outline of the genus *Juniperus*
(from Gaussen)

(The outline contains only those species covered in this book; the nomenclature of Gaussen is not retained in all cases)

Subgenus I. **Caryocedrus** (Endl.) Gaussen

Leaves all needle-like, 3–4 mm wide, in whorls of 3, spreading, segmented at the base, base decurrent on the twig, stiff and sharp tipped; male flowers 3–6 in the leaf axils; berry-cones to 2.5 cm thick, seeds connate in a seed pit:

J. drupaceae

Subgenus II. **Oxycedrus** (Spach) Gaussen
Leaves all needle-like, 1.5–3 mm wide, in whorls of 3, spreading, segmented at the base, base never decurrent on the twig; berry-cones small, seed not fused;

Section **Oxycedroides** Gaussen
Leaves with 2 white stomatal bands on the upper side, separated by a green midline, cones not blue:
J. brevifolia, cedrus, formosana, oxycedrus ssp. *macrocarpa, taxifolia*

Section **Rigidoides** Gaussen
Leaves with a broad white midstripe above:
J. communis, conferta, procumbens, rigida

Section **Recurvoides** Gaussen
Leaves decurrent; fruits blue-black, with 1 seed, smooth; Asiatic species:
J. kansuensis, morrisonicola, recurva, squamata

Subgenus III. **Sabina** (Spach) Gaussen
Juvenile foliage needle-like, in whorls of 3, the mature form all or partly scale-like, less often all needle-like, not segmented at the base, decurrent, without distinct winter buds; plants dioecious or monoecious, male flowers solitary, axillary; ovules 3–6 (10), 1–2 before the carpels or solitary, terminal; fruit cones usually composed of 6 scales:

● Leaves very finely dentate (visible with hand lens)

Section **Phoenicioides** Gaussen
Fruits red when ripe, then dark red to black, with only one seed; Eurasia, Central Asia:
J. convallium, mekongensis, phoenicia, pseudosabina, saltuaria, seravshanica, wallichiana, zaidamensis

Section **Pachyphlaeoides** Gaussen
American species with dentate leaves. No blue fruits:
J. californica, deppeana, durangensis, flaccida, pachyphlaea, pinchotii

Section **Occidentalis** Gaussen
American species with dentate leaves and blue fruits:
J. ashei, occidentalism monosperma

● ● Leaves entire
Section **Excelsoides** Gaussen
Fruits red, black or blue-black, with 1–3 seeds; Africa, Orient, Central Asia:
J. centrasiatica, distans, excelsa, foetidissima, glaucescens, komarovii, macropoda, potaninii, procera, przewalskii, ramulosa, semiglobosa, tibetica

Section **Chinensioides** Gaussen
Fruits blue; Europe to E. Asia:
J. chinensis, davurica, sabina, thurifera

Section **Virginioides** Gaussen
Fruits blue or brown, with several seeds; N. America:
J. barbadensis, bermudiana, horizontalis, scopulorum, silicicola, virginiana

Outline of the relationships of the prominent cultivars
to species of *Juniperus*

'Admirabilis'	→ *horizontalis*
'Admiral'	→ *scopulorum*
'Adpressa'	→ *horizontalis*
'Albospica'	→ *virginiana*
'Alpina'	→ *horizontalis*
'Ames'	→ *chinensis*
'Andorra'	= *horizontalis* **'Plumosa'**
'Andorra Compact'	→ *horizontalis*
'Arbuscula'	→ *chinensis*
'Arcadia'	→ *sabina*
'Argentea'	→ *horizontalis*
'Armstrongii'	→ × *media*
"B 2"	= *communis* **'Suecica'**
'Bar Harbor'	→ *horizontalis*
'Belvedere'	→ *chinensis* **'Echiniformis'**
'Berkshire'	→ *communis*
'Berry Hill'	→ × *media*
'Blaauw'	→ × *media*
'Blaue Donau'	= *sabina* **'Blue Danube'**
'Black Hill's Creeper'	= **'Emerson'**
'Blue Alps'	→ *chinensis*
'Blue Carpet'	→ *squamata*
'Blue Chip'	→ *horizontalis*
'Blue Cloud'	→ × *media*
'Blue Danube'	→ *sabina*
'Blue Heaven'	→ *scopulorum*
'Blue Moon'	→ *horizontalis*
'Blue Pacific'	→ *conferta*
'Blue Point'	→ *chinensis*
'Blue Rug'	= **'Wiltonii'**
'Blue Star'	→ *squamata*
'Blue Wiltonii'	= **'Wiltonii'**
'Bonin Isles'	→ *procumbens*
'Boskoop Purple'	→ *virginiana*
'Broadmoor'	→ *sabina*
'Bruns'	→ *communis* 'Suecica'
'Buffalo'	→ *sabina*
'Burkii'	→ *virginiana*
'Campbellii'	= *chinensis* **'Stricta'**
'Canaertii'	→ *virginiana*
'Castlewellan'	→ *recurva*
'Chamberlaynii'	→ *virginiana*
'Chandler's Silver'	→ *scopulorum*
'Cinerascens'	→ *squamata*
'Chinese Silver'	→ *virginiana*
'Cologreen'	→ *scopulorum*
'Columnaris' (*comm.*)	= **'Suecica Nana'**
'Columnaris' (*chinensis*)	→ *chinensis*
'Columnaris Glauca'	→ *chinensis*
'Compressa'	→ *communis*
'Cracovica'	→ *communis*
'Cupressifolia'	→ *sabina*
'Cupressifolia'	→ *virginiana*
'Den Boer'	→ × *media*
'Densa'	→ *recurva*
'Depressa Aurea'	→ *communis*
'Douglasii'	→ *horizontalis*
'Echiniformis'	→ *chinensis*
'Elegantissima'	→ *virginiana*
'Embley Park'	→ *recurva*
'Emerald Sea'	→ *conferta*
'Emerald Spreader'	→ *horizontalis*
'Emerson'	→ *horizontalis*
'Erecta' (*communis*)	→ *communis*
'Erecta' (*sabina*)	→ *sabina*
'Expansa'	→ *dahurica*
'Expansa Variegata'	→ *dahurica*

'Fairview'	→ *chinensis*
'Fastigiata' (*sabina*)	→ *sabina*
'Fastigiata' (*virginiana*)	→ *virginiana*
'Filicina'	→ *horizontalis*
'Filifera'	→ *virginiana*
'Fruitlandii'	→ × *media*
'Gareei'	→ *scopulorum*
'Glauca Major'	= *horizontalis* **'Douglasii'**
'Glenmore'	→ *horizontalis*
'Globe'	→ *scopulorum*
'Globosa'	→ × *media*
'Globosa' (*virginiana*)	→ *virginiana*
'Globosa Cinerea'	→ × *media*
'Gold Beach'	→ *communis*
'Gold Coast'	→ *chinensis*
'Golden'	→ *procumbens*
'Golden Flame'	→ *squamata*
'Golden Saucer'	→ × *media*
'Graciosa'	→ *communis*
'Gray Gleam'	→ *scopulorum*
'Grey Owl'	→ *virginiana*
'Haverbeck'	→ *communis*
'Heidegeist'	→ *communis*
'Helle'	→ *chinensis* 'Spartan'
'Hetzii'	→ × *media*
'Hetz's Columnaris'	= **'Fairview'**
'Hibernica'	→ *communis*
"Hibernica Erecta"	= **'Erecta'** (*communis*)
"Hibernica Excelsa Pyramidalis"	= **'Pyramidalis'** (*comm.*)
"Hibernica Pyramidalis"	= **'Pyramidalis'** (*comm.*)
'Hicksii'	→ *sabina*
'Hillii'	→ *virginiana*
'Hillspire'	→ *virginiana*
'Holger'	→ *squamata*
'Holmes Silver'	→ *scopulorum*
"Hollywood Juniper"	= **'Kaizuka'**
'Hornibrookii'	→ *communis*
'Hornibrook's Gold'	→ *communis*
'Horstmann'	→ *communis*
'Hughes'	→ *horizontalis*
'Hulkjaerhus'	→ *communis*
'Iowa'	→ *chinensis*
'Jade	→ *sabina*
'Japonica'	→ *chinensis*
'Kaizuka'	→ *chinensis*
'Kenyonii'	→ *scopulorum*
'Keteleerii'	→ *chinensis*
'Kobold'	→ *virginiana*
'Kosteri'	→ *chinensis*
'Lakewood Globe'	→ *scopulorum*
'Lividus'	→ *horizontalis*
'Loderi'	→ *squamata*
'Lönsgrab'	→ *communis*
'Laney'	→ *chinensis*
'Manhattan Blue'	→ *virginiana*
'Marcellus'	→ *horizontalis*
"Marshall"	= **'Emerson'**
'Mathot'	→ × *media*
'Meyer'	→ *communis*
'Meyeri'	→ *squamata*
'Mint Julep'	→ × *media*
'Moffetii'	→ *scopulorum*
'Monarch'	→ *chinensis*
'Monstrosa'	→ *virginiana*
'Montana'	→ *scopulorum*
'Moraine'	→ × *media*
'Mordigan Aurea'	→ *chinensis*
'Mountbatten'	→ *chinensis*

'Musgrave'	→ *sabina*
'Myosurus'	→ *phoenicia*
'Nana'(*communis*)	= *communis* **montana**
'Nana'	→ *procumbens*
'Nana'	→ *recurva*
'Nana Aurea'	→ *communis*
'Neaboriensis'	→ *chinensis*
'New Blue'	of **'Tamariscifolia'**
'Nick's Compact'	→ × *media*
'Obelisk'	→ *chinensis*
'Obergärtner Bruns'	= **'Bruns'**
'Oblonga Pendula'	→ *communis*
'O'Connor'	→ *scopulorum*
'Old Gold'	→ × *media*
'Olympia'	→ *chinensis*
'Palmeri'	→ *scopulorum* **'Repens'**
'Pathfinder'	→ *scopulorum*
'Petraeus'	→ *horizontalis*
'Pfitzeriana'	→ × *media*
'Pfitzeriana Aurea'	→ × *media*
'Pfitzeriana Compacta'	→ × *media*
'Pfitzeriana Glauca'	→ × *media*
'Planifolia'	→ *horizontalis*
'Platinum'	→ *scopulorum*
'Plumosa' (*horizontalis*)	→ *horizontalis*
'Plumosa'	→ × *media*
'Plumosa Albovariegata'	→ × *media*
'Plumosa Aurea'	→ × *media*
'Plumosa Aureovariegata'	→ × *media*
'Plumosa Tremonia'	→ × *media*
'Prostrata' (*horizontalis*)	→ *horizontalis*
'Pseudocupressus'	→ *virginiana*
'Pulchella'	→ *horizontalis*
'Pyramidalis'	→ *chinensis*
'Pyramidalis' (*communis*)	→ *communis*
'Pyramidiformis'	→ *virginiana*
'Repanda'	→ *communis*
'Repens'	→ *scopulorum*
'Richeson'	→ × *media*
'Robusta Green'	→ *virginiana*
'Rockery Gem'	→ *chinensis*
'Santa Rosa'	→ *procumbens*
saxatilis	= *communis* **montana**
'Scandens'	→ **'Skandia'**
'Schneverdinger Goldmachangel'	→ *communis*
'Schottii'	→ *virginiana*
'Sea Spray'	→ *horizontalis*
'Sentinel'	→ *communis*
'Sherwoodii'	→ *virginiana*
'Shimpaku'	→ × *media*
'Shimpaku Gold'	→ × *media*
'Shoosmith'	→ *chinensis*
'Sierra Silver'	→ *occidentalis*
'Silver Beauty'	→ *scopulorum*
'Silver Cord'	→ *scopulorum*
'Silver King'	→ *scopulorum*
"Silver Lining"	→ **'Minima'**(*communis*)
'Silver Spreader'	→ *virginiana*
'Silver Star'	→ *scopulorum*
'Skandia'	→ *sabina*
'Skyrocket'	→ *scopulorum*
'Springbank'	→ *scopulorum*
'Spartan'	→ *chinensis*
'Steel Blue'	→ *scopulorum*
'Stricta' (*chinensis*)	→ *chinensis*
'Stricta' (*communis*)	= **'Hibernica'**
'Suecica'	→ *communis*
'Suecica Aurea'	→ *communis*

'Suecica Major'	= 'Meyer'
'Suecica Nana'	→ communis
'Sulphur Spray'	→ × media
'Sutherland'	→ scopulorum
'Tabletop'	→ scopulorum
'Tage Lundell'	→ comunis
'Tamariscifolia'	→ sabina
'Tamariscifolia New Blue'	→ sabina
'Thomsen'	→ sabina
'Titlis'	→ chinensis
'Tolleson's Weeping'	→ scopulorum
'Tremonia'	= 'Plumosa Tremonia'
'Triomphe d'Angers'	→ virginiana
'Tripartita'	→ virginiana
'Turquoise Spreader'	→ horizontalis
'Viridifolia'	→ scopulorum
'Von Ehren'	→ sabina
'Waukegan Juniper'	= horizontalis 'Douglasii'
'Welchii'	→ scopulorum
'Wichita Blue'	→ scopulorum
'Wilseder Berg'	→ communis
'Wilsonii'	→ squamata
'Wilton Carpet'	= 'Wiltonii'
'Wiltonii'	→ horizontalis
'Winter Surprise'	→ × media
'Youngstown'	→ horizontalis
'Yukon Belle'	→ horizontalis

Juniperus ashei Buchh. Large, dioecious shrub or small, shrubby tree, to 6 m high, normally multistemmed, branches gray-white with age, spreading, branchlets 4 sided; leaves scale-like, ovate, acute, dark gray-green, 1–2 mm long, with or without dorsal glands; ripe fruits dark blue, pruinose, oval, 8 × 7 mm in size, with 1–2 seeds, these without angles and furrows. GGy 495; CB III 19, 31 (as *J. tetragona* Schlechtend.) (= *J. mexicana* Schlechtend.). USA; Oklahoma to Texas. 1925. z9

J. barbadensis L. A tree in its habitat, to 15 m high, branches rather thin; leaves ovate, about 1.5 mm long, usually light green, acute or obtuse, rounded on the dorsal side, apex curving inward, with a narrow ovate oil gland; fruits flat-globose to kidney-shaped (!!), blue-green, 6 mm wide. GGy 510 (= *J. lucayana* Britt. p. p.; *J. virginiana* var. *australis* Endl.; *J. virginiana* var. *barbadensis* Gord.). Barbados, Bahamas, Cuba, Haiti, Jamaica. Often confused with *J. bermudiana* (differing in the 4 sided, stiff branches) and *J. silicicola* (fruits ovate). z9

J. bermudiana L. Bermuda Juniper. A tree in its habitat, 12–15 m high, bark dark red, crown stoutly branched, branchlets 4 sided, stiff, to 2 mm thick; leaves scale-like and in 4 rows, ovate, obtuse, 1.5–2 mm long, curving inward at the apex, gray-green to blue-green, usually distinctly furrowed on the dorsal side; juvenile foliage awl-shaped (subulate), to 12 mm long; fruits more or less globose, blue-green, ripening the 1st year, with 2–3 glossy, brown, furrowed seeds. CB III 6 and 49 (as *Diselma archeri*); CCE 191. Bermuda Islands. Fig 94C. z9

J. brevifolia (Seub.) Antoine. Small tree or only a shrub (at high altitudes in its habitat), branches short and very numerous, densely foliate; all leaves needle-like, in whorls of 3, 6–9 mm long and 1–2 mm wide, base thickened, apex round or short acuminate, with 2 broad, white stomatal bands above, midrib and margin green, the keeled underside likewise green; fruits globose, red-brown, 8 to 10 mm thick, with 3 seeds. CB III 7; OCC 147; Antoine, Kupr. Gatt; Pl. 20–22 (= *J. oxycedrus* var. *brevifolia* Seub.). Known only in the Azores, in mountains from 600 to 1500 m. Fig. 80C. z9

J. californica. Carr. Shrub, occasionally also a tree, to 12 m, conical, stem irregularly twisted, bark brown to ash-gray, exfoliating in long, thin strips, branches very flexible, branchlets stiff, thickish; needles in whorls of 3, scale-like, yellow-green, 1.5–2 mm long, usually round on the dorsal side and with a distinct gland, margin very finely dentate; fruits ovate, 1.5–2 cm long, red-brown, bluish pruinose, edible, dry and somewhat sweet, with 1–2 large seeds. CB III 8; GGy 507, 508; OCC 148. SW. USA, S. Oregon to S. California, Mexico, in the coastal mountains. 1853. Plate 68. z9

J. cedrus Webb & Berthelot. Tree, to 30 m, but usually much lower, with a short, thick trunk and outspread branches, twigs pendulous, well branched, limp, angular, blue-green; needles in whorls of 3, stiff, narrow lanceolate, outspread, directed forward on the short branchlets, 15–20 mm long, blue-green, with distinct midrib above, this only half as wide as the white stomatal bands; plants dioecious; fruits globose, 10–12 mm thick, red-brown, bluish pruinose. OCC 148; CB III 9; CCE 194. Canary Islands; growing as a tree on the edges of volcanic crater pits and other such inaccessible places, has been eradicated elsewhere. Fig. 90B. z9

J. centrasiatica Komar. Tree, to 12 m high, densely gray-green foliate crown, branchlets erect, 2 mm thick; leaves scale-like, triangular with a broad base, apex obtuse, gray-green, keeled on the dorsal side and usually without glands; fruits globose to more oblong, about 1 cm long, black, with only 1 seed. GGy 504. Central Asia, Kuen-lun-Mountains, at 3000–4000 m. z5?

J. chinensis L. Tree or shrub, to 20 m high in its habitat, crown broad or narrowly conical or also shrubby or procumbent, branchlets thin and with 2 leaf forms; the scale leaves narrow-rhombic, tightly appressed, about 1.5 mm long, obtuse, arranged in 4 rows, green with a light border and indented glands on the dorsal side, needle-like leaves also occurring on wild plants and occasionally found over the entire plant of both sexes, in whorls of 3 or in decussate pairs, about 8–12 mm long, with a green midrib above and 2 blue-white stomatal bands, apex prickly; plants dioecious, male flowers yellow; fruits globose, 6–8 mm thick, brown, mealy pruinose, ripening the 2nd year, with 2–3 seeds. x = 22. CB II 75; MJu 12; CCE 196, 197. China, Mongolia and Japan. Before 1767. Plate 68; Fig. 79A. z3–9.

Including many cultivars:

'Ames' (Many). Broadly conical, upright habit; all leaves subulate, steel blue, but eventually becoming more green. Selected by F. J. Maney, Iowa State College, 1935, but first introduced in 1947.

'Arbuscula'. Female, possibly *J. chinensis* × *J. sabina*. Conical habit; all leaves scale-like, unpleasant scent when crushed (= *J.*

Plate 49

Cryptomeria japonica 'Viminalis'
in Wakehurst Place, England

Cryptomeria japonica 'Dacrydioides
in the Copenhagen Bot. Garden, Denmark

Cryptomeria japonica 'Monstrosa Nana'
in the Breda Nursery, Spain

Cryptomeria japonica 'Spiralis'
in the Villa Maria Park, Cadenabbia, Italy

Plate 50

Cryptomera japonica 'Kilmacurragh'
in the Royal Bot. Garden, Edinburgh, Scotland

Cryptomeria japonica 'Vilmoriniana'
in the Blijdenstein Arboretum, Holland

× *Cupressocyparis leylandii*
in RHS Gardens, Wisley, England
Photo: N. K. Gould

Cryptomeria japonica 'Ashio-sugi'
in its native habitat, Japan
Photo: Prof. Dr. H. Kruse, Tokyo

Plate 51

Cryptomeria japonica
in a natural forest, Japan
Photo: Forest Agency, Tokyo

Cryptomeria japonica 'Nana Albospica'
in the Taranto Gardens, Pallanza, Italy

Cunninghamia lanceolata
in Les Barres Arboretum, France

Cunninghamia lanceolata,
staminate flowers, enlarged
Photo: G. Varga, Ungarn

Plate 52

Cunninghamia lanceolata in China;
4 years old but 5 m high!
Photo: F. Bencat, USSR

Cunninghamia lanceolata with beautiful habit
in the Pietermaritzburg Bot. Garden, Natal,
South Africa

Cupressus forbesii
in the Hillier Arboretum, England

Cupressus guadalupensis
in the Nikita Bot. Garden,
Jalta, Crimea, USSR

Cupressus arizonica in Orselina,
near Muralto, Switzerland

Plate 53

Cupressus arizonica
in its native habitat in Arizona, USA
Photo: U.S. Forest Service

Cupressus lusitanica
in Crarae, Scotland

Cupressus macrocarpa in its native habitat in Monterey, California
Photo: U.S. Forest Service

Plate 54

Cupressus sempervirens, extra narrow,
in the Horticultural Research Station, Pretoria,
S. Africa

Cupressus sempervirens,
branch with cones
Photo: G. Varga, Hungary

Cupressus sempervirens in the Marimurtra Garden in Blanes, Gerona Province, Spain

Plate 55

Cupressus arizonica 'Compacta'
in the Hillier Arboretum, England

Cunninghamia lanceolata 'Compacta'
in the Kámoni Arboretum, Hungary

Dacrydium cupressinum on Garnish Island, Ireland

Plate 56

Ephedra lomatolepis
in its native habitat in the Prilijska Desert,
Central Asia (USSR)
Photo: F. Bencat

Ephedra intermedia
in its native habitat in Tien Shan Mts., Central Asia
Photo: K. Browicz

Ephedra major
in the Geneva Botanic Garden, Switzerland

Ephedra americana var. *andina*
in the Lyon Botanic Garden, France

Ephedra distachya ssp. *helvetica*
in the Hanover Botanic Garden, W. Germany

Ephedra equisetina
in the Blijdenstein Pinetum, Hilversum, Holland

Plate 57

Ephedra minuta
in the Göteborg Botanic Garden, Sweden

Glyptostrobus lineatus in its habitat
Photo: B. Rollet

Juniperus recurva 'Castlewellan'
in the Castlewellan Park, N. Ireland

Juniperus recurva var. *coxii*
in the Exeter Botanic Garden, England

Plate 58

Ginkgo biloba in the Hluboká Castle Park, Vltavou, Czechoslovakia
Photo: G. Hiekova

Plate 59

Pyramidal forms of *Juniperus chinensis* 'Kaizuka' (trimmed)
in a public park in Hang-tschou, China
Photo: F. Bencat

Juniperus chinensis 'Kaizuka', growing in the open and untrimmed in the Hillier Arboretum, England

Plate 60

Juniperus communis 'Suecica'
in the Boskoop Experiment Station, Holland

Juniperus communis,
fruiting branch

Juniperus communis; typical juniper landscape in the Lueneburg Heath, W. Germany
Photo: Landesbildstelle Hanover

Plate 61

Juniperus phoenicia
in its native habitat near Dubrovnik, Yugoslavia

Juniperus oxycedrus, branch,
in the Bern Botanic Garden, Switzerland

Juniperus thurifera in its native habitat
in St. Crépien, near Briancon, S. Africa
Photo: R. Ruffier-Lanche

Juniperus excelsa
in its native habitat in the Cilician Taurus Mts.
Photo: W. Schacht

Plate 62

Cryptomeria japonica
in the U. S. National Arboretum
Washington, D. C., USA

Cryptomeria japonica 'Globosa Nana',
a very winter hardy dwarf form

Cryptomeria japonica 'Cristata'
in the Hamburg Botanic Garden, W. Germany

Cryptomeria japonica 'Compacta'
in the Royal Botanic Garden, Edinburgh, Scotland

Plate 63

Cephalotaxus fortunei
in the park of the Eden-Panorama Hotel
(earlier the Hortus Rovelli) in Pallanza, Italy

Cephalotaxus harringtonia 'Fastigiata'
in the Thiensen Arboretum, Ellerhoop, Holland

Cupressuss arizonica 'Fastigiata'
branch with young cones,
Hamburg Botanic Garden, W. Germany

Cupressus guadalupensis
has a smooth bark exfoliating
in thin plates and strips

Plate 64

Ginkgo biloba with "aerial roots",
at Mount Congreve, Kilmeaden, South Ireland

Glyptostrobus lineatus, branch with young cones
at the Hamburg Botanic Garden, W. Germany

Ginkgo biloba in fall foliage as a street tree in Washington D. C., USA

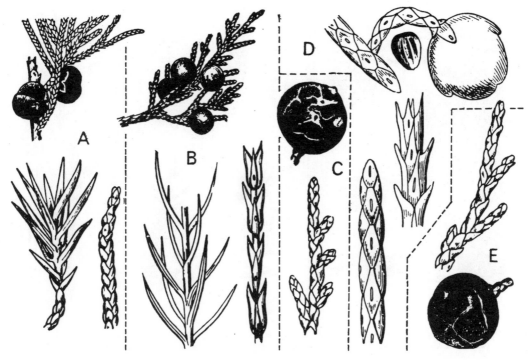

Fig. 79. **Juniperus,** parts of branches and cones, enlarged.
(A. *J. chinensis,* B. *J. virginiana,* C. *J. excelsa,* D. *J. sabina,* E. *J. foetidissima*)

chinensis var. *arbuscula* [van Melle] Cornman; *J. × media* var. *arbuscula* van Melle).

'Aurea' (Young). Male, slender conical, slow growing, to 5 m or more high, branches ascending, branchlets with 2 needle-forms; subulate needles with 2 indistinct blue-white stomatal bands above, midrib and margin yellow-green, scale needles golden-yellow. SN 116 (H); WDw 121 (H), Pl. 9A (Br); CCE 195. Developed about 1855 in the Maurice Young Nursery, Milford Surrey, England. Introduced in 1972. An attractive yellow form, but susceptible to sunscald as a young plant.

'Blue Alps' (F. J. Grootendorst 1978). Strong upright grower, branches more or less nodding; foliage blue-green, similar to *J. squamata* 'Holger' in color, needles sharp.

'Blue Point'. Very regular, acute conical form with ovate spreading base, very densely branched; foliage blue-gray.

'Columnaris'. Habit open columnar, to 8 m high, branches and twigs upright; needles awl-shaped. OCC 150; CCE 195 (= *J. chinensis columnaris* Fairchild; *J. chinensis pyramidalis* Kumlien). Selected from seed introduced from Hupeh, China, in 1905 at Glenn Dale, Md., USA. Very similar to 'Mas'.

'Columnaris Glauca'. Columnar habit, like the above, but more densely branched; needles awl-shaped, to 12 mm long and 1.5 mm wide, sharp acuminate, but silver-gray. Developed by the same selection process as the above form. Widely grown in the USA as "Blue Column Juniper".

'Dropmore'. Dwarf form, broad hemispherical habit, very densely branched, exceptionally slow growing; mature leaves decussate, needle leaves only 3 mm long, not spreading at the tips. WM 201 (H). Introduced by F. L. Skinner, Dropmore, Manitoba, Canada. 1938.

'Echiniformis'. Dwarf form, globose to more flat-globose, branches very short, densely crowded; all leaves needle-like, very small, spreading on the branch tips. WM 81C (Br), 200, 202 (H) (= *J. communis echinoformis* Beissn., *J. oxycedrus*

echinoformis Van Houtte). Origin unknown, presumably introduced however, by Rinz of Frankfurt, W. Germany before 1887. A specimen is growing in the Belvedere Alpine Garden, Vienna, Austria; see illustration in WM 201 (H). Plate 69; Fig. 84C.

'Excelsior'. Female, American form, columnar, to 4 m high, similar to 'Keteleerii', but growth less regular; all leaves on the lower portion of the plant awl-shaped, scale-like on the upper half, dark green. Morris Arboretum, Philadelphia, USA, before 1943.

'Fairview'. Narrow-conical habit, growth vigorous; leaves mostly awl-shaped, occasionally scale-like on individual branches, light green (= *J. sinensis pyramidalis* 'Fairview' Grootendorst). Developed from seed in the Evergreen Nurseries, Fairview, Pennsylvania, USA, about 1930.

'Femina'. Female, conical, to 5 m high, branches spreading, thin, limp, numerous branchlets; leaves scale-like, appressed, blue pruinose, occasionally awl-shaped leaves present; fruits globose to irregular-oblong, 5–7 mm thick, blue-white pruinose at first, later dark blue. OCC 151; CCE 199 (= *J. reevesiana* Hort.; *J. sphaerica* var. *dioica* van Melle). Presumably brought to England in 1861 by R. Fortune.

'Helle' see **'Spartan'.**

'Iowa' (Maney). Female, similar to 'Ames', and of the same origin, but taller and wider; leaves partly subulate, partly scale-like, bluish-green. KN104. Developed from seed about 1937 by T. J. Maney, but first introduced in 1947.

'Jacobiniana'. Regular columnar habit, to 2.5 m high, branches erect, secondary branches short, branchlets numerous, thin; leaves awl-shaped, blue-green, also with scale-leaves on older plants, these more gray-green, monoecious (= *J. jacobiniana* de Vos). Known in cultivation before 1887 but origin unknown.

'Japonica'. Wide dwarf form, occasionally also procumbent or irregularly conical, to 2 m high, often with a single main stem,

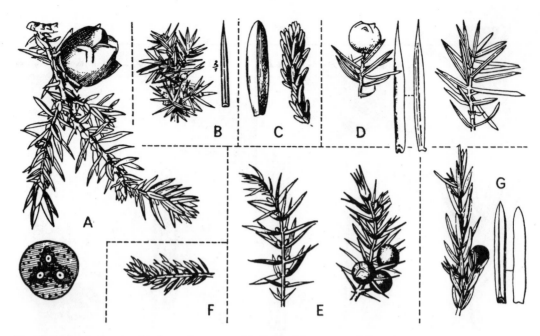

Fig. 80 **Juniperus**, parts of twigs and cones and individual leaves, partially enlarged (A. *J. drupaceae*, B. *J. oxycedrus*, C. *J. brevifolia*, D. *J. formosana*, E. *J. communis*, F. *J. communis* ssp. *nana*, G. *J. taxifolia*)

branches ascending, older plants with yellow-green scale-leaves at the branch tips, tips drooping, especially the twigs with scale-leaves, twigs short and densely arranged, most densely covered with needle-like leaves, these in whorls of 3, very sharply acuminate and prickly, with 2 blue-stomatal bands above, lightly keeled beneath and light green. WDw 122 (H); WM 15A (Br) (= *J. chinensis japonica* [Carr.] Lav.; *J. chinensis procumbens* Beissn.). Not to be confused with *J. chinensis* 'Plumosa' as is often done in the trade.

'**Kaizuka**'. "Hollywood Juniper". Broad, shrubby, upright habit, 3–4 m high or more, branches spreading very irregularly and gracefully, twigs arranged in groups along the branches; leaves bright green, scale-like, occasionally with a few needle leaves; fruits ovate, most longer than wide, distinctly violet pruinose. WDw 123 (H), Pl. 9C (Br); DB 1962: 158; LT 53; MJu 9; WM 15B (Br) (= *J. chinensis* var. *torulosa* Bail.; *J. sheppardii* var. *torulosa* [Bail.] van Melle). Exported from Japan to the USA by the Yokohama Nursery about 1920. This plant, with its interesting habit, has great promise for the future. Plate 59.

A yellow variegated form is also available, '**Variegated Kaizuka**'.

'**Keteleeri**'. Female, dense columnar form or also more conical, to 10 m high, occasionally higher, branches ascending, secondary branches numerous, short, very thin; leaves scale-like, very acute, green, light bluish pruinose; fruits irregularly globose, 12–15 mm thick, blue-white pruinose, on reflexed stalks, fruits abundantly. KEv 169. Cultivated before 1910, presumably developed or imported by Keteleer.

'**Leeana**' (Lee). Male, slender columnar form, very densely branched, branches horizontal, tips lightly nodding; leaves mostly scale-like, but also needle-like, then to 12 mm long, bright green on both sides (= *J. leeana* R. Smith). Developed before 1865 in the Lee Nursery, Hammersmith, London.

'**Maney**'. (Maney). Broad upright habit, irregular; leaves all subulate, bluish and pruinose. WM 205 (H). Selected by F. J. Maney in 1935, introduced in 1947 but surpassed now by better forms.

'**Mas**'. Tree-like, columnar, to 20 m high, branches outspread and ascending, with numerous short twigs very close to the trunk; needles partly subulate and in whorls of 3, stiff, sharply acuminate and prickly, distinctly bluish-white striped above, green beneath, partly with yellow-green scale leaves, especially on the flowering shoots; flowers abundantly in spring. BFN 604(H).

'**Mission Spire**'. Seedling selection, broad, compact columnar form supposedly about 3–4 m high in 15 years, 1.2 m wide at the base; needles glossy bluish-green, but with a distinct lilac-tone in winter and spring. Introduced to the trade by the Mission Gardens, Techny, Ill., USA.

'**Monarch**' (Grootendorst). Narrowly conical; all leaves subulate, blue-green, sharply acuminate. KN 105; WM 14C (Br), 206 (H). Selected by F. J. Grootendorst, Boskoop, Holland from Japanese seed, before 1965.

'**Mordigan Aurea**'. Compact habit; golden-yellow needles. From the USA. (Minier 1976).

'**Mountbatten**' (Sheridan). Female, narrow conical form or columnar, 4 m high in 15 years, resembling *J. communis* 'Hibernica' in form, very dense and short branched; leaves mostly needle-like, gray-green; fruits very abundantly. From seed in the Sheridan Nurseries, Canada; introduced to the trade in 1948.

'**Neaboriensis**'. Columnar form, 3–5 m high; with needle and scale leaves, needle leaves widely spaced, more or less stiff and prickly, wide spreading, often short or very short, silvery-green, scale leaves green to blue-green. OCC 154 (= *J. chinensis neaboriensis* [Veitch] Beissn.; *J. sphaerica* var. *neaboriensis* [Veitch] van Melle). Origin unknown; according to van Melle possibly collected by Father A. David in Shensi, China. 1881. Fig. 82B.

'**Obelisk**' (Grootendorst 1946). Slender, often somewhat irregular columnar form, 3 m high or higher, by about 1 m wide, branches ascending, short, twigs develop in the same manner, branch tips erect; all leaves needle-like, erect and directed

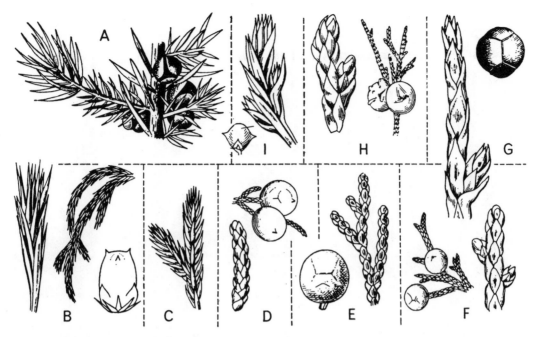

Fig. 81. **Juniperus,** parts of twigs and cones; some enlarged (A. *J. rigida,* B. *J. recurva,* C. *J. procumbens,* D. *J. osteosperma,* E. *J. phoenicia,* F. *J. occidentalis,* G. *J. thurifera,* H. *J. deppeana,* I. *J. squamata)*

forward, lightly bowed, 10–15 mm long, 1.5–2 mm wide at the middle, with 2 blue-white stomatal bands above, blue pruinose beneath, long and sharply acuminate. WDw 124 (H), Pl. 9E (BR); OCC 155; KN 106; CCE 199; WMK 14D (Br). Developed by F. J. Grootendorst about 1930 from Japanese seed, but first introduced in 1946. Holds its typical form without any trimming, slow growing, about 3 m high in 20 years.

'Olympia' (Grootendorst 1956). Slender columnar form, branches ascending, branchlets short, with scale and needle leaves, the former tightly appressed and bluish, the latter to 12 mm long, with 2 white stomatal bands above, greenish-blue beneath, sharply acuminate, prickly. CCE 199. Developed by F. J. Grootendorst, Boskoop, Holland from Japanese seed around 1930; introduced in 1956. Fig. 82C.

'Pyramidalis'. Male, dense and narrow columnar, blue-green, branches ascending; leaves mostly needle-like and prickly sharp. WM 14A (Br), 208 (H). Imported into Belgium from Japan in 1843.

'Rockery Gem' (Lefeber). Habit dense and very low, becoming somewhat taller than *J. sabina* 'Tamariscifolia'. Introduced by Lefeber & Co., Boskoop, Holland. 1967.

'San Jose' (Clarke). Procumbent, dwarf form, growth irregular in all directions, branchlets and leaves blue-green, the latter scale and awl-shaped, but soft and not prickly. WM 14E (Br), 210 (H). Originated in San Jose, California, USA by W. B. Clarke in 1935. Much used in California.

var. *sargentii* see **J. sargentii**

'Sheppardii'. Multistemmed shrub, 3–4 m high, young plants differ from old in habit, young plants usually regular conical, old plants irregularly conical, open branched, twigs partly crowded, partly sparse, occasionally with long, filamentous branch tips; leaves needle and scale-like, mostly gray-green; plants mono- or dioecious; fruits with 2–4 (6) seeds. MJu 4 and 5 (H) (= *J. sheppardii* [Veitch] van Melle). Presumably introduced before 1850 by Fortune, from China.

'Shoosmith'. Dwarf form, globose or conical habit, very dense and compact; leaves needle-like, 5–10 mm long, 0.6–0.8 mm wide, very thin, prickly acuminate, with 2 indistinct stomatal bands above, dark green beneath. KN 107. Developed about 1930 in the Southside Nursery, Pennsylvania, USA. Introduced to the trade by F. Shoosmith.

'Spartan'. Slender conical habit, tall, densely branched, a beautiful green (= *J. chinensis* 'Densaerecta'; 'Helle'). Introduced by the Monrovia Nurseries of California, USA in 1961.

'Stricta'. Narrowly conical, acute, very densely branched, branches ascending, regularly arranged, twigs also erect, rather short; leaves only needle-like, blue-green above, pruinose beneath, steel-blue in winter, soft to the touch. WDw 125 (H), Pl. 9G (Br); MJu 607 (as *J. sheppardii* var. *pyramidalis*); KN 102; CCE 121; WM 209 (H) (= *J. chinensis stricta* den Ouden; *J. excelsa stricta* Hort. Americ.; *J. chinensis* 'Campbellii'). Very popular and much planted form, first disseminated from Holland in 1945.

'Titlis' (Draijer 1972). Compact columnar habit, but more or less open and irregularly branched; foliage silvery-blue, sharp to the touch.

'Variegata'. Conical habit, densely branched, twigs ascending, new shoots thick, some white or with white markings; leaves mostly awl-shaped, bluish pruinose, green beneath, very similar to 'Stricta' in color. WDw Pl. 9B (Br); CCE 201. Imported from Japan to Holland by Siebold about 1860. A very pretty form; must be propagated from the variegated twigs to retain white markings.

'Wilson's Weeping' (Clarke). Variable form, mostly flat, broad, vase-shaped, to 2 m wide and 1 m high, branch tips more or less filamentous and nodding, originating from tip cuttings, but also seen as a broad conical form, hardly distinguishable from *J. chinensis;* leaves partly needle-, partly scale-like, gray-green with a bluish trace. Introduced in 1934 by W. B. Clarke, San Jose, California, USA.

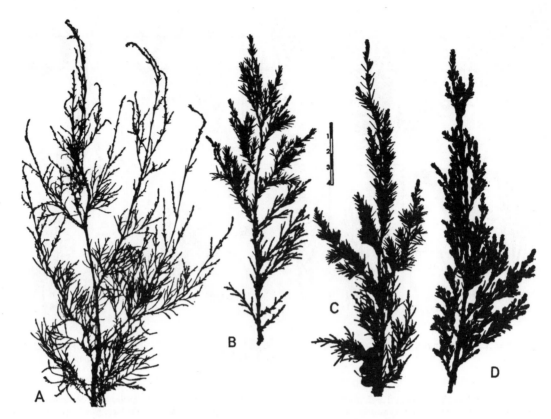

Fig. 82. **Juniperus**. A. *J.* × *media* 'Blue Cloud'; B. *J. chinensis* 'Neaboriensis';
C. *J. chinensis* 'Olympia'; D. *J. sargentii* (Original)

J. communis L. Common Juniper. Tree-like, to 15 m
high, or only a shrub, usually multistemmed, 3 to 5 m
high, habit quite variable, bark smooth at first, later
fibrous, gray-brown, young shoots triangular, with
longitudinal ridges; leaves always needle-like, 3–15 mm
long, 1–2 mm wide, straight, usually gray-green,
shallowly grooved above and with a broad white band,
limb green; plants usually dioecious; fruits ripening the
2nd or 3rd year, globose to more oval, green in the first
year, then white-blue pruinose, black when fully ripe, 6–
9 mm thick, short stalked; seeds in 3's, distinct. CCE 204.
Europe, N. Asia to N. China, N. Africa, N. America. Plate
42 and 60; Fig. 80E and 84B. z2–6

Includes many cultivars:

'Arnold' (Arnold). Mutation of *J. communis* 'Suecica', very
narrow columnar habit, fast growing; needles pale green, like
those of 'Hibernica', but shorter. CCE 206. Discovered in 1951,
introduced to the trade in 1958. R. Arnold, Alveslohe, Holstein,
W. Germany.

'Aurea' Normal habit; needles yellow at first, later greening (=
J. communis f. *aureovariegata* Beissn.). (VR)

'Berkshire'. A ssp. *nana* type, very slow growing, nearly
cushion-like, spreading, short branched. WM213(H). Found in
the Arnold Arboretum, USA and disseminated from there.
Very meritorious.

'Bruns'. Columnar form, strictly upright, similar to 'Suecica',
but more openly branched at the peak, twigs light brown;
needles blue-green, concave above, distinctly keeled beneath

and glossy bright green. CCE 205. Introduced to the trade
about 1930 by Heinr. Bruns, of Westerstede, W. Germany, as a
wild selection obtained from Sweden. Supposedly very
resistant to rust.

'Candelabrica'. Conical habit, branches spreading candelabra-
like, ascending at the tips. Observed in 1909 in Switzerland
(Solothurner Jura) by Luescher.

'Candelabriformis'. Tree, 3–4 m high, branches horizontal and
twigs more or less pendulous, crown compact. Discovered by
G. Kuphaldt before 1937 in Lithuania. (EX?)

'Compressa'. Dwarf form, spindle form or very narrowly
conical, very slow growing (2–3 cm per year), seldom higher
than 80 cm, branches all narrowly upright, peak very acute;
needles very fine, 4–5 mm long, thin, light green, with a distinct
white stomatal band above, dark green beneath. WDw 128 (H),
Pl. 10A (Br); HD 13; CC 12 (H); KN Pl.4; CCE 205; WM 16C
(Br). Origin unknown, but cultivated before 1855. Often
confused with the much coarser 'Suecica Nana'. z7

'Conspicua'. Upright, broad, 3–5 m high, branches spreading,
tips nodding, branchlets 5–10 cm long, yellow-brown; needles
rather widely spaced, 1.5 cm long, with white stomatal bands
above and a quite narrow, light green limb, green beneath.
OCC 162 (H) (= *J. communis* 'den Ouden' 1934; *J. communis
conspicua* den Ouden 1949).

'Controversa'. Densely columnar, branches ascending, tips
nodding, branchlets bowed; needles straight, upper side
twisted outward, 12–14 mm long, blue-green beneath.
Developed in the Gimborn Arboretum, Doorn, Holland;
introduced by H. den Ouden & Zoon in 1949.

'Cracovica'. Conical form, rather open, vigorous, fast growing, to 3 m high, perhaps higher, branches partly upright, partly spreading, light brown, tips nodding; needles rather short, about 1 cm long and 1.7 mm wide, midrib blue-green, both stomatal bands blue-white, limb light green, glossy green beneath with a distinct midrib. CCE 206. Discovered before 1855 in the vicinity of Krakow, Poland. Not unusual in cultivation. Fig. 83C.

var. **depressa** Pursh. Canadian Juniper. Procumbent habit, main branches ascending, to 1 m high on old plants; needles to 15 mm long and 1.5 mm wide, often directed upward, with white stomatal band beneath. WM 17A (Br), 215 (H) (= *J. canadensis* Lodd. ex Burgsd.; *J. nana canadensis* Loud.; *J. communis* var. *canadensis* Loud.). Eastern N. America and Canada, in the mountains.

The above variety is considered a geographical variety in this work; plants labeled with this name in the nursery trade have originated from clonal propagation and therefore must carry the corresponding name. Dr. Boom called these plants 'Depressed Star' where practical. We consider other *depressa* clones to fall in the following groups:

Clones of var. *depressa*

Name	Habit	Foliage color
'Depressed Star'	flat and wide	green, brown in winter
'Depressa Aurea'	flat, medium height	bronze-yellow
'Prostrata'	creeping	green, brown in winter
'Dumosa'	flat, to 1 m high	green, brown in winter
'Gimborn'	creeping, branches ascending	green
'Vase'	nest-form	deep green, dark brown in winter

'Depressa Aurea'. Dwarf form, branches spreading, main branches ascending, middle of the plant convex or also concave; needles yellow on the branch base, the branch tips yellow in spring, later bronze. WDw 127 (H), Pl. 10K (Br); WM 216 (H); CCE 207. (= *J. communis depressa aurea* Hornibr.; *J. canadensis aurea* de Vos; *J. communis* var. *aureospica* Rehd. In cultivation before 1887. Plate 70.

'Depressed Star'. This is the plant grown in most nurseries as var. *depressa*. Growth broad and flat, branches more or less ascending, branchlets regularly arranged, about 5–10 cm long; needles green, somewhat brownish in winter. WDw 126 (H), Pl. 10E (Br); WM 217 (H). Plate 70.

'Dumosa'. Broad, low habit, branches ascending to 1 m high, secondary branches spreading with the tips somewhat drooping, young branchlets 4 sided and green, older ones cylindrical and glossy brown; needles 10 mm long and 1.5 mm wide at the base, green, with a distinct midrib beneath, stomatal bands white. OCC 163 (H); WM 218 (H). A *depressa* form originating in the Gimborn Arboretum, Doorn, Holland; introduced by H. den Ouden & Zoon, 1934.

'Echiniformis'. Plants labeled with this name in modern cultivation are, according to Welch, always *J. chinensis* 'Echiniformis'. Plate 65.

"Effusa". Plants labeled with this name in Dutch and English nurseries are practically identical to 'Rependa'. CCE 208 (= *J. communis depressa effusa* den Ouden 1949). Discovered in the Gimborn Arboretum; introduced by den Ouden about 1944.

'Erecta'. (H. A. Hesse). Columnar form, similar to 'Hibernica', but narrower, branches upright; needles 8 mm long and 1 mm wide(= *J. communis hibernica erecta* Hesse). Introduced by Herm. A. Hesse in 1896.

'Gimborn'. Clone of var. *depressa*, creeping habit, densely branched, to 1.5 m wide, branches procumbent, tips ascending, twigs numerous, short, angular, light brown; needles densely arranged, 5 to 8 mm long, 1 mm wide at the base, flat with silvery stomatal bands above, convex beneath, green (= *J. communis depressa* 'Gimborn' den Ouden 1949). Developed in the Gimborn Arboretum; introduced by H. den Ouden & Zoon.

'Gold Beach'. Dwarf form, growth quite flat, dense and wide; foliage green. Described by D. Wyman as "excellent" (Arnoldia 1968: 19) The plant in the Arnold Arboretum is only 15 cm high and 60 cm wide; said to originate from the west coast of N. America.

'Graciosa' (Konijn). Broad shrubby habit, finely branched, young bark light brown; needles fine, narrow, 5–10 mm long, light green, wtih bluish lines above, sharply pointed. Selected from a seedling by L. Konijn & Co., Reeuwijk, Holland. Before 1968.

'Haverbeck'. Very dense habit, "witches'-broom-like", distinctly dwarf, 35 cm high and 20 cm wide in 10 years; evenly covered in winter with very prickly "long needles", and tiny "bud needles" and buds, needles light blue-gray, needle length 14 and 3 mm respectively. Selected by G. Horstmann. A good substitute for 'Echiniformis' which often grows poorly. 1983.

'Heidegeist'. (G. Horstmann 1982). Strict upright habit, columnar, opening slightly at the apex; needles silver-blue. A new, exceptionally healthy form.

ssp. **hemisphaerica** (J. & C. Presl). Nyman. An alpine variety, low, dense shrub, more or less globose-bushy, to 2.5 m high, but usually lower; needles linear-oblong, 5–12 mm long and 1.3–2 mm wide, sharply acuminate, with broad white stomatal bands. WM 17D (Br), 211 (H) (= *J. hemisphaerica* Presl). High mountainous areas in the Mediterranean region. z9

'Hibernica'. Irish Juniper. Very popular, narrow, conical or columnar form, very densely branched, 3–5 m high, branch tips stiffly erect (not nodding, like 'Suecica'); needles 5–7 mm long, 1 mm wide, abruptly sharply acuminate (but not prickly like 'Suecica'), both sides bluish-green. WDw 130 (Br); BFN 581 (H); WM 16A (Br) (= *J. communis hibernica* Lodd. ex Gord.; *J. hibernica* Lodd.; *J. communis stricta* Carr.) Originally from Ireland, but now widely disseminated in cultivation.

var. **hondoensis** Satake. Very similar to var. *nipponica*, procumbent, but with wider leaves, 1.7–2 mm wide, flat, with a 0.7 to 0.9 mm wide, somewhat indented white stomatal band on the upper side; fruits globose, but flat on the apex (= *J. communis* var. *nipponica sensu auct.* Japan. p.p. non Wils). Japan; mountain slopes of Hokkaido and Honshu.

'Hornibrookii'. Dwarf form, creeping, to 2 m wide, eventually about 50 cm high (in 15 years), branches lying flat on the ground at first, tips ascending slightly, glossy dark brown, branchlets of uneven length; needles densely arranged, 5–6 mm long, prickly (!), flat above, with a broad, silver-white stomatal band, margin light green, green beneath with a distinct keel, somewhat brownish in winter. WDw 133 (H), Pl. 10L (Br); CCE 205; WM 17E (Br) (= *J. communis hornibrookii* Grootend.; *J. communis prostrata* Hornibr. non Beissn.). Discovered about 1923 by M. Hornibrook in County Galway, West Ireland. Widely cultivated today. Fig. 83A, 84A.

'Hornibrook's Gold' (M. van Klaveren & Zoon, Boskoop, 1979). Sport of 'Hornibrookii'. Quite flat, broad to creeping, branch tips more or less directed upward, branches orange-

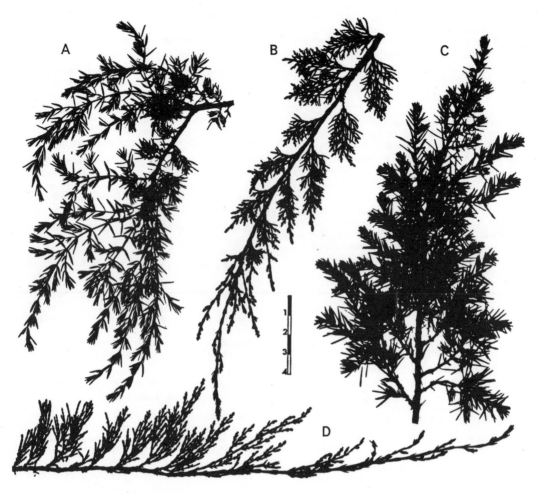

Fig. 83. **Juniperus.** A. *J. communis* 'Hornibrookii'; B. *J.* × *media* 'Blaauw';
C. *J. communis* 'Cracovica'; D. *J. horizontalis* (Original)

brown; needles in whorls of 3, sharply acuminate, 5–8 mm
long, green-yellow beneath, bronze golden-yellow in winter.
Found as a mutation in 1970. Meritorious.

'Horstmann'. Similar to *J. rigida,* with wide arching, irregularly
arranged branches, from which the twigs hang "mane-like".
Selection of G. Horstmann, Schneverdingen, W. Germany
(1982). Must be staked for the first few years. Meritorious, very
decorative novelty plant!

'Hulkjaerhus' (Thomsen). Columnar form, like 'Suecica', but
as a young plant somewhat lower and wider, older plants
hardly distinguishable from 'Suecica'; needles greener and less
prickly. Selected by Thomsen Plantskole, Skalborg, Denmark,
1962.

var. **jackii** Rehd. Procumbent, branches to 1 m long, only
sparsely branched, "whip-like" (flagellate), the branchlets
usually only a few centimeters long; needles linear-lanceolate,
thick, 10 mm long, 2.2 mm wide, sickle-shaped curving inward,
with sharp tips, distinct blue-white stomatal bands. OCC 167
(H). Mountain form from California (Siskiyou Mts.) and
Washington (Mt. Rainier) USA; in cultivation since 1907, but
quite rare.

'Jensen'. Weeping form, similar to 'Pendula', but growth
stronger; leaves shorter, arranged in dense whorls (= *J. communis pendula* 'Jensen' A. M. Jensen). Developed in the nursery
of Asger M. Jensen of Holmstrup, Denmark. Introduced in
1944.

'Laxa'. Upright, columnar, somewhat open; foliage conspicuously yellow-green. Developed about 1930 by G. D.
Boehlje.

'Loensgrab'. Broad form, 65 cm high and 50 cm wide in 10
years, branching obliquely upward, twigs numerous, very
dense, pendulous, totally covering the branches; needles light
green, white stomatal bands, 6 mm long. Selected by G.
Horstmann, Schneverdingen, W. Germany (1982).

'Meyer'. (Timm & Co. 1958). Broadly conical, to 3 m high;
foliage silvery-green. CCE 206; WM 16B (Br) (= *J. communis
suecica major* Grootendorst). Selected by Erich Meyer,
Barmstedt, W. Germany, about 1945. The spelling "Mayer" by
Boom and Welch is incorrect.

'Minima'. Dwarf form, procumbent habit, irregular, strongly
branched, branches short, brown-purple, young shoots
distinctly 3 sided, reddish above, green beneath, internodes
about 1 cm long, shorter toward the branch tips; leaves 5–8 mm
long and 1.5–2 mm wide, densely arranged at the branch tips,
obtuse (not prickly), very broad blue-white striped above,
green beneath, bluish pruinose, convex, obtuse keeled. WDw
Pl. 10F and G (Br), 136 (H); WM 16F (Br), 222 (H) (= *J. communis nana prostrata* Horn.; *J. communis prostrata* Hort. Holl. non
Pers.; *J. communis* var. *minima* Grootend.; *J. communis* 'Silver
Lining' Welch). Cultivated for over l00 years in Boskoop,
Holland.

Fig. 84. **Juniperus.** A. *J. communis* 'Hornibrookii'; B. *J. communis*;, C. *J*; *chinensis* 'Echiniformis';
D. *J. communis* 'Repanda'; E. *J. communis* ssp. *nana* (Original)

ssp. **nana** Syme. Mountain Juniper. Procumbent, often mat-forming, 20–30 cm high, branches densely arranged, short, thick, 3 sided, often wavy, whorls usually only 1 mm apart, up to 3 mm apart on the major branches; needles usually bowed upward or curving, linear-lanceolate, 4–8 mm long, 1–2 mm wide, abruptly acuminate, distinctly concave above, with a broad, white stomatal band, rounded beneath, dark green glossy; fruits oval to nearly globose. OCC 170; WM 15D (Br), 212 (H) (= *J. communis* var. *nana* [Willd.] Baumg.; *J. nana* Willd.; *J. communis* var. *saxatilis* Pall.; *J. communis* var. *montana* Ait.; *J. sibirica* Burgsd.). Europe, alpine regions, also often on the moors; also in N. Asia and N. America. Fig. 80F, 84E.

An outline of the taxa closely related to ssp. *nana*:

Name	Characteristics
var. *hondoensis*	geographical variety, known only in Japan
'Minima'	cultivar, needles blue-white
'Nana Aurea'	cultivar, needles yellow to yellow-bronze
'Repanda'	cultivar, needles smaller, green

'Nana Aurea'. Dwarf form, procumbent, to 0.5 m high as an old plant, densely branched, covering the ground with downward directed branch tips, branchlets broadly fan-like spreading; needles silver-white striped above with a green margin, golden-yellow beneath to more bronze-yellow (in winter), easily distinguished from the other forms by this coloration. WDw Pl. 10J (Br); KN Plate 4; WM 223 (H). Unfortunately this cultivar suffers from a twig blight.

f. **oblonga** (Bieb.) Loud. Growth upright; needles 15 to 22 mm long, often reflexed; fruits only 4–5 mm thick (= *J. communis* var. *caucasica* Endl.). Transcaucasus. 1830.

'Oblonga Pendula'. Broad and open upright habit, 3–4 m high, branches upright at first, then long, nodding gracefully at the tips, branchlets 10–20 cm long, pendulous; needles 15–20 mm long, thin, stiff, sharply acuminate, prickly, with an indistinct stomatal band above, green beneath. OC 162. DJ 241; CCE 208 (= *J. communis* f. *oblongopendula* [Loud.] Beissn.). Cultivated since 1898 and still much prized. Somewhat sensitive in cultivation. z7

'Pendula'. Open upright habit, branches spreading and drooping, long pendulous; needles 10–12 mm long, in widely spaced whorls (= *J. communis reflexa* de Vos; *J. communis reflexa pendula* Carr.). Before 1855. (VR)

'Pendulina'. Habit tree-like, with a stem, branches horizontal to slightly ascending, twigs weeping, plants resembling the habit

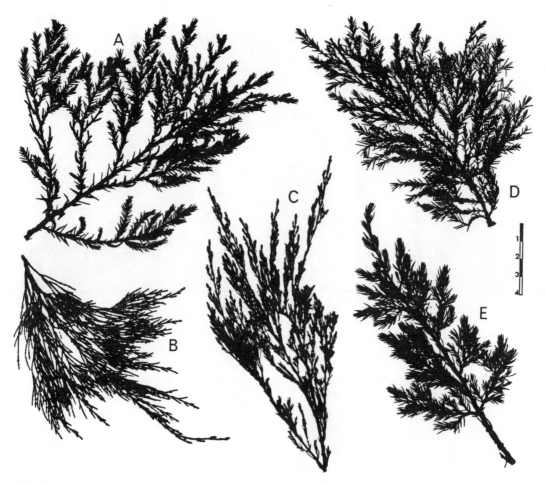

Fig. 85. **Juniperus** A. *J. distans*; B. *J. scopulorum* 'Blue Heaven'; C. *J. horizontalis* 'Andorra Compacta,; D. *J. × media* 'Pfitzeriana Compacta'; E. *J. procumbens* 'Nana' (Original)

of *Picea breweriana* in appearance (= *J. communis* var. *arborea* f. *pendulina* Kuphaldt; *J. communis pendens* den Ouden non Sudw.; *J. communis arborea pyramidalis pendula* H. A. Hesse). Found in Lithuania (presently Polland) by Kuphaldt before 1937. Introduced to the trade by H. A. Hesse in 1949.

'Prostrata'. Dwarf form, procumbent habit, 1.5–2 m wide, and only 20–30 cm high, branches radiating from a central stem; needles somewhat bowed, with a distinct silvery stomatal band above, limb and dorsal side green, brownish in late fall. CCE 207 (= *J. communis prostrata* Beissn. non Hornibr.). Discovered about 1894 by Rettig in the limestone mountains near Jena, Thueringia, E. Germany.

'Pyramidalis'. Columnar form similar to 'Hibernica', but broader growing, leaves less blue (= *J. communis hibernica excelsa pyramidalis* Hesse, 1908; *J. communis hibernica pyramidalis* Hesse 1939). Introduced by Herm. A. Hesse in 1908.

'Repanda'. Dwarf form, creeping, round and flat to 1.5 m wide and only 30–40 cm high, branches spreading radially, twigs thin, densely arranged, brown; needles 5–8 mm long, densely arranged, somewhat bowed inward, quite soft and not sharp to the touch (!), arising radially around the branch, silvery striped above, green beneath and always convex. WDw 134 (H), Pl.

10H (Br); CCE 205; WM 17G (Br), 224 (H). Discovered by M. Prichard (of M. Prichard & Sons, Nurseries, Christchurch, Hampshire, England) in Ireland; introduced in 1934 by M. Koster & Zonen, Boskoop, Holland. One of the foremost cultivars today. Fig. 84D.

'Schneverdinger Goldmachangel' (G. Horstmann, Schneverdingen 1979). Similar to 'Hibernica', branch tips remaining bright golden-yellow well into the summer; needles very large and lush, 11 mm long. This plant is not susceptible to fungal attack.

'Sentinel'. Very narrow columnar form, long acuminate. WM 16E (Br) (= *J. communis* 'Pencil Point' Sheridan Nurseries 1963). Developed in the Sheridan Nurseries, Canada before 1961.

'Suecica'. Swedish Juniper. Habit variable in its native habitat (see plate 42) and to 10 m high; plants found under this name in gardens are usually broadly columnar, but very narrow selections have been made (in Sweden), branches upright, branch tips nodding (!); leaves bluish-green, prickly; fruits oblong. WDw 132 (Br); OC 134m (H); CCE 207 (= *J. suecica* Mill.; *J. communis* var. *suecica* [Mill.] Ait.). Grows wild from Scandinavia to eastern Russia.

Outline of the more prominent Columnar Forms
('Suecica' group by Welch)

Narrowly Columnar	Broadly Columnar	Dwarf forms
'Arnold'	'Bruns'	'Compressa'
'Erecta'	'Conspicua'	'Suecica Nana'
'Hibernica'	'Cracovica'	
'Pyramidalis'	'Meyer'	
'Sentinel'	'Suecica'	
'Suecica'		

'Suecica Aurea'. New growth yellow, later yellow-green. KN Plate 5. This form is unfortunately disease prone.

'Suecica Nana'. Dwarf form, actually only a fast growing, open type of 'Compressa', columnar, narrow and dense, generally not over 1–1.5 m high and to 30 cm wide, with obtuse (!) peak, often somewhat irregular, branches and twigs ascending; needles short, blue-white striped above, blue-green beneath. WDw 129 (H), Pl. 10B (Br); WM 16D (Br), 225 (H) (= *J. communis columnaris* Hornibr.). Known in cultivation before 1929. Plate 67.

'Tage Lundell'. Dwarf form, 100 cm high and 20 cm wide in 10 years; branches and needles alternately golden-yellow, yellow variegated or green. Discovered in Sweden by Tage Lundell. 1982.

'Vase'. Low form, branches spreading wide from the very narrow middle ("vase-shaped"), to 1 m high, tips nodding, branchlets 5–10 cm long; needles 8–12 mm long, white striped above, flat, dark green beneath, chocolate-brown in winter (= *J. communis* 'Vase Shaped' Kumlien). Introduced into the trade by the D. Hill Nursery of Illinois, USA before 1936 ('Depressa' type).

'Weckii'. Slender upright, needle whorls occasionally 2 or 4 parted, spaced 5–10 mm apart; needles 15–22 mm long, usually reflexed; fruits only 4–5, thick (= *J. communis weckii* Aschers. & Graeb.). Can be observed in the wild in Hungary; Switzerland; Germany near Stuttgart, Kissingen and Berlin. Introduced 1897.

'Wilseder Berg' (G. Horstmann, Schneverdingen 1982). Very dense upright habit, narrowly columnar; needles bright green, holding their color well in winter, 12–14 mm long. Can be considered as a substitute for 'Hibernica'. Not susceptible to fungal attack.

J. conferta Parl. Shrub, procumbent, branches long and forward creeping, spreading mat-like, red-brown, tips of the branchlets erect; all leaves needle-like, in dense whorls of 3, bright green, often more gray-green in the 2nd year, 10–15 mm long, 1 mm wide, long and prickly acuminate, grooved above with 1 (not 2!) white band, without a green midrib, convex beneath; fruits globose, 8–12 mm thick, deep dark blue, gray pruinose, smooth. CB III 18; OCC 171; WDw Pl. 9H (Br); CCE 210; WM 18 A (Br) (= *J. litoralis* Maxim.). In Japan and Sachalin, developing as a dense groundcover in the sand along the sea shore. Fig. 90C. z6

'Blue Pacific'. Differing from the type in the more procumbent habit and attractive blue-green needle color. Good groundcover.

'Emerald Sea'. Forming an enduring dense mat, branches nearly spruce-like in appearance with awl-like needles, in whorls of 3, equally spaced, 1–1.5 cm long, and emerald-green, with a gray-green band above, needles yellow-green in winter. Collected by J. L. Creech as cuttings on the coast of Honshu, Japan in 1957. Very salt tolerant. Disseminated by the US National Arboretum, Washington D.C., USA 1977.

J. convallium Rehd. & Wils. Small tree, 4–9 m high in its habitat, bark gray; leaves scale-form, opposite, appressed, ovate, 1 mm long, obtuse or acute at the apex, convex and with a dorsal gland; fruits rounded, 6–8 mm long, single seeded; GGy 489. SW. China; Szechwan, in dry mountainous sites. Introduced in 1904, but rare in cultivation today. z6

J. davurica Pall. Shrub, procumbent, bark ash-gray, exfoliating, branches cylindrical, spreading, branchlets 4 sided, about 1 mm thick; leaves scale- and needle-like, opposite, the scale leaves appressed, ovate-rhombic, obtuse or somewhat acuminate, dorsally convex, with a gland, needle leaves usually spreading, sharply acuminate, grooved above, convex beneath; fruits solitary, axillary, globose, 5–6 mm thick, brown, blue pruinose, seeds 1 or 2–4–6. CCE 211. Siberia; in the highest parts of the Baikal and Sondochai Mts.; as well as along sandy river banks of the Katunja to the Amur region. Closely related to *J. sabina*. It is not certain if the type is in cultivation. z6

'Expansa'. Branches nearly table-like, flat, spreading and very stiff, densely covering the ground, but not lying down(!), branches densely covered with short twigs, twig tips often nearly filamentous; needles partly scale-like, partly subulate, green, somewhat bluish pruinose; fruits often with 6 seeds. WDw 138 (H); WM 18C (Br) (= *J. chinensis* var. *expansa* Grootend.; *J. davurica* var. *parsonii* van Melle; *J. chinensis* var. *parsonii* Hornibr.). Presumably brought from Japan to the USA and distributed by the Parsons Nurseries, Flushing, NY, about 1862. Fig. 86A.

'Expansa Aureospicata'. Like 'Expansa', but the branches partly yellow variegated; leaves needle- and scale-like, the former predominating. Introduced in the USA before 1938.

'Expansa Variegata'. Like 'Expansa', but taller and denser, not so flat, branches with larger and smaller cream-white parts; needles more blue-green, some scale-, some needle-like (= *J. chinensis* var. *expansa variegata* Hornibr.). Very attractive, widely disseminated cultivar. Plate 69.

J. deppeana Steud. Alligator Juniper. Tree, to 20 m high, broadly conical, stem short and thick, bark oak-like, thick and checkered (hence "Alligator Juniper"), very hard, grooved, gray; branches 4 sided, 1 mm thick; needles usually only scale-form, opposite oval-rhombic, tightly appressed, acute, blue-green, indistinctly keeled in the dorsal side, with a gland, young plants with needle leaves, 2–3 together, long acuminate, concave and whitish above, keeled beneath; plants dioecious; fruits globose to broad ellipsoid, 10–12 mm long, red-brown, pruinose, ripening the 2nd year, flesh thick, mealy-dry, usually with 4 sides, brown seeds. CB III 23; GGy Pl. 53, 479, 481; CCE 217 (= *J. pachyphlaea* Torr.). SW. USA, on limestone. Found with *Pinus ponderosa*, in dry, sunny areas. Hardly any other *Juniperus* is so silvery-gray! Plate 70; Fig. 81H and 91B. z8–9

'Ericoides' (Barbier). Mutation with only awl-shaped, blue-green needle leaves. RH 1914: 343 (= *J. pachyphlaea ericoides* Barbier). Developed before 1909 by Barbier, Orléans, France. (EX?)

Fig. 86. **Juniperus.** A. *J. davurica* 'Expansa'; B. *J.* × *media* 'Plumosa'; C. *J.* × *media* 'Hetzii';
D. *J. virginiana* 'Grey Owl' (Original)

J. distans Florin. Small shrub, to 2 m high, usually lower, open, branches horizontal or bowed outward, branchlets pendulous; needles scale- or needle-like, needle leaves in whorls of 3 on the base of the branclets, appressed or spreading, lanceolate, 6 mm long, becoming scale-like toward the branchlet tips, ovate-triangular, 2–3 mm long, tightly appressed; fruits red-brown, oval, 8–12 mm long, the scales distinct, seeds solitary, large, ovate, furrowed. GGy 503, 488. SW. China. W. Szechwan Province. 1926. Presumably quite hardy. Fig. 85A. z5–6.

J. drupaceae Labill. Syrian Juniper. Tree, 10–12 m high, trunk branched on plants in the wild, upright, broadly conical, cultivated plants more broadly columnar, bark ash-gray, branches ascending to horizontal; all leaves needle-like, in whorls of 3, decurrent, lanceolate, stiff, 15–25 mm long, 3–4 mm wide, sharply pointed, slightly channeled above, with 2 white bands and a green midrib, keeled beneath; plants dioecious; fruits globose to oval, with 6–9 fleshy scales, 15 to 25 mm long, bluish, pruinose, edible, ripening the 2nd year, with 3 seeds, these however, usually fused into a seed pit. CB III 14; KN 175; OCC 174; CCE 217 (= *Arceuthos drupaceae* Ant. & Kotschy). Asia Minor, Greece. Easily distinguished from all the other species by the very wide and long leaves. Plate 67; Fig. 80A, 87. z8–9

J. durangensis Martinez. Small tree or shrub, 2–4 m high, open crown, with irregularly arranged and twisted branches, bark gray, fibrous-striated, branchlets very densely arranged, short, widely spaced, 4 sided in cross section; leaves usually opposite, broadly ovate, with obtuse tips, yellowish-green, with narrow oil glands; fruits globose to wide 2 lobed, about 5 mm wide, orange to reddish, bluish pruinose, seeds 2–3. GGy Pl. 53, 478. Mexico. z9

J. excelsa Bieb. Grecian Juniper. Tree, 10–20 m high, monoecious, crown conical at first, later more globose, bark brown, exfoliating in strips, branches very thin; needles usually scale-like, opposite, oval-rhombic, densely appressed, apex distinct, with a gland, dorsal side convex, leaves in whorls of 3 on the leading branch, needle-like only on older shoots, but rare, 5–6 mm long, opposite, with 2 blue bands above; fruits globose, 8 mm thick, dark brown, bluish pruinose, ripening the 2nd year, seeds 5–6. GGy Pl. 54; BC II 75; SN 70 (H); CCE 213. SW. Europe, Asia Minor to the Caucasus, developing forests in the mountains. Plate 61; Fig. 79C, 94E. z7

J. flaccida Schlechtend. Mexican Juniper. An 8–12 m tree in its habitat, bark with long, narrow scales, branches spreading widely and irregularly arranged, branchlets pendulous; leaves scale- and needle-like, scale leaves opposite, somewhat spreading, oval-lanceolate, 1.5–2 mm long, base stem clasping, acute, with an indented oil gland on the dorsal side, needle leaves occasionally appearing at the branch tips, usually in whorls of 3, about

6 mm long, gradually drawn out to a horn-like tip, concave above with an inward curving limb and 2 narrow stomatal bands, with a gland at the base beneath; fruits globose, red-brown, with a waxy coating, 10–15 mm thick, ripening in the 2nd year, monoecious, but with male and female flowers on different branches. GGy 479–80; CB III 15; CCE 210. Mexico, in the mountains. Fig. 94A. z9

var. **poblana** Martinez. Leaves ovate to nearly elliptic, acute, but not acuminate; fruits often to 2 cm thick. GGy 480 (= *Cupressus thurifera* HKB). Mexico. z9

J. foetidissima Willd. Tree, 5–15 m high, living to be very old, stem quite straight, crown slender conical, branched to the ground, branches upright, bark gray, branchlets short, thickish, distinctly 4 sided, similar to those of *J. excelsa*, but thicker; leaves having an unpleasant odor when crushed (hence "Stinking Juniper"), partly needle-form, loosely appressed or spreading, mucronulate, sharp keeled on the dorsal side, partly scale-like, ovate-rhombic, acutish, convex on the dorsal side, usually without glands; plants mono- or dioecious; fruits solitary, but numerous, on short branches, globose, 6–12 mm thick, red-brown to black, pruinose, usually with 1–2 seeds. Mountains of Greece, Albania, Yugoslavia, Asia Minor to Transcaucasus; rocky areas. Fig. 79E. z9

var. **pindicola** Formanek. Differs from the species principally in characteristics of the fruits, these rugose, lower scales "hunchbacked-acutish". Pindus Mts. 1895

J. formosana Hayata. Tree. 8–15 m high, often multi-stemmed, narrow crown, outspread branches, secondary branches pendulous, bark brown, exfoliating in fibrous strips; all leaves needle-like, similar to *J. rigida* (but without groove-like indentations on the upper surface of the leaves and lacking black fruits!), in whorls of 3, about 2 mm wide and 12 mm long, with 2 white stomatal bands above, midrib bluish or green, thickened at the base and connate; fruits dark red-brown to orange, pea-sized, with 3 furrows on the apex. LT 55; CB III 17;

SH 31 (H); CCE 208 + 211. China and Taiwan, widely distributed in the mountains. 1844. Fig. 80D and 88. z9

J. glaucescens Florin. Small tree, crown dense, bark gray, most branches outspread, but some bowed downward, branchlets usually pendulous, 4 sided in cross section; leaves scale-like, opposite, tightly appressed, gray-green, triangular-ovate, obtuse, with a distinct gland on the convex dorsal side, also with needle leaves in whorls of 3 on young plants and long shoots; fruits oval-rounded, blue-black, bluish pruinose, 6–8 mm thick, seeds with about 6 shallow furrows on either side. NW.China; NW.Szechwan, in the mountains. z9?

J. horizontalis Moench. Creeping Juniper. Shrub, long branches, creeping widely along the ground, secondary branches very numerous, short, dense; leaves on plants in cultivation nearly all needle-like, often in 3's, blue-green to steel green, 2–6 mm long, somewhat spreading, scale leaves narrow elliptic, sharply acuminate, with awn tips not appressed, convex on the dorsal side, with a gland; fruits globose, blue-black, somewhat bluish pruinose, 7–9 mm thick, fruit not found on cultivated plants. WDw 131, 140 (H) (= *J. prostrata* Pers.; *J. sabina* var. *prostrata* [Michx.] Loud.; *J. sabina* var. *humilis* Hook.). N. America, Nova Scotia to British Columbia, in the mountains and on the sandy shores of the Great Lakes. 1840. Fig. 83D. z3–9

Includes many Cultivars:

'Admirabilis'. Strong growing male form, otherwise similar to 'Emerson', major branches spreading horizontally over the ground; leaves all needle form, yellow-green, distinctly gray pruinose, especially on the upper side. Introduced in 1935 by the Plumfield Nurseries, Fremont, Nebraska, USA.

'Adpressa'. Dense mat form habit, only 10–15 cm high, grows very fast; foliage more green with very conspicuous, white-green tips. (Plumfield Nurseries).

Fig. 87 *Juniperus drupacea* (Original)

Fig. 88. *Juniperus formosana* (Original)

Fig. 89. **Juniperus.** A. *J. horizontalis* 'Prostrata'; B. and C. *J. horizontalis* 'Douglasii';
D. *J. horizontalis* 'Glauca'; E. *J. horizontalis* 'Plumosa' (Original)

'Alpina'. Creeping form, 1–2 m wide, branches erect at first, but gradually drooping and creeping, to 60 cm high; all leaves needle form, 3–4 mm long, more or less blue-green, purple in fall and winter (= *J. horizontalis* f. *alpina* [Loud.] Rehd.; *J. sabina* var. *alpina* Loud.). In cultivation since 1836, but not especially valuable. Plate 69.

'Andorra' (in USA) see *J. horizontalis* 'Plumosa'

'Andorra Compact'. Differing from 'Plumosa' in the denser habit, narrower needles, otherwise very similar, nearly cushion form, 30–40 cm high and about 1 m wide, all branches ascending obliquely from the center of the plant. American selection. Fig. 85C.

'Argentea'. Mat-like habit, 15–20 cm high, very dense; foliage blue-silvery. (Plumfield Nurseries).

'Bar Harbor'. Procumbent, dense, branches very thin, less than 1.5 mm thick, main branches procumbent for their entire length including the tips, lateral branches distinctly oblique-ascending, young shoots orange-brown, lilac toward the tips; leaves very small, all appressed, dark green, dense gray-green pruinose, with a purple cast in the winter. WM 232 (H). The original description from Hornibrook is too general to make a positive identification of the plant. Moreover, several types are grown in America so that the original type is impossible to distinguish.

'Blue Chip'. Low growing, lying on the ground, but with a high center; foliage a good silver-blue. Very good groundcover.

'Blue Moon'. Grows as a mat form along the ground, very finely branched, an attractive blue-green, brownish in winter. (Minier 1976).

'Douglasii' (Waukegan Juniper). Mat-like habit, procumbent, long branched, 2–3 m wide with age, center sometimes mounding to 30–40 cm high with layered branches, branch tips long and straight, branchlets 5–8 cm long, directed forward, ascending; leaves scale- and needle-like, scale leaves very densely arranged, appressed, gray-green, blue-pruinose, turning light purple in late fall and winter, needle leaves appearing in large numbers on the branchlets. DB 20: 254; OCC 177; DDG 1940: 52; WM 19E (Br), 233 (H) (= *J. horizontalis douglasii* Rehd.; *J. horizontalis glauca major* Grootend.). Named for the site of origin near the Douglas Nurseries in Waukegan, Ill., USA. Before 1916. Plate 69; Fig. 89B and C.

'Emerald Spreader'. Procumbent habit; foliage emerald-green. Introduced by Monrovia Nurseries, California, USA. Not yet widely distributed.

'Emerson'. Female, creeping habit, very slow growing and not over 30 cm high; foliage blue-green, needle- and scale-form, retaining its color throughout the winter (= *J. horizontalis* 'Marshall'; *J. horizontalis* 'Black Hill's Creeper'). Introduced about 1915 by G. A. Marshall, Marshall Nurseries, Arlington, Nebraska, USA. Discovered by and named for Prof. Emerson.

'Filicina'. Female, creeping habit and very slow growing, branches light brown, branchlets directed upward and forward; needles blue, with a purple cast in winter. Introduced by the Plumfield Nurseries, Fremont, Nebraska, USA.

'Glauca'. Dense mat form, prostrate habit, main branches straight, tightly appressed to the ground at first, eventually layered to 30 cm high in the center, branchlets numerous, 2 mm thick, directed forward, filamentous with the tightly appressed leaves, steel-blue, not changing color in the winter(!), awl-shaped leaves primarily in the center of the plant and on the less vigorous shoots, then rather densely arranged, in 4 rows. WDw 142 (H), Pl. 11E (Br). Selected in the Arnold Arboretum, before 1939. Fig. 89D.

'Glenmore'. Female, one of the lowest and slowest growing cultivars of the species, branches creeping, side shoots nearly erect, thin, dull light brown; leaves deep green, tips more brownish in winter. Found in the wild in 1932 by Robert E. Moore in Wyoming. Introduced in 1950 through the Marshall Nursery, of Denver, Colorado, USA.

'Glomerata'. Dwarf form, all branches erect, but not over 20 cm high, frequently twisted, densely crowded, with appressed needle leaves on the main branches, branchlets very short, and also growing upward, very dense and bright green foliate, somewhat bluish only on the inside of the plant, purple-violet in winter. From the USA, before 1925.

'Gracilis'. Selected in the Brooklyn Botanic Garden, about 1937, character is not particularly "graceful" and not commonly found in the trade.

'Hughes'. Quite flat, vigorous grower, whitish-blue. Considered the bluest of the *horizontalis* forms. (H. Kordes 1976).

'Humilis'. Creeping habit, mat form, dense, to 2 m wide and 0.3 m high with age, the long branches lying flat on the ground, secondary branches only 3–5 cm long, nearly vertically arranged, branchlets laterally arranged, outspread, overlapping, tips somewhat recurved; needles scale-like, green. In the trade since 1939, but not common in cultivation.

'Jade Spreader' (Monrovia). Mat form habit; leaves jade green (sea-green). Recently introduced by the Monrovia Nurseries, California, USA.

'Livida'. Dense mat form habit, main branches yellow-brown, and, like the side branches, procumbent along their entire length, twigs very short; needles dark gray-green, gray pruinose.

'Marcellus'. All branches procumbent, gray-blue, purple in winter. Selected in the USA before 1960.

'Petraeus'. Vigorous habit, flat, 18–25 cm high; foliage dull silver-green, retaining this color in winter. (Plumfield Nursery).

'Planifolia'. Very fast growing form, 20–25 cm high, with long, stout shoots, penniform, covered with short shoots; foliage silver-blue, excellent groundcover. (Plumfield Nursery).

'Plumosa' (Andorra Juniper in the USA). Procumbent habit, 2–2.5 m wide, old plants to 0.6 m high in the center, main branches lying on the ground, secondary branches ascending at a 45° angle, branchlets in a penniform arrangement; leaves all subulate (awl-shaped), very densely arranged and loosely appressed, light gray-green, with a distinct purple tone in fall and winter. WDw 143 (H); WM 19B (Br), 236 (H). Discovered in 1907 along the coast of Maine, USA and introduced by the Andorra Nurseries of Philadelphia, USA in 1919. One of the most popular forms. Fig. 89E.

'Procumbens'. Very prostrate habit, mat form, to 4 m wide, to 20 cm high in the center, branches spreading irregularly, branchlets numerous, short, erect or procumbent; needles awl-shaped, 4–5 mm long, more or less appressed, green at first with a bluish trace, later more intensive blue-green. Introduced before 1932 by Ellwanger & Barry, USA.

'Prostrata'. Procumbent, mat form, 3–4 m wide, 20–30 cm high in the center, the main branches rather stiff, very long, procumbent, but ascending on the outermost tips, the densely packed branchlets lying on the ground, blue-green with purple tips; needles mostly awl-shaped, blue-green, more scale-like toward the branch tips. WDw Pl. 11D (Br); WM 19D (Br), 238 (H) (= *J. horizontalis* var. *prostrata* Grootend.; *J. sabina prostrata* Hort. non Loud.). Cultivated for more than 100 years, but better known by the erroneous name of *J. sabina prostrata*. Fig. 89A.

'Pulchella'. Procumbent, mat form, but only 1 m wide and 10–15 cm high, very slow growing, symmetrical, branches creeping; needles all subulate (awl-shaped), gray-green, the branch tips more blue-green. Introduced in 1935 by the Plumfield Nurseries, Fremont, Nebraska, USA. Said to be exceptionally tolerant of sun, shade or dryness.

'Sea Spray'. American selection. Introduced by Frank F. Serpa, Hines Wholesale Nurseries, Santa Ana, California, US Plant Pat. Nr. 3140.

'Turquoise Spreader' (Monrovia). Lying especially flat, branchlets penniform spreading, turquoise-green. Selected by the Monrovia Nurseries, USA.

'Variegata'. Procumbent habit, to 2 m wide with a 30 cm high center, branchlets erect, with cream-white tips; all leaves needle-like, 2–4 mm long, blue-green. Introduced in 1932 by Highland Park, Rochester, New York, USA.

'Viridis'. Female, procumbent, densely branched, wide, 50–60 cm high, the branches spreading horizontally, also the branchlets, densely covering the plant; needles mostly awl-shaped, acute, bright green above, occasionally bluish pruinose beneath. Distinguished from other forms by the bright green needle color.

'Wapiti'. Procumbent, very strong grower (considered the most vigorous of all the *horizontalis* types), covering 5–6 m² in 6 years, then about 30 cm high in the center, densely branched. Discovered in Beaverlodge, Alberta, Canada.

'Wiltonii'. Very dense habit, carpet-like, very slow growing and only 10 cm high, very densely branched; needles mostly awl-shaped, very small, silver-blue. WDw Pl. 11G (Br); WM 19A (Br), 239 (H) (= *J. horizontalis* 'Blue Wiltonii' More; *J. horizontalis* 'Wilton Carpet'; *J. horizontalis* 'Blue Rug'). Discovered in 1914 by J. C. Van Heiningen of South Wilton, Conn., USA on the Vinal Haven Island, Maine. Very desirable rock garden plant for its dwarf habit and attractive color.

'Youngstown'. A selection of 'Plumosa Compacta', but lower growing, very flat, bright green. Plumfield Nurseries, Fremont, Nebraska, USA.

'Yukon Belle'. Mat form habit, broad; foliage silver-blue. Notable for its hardiness. Plumfield Nurseries, Fremont, Nebraska, USA.

J. × kanitzii Csató (*J. communis* × *J. sabina*). Superficially indistinguishable from *J. sabina* 'Tamariscifolia,' but differing microscopically in the needles. Discovered in 1886 by Csató in Remete, Hungary. Beissner considers this a *sabina* form, not a hybrid.

J. kansuensis Komar. Low shrub, very densely branched; all leaves needle-like, oblong-lanceolate, without glands, prickly acuminate; fruits small, blackish, dull, seeds only 3–5 mm long. China. Scarce in cultivation. z6

J. komarovii Florin. Tree-like habit, 3–8 m high, crown dense, gray-green, branches ascending, straight and directed upward; leaves scale-like, ovate-triangular, in 4 rows, 1–3.5 mm long, appressed, acute, juvenile foliage needle-like, in whorls of 3; fruits globose, about 10 mm long, deep brown to black-blue, pruinose, seeds solitary, 7 mm long. China; NW. Szechwan Province, in the mountains at 4000 m. Not well known. z5

J. macrocarpa see: **J. oxycedrus** ssp. **macrocarpa**

J. macrocarpoda Boiss. Shrub or small tree, 10–12 m high, stem 60–70 cm thick; foliage similar to that of *J. excelsa*, but coarser; fruits globose, 8 mm thick, purple-brown, blue pruinose, with 4–6 scales, these with a distinct umbo, seeds 2–4. Iran, Afghanistan, Belutchistan; develops forests. z9

J. × media van Melle (1947). This name was given by Van Melle for hybrids of *J. sabina× J. sphaerica*, but *J. sphaerica* is often considered a synonym for *J. chinensis*. The name is still in contention among various authors, so the classification of its form 'Pfitzeriana' is not yet conclusive. Detailed cytological investigation could determine if it is a hybrid or a form of *J. sabina* for example; or if *J.* 'Pfitzeriana' could be elevated to species rank. Considering the questionable classification of this complex, only the forms of 'Pfitzeriana' and 'Plumosa' should be included. The nursery trade has retained the original nomenclature as follows:

'Armstrongii' (Armstrong). Low, slow growing 'Pfitzeriana' type, to 1.2 m high and wide, branches spreading; needles like 'Pfitzeriana', but finer, softer, gray-blue to gray-green, more scale-like, acuminate to prickly. WM 240 (H). (= *J. media* f. *armstrongii* [Bailey] van Melle). Developed in 1932 at the Armstrong Nurseries, Ontario, California USA and widely distributed.

'Berry Hill'. Similar to 'Pfitzeriana'; but flatter, growth wider. (Minier 1976).

'Blaauw'. Dwarf form, shrubby, like a blue-green 'Plumosa' form, main branches mostly arising to one side, the twigs regularly ascending, penniform in arrangement, but also tight, nearly columnar narrow types in cultivation (Bot. Gard. Dortmund!); branchlets numerous; all needles scale-like, dense, gray-blue, interior of the plant occasionally displaying scattered awl-like needles. WM 241 (H). Introduced from Japan around 1924 by J. Blaauw & Co., Boskoop, Holland. See also 'Globosa Cinerea'. Fig. 83B.

'Blue Cloud' (F. J. Grootendorst). Growth wide and low, shrubby, branchlets very thin and nearly filamentous, steel-blue, unpleasant odor when crushed. KN 103 (= *J. media* 'Blue Cloud' Hillier). Developed about 1955 by F. J. Grootendorst, Boskoop, Holland. Fig. 82A.

'Den Boer' (Den Boer 1930). Mutation of 'Pfitzeriana' with a lower growth habit and greener foliage, only about 25 cm high and 2 m wide. Discovered by A. F. Den Boer, Des Moines, Iowa USA in 1930; introduced to the trade by Heard's Landscape Nurseries, Des Moines Iowa, USA. (Patented.)

'Fruitlandii'. Broad and flat, spreading, compact, very densely branched, green. Called 'Improved Pfitzer Compacta' in the USA.

'Globosa'. Female, dwarf form, open shrubby, occasionally somewhat globose, to 1 m high, branches spreading, exserted beyond the globose form, thin; needles scale-like, appressed, light green, with some awl-shaped needles inside the plant. Exported by the Yokohama Nursery, Japan before 1911 under the name *J. "virginalis globosa"* and brought into the trade in England as *J. "virginiana globosa"* but recognized by Hornibrook

as a form of *J. chinensis*. At the same time, a yellow form ('Aurea-globosa' = 'Plumosa Aurea') and a more gray-green form ('Globosa Cinerea') were imported, all of which are still in cultivation.

'Globosa Cinerea'. This form is so similar to 'Blaauw' that it can practically be considered a synonym. They can not be differentiated in foliage or in habit. Since both plants were imported from Japan, together with 'Globosa' in 1916 (by Wallace & Co., Tunbridge Wells, England), the name 'Blaauw' should be discontinued. WDw Pl. 13F (Br)

'Golden Saucer'. (Nic. Bosman, Boskoop). A sport of 'Pfitzeriana Aurea', very compact, yellower in winter than in summer. Distributed after 1976 by M. W. Van Nierop, Boskoop, Holland. The prettiest yellow 'Pfitzeriana' type.

'Hetzii' (Hetz). Female, shrubby, main stem ascending obliquely, 4–5 m high, branches arising on all sides, thin twigs, light brown, branch tips thin, blue-green; leaves scale-like, small, distinctly blue-green, with needle-leaves inside the plant. WM 242 (H) (= *J. glauca hetzii* Hetz). Originated from seed, around 1920; brought into the trade by Fairview Evergreen Nurseries, Fairview, Pa., USA, about 1930. Fig. 86C.

'Mathot' (Mathot 1940). Mutation of 'Pfitzeriana' and similar in habit, but more densely branched; all leaves subulate and opposite, to 7.5 mm long, with blue-green stomatal bands above, green beneath, upper surface twists outward and gives the plant a blue-green effect (= *J. chinensis* 'Mathot' den Ouden). Developed in the nursery of Gebr. Mathot in Boskoop, Holland. Introduced to the trade in 1947.

'Mint Julep' (Monrovia). Broad with bowed, spreading branches, general impression like that of a bright green 'Pfitzeriana'; needles bright green. Developed in the Monrovia Nurseries, Saratoga, California USA. Introduced in 1960.

'Moraine' (Siebenthaler). Sport of 'Pfitzeriana', more compact habit, very similar to 'Nick's Compact'. Developed by Siebenthaler, Ohio USA, 1932; introduced in 1949. (Patented.)

'Nick's Compact' is the commonly used name in the USA for *J. chinensis* 'Pfitzeriana Compacta', which see.

'Old Gold' (Grootendorst 1958). Mutation of 'Pfitzeriana Aurea', but much flatter in habit; leaves bronze-yellow, retaining this color in winter. WDw 145 (H); CCE 200; WM 244 (H). Developed in the nursery of F. J. Grootendorst, Boskoop, Holland and introduced in 1958.

'Pendula'. Open branched weeping form, branches ascending in a wide bow, but the tips pendulous; needles gray-green (= *J. chinensis pendula* Franch. 1884; *J. sphaerica* var. *pendula* [Franch.] van Melle). Probably imported around 1882 into France from W. China by Fr. Armand David. (VR)

'Pfitzeriana'. Only male plant known, normally wide arching, to 3 m high and equally wide or (rarely) to 5 m wide, branches wide spreading and bowed, often trained up in culture, tips drooping; leaves partly scale-like and light green, but needle-like in whorls of 4 inside the plant, bluish striped above, sharply acuminate. BFN 605 (H); WDw 147 (H); WM 22A (Br) (= *J. chinensis pfitzeriana* Späth; *J. chinensis* var. *pendula* Beissn. [without a description]; *J. sabina* 'Knap Hill' Fitsch.). Introduced to the trade by L. Späth in 1899 and one of the most frequently planted conifers today with numerous mutations.

A historical note: Although there is no conclusive evidence as to the origin of this plant, Van Melle's research (1947) is very compelling. According to Van Melle (p. 82) the plant was found in 1866 by the French missionary and botanist Armand David in the Ho Lan Shan Mountains in inner Mongolia. He could have (as often before) collected seed and sent it on to Paris. (Unfortunately most of his herbarium notes have been lost). In any case, plants were purchased under the name of *Juniperus chinensis pendula* in 1876 by the Simon Louis Nursery in Metz, France. These plants, during the decade from 1870 to 1880, became well known in French and Belgian nurseries.

As to the nomenclature, Van Melle's combination, *J. × media* var. *pfitzeriana* (Späth) van Melle, 1946, has by no means met with general acceptance. See also the notes at *J. × media*.

Outline of the 'Pfitzeriana' Group

Habit like 'Pfitzeriana'
    Needles green:
        'Mathot', 'Mint Julep'
    Needles blue:
        'Hetzii', 'Pfitzeriana Glauca'
        ("Silver-Blue Juniper")
    Needles yellow:
        'Pfitzeriana Aurea'
Habit lower and wider
    Needles green:
        'Armstrongii', 'Den Boer', 'Pfitzeriana
        Compacta' ("Nick's Compact")
    Needles blue:
        'Moraine', 'Richeson'
    Needles yellow:
        'Old Gold'

'Pfitzeriana Aurea' (Hill). Mutation of 'Pfitzeriana', similar to the type, but young shoots yellow, especially intensive on clay soil, but gradually greening in summer, yellow-green in winter (= *J. chinensis pfitzeriana aurea* Hill; *J. media* var. *pfitzeriana* f. *aurea* van Melle). Developed in 1923 at the D. Hill Nursery, Dundee, Ill., USA. Introduced in 1937. Generally surpassed today by 'Old Gold'.

'Pfitzeriana Compacta' (Bobbink & Atkins). Very compact and flat growing, without the typical stout branches of 'Pfitzeriana', about 1.8 m wide in 12 years, but only 30–50 cm high; a portion of the needle leaves distinctly larger than those of 'Pfitzeriana', these short, rather soft and light green. WDw Pl. 13D (Br); WM 22B (Br) (= *J. × media* var. *pfitzeriana* f. *compacta* van Melle). Developed about 1930 by Bobbink & Atkins, Rutherford, Vermont USA; but known in the trade as *J. chinensis* 'Nick's Compact'. Fig. 85D.

'Pfitzeriana Glauca' (Haygood). Growth like 'Pfitzeriana', but more densely branched; leaves usually needle-like, sharply acuminate and prickly, silvery-gray to gray-green, with a somewhat purple-blue trace in winter (= *J. × media* var. *pfitzeriana* f. *glauca* van Melle). Developed by R. W. Haygood in Keithville, Louisiana USA; introduced to the trade by the Texas Nursery Co., Sherman, Texas USA (Plant Pat. Nr. 422). Often sold in the American nursery trade as 'Silver Blue Juniper'.

Outline of the Forms of the 'Plumosa' Group

Tall growing, over 1 m high
    green:
        'Plumosa'
    gray-green:
        'Blaauw' (= 'Globosa Cinerea')
    yellow and yellow variegated:
        'Tremonia'

Growth to or less than 1 m high
    green:
        'Globosa', 'Shimpaku'
    yellow and yellow variegated:
        'Plumosa Aurea',
        'Plumosa Aureovariegata',
        'Shimpaku Gold'
    white variegated:
        'Plumosa Albovariegata'

'Plumosa'. Male, dwarf form, broad, 1–1.5 m high, branches ascending, main stem occasionally growing to one side, branches rather equal in length, directed forward, penniform; leaves scale-like, dense, dark green, also with a few needle leaves inside the plant. CCE 203 (= *J. chinensis plumosa* Hornibr.; *J. × media* var. *plumosa* [Hornibr.] van Melle; *J. "chinensis procumbens"*). Introduced from Japan, presumably between 1900 and 1910 as "*J. japonica*". Fig. 86B.

'Plumosa Albovariegata'. Dwarf form, like 'Plumosa', scarcely over 1 m high, usually lower, branches with small, white tips; all needles scale-like, bluish-green. WDw 148 (H); WM 249 (H) (= *J. chinensis plumosa albovariegata* [Otto] Hornibr.; *J. × media* var. *plumosa* f. *albovariegata* [Beissn.] van Melle). Cultivated before 1867 in Holland as *J. "japonica argenteovariegata"*.

'Plumosa Aurea'. Dwarf form, habit generally broad, shrubby, to about 1 m high, branches ascending, irregular, twigs short and densely arranged, tips nodding; nearly all needles scale-like, a good gold-yellow especially in spring, more bronze-yellow in winter. WDw 149 (H); WM 22E (Br); CCE 201 (= *J. chinensis procumbens aurea* Beissn.; *J. chinensis* var. *globosa aurea* Hornibr.; *J. chinensis aurea* Nich.). Cultivated since before 1885 in England. Plate 65.

A strict upright form of this plant is growing in the Dortmund Botanic Garden, W. Germany. Originating in the State Conifer Nursery in Zehusice, Czechoslovakia, it is 2 m high and vigorous. It has been given the provisional name of 'Plumosa Tremonia'. Possibly propagated from a tip shoot of the above cultivar.

'Plumosa Aureovariegata'. Lower than the above, only 50–80 cm high, slow growing, branches shorter, twigs and branchlets scattered yellow variegated, also with individual yellow branchlets; needles usually scale-like and dark green. CCE 201 (= *J. chinensis procumbens aureovariegata* Beissn.; *J. × media* var. *plumosa* f. *aureovariegata* [Otto] van Melle). 1873.

'Richeson' (Armstrong 1941). Low and broad, 14-year old plants only 30 cm high but 1.2 m wide; most leaves needle-like, blue-green. 'Pfitzeriana' mutation. Discovered in 1941 by L. J. Richeson, Ontario, California, USA; introduced by Armstrong Nurseries, California, USA in 1946.

'Shimpaku'. Dwarf form of the 'Plumosa' group, very slow growing and therefore much used in Japan in the creation of bonsai. WM 22D. Not often found in cultivation but available in 3 forms according to Hillier and Welch, England.

'Shimpaku Gold', yellow variegated.

'Sulphur Spray' (Konijn). Mutation on 'Hetzii' with sulfur-yellow color. CCE 203. Discovered in 1962 by L. Konijn, Reeuwijk, Holland.

'Winter Surprise' (K. W. van Klaveren, Boskoop, 1979). Sport of 'Pfitzeriana Aurea'; foliage bright green, with numerous, large and small, gold-yellow spots and tips, especially conspicuous in winter, less so in summer.

J. mekongensis Komar. Tree, to 12 m high in its habitat, with a dense crown and widely spreading thin branches; needles scale-like, in 4 rows, ovate, about 2 mm long, obtuse, with a distinct, indented gland on the dorsal side; fruits ovate, black, with only 1 seed, these about 6 mm long, pitted. E. Tibet; at 3000 m. z6

J. monosperma (Engelm.) Sarg. Tree with open, strongly branched crown, 10 m high, bark exfoliating in strips, densely branched from the ground up, new shoots 4 sided, 1 mm thick; leaves usually scale-like, grouped 2 or 3 together, appressed, short or long acuminate and slightly spreading, rounded on the dorsal side, gray-green, with a distinct gland, needle leaves in 3's on young plants, to 15 mm long, green, keeled, with a broad, white stomatal band above; fruits globose to ovate, 5–6 mm long, dark blue and pruinose, seeds solitary, occasionally in 2's or 3, more or less exserted. GGy 477, 483. Colorado to W. Texas, New Mexico, Nevada, USA, Northern Mexico. Around 1900. Of only slight garden merit. Fig. 90D. z7

var. **gracilia** Martinez. Shrub, branches very thin, bark exfoliating occasionally in long plates rather than strips; fruits somewhat smaller than those of the species. GGy 483. Mexico. z9

J. morrisonicola Hayata. Upright shrub, resembling *J. squamata* var. *fargesii*, the needle-like leaves lanceolate, very narrow, 6–7 mm long, conspicuously silver-gray above, green beneath, densely arranged on rather short branchlets; fruits globose to oblong, about 8 mm long, black, smooth. LT 57; LWT 16; CCE 217. Mount Morrison, Taiwan. z7

J. occidentalis Hook. f. Tree, 12(20) m high or only shrubby, stem columnar and straight, crown wide spreading, branches thick, horizontal or also pendulous, bark light brown, scaly, branchlets yellow-green, short-stout, to 2 mm thick; needles usually scale-like, in whorls of 3, arranged in 6 rows, tightly appressed, oval-rhombic, usually acute or acuminate, gray-green, 3 mm long, with a distinct gland; plants monoecious; fruits numerous, but solitary, globose, 7 to 8 mm thick, blue-black with blue-white pruinose, 2–3 seeds. CB III 21; SN 191 (H); SPa 71–72. Western N. America, British Columbia to California, in the higher mountains. Plate 68; Fig. 81F. z7

'**Sierra Silver**'. Twisted habit; foliage very conspicuously gray-green. Found in the mountains of California and clonally propagated; introduced by the Monrovia Nursery, California, USA in 1960.

J. osteosperma (Torr.) Little. Shrub, occasionally a small tree, to 7 m high, with a short, thick trunk and bark exfoliating in long strips, branches dense, covering the ground, ascending, crown broad and open, twigs outspread, branchlets about 2 mm thick, yellow-green; leaves scale-like, short acuminate, finely dentate, indistinctly glandular, usually opposite, but also in whorls of 3; plants monoecious; fruits globose, 6–15 mm thick, red-brown, blue-pruinose. GGy Pl. 52; BCC 40 (H); SPa 73 (= *J. utahensis* Lemm.; *J. californica* var. *utahensis* Engelm.; *J. megalocarpa* Sudw.). USA; from SW. Wyoming to S. Idaho and Nevada, Arizona, California, New Mexico; mainly in the dry mountains and deserts. Fig. 81D. z6

J. oxycedrus L. Large shrub or small tree, to 10 m in its habitat, occasionally growing to 14 m; needles flat-grooved above with 2 white bands; cones globose to pear-shaped, ripening the second year, seeds usually 3. Mediterranean region to Bulgaria, Syria and Iran. z9

ssp. **oxycedrus** L. Dense shrub or also a small tree, occasionally to 14 m high, bark gray-brown, branchlets angular; needles all subulate, 12–18 mm long, outspread, sharply mucronulate, flat-grooved above with 2 white bands, margin smooth, green, midrib green, convex beneath, green keeled; plants dioecious; fruits solitary, in the leaf axils, short stalked, globose to

obovoid, also 3–6 scales, glossy red-brown, when ripe, seeds usually 3, red-brown. CB III 22; DJ 50; CCE 215. Over the entire Mediterranean region to Syria and Iran. Of no importance in gardens, but valued in its habitat. Plate 61; Fig. 80B, 90E. z9

var. **brachyphylla** Loret. Leaves shorter, not so sharply acuminate, more blue-green. France; Haute Garonne, on limestone soil near St. Bét.

ssp. **macrocarpa** (Sibth. & Sm.) Ball. Bushy shrub or small tree, 3–6 m high, dense conical habit; leaves all linear, tapering from the base to the sharp, prickly tip, 2–2.5 cm long, flexible, outspread, 1–2 mm wide at the base; fruits globose to ovate, 12–15 mm thick, blue pruinose when young, eventually red-brown to black-brown. OCC 180; CB III 16; CCE 215 (= *J. macrocarpa* Sibth. & Sm.). Mediterranean region, from Spain to Syria, also in Bulgaria. Introduced about 1600. Very similar to *J. oxycedrus*, but with larger fruits and longer leaves. z9

J. phoenicia L. Shrub or small tree, to 6 m high, dense bushy or conical, bark dark brown, branchlets scarcely 1 mm thick; leaves scale-like, on young plants needle-like, needle leaves in whorls of 3, about 6 mm long, with 2 stomatal lines on both sides, scale leaves oval-rhombic, either in 4 rows with the opposite leaves or 6 rows with the whorled leaves, obtuse, green to blue-green, convex beneath; plants normally monoecious, occasionally also dioecious; fruits globose, ripening the 2nd year, 6–12 mm thick, yellowish to red-brown, glossy, hardly pruinose, with 3–9 seeds, flesh dry and fibrous. CB III 13; CCE 215, 218 (= *J. tetragona* Mnch.). Mediterranean region, on dry, gravelly hills, near the coast. Plate 61; Fig. 81E and 90A. z8–9

The original spelling, *phoenicea*, by Linnaeus is considered by many botanists (Erdtman, Laurent, Coltman-Rogers, Gaussen) to be an unintentional error. It is generally assumed that Linnaeus meant, *phoenicia*, meaning Phoenician since this species is indigenous to the Mediterranean region; not that it has scarlet red fruit as is meant by *phoenicea* (phoeniceous).

'**Myosurus**'. Bushy shrub, branches wavy-bowed, twisted, spreading-nodding, twigs long "whip-like"; needles usually scale-like (= *J. myosurus* Sénécl.). Found as a seedling among *J. phoenicia* by Sénéclauze in 1854.

var. **turbinata** (Guss.) Parl. Habit usually procumbent; fruits shaped like a top or ovate, seeds deep longitudinally furrowed (= *J. turbinata* Guss.). Occurs with the type, primarily on the western Mediterranean Sea coast.

J. pinchotii Sudw. Shrub or small tree, to 6 m high, similar to *J. osteosperma*, but bushier, branches wide spreading, forming an irregular crown, bark thin, light brown; leaves on young plants in whorls of 3, awl-shaped, 6–8 mm long, grouped 2 or 3 together on older plants, scale-like, in 3 rows, 2 mm long, dark yellow-green, with a glandular pit on the dorsal side; fruits ripening the first year, globose, 6 mm thick, bright red, seeds solitary, obtuse-ovate, deeply furrowed. GGy 486. Texas, USA; dry, gravelly slopes. Fig. 91D. z9

J. potaninii Komar. Tree, to 15 m high in its habitat, branches erect, branchlets very thin; scale leaves densely appressed, dark green, obtuse; fruits blue-black, globose, about 5 mm thick, glossy, seeds acute-conical at both ends. GGy 488 and 502. China; Szechwan. Considered *J. distans* by many authors, due to the

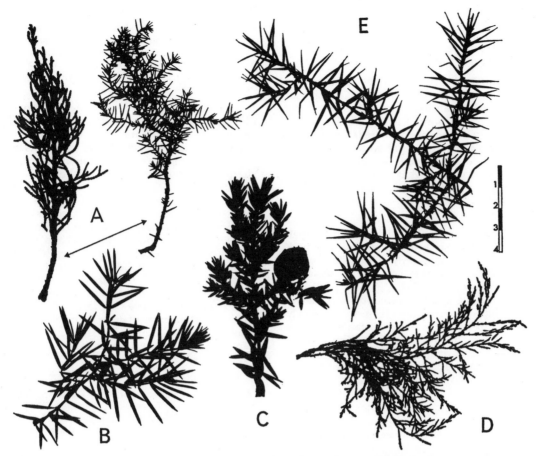

Fig. 90. **Juniperus.** A. *J. phoenicia* (left mature, right juvenile); B. *J. cedrus;*
C. *J. conferta;* D. *J. monosperma;* E. *J. oxycedrus* (Original)

persistance of the juvenile leaves, but *J. distans* has red-brown fruit.

J. procera Hochst. ex Endl. African Juniper. Tall tree, 20–30 m in its habitat, straight stem, branchlets irregularly penniform, very slender, 4 sided; leaves lanceolate on the main shoots, drawn out to a sharp tip, tightly appressed, about 4 mm long, becoming smaller toward the branch tips, often furrowed on the dorsal side, juvenile foliage rare on older plants; fruits globose, 5 mm thick, black-blue, very pruinose, with 2–3 ovate seeds. CB III 24; GGy 493, 497; CC 80–81 (H). E. Africa; Kenya to Ethiopia; common forest tree. z9

J. procumbens (Endl.) Miq. Small shrub, procumbent spreading habit, to 2 m wide and 50–75 cm high as an old plant, branches somewhat stiff, turned upward at the tips, blue-green furrowed; needles in whorls of 3, linear-lanceolate, 6–8 mm long, gradually becoming sharply acuminate, concave above with a green midrib, otherwise bluish with 2 white spots near the base; fruits nearly globose, 8–9 mm thick, usually with 3 seeds. CB III 25; MJu 2; WDw 150 (H), Pl. 12B (Br); DDG 1940: 53. Japan; in the mountains. Introduced into Holland in 1843. Plate 70; Fig. 81C. z4–9

'Bonin Isles'. Habit mat form and very dense, but intermediate between the species and 'Nana' in growth rate; needle leaves

somewhat larger than those of 'Nana'. WM 18E (Br). Originally from the Bonin Islands of Japan. Cultivated in England erroneously as 'Nana'.

'Golden'. Branch tips a good golden-yellow; foliage gray-green. Cultivated only in the USA.

'Nana'. Like the species, but lower, denser, stem shorter and thicker, internodes shorter, annual growth only about 15 cm long, basal part of the branches densely padded with erect short shoots; leaves broader than those of the species, stomatal bands not so conspicuous and sometimes absent. WDw 151 (H), Pl. 12A (Br); WLM 218D (Br). Introduced from Japan about 1922 by D. Hill of Dundee, Illinois, USA.

'Santa Rosa'. Totally dwarf form. Developed in the USA before 1963.

J. przewalskii Komar. Medium size tree, to 12 m in its habitat, branches erect to horizontal; leaves scale-like, outspread or appressed, gray-green, about 2.5 mm long, rather acute, papillose on the dorsal side; fruits globose, 10–15 mm thick, reddish-brown, seeds irregularly globose, keeled, 1 cm long, rugose on both sides. GGy 500. W.China; Kansu. z9

J. pseudosabina Fisch. & C. A. Mey. Small, upright shrub, branches round, erect to horizontal, branchlets short, thick, 4 sided, about 2 mm thick; leaves scale-like, opposite, oval-rhombic, 1–3 mm long, obtuse, gray-green, convex to obtusely keeled on the dorsal side, with a gland, needle-like leaves on young plants and partly on older plants; fruits ovate, 10–12 mm long and 6–8 mm thick, black, with 1 large seed. GGy 487. Turkestan; in the Altai and Targabatai Mts. In cultivation? z6

J. ramulosa Florin. Tree, to 10 m in its habitat, crown very dense, gray-green, branches bowed upward, those with male flowers well branched, branchlets erect or somewhat bowed, thin, round; leaves scale-like, in 3's, tightly appressed, rather obtuse, with linear gland, awl-shaped on young plants and dark green on both sides, 3–7 mm long; fruits oval-rounded, 6–8 mm long, red-brown to black-brown, somewhat pruinose, seeds to 6 mm long, deeply furrowed. GGy 501. China; NE. Szechwan Province, at about 3000 m in the mountains. Similar to *J. convallium*. z6

J. recurva Buch.-Ham. ex D. Don. Himalayan Juniper. Tree, to 10 m, or a shrub, broad conical crown, bark shredding in thin strips, gray-brown, branches bowed outward and nodding, branchlets pendulous; leaves in whorls of 3, linear-lanceolate, 3–6 mm long, 0.5–1 mm wide, tightly imbricate and appressed, distinct on the apical portion, blue-green or gray-green, sharp, prickly tip, channeled above with 2 white bands, convex beneath, dull green, furrowed nearly to the middle; monoecious; fruits oval, ripening the 2nd year, 8–10 mm long, dark olive brown, glossy, with 1 large seed. CB II 75. SW. China; Himalaya. 1830. Plate 57; Fig. 82B and 91C. z8–9

'Castlewellan'. Differing from the type in the taller growth habit, the branchlets "whip-like" pendulous; leaves finer. DB 14: 187; KN Plate 5. Originated in Castlewellan, N. Ireland.

var. coxii (Jacks.) Melv. Crown of older plants narrowly conical, with graceful pendulous branches, bark of young shoots an attractive red-brown; leaves 6–8 mm long and loosely arranged, dark green, with distinctly darker midrib above. CBJ 50; JRHS 67: 128; WDw 152 (H), Pl. 11A (Br); WM 20E (Br) (= *J. coxii* Jacks.). Burma, SW. China. Plate 57; Fig. 91A.

'Densa'. Low growing, spreading always much wider than high, branch tips always directed upward; needles longer than those of var. *coxii*, but similar in color, distinctly green (not gray-green), with an intense turpentine odor. WM 20F (Br), 255 (H) (= *J. recurva* var. *densa* Carr.; *J. recurva* var. *squamata* Veitch; *J. recurva* 'Nana'). In cultivation before 1855.

'Embley Park'. Low, wide shrub, to 1.5 m high and twice as wide, bark of the young shoots yellow-green; leaves bright green, loosely arranged, 6–8 mm long, lanceolate, needle-form acuminate. WDw 153 (H); WM 21B (Br), 256 (H) (= *J. recurva* var. *viridis* Hillier). Found in Embley Park, Romsey, England but originally brought to England in 1929 by G. Forrest.

J. rigida S. & Z. Shrub or a small tree, conical, 6 m high or more, branches brown-red to yellow-brown, wide spreading, arching, branchlets hanging "mane-like"; needles awl-shaped, in whorls of 3, outspread, stiff, with sharp tips, prickly, 15–25 mm long, to 1 mm wide, deeply grooved above with a narrow white middle band, with a wide green margin, distinctly keeled and green beneath; fruits ripening the 2nd year, solitary globose, 6–8 mm thick, black-brown and pruinose, composed of 3 scales, with 2–3 seeds, these oblong and angular, with 3–4 resin pits. OCC 173; CB III 12; WDw Pl. 9 (Br), 156 (Br); CCE 216, 219. Korea, Manchuria. Planted particularly near temples in Japan. 1861. Plate 65; Fig. 82A. z6

ssp. nipponica (Maxim.) Franco. Procumbent habit; leaves densely arranged, only 6–10 mm long, deeply furrowed above and with a narrow stomatal band, distinctly keeled beneath; fruits with 1 seed. OCC 187 (Br) (= *J. nipponica* Maxim.; *J. communis* var. *nipponica* [Maxim.] Wils.). N.Japan; in the mountains. 1915.

J. sabina L. Normally a low shrub with procumbent or obliquely ascending branches, or rarely a small tree, to about 4 m, with oblique stem, older bark red-brown, exfoliating, branches very dense, branchlets thin, hardly 1 mm thick, more rounded than angular; leaves very sharp, unpleasant odor when crushed (typical of all the *sabina* forms!), with needle and scale-like leaves, these awl-shaped on young plants, outspread, straight, 4 mm long, sharply acuminate, blue-green above, with a distinctly raised midrib, scale leaves opposite, ovate, 1 mm long, obtuse (but 3 mm long and acute on main shoots), dorsal side convex, usually with 1 gland; mono- or dioecious; fruits nodding on short, curving stalks, globose to oval, 5–7 mm thick, blue-black, pruinose, ripening in the fall of the 1st or spring of the 2nd year, with 1–3 ovate, furrowed seeds. CB III 26; SN 190 (H); CCE 219. Mountains of central and S. Europe, Siberia, Caucasus, Asia Minor. In cultivation for centuries, generally only the low, procumbent types. Plate 67; Fig. 79D, 92A. z3–7

Includes the following cultivars:

'Arcadia'. Dwarf form, similar to 'Tamariscifolia', but lower, leaves predominantly scale-like, light green. WM 257 (H). Like 'Broadmoor' and 'Skandia', a selection of F. J. Grootendorst & Zonen, Boskoop, Holland, from seedling plants of D. Hill Nurseries, USA. The latter firm obtained the seed from the Ural Mts. in 1933. Fig. 92B.

'Aureovariegata'. Very similar to 'Cupressifolia', but with scale leaves primary and yellow branch tips (= *J. sabina humilis aureovariegata* Hornibr.). Originated as a mutation on an old plant of *J. sabina* before 1923 in Abbeyleix House, Queen's Co., Ireland.

'Blue Danube'. Broad, low habit, branch tips bowed upward, branchlets clustered; leaves mostly scale-like, also needle-like inside the plant, light gray-blue. Introduced to the trade as a nameless seedling by L. Visser of Pressbaum, Austria; introduced under the current name by Blaauw & Co., of Boskoop, Holland in 1956.

'Broadmoor'. Low, broad, to 60 cm high, male very similar to 'Tamariscifolia', but with finer foliage, main branches stout, horizontal, branchlets short and directed upward; needles 3–4 mm long, gray-green. For the origin, see 'Arcadia'.

'Buffalo'. Similar to 'Tamariscifolia', but lower and wider; foliage bright green. Exceptionally frost hardy.

'Cupressifolia'. Very low, compact habit, horizontally branched, occasionally somewhat ascending, but never erect (sometimes confused with 'Erecta'!); all leaves scale-like, appressed, blue-green, inside, occasionally the basal part of the plant with needle leaves; female form fruits abundantly. WDw 155 (H), Pl. 12C (Br); CCE 220 (= *J. sabina nana* Carr.). Known in English gardens since 1789.

'Erecta'. Upright habit, open, a few meters high and equally wide, branches thin, ascending, tips nodding, branchlets clustered; leaves predominantly scale-like, dark green. WDw 159 (H). Origin of this type (or clone) unknown. This is actually nothing more than the normal wild *J. sabina*; however, often

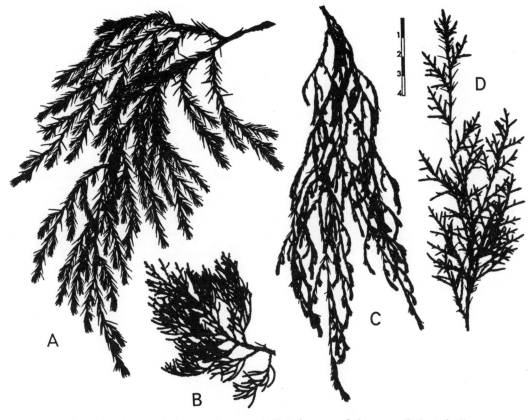

Fig. 91. **Juniperus**. A. *J. recurvata* var. *coxii*; B. *J. deppeana*; C. *J. recurva*; D. *J. pinchotii*
(Original)

erroneously labeled as *J. sabina* 'Cupressifolia'.

'Fastigiata'. Irregular columnar form, 5–6 m high, very narrow and dense, branches all upright, clustered; leaves mostly scale-like, deep green, bluish pruinose. WDw 161 (H); WM 258 (H); CCE 219 (= *J. sabina pyramidalis* Hort.). Originated in Holland before 1891.

'Femina'. Female form, low growing, branches and branchlets ascending; needles mostly scale-like, dark green. Selected by Herm. A. Hesse.

'Hicksii'. Strong grower, to 1.3 m, branches ascending at first, later procumbent with ascending tips; leaves mostly needle-like and distinctly blue-gray, with a trace of lilac in the winter. WDw Pl. 12F (Br); TC 134 (= *J. sabina* var. *hicksii* Grootend.; *J. horizontalis hicksii* Hort. Americ.). Developed by I. Hicks & Son, USA before 1940.

'Jade'. Slow growing, differing from the type in the finer, blue-green foliage. (Fairview).

'Mas'. Shrub, to 1.3 m high, branches ascending; needles usually needle-like, bluish above, green beneath, with a somewhat purple cast in winter; regarded as a male plant, but producing scattered fruit on older plants. Developed by Herm. A. Hesse before 1940.

'Musgrave' (C. Musgrave). Dwarf form, branches lying on the ground, about 20 cm high and 1.2 m wide in 10 years; leaves partly needle-like, partly scale-like, blue-green, needle leaves on the younger and interior leaves, otherwise predominantly scale leaves, tightly appressed. Found in the garden of Ch. Musgrave, Hascombe Place, Godalming, Surrey, England; introduced in 1961 by W. E. Th. Ingwersen, East Grinstead, England as 'Musgrave Variety'.

'Skandia'. Very similar to 'Arcadia' (and of the same origin, which see), but flatter growing; leaves usually needle-like, more gray-blue or also yellowish-green. WM 260 (H) (= *J. sabina* 'Scandens' Hillier).

'Tamariscifolia'. Low, spreading shrub, to 1 m high a 2 m wide when very old, branches horizontal, layered on each other, branchlets compact, short, spreading; leaves mostly needle-form, very short, sharp tipped, outspread, light bluish-green, with a dorsal gland. WDw 157 (H); WM 21C (Br) (= *J. sabina* var. *tamariscifolia* Ait.). This botanical variety is treated here as a cultivar because the garden plants are so consistent as to indicate a clonal origin. Fig. 92C.

'Tamariscifolia New Blue'. In USA. Differentiated from the type only in a distinct bluish tone to the needles.

'Thomsen'. Dwarf habit, very compact, only 10–20 cm high, branches horizontal or prostrate, branchlets thin, but firm, gray-brown, new shoots 5–6 cm long, filamentous, dense feathery; leaves scale-like, dark green, tightly appressed. Introduced by Thomsen, of Skalborg, Denmark in 1964.

'Variegata'. Slower growing than the species, but also to 1.5 m wide and 1 m high, branches horizontal, tips nodding, branchlets white variegated; leaves mostly scale-like. WDw 158 (H), Pl. 12E (Br); CCE 220. Very attractive form.

'Von Ehren'. Shrub, to 1.5 m high and wide, branches vase-like spreading-ascending, only sparsely branched inside the plant; needles awl-shaped, 3–5 mm long, acute, light green. KEv 178. Imported into the USA in 1908 by D. Hill of Dundee, Ill. from the L. Von Ehren Nursery of Hamburg, Germany. Widely disseminated in the USA under the erroneous spelling of "Vonehron".

J. saltuaria Rehd. & Wils. A tree in its habitat, to 15 m, crown conical, densely branched, branches and twigs upright or ascending, bark gray-brown to cinnamon-brown, branchlets short, somewhat reflexed, rectangular in cross section; leaves scale-like, opposite, densely appressed, ovate and short acuminate or also obtuse, incurved somewhat at the apex, dark green, 2 mm long, but also larger on the terminal shoot; plants monoecious; fruits oval, about 6 mm thick, glossy black, not pruinose, with only one seed, these ovate, 3 mm long. GGy 491. China; NW. Szechwan, develops dense forests. 1904. z6

J. sargentii (Henry). Takeda. Shrub, procumbent, 2–3 m wide and 0.5–0.8 m high, branches creeping or spreading over the ground, stiff, branchlets 4 sided, upright; nearly all leaves scale-like, small, bluish-green, more grass-green on young shoots, slightly furrowed on the dorsal side; fruits blue, light pruinose, seeds 3. WDw Pl. 12G (Br); LT 56; BCC 39 (H) (= *J. chinensis* var. *sargentii* Henry). Japan, Sachalin, Kurilen. Excellent groundcover, good plant for poor soils. Plate 69; Fig. 82D. z4

'Compacta'. More compact habit; scale leaves light green, needle leaves dark green with very blue-green tips, margin dark green. Distributed in California, USA since about 1950.

'Glauca'. Like *J. sargentii*, but needles conspicuously blue pruinose, branchlets thin, penniform, better growth habit. Cultivated before 1940 in Boskoop, Holland.

'Viridis'. Like *J. sargentii*, but with light green foliage. Cultivated in Boskoop, before 1940.

J. scopulorum Sarg. Rocky Mountain Juniper. Tree, 10–13 m high, often multistemmed from the base, broad crown formed by horizontal branches, bark brown to gray, in narrow strips, but not exfoliating, branches thinner than those of *J. virginiana*, but stiffer, not distinctly 4 sided; leaves scale-like, opposite, tightly appressed, tips not or slightly distinct, dark green or more yellowish or bluish, with an oblong, indistinct dorsal gland; fruits globose, ripening at the end of the 2nd year, 6 mm thick, dark blue and pruinose, flesh sweetish, with (1–)2 seeds, these red-brown, triangular. SPa 69–70; CB III 28; GGy 510. Western N. America, in dry rock outcroppings in Texas to Oregon and British Columbia. 1839. Plate 66. z6

> Also includes a large number of cultivars (40 to date!); most introduced by D. Hill Nurseries of Dundee, Illinois, USA. Only the most important forms are described.

'Admiral' (Mount Arbor Nurseries). Conical and broad; foliage gray-green. 1956.

'Blue Heaven' (Plumfield Nurseries). Conical habit, color a persistent blue-green; fruits abundantly all year. Introduced by the Plumfield Nurseries, Fremont, Nebraska, USA before 1963. Fig. 85B.

'Chandler's Silver'. Loose conical habit, tall, branches wide spreading, branchlets 7–8 cm long; leaves awl-shaped, very narrow, appressed, silver-gray above, green beneath. KEv 171. Discovered in the wild about 1936 in the Black Hills of South Dakota, USA.

'Columnaris'. Broadly upright, about 3 times as high as wide. Found wild in N. Dakota about 1941.

'Cologreen' (Marshall Nurseries). Upright habit, medium size, columnar, with a strong terminal leader; foliage always green (= *J. scopulorum* 'Colorado Green' Hort. Amer.). Found in the wild by Marshall about 1935.

'Gareei'. Dwarf form, hemispherical habit, to 1.5 m high and wide, branches horizontal, intermediate between *J. sabina* and *J. chinensis* 'Pfitzeriana' in habit; foliage silver-blue. KEv 171. Found in the wild by Garee, Noble, Oklahoma, USA, in the mountains of South Dakota about 1935.

'Globe'. Globose habit (without pruning!), to 2 m high and wide; foliage silvery and green (= *J. scopulorum globosa* Wyman 1963).

'Gray Gleam'. Very attractive, symmetrical columnar, densely and finely branched; foliage a good silver-gray. Found in 1944 in Wheat Ridge, Colorado, USA; introduced in 1949 by the W. W. Wilmore Nurseries. (Patented.)

'Hill's Silver'. Narrow conical form, to 6 m high; foliage silvery-blue, especially in summer. KEv 171 (= *J. scopulorum argentea* D. Hill ex Rehd.). Found in the wild in the mountains of S. Dakota, USA; introduced by D. Hill of Ill., USA in 1922. No longer cultivated.

'Horizontalis' (Hill). Upright form with horizontally spreading branches; leaves silvery-blue. 1923.

'Kenyonii'. Compact upright habit, 3–3.5 m high, steel-blue (= 'Dew Drop'). Selected in Kenyon's Nursery, Dover, Oklahoma, USA.

'Lakewood Globe'. Rather globose habit (this form must be maintained by an occasional pruning); foliage a good blue-green.

'Moffetii'. Regular upright, conical habit, very densely branched, annual growth about 30 cm; foliage light green and silvery, the branch tips more silvery. Found by L. A. Moffet of Plumfield Nurseries in the Rocky Mountains of Colorado, USA 1937.

'Montana'. Very slow growing, low or medium size conical form, densely branched; foliage deep green. Not a new form, but only recently reintroduced by the Plumfield Nurseries.

'O'Connor'. A wider, upright, densely branched form; foliage blue. Good winter hardiness.

'Pathfinder'. Broadly conical in habit, 6–9 m high, annual growth about 30 cm, densely branched, branches upright, also dense at the base, silver-blue. Selected by L. A. Moffet, Plumfield Nurseries, 1937.

'Platinum'. Dense conical habit, upright, attractively silver-blue foliage during the entire year. Selected by Willis Nurseries, Ottawa, Kansas, USA 1958. (Patented.)

'Repens'. Dwarf form, creeping habit, branches procumbent (very similar to *J. horizontalis* 'Prostrata'), branchlets directed forward, feathery, tips curved upward; leaves needle-like, 5 mm long, blue-green, later more green; often fruits abundantly. KN 124 (= *J. scopulorum repens* Hornibr.; *J. scopulorum palmeri* Grootend.). Found by R. C. Palmer at Lake Windermere, British Columbia, Canada, before 1938.

'Silver Beauty'. Regular conical-upright habit, 6–9 m high, annual growth 30 cm, branches narrowly ascending; foliage greenish-silver, more silvery on the branch tips. Selected by the D. Hill Nurseries of Dundee, Illinois, USA in 1932. Not widely cultivated.

'Silver Cord'. Habit very narrow and upright, compact; foliage bluish-silver. (Plumfield).

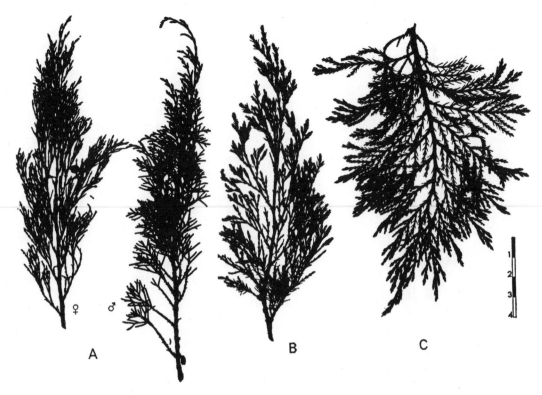

Fig. 92. **Juniperus.**
A. *J. sabina*, male and female; B. *J. sabina* 'Arcadia'; C. *J. sabina* 'Tamariscifolia' (Original)

'Silver King'. Low and shrubby, only to 50 cm high, but 2 m wide, densely branched, branch tips thin, filamentous; foliage silver-blue. Originated as a seedling in the nursery of C. White, Walla Walla, Washington, USA. (Patented.)

'Silver Star'. Broad, low habit, slow growing, to 40 cm high and 125 cm wide, young shoots bright green at first, but soon becoming silvery. USA, before 1965.

'Skyrocket'. One of the narrowest columnar forms, at least 4 m high (then only 40 cm wide!), all branches and twigs ascend vertically. WDw 173 (H) (= *J. virginiana* 'Skyrocket' F. J. Grootendorst; *J. chinensis* 'Skyrocket' F. J. Grootendorst; *J. scopulorum pillaris* Wyman). Found in the wild before 1949 and first propagated without a name at the former Schuel Nursery in South Bend, Indiana, USA. Fig. 93.

'Springbank'. Narrow, conical habit, to about 2 m high, upper branches loose and spreading gracefully, branch tips very thin, nearly filamentous; foliage intense silver-blue. Very vigorous and particularly winter hardy.

'Steel Blue'. Flat growing; foliage blue-green. Hardly disseminated. (Minier catalogue 1977).

'Sutherland'. Broadly conical habit, tall but slow growing, branches upright, rather thin, but stiff; leaves small, tightly appressed, deep green. Introduced in 1925 by the Sutherland Nurseries of Boulder, Colorado, USA.

'Tabletop'. Shrubby habit, to about 2 m high, then 5 m wide, branches spreading and dense, thin, yellowish-brown; leaves very small, tightly appressed, a good silver-blue. 1956.

'Tolleson's Weeping'. Broad and open conical upright, but all branches limply spreading in narrow or wide bows, the twigs nearly "mane-like" pendulous and very dense. Distributed by the Monrovia Nurseries of California, USA since 1973 but certainly cultivated in the United States before that. Extraordinarily attractive form with silver-blue foliage.

'Viridifolia' (D. Hill). Tall, narrow form with bright green foliage. D. Hill, Dundee, Illinois, USA. 1923

'Welchii' (Plumfield, before 1940). Compact narrow-conical habit; foliage silvery, especially on young plants. KEv 172.

'Wichita Blue'. Medium high, broad conical-upright; foliage blue-green during the entire year.

J. semiglobosa Regel. Tree, to 10 m high in its habitat, crown narrow and open, occasionally pendulous, branchlets rather short, thin, pendulous; leaves scale-like, glossy green, white beneath, very acute, rhombic, tightly appressed, entire; fruit at the apex, hemispherical, 5 to 8 mm thick, dark brown to black, fleshy, but not sweet. Central Asia; Tien-Shan, Turkestan, Kokania Valley in Sarawchan, Kasachstan, USSR. Plate 66. z6

J. seravshanica Komar. Low shrub, branches often lying on the ground, or also a small tree, 5–10 m high, bark reddish or gray-red, branchlets short, 1.5 mm thick, yellowish or bluish-green; leaves scale-like, acute, slightly dentate, with an elongated dorsal gland; fruit globose, 1.2 cm thick, blue and pruinose, hard and woody (= *J. polycarpos* Haeckel non Kosch). Central Asia, Pakistan, on Mt. Noshaq, between 3800 and 4000 m. Plate 66. z6

J. silicicola (Small) Bail. Southern Juniper. Conical tree,

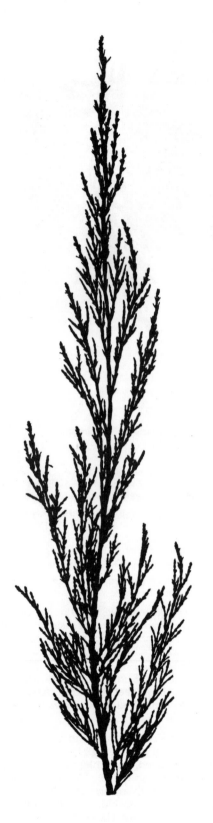

Fig. 93. *Juniperus scopulorum* 'Skyrocket' (Original)

with wide spreading branches on older plants, or only an erect shrub, branchlets thin; leaves scale-like, ovate to more triangular, acute to truncate, appressed, but the tips often distinct; plants usually dioecious; fruits oval, about 5 mm long, more or less pruinose when ripe (= *J. barbadensis* Michx. p.p. non L.; *J. lucayana* Britt. p.p.). N. America, coastal plains of S. Carolina to Florida and Texas. Occasionally confused with *J. barbadensis* which has kidney-shaped fruits; and with *J. virginiana* which has thicker twigs and larger fruits. Plate 66. z9

J. squamata D. Don. Shrub, usually procumbent, main stem short and more or less ascending or upright, bark reddish-brown, young shoots green and furrowed, tips nodding (!!); leaves in whorls of 3, needle-like, densely arranged, loosely appressed or somewhat spreading, finely and sharply acuminate, stiff, concave above and white, with a slightly conspicuous midrib, convex beneath and green, furrowed from the base nearly to the apex, 4–5 mm long, old dry and brown leaves remaining on the twigs for several years; fruits ellipsoid, 6–8 mm long, ripening the 2nd year, red-brown, eventually black, composed of 3–6 scales, single seeded, ovate. SN 192 (H); EH (6) l420; MJu 11; CB III 29. Afghanistan to Taiwan, in the mountains. 1824. Its forms are often found in cultivation, but rarely the type; often confused with *J. procumbens*, but easily distinguished by the nodding branch tips (also typical of the forms). Fig. 81. z4–8

'Blue Carpet' (J. Schoemaker). Mutation of 'Meyeri', very vigorous, but quite flat and broad, about 30 cm high and 1.2–1.5 m wide after 10 years, very densely branched; needles like those of 'Meyeri', blue-gray, 6–9 mm long, 1.5–2 mm wide, acute and sharp. Developed before 1972 by Jac. Schoemaker, Boskoop, Holland.

'Blue Star' (Hoogeveen). Dwarf form, broad and hemispherical, very dense; foliage exactly like that of 'Meyeri'. Originated as a witches'-broom on 'Meyeri', about 1950 in the Gebr. Hoogeveen Nursery in Reeuwijk, Holland. First introduced in 1964. Plate 70.

'Chinese Silver'. Broad, bushy, with pendulous branches; needles intense silver-blue. Meritorious novelty from the USA.

var. **fargesii** Rehd. & Wils. Tree, 5–20 m high, often multistemmed from the ground, bark brown, shredding in long strips, branches upright and spreading, branchlets pendulous; needles longer and narrower than the type, to 8 mm long, prickly acuminate, pale or blue-green; fruits ovate, 5–6 mm long, obtuse black-blue. SN 193 (H), CC 30 (H) (= *J. fargesii* Komar; *J. kansuensis* Komar). Forests on the Chinese-Tibetan border. 1907. Rare in cultivation. Fig. 95E.

'Forrestii'. Similar to 'Wilsonii', but more upright, not so narrowly conical as 'Loderi'. Cultivated by Hillier and Welch, England, but the origin is unknown.

'Glassell'. Dwarf form, quite low, very slow growing, nearly hemispherical, branchlets short, tips curved downward; needles gray-green, like 'Wilsonii', but shorter and denser. WDw 165 (H); Pl. 11f (Br); WM 20A (Br). Distributed by H. J. Welch, England.

'Golden Flame'. A 'Meyeri' with yellow spots in the branches. Discovered by L. Konijn & Co., Reeuwijk, Holland; introduced in 1968.

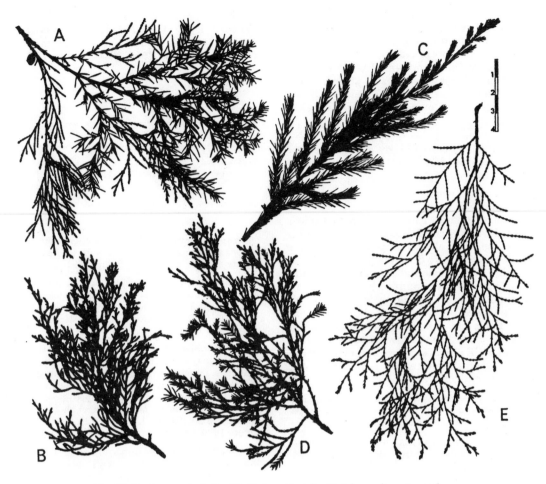

Fig. 94. **Juniperus.** A. *J. flaccida*; B. *J. occidentalis*; C. *J. bermudiana*, juvenile;
D. *J. thurifera*; E. *J. excelsa* (Original)

'Holger' (Holger Jensen, Helsingborg, Sweden, 1946). Alleged hybrid between *J. squamata* and *J.* 'Pfitzeriana Aurea', intermediate between the parents in appearance, but closer to *J. squamata*, broad and flat, about 2 × 2 m, new growth yellow, older foliage gray-green, therefore bicolored in spring. WM 265 (H).

'Loderi'. Low columnar form, 1–1.5 m high, branches and twigs very densely arranged, upright, tips nodding; leaves needle-like, acute, blue-green above, green beneath, 2nd year needles become dry and brown. WDw 164 (H), Pl. 11B (Br); WM 20B (Br), 266 (H) (= *J. wallichiana* var. *loderi* Hornibr.; *J. squamata* var. *loderi* Hornibr.). Developed by Sir Edmund Loder about 1926.

'Meyeri'. Not a dwarf shrub! Reaches height of 5–6 m (perhaps higher), usually with a central stem, upright branches and short, ascending twigs, branchlets with very dense foliage, red-brown, branch tips curved; leaves narrow-lanceolate, 6–10 mm long, to 1.5 mm wide, very densely arranged, straight, impressive blue-white; fruits oval-oblong, 5–6 mm long, deep brown, eventually black, pruinose. WM 20C (Br). China, but only in cultivation; probably disseminated from the Chinese gardening center, Tsaochan, SW. Shantung Province. Brought to the USA (Arnold Arboretum) in 1914 by F. N. Meyer. Widely grown today despite the ugly brown color of the old needles. Plate 67; Fig. 95C.

'Prostrata'. Shrub, dwarf, procumbent, slow growing, branches and branchlets horizontal, with nodding tips; leaves needle-like, outspread, with blue-white stomatal bands above and a wide green margin, green and somewhat keeled beneath. NF 8: 195; CCE 222 (= *J. squamata prostrata* Hornibr.). Developed from Chinese seed collected by E. H. Wilson about 1909 by Hornibrook. It is therefore possible, as noted by Welch, that this could be the type of the species.

'Pygmaea'. Shrub, very similar to 'Wilsonii', but much lower, scarcely over 1 m high, main branches narrowly upright; foliage also like that of 'Wilsonii', but the branch tips less nodding. WDw 167 (H); WM 268 (H). Only cultivated in England. Plate 70.

'Wilsonii'. Upright, dense, conical form shrub, 2–3 m high, branches and twigs very densely arranged, branchlets short and compact, branch tips nodding, turning somewhat purple in winter; needles awl-shaped, very much bowed, 5–6 mm long, 1 mm wide, with 2 blue-white stomatal bands above, midrib green, also a narrow green margin, keeled and green beneath. WDw 166 (H), Pl. 11J (Br); WM 20D (Br), 269 (H) (= *J. squamata* f. *wilsonii* Rehd.). Collected by Wilson in China in 1909 and imported to the USA. Fig. 95D.

J. taxifolia Hook. & Arn., non Parl. Tree, to 12 m high, or only a shrub, stem more or less twisting, branches spreading horizontally, branchlets pendulous, young shoots with narrow wing-like ridges; leaves in widely spaced whorls of 3, light green, usually straight and equally wide to the apex, not prickly(!), 10(20) mm long, 2 mm wide, concave above and with 2 white stomatal bands, midrib green, convex beneath, keeled; fruits globose, glossy blue, 6 mm thick, with 3 seeds. CB III 30. Japan; Ogasawara-Gunta, Bonin Islands. Fig. 80G. z9

var. **luchuenensis** (Koidz.) Satake. Procumbent, resembling J. *conferta*, but needles flatter and not so deeply furrowed above, often with a distinct midrib, but not prickly, grass green. WDw 137 (H), Pl. 9F (Br); WM 18B (Br), 270 (H). Japan, Ryukyu Island. z9

J. thurifera L. Conical when young, older trees often more or less round crowned, to 15 m high, branches horizontal, branchlets hardly 1 mm thick, nearly 4 sided, strongly scented when crushed; leaves partly scale-like, partly needle-like, but always opposite, the latter outspread, 2–4 mm long, also occurring on older plants, gray-green, with a white band above, green beneath, scale leaves usually with the penniform branchlets on an even plane, about 1.5 mm long, tightly appressed, with distinct tips, furrowed beneath; plants dioecious; fruit globose, 8 mm thick, dark blue, pruinose, composed of 6 scales, with 2 to 4 ovate, glossy brown seeds. OCC 197; CB III 11; DJ 56; CCE 223, 224. Spain, mountains in the center and to the south; S. France; NW. Africa, Atlas Mts. Plate 61; Fig. 81G and 94D. z9

var. **gallica** de Coincy. Differing primarily in the smaller, less angular fruit, striped seeds, not as glossy as those of the type. GGy 505. S. France, Corsica, N. Spain (near Saragossa).

J. tibetica Komar. Tree, 10–30 m high in its habitat, with a densely branched crown; stem gray-brown, bark exfoliating, branchlets rather thin, brownish, horizontally arranged; leaves opposite, nearly triangular, brownish; flowers very small, yellow-green; fruits oval to globose, 10 mm high and wide, yellow-green, seeds 4 sided (important distinction!), pitted and rugose. GGy 498. Tibet, China; W. Szechwan, in the mountains between 3000–4000 m. 1926. Presumably winter hardy.

J. turkestanica Komar. Shrub or tree, 3 to 12 m high, with a dense crown, stem gray, bark scaly, exfoliating, twigs upright or spreading; leaves scale-like or needle-like, scale leaves 2 mm long, 8–10 mm thick, blackish, glossy, somewhat pruinose, succulent, with 1 seed, these oblong-spathulate, 6–10 mm long, furrowed. DB 1970: 66 (H). Central Asia; Turkestan, in the mountains at 3000–4000 m. z6

J. virginiana L. "Red Cedar". Tree, to 30 m high, quite variable in habit, usually slender ovate to conical at first, later with horizontally spreading branches, also nodding, stem to 1 m thick, bark gray to red-brown, exfoliating in long strips, branchlets indistinctly 4 sided, thin; leaves mostly scale-like, but needle leaves frequently found on older trees, these to 10 mm long, prickly acuminate, grooved above with white markings, green beneath, opposite, scale leaves in 4 rows, oval-rhombic to lanceolate, 1.5 mm long, short or longer acuminate, with an indented gland on the dorsal side; plants usually monoecious; fruits ripening the 1st year,

oval, to 6 mm thick, dark blue, glossy or also pruinose. CB II 75; DJ 57; CCE 224–226. N. America; Canada to Florida, widely distributed east of the Rocky Mts. Introduced before 1664. Plate 65; Fig. 75B. z9

With numerous cultivars.

To help distinguish J. *virginiana* from J. *chinensis* cultivars:

	J. *chinensis*	J. *virginiana*
Juvenile leaves ("Needle leaves")	usually in whorls of 3	usually paired, whorled on the terminal shoot
Scale leaves	apex obtuse and bowed inward	acute on the apex, not incurved

'Albospica'. Branch tips conspicuously white (= J. *virginiana albospica* Beissn.; J. *virginiana albospicata* Beissn.; J. *virginiana* 'White Tip' Hort. Americ.). Before 1891. z7

'Boskoop Purple' (Grootend.). Narrow columnar form, fast growing and tall, mutation of 'Hillii', but taller, faster growing and colored a more intense purple-brown in winter. Otherwise, see 'Hillii'. Developed by F. J. Grootendorst in 1960, introduced in 1963.

'Burkii' (Bobbink & Atkins). Broad columnar or also a more conical habit, to 3 m high, branches densely arranged, erect, branches numerous, short, evenly arranged; needles awl-shaped, narrow, 5 to 7 mm long, gradually fine acuminate, sharp, but not prickly, dull blue striped above, margin narrow, green, green beneath, fall color steel-blue, turning purple in winter. DB 20:252; TC 137; CCE 225. Originated in the USA before 1930. Often seen in cultivation today.

'Canaertii'. Slender columnar to conical habit, to 8 m high, branches ascending, thick, twigs short, densely crowded; needles scale-like on young shoots, often awl-shaped on older plants, dark green; fruits very numerous, small, blue-white, contrasting well with the dark green foliage. KEv 166; MC 151; CCE 228. Named in honor of Canaert D'Hamale, Mechelen, Belgium. Before 1868.

'Chamberlaynii'. Broad, branches horizontal to procumbent, stout, elongated with nodding tips, main branches with long needle leaves, these tightly appressed to the twigs up to the terminal 3–5 mm, then acute and spreading, slightly spreading on weaker shoots, gray-blue pruinose, scale leaves in the center of the plant dark green, with an oval gland on the dorsal side. WDw 168 (H). Cultivated in England since 1850.

'Cinerascens'. Conical habit, open, growth vigorous, branches long, horizontal, branchlets numerous, crowded, short; needles subulate, short acuminate, the scale needles small and appressed, ash gray to silver-white (= J. *virginiana cinerascens* Carr.; J. *virginiana argentea* Hort.). Cultivated in France before 1855; but today (EX?).

var. **creba** Fern. & Griscom. Narrow conical to columnar habit, tall, branches ascending; leaves narrow ovate, acute, loosely appressed; seeds somewhat pitted. Rhodora Pl. 332. This is the slender growing type encountered in the NE. USA as opposed to the broader growing southern type.

'Cupressifolia'. Conical habit, rather loose; needles yellowish-green, scale-like (= J. *virginiana cupressifolia* Kammerer, non Kumlien!). See also 'Hillspire'.

'Elegantissima'. Conical habit, 2–3 m high, light and elegant branching, branches slightly pendulous, branch tips yellow, older branches dark green; leaves needle- and scale-like. KEv

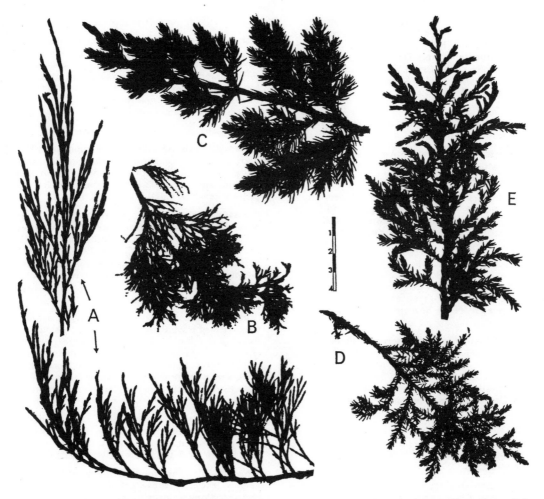

Fig. 95. **Juniperus.** A. *J. "virginiana* Reptans" (in German nurseries), viewed from the side and from above; B. *J. virginiana* 'Globosa'; C. *J. squamata* 'Meyeri'; D. *J. squamata* 'Wilsonii'; E. *J. squamata* var. *fargesii* (Original)

168 (= *J. virginiana elegantissima* Hochst.; *J. virginiana elegans* Nichols.). Cultivated before 1882. One of the most beautiful forms today.

'Fastigiata' (Hesse). Narrow columnar form, 5–6 m high, peak with several tips, branches ascending, twigs very thin, blue-green; all leaves scale-like, tightly appressed, very small, acute, blue-green with narrow white stomatal lines. CCE 227. Origin unknown. Introduced in 1933 by Herm A. Hesse. Similar to *J. sabina* 'Fastigiata', but the crushed twigs do not have an unpleasant smell.

'Filifera' (D. Hill). Broadly conical, branchlets long and thin, often filamentous; leaves blue-green. Introduced by D. Hill, Dundee, Illinois, USA before 1923.

'Glauca'. Columnar form, fast and vigorous grower, 5(10) m high, densely branched, narrow, branch tips exserted from the columnar form; leaves scale-like, small, appressed, occasionally needle-like inside the plant. TC 125; KEv 167; MC 155. Very popular form, should be propagated only from the best steel-blue branchlets.

'Glauca Pendula' (Simon Louis Frères). Conical habit, branches spread horizontally, branch tips and branchlets gracefully nodding; leaves scale-like, blue-green; male flowers very numerous, yellow, in May. Cultivated before 1909 in France, but no longer in culture.

'Globosa'. Globose, scarcely over 1 m high, compact, very densely branched, branchlets short and clustered, thin; leaves all scale-like, small, dark green, more brown in winter. SN 63 (H); Gs 1926: 39 (H); WDw 169 (H); CCE 229; WM 21F (Br), 272 (H). Known since 1891. Welch reported a 50-year old plant in the Arnold Arboretum at 4.5 m high, globose and quite dense. Fig. 95B.

'Grey Owl' (Gebr. Caam). Shrubby, branches ascending, stout, like *J.* × *media* 'Pfitzeriana', but branches spread more horizontally blue-pruinose, branchlets rather thin, branch tips occasionally somewhat purple in winter. MC 154; CCE 225; WM 273 (H). Developed in 1938 by Gebr. Caam, Oudenbosch, Holland from seed of *J. virginiana* 'Glauca', growing near *J.* × *media* 'Pfitzeriana'. Introduced by F. J. Grootendorst in 1949. Fig. 86D.

'Helle' see: **J. chinensis 'Spartan'**

'Hillii' (D. Hill). Columnar form, dense, 2–4 m high, branches and twigs horizontal, short, branchlets 5–10 cm long; leaves subulate, 5–8 mm long, with rather broad blue-white stomatal bands above, margin blue-green, greenish-blue beneath, entire plant turning distinctly purple in winter. KEv 170; MC 153 (= *J. virginiana hillii* D. Hill 1944; *J. virginiana pyramidiformis hillii* D. Hill 1922). Originated by D. Hill, USA about 1916.

'**Hillspire**' (D. Hill). Symmetrically conical habit, male form with especially bright green foliage, retained in winter. OCC 201; KEv 168 (= *J. virginiana* 'Hillspire' D. Hill 1963; *J. virginiana cupressifolia* Kuml. non Kammerer). Developed about 1925 by D. Hill, USA and mistakenly named 'Cupressifolia' in 1946. Since this name was already used by Kammerer in 1932, a new name had to be assigned.

"Horizontalis". Plants in the nursery under this name have been shown by Hillier and Welch consistently to be *J. horizontalis* or a form thereof.

"Horizontalis Glauca". Also known in American nurseries as 'Blue Coast Juniper' (see illust. in KEv 183); is actually *J. virginiana* Chamberlaynii'!

'**Kobendzii**'. Narrow, densely branched, small tree, young shoots only with needle leaves, these blue-green and prickly (= *J. virginiana* f. *kobendzii* Wroblewski ex Browicz & Bugala). Selected as a seedling in 1932 at the Kornik Arboretum, Poland.

'**Kobold**' (N. Th. Bosman). Globose dwarf form, very dense, branches thin, but stiff, branchlets upright to horizontal, 1–1.5 cm long; leaves needle-like, very densely arranged, 0.5–1 cm long and 0.5 mm wide, blue-green above, green beneath. Originated from seed by N. Th. Bosman, Boskoop, Holland in 1952.

"Kosteri". Plants of this name in the nursery look almost exactly like *J.* × *media* 'Pfitzeriana', distinguished only by a wide, flat habit. It remains to be seen whether or not the plant introduced about 1870 by M. Koster & Zonen, Boskoop, Holland is truly different. Lacks the strong *sabina* scent of 'Pfitzeriana'. The illustration in WDw 171 shows a × *media* form; totally different from that in OCC 202.

'**Manhattan Blue**' (R. Scott). Male, conical form, compact, similar to 'Glauca', but with a more blue-green foliage (more gray-green on 'Glauca'). Introduced before 1963 by R. Scott, Manhattan, Kansas, USA.

'**Monstrosa**'. Very slow growing, low and wide, with witches'-broom-like branching. Known since 1867.

'**Nana Compacta**'. Dwarf globose form, but somewhat irregular, 0.8–1.0 m high, branches horizontal and ascending, not so com-pressed as those of 'Globosa', branchlets numerous, densely feathery; needles partly subulate and 2–4 mm long, partly scale-like, greenish-blue above, green beneath, winter color dull purple-green. WDw 170 (H); WM 274 (H) (= *J. virginiana tripartita nana* Hort. Angl.). Introduced before 1887 by C. G. Overeynder, Boskoop.

'**Pendula**'. Weeping form, tree-like, to 10 m high or higher, branches horizontal-nodding, secondary branches and branchlets hanging downward; needles usually scale-like, obtuse, bright green, the needle-like leaves narrow, tightly appressed; fruits abundantly, fruits small, blue-white pruinose. BFN 611 (H). Cultivated in England before 1850. Plate 68.

'**Pendula Nana**'. Dwarf form, quite low growing, scarcely 60 cm high, branches horizontal and distinctly nodding; leaves scale-like, gray-green. WDw 174 (H). Distributed by Hillier, 1928.

'**Pendula Viridis**'. Female, weeping form, branches and twigs limp and arching, branchlets limp downward; leaves all scale-like, bright green (= *J. virginiana viridis pendula* R. Sm.; *J. virginiana* f. *smithii pendula* Beissn.). Known in England before 1862.

'**Plumosa Argentea**'. Graceful habit, conical, branches horizontal, lightly branched, branchlets short, tips white variegated or sometimes sulfur-yellow and gray-green, eventually greenish; leaves predominantly needle-like. SH 63 (H) (= *J. virginiana plumosa alba* Beissn.). Developed before

1887 by H. Van Nes, Boskoop, Holland.

'**Pseudocupressus**'. Columnar, very slender acuminate peak, 3–4 m high, branches and twigs narrowly upright, densely covering the stem; needles usually subulate, mostly appressed on the branch tips, spreading toward the branch base, to 6 mm long, acute, concave above and light green, keeled beneath and blue-green. Origin unknown; first described at the Morton Arboretum by Kammerer in 1932.

'Pyramidalis' is only a collective name.

'**Pyramidiformis**' (D. Hill). Very slender conical form, to 15 m high, similar to 'Canaertii' in habit, branches ascending and outspread, branchlets upright, short, thin, loose; leaves scale-like and appressed, dark green, very small (= *J. virginiana pyramidiformis* D. Hill.). Introduced in 1922.

'**Reptans**'. Male, dwarf form, creeping, spreading across the ground, branch tips nodding gracefully; leaves inside the plant needle-like and faintly bluish, more scale-like and bright green toward the branch tips. MG 1896:296. Described by Beissner (1896) from a plant growing in the Botanic Garden of Jena, E. Germany, since 1918. This is not, however, the plant generally found in cultivation, which is nothing more than a *J. horizontalis*. Fig. 95A.

'**Robusta Green**'. Narrow columnar habit, densely branched, twigs curved inward and more or less twisted; leaves needle-like, 5–8 mm long, 1–1.5 mm wide, blue-green(!), somewhat curving inward and more or less twisted; prickly tips, occasionally small shoots with needle leaves inside the plant. From USA, origin unknown. Cultivated in Boskoop, Holland. Very attractive compact columnar plant, very vigorous, good winter hardiness.

'**Schottii**'. Narrow conical habit, 2–3 m high, ascending branches, twigs very thin, yellow-green; all needles scale-like, tightly appressed, light green to yellow-green. Known in England before 1855 and still widely cultivated.

'**Sherwoodii**' (Sherwood Nursery 1943). Conical habit, narrow; leaves like those of 'Canaertii', dark green, but branch tips on the long shoots are cream-yellow in spring, bright green in summer, violet in winter. Developed in 1935 at the Sherwood Nursery Company, Portland, Oregon, USA.

'**Silver Spreader**'. Low flat habit, similar to 'Grey Owl', but with more greenish-silver foliage (= *J. virginiana dammii* 1955; *J. virginiana prostrata* 'Silver Spreader' 1963). Both names were given by Monrovia Nurseries in Azusa, California, USA, who obtained the plant as a seedling about 1954. Very popular in the USA.

'Skyrocket' see: **J. scopulorum 'Skyrocket'**

'**Triomphe d'Angers**'. Conical form, slow growing, open branching, branches and twigs thin, regularly arranged, branchlets very even in length, rather short, white variegated, the white variegated tips evenly distributed over the entire plant, the other needles blue-green, small. Before 1891. z8

'**Tripartita**'. Low growing, but to 2 m high and at least as wide on older plants, usually with a few, stiff, irregularly arranged branches, twigs horizontal to upright, tips partly nodding; leaves mostly needle-like, more appressed at the branch tips, but spreading toward the base, blue-green. WDw Pl. 13J (Br); CCE 229 (= *J. tripartita* de Vos). Known since 1867.

J. wallichiana Hook. f. ex Brandis. Black Juniper. Tall tree, dioecious, 10–15 m high, loosely branched, bark brown, very rough, exfoliating in papery scales, branch tips 4 sided, over 1 mm thick; leaves needle-like and in whorls of 3 on young shoots and partly also on older shoots, directed forward, 3–6 mm long, acuminate, concave and bluish above, furrowed and green beneath, scale leaves opposite, narrowly ovate, furrowed on the dorsal side; fruits ovate, 9 mm long, 8 mm thick, with 3–5 scales, blue, ripening the 2nd year. OCC 206 (Br); CB III 22; GGy 410; DJ 58. The Himalayan mountains. 1849. z9

J. zaidamensis Komar. Small tree, 9–12 m high, bark cinnamon-brown, exfoliating in thin strips, branches horizontal to pendulous; branchlets thin, crowded; leaves needle-like, small, tightly appressed, truncate, gray-green, with a linear gland; fruits globose, dark brown, to 10 m thick, seeds very rugose. GGy 492. China; Kansu Province, in the mountains of southern Kukunor. z6

Lit. Antoine, F.: Die Kupressineen-Gattungen *Arceuthos, Juniperus* and *Sabina*. Vienna 1857. ● Gaussen, H.: Les Gymnospermes, actuelles et fossiles. 1943–1955 (chapter XII: *Juniperus*, 81–220). ● Kuphaldt G.: Der Baumwacholder. Mitt. DDG 1933, 112–115 (with 4 ills.). ● Pilger, R.: Die Gattung *Juniperus*. Mitt. Deutsch. Dendr. Ges. **43**, 265–269, 1931. ● Spach, E.: Révision des *Juniperus*. Ann. Sci. Nat. sér. 2, **16**, 282–305, 1841. ● Van Melle, P.J.: The Junipers commonly included in *Juniperus chinensis*. Phytologia **2**, 185–195, 1946. New York. ● Van Melle, P. J.: A Review of *Juniperus chinensis* et al. New York 1947 (108 pp., 12 plates). ● Wyman, D.: Many excellent Forms and much Confusion in the variable Junipers. Part I: American Nurseryman 1963, I, 13–16, 115–123; part II: 1963, II, 12–13, 56–76.

KETELEERIA Carr—PINACEAE

Tall evergreen trees (often only shrubby in cultivation) of *Abies*-like appearance, branches whorled, spreading, irregularly branched, crown more umbrella-shaped with age, conical when young; buds ovate to globose, not resinous; leaves needle-like, linear, stiff, nearly 2 ranked and loosely arranged, flat on both sides with a protruding midrib, glossy green above, pale green beneath, with indistinct stomatal bands, usually acutely thorned on young plants, obtuse on older plants, with 2 marginal resin ducts on the lower epidermis at the leaf edges; leaf scar circular, like *Abies*; plants monoecious; male flowers clustered, axillary or terminal, emerging from a scaly bud; female flowers terminal and erect on short foliate, lateral branches, the stout cone rachis is later developed from this shoot; cones like those of *Abies*, erect, ovate to cylindrical, but totally abscising when ripe (in the 1st year; whereas *Abies* disintegrates leaving the rachis!); seed scales large, wide, leathery-woody; bract scales half as long as the seed scales; seeds in 2's, with resin pits large, winged, wing as long or nearly as long as the scale; and somewhat exserted when ripe; cotyledons 2, remaining underground. x = 12.—4–8 species in China and Taiwan. Better suited to dry climates than *Abies*. Range map Fig. 96.

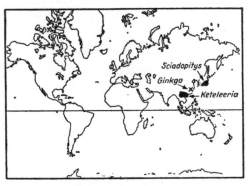

Fig. 96. Range of the genus *Keteleeria*, *Ginkgo* and *Sciadopitys*

Outline of the morphological characteristics of the species (from Flous)

Leaves mucronulate. 1

Leaves not mucronulate 2

1. Leaves long, with numerous stomata on the upper side; cones large, cylindrical; fruit scales pubescent, rhombic, limb toothed, bract scales compact, base very wide, but blade very constricted; Yunnan Province:
K. evelyniana

   Leaves short, only rarely with stomata above; cones small, ovate; seed scales not pubescent, pentangular, entire; bract scales narrow, base linear, much narrower than the blade; Kwangsi, Kweichow Provinces:
K. chien peii

2. Leaves long, to 4.5 cm. 3

   Leaves short, to 2.5 cm 5

3. Leaves narrow, scarcely 2.5 mm wide; seeds scales about as long as wide; Laos:
K. roulletii var. *dopiana*
(not dealt with here)

   Leaves wide, 3.5 mm wide and more; seed scales elongated, seeds with long, narrow wing: 4

4. Young shoots glabrous; with long stomatal lines above; apex tapered; Vietnam:
K. roulletii

   Young shoots pubescent; rarely with stomatal lines above but only on the apex; apex wide, more or less round; N. China:
K. davidiana

5. Bract scales with only 1 lobe on the apex; stomata rare, only on the apex; Kwangsi, Kweichow Provinces:
K. esquirolii

   Bract scales with 3 lobes on the apex 6

6. Upper side of the leaves without stomata; Chekiang Province:
K. fortunei

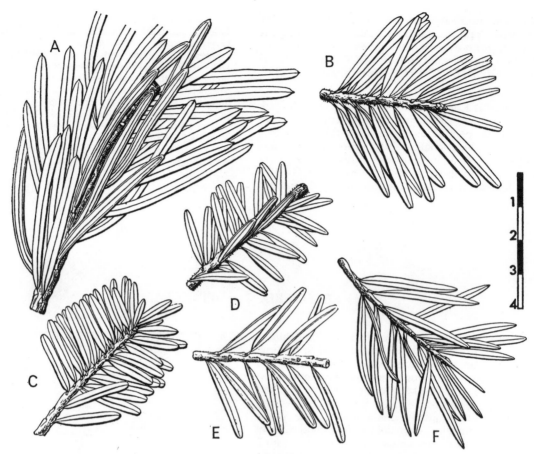

Fig. 97. **Keteleeria** branch. A. *K. evelyniana*; B. *K. davidiana*; C. *K. fortunei*;
D. *K. esquirolii*; E. *K. davidiana* var. *formosana*; F. *K. roulletii* (compiled by Flous)

7. Stomata very numerous; young shoots distinctly
    pubescent; seed scales nearly circular; Kwangsi Province:
    K. cyclolepis

    Stomata less numerous; seed scales pentangular to
    rhombic; Taiwan: *K. davidiana* var. *formosana*

Keteleeria chien peii Flous. Tree, 7–10 m high, bark gray
to gray-brown, young shoots red-brown, very
pubescent, leaf scars circular and arranged in narrow
spirals; leaves of sterile shoots straight, 15–30 mm long,
about 2.5 mm wide, limb slightly involute, bright green
above, with 2–3 intermittent stomatal lines at the apex,
underside with 2 stomatal bands, each with 8–15 lines,
leaves acuminate in fertile shoots; cones ovate-
cylindrical, curved, about 8 cm long, 3.5 cm thick; seed
scales and bract scales, see Fig. 99G; 100D (C). FK 35.
China; Kwangsi, and Kweichow Provinces. z7

K. cyclolepis Flous. Tree, to about 11 m high; young
shoots red-brown, short and densely pubescent; leaves
on sterile shoots straight or slightly sickle-shaped, apical
half wider than the basal half, limb not involute, about
15–20 mm long, 2.5–3 mm wide, with 2 stomatal bands
on the upper side, each with 6–8 lines, underside with
12–20 lines; cones not completely known, seed scales
nearly circular. FK 39. China; Kwangsi Province. Fig.
98E. z7

K. davidiana (Bertr.) Beissn. Tree, 10–20 m high in its
habitat (to 30 m according to Lee), habit *Abies*-like at first,
more irregular with age, bark dark gray, rough and split,
young shoots chestnut-brown, short and frequently
very distinctly pubescent, buds rather globose, reddish;
needles nearly 2 ranked, widely spaced, straight or
somewhat sickle-shaped, somewhat wider toward the
base, 15–40 mm long, 3.5–4 mm wide, stiff, sharp tipped
and prickly on young plants, obtuse or slightly
emarginate on older plants, both sides glossy green or
more blue-green beneath, with a few stomata on the
apex above, 2 stomatal bands beneath, each with 12–15
lines; seed scales (Fig. 98C) chestnut-brown, margin
reflexed on older cones, cones 8–15 cm long and 5 cm
thick. FK 43; CB I 72., CIS 11. China; Central and W.
Szechwan Provinces. 1888. Fig. 97B and 99C (C). z9

var. **formosana** Hayata. Tree, to 35 m high and trunk to 2.5 m in
diameter, young shoots short haired or glabrous; leaves 20–40
mm long, 3–4 mm wide, keeled on both sides, margin more or
less involute; cones cylindrical, 5–15 cm long, about 4 cm thick,
bract scales abruptly broad rounded past the middle. FK 63;
LWT 7; LT 25 (= *K. formosana* Hayata). Taiwan, but also in central and W. China. Fig. 97E, 98H, 99E (C). (R)

K. esquirolii Lév. Tree, 25–30 m high, bark gray, rough,
young shoots red-brown, nearly glabrous or with
scattered, short pubescence; leaves straight, 15–20 mm

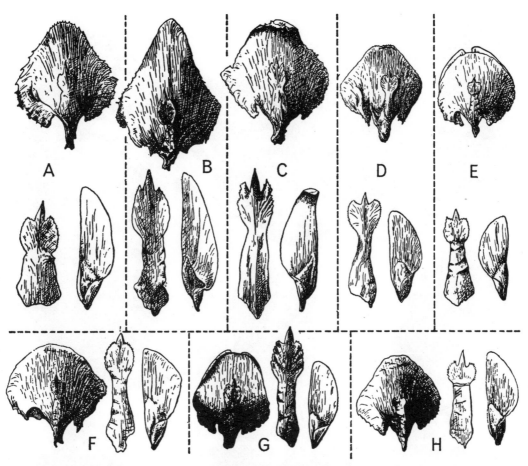

Fig. 98. **Keteleeria**. A. *K. evelyniana;* B. *K. roulletii;* C. *K. davidiana;* D. *K. fortunei;* E. *K. cyclolepis;* F. *K. esquirolii;* G. *K. chien pei;* H. *K. davidianna* var. *formosana* (each with a seed scale, bract scale and seed with wing, about natural size; compiled by Flous)

long, margin not involute, 2.2–3 mm wide, both sides green, lighter beneath, only 2–3 intermittent stomatal lines on each blade half above, 12–16 stomatal lines beneath; cones cylindrical and usually curved, 12–13 cm long, 4 cm thick. FK 53. China; Kweichow and Kwangsi Provinces. Fig. 97D, 98F and 99G (C). z7

K. evelyniana Mast. Tree, to 12 m high, young shoots red-brown, more or less pubescent; leaves linear, slightly sickle-shaped, 20–60 cm long, 3.5 mm wide, both sides dull green, with 2 distinct whitish stomatal bands above, each with 10–20 lines, 10–15 lines on either blade half beneath, short acuminate; cones cylindrical, 12–20 cm long, 3.5–4.5 cm thick. FK 58–59. China; Yunnan Province. Fig. 97D, 98F and 99G (C). z7

K. fortunei (Murr.) Carr. Tree, to 30 m high in its habitat, branches horizontal, crown conical at first, but flat rounded and very wide with age, bark very thick, corky, fissured, young shoots on young trees very pubescent, somewhat glabrous on older trees, buds oval; leaves linear, straight, nearly 2 ranked, widely spaced, 15–25 mm long, 3 mm wide, stiff, "dagger-like" acute on young plants, obtuse on older plants, glossy green above and totally without stomata, light green beneath with 2

stomatal bands, each with 15–20 lines; cones ovate-cylindrical, 8–12 cm long, purple before ripening, bract scales linear, rounded at the apex, seed scales, see Fig. 98D, seeds yellow, 13 mm long, with wings 28 mm long. FK 67; CB I 73; CIS 73. China; Chekiang Province. 1846. Plate 71 and 72; Fig. 97C, 98D and 99A (C). z7

K. roulletii (Chev.) Flous. A large, beautiful tree in its habitat, conical crown, 20–25 m high, young shoots red-brown, pubescent on young trees, glabrous with age, buds oblong-ovate; leaves linear on young shoots, straight to slightly sickle-shaped, 60–80 mm long, 3.5 mm wide, only 35–50 mm long on older trees, with 1–5 stomatal lines above only on older trees, 2 bands beneath, each with 10–15 lines; cones cylindrical, 12–18 cm long and 6–7 cm thick. FK 73,79. Vietnam. (The rather globose cone form illustrated in Fig.99B is not typical.) Fig. 97F, 98B and 99B (C). z10

Lit. Flous, F.: Espèces nouvelles de *Keteleeria.* Bull. Soc. Hist. Nat. Toulouse 69, 399–408, 1936. ● Flous, F.: Revision du genre *Keteleeria.* Bull. Soc. Hist. Nat. Toulouse 70, 273–348, 1936. (ill.) ● Ferre, Y. de: Additions et corrections à l'étude du genre *Keteleeria.* I. *Keteleeria roulletii.* Bull. Soc. Hist. Nat. Toulouse 87, 340–342, 1952. ● Gaussen, H.: Genre *Keteleeria.* In: Les Gymnospermes XI, 487–502, 1966.

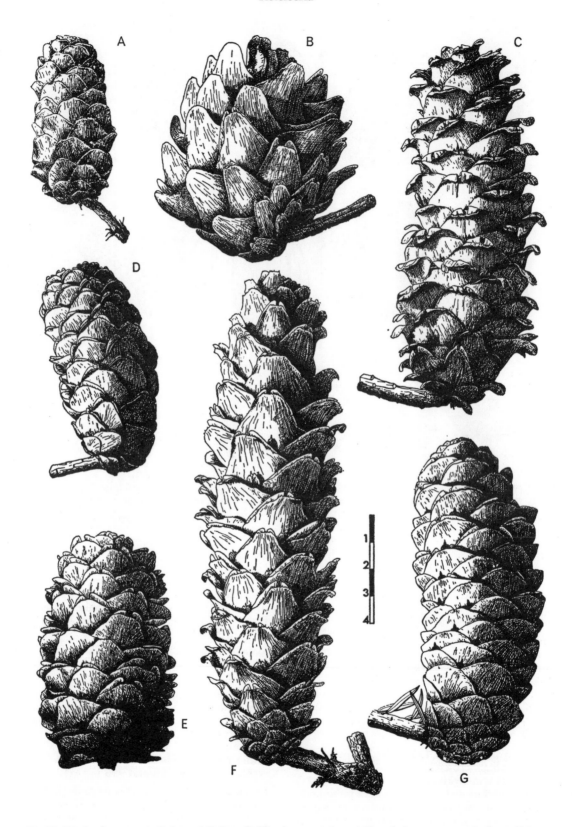

Fig 99. **Keteleeria** cones. A. *K. fortunei;* B. *K. roulletii* (only a partial cone! The whole cone more similar to F. in size); C. *K. davidiana;* D. *K. chien peii;* E. *K. davidiana* var. *formosana;* F. *K. evelyniana;* G. *K. esquirolii* (compiled by Flous)

LARIX MILLER—Larch—PINACEAE

Deciduous trees with horizontally spreading or pendulous branches in irregular whorls, fissured bark, small, ovate buds with small, imbricate scales; leaves needle-like, soft, thin, keeled beneath or on both sides, with stomata beneath or on both sides, with 2 lateral resin ducts, spiraling and widely spaced on long shoots, in dense clusters on short shoots; plants monoecious; male flowers solitary, terminal, on short, thick, axillary shoots, globose to ovate, stalked or sessile, yellow, composed of numerous, dense and spirally arranged stamens; female flowers nearly globose, terminal on short shoots, erect, surrounded by a ring of needles; cones cylindrical or ovate to globose, green, reddish or purple at flowering time, brown and woody when ripe; always 2 seeds under each seed scale, nearly triangular, with a membranous wing. x = 12.—About 10 species in the colder regions of the Northern Hemisphere. Range map at Fig. 100.

Outline of the Genus
(from Ostenfeld/Syragh Larsen, expanded)

Section 1. **Multiseriales** Patschke
Bract scales exserted past the seed scales; cones rather large, many scaled; leaves more or less keeled on both sides, occasionally not keeled above;

- ● Bract scales reflexed;
  - + Bract scales much longer than the seed scales; cones 5–11 cm long:
    L. griffithiana

  - ++ Bract scales only slightly longer than the seed scales; cones 3–4 cm long:
    L. mastersiana

- ● ● Bract scales erect or only slightly reflexed;
  - + Cones 3–4.5 cm long and narrow (to 2.5 cm wide);

bract scales 0–2 mm longer than the seed scales; leaves distinctly keeled beneath, only slightly keeled above, 1.5–3 cm long:
  L. potaninii

- ++ Cones short and wide; length to width ratio 1:1.5, leaves 2.5–4 cm long;

  - ○ Leaves very distinctly keeled on both sides; young shoots covered with especially dense short hairs; cones 3–4.5 cm long; bract scales erect:
    L. lyallii

  - ○ ○ Leaves only keeled on the underside; young shoots pubescent at first, later glabrous; cones 2.5–4 cm long; bract scales straight or slightly reflexed:
    L. occidentalis

Section 2. **Pauciseriales** Patschke
Bract scales shorter than the seed scales, not visible on ripe cones; cones ovate, nearly globose or conical; leaves not keeled above, often flat;

- ● Seed scales reflexed; leaves wide, distinctly keeled beneath; with stomata on both sides; young shoots stiff and reddish-brown:
    L. kaempferi

- ● ● Seed scales erect or somewhat concave; leaves flat or slightly keeled beneath;

  - + Seed scales distinctly concave;

  - ○ Cones 1.0–1.5 cm long; seed scales glabrous, often also glossy:
    L. laricina

  - ○ ○ Cones narrow, 2.5–4 cm long; seed scales short pubescent, usually especially so on the exterior at the base, not glossy:
    L. russica

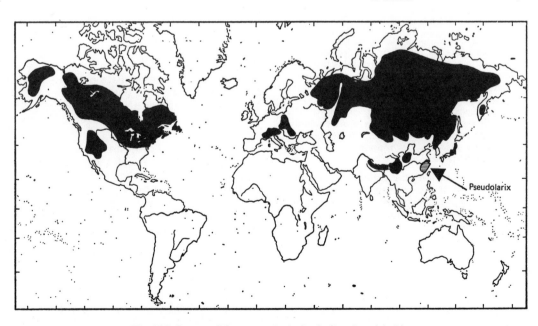

Fig. 100. Range of the genus *Larix* (including *Psuedolarix*)

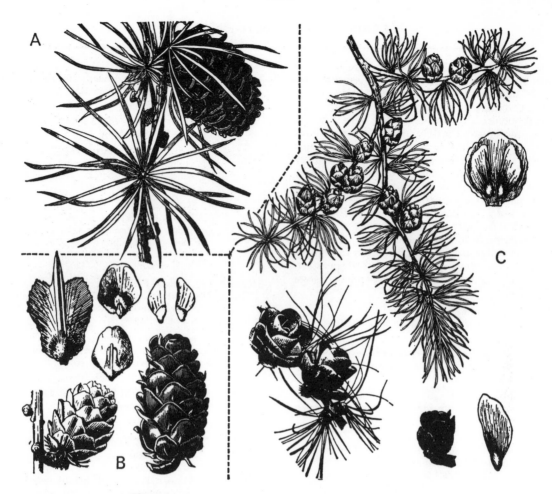

Fig. 101. **Larix.** A. *L. kaempferi;* B. *L. decidua;* C. *L. laricina;*
branches and cones about actual size; scales and seeds enlarged.

++ Seed scales straight upright;

    ○ Cones 2.5–4 cm long, narrow; scales dull, the
free limb evenly round or emarginate; bract
scales the same color as the seed scales, the latter
glabrous or short pubescent on the exterior;
cones compact; scales open somewhat only
when ripe:

        L. decidua
On ssp. *polonica* the cones are frequently
smaller, shorter and thicker; the free margin
of the seed scale is rounder, the exterior
frequently pubescent.

  ○○ Cones 2–3.5 cm long; the distinct margin of the
seed scales truncate or emarginate; bract scales
darker than the light colored, glossy seed scales;
the latter usually glabrous on the exterior or
occasionally lightly pubescent; cones light and
loosely constructed; seed scales wide open
when ripe:

        L. gmelinii
On the var. *olgensis* the cones are shorter and
more cylindrical, the free limb of the seed
scales rounded or truncate; the normally
erect seed scales can also be somewhat
concave or slightly reflexed; the young
shoots are usually conspicuously pubescent.

On var. *principis-rupprechtii* the cones are
longer, more cylindrical than on var. *olgensis;*
to 4 cm long.

Larix × czekanowskii Szafer (*L. gmelinii × L. russica*).
Natural hybrid, intermediate between the parents in
appearance. OSL 32–33 (C). Known since 1913. Occurs
over a large range from the region around the Baikal Sea
to the mouth of the Yenisey River in Siberia. z4 ?

L. decidua Miller. European Larch. Tree, to 35 m high,
stem straight, crown slender, conical, occasionally also
irregular, bark gray, exfoliating, later brown, branches in
horizontal whorls or nodding with ascending tips, twigs
thin, gracefully pendulous, yellowish(!), glabrous, short
shoots black-brown, terminal buds resinous; leaves
always light green, 30–40 in clusters, 10–30 mm long, flat
above, keeled beneath; female flowers oblong-
cylindrical, purple-red; cones narrowly ovate, 2.5 to 4 cm
long, with 40–50 seed scales, these straight upright, light
brown, not involute on the margin, exterior glabrous or
short pubescent, limb evenly rounded or somewhat
emarginate, bract scales the same color as the seed
scales, seeds small, with brown wings. OSL 22–23 (C);
CCE 232 (= *L. europaea* DC.). Alps, Carpathians,

Plate 65

Juniperus × media 'Plumosa Aurea'
in the Hamburg Botanic Garden, W. Germany

Juniperus rigida in the park at Birr Castle, County Offaly,
Ireland; this species was introduced into culture in
1861 and is by far the most beautiful of all;
unfortunately it is rarely found in cultivation

Juniperus virginiana in its native habitat
near Frederick, Maryland, USA

Juniperus virginiana
near Hildesheim, W. Germany

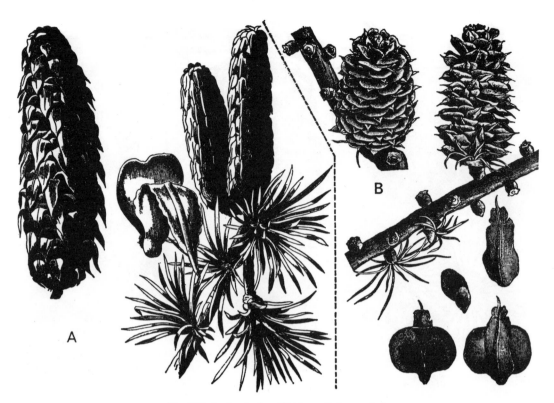

Fig. 103. **Larix.** A. *L. griffithiana;* B. *L.potaninii;*
the branches and cones about actual size; the scales enlarged (from Regel)

like'', sparsely branched. Found about 1892 in Upper Steiermark, W. Germany and in Austria.

L. × eurokurilensis Rohm & Dimpflmeier (*L. decidua × L. gmelinii* var. *japonica*). Tall tree, conical crown, lower branches horizontal with ascending tips, upper branches ascending, young shoots yellowish with a reddish trace, glabrous; cones short stalked, about 3 cm long, scales nearly like those of *L. gmelinii* var. *japonica*, but not so outspread (at about a 50–70° angle). KN 207. Originated in 1952 in the Forestry Trial Garden near Munich, W. Germany.

L. × eurolepis A. Henry (*L. kaempferi × L. decidua*). Tree, habit resembling *L. kaempferi*, but with a somewhat narrower crown, branches ascending at the tips, twigs yellow, glabrous or slightly pubescent, less pruinose than *L. kaempferi*, buds not resinous; leaves bluish-green, to 36 mm long, stomatal bands beneath; cones narrowly conical, stalk yellow, seed scales with slightly reflexed margin (similar to that of *L. kaempferi*). OCC 211 (C); CB III 51 (C); BFN 304 (H); CCE 235 (C) (= *L. henryana* Rehd.). Originated about 1900 in Dunkeld, Scotland. Distinguished from *L. kaempferi* by the yellower, stiffer, less pruinose twigs, shorter leaves, fewer stomatal bands on the underside, more cylindrical to conical cones with indistinctly reflexed seed scales and somewhat exserted bract scales. z5

L. gmelinii (Rupr.) Kuzeneva. Tall tree, 30–50 m, but only shrubby in the northern part of its range (north of the polar circle and in the mountains), slender crown,

winter buds globose, resin free, bud scales distinct at the tips; leaves abscising late, both sides with distinct gray-green stomatal lines; cones 15–30 mm long, seed scales nearly flat, glabrous glossy brown, usually erect, bract scales 5 mm long, about ⅓ shorter than the seed scales, seeds small. E. Asia. z1

This species includes the following geographical varieties:

var. **gmelinii.** Dahurian Larch. Regular conical habit, branches rather long, horizontal, young shoots somewhat pendulous, glabrous or somewhat pubescent, yellowish, often reddish in winter, buds yellow-brown, darker to nearly black on the base; leaves on short shoots cup form spreading, 25–35 mm long, bright green, flat above, keeled beneath, with distinct stomatal bands, apex obtuse; cones ovate, 20–35 mm long, with 20–40 scales, gaping widely when ripe. OSL 13 (H), 14–15 (C) (= *L. cajanderi* Mayr; *L. dahurica* Turcz. ex Trautv.; *L. davurica* Trautv.; *L. amurensis* Hort.). NE. Asia, E. Siberia, Manchuria to Kamchatka, developing forests. Introduced 1827. Quite hardy, but rarely found true to name; remains green well into fall. Fig. 102A (C), 102E (C) z2

var. **japonica** (Regel) Pilg. Kurilen Larch. Habit like the type, horizontally branched, short shoots very thick and strong, young shoots brown-red to violet, pruinose; leaves 15–25(–30), rather wide, spreading horizontally, stiff, sickle-shaped, 12–25 mm long; cones oval, 15–25 mm long, with 12–18 seed scales, gaping open long before ripening. OSL 14; BMns 159; CCE 233–235 (= *L. kamtschatika* [Rupr.] Carr.;*L. dahurica japonica* Maxim.; *L. kurilensis* Mayr; *L. dahurica* var. *kurilensis* [Mayr] Sarg.). Sachalin; Kurilen, USSR. 1888. Rarely found in cultivation, quite hardy and the first larch to leaf out in spring. Plate 73; Fig. 102B. z3

tips, terminal 4–6 mm long, the other buds 2–4 mm long, branch tips with 5–8 buds clustered together, small scales, fringed, loosely appressed; needles very densely crowded, stiff, directed forward on the branch tips, not enclosing the bud, bright green, glossy, 6–8 mm long, longest in the middle of the shoot, not totally radial in arrangement, curved like an elongated "S" with the tips curving slightly inward, rhombic in cross section, with sharp tips and 1–3 stomatal lines. WDw 190 (H); BCC 24 (H); WM 295 (H) (= *P. abies* f. *microsperma* [Hornib.] Rehd.). Origin unknown, but cultivated in 1923 in Ireland (Glasnevin) and the USA (Rochester).

'Minutifolia'. Dwarf form similar to 'Crippsii', conical habit, branches thin, short, stiff, ascending, with very narrow shoots, only 3–6 mm wide (!), twigs very densely clustered, fine, short, annual growth 1–2.5 cm, gray-yellow, with very conspicuous leaf cushions; needles directed forward, tiny, only 2–3 mm long, occasionally to 6–7 mm long on strong shoots, radially arranged and very densely crowded, all leaning forward at very acute angles (30°), the buds not enclosed, dark green (= *P. abies* var. *minutifolia* Hornib.). Discovered and introduced by H. J. Grootendorst in a Dutch nursery before 1923.

'Monstrosa'. Branchless Spruce. Upright stem, branches totally absent, rod-like, apical portions with radially arranged needles, these thick, stiff, to 3.5 cm long, obtuse or sharp acuminate (= *P. abies* f. *monstrosa* [Loud.] Rehd.; *P. excelsa* var. *monocaulis* Noerdlinger ex Willk.). Observed in the wild repeatedly since 1838, also cultivated on Bella Island, Italy, about 1898. (EX?)

'Mucronata'. Low form, growth strong, to 5 m high or more, regular, very densely branched, vigorous, branches horizontal to ascending, the coarse branches with radially arranged needles, twigs orange-brown, 4–6 mm long, terminal buds 7–8 mm long, standing alone, not hidden by the needles, but with numerous lateral buds near the terminal (!), bud scales large, acute, fringed and tightly appressed; needles widely spaced, nearly radial, directed forward at the branch tips, 10–17 mm long, 1 mm wide, blue-green, glossy, thick and flat, straight, but ending abruptly in small, sharp, somewhat outspread tips, with 1–3 stomatal lines. CCE 256 (= *P. abies* f. *mucronata* [Loud.] Rehd.). Discovered about 1835 by Briot in the Trianon-Garden, Versailles, France and still in cultivation. (The description by Beissner is imprecise and incorrect.)

'Mutabilis'. Growth normal, twigs and needles on new growth an attractive golden-yellow and spreading widely, later changing to light yellow. KN 238 (Br); CCE 256 (= *P. abies* var. *mutabilis* [Carr.] Dallim. & Jacks.). Developed before 1867 by André Leroy in Angers, France. Developed later in other areas. (R)

'Nana'. Dwarf form, growth broadly conical to 1.5 m high, irregular, especially at the peak with strong upright shoots, young shoots orange on both sides, glabrous and glossy, with very conspicuous leaf cushions, very thick and stiff, frequently also swollen or contorted, annual growth quite variable, from 5–50 mm, but to 10 cm long on the coarser branch tips, buds orange-brown, obtuse-oval, very slender, terminal from 2–6 mm long, the others 1–2 mm, bud scales large, acute, thick, fringed, loosely appressed; needles radially arranged, densely crowded on the weaker shoots, but widely spaced on the vigorous shoots, bright green, glossy, variable in size, 2–16 mm long, usually straight, but curved outward on the strong shoots, cylindrical in cross section, otherwise directed forward and completely covering the terminal bud, with short, fine, sharp tips, 2–4 stomatal lines on either side, these however not reaching to the apex. WDw 191 (H); Gs 1926: 38 (H); HD 141 (H); WM 296 (H) (= *P. abies* var. *nana* [Carr] Rehd.). Origin unknown, but cultivated in France in 1855, rare today. Plants cultivated by this name in the trade are usually incorrect (perhaps 'Pygmaea').

'Nana Compacta'. Dwarf form, flat-globose, as high as wide, very compact, densely branched, branches strong, thick, ascending obliquely at the peak (never vertical!), twigs gray-yellow or gray-green, more whitish beneath, glabrous, glossy, thin and flexible, but the above-mentioned stout shoots very thick, annual growth of the side shoots 2–3 cm, coarse shoots 4–6 cm, leaf cushions distinctly developed and orange-brown, buds obtuse ovate, dark red-brown, terminal 4–5 mm long, the others 2–3 mm, the conspicuous large buds at the branch tips grouped 1–5 or more, bud scales acute, often with resinous margins, tightly appressed; needles nearly all radially arranged, on main branches as well as side shoots, dense, stiff and prickly to the touch, 4–7 mm long and 0.5 mm wide, bright green, rather straight, 4 sided in cross section, with 1–2 stomatal lines on either side, a few loosely arranged needles at the branch tips. WDw 192 (H), Pl. 14H (Br). Developed by Hesse, Weener (near Hanover), W. Germany and introduced in 1950. Occasionally confused with 'Ohlendorfii', which grows more tightly upright, and has more yellow-green needles and fewer buds. (VR)

'Nidiformis'. Dwarf form, growth broad and dense, regular, with a more or less conspicuous nest form depression in the center, caused by the branches ascending obliquely from the middle, twigs very numerous, outspread with nodding tips, yellow-gray above, nearly white beneath, glabrous, glossy, thin and very flexible, annual growth 3–4 cm, leaf cushions conspicuous, buds obtuse-ovate, small, terminal bud 1–2 mm long, the others only slightly smaller, dark brown, terminal buds usually solitary or with 2 adjacent buds, round bud scales, tightly appressed; needles not completely radial, underside more or less parted, 7–10 mm long, gradually becoming shorter from the branch base to the apex, somewhat light green in color, flat, angular, with 8–10 sharp, more or less appressed teeth on the margin, distinctly visible with a hand lens (20X), very reliably distinguished from the other forms by this characteristic (Fig. 122A), with 1–2 stomatal lines running to the apex. WDw193 (H), Pl. 14E (Br); KN 242 (H); CCE 252; WM 24A (Br), 297 (H). Discovered before 1904 in the Rulemann Grisson Nursery near Hamburg, W. Germany; named by Beissner in 1906. One of the most widely distributed dwarf conifers. Plate 93; Fig. 122A.

f. nigra (Loud.) Th. Fries. "Double Fir". Normal tree; but the needles on the lateral shoots very densely arranged, sword-like and curving upward, very thick, dull dark green (= *Abies excelsa* f. *nigra* Loud.). Named by Loudon in 1838. Occurs occasionally with the species but not in cultivation.

'Ohlendorffii'. Dwarf form, globose when young, but becoming broadly conical with age, branches ascending and spreading, densely branched, twigs not spreading flat (fan-like), rather irregular, light brown, lighter beneath, glossy, glabrous, thin, flexible, not in an even plane, annual growth 3–6 cm, buds dark orange-brown, acutely conical, terminal bud usually only 2–3 mm long, the others smaller, usually 3–5 in irregular terminal groups, up to 10 on very strong shoots, buds attractive on young shoots; needles on young shoots and the terminal leader radially arranged, otherwise semi-radial on the upper side, parted beneath, yellow-green, 4–8 mm long, glossy, very thin, 4 sided in cross section or round, pointed on both ends, sharp at the apex, both sides with 1–4 irregular rows of very small stomata, stiff, densely arranged, terminal bud visible. WDw 194 (H), Pl. 14J (Br); Gs 1925: 204 (H); SN 220 (H); BFN 53 (H); CCE 259; WM 298 (H) (= *P. abies* var. *ohlendorffii* [Späth] Bail.; *P. orientalis pygmaea* Th. Ohlendorff). Developed between 1840 and 1850 by Th. Ohlendorff, Hamburg, W. Germany from seed obtained from Nikita, Crimea (USSR). Introduced in 1904 by Späth. Plate 90.

'Pachyphylla'. Dwarf form, exceptionally slow growing, irregular and open, but very short branched, very old plants to

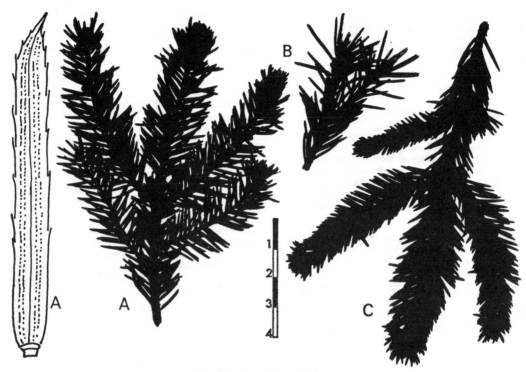

Fig. 122. *Picea abies*—Cultivars.
A. 'Nidiformis' with enlarged leaf; B. 'Gregoryana': C. 'Pumila Glauca'

'Loreley' (Grootendorst). Slow growing weeping form, stem more or less bowed, lowest branches creeping along the ground, buds light brown, scales reflexed, but not as distinctly so as those of 'Inversa'; needles small, 10–16 mm long, dull green. Origin unknown; introduced by F. G. Grootendorst in 1975.

'Lubecensis'. Regular habit, growth strong but graceful, very much resembling *P. orientalis;* needles only half as long as those of the type, golden-yellow on new growth, greening in summer (= *P. abies lubecensis* [Rose] Krüssm.). Developed before 1903 by W. Rose in Lübeck, W. Germany. Suffers from sunscald. (EX?)

'Mariae-Orffiae'. Dwarf form, oval, branches crowded, upright, twigs densely crowded and wide spreading, yellow-white, very small and thin, annual growth 5–10 mm, buds very small, globose, enveloped by the needles, yellow-brown, lateral buds outspread; needles usually radially arranged on the branch tips, but more parted on the older shoots, 4 to 8 mm long, light yellow-green with distinctly yellow tips, stiff and thick, often curved somewhat sickle-shape. Gs 1929: 304 (H); CCE 253 (= *P. excelsa* var. *Mariae-Orffii* Hornib. apud Schneid.). Discovered in 1928 by the wife of Prof. Alwin Seifert (Maria Orff), Upper Bavaria, W. Germany; introduced by Herm. A. Hesse, 1936. Plate 89.

'Maxwellii'. 3 different dwarf forms are described by this name, thereby creating considerable confusion.

Beissner's 'Maxwellii', illustrated in BFN 51: (H) is now *P. abies* 'Beissneri' (see p. 177); *P. abies* 'Maxwellii' Hort. Europ. is = *P. abies* 'Psuedo-Maxwellii' (see p. 185).

The true plant is described by Hornibrook as follows (in summary): Dwarf form, round, cushion form habit, with a large number of very short, thick shoots at the apex and radially arranged needles, buds thick, ovate, rounded, dark brown, scales appressed, twigs short and stiff, white or yellow brown, annual growth 20–25 mm; needles radially arranged on upright shoots and directed somewhat forward, rather widely spaced, incompletely radial on the lower branches, the apical ones pointing straight forward, thick and stiff, rounded in cross section, somewhat curved, narrower on the apical ⅓, abruptly drawn out in a rather long hair-like tip, occasionally terminating in a hook, bright green, with about 3 stomatal lines on either side. HD 140 (H); KN 241 (H); CCE 251; WM 293 (H) (= *P. abies* var. *maxwellii* [R. Smith] Nash). Developed about 1860 in the T. C. Maxwell Bros. Nursery, Geneva, New York USA. Only grown in American gardens.

'Merkii'. Dwarf form, globose habit, or also broadly conical, compact, short branched, branches somewhat more horizontal, main branches horizontal and ascending somewhat, but the tips pendulous, twigs very irregular in size and numbers, yellow-white, usually very thin, flexible, annual growth 6–24 mm, buds 1.5–3 mm long, conical, light brown, scales somewhat loose; needles parted or nearly so on the underside of the branch, semi-radial above, straight, very thin, narrow, flat, grass green, gradually tapering to a long, hair-thin tip, about 12 mm long, with 1–3 stomatal lines on either side. DB 1970: 87–88 (H); CCE 257; WM 294 (H) (= *P. abies* f. *merkii* [Beissn.] Rehd.). Cultivated since 1884, but often mislabeled.

'Microphylla'. Normal vigor, but graceful, twigs somewhat nodding; needles very short and fine, somewhat resembling those of *P. orientalis* (= *P. abies microphylla* [Carr.] Krüssm.). Known since 1855. Occurs occasionally as a chance seedling.

'Microsperma'. Dwarf form, regular broad conical habit, branches horizontal to steeply ascending, branch tips nodding slightly (!), twigs brown above, gray-brown beneath, glossy, slightly pubescent, terminal shoot very thick, lateral shoots thin and flexible, annual growth 3–5 cm, scales of the previous year's buds persisting, dark brown, buds conical, with sharp

PHYLLOCLADUS L. C. & A. Rich.— PHYLLOCLADACEAE

Evergreen trees or shrubs with long shoots and leaf-like short shoots (phylloclades); long shoots terminated by a vegetative bud, with rudimentary leaves reduced to small scales, these spirally arranged and inconspicuous, in the axil of leathery, leaf-like, short branches, differing in form and size for each species, cuneate tapered at the base and very narrow at the point of attachment, therefore appearing nearly petioled, basal half entire, apical portion more or less deep, coarsely dentate or sinuately incised; plants monoecious or dioecious, the male catkins cylindrical, stalked, clustered on the branch tips; female flowers solitary in the axis of the scale leaves or sessile on the margin of reshaped phylloclades; fruit a small, sessile nut in a cupulate aril, these as long or shorter than the seed.—5 species on the Phillipines, Borneo, Moluccas, New Guinea, Tasmania and New Zealand. Range map Fig. 117.

Phyllocladus alpinus Hook. f. Evergreen tree or shrub, to 9 m in its habitat, stem short, stiff, phylloclades alternate to nearly opposite, with a short axis, green, irregular in form and size, often narrow and rhombic, to 2 cm long on young plants, deeply incised, thin, segments narrow-linear, blue-green beneath, thick and leathery on older plants, 2.5 to (occasionally) 6 cm long and to 2 cm wide; also with true leaves on young seedlings, these narrow-linear, acute, abscising, to 1.5 cm long, much shorter on old plants; male flower catkins 5–6 mm long, 2–5 in clusters at the branch tips, nearly sessile, carmine-red; fruits red, in globose heads on misshapen phylloclades, either on the base or on the margin, seeds ovate, exserted, black, 2.5 mm long, cupule white. KF 100: CC 50; CBJ 58; CCE 245 (= *P. trichomanoides* var. *alpina* Parl.). New Zealand, both lslands, in subalpine forests and thickets. Fig. 118. z9.

'Silver Blades'. Phylloclades silvery-blue on both sides. Selected by Hillier, Winchester, England. Fig. 116 B.

P. asplenifolius (Labill.) Hook. f. A tree in its habitat, 15 m or taller, but at higher altitudes only a low shrub, bark to nearly 3 cm thick, hard and scaly, branches short, thick and irregularly distributed, phylloclades very distinctive in size and form, often rhombic or fan-shaped, base cuneate, 3–5 cm long, and half as wide, margin irregular and obtuse dentate or lobed, the uppermost phylloclades containing the 8 mm long, carmine-red fruits; seeds small, otherwise similar to those of *P. alpinus*. BAu 414; CFTa 60; CTa 2; LNH 221; CCE 245 (= *P. rhomboidalis* L. C. & A. Rich.; *P. billardieri* Mirb.; *P. serratifolius* Noisette ex Carr.). Tasmania, in the vicinity of Williamsford. 1825. Plate 79; Fig. 116 A. z9

P. glaucus Carr. Tree, 12 (15) m in its habitat, trunk to 60 cm in diameter, branches short and stiff, usually in whorls, phylloclades alternate, pinnate and to 40 cm long; about 10–12 on each axis, rhombic, base unevenly

Fig. 116 **Phyllocladus.**
A. *P. asplenifolius*; B. *P. alpinus* 'Silver Blades'; C. *P. trichomanoides* (Original)

cuneate to broadly ovate or oblong, 4–6 × 2–4 cm in size, underside blue green when young, shallow or deeply lobed, margin wide crenate lobed; true leaves on young plants linear, obtuse to acute, to 15 mm long, inconspicuous, much shorter on older plants; plants mono- or dioecious, male flowers 10–20 in dense, terminal clusters, 10–25 mm long; fruits 4–7 in globose heads, near the base of the rachis, ripe capitulum about 15 mm long, on a 5 mm long stalk, seeds 3 mm long, in a white cupule. KF 98–99; CC 42; CBJ 59–60; CCE 245; SFP 80 (= *P. trichomanoides* var. *glauca* Parl.). New Zealand; plains and mountain forests. Fig. 118. z9

Fig. 117. Range of the genus *Phyllocladus*
(Original)

P. hypophyllus Hook. f. Tree or shrub, 1.5–10 m high, quite variable in habit, branches stiff and whorled, phylloclades blue-green, quite variable in size and form, lateral phylloclades spirally arranged, 2–8 × 1.5–4 cm in size, on a 6–12 mm long stalk, ovate, obovate to fan-shaped, irregular and coarsely crenate or serrate on the margin (but not toward the base) or deeply lobed, margin thickened, often divided into 2 large lobes at the apex, terminal phylloclades pinnately arranged on an axis, in whorls, the solitary phylloclades normally smaller than the lateral ones; male catkins narrow, cylindrical, clustered, on about a 2.5 cm long stalk; fruits about like those of *P. glaucus*, seeds about 5 mm long. HI 889; CCE 243 (= *P. prostratus* [Warb.] Pilg.; *P. major* Pilg.). Luzon and Borneo to New Guinea. Fig. 119. z9

P. trichomanoides D. Don. Tree, to 20 m high in its habitat, bark thick, exterior black, interior red, branches arranged in whorls, phylloclades alternate and pinnate, rachis to 30 cm long, 10–15 on an axis, irregular and broadly rhombic, 10–25 mm long, the terminal one fan-shaped, the lateral phylloclades somewhat smaller and narrower, finely crenate on the margin, an attractive red-brown on the new growth; leaves on young plants to 2 cm long, narrow-linear, abscising, much smaller on older plants; male catkins in clusters of 5–10 together on 3–10 mm long stalks, plants monoecious; fruits 6–8 together on reduced phylloclades, nearly terminal, seeds 3 mm long. KF 6–7; HI 549–550; CBJ 61; DJ 36; CCE 245; SFP 96 (= *P. cunninghamii* Hort.). New Zealand, in the forests on the plains. Plate 77; Fig 116 C. z9.

Hybrids. According to Allan (Fl. N. Z. 112) hybrids have been developed between the New Zealand species *P. glaucus* and *P. trichomanoides*, but both species are quite variable and in this respect, not yet sufficiently investigated. *P. alpinus* is also polymorphic, but here there possibly exist varieties (see *P. alpinus* var. *minor*; illust. in HiD 43).

Lit Laubenfels, D. J. De: A revision of the Malesian and Pacific Rainforest Conifers. I. Podocarpaceae. *Phyllocladus*. Jour. Arnold Arboretum **50**, 277–282, 1969.

Fig. 118. **Phyllocladus.**
Left, *P. glaucus;* right, *P. alpinus;* the twigs somewhat reduced, fruits enlarged
(from Adams; Hooker)

Fig. 119. *Phyllocladus hypophyllus*
(from Womersley)

PICEA A. Dietr.—Spruce—PINACEAE

Tall or medium size, evergreen, conical growing trees, bark scaly, occasionally furrowed on older trees; branches usually rather short, whorled; young shoots thin furrowed, rough from distinctly raised leaf bases; winter buds often not resinous; leaves needle-like, 4 sided or flat with 2 resin ducts, persisting for several years on the tree, with stomatal lines on all sides or only those facing downward, a short, brownish petiole, remains on the leaf petiole base after leaf drop; plants monoecious; male flowers on the previous year's shoots in the axils of the uppermost needles, with numerous, spirally arranged stamens, pollen grains with wings; female flowers solitary on the tips of the previous year's growth, erect or outspread, surrounded by a few imbricate scales at the base; cones usually pendulous, ripening in the first year, oval to oblong-cylindrical, green to purple before ripening, abscising when ripe; seed scales numerous, persistent, bract scales small and narrow, hidden between the seed scales; seeds without resin blisters, 2 under each seed scale, small, winged, the wing easily detached, concave and covering the upper side of the seed; cotyledons 4–15. x = 12.—About 50 species (depending on the interpretation, 36–80) in the Northern Hemisphere, half being from W. and Central China.

Because of some wide variations in appearance, the positive identification of many East Asiatic species is not easy.

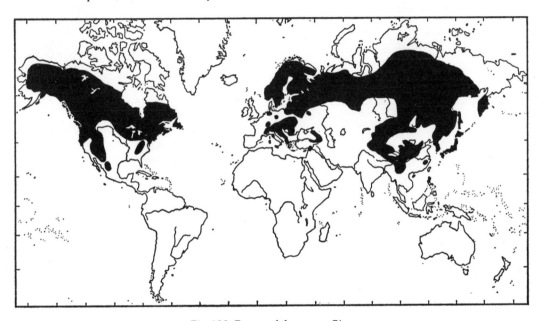

Fig. 120. Range of the genus *Picea*

Outline of the Genus

Section 1. **Picea**

Needles 4 sided, with stomatal lines on all sides, forming oblique or nearly right angles in cross section; cones pendulous; cone scales tight, tightly appressed before ripe, usually rounded and entire on the apex:

P. abies	maximowiczii	retroflexa
alcoquiana	meyeri	rubens
asperata	morrisonicola	schrenkiana
gemmata	neoveitchii	smithiana
glauca	obovata	wilsonii
glehnii	orientalis	
koyamai	polita	
mariana	pungsaniensis	

Section 2. **Casicta** Mayr.

Needles 4 sided and with stomatal lines on all sides or compressed and without or with fewer stomatal lines beneath than above; cone scales loosely appressed before ripening, thin and flexible when ripe, usually rhombic, with a wavy or "eroded" margin:

P. chihuahuana	likiangensis	montigena
engelmannii	—balfouriana	pungens
hirtella	—purpurea	sitchensis
jezoensis	mexicana	

Section 3. **Omorika** Willk.

Needles fir-like compressed, with stomatal lines only on the underside (the morphological dorsal side); cones all pendulous or the uppermost, outspread:

P. brachytyla	omorika
breweriana	spinulosa

For practical purposes of identification of the species of this genus a table will be found at *Picea asperata* (at the end of the cultivars of *Picea abies*).

Picea abies (L.) Karst. Norway Spruce. Tree, 30–50 m, stem straight, columnar, to 2 m thick, bark red-brown to gray, exfoliating in thin scales, crown acutely conical, branches horizontal or bowed downward with more or less ascending tips, young shoots brown to reddish-yellow, glabrous to lightly pubescent, buds slender conical, acute, light brown, not resinous; needles pectinate parted on the branch underside, 1.2 cm long, evenly acuminate, 4 sided, with stomata on all 4 sides, dark green; cones pendulous, cylindrical, 10–15 cm long, 3–4 cm wide, green or red when young, seed scales rather hard, rhombic, tapering toward the apical end, truncate on the tip or emarginate (= *P. excelsa* [Lam.] Link). N. and Central Europe. In cultivation for centuries. Valuable lumber tree in Europe. Prefers cool, humid air, a good, moist clay soil or sandy clay. Plate 80; Fig. 121, 124 and 127. z5

Tncludes a 1arge number of cultivars; please refer to the following outline.

Outline of the Cultivars and Forms of *Picea abies*

Group 1. Habit normal, strong upright
(except for 3)

1. Columnar and conical forms:

var. *carpathica*   'Pruhoniciana'
'Columnaris'   'Rothenhaus'
'Cupressina'   'Viminalis'
'Falcata'
'Falcato-viminalis'   4. Variant needles:
f. *gigantea*
'Interrupta'   'Acutissima'
'Pyramidata'   'Cincinnata'
f. *strigosa*   'Microphylla'
                           f. *nigra*

2. Sparsely branched forms:

'Araucarioides'   5. Colored needles:
'Cranstonii'
'Denudata'   'Argentea'
'Dicksonii'   'Argenteospica'
'Eremita'   'Aurea'
f. *glomerulans*   'Aurescens'
'Intermedia'   'Coerulea'
'Monstrosa'   'Finedonensis'
'Virgata'   'Mutabilis'

3. Weeping forms: 6. Variant cone forms:

'Aarburg'   f. *acuminata*
'Frohburg'   f. *apiculata*
'Inversa'   f. *chlorocarpa*
'Loreley'   f. *deflexa*
('Pendula')   f. *erythrocarpa*
'Pendula Bohemica'   f. *squarrosa*
'Pendula Major'   f. *triloba*
'Pendula Monstrosa'
'Plumosa'   7. Variant bark and trunk:

                           'Corticata'
                           'Tuberculata'

Group 2. Low growing, normally 3–5 m high when mature

1. Narrowly conical: 3. Globose form:

var. *alpestris*   'Globosa'
'Concinna'
('Densa')   4. Weeping form:
'Phylicoides'
                           'Acrocona'
2. Broadly conical: 'Depressa'
                           f. *palustris*
'Compressa'   'Reflexa'
'Conica'
f. *hercynica*   5. Colored needles:
'Mucronata'
'Sibirica'   'Aurea Magnifica'
'Wills Zwerg'   'Diedorfiana'

Group 3. Dwarf forms less than 3 m high.
Since these forms are not always constant in habit, some being either more conical or more globose, such forms are noted in the outline by "1–2" (applying to both groups); I = irregular habit; ! = especially irregular

1. Conical form:

'Archangelica'
'Bennett's Miniature'
'Capitata' I
'Clanbrassiliana Elegans' I
'Clanbrassiliana Plumosa'
'Decumbens' (1–2) I
'Elegans'
'Ellwangeriana' (1–2) I
'Globosa Nana' (1–2) I
'Gymnoclada' I!
'Holmstrup'
'Humilis'
'Knaptonensis' (1–2) I
'Maxwellii' (1–2) I
'Microsperma'
'Minutifolia' I!
'Nana' (1–2) I
'Ohlendorffii'
'Pachyphylla' I
'Plumosa'
'Pseudo-Maxwellii' (1–2) I
'Pumila Argentea' I
'Pygmaea' I
'Pyramidalis Gracilis'
'Pyramidalis Robusta'
'Remontii'
'Turfosa'
'Wansdyke Miniature'
'Waugh'

2. Globose form,
stoutly branched:

'Compacta'
'Compacta Asselyn'
'Cripsii' I!
'Merkii' (1-2)
'Nana Compacta'
'Parviformis'
'Pyramidalis Gracilis'
'Sherwood'

3. Globose form,
finely branched:

'Clanbrassiliana'
'Echiniformis' I
'Gregoryana'
'Gregoriana Parsonii' I
'Gregoryana Veitchii' I!
'Hystrix' I
'Mariae-Orffiae'

4. Flat, broad rounded forms
(wider than high):

'Abbeyleixensis'
'Beissneri' I!
'Diffusa'
'Dumosa'
'Highlandia'
('Horizontalis')
'Hornibrookii'
'Kamon'
'Little Gem'
'Nidiformis'
'Procumbens'
'Pseudoprostrata'
'Pumila' I
'Pumila Glauca' I
'Pumila Nigra' I
'Ramosa'
'Repens'
'Sargentii'
'Spathulifolia'
'Tabuliformis'

5. Colored needles:

'Cellensis'
'Lubecensis'
'Helene Cordes'

Spruce and Fir blight: Since about 1979/80 a blight phenomenon has threatened the *Picea abies* and *Abies alba* of European forests. The primary cause is presumed to be pollutants carried by "acid rain." This causes excessive acid accumulation in the already acidic coniferous forest soil. The damage to the crown through air pollution is intensified by the disturbed roots; that is, because of over-acidification they cannot absorb calcium and magnesium, essential to proper plant nutrition. In nurseries, parks and gardens, the soil can be amended with lime and fertilizer to reduce or prevent excessive damage.

'Aarburg' (Haller). Irregular habit, not tightly upright, 8 m or taller, branches irregularly arranged, twigs outspread or pendulous, rather densely branched: needles deep green, rather small, 10–15 mm long on the stout shoots, 8–10 mm on lateral shoots. Introduced by Haller AG, Switzerland in 1965. New growth appears very late, thereby avoiding frost damage.

'Abbeyleixensis'. Dwarf, cushion-form habit, very weak and slow growing, about 25 cm high and 50 cm wide in 16 years, branch tips curved downward; needles long and thin, loosely twisted (similar to 'Cincinnata'). HD 161 (H) (= *P. abies* var. *abbeyleixensis* Hornibr.). Discovered as a seedling in 1916 by Hornibrook in Abbeyleix, Ireland. (EX)

f. **acuminata** (Beck) Dall. & Jacks. Normal tree with deviant cone form, seed scales with very undulate margins, apex long and curving upward hook-like, finely toothed. OCC 227 (C) (= *P. excelsa acuminata* Beck, *P. abies* f. *acuminata* Beck] Dall & Jacks). Repeatedly found in Poland ("Galicia"), Yugoslavia, Sweden. 1887.

'Acrocona'. Low form, but becoming a few meters high, branches rather stiff, spreading horizontally to pendulous, the side branches with normal cones, the branch tips of most shoots with long, extended, contorted cones, the very young cones with tough, short, sharp tipped needles between the soft, recurved seed scales. WDw 177 (H); KN 232 (H) (= *P. abies* f. *acrocona* [Fries] Fries). Originated spontaneously in the forest near Uppsala, Sweden before 1890; widely disseminated in cultivation today. Plate 85.

'Acutissima'. Growth to normal height, but slow, differing in the very long, thin, very acute, laterally compressed needles (= *P. abies acutissima* [Wittr.] den Ouden). Discovered in the Stockholm Botanic Garden, Sweden as a seedling in 1879.

var. **alpestris** (Bruegg.) Krüssm. Alpine Spruce. Alpine form of compact conical habit, bark gray-white, branches widely spaced, twigs short and stiff, densely short pubescent; needles at nearly right angles to the shoot, some incurved, short, tough, 4 sided, appearing bluish from the stomatal development, therefore resembling *Picea glauca* (= *P. excelsa* var. *alpestris* Bruegg.; *P. obvata* var. *alpestris* Henry). Switzerland; in the Graubuenden Alps, around Paryan and on the Lenzerheide, developing forests at 1300–1600 m.

f. **apiculata** (Beck) Krüssm. Normal, like the type in all respects except the seed scales on the cones taper from the middle outward (= *P. excelsa* var. *apiculata* Beck). Repeatedly observed in Poland, Southern Austria, Bosnia (Yugoslavia), Siebenbirge (W. Germ.). Introduced in 1890.

Araucarioides'. Normal upright habit, growth rapid, stem normally branched on the lower portion, but the apical part with branches in widely spaced whorls. MD 1905: 73 (H) (= *P. excelsa* var. *araucarioides* Beissn.). Discovered before 1905 by Saachy in Kamon, Hungary.

'Archangelica'. Dwarf form, compact conical habit, branches short and stiff; needles rigid and prickly, 6–15 mm long. Introduced before 1867 by Lawson. (EX)

'Argentea'. Normal habit; needles white variegated, but not very conspicuous (= *P. abies* f. *argentea* [Beissn.] Rehd.). Known in 1887. (EX)

'Argenteospica'. Normal habit, young shoots with long white tips, later greening. SN 221: BFN 54 (H): Gs 1935: 106 (Br) (= *P. abies* f. *argenteospica* [Beissn.] Rehd.). Developed in Hesse Nursery; known before 1891. Plate 80.

'Aurea'. Grows like the species, but lower, to about 10 m, branches spreading horizontally; needles glossy yellowish-white, but easily scalded in bright sun, becoming paler in shady locations. CCe 255 (= *P. abies* var. *aurea* [Carr.] Rehd.). 1855.

'Aurea Magnifica'. Lower than 'Aurea', wider, occasionally also shrubby, branches and twigs rather horizontal; needles conspicuously bright golden-yellow, more orange-yellow in winter. Introduced into the trade about 1899 by Ottolander & Hooftman, Boskoop, Holland. One of the best yellow forms.

'Aurescens'. Normal habit, branches more or less ascending, but not so densely compact; young needles golden-yellow, later yellowish-green (= *P. abies* f. *aurescens* Slavin.). Distributed before 1920 by the Westbrook Gardens, Long Island, New York. (VR)

'Barryi'. Vigorous dwarf form, often more globose as a young plant, but becoming conical with age, very irregular, branches rather long, ascending, twigs outspread, stout, young shoots orange-brown, with very large terminal buds on the branch tips (!), surrounded by needles, with a lower ring of smaller buds; needles glossy dark green, about 10 mm long, obtuse, directed forward and upward. Gs 1933: 244 (H); BFN 45 (H); SN 48 (H) (= *P. abies* f. *barryi* [Beissn.] Rehd.). Known since 1891. Fig. 123B.

'Beissneri'. Dwarf form, compact habit, flat, branches thick, conspicuously brown, often with contorted short shoots, buds disproportionately large, globose to broadly ovate, light brown; needles clustered and radially arranged, short, very thick, prickly. WDw 178 (H); WM 279 (H) (= *P. abies* var. *beissneri* Hornib.; *P. excelsa* 'Maxwellii' Beissn. 1891 non Hornib. nec Hort.). Origin unknown. Somewhat resembles 'Barryi', but flatter, needles nearly like those of *P. polita*. (VR)

'Bennett's Miniature'. Dwarf form, originated from a terminal witches'-broom on a normal *Picea abies*, about 75 cm high in 20 years, conical, narrow, very dense, annual growth only about 15 mm; needles deep green, 6 mm long. JA 27: Pl. 20. Discovered in 1964 in Princeton, W. Virginia; introduced by Wm. M. Bennett, Christiansburg, Virginia, USA.

'Capitata'. Dwarf form, irregular and broadly conical, branches thick, ascending, twigs variably long, but evenly thick, clustered or capitate at the ends of the secondary branches, flexible, orange above, more yellow beneath, annual growth 5–6 cm, buds oval to globose, terminal buds 3–5 mm long, the axillary buds shorter, dull orange-brown, few or many (1–10) densely clustered around the terminal bud; needles radially arranged, directed forward, 10–15 mm long, very thick and wide, drawn out to a short sharp tip (not prickly), stiff, with stomatal lines on both sides, glossy light green. WDw 179 (H); CCE 252; WM 280 (H) (= *P. abies* var. *capitata* Bailly] Bail.). Originated before 1889 in the Croux Nursery at Sceaux, France. Occasionally confused with 'Beissneri'.

var. **carpathica** (Willk.) Krüssm. Carpathian Spruce. Tree, lower growing than the species, branches finely pubescent; needles shorter, thinner, glossier dark green, tightly appressed to the twig; cones smaller (= *P. excelsa* var. *carpathica* Willk.; *P. excelsa tenuifolia* Carr.). Carpathian Mts.

'Cellensis'. Dwarf form, regular conical habit, branches very fine and delicate; needles only 3–4 mm long, very densely arranged, yellow variegated on new growth (= *P. excelsa* f. *cellensis* Beissn.). Developed in the nursery of L. Schiebler & Son, Celle, W. Germany; before 1903.

f. **chlorocarpa** (Purkyne) Fries. Normal spruce with cones remaining bright green until fall, seed scales thin and flat. Occasionally occurring with the type.

'Cincinnata'. Curly Spruce. Normal, tree-like and vigorous, lower branches bowed downward, shoots more or less pendulous, the young shoots with 4–6 cm long side branches; needles very long, bright green, more or less curving upward (but not "curly" as the name would imply). DB 20: 307 (Br);

Fig 121. *Picea abies.* Above, branch with male flowers, next right, the same enlarged; beneath, female inflorescence, with individual seed scale and 2 seeds; a. terminal shoot; b. branch tip from the crown of an older tree; c. partial branch from a young tree (from Beissner)

CCE 251 (= *P. abies* var. *cincinnata* [Beissn.] Rehd.). Developed in the Hesse Nursery, Weener, W. Germany; introduced in 1897. Plate 88.

'Clanbrassiliana'. Dwarf form, habit more or less "bee hive"-shaped, old plants seldom over 1.5 m high (the original plant is about 3 m high and 180 years old!), branches thin and flexible, annual growth about 2–5 cm, light gray-brown above, cream-white to greenish-white beneath, glossy, glabrous, distinct difference between the strong shoots with long needles and weak shoots with short needles (!!), buds acutely ovate, 4–5 mm long, axillary buds only 2–3, long, red-brown, glossy very resinous in winter and then gray, terminal buds 1–3 (4); needles spreading nearly radially, about 5–10 mm long, glossy light green, densely arranged, widest in the middle, thick, flat in cross section, keeled, apical half drawn out to a long sharp tip, these however are not stiff. WDw 180–181 (H); Gs 1933: 232 (H); HD 160 (H); CCE 261; WM 23E (Br). The oldest known dwarf form; found about 1780 or earlier on the Moira Estate, near Belfast, N. Ireland. Lord Clanbrassil brought it to his country residence, Tolleymore in County Down, where the plant stands now at about 3 m high. Frequently found in cultivation today but often incorrectly labeled. The coarse reverting branches should be pruned out as soon as they develop. Plate 90.

'Clanbrassiliana Elegans'. Dwarf form, broadly conical habit, very dense and irregular, shoots thin and very flexible, yellow above, cream-yellow beneath, glossy, annual growth 2–3 cm, buds ovate, red-brown, obtuse, 2–3 mm long, axillary buds 1.5–2 mm long, terminal buds usually with only 2 side buds, bud

scales not fringed; needles densely arranged, stiff, 6–8 mm long, glossy light green, incompletely radially arranged, widest at the middle, drawn out to a long, fine, translucent, sharp apex, mjd rib above and beneath with 1–2 rows of very small stomata. WDw 182 (H), Pl. 14B (Br) (= *P. excelsa* var. *Clanbrassiliana elegans* Sénécl.). There is still some difference of opinion concerning the genuineness of this plant (see Welch, p. 226).

'Clanbrassiliana Plumosa'. Dwarf form, compact conical habit, branches short and tough; needles stout, somewhat bowed, spiraling toward the branch tips, thereby covering the buds, the total plant is ruffled (crispate) in appearance (= *P. excelsa Clanbrassiliana plumosa* Beissn.). An uncertain form, which because of its coarse shoots and stout needles, can hardly be classed as 'Clanbrassiliana'.

"Clanbrassiliana Stricta" is practically identical to 'Clanbrassiliana Elegans'. As older plants, they can not be distinguished (according to Welch).

'Coerulea'. Tree, normal habit, young shoots conspicuously luxuriant, with steel-blue needles (= *P. abies coerulea* [Beissn.] Krüssm.). Repeatedly found both in cultivation and in the wild; first discovered by Breinig near Cologne, W. Germany and introduced before 1891.

'Columnaris'. Tree, grows to normal height, but the main branches are very short, horizontal or somewhat inclined downward, side shoots densely branched, therefore developing a dense, narrow column. OCC 229 (the illust. in BFN 48 and SN 120 are incorrect!!); CCE 225 (= *P. abies* f. *columnaris* [Jacques] Rehd.). Found among the species, especially in Finland and Switzerland.

Fig. 106. **Libocedrus.** A. *L. plumosa,* 3 twigs; B. *L. bidwillii;* F. cones enlarged;
S. seed; juv., juvenile branch sections (Original, the enlarged parts from Hooker)

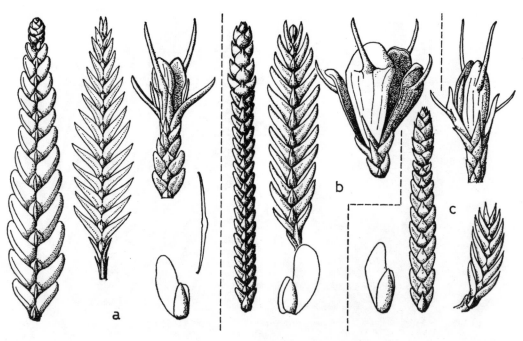

Fig. 107. **Libocedrus**. a. *L. austro-caledonica;* b. *L. chevalieri;*
c. *L. yateensis;* mature shoot at left, right juvenile (from De Laubenfels, modified)

L. chevalieri Buchholz. Shrub or small tree, 1–5 m high, branchlets nearly rhombic in cross section; leaves decussate, not completed identical in form, lateral leaves broadly triangular, 3–4 mm long, facial leaves 2–3 mm long, but only distinct to ⅔ of their length, lateral leaves with stomatal bands on both sides, but only at the base on the underside; cones about 1.5 cm long or shorter, cone scales with 6–8 mm long, straight or slightly curving thorn, seed 2–3 mm long, with uneven wings. GGy 521 (C and Br); LG 40. New Caledonia; Western slope of Mt. Humboldt. Plate 75; Fig. 107. z9

L. plumosa (D. Don) Sarg. Kawaka. Tree, to 25 m, stem to 1.2 m in diameter, bark exfoliating in narrow, thin strips, branchlets 2 ranked, flattened in the juvenile stage and then to 7 mm wide, less distinctly compressed with age and then only 3 mm wide; leaves on older plants all approaching similar size, the lateral leaves then to 5 mm long and spreading, the facial leaves 2.5 mm long, triangular and appressed; cones 8–12 mm long, with 4 scales and a dorsal thorn, 1 seed under each of the 2 fertile scales. CBJ 55 (Br); KF 82; CCE 240 (= *L. doniana*

[Hook.] Endl.; *Thuja doniana* Hook.). New Zealand, particularly in forests on the North Island, at 600 m in the mountains. Very young seedlings have narrow, linear-subulate leaves spreading on all sides, but soon changing to the 4 ranked stage. Fig. 106A. z9

L. yateensis Guillaumin. Tree or shrub, to 8 m, branches to 1.2 m long, the lower ones horizontal, the upper ones rather steeply upright, the apexes much and finely branched, branchlets flattened; leaves decussate, the lateral leaves on older plants 3–4 mm long, acute, dorsal side vaulted, the facial leaves 2–3 mm long, acute; plants monoecious; cones ovate, about 1 cm long, the 2 sterile scales 7 mm long, the fertile ones 10 mm long, each with one, 12 mm long, prickly thorn. LG 39; CCE 240. New Caledonia; Rivière Bleu. Not cultivated. Plate 75; Fig. 107. z9 (R)

Lit. Florin, R.: Die Koniferengattung *Libocedrus*. Svensk Bot. Tidskr. **24**, 117–131, 1930. ● Florin, R., & J. B. Boutelje: External morphology and epidermal structure of leaves in the genus *Libocedrus* s. lat. Acta Horti Bergian. **17**, 7–37, 1954. Stockholm. ● Li, Hui-Lin: A reclassification of *Libocedrus* and Cupressaceae. Jour. Arnold Arboretum **34**, 17–36, 1963.

METASEQUOIA Miki ex Hu & Cheng—Dawn Redwood—TAXODIACEAE

Deciduous tree, closely related to *Taxodium;* branches opposite; young shoots 2 ranked and opposite, the very youngest shoots abscising in fall; leaves opposite, sessile to nearly sessile, linear, with 2 stomatal bands beneath with 4–6 rows each; monoecious; male flowers axillary or terminal in racemes or panicles, opposite, with about 20 stamens; female flowers with about 22–26 decussate seed scales, of these the uppermost and lower ones sterile; cones nearly globose, pendulous, long stalked; seeds 5–6, compressed, with encircling wing; cotyledons 2. $x = 11$.—Only 1 species in China; first discovered in 1945. Widely cultivated today. Range map Fig. 109.

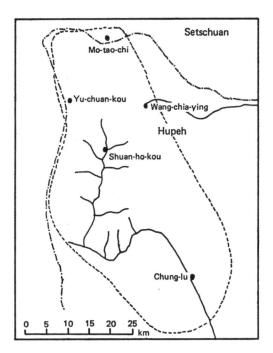

Fig. 109. Range of *Metasequoia* (- - - - -); the map depicts the NW corner of Hupeh Province
(—.—.—.)
(from Hui-Lin Li)

Fig. 108. *Metasequoia glyptostroboides,*
partial branch, ½ actual size (natural pressing)

Metasequoia glyptostroboides Hu & Cheng. A tree to 35 m in its habitat, trunk to 2 m in diameter, gradually tapering toward the peak, base with flared ridges, bark dark gray, fissured, exfoliating in thin strips, twigs opposite, glabrous, smooth, green at first, later red-brown; needles opposite, 2 ranked, sessile or nearly so, linear, 8 to 25 mm long, somewhat blue-green above, light green beneath with 2 stomatal bands, each with 4–6 rows of stomata, deciduous; cones rather globose, about 25 mm thick, the fertile seed scales with 2–9, but usually 5–6 seeds, these light brown, 5 mm long, with a light and wide encircling wing (= *Sequoia glyptostroboides* [Hu &

Cheng] Weide). China; E. Szechwan and W. Hupeh. Completely winter hardy and fast growing; easily propagated from cuttings. Plate 76; Fig. 108. z5

Some clones have been selected from seedling plants:

'National'. Narrow conical form. Selected from Chinese seed in the US National Arboretum, Washington, D.C., in 1958, named in 1963.

Some other selections have been 'Moerheim' and 'Vada', both from Holland; also 'Emerald Feathers'.

Lit. Of the many publications dealing with this plant, only a few will be mentioned: Hu, H. H., & W. C. Cheng: On the new family Metasequoiaceae, and on *Metasequoia glyptostroboides,* a living species of the genus *Metasequoia* found in Szechuan and Hupeh. Bull. Fan. Mem. Inst. Biol. N. S. **1**, 153–161, 1948. ● Florin, R.: On *Metasequoia,* living and fossil. Bot. Notiser 1952, 1–29. ● Burrichter, E., & W. Schoenwald: Forstliche Anbauversuche mit der *Metasequoia glypt.* im Raum Westfalen. Opladen 1968 (36pp. with 3pp. Lit. Ref.). ● Wyman, D.: The complete *Metasequoia* Story. American Nurseryman 1970 (June 15), 12–13, 28–36.

MICROBIOTA Komar.—CUPRESSACEAE

Shrub; usually dioecious; branchlets 4 sided, flattened, short; all leaves scale-like, facial leaves broadly triangular, acute, with easily visible glands, lateral leaves thick, somewhat convex, apexes curved inward; cones horizontally arranged, terminal on short branchlets, outspread, globose, 3 × 6 mm in size, with 2–4 seed scales, these leathery or more woody, of these only 1 fertile and that with only 1 seed; seed erect, elliptic, not winged, with large resin gland. x = 11.—Only 1 species; SE. Siberia. Range map Fig. 2.

Microbiota decussata Komar. Shrub, scarcely over 60 cm high, but to 1.5 m wide, very stoutly branched, branch tips more or less nodding; leaves very small, usually triangular, occasionally also needle-like, yellowish-green in summer, somewhat brownish in winter, like *Thuja*. DB 1969: 42–44; KN Plate 5. SE. Siberia; Primorskaja Province (east of Vladivostock), Olga region, in the Suchan River Valley, the upper course of the Anjuja and Chora Rivers near Chernigovka, USSR; common in the mountains over the timber line. Very winter hardy. Plate 77. z2

Lit. Zamjatin, B.: Observationes nonnullae de *Microbiota decussata*. Notul. Syst. Herb. Inst. Komarov, Leningrad, **22**, 43–50, 1963

MICROCACHRYS Hook f.—PODOCARPACEAE

Monotypic genus. Low, evergreen shrub, twigs 4 sided; leaves small, scale-like, arranged in 4 rows; male flowers terminal, ovate, female flowers terminal, ovate-globose, carpels numerous, imbricately overlapping, each with 1 ovule, these adnate to the upper side of the carpel, micropyle twisted at the base, exterior surrounded by the receptacle; fruit a small cone, mulberry-like in appearance, the individual carpels not connate.—Tasmania. Range map Fig. 111.

Microcachrys tetragona Hook. f. Small, evergreen shrub, branches procumbent, long, thin, "whip-like", 4 sided, strongly branched; leaves scale-like, 2–3 mm long, tightly appressed in 4 rows, overlapping, all of similar form, finely ciliate, persisting several years on the main shoots; male and female flowers on the same plant, but on different branches; fruit cones mulberry-like in appearance, with 20–28 fertile scales, red when ripe, translucent, 6–8 mm long, seeds surrounded by the receptacle only at the base. CFTa 61; CBJ 57; CTa 1. Tasmania; in the mountains on wet, swampy soil. 1845. Plate 77; Fig. 110. z9

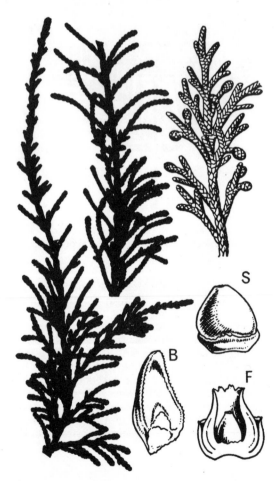

Fig. 110 *Microcachrys tetragona* 3 twigs, nearly actual size; B. leaf; S. ovule with receptacle; F. same in cross section (from Hooker; both twigs at left Original)

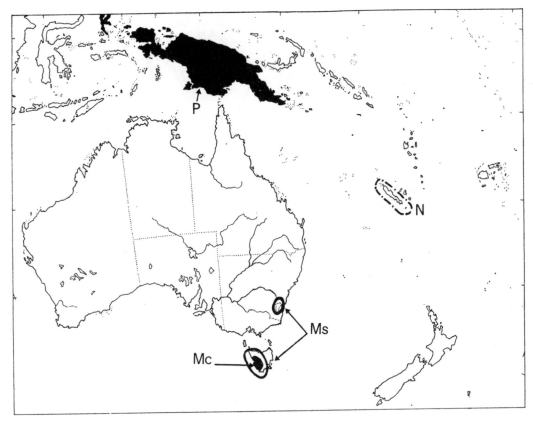

Fig. 111. Range of the genus *Microcachrys* (Mc), *Microstrobus* (Ms), *Neocallitropsis* (N) and *Papuacedrus* (P) (Original)

MICROSTROBOS J. Garden & L. S. Johnson— PODOCARPACEAE

Evergreen, moisture loving shrubs, closely related to *Dacrydium, Diselma* and *Microcachrys*; branches either short and stiff or long and thin; leaves scale-like, spirally arranged, in 4 or 5 rows, densely crowded and overlapping; plants dioecious; male flowers terminal, globose to ovate, erect, very small, composed of 10–15 stamens; female flowers also terminal, short and recurved, carpels not numerous, loosely arranged, with 1 ovule each, seed scales, as contrasted with *Podocarpus*, only thickened at the base, but not fleshy; ovules erect, without a receptacle, integument drawn out to a short, wide micropyle; actual seed very small, about 1 mm long, light brown or gray (= *Pherosphaera* Hook. non Archer).—2 species in Tasmania and Australia. Range map Fig. 111.

Microstrobus fitzgeraldii (F. Muell.) Garden & Johnson. Low shrub, abundantly branched, twigs long and thin, densely covered with small, narrow, acute leaves, 2.5 mm long, curved inward at the tips, dorsally keeled, spreading in all directions, interior with white stomatal lines, exterior olive-green, more blue-gray in appearance resulting from the white upper surface. BAu 411; HI 1383; CCE 243 (= *Pherosphaera fitzgeraldii* [F. Muell.] F. Muell.). New South Wales, Australia; only in a limited area in the Blue Mountains, mostly at the base of large waterfalls. Cultivated in the Royal Botanic Garden, Edinburgh. Plate 78; Fig. 112A. z9

M. niphophilus Garden & Johnson. Erect, dense shrub, 1–2 mm high, branches short and stiff, shoots densely covered with scale-like leaves, densely overlapping, 1.5 mm long and arranged in 4–5 rows; leaves thick, distinctly keeled on the dorsal side, apex obtuse and curving inward; plants dioecious, male flowers 2–3 mm long with 8–15 stamens, female flowers terminal in small cones on short, nodding branchlets, with 3–5 fertile seed scales, about 3 mm long. CTa 2; CCE 243 (= *Pherosphaera hookeriana* J. D. Hook. non Archer). Tasmania; only in the alpine region from 1000–1300 m. Fig. 112 B and C. z9

Fig. 112. **Microstrobos.** A. *M. fitzgeraldii,* nearly actual size; B–C. *M. niphophilus;*
B. twig with fruits, 3× enlarged; twig beneath reduced (from Hooker, Maloney, left Original)

NEOCALLITROPSIS Florin—CUPRESSACEAE

Evergreen tree, similar to *Callitris,* but differing in the
densely foliate, cylindrical, unsegmented branchlets;
leaves similar to those of *Araucaria,* arranged in 8 evenly
spaced rows; cones small, composed of 2 whorls of 4
seed scales, opening widely when ripe with 1 form more
cupulate; seeds angular, scarcely winged.—1 species in
New Caledonia. Range map Fig. 111.

Neocallitropsis araucarioides (Compton) Florin. Tree,
8–10 m high, crown conical, stem straight upright, bark
gray and resinous, branches spreading horizontally,
branchlets cylindrical, similar to *Araucaria* in
appearance, forked; leaves in 8 regularly arranged rows,
6 mm long, about 3 mm wide, stiff, curving inward, short
acuminate, margin very finely dentate, distinctly keeled
on the dorsal side, juvenile foliage needle-like, about 1.5
cm long and spreading; male flowers terminal on long
branchlets, composed of 8 rowed pollen sacs on the
individual bracts; cones terminal on short side branches,
composed of 2 whorls of 4 carpels. GGy 516; J. Linn. Soc.
1922: Pl. 27; LG 43; CCE 243 (= *Callitropsis araucarioides*
Compton). New Caledonia; 1914, found in one location
in the mountains. Fig. 113. z9

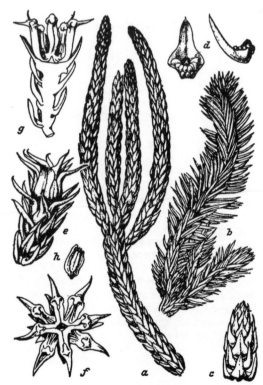

Fig 113. *Neocallitropsis araucarioides.* a. mature twig; b.
juvenile form; c. male inflorescence; d. stamens; e–g.
cones from the side, in longitudinal section and from
above; h. seed (from Compton)

PAPUACEDRUS Li—CUPRESSACEAE

Evergreen trees, closely related to *Libocedrus*, but anatomically and morphologically different; mature leaves decussate and usually somewhat dimorphic, scale-like, leathery, the lateral leaves appressed and curving inward, with subdivided stomatal bands on the underside; facial leaves small, rhombic, convex, dorsally keeled, base short decurrent; outer walls of the guard cells bordering the stomata much less cutinized (except in the papillae) than the normal epidermal cells surrounding the stomata; juvenile foliage nearly herbaceous, very dimorphic, facial leaves small, lateral leaves very large, quite flat, lanceolate, sharp and spreading acuminate, adnate to the twig for much of its length; male inflorescence with pollen sacs in whorls of 4; female cones ovate, with 4 leathery, valvate seed scales, each with a dorsal ovate or triangular appendage on the base or basal half; the 2 outer, ovate or oblong scales sterile, both inner scales lanceolate, 2–3 times larger and each with 2 ellipsoid, very unevenly winged seeds.—3 tropical species on New Guinea and the Moluccas in forested mountains from 900–3000 m. Range map Fig. 111.

Papuacedrus arfakensis (Gibb.) Li Tree, 25–35 m, crown more or less conical, stem with red-brown, scaly bark, branchlets segmented; juvenile leaves dimorphic, facial leaves in widely spaced pairs, very small, rhombic to cuneate, but visible, light green, lateral leaves very flattened, light green, to 20 mm long (very large in relation to the mature foliage), generally widening from the base, the apex spreading, gradually becoming smaller and changing to the mature form, these likewise dimorphic, dark green, narrow at the base, widening toward the obtuse tip, not spreading, with a few faint stomatal lines; male and female flowers on the same tree, but on different branches; cones about 13 mm long, both fertile carpels 2–3 times as large as the sterile ones, with a triangular dorsal appendage: CCE 244 (= *Libocedrus arfakensis* Gibbs). New Guinea; in state protected forests at 900–3800 m in the Arfak Mts. Fig. 115A. z9

P. papuana (F. Muell.) Li Not yet fully known, but differing primarily in the nearly evenly formed leaves at the branch tips, lateral leaves only partly covering the facial leaves, the latter visible to the base and then

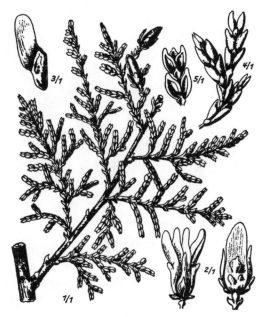

Fig. 114. *Papuacedrus torricellensis.*
Partial branch enlarged above right,
cone below right
seed above left (from Lauterbach)

covered by the tip of the next lower facial leaf, juvenile leaves similar to those of *P. arfakensis* (see Fig. 115A). CCE 244 (= *Libocedrus papuana* F. Muell.). New Guinea; Papua Territories. Plate 78; Fig. 114 B and C. z9

P. torricellensis (Schlechter ex Lauterbach) Li Not completely known, branchlets distinctly flattened, leaves clearly dimorphic, with large stomatal surfaces, lateral leaves 3 mm long, concave above, convex beneath, facial leaves only 1.5 mm long. Juvenile leaves not known. CCE 244 (= *Libocedrus torricellensis* Schlecht. ex Lauterbach). N. New Guinea; Torricelli Mts. Fig. 144. z9

Lit. Florin, R., & J. B. Boutelje: External Morphology and Epidermal Structure of Leaves in the Genus *Libocedrus*, s. lat. Acta Hort. Bergian. **17**, 21–24, 1954 (with plates).

Fig. 115. Papuacedrus.
A. *P. arfakensis,* mature branch; B–C. *P. papuana,* B. mature branch, C. juvenile form (Original)

'**Compacta**'. Dwarf form, broadly conical and compact, to about 1.5 m high, to 6 m high and as wide as very old plants, branches numerous, short, horizontal near the base, but ascending toward the peak, brown, buds distinct, 3–4 mm long, obtuse, glossy brown, scales appressed; needles about 9 mm long, generally becoming smaller toward the branch tips, about 6 mm long, 4 sided, glossy green. CCE 259 (= *P. excelsa compacta* Sénécl.). Known since 1864; presumably introduced by Booth. Plate 89.

'**Compacta Asselyn**'. Very similar to 'Compacta', but more compact as a young plant, needles shorter (6–9 mm long) and somewhat bluish beneath in early summer, hard to distinguish from 'Compacta' as older plants. OCC 230(H).

'**Compressa**'. Dwarf form, compact conical habit, regular, branches densely crowded, ascending, covered with branchlets, flat, all nearly equally long; needles very densely arranged, 5 to 10 mm long, glossy dark green (= *P. abies* var. *compressa* Schwerin] Hornib.). Discovered in the Diedorf Forestry Garden near Augsburg, W. Germany about 1903. (EX?)

'**Concinna**'. Low form, conical habit, branches ascending, twigs exceptionally thin, whitish; needles very densely arranged, thin, short, nearly cylindrical, tightly appressed to the branches (= *P. abies conica* [Endl.] Fries). In cultivation before 1847. (EX)

'**Conica**'. Dwarf form, compact conical, but rather strong grower, annual growth 3–6 cm, branchlets ascending, tightly crowded, thin, lighter or darker brown; needles radial and densely arranged, soft, thin, light green, 3–6 mm long (= *P. abies conica* [Endl.] Fries). In cultivation before 1847. (EX?)

'**Cortica**'. Normal growth habit, differing only in the bark which develops to 9 cm thick and is longitudinally fissured, like pine and larch (= *P. excelsa* var. *corticata* Schroet.). Repeatedly observed near Lausanne, Switzerland, Southern Austria, near Frankfurt, W. Germany, etc. First observed in 1898.

'**Cranstonii**'. Tree-like habit, 10–15 m high, very openly branched, branches long and thick, with only a few lateral branches, often crossing one another, buds to 15 mm long, conical; needles radial and widely spaced, to 30 mm long, often somewhat wavy, dark green, very similar to those of 'Virgata', but much more laterally compressed. OCC 231 (H); CCE 254 (= *P. abies cranstonii* [Carr.] den Ouden). Originated from seed in the Cranston Nursery of Herefeld, England about 1840. Plate 91.

'**Crippsii**'. Dwarf form, conical, very slow growing, branches horizontal, slightly ascending, twigs spreading at acute angles and very densely crowded, very thin, but stiff, light yellow, gray-yellow in the 2nd year, very uneven in length, to 5 cm long, solitary or in groups, buds small, conical, acute, 3–4 mm long, light brown; needles radially arranged and very dense, but less dense on the branch underside, thin, 4–6 mm long, yellow-green, drawn out to a fine tip (= *P. abies* var. *crippsii* Hornib.; *P. abies brevifolia* Hornib.; *Abies excelsa brevifolia* Cripps ex Gord.). In cultivation before 1875. (VR)

'**Cupressina**'. Tree, 10–20 m, broadly conical crown (like a wide *Cupressus sempervirens*), branches rather densely arranged, ascending steeply, densely branched toward the apex, twigs short, flexible, light orange, sparsely short pubescent, buds small, surrounded by the needles; needles 12 to 14 mm long, dark green, somewhat bluish-green in winter; cones 8–10 cm long, 2.5–3 cm thick, otherwise normal. OCC 232 (H); MD 1904: 252 (H); KN 14; CCE 262 (= *P. abies* f. *cupressina* [Thomas[Rehd.). Discovered before 1904 in the Thuringian Forest, W. Germany.

'**Decumbens**'. Dwarf form, broad and flat habit, scarcely over 30 cm high and 1 m wide, very similar to 'Nidiformis', but flatter and without the nest form depression, habit also more irregular, denser, branches dull brown, glabrous, thin, flexible, annual growth 4–7 cm, all young shoots slightly pendulous, buds conical, acute, 2–3 mm long, all equal in size, red-brown, resinous in winter; needles lighter and more yellow-green, 12–20 mm long, shortest at the branch tips and semi-radially arranged, densely crowded, flexible, but with sharp tips, both sides with 1–3 stomatal bands. WDw 183 (H); WM 24C (Br). Often confused in the literature with 'Dumosa' because of the inconclusive description by Hornibrook. (R)

f. **deflexa** (Tyszkiewicz) Krüssm. Normal tree, differing only in the cones whose seed scales are long acuminate and reflexed. OCC 233 (C) (= *P. excelsa* f. *deflexa* Tyszk.). Poland; found in the forest near Bialowies. Before 1934. Not in cultivation.

"**Densa**". Compact conical form, which cannot be found or identified today because of incomplete descriptions. (= *P. excelsa densa* Carr. 1867).

'**Denudata**'. Transition form between the sparsely branched 'Cranstonii' and the nearly unbranched 'Monstrosa', stem vertical with only a few branches. Rev. Hort. 1854, Fig. 7 (also in Berg, Pl. 5) (= *P. excelsa* var. *denudata* Carr.). Repeatedly found in the wild. Before 1854 in Livonia (now Estonia & N. Latvia) and elsewhere. Not in cultivation.

'**Depressa**'. Weeping form, branches densely crowded, long, pendulous from the stem, lying on the ground on old plants where the tips then commence to grow upward again, branchlets densely covering the plant; needles very densely arranged, 10–12 mm long (= *P. excelsa depressa* Berg). An old specimen stands in the Geneva Botanic Garden, Switzerland.

'**Dicksonii**'. Sparsely branched form, similar to 'Cranstonii', but somewhat more fully branched and with reddish young twigs; needles more densely arranged (= *P. abies dicksonii* [Beissn.] Krüssm.). Known before 1891. (R)

'**Diedorfiana**'. Delicate form with very short needles, the first shoots a persistent golden-yellow, even in the shade, the later shoots a contrasting green, therefore with alternating yellow and green branch segments (= *P. abies diedorfiana* [Schwer.] Krüssm.). Originated in the Diedorf Forestry Garden, W. Germany before 1903. (EX?)

'**Diffusa**'. Dwarf form, similar to 'Pumila', low, wide spreading and very densely branched ("bee hive" form according to Welch!), branches orange-brown, fine, flexible, annual growth 5–6 cm long; leaves radially arranged on the tips, but only semi-radial on the side shoots, thin and flat, 6–9 mm long, conspicuously yellow-green, midrib slightly raised, apex straight and normally translucent. WDw 184 (H), Pl. 14K (Br); WM 284 (H) (= *P. abies* var. *diffusa* [Hornib.] Hornib.). (VR)

'**Dumosa**'. Dwarf form, broad to conical upright, to 1.5 m high, branches partly in horizontal layers, some slightly ascending, twigs yellow above, gray beneath, somewhat glossy and slightly pubescent, leaf cushions hard, shoots thin and very flexible, annual growth 5–7 cm, spreading at various angles, buds light orange, obtuse oval-oblong, terminal bud 5–6 mm long, the others 3–4 mm, glossy; needles dark green, straight, thick and flat, midrib indented, quite short acuminate, not sharp, 10–15 mm long, radially arranged, shortest at the branch tips. WDw 185 (H), Pl. 14G (Br); CCE 252, 253 (= *P. abies* var. *dumosa* [Carr.] Bail.). Frequently mislabeled as 'Decumbens'. (R)

'**Echiniformis**'. Dwarf form, very slow growing, globose to cushion form, growth dense and irregular, to about 20 cm high and 40 cm wide in 30 years, shoots rather stiff and thick, light brown, glabrous, somewhat glossy, leaf cushions quite flat, buds light brown, the larger ones cylindrical with rounded tips, 1–3 mm long, quite variable in size, annual growth very stunted and irregular, 15–20 mm long with normal needles and 3–5 buds or a cluster of compressed, only 3–5 mm, long shoots with thin leaves, each with a single terminal bud, occasionally with a large axillary bud on a long shoot near the base; needles medium size, 12–15 mm long, dull yellow-green to gray-green, 1–1.25 mm thick, very narrow, but thick, rhombic in cross section, flatly arranged, with a short, very sharp apex, the uppermost needles stellately arranged under the terminal bud, the strong shoots always with a few widely spaced needles, these stiff and prickly. HD 146 (H): CCE 253; WM 23B (Br) (= *P. abies* var. *echiniformis* [Gord.] Bail.). Known before 1875. Almost never true in cultivation and always confused with 'Gregoryana' or 'Veitchii'. Plate 89.

'Elegans'. Dwarf form, conical, to 1.5 m high, branches numerous and quite regularly arranged, twigs short, yellow-brown, thin, buds short, acute, dull brown; needles dense and radially arranged, 8 mm long at the branch base, gradually becoming shorter toward the tips (4 mm), acute, light green. WM 23F (Br), 285 (H) (= *P. abies* f. *elegans* [Forbes] Rehd.; *P. excelsa conica elegans* Hort. ex Hornib.). Known before 1839. (VR)

'Ellwangeriana'. Dwarf form, broad habit, dense, but vigorous, with ascending branches, but without a central leader, annual growth very thick and stiff, 4–6 cm long, with distinct leaf cushions, orange-brown and pubescent, buds orange-brown, conical, sharply acuminate, 3–5 mm long, all equal in size, resinous in winter, up to 10 buds together at the branch tips, bud scales fringed on the margin; needles glossy dark green, thick and stiff, usually straight, occasionally somewhat bowed upward, keeled on both sides, 12–15 mm long, 1 mm wide, on strong shoots nearly radial, otherwise semi-radial, densely arranged, very stiff to the touch, both sides with 2–3 rows of glossy stomatal lines. WDw 186 (H); KN 237 (H), 150; WM 286 (H) (= *P. abies* f. *ellwangeriana* [Beissn.] Rehd.). Originated before 1890 in Highland Park, Rochester, New York, USA.

'Eremita'. Eventually a small tree, slow growing at first, later faster, conical, coarse, open, irregular, branches numerous, ascending, twigs short, thick, sparsely branched, the new shoots orange-red, buds large and thick, nearly totally hidden under the needles; needles densely arranged, 15 mm long, thick, stiff, prickly, outspread, bluish-green, directed forward on older shoots (= *P. abies* var. *eremita* [Carr.] Dallim & Jacks.; *P. excelsa crassifolia* Sénécl.). Known before 1855, in France.

f. erythrocarpa (Purk.) Rehd. Normal growth habit, differing only in the color of the cone scales, these dark violet until September. Occurs occasionally among the species.

'Falcata'. Tree, normal habit, branches declining obliquely downward and then curved upward in a sickle-shape. MD 1912: 263 (H). This form is found occasionally in the wild and also nursery beds.

'Falcato-viminalis'. Similar to 'Falcata', a normal tree, but displaying upward curving branches with limply pendulous branchlets. MD 1928: Pl. 64 (H) (= *P. abies falcato-viminalis* [Schwer.] Krüssm.; *P. excelsa bella* Schwer.). Known before 1919.

'Finedonensis'. Tree, 10–15 m high, conical, branches and twigs spreading nearly horizontally; needles pale yellow on young shoots, later more brownish, susceptible to sunscald and then browning. OCC 235 (H); KN 238 (Br); CCE 254 (= *P. abies* var. *finedonensis* [Gord.] Rehd.). Originated from seed before 1862 in the Finedon Hall Park, Northamptonshire, England.

'Frohburg'. Weeping form of the 'Inversa' type, stem erect, side branches limply pendulous. KN 151; CCE 263. Discovered by

Haller (Switzerland), introduced by C. Esveld, Boskoop, Holland.

f. gigantea (Beissn.) Boom. Tree, luxuriant and very fast growing, slender branches; needles longer and wider (= *P. excelsa* f. *gigantea* Beissn.). Before 1891.

'Globosa'. Globe Spruce. Tree, basal portion grows normally, peak however, a large globe, also with individual branches having sporadic, globose clusters of twigs. Illustrated in Berg, Pl. 19–20 (= *P. excelsa* var. *globosa* Berg.). Repeatedly observed in Switzerland and elsewhere. Before 1887. Seed from the cones of about 150 cm wide globes on 10 m high or taller stems will produce dwarf forms. Examination has revealed no parasites, but such witches'-brooms are in all probability caused by parasites. Not in cultivation.

'Globosa Nana'. Dwarf form, globose to broadly conical, very dense, branches spreading in all directions, occasionally even growing inward, annual growth 3–6 cm, young shoots partly thin, partly very thick, flexible, orange-brown on both sides, lightly pubescent, lateral branches very irregularly spreading, buds dull dark-brown, oval, terminal buds 3–5 mm long, the others 2–3 mm long, the terminal buds usually surrounded by 4–6 neighboring buds, but not crowded; needles 6–8 mm long, nearly gray-green, glossy, widest in the middle, occasionally slightly recurved, otherwise straight, apexes obtuse with a fine tip, both sides with 3–4 stomatal lines to the apex, radially arranged, leaning forward at the branch tips, but not hiding the terminal, densely arranged, stiff to the touch (= *P. abies* var. *globosa nana* Hornib.).

f. glomerulans (Kihlm.) Krüssm. Tree-like, but sparsely branched, main branches very twiggy, the twigs poorly developed and forming small knots all along the branches (= *P. excelsa glomerulans* Kihlm.). Found in the forests of Finland, before 1905. Not in cultivation.

'Gregoryana'. Dwarf form, exceptionally slow growing, globose to broadly globose when young and very densely branched, differing from the much rarer 'Echiniformis' in the shorter needles (8–12 mm long), more densely arranged, otherwise differing in the absence of strong shoots which break out of the globose form (very typical of 'Echiniformis'); habit more or less globose-cushion form, with occasional indentions with age, 60–80 cm high, annual growth 5–20 mm, shoots rather thick, but flexible, light brown, lightly pubescent, leaf cushions well developed, brown, buds very light yellow-green, globose, only 1–1.5 mm thick, grouped to 10 together on the branch tips; needles dull gray-green, straight, with a fine, sharp tip, and 1–2 stomatal lines running to the apex on both sides, radially arranged, the uppermost leaves radiating so all buds can be clearly seen. WDw 187 (H), Pl. 14C (Br); OCC 236 (H); HD 147 (H); CCE 258; WM 23A (Br), 287 (H) (= *P. abies* var. *gregoryana* [Gord.] Rehd.). Very popular form, but often incorrectly labeled as 'Echiniformis'. Plate 89; Fig. 122B.

'Gregoryana Parsonsii'. To 90 cm high and 150 cm wide, similar to 'Gregoryana', but much more open, especially at the base; needles longer, flatter, never completely radially arranged, rather parted beneath, but otherwise the color and form of the needles, buds and twigs the same as that of 'Gregoryana'. HD 146 (H) (= *P. abies* var. *gregoryana parsonsii* [Hornib.] Hornib.). Introduced before 1923 by the S. B. Parsons Nursery in Flushing, New York, USA under the incorrect name of 'Clanbrassiliana'. (VR)

'Gregoryana Veitchii'. Dwarf form, again very similar to 'Gregoryana', but differing in the radial arrangement of the needles on the erect central leader, thinner and flatter on the lateral shoots, also only semi-radial or parted, new shoots longer with annual growth of 12–35 mm, very flexible, often inclined downward; strongly growing plant, not so compact,

'**Remontii**'. Dwarf form, but to 3 m high, regularly conical, branches spreading at acute angles, twigs brown, lighter beneath, glabrous, rather thin, annual growth about 2–3 cm, buds orange, obtuse-conical or ovate, terminal buds 2–3 mm long, the others only 1–2 mm, glossy, terminal usually with 1–2 side buds; leaves bright green, incompletely radial, 5–7 mm long, the longest basal on the twigs and directed downward, shorter and directed forward at the branch tips, visible buds, flexible to the touch, bowed at the base, otherwise straight, with 1–3 intermittent stomatal lines on either side. WDw 201 (H); DB 15: 174 (H); MG 1906: 557; SN 206; CCE 259; WM 306 (H) (= *P. abies* f. *remontii* [R. Smith] Rehd.). Known since 1874. Common in cultivation. Plate 90; Fig. 123A.

'**Repens**'. This is another form about which authors disagree: Beissner-Fitschen (p. 209), Hornibrook (p. 169) and den Ouden-Boom (p. 248) all refer to the plant as being so vaguely described as to be considered invalid. Moreover, the illustration on p. 248 of den Ouden-Boom is incorrect; the fig. 50 in Beissner-Fitschen is presumably 'Repens' (but illustrated as 'Procumbens'). It is therefore sensible to follow the description by Welch of the original plant from Hornibrook as a valid description.—Dwarf form, procumbent to spreading, branches layered from the middle of the plant outward, regular, dense and evenly formed, shoots orange-brown, glabrous, thin and very flexible, horizontally outspread, tips nodding slightly,

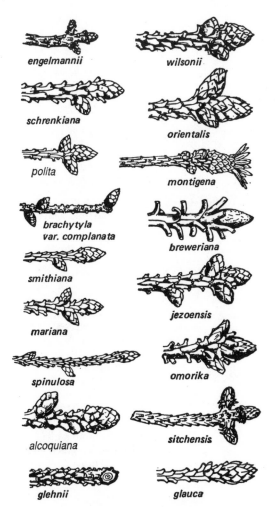

engelmannii
wilsonii
schrenkiana
orientalis
polita
montigena
brachytyla var. complanata
breweriana
smithiana
jezoensis
mariana
spinulosa
omorika
alcoquiana
sitchensis
glehnii
glauca

Fig. 126. Needle-less shoots of *Picea* species. Form and size of the leaf cushions are easily visible.

annual growth 3–5 cm, leaf cushions not conspicuous, buds orange, oval-conical, with sharp tips, terminal 3–4 mm long, the others 2–3 mm, usually 3 buds together at the branch tips; needles bright green to yellow-green (color variable!), semi-radially arranged, but very flat, twigs openly visible from beneath, very densely arranged and flexible to the touch, 8–10 mm long, straight, widest at the base, with a distinct midrib, drawn out to a small, sharp apex, with 1–2 intermittent stomatal lines on either side. WDw 202 (H), Pl. 14M (Br); DB 1970: 170; CCE 261; WM 307 (H). Plate 89.

'**Rothenhaus**'. Tall tree, narrow, somewhat resembling *P. orientalis* in habit and in the short needles, but twigs more spirally arranged and pendulous (= *P. excelsa rothenhausii* Hahn). Discovered before 1900 in the forest at Rothenhaus Castle near Eisenburg, Czechoslovakia; brought to the Pruinitz Park near Prague. Very decorative. Plate 80.

'**Sargentii**'. Dwarf form, twigs thin and densely crowded, light yellow, directed obliquely forward, annual growth about 2.5 cm, buds small, conical, red-brown, somewhat resinous; needles irregularly arranged, parted or radial, rather thin, consistently formed, 8 mm long, abruptly tapered at the apex, obtuse, soft, occasionally yellow tipped in winter. CCE 260; WM 308 (H) (= *P. abies* var. *sargentii* [Hornib.] Hornib.). Distributed by the Arnold Arboretum, before 1923. USA.

'**Sibirica**'. Compact, lower than the type, broadly conical, densely branched, young shoots light brown, glabrous, buds conical, rather large, brown; needles fine, sharply acuminate, 10–15 mm long (= *P. excelsa sibirica* Carr.). Known since 1855; presumably EX.

'**Sherwood**'. Dwarf form, compact and flat habit, irregular, occasionally more globose, 1.2 m high and 2.4 m wide in 30 years (= *P. abies sherwoodii* Sherwood). Introduced in 1945 by the H. M. Sherwood Nursery, Portland, Oregon, USA.

'**Spathulifolia**'. Dwarf form, broad and low, twigs light and glossy orange, very conspicuous leaf cushions, buds small, acutely conical, light brown; needles semi-radial and more parted, thin, yellow-green, narrowest at the base, then becoming flatter, apex cut off at an angle as if with a knife (= *P. abies* var. *spathulifolia* [Hornib.] Hornib.). Originated in Kew Gardens, but named by Hornibrook in 1923. (VR)

f. **squarrosa** (Jacobasch) den Oud. & Boom. Like the normal type in all respects, except the margins of the cone scales on the apical portion of the cones are bowed divaricately downward, further appressed at the apex. Discovered before 1883. Not in cultivation.

f. **strigosa** (Christ) Dallim. & Jacks. Normal size trees, like the species, twigs very numerous, spreading horizontally in all directions, resembling a larch in habit (= *P. excelsa* f. *strigosa* Christ). Discovered before 1895 in St. Gallen Canton, Switzerland. Not in cultivation.

'**Tabuliformis**'. Dwarf form, wide spreading habit, mat-form at first, mounding in layers with age, then flat-globose, but loose, peak of the plant always quite flat(!), branches spreading flatly, tips slightly nodding, twigs light brown above, more gray beneath, glabrous, glossy, very thin and flexible, annual growth about 2–3 cm, all side shoots very consistently formed, buds orange-brown, oval, 2–3 mm long, with 1–2 smaller side buds; needles semi-radial, rather widely spaced, flexible to the touch, light yellow-green, straight, but twisted at the base, 7–10 mm long, distinct midrib, drawn out to a long tip, with 1–4 stomatal lines running to the apex. WDw 203 (H); HiD 47 (H); CCE 261; WM 24D (Br), 309 (H) (= *P. abies* f. *tabulaeformis* [Carr.] Rehd.). Found as a witches'-broom before 1865 in Trianon, Versailles, France; also in Sweden.

Outline of the *Picea* species covered (without hybrids)

Species	Young Shoots pubescent	Young Shoots glabrous	Young Shoots Color	Buds resinous	Buds resin free	Needles Length (mm)	Needles 4 sided	Needles flat	Stomata above	Stomata beneath	Characteristics

Section 1. Picea. Needles 4 sided, with stomatal lines on all sides; forming right or obtuse angles in cross section; cones pendulous; cone scales tight, tightly appressed before ripening, usually rounded at the apex and entire

Species	pubescent	glabrous	Color	resinous	resin free	Length (mm)	4 sided	flat	above	beneath	Characteristics
smithiana		×	gray	×		20–40	×		×	×	shoots pendulous
schrenkiana		×	gray		×	20–35	×		×	×	
wilsonii		×	gray-white		×	10–20	×		×	×	thin shoots
maximowiczii		×	light brown	×		8–15	×		×	×	
polita		×	light yellow		×	15–20	×		×	×	needles stiff, prickly
neoveitchii		×	light brown			12–15	×		×	×	
asperata	×—×		yellowish	×		10–18	×		×	×	similar to *P. abies*
gemmata	×		reddish yellow	×		8–17	×		×	×	shoots densely pubescent
meyeri	×		yellowish	×		8–20	×		×	×	needles not prickly
retroflexa		×	yellow		×	10–25	×		×	×	needles prickly
abies	×—×		brown		×	10–20	×		×	×	
obovata	×		brown		×	10–18	×		×	×	
orientalis	×		light brown		×	6–10	×		×	×	needles very glossy
koyamai	×		brown, pruinose	×		8–12	×—×		×	×	most stomata above
pungsaniensis		×	yellow-brown	×		12–25	×		×	×	
alcoquiana		×	brownish		×	10–20	×—×		×	×	
glehnii	×		reddish brown	×		6–12	×—×		×	×	
morrisonicola		×	yellow		×	10–20	×		×	×	needles thin, acute
rubens	×		brown		×	10–15	×		×	×	needles glossy
mariana	×		brown		×	6–18	×		×	×	needles blue-gray
glauca		×	gray-brown		×	8–18	×		×	×	needles bluish

Section 2. Casicta Mayr. Needles 4 sided and with stomatal lines on all sides or compressed and without or with fewer stomatal lines beneath than above; cone scales loosely appressed before ripening, thin and flexible when ripe, usually rhombic, with undulate or eroded margins

Species	pubescent	glabrous	Color	resinous	resin free	Length (mm)	4 sided	flat	above	beneath	Characteristics
engelmannii	×		yellow-brown		×	15–25	×		×	×	needles bluish, bowed
mexicana	×		yellow-brown		×	20–35	×		×	×	
pungens		×	yellow-brown		×	20–30	×		×	×	needles outspread
chihuahuana						15–21	×		×	×	
likiangensis	×		yellow-orange	×		8–15	×—×		×	×	needle cushions yellow
—balfouriana	×		yellowish	×		8–15	×		×	×	branches very short
—purpurea	×		gray-yellow	×—×		8–12	×		×	×	twigs widely spaced
hirtella	×		light yellow			10–20	×		×	×	needles prickly
montigena	×		yellow-brown	×		8–15	×		×	×	
jezoensis		×	yellow-brown	×		10–20		×		×	needles not prickly
sitchensis		×	yellow-brown	×		15–25		×		×	needles prickly

Section 3. Omorika Willk. Needles *Abies*-like compressed, with stomatal lines only on the dorsal (outer) side; cones all pendulous or the uppermost outspread

Species	pubescent	glabrous	Color	resinous	resin free	Length (mm)	4 sided	flat	above	beneath	Characteristics
brachytyla		×	yellow-brown		×	10–24		×		×	needles without a green midline
omorika	×		brown		×	8–18		×		×	needles with a green midline
breweriana	×		red-brown		×	20–25		×		×	needles obtuse
spinulosa		×	yellow-gray		×	20–35		×		×	needles prickly

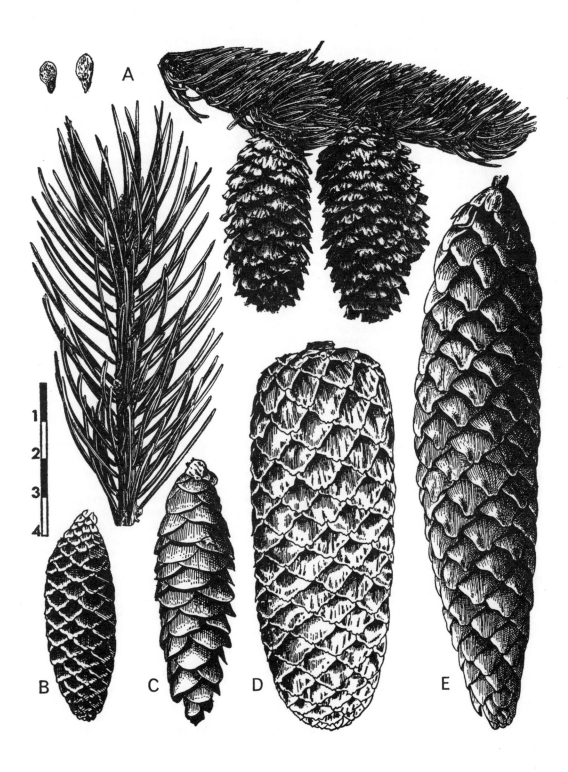

Fig. 127. **Picea.** A. *P. engelmannii,* left terminal branch and 2 seeds;
B. *P. glehnii;* C. *P. orientalis;* D. *P. hirtella;* E. *P. abies*

f. **triloba** (Aschers & Graebn.) den Oud. & Boom. Like the normal species in all respects, but the cone scales (at least the basal ones) deeply 3 lobed. Discovered before 1897 in the Harz Mts., Germany; also in Czechoslovakia and in Switzerland. Not in cultivation.

'**Tuberculata**'. Grows like the species, but recognizable by the numerous conical outgrowths from the stem or the swollen branch bases. OCC 521 (= *P. abies tuberculata* [Schroet.] den Oud.). Discovered before 1898 in Switzerland. Plate 81.

'**Turfosa**'. Dwarf form, to 5 m or more, shrubby, slender to conical or also globose, main branches often forked, lower branches lying on the ground, twigs very dense and consistently long. MD 1916: Pl. 56–57 (H) (= *P. excelsa* var. *turfosa* Lingelsh.). Discovered before 1875 in the Ore Mts., E. Germany and again in 1916 in Silesia (now Poland and Czech.).

'**Viminalis**'. Tree, to 20 m, broad conical habit, branches long and horizontal, later more drooping, long twigs, nearly vertically weeping, flexible; needles 2.5–3 cm long, light green, somewhat sickle-shaped. BFN 47 (H); CCE 262 (= *P. abies* f. *viminalis* [Alstroem.] Lindman). Repeatedly found in various places in Germany, Austria, Switzerland, Scandinavia and Poland; first in 1741 in the vicinity of Stockholm. Plate 91.

'**Virgata**'. A tall tree as well as a shrubby form, generally with a central leader, branch arrangement usually solitary or in irregular whorls, long, horizontal, often intertwining, chaotic and "snake-like", the uppermost directed upward, the lower ones more pendulous, usually without side buds, therefore normally only growing from the branch tips; radially arranged needles, of variable length, about 26 mm, thick, acute, often curving upward, usually persisting for 10 years on the branch. DB 20: 105 (H); CCE 256, 263 (= *P. abies* f. *virgata* [Jacques] Rehd.). Frequently found; first well before 1853 in France, later in Germany, Scandinavia, Bohemia, Switzerland and Tirol. Plate 91.

'**Wansdyke Miniature**'. Dwarf form, growth compact and regular, with a short, thick stem, but otherwise like a miniature form of the type; needles dense, bluish-green. Discovered by H. J. Welch, Wansdyke Nurseries, Devizes, Wiltshire, England.

'**Wartburg**' (Haller). Growth upright with a dominant central leader, tall, branches horizontal or bowing to the ground, side branches obliquely ascending, or descending (looks like "several umbrellas stacked up"); foliage like that of 'Frohburg', which is very similar as a young plant but differing with age. Introduced by Haller AG, Switzerland. 1965.

'**Waugh**'. Dwarf form, very similar to 'Pachyphylla', sparsely branched, twigs relatively thick; leaves arranged radially, widely spaced, thick. Cultivated by Hillier.

'**Wills Dwarf**'. Low form, about 2 m high in 30 years, regular and very densely growing; interesting for the light green foliage on the summer shoots, these much lighter than the dark green older needles. DB 1956: 80 (H). Developed about 1936 in the nursery of Hans Will, Barmstedt, Holstein, W. Germany; introduced in 1956. Plate 90.

P. alcoquiana (J. G. Veitch ex Lindl.) Carr. Alcock Spruce. Tall tree, to 25 m or more in its habitat, crown acutely conical, bark gray and fissured, branches horizontal and bowed somewhat upward, rather thin, twigs yellow to reddish-yellow, previous year's twigs red-brown and deeply furrowed, main shoots frequently pubescent, but side shoots glabrous(!), buds ovate, brown, not resinous or lightly so, scales mostly appressed, split at the apex; needles 10–20 mm long, appressed to the twig and directed forward, blue-green beneath, dark green above (hence perhaps "bicolor"?), somewhat curved and compressed, 4 sided in cross section, with 5–6 white stomatal lines beneath, upper side with only 2–3 indistinct stomatal lines, needles producing an unpleasant odor when crushed; cones sessile, cylindrical, 6–10–12 cm long, purple when young, brown when ripe, seed scales soft, obovate, rounded or somewhat tapered at the apex, bract scales very small, seeds black-brown. SN 14 (H); GGy 425; CCE 267, 268; KIF 1: 22 (= *P. bicolor* [Maxim.] Mayr.). Central Japan. Plate 92; Fig. 124, 126, and 131. z6

var. **acicularis** Shiras. & Koyama. Young shoots fine brown pubescent, buds densely gray-white pubescent; needles more densely arranged than those of the type, narrow, curved, blue-white; cones always smaller than those of the type, seed scales always entire, never undulate. OCC 255 (C); CCE 268. Japan, only on Yatsuga-take Mt. 1868. z6

var. **alcoquiana**. Young shoots glabrous or lightly pubescent, seed scales on the cones always finely dentate and with wavy margins.

var. **reflexa** Shiras. & Koyama. Young shoots always pubescent, buds not resinous; needles more or less curved and shorter than those of the type, only 10–15 mm long; seed scales very thin on the margin, never undulate, apex ligulate and reflexed. Japan; only in the higher river valleys of the Oi River, 1500–1800 m.

P. asperata Mast. Tall tree, crown broadly conical, to 25 m high, bark gray-brown, branches horizontal, more pendulous on older trees, tips ascending, young shoots thin, gray-yellow, glossy, pubescent, deeply furrowed (often also glabrous in cultivation), swollen leaf cushions; buds oval-conical, 8–15 mm long(!), yellow-brown, resinous, scales loosely appressed and somewhat recurved at the apex (very important characteristic!); needles radially arranged, bluish-green, 10–20 mm long, 1 mm thick, stiff and prickly, often curved, directed forward, 4 sided in cross section, with 3–4 stomatal lines on either side; cones cylindrical, 8–10 cm long, light brown at first, eventually chestnut-brown, scales obovate, stiff and woody, seeds oblong, red-brown, somewhat shorter than the seed scales. CBI 62 (C and Br); SN 219 (H); GGy 429; DJ 66 (Br); OCC 252 (C and H); CCE 264, 265. W. China. Commonly develops forests in Asia. z6

var. **asperata**. Young shoots gray-yellow, pubescent, occasionally also glabrous on cultivated plants, buds conical; cones 8–10 cm long, seed scales round, entire on the tips.

var. **heterolepis** (Rehd. & Wils.) Cheng ex Rehd. Young shoots glossy reddish- or yellowish-brown, glabrous, older shoots more black-brown, buds more oval-oblong, obtuse, light brown, resinous, scales reflexed at the tips; needles blue-green, often with a more bluish trace, prickly, 10–20 mm long; cones 9–14 cm long, scales oval-rhombic, stiff, tight, the basal scales deeply emarginate, glossy rust-brown. GGy 429; CC 34 (H) (= *P. heterolepis* Rehd. & Wils.). Occurs with the species. Rare in cultivation.

var. **notabilis** Rehd. & Wils. Needles somewhat larger, 12–20 mm long; cones 9–14 cm long, seed scales rhombic-obovate, gradually tapering to the tip or abruptly pointed. OCC 254 (C); GGy 428; CCE 266. Occurs with the species. Rare in cultivation.

Plate 81

Picea abies 'Pendula Bohemica'
in the Zehusice Park, Czechoslovakia

Picea abies 'Pendula'
in Biella, Italy

Picea abies 'Pruhoniceana' in the
Pruhonice Park, Czechoslovakia

Picea abies 'Tuberculata'
in Hainberg near Göttingen, W. Germany
Photo: Schomaekers

Picea abies 'Humilis'
in the Dortmund Bot. Garden, W. Germany

Plate 82

Cupressus cashmeriana
on Madre Island, Lake Maggiore, Italy,
trunk circumference at 90 cm high about 7.3 m

Dacrydium cupressinum
Mount Congreve, Kilmeaden, Ireland

Fitzroya cupressoides in Benmore, Scotland;
in its habitat, western Patagonia (South America),
trees over 2000 years old have been found

Larix decidua in Dawyck, Scotland

Plate 83

Picea breweriana
in the Klamath National Forest, California, USA
Photo: Uwe Horstmann

Picea jezoensis
in the Thiensen Arboretum, Ellerhoop, Holland

Picea breweriana,
this beautiful specimen stands in Dawyck, Scotland; it was planted in 1911.

Plate 84

Picea engelmannii
near Aspen, Colorado, USA
Photo: Karl Fuchs

Picea sitchuensis
as a windbreak in Utersum, North Friesland,
Holland

Picea engelmannii in its native habitat near Aspen, Colorado
Photo: Karl Fuchs

Plate 85

Picea abies 'Acrocona'
bears cones on most of the branch tips
Photo: Krüssmann

Staminate inflorescences on *pinus densiflora*
Photo: Krüssmann

Pinus aristata
with the distinctive white resin spots on its needles

Pinus hakkodensis
of Japan is quite rare in cultivation
Photo: Krüssmann

Plate 86

Pinus aristata
in the Weston Pass, Colorado, USA
Photo: Karl Fuchs

Pinus balfouriana
in Onion Valley, California, USA
Photo: Karl Fuchs

Pinus bungeana
with its conspicuously colorful bark; this tree in the
Bonn Botanic Garden, W. Germany, is about 90 years
old, 22 m high with a trunk diameter of 34 cm at 1 m
high. (1983)

Pinus densiflora 'Umbraculifera'
in the Royal Botanic Garden, Edinburgh, Scotland

Plate 87

Pinus aristata var. *longaeva;* in the White Mountains of California, USA. These trees are about 4600 years old; therefore they are the oldest living things on earth. Dead branches persist for centuries since fungi and insects cannot withstand the extremely dry and cold climate (annual rainfall, 200 mm and temperatures to −30F°).
Photo: Karl Fuchs

Pinus aristata var. *longaeva*
in its native habitat
Photo: Karl Fuchs

Pinus aristata var. *longaeva*
as a young plant in its native habitat
Photo: Karl Fuchs

Plate 88

Picea abies 'Cincinnata'
in the Grüningen Arboretum, Switzerland

Picea abies 'Pyramidata'
on Mainau Island, W. Germany

Picea abies 'Reflexa' in the Hillier Arboretum, England

Plate 89

Picea abies 'Gregoryana'
in the Boskoop Experiment Station, Holland

Picea abies 'Echiniformis' in
Pygmy Pinetum, Devizes, England

Picea abies 'Gregoryana Veitchii'
Photo: M. Hornibrook

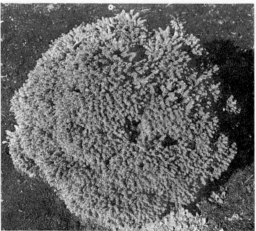

Picea abies 'Mariae-Orffiae'
in the Thiesen Arboretum, W. Germany

Picea abies 'Repens' in the
Frohnleiten Alpengarten, Steiermark, W. Germany

Picea abies 'Compacta'
in the Villa Huegel Park, Essen, W. Germany;
this specimen was planted in 1890.
It was 6 m high and wide in 1983.

Plate 90

Picea abies 'Clanbrassiliana',
original plant in Tolleymore Forest Park, N. Ireland

Picea abies 'Wills Zwerg'
in the Dortmund Bot. Garden, W. Germany

Picea abies 'Remontii'
in Shane's Park, N. Ireland

Picea abies 'Ohlendorffii'
in the St. Gallen Bot. Garden, Switzerland

Plate 91

Picea abies 'Virgata'
in the Wildungen town park, Germany

Picea abies 'Cranstonii'
in the Dortmund Bot. Garden, W. Germany

Picea abies 'Viminalis'
in the Munchen Bot. Garden, W. Germany

Picea abies 'Phylocoides'
in RHS Gardens, Wisley, England

Plate 92

Picea asperata
in the Hoersholm Arboretum, Denmark

Picea alcoquiana
in the Aurich Arboretum, Holland

Picea engelmannii
in the Doorn Arboretum, Holland

Picea engelmannii
in the Boysen Nursery, Husum, W. Germany

Plate 93

Picea abies 'Parviformis'
in the Aurich Arboretum, Holland

Picea abies 'Procumbens'
in the Blijdenstein Arboretum, Holland

Picea abies 'Hornibrookii'
in the Dortmund Bot. Garden, W. Germany

Picea abies 'Nidiformis'
in the St. Gallen Bot. Garden, Switzerland

Picea abies 'Little Gem'
in the Jeddeloh Nursery, W. Germany

Picea abies 'Pumila Nigra'
in the Dortmund Bot. Garden, W. Germany

Plate 94

Picea koyamai in its native habitat
on Mt. Yatsuga-take, Japan at 1750 m.
Photo: E. H. Wilson

Picea likiangensis
in the Bedgebury National Arboretum, England

Picea likiangensis
in RHS Gardens, Wisley, England

Picea likiangensis var. *purpurea*
in the Aurich Arboretum, E. Friesland, Holland

Plate 95

Picea mariana 'Beissneri'
in the St. Gallen Bot. Garden, Switzerland

Picea × *mariorika*
in the Jeddeloh Nursery, W. Germany

Picea maximowiczii
in its native habitat on Hondo Island,
Japan at 1600 m
Photo: E. H. Wilson; Arnold Arboretum

Picea morrisonicola
at Crarae, Scotland

Plate 96

Picea mariana 'Nana'
in the Jeddeloh Nursery, W. Germany

Picea pungens 'Glauca Globosa'
in the Dortmund Bot. Garden, W. Germany

Picea pungens in its native habitat
in the Pika National Park, Colorado, USA
Photo: U.S. Forest Service

Picea omorika in its habitat
in the Tara Mts., Yugoslavia
Photo: S. Kolarovic

var. **ponderosa** Rehd. & Wils. Young shoots yellowish, nearly totally glabrous; cones 12–15 cm long, seed scales ovate to rhombic, light brown. GGy 429; CC 71 (H). Occurs with the species. Rarely found in cultivation.

P. aurantiaca M. T. Mast. Tall tree, 20–28 m in its habitat, trunk 80–130 cm thick, narrowly conical crown, young shoots yellow or orange, occasionally lightly pruinose, finely pubescent or also glabrous, occasionally glabrous for one year, pubescent the next, and so on alternately, buds conical, resinous, scales later reflexed at the tips; needles 8–18 mm long, gray-green or more blue-green, 4 sided, directed forward, usually with 3–5 stomatal lines on either side; cones cylindrical, 10–12 cm long, glossy brown, scales hard, wide, round, margin eroded at the apex. OCC 253 (H); GGy 429; CCE 274 (= *P. asperata* var. *aurantiaca* [Mast.] Boom). China; W. Szechwan, in the mountains at 4000–4800 m. 1910. Hardy. z5

P. bicolor = **P. alcoquiana.**

P. brachytyla (Franch.) Pritz. Tall tree, 20–25 m (to 40 m in its habitat), stem to 1.5 m in diameter, bark of younger trees red-brown and deeply furrowed, splitting irregularly on older trees, branches rather long, horizontal, tips ascending, young shoots thin, older branches more or less pendulous, orange-yellow, glabrous or somewhat pubescent, very small leaf cushions, buds ovate, 5 mm long, red-brown, slightly resinous, scales tightly appressed; needles obtuse or acute, green and distinctly keeled, snowy-white beneath with 10–12 stomatal lines, without a distinct midrib; cones cylindrical, dark brown, green when young, scales broadly obovate, woody. CC 70 (H), 78 (H); DJ 67; NFG 12; GGy 443; CCE 268 to 270. Western and Central China, in the mountains between 2000 and 4000 m. One of the most beautiful chinese *Picea* species and totally winter hardy. z6

var. **brachytyla.** Bark gray-brown; needles 10–20 mm long, 1–2 mm wide, finely crenate on the margin; cones 8–10 cm long, scales obovate, rounded and entire on the apex. GGy 433 (= f. *latisquama* Dallim. & Jacks.). Introduced in 1901 by E. H. Wilson through England. The type of the species. Fig. 125, 128D.

var. **complanata** (Mast.) Rehd. Bark light gray; cones larger, 12–16 cm long, seed scales truncate or rounded on the apex. BM 8969; SN 33 (H); OCC 257 (H); GGy 433; CCE 269, 271 (= *P. complanata* Mast.). W. China. Fig. 126.

var. **rhombisquamea** Stapf. Young shoots all pendulous; needles very flat, 10–18 mm long, 1 mm wide, dark green above with a distinct keel, snowy-white beneath; cones 7–10 cm long, seed scales rhombic, tightly appressed, apex truncate or emarginate. BM 8969; GGy 433 (= *P. ascendens* Patschke). W. China; Szechwan; in the mountains at 2400–3500 m. Introduced in 1903 by E. H. Wilson.

P. × brewentalis G. Horstm. (*P. breweriana* × *P. orientalis* 'Nutans'). Habit and foliage like *P. orientalis* 'Nutans', but with more pendulous twigs. Developed in 1973 by G. Horstmann and introduced to the trade in 1983.

P. breweriana S. Wats. Siskiyou Spruce. Tree, 20–25 m, occasionally to 35 m high in its habitat, branches spread horizontally, ascending slightly at the tips, twigs vertical and whip-like pendulous, to 2.5 m long on very old trees, young shoots reddish-brown, pubescent, shaggy, deeply furrowed, later silver-gray, buds ovate to spindle-form, 6 mm long, reddish-yellow, resinous; needles usually radially arranged, but also parted beneath, 20–25 mm long, somewhat compressed, obtuse, straight or somewhat bowed, flat beneath with 5–6 stomatal lines, midrib green, rounded above and dark green, glossy, without stomata; cones cylindrical, 8–10 cm long, 2–3 cm wide, green at first, then purple, eventually yellow-brown, scales obovate, very thick, open widely when ripe, seeds red-brown. DJ 68; KN 251 (H); GGy 423; CCE 272. USA; NW. California (Siskiyou Mts.) and SW. Oregon (Klamath Mts.). Discovered in 1863. Extraordinarily decorative spruce with pendulous branches; grows on dry, gravelly soil in deep ravines at high altitudes in its native habitat. Plate 83; Fig. 125, 126 and 132. z6

P. chihuahuana Martinez. Tree, 18–25 m, crown conical, bark gray, furrowed, conspicuous leaf cushions, bud scales ovate, ciliate, the basal scales rather acute; needles 15–20 mm long, stiff, somewhat bowed, sharply acuminate, 4 sided in cross section, bright green and somewhat bluish, with 3–6 stomatal lines on either side; cones cylindrical, yellow-brown, 10–12 cm long, 3.5 cm thick, seed scales broadly obovate, tough and stiff, apical limb round and entire. GGy 427. Mexico; found in Chihuahua, before 1942. Resembles *P. pungens*, but without the reflexed bud scales and with entire, rounded seed scales. Rarely found in cultivation; not well known. Fig. 125. z7

P. engelmannii (Parry) ex Engelm. Engelmann Spruce. Tall tree, 20–40 m or taller, grows slowly, crown very dense, conical or also narrow and acute, bark thin, light brown, resinous, branches in dense whorls, spreading horizontally or slightly ascending, twigs yellow-brown and very finely glandular pubescent, glabrous after about 3 years, buds conical, brown, scales appressed, the apical ones round, the basal long acuminate; needles thin, 15–25 mm long, straight or somewhat curved, flexible (not stiff like *P. pungens*!), bluish-green to steel-blue, 4 sided in cross section, with 2–4 stomatal lines above, 3–6 beneath, partly radially arranged, some more parted on the branch underside, unpleasant odor when crushed; cones nearly sessile, ovate to cylindrical, 4–8 cm long, 2.5–3 cm wide, light brown, greenish-red before ripening, scales paper thin, rhombic-oblong, tapering toward the tip and split, apex truncate and finely dentate, bract scales small, light yellow, seeds black, 1.5 mm long, with 10 mm long wings. GGy 431; CCE 273. Western N. America, tall mountain tree with a wide range, growing between 1000 and 4000 m. 1862. Thriving in all soils, if sufficiently moist. Plate 84 and 92; Fig. 125, 126 and 127. z3

'**Argentea**'. Needles silver-gray. MG 21: 557 (H). 1891. Occurs occasionally from seed.

'**Fendleri**'. Branches pendulous; needles thin, to 28 mm long, 4 sided, with 4 blue-white stomatal lines above, only 2 beneath (= *P. engelmannii* var. *fendleri* Henry). Probably found in New Mexico. Before 1912.

'**Glauca**'. Needles intensely blue-green (= *P. engelmannii* f. *glauca* [R. Smith] Beissn.). Before 1874. The most common cultivar.

'**Microphylla**'. Dwarf form, bushy compact habit; needles much shorter. Developed by Hesse before 1891. (EX?)

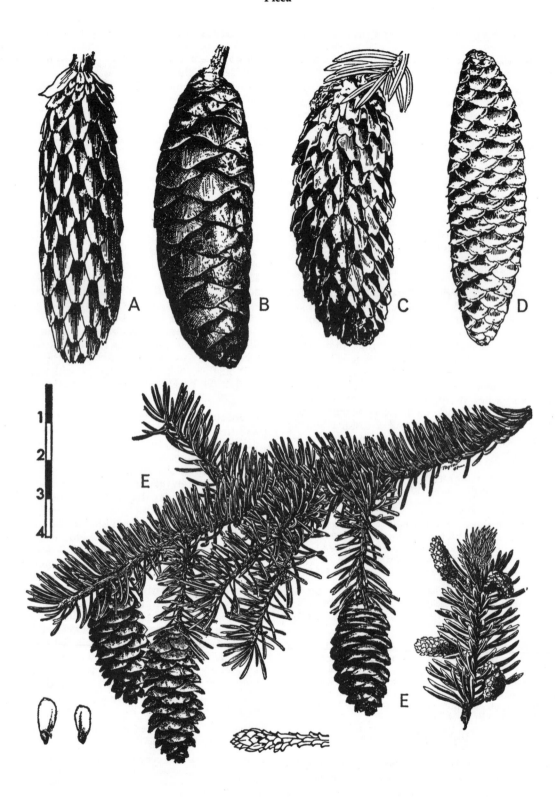

Fig. 128. **Picea.** A. *P. jezoensis;* B. *P. neoveitchii;* C. *P. pungens;* D. *P. brachytyla;*
E. *P. glauca* (right twig with male flowers, needle-less branch tip below, seed at left)

P. gemmata Rehd. & Wils. Tall tree, 20–40 m, bark gray or more brown, horizontal branches with nodding tips, twigs light brown to gray-yellow, often pruinose (distinction from the very similar *P. asperata*); needles 4 sided, 6–18 mm long, but usually 8 to 15 mm long, 1–2 mm wide, straight or also bowed, abruptly acuminate, prickly, with 4–6 stomatal lines; cones cylindrical, tapering to the tip, 8–12 cm long, about 3.5 cm thick, smooth and glossy, scales leathery, wide, rounded. GGy 428; CCE 274. W. China; W. Szechwan; in the mountains from 3300 to 3600 m. 1908. The peculiarity of this species is in the needles surrounding the buds, which appear almost as bud scales and have a pubescent exterior. Fig. 124. z6

P. glauca (Moench) Voss. White Spruce. Tree, to 25 m, conical growth, stem 1–2 m in diameter, bark thin, gray-brown, scaly, branches rather distinctly pendulous, close to the stem, tips then ascending, rather horizontal and densely arranged on younger trees, young shoots white-yellow to yellow-brown, purinose at first, later glossy, glabrous, stout, buds oval, to 6 mm long, light brown, lower scales keeled and with a very fine tip, upper scales loosely appressed, obtuse, not resinous; needles dull blue-green to white-gray, 10–18 mm long, with 2–3 stomatal lines above, 3–4 beneath, very densely arranged, rather stiff, odor resembles *Ribies nigrum* when crushed; cones cylindrical, of varying length on the same branch, 3.5–5 cm long, 1.2–2 cm wide, green when young, light brown when ripe, scales soft, flexible, margin round and entire, bract scales small and enclosed. OCC 259 (C); GGy 426; SN 40 (H); CCE 275, 276 (= *P. canadensis* B. S. P.; *P. alba* Link). Eastern N. America. Tolerant of coastal sites and strong wind; prefers a moderately moist soil. Fig. 124, 126, 128E. z3

'Alberta Globe' (Streng). Mutation of *P. glauca* 'Conica', but globose in habit; needles green, 6–9 mm long, thin like 'Conica'. WM 312 (H). Developed before 1967 by C. Streng Jr. in Boskoop, Holland.

var. **albertiana** (S. Brown) Sarg. The western form of the White Spruce and at 50 m, the second tallest *Picea* in N. America (after *P. sitchensis*), narrow crown, young shoots darker than those of the type, somewhat pubescent, buds slightly resinous, scales lacking a slit on the apical margin; needles larger, 12–24 mm long, short acuminate at the apex; cones more oval, never over 4 cm long, scales stiffer and limb toothed. SN 217 (H); DJ 69 (Br); GGy 426 (= *P. alba albertiana* [S. Brown] Beissn.; *P. albertiana* S. Brown). Northwest N. America, especially in Alberta, Canada. z3

'Aurea'. Strong grower; needles golden-yellow above. CCE 277 (= *P. glauca* f. *aurea* [Nels.] Rehd.). Known since 1866.

'Aureospicata'. Of normal vigor, young shoots yellow, but greening over the course of the summer (= *P. alba aureospicata* Beissn.) Originated before 1890 from seed in Karlsruhe, W. Germany.

'Coerulea'. Habit somewhat more compact than the type, conical, very dense; needles shorter, very densely crowded, distinctly blue-gray to silvery (= *P. alba* var. *coerulea* Nels.). 1866. (R)

'Conica'. Dwarf Alberta Spruce. Dwarf form, a 60-year-old plant in France is about 4 m high, another in Germany is 3.6 m high after 35 years, growth stiff and regularly conical, quite dense and narrow, twigs very finely textured, flexible, somewhat pubescent in the furrows, branches stiff, very thin,

cream-white; needles radial, loosely arranged, 10 mm long, light green new growth, later light bluish-green. WM 25A (Br); CCE 278 (= *P. glauca* var. *albertiana* f. *conica* Rehd.; *P. albertiana conica* Bean). Discovered growing in the wild in 1904 by A. Rehder and J. G. Jack in the mountains near Lake Laggan, in Canada. One of the most frequently cultivated conifers today; unfortunately suffers from red spider mite damage in dry heat.

Several other forms have occurred as mutations on this cultivar.

Outline of the Forms of *P. glauca* 'Conica'

	Annual growth (cm)	Needle length (mm)	Needle color
'Alberta Globe'	2–4	6–9	light green
'Laurin'	1.5–2.5	5–10	dark green
'Elegans Compacta'	3–4	8–10	bright green
'Conica'	2–4	12–15	light green
'Gnom'	3–5	8–10	gray-green
'Gracilis Compacta'	4–7	7–10	gray-green

'Echiniformis'. Dwarf form, quite flat globose to cushion-form, to about 1 m wide and 0.5 m high, young shoots very short, annual growth about 1.5–3 cm, brown, very flexible, buds brown, oblong to globose, terminal 2–3 mm long, the other buds somewhat smaller; needles radially arranged, 5–7 mm long, very narrow, round in cross section, yellow-green, but appearing blue-gray or gray from the heavy pruinose coating. WDw 205 (H); DB 1961: 161 (as *P. glauca* 'Nana'); CCE 277; WM 314 (H) (= *P. alba* var. *echiniformis* Carr.). Developed in France before 1955. Very widely distributed today.

'Elegans Compacta'. A mutation of *P. glauca* 'Conica', conical like 'Conica', perhaps more distinctly conical, twigs yellow-brown, as are the buds; needles bright green, 8–10 mm long. DB 1969: 272 (H). Developed in the State Conifer Nursery, Jehusice, Czechoslovakia about 1950.

'Gnom'. Mutation of *P. glauca* 'Conica', strictly conical, annual growth 3–5 cm; needles distinctly gray-green, 8–10 mm long. DM 1962 (January cover) and DB 1969: 273 (H). Developed in the State Conifer Nursery, Jehusice, Czechoslovakia before 1960.

'Laurin' (Arnold). Mutation of *P. glauca* 'Conica', dwarf, exceptionally slow growing, annual growth only 15–25 mm, dark green. DB 1970: 71–73 (H). Developed in 1952 by R. Arnold, Holstein, W. Germany; introduced in 1970.

'Hendersonii'. Very similar to 'Coerulea', but young shoots horizontal, older ones pendulous; needles silver-blue (= *P. alba* var *coerulea hendersonii* Dall. & Jacks.). Before 1923. (R)

'Nana'. Dwarf form, globose habit, main shoot upright, to 2 m high and as wide on an old plant, branches irregularly arranged, densely crowded twigs, shoots gray, glabrous, very flexible, annual growth 2.5–4.5 cm, buds brown, terminal 4–5 mm long, the others 1–4 mm long, bud scales paper thin, loosely appressed; needles very light gray-green, 5–7 mm long, radial on the upright shoots, semi-radial on the lateral shoots, directed forward on the branch tips, densely arranged and stiff to the touch, with 3–4 stomatal lines above, 2–3 of which do not reach the apex. WM 317 (H); CCE 277 (= *P. glauca* f. *nana* [Jacques] Rehd.). Known in cultivation since 1828, but not as well distributed as *P. glauca* 'Echiniformis'.

'Parva'. Dwarf form, branches dense and spreading horizontally, lying on the ground, developing a "flat crown", twigs short, light brown, glabrous, somewhat nodding; needles densely arranged, radial, bluish-green. Gw 38: 206 (H) (= *P. glauca* f. *parva* [Vict.] Fern. & Weatherby; *P. glauca* var. *procumbens* F. Meyer). (VR)

'Pendula'. Weeping form, branches very pendulous, bark red, very thick, densely branched; blue-green needles densely arranged (= *P. glauca* var. *pendula* [Carr.] Hornib.). Discovered before 1867 by A. Carrière in Trianon Park, Versailles, France.

'Pinsapoides'. Growth normal, ascending, twigs short, somewhat contorted, buds thick, light brown; needles radially arranged, thick, tough, 6–12 mm long, acute, blue-gray (= *P. glauca pinsapoides* den Ouden). Developed before 1897 by V. D. Elst in Dedemsvaart, Holland (EX?)

var. **porsildii** Raup. Form with glossy bark and resin blisters, broad crowned. NW. Canada to Alaska. Discovered in 1947.

P. glehnii (Fr. Schmidt) Mast. Sachalin Spruce. Tall tree, to 30 m or taller in its habitat, narrowly conical crown, bark chocolate-brown (thereby differing from all the other *Picea* species), exfoliating in thin scales, branches thin, short, shoots red, densely bristly pubescent, but usually only in the furrows, buds oval-conical, resinous, brown, terminal buds with awl-shaped basal scales, these protruding past the bud apex, tightly appressed, 8–15 mm long, bright green above with only 1 stomatal line, dull green beneath with 3 (2–5) stomatal lines, obtuse, but usually acute on young plants, 4 sided in cross section, as high as wide; cones cylindrical-oblong, 4–8 cm long, glossy brown when ripe, scales round and woody, entire to slightly eroded, seeds with a 1 cm long wing. TC 22; CC 75 (H); GGy 425; BM 9020; CCE 279, 281: KIF 1: 22. Sachalin; Japan (Hokkaido). Very hardy; in its habitat often growing in cold, marshy soil. New growth appears late. Easily recognizable by the red, pubescent young shoots. Fig. 124, 126 and 127. z6

P. hirtella Rehd. & Wils. Tree, to 16 m, stem 0.3–0.6 m in diameter, branches long and spreading horizontally, twigs thin, light yellow, densely pubescent when young, bud scales densely appressed; needles outspread, nearly straight or somewhat bowed at the base, 10–20 mm long, 1–2 mm wide, 4 sided in cross section, with 4–5 indistinct stomatal lines on either side; cones oval-oblong or more cylindrical, 6–8 cm long, glossy yellow-brown when ripe, scales leathery, broadly ovate to rhombic, apex obtuse to round, 10–20 mm long and 10–15 mm wide, base broadly cuneate, limb somewhat undulate, finely dentate, bract scales linear, 3–4 mm long. GGy 430; CCE 284. W. China; W. Szechwan Province, in the mountains at 3500–4000 m. Similar to *P. likiangensis*, but the twigs densely pubescent, needles more compressed, longer and prickly, leaf cushions less conspicuous, cones totally different. Fig. 125 and 127. z6

P. × hurstii De Hurst (*P. engelmannii* × *P. pungens*). Tree, conical crown, branches rather upright, young shoots thin, white, glabrous, buds small, light brown, leaf cushions nearly totally absent; needles densely arranged, 10–12 mm long, thin, finely acuminate, prickly to the touch, light green; cones similar to those of *P. pungens*. CCE 280, 281. Introduced to the trade in the USA in 1938.

P. jezoensis (S. & Z.) Carr. Yedo Spruce. Tree, 50–60 m in its habitat, habit similar to *P. abies*, conical crown, bark gray, exfoliating in round scales, but deeply furrowed on older trees, branches eventually more pendulous, but with ascending tips, young shoots light yellowish-greenish, glabrous and glossy, also light colored in the second year, leaf cushions without a lateral bulge, buds broadly conical, scales ovate, glossy, resinous, yellow-brown; needles rather straight, 10–20 mm long, long acuminate, slightly keeled on both sides, glossy dark green above, with 2 wide stomatal bands beneath; cones cylindrical-oblong, 4–7.5 cm long, straight, carmine when young, leathery brown when ripe, scales narrowly oblong, margin dentate, bract scales tiny, seed scales 2–3 times longer than the seed. OCC 263 (C); SN 238, 241; DJ 60 (Br); GGy 431; BM 9020; CCE 282; KIF 1: 24 (= *P. ajanensis* Fisch.; *P. kamtschatkensis* Lacassagne). Sachalin, N. Korea, Kurilen, Japan (only Hokkaido). 1878. Plate 83; Fig. 125, 126 and 128. z5

var. **hondoensis** (Mayr) Rehd. Hondo Spruce. Differing from the type in its lower ultimate height, 30 m, darker older branches, young shoots more red-brown, buds violet and very resinous, leaf cushions more swollen on the sides; needles deep green above, nearly white beneath (!), more appressed to the branch, shorter, with shorter tips. BM 6743; GGy 431; CCE 280, 281; KIF 1: 24 (= *P. hondoensis* Mayr). Japan; only the central mountains of Hondo. New growth appears later than on the species, therefore more frost tolerant. Prof. Kruse, Tokyo (personal correspondence) suggests that it is possible that the true *hondoensis* does not exist in Europe, since it is never correctly described, or that it has degenerated so much as to have lost many of its original characteristics.

'Aurea'. Young needles golden-yellow, in summer, then more brownish, eventually green, apparently not consistent since older plants lose their yellow color (= *P. ajanensis* var. *aurea* P. Smith). Developed before 1891 by P. Smith, near Hamburg, W. Germany.

P. koyamai Shiras. Tree, 18–20 m in its habitat, trunk to 50 cm in diameter, narrowly conical crown, bark gray-brown, lightly furrowed, exfoliating in paper thin, oblong pieces, branches dense and spreading horizontally, tips ascending, young shoots red-brown, usually slightly pruinose, terminal shoot nearly glabrous, lateral shoots glandular pubescent, especially in the furrows, buds conical, brown, resinous, scales acuminate, basal scales long acuminate; needles straight or bowed, very densely arranged, directed forward and upward, 7–12 mm long, 1–1.5 mm thick, obtuse or acute, 4 sided, somewhat wider than high in cross section, with 2–4 indistinct stomatal lines above, 5–8 distinct stomatal lines beneath; cones elliptic-ovate, 4–10 cm long, light green when young, glossy brown when ripe, scales thin, obovate, 15 mm wide, 18 mm long, round above and very fine dentate. SN 218 (H); OCC 265 (C); CBI 63; GGy 425; CCE 283, 284; KIF 2: 2. Japan; Central Honshu; the rarest of all the Japanese spruces, only about 100 trees on Mt. Yatsuga-take. 1914. Hardy but rare and apparently short lived. Plate 94; Fig. 124. z6

P. likiangensis (Franch.) Pritz. Tree, to 40 m in its habitat, trunk with gray, deeply fissured bark, branches spreading horizontally to slightly ascending, young shoots gray-yellow to more brownish or reddish, twisted leaf cushions, buds ovate to conical, 4–6 mm long, resinous, scales small, short acuminate; needles directed forward on the upper side of the branch, loosely appressed, parted beneath, somewhat compressed, acuminate, dark green, keeled on both sides, with 1–2, occasionally 3–4 intermittent stomatal lines beneath; cones oblong-ovate, seed scales soft, leathery, ovate-cordate, split at the apex or rounded, margin serrate or undulate, horizontal on ripe cones, seeds about 10 mm long with the wing. W. China; N. Yunnan and W. Szechwan, in the mountains at 3000–4000 m. Cultivated since about 1925. Hardy. Plate 94: Fig. 125. z6

var. **balfouriana** (Rehd. & Wils.) Hillier ex Slavin. Differing in the shorter branches, producing a narrower crown, young shoots yellowish, densely shaggy pubescent when young; needles 8–15 mm long, 1.5 mm wide, stomatal lines less distinct; cones 5–9 cm long, purple-violet before ripening, seed scales paper thin, rhombic-ovate and stretched upward, margin undulate. OCC 266 (Br); GGy 430; TC 18; CCE 285, 286 (= *P. balfouriana* Rehd.; *P. sikangensis* Cheng; *P. yunnanensis* [Forrest] Vilm.). W. China; W. Szechwan, 3000–4000 m. Introduced by E. H. Wilson, 1910. Fig. 125.

var. **likiangensis.** The type of the species, branches long and relatively slender, tips ascending, annual shoots gray-yellow, only slightly pubescent when young; needles 10–18 mm long, 1 mm wide, distinctly keeled; cones 5–8 cm long, brownish, seed scales leathery and soft, undulate on the margin and finely dentate, horizontal and gaping open when ripe. OCC 266 (Br); DJ 71 (Br); GGy 430; CBI 64; NF 6: 14. W. China; W. Szechwan, 3300–4000 m. Introduced in 1908 by E. H. Wilson.

var. **purpurea** (Mast.) Dall. & Jacks. Purple Spruce. Branches thick, spreading widely and horizontally, young shoots yellowish-gray, very densely pubescent when young, buds conical, acute, dark brown, resinous; leaves 8–12 mm long, 1 mm wide, keeled, obtuse, very compressed, gray-green, with 1–2 slightly protruding stomatal lines above, 2–3 beneath; cones small, only 4–6 cm long, purple-violet before ripening, scales abruptly constricted past the middle and acute or more rhombic. SN 237 (H); OCC 267 (C); DJ 72 (Br); GGy 433; CBI 65; CCE 286 (= *P. purpurea* Mast.). W. China; W. Szechwan, Kansu, in the mountains at 3000–4000 m. Introduced in 1910 by E. H. Wilson. Plate 94; Fig. 125.

P. × lutzii Little. (*P. glauca × P. sitchensis*). Tree, to 20 m, trunk to 0.3 m in diameter, young shoots yellowish, glabrous, needles and cones intermediate between the parents; needles spirally arranged, 10–16 mm long, linear, about 1.5 mm wide and nearly as thick, acute, slightly 4 sided or somewhat keeled on both sides, with 2–4 stomatal lines above, 5–8 beneath; cones oblong-cylindrical, 3–6 cm long, 2.5–3 cm wide, scales round, 12–14 mm long, 10–11 mm wide, yellowish-brown, limb dentate, bract scales ovate, 4–5 mm long, 2–3 mm wide, obtuse, dentate. S. Alaska, in the overlapping range of the parents; discovered in 1950 by H. Lutz, Yale University. z5?

P. mariana (Mill.) B.S.P. Black Spruce. Tree, 6–20 m, rarely to 30 m, narrowly conical crown, frequently irregular, bark red-brown, scaly, branches thin, often pendulous, young shoots red-brown, densely glandular pubescent, leaf cushions flat, not swollen, buds thick, about 5 mm long, acute or obtuse, bright red, not resinous, basal scales subulate, protruding past the bud tip; needles very densely arranged, 7–12 (–18) mm long, dull green to blue-green, stiff, 4 sided, straight or slightly curved, aromatic when crushed (!), not parted beneath the branch, with 1–2 stomatal lines above, 3–4 beneath,

whitish; cones ovate to spindle-shaped, red-blue when closed, later more gray-brown, 2–3 cm long, to 1.5 cm thick, persisting for several years on the tree, seed scales stiff, woody, circular apex, margin finely dentate, bract scales much shorter, seeds chocolate-brown, with wings 10 mm long. OCC 268 (C); DJ 73 (Br and C); GGy 426; GTP 72; SPa 32; CCE 287 (= *P. nigra* Ait.; *P. brevifolia* Peck). N. America; Labrador to Alaska, south to Wisconsin and Michigan. Hardy and very attractive as a young tree, but less decorative with age; easily cultivated, thrives in cold, swampy areas, develops large forests in its habitat. "Spruce beer" is made in Newfoundland by boiling the branches in water. Fig. 124, 126 and 131. z3

'**Argenteovariegata**'. Growth normal; needles white variegated (= *P. nigra* f. *argenteovariegata* Hesse ex Beissn.). Introduced to the trade in 1891 by Hesse. (EX)

'**Aurea**'. More graceful habit than the species; needles with a golden glow (= *P. mariana* var. *aurea* [Beissn.] Fitsch.). Developed before 1891 by Hesse.

'**Beissneri**'. Dwarf form, but growing to 5 m high, similar to 'Doumetii' in habit, but wider at the base; needles often steel-blue. BFN 62 (H); DB 1969: 260 (H); SN 216 (= *P. mariana* var. *beissneri* Rehd.; in BFN 249 incorrectly quoted as "Beissneriana"). Presumably distributed from Cassel, W. Germany before 1915.

'**Beissneri Compacta**'. Dwarf form, to 2 m high and at least as wide or wider, without a central leader; needles like 'Beissneri' in form and color. WDw 206–207 (H and Br); WM 315 (H); CCE 281 (= *P. mariana beissneri compacta* Hesse). Developed by Hesse, W. Germany; introduced in 1954.

'**Doumetii**'. Dwarf form, but 5–6 m high as old plants, habit rather regular broadly conical, but globose as young plants, branches outspread, orange-yellow and somewhat glossy, twigs very densely arranged, thin, orange-yellow, buds conical, small, dull brown; needles dense and radially arranged, thin, silvery gray-green. OCC 268 (C); KN 260 (H); TC 24; CCE 288, 289 (= *P. mariana* var. *doumetii* [Carr.] Sudw.). Originated around 1850 in the park of Chateau de Balène near Moulins, France.

'**Empetroides**'. Dwarf form, totally procumbent, thinly branched, finely textured, like an *Empetrum* in appearance; needles 3–6 mm long (= *P. mariana empetroides* Rousseau). Discovered about 1930 on Mt. Sterling, Quebec, Canada.

'**Ericoides**'. Dwarf form, conical habit or more globose, very slow growing, terminal shoot glabrous; needles nearly *Erica*-like, very thin, finely acuminate, deep blue-green. WM 316 (H) (= *P. mariana* f. *ericoides* Rehd.). Originated in England before 1914. (VR)

'**Fastigiata**'. Dwarf columnar form, branches slender, ascending; needles thinner than those of the type, acute, only 6–10 mm long (= *P. mariana* var. *fastigiata* [Carr.] Rehd.). Discovered before 1855 by Briot in Trianon Park, Versailles, France.

'**Nana**'. Dwarf form, broad globose habit, seldom over 50 cm high, but much wider, somewhat open, but very regularly branched, twigs brown, very pubescent, thin and very flexible, annual growth 2 to 3 cm, inconspicuous leaf cushions, buds brown, globose, terminal 2 mm long, other buds only 1 mm long, not resinous; needles very densely crowded, more or less radially arranged, 5–7 mm long, dull blue-green, round in cross section, with 2–4 very conspicuous stomatal lines on either side, running to the apex, finely acuminate. DB 1969: 243 (H); WDw Pl. 15C (Br), 209 (H); CCE 288, 289; WM 25C (Br), 317

(H) (= *P. mariana* var. *nana* [Beissn.] Rehd.). Cultivated since 1884, but origin unknown. Very attractive form! Plate 96.

'Pendula'. Weeping form, stem upright, branches pendulous along the stem, otherwise like the type (= *P. mariana* var. *pendula* [Schwerin] Fitsch.). Selected before 1903 by Ganghofer in the Diedorf Forestry Garden near Augsburg, W. Germany; 5 m high at the time. (EX?)

"Pumila" is an uncertain form, apparently identical to 'Nana', in any case, hardly distinguishable (= *P. mariana* var. *pumila* Hornib.). Known by this name since 1875.

'Semiprostrata'. Dwarf form with a short stem, branches short and strong, distinctly different from 'Empetroides' (= *P. mariana semiprostrata* Blake). Discovered before 1955 on the top of Mt. Sterling in Quebec, Canada.

P. × mariorika Boom (*P. mariana × P. omorika*). The type of this cross is intermediate between the parents, differing from *P. omorika* in the broadly conical habit, short pubescent twigs with scattered glands; needles narrower, more blue-green, with sharp, prickly tips, with 4–6 stomatal lines beneath, with only 1 or no stomatal line above; cones 3.5–5 cm long, purple when young (brown when young and 4–6 cm long on *P. omorika*). Plate 95.

> Included in this category by Boom were all the broad growing plants with the various transition form characteristics (as regards habit); i.e. those not displaying the typical narrow, nearly columnar growth habit of *P. omorika*. According to Boom, this hybrid was first developed in and distributed from the G. D. Boehlje Nursery of Westerstede, W. Germany about 1925. This opinion must, however, be contested since many, perhaps most, of the wide growing plants are not hybrids at all, but simply wide growing *omorika* types which occur naturally in Yugoslavia, particularly at lower altitudes. They may also have simply originated from degenerate germ plasm of plants in cultivation. See also *P. omorika*.

'Kobold' (Jeddeloh). (*P. mariana* 'Doumetii' × *P. omorika*). Globose habit, dense, about 1 m high and wide in 20 years, very densely branched, annual growth about 5 cm, shoots rather thick and stiff, red-brown, furrowed, short scattered pubescent, buds obtuse-ovate, 2–3 mm long, terminal bud usually solitary, often totally enclosed by the needles, basal scales often exserted past the tip; needles radially arranged, directed strictly forward, 8–12 mm long, about 0.5 mm wide, straight to slightly curved, deep green beneath, with 3–4 stomatal lines above. WM 319 (H). Selected by Jeddeloh in 1951.

'Machala' (Machala). Dwarf, spreading to flat-globose, about 1 m wide (or more) and 30–50 cm high, twigs partly horizontal, to more vertical in the middle, annual growth about 10 cm, rather stiff, buds medium brown, ovate, acute; needles usually 10–15 mm long, rather stiff and very acute, about 0.8 mm wide, dark green, but often effectively silver-white to gray-blue with the 2 single stomatal rows above and 2 stomatal bands beneath. First distributed in 1963 from Zehusize, Czechoslovakia as *P. omorika* 'Compacta'. Selected from *P. omorika*, but because of the acute needles, perhaps a hybrid with *P. sitchensis* (instead of *P. glauca?*).

P. maximowiczii Regel ex Mast. Medium tall tree, scarcely over 25 m, very dense crown, trunk with gray-brown, rough, fissured bark, branches horizontal, thin, ascending tips, young shoots thick and glabrous, brown in the first year, gray-white in the 2nd year, buds oval, 4 mm long, red-brown, very resinous, with tightly appressed scales; needles loosely arranged, very stiff,

sharp-prickly, 7–15 mm long, rather straight, stout, usually radial above, usually somewhat parted beneath, spreading nearly vertically, 4 sided, with 3–4 stomatal lines on all sides; cones cylindrical, 3–6 cm long, green-yellow when young, glossy brown when ripe, limb of the seed scales rounded, entire, bract scales 4 mm long, seeds 3 mm long. OCC 270 (C and Br); GGy 425; SN 219 (H); CCE 291; KIF 2: 14 (= *P. tschonoskii* Mayr). Japan; in only 2 locations: on Mt. Yatsuga-take, at 1200–1600 m; and on Mt. Fuji. 1861. Plate 95: Fig. 124. (VR) z7

P. mexicana Martinez. Conical tree, 20–25 m in its habitat, bark thin and scaly, young shoots light yellowish-brown, with numerous tiny hairs; needles 4 sided, directed forward, 20–35 mm long, 1 mm wide, bowed, sharply acuminate, without resin ducts; cones oval-oblong, yellowish, 5–7 cm long, seed scales nearly rhombic, thin, dentate on the apical margin, bract scales acute-elliptic, only half as long as the seed scales, seeds 3 mm long. Mexico, N. Leon, in the mountains at 3000 m. Growing among *P. engelmannii* and *P. pungens*. z7

P. meyeri Rehd. & Wils. Medium tall tree, similar to *P. gemmata*, young shoots yellow-brown or cinnamon-brown, very pubescent, but the density of the pubescence quite variable from year to year on similar shoots, buds conical, light brown, resinous, but without awl-shaped basal scales; needles 4 sided in cross section, slightly compressed, 8–18 mm long, stout, obtuse, straight or bowed, with 5–8 stomatal lines on either side; cones cylindrical-oblong, 6–7 cm long, glossy brown, seed scales stiff, stout, obovate, apical margin round. GGy 428, CCE 291, 292. China; Shansi, Kansu, in the mountains at 3000 m. 1905. (VR) z6

P. montana Schur. The East Carpathian Spruce, which should be considered an independent species in the opinion of Kondratjuk (Moscow 1958).

P. montigena Mast. Tree to 30 m, branches spreading horizontally, rather long, tips bowed upward, young shoots pubescent, yellowish or brownish, buds ovate, acute, resinous, basal scales of the terminal bud long pointed and keeled; needles 4 sided in cross section, but wider than high, 8–15 mm long, obtuse or acute, with 2 distinctly white stomatal bands beneath, each with 5 lines, glossy green above, with 2–3 indistinct stomatal bands; cones oblong-cylindrical, 7–10 cm long, glossy cinnamon-brown, scales rhombic-ovate, thin, limb somewhat eroded, but not undulate. GGy 430; CCE 293, 294. China; NW. Szechwan Province. 1908. Hardy. Fig. 125 and 126. (R) z5

P. morrisonicola Hayata. Taiwan Spruce. Tree, reaching 40 m in its habitat, similar to *P. glehnii*, but the young shoots are glabrous, buds conical-ovate, only 3 mm long, not so resinous, scales brown and appressed; needles 8–18 mm long, thin, 4 sided in cross section, long and sharply acuminate, prickly, with 2–4 stomatal lines on all sides; cones oblong-cylindrical, 4–6 cm long, scales ovate to circular, apical limb round to truncate, entire. OCC 271 (H), 272 (C); GGy 425; LT 26; LWT 8; CCE 294, 295 (= *P. glehnii* var. *morrisonicola* Hayata). Mt. Morrison, Taiwan. Discovered in 1900. Plate 95; Fig. 124. (VR) z7

Fig. 129. Cones of **Picea**.
A. *P. smithiana*; B. *P. obovata*; C. *P. spinulosa*; D. *P. polita*; E. *P. schrenkiana*; F. *P. wilsonii*

P. × moseri Mast. (*P. jezoensis × P. mariana*). Tree, twigs glabrous, greenish or olive-green, needles densely crowded, in many rows, lateral needles sharp angular, the upper and middle ones convex, all about equal in length, about 16 mm, sharply pointed, thin, linear, acute, blue-green above, with silvery stomatal bands beneath. Developed by Moser of Versailles, France about 1900 from *P. jezoensis × P. mariana* 'Doumetii'.

P. neoveitchii Mast. Small tree, 8–15 m, stem with rough, gray bark, branches usually rather short and directed upward, twigs light brown, glabrous when young, buds conical, 5 mm long, dark brown, scales tightly appressed, the apical ones broad rounded; needles densely arranged, about 15 mm long, prickly acuminate, 4 sided, dark green, with stomata on every side; cones oblong-cylindrical, tapering to both ends, 12 cm long, 4 cm wide, seed scales tightly appressed, ovate to round, leathery, yellow-brown, margin undulate, entire, seeds with the wing 2.5 cm long. GGy 428. W. China; Hupeh Province. Fig. 124, 128. z7

P. × notha Rehd. (*P. glehnii × P. jezoensis*). Tree, similar to *P. jezoensis* in appearance, young shoots brown, scattered pubescent, buds obtuse oval-conical, black-brown, somewhat resinous, with a few acute scales, these half as long as the buds; needles about 15 mm long on older twigs, 1.2 mm wide, shorter on young shoots, apex abruptly reduced to an obtuse tip, bowed, dense and appressed on the upper side of the branch, more parted beneath, glossy light green above and obtusely keeled, with 1–2 indistinct stomatal lines, 2 white stomatal bands beneath with 5–7 lines; cones oblong-cylindrical, 4.5–5.5 cm long, scales more loosely appressed, flexible, rhombic-ovate, 1 cm long, 7–8 mm wide, margin undulate and incised in the middle. Grown in the Arnold Arboretum in 1894 from Japanese seed. z6

P. obovata Ledeb. Siberian Spruce. Tall tree, similar to *P. abies*, but with slightly pendulous branches, twigs thinner, yellow-green, only slightly glossy, densely glandular pubescent, leaf cushions less prominent, buds conical, somewhat resinous, the basal scales somewhat cuspidate and shorter; needles short, 10–18 mm long, dull green, more appressed to the upper branch surface and directed forward, somewhat parted beneath and some spreading downward, with 2–3 faint stomatal lines on either side; cones cylindrical-ovate, 6–8 cm long, purple when young, scales broad rounded at the apex, entire or somewhat emarginate. GGy 426; KN 263 (Br and C); CCE 295, 296 (= *P. abies* f. *obovata* [Ledeb.] Lindm.). N. Europe to Siberia and Kamchatka. 1852. Very winter hardy. Fig. 124 and 129. z2

var. **coerulea** Tigerstedt. Young shoots glabrous; needles radially arranged, blue-green. Altai Mts.

var. **fennica** (Regel) Henry. Finnish Spruce. Needles deep green; cones with rounded seed scales, always finely toothed on the margin (= *P. abies* var. *fennica* Regel). N. Sweden, N. Finland. Not totally certain, perhaps belonging to *P. abies*.

> Note: In the Flora Europaea, *P. obovata* is treated as a subspecies of *Picea abies*. The questionable status of *P. obovata* var. *fennica* is related to this classification problem.

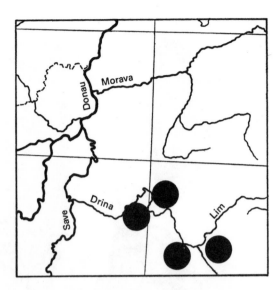

Fig. 130. Native stands of *Picea omorika* in Yugoslavia (from Fukarek)

P. omorika (Pancic) Purkyne. Serbian Spruce. Tree, to 30 m in its habitat, narrowly conical crown, usually nearly columnar, branches rather short, horizontal and ascending at the tips, young shoots light brown, densely glandular pubescent, buds globose to acutely ovate, dark brown, not resinous, basal scales long, subulate; needles compressed, 8–18 mm long, both sides keeled, obtuse with a small apical tip, 2 broad white stomatal bands beneath, each with 5–6 lines, glossy green above and without stomatal lines; cones ovate-oblong, 3–6 cm long, about 1 cm thick, violet-purple at first, then glossy cinnamon-brown, numerous even on young plants, scales with a 2 mm wide, red, regularly dentate limb, very convex, seeds black-brown, 2.5–3 mm long, wings 8 mm long. BM 9163; GGy 432; KN 262, 265; CCE 296–299. Yugoslavia; Bosnia and Serbia, on the steep limestone banks of the middle Drina River. Widely planted and admired throughout the world. Plate 96; Fig. 125, 126, 131. z5

> Discovered in 1877 by Prof. Pancic near Zaovina, although described by him from twigs and cones in 1875. The natural range today includes some locations in the middle and upper Drina River valley near Visegrad, in the Viogora Mts. above the mouth of the Lim River and in the Zelengora Mts. Earlier reports of the plant's occurrence in Montenegro, Bosnia and Herzegowina are incorrect and based on the fact that the word "omorika" in the Serbian language simply means "spruce" and so was used for both *P. omorika* and *P. abies*.

> The plants in cultivation today no longer display the typical "spire-shape". They are, rather, narrow or widely conical as is more commonly found in the lower altitudes of the native range. The wide crowned type predominates in the plains where the seed is more easily obtained and therefore less expensive than that taken from the "spire-shaped" plants of the high mountains.

'Expansa'. Dwarf form, without a trunk, spreading along the ground, but a strong grower, branch tips slightly ascending, otherwise like the species. OCC 275 (H); CCE 295 (= *P. omorika expansa* den Ouden). Originated as a seedling in the Boehlje

Nursery in Westerstede, Holland in 1930. The original plant is still alive in the Van Hoey Smith Park in Rotterdam, and is about 4 m wide by 80 cm high.

'Frohnleiten'. Dwarf form, irregular and shrubby, loose, 40 cm high at 10 years old; needles much shorter than those of the species. DB 21: 166 (H). Originated in the Frohnleiten Alpengarten, Steiermark, W. Germany around 1958.

'Gnom' (Jeddeloh). Dwarf form, broadly conical, to about 1.5 m high in 20 years, very densely branched, annual growth about 2–3 cm on older plants, twigs thin, flexible, gray-yellow, with scattered short pubescence, inconspicuous leaf cushions, terminal buds 3–4 mm long, usually surrounded by 1–3 somewhat smaller side buds, intermixed with solitary needles, scales narrowly subulate, long, red-brown, loosely appressed, not resinous; needles very densely arranged, more or less radial, directed forward, 10–15 mm long, somewhat curved, acute, but not sharp, with 4–5 white stomatal lines above, glossy green beneath, 4 sided in cross section. CCE 297. Selected by Jeddeloh in 1951. Supposedly very resistant to red spider mite damage.

'Minima'. Quite dwarf, very short branched, otherwise like *P. omorika* 'Nana', on which it was found as a witches'-broom by Jeddeloh.

'Nana' (Goudkade). Mutation, dwarf form, 3 m high as an old plant (perhaps also higher), growth broadly conical, very dense, branches irregular in length, therefore lacking a regular habit, twigs thick, but not stiff, light brown, annual growth 2–4 cm, buds obtusely ovate, brown, terminal 3–4 mm long, the others 1 mm shorter, not resinous; needles more or less radial to semi-radially arranged, 7–8 mm long, 1.5 mm wide, very densely crowded and stiff, obtuse, yellow-green above and without stomata, with 2 broad, white stomatal bands beneath, each with 5–7 stomatal lines. KN 271 (H); CCE 299; WM 25C (Br), 321 (H). Developed about 1930 by Goudkade, Boskoop, Holland. Very popular form in cultivation today.

'Pendula'. Now and then, forms of varying appearance are found under this name; either as erect stems with pendulous branches or as a drooping stem. CCE 297. Best considered as a collective name.

'Pimoko'. Dwarf form, dense, irregular habit, 30 cm high and 40 cm wide in 10 years, annual growth to 7 cm, twigs conspicuously covered with numerous dark red-brown buds, terminal buds nearly totally hidden by needles; needles emerald-green with white stomatal bands, 1.2 cm long. Very beautiful, new dwarf form. Originated as a witches'-broom in the W. Wuestemeyer Nursery in W. Germany. 1980.

P. orientalis (L.) Link. Oriental Spruce. Tree, to 50 m or more in its habitat, stem to 1.2 m in diameter, conical crown, densely branched to the ground, bark thin, scaly, branches irregular, in whorls, ascending or horizontal, young shoots light brown to light yellow, thin, fine bristly pubescent, spreading fan-like in an even plane, very conspicuous leaf cushions, buds oval, red-brown, not resinous, 3 mm long; needles dark green, very glossy, 6–8 mm long, quite obtuse, 4 sided in cross section, densely arranged and rather stiff, with 1–4 stomatal lines on all sides, but as wide bands only beneath; female flowers violet-purple; cones cylindrical-ovate, about 2 cm in diameter, violet before ripening, brown when ripe, scales obovate, 15 mm wide, semicircular on the apex and entire, seeds black, 5 mm long, 12 mm long with the wing. SN 16 (H); BFN 241 (H); DJ 78; GGy 432; CCE 299, 300. Caucasus and northern Asia Minor, in the mountains. Very beautiful and popular ornamental. Fig. 124, 126 and 127. z5

'Atrovirens'. Needles especially deep dark green (= *P. orientalis* f. *atrovirens* Beissn.) Developed by den Ouden, Boskoop, Holland before 1911.

'Aurea.' Normal habit, young shoots cream-yellow in spring, later greening, occasionally retaining a yellowish glow. SH 121 (H) (= *P. orientalis aurea* Otto; *P. orientalis aureospicata* Beissn.). Numerous origins, first by P. Smith near Hamburg, W. Germany before 1873. Plate 98.

'Aurea Compacta'. (Jeddeloh). Very compact, annual growth 4–7 cm; needles, at least on the branch upper side, lighter or darker yellow for the entire year, always green beneath. (R)

'Compacta'. Dwarf form, broad conical habit, as high as wide, branches nearly horizontally arranged and open. DB 1969: 270 (H) (as "*P. orientalis* 'Echiniformis' "). Introduced by Hillier, 1969.

'Early Gold'. Needles yellow on new growth, later greening. Introduced by Konijn, Reeuwijk, Holland. Seldom found in cultivation.

'Gracilis'. Dwarf form, oval habit, to 6 m high, branches very densely arranged, twigs variable in length, light brown, pubescent, glossy, annual growth 3–7 cm, thin and very flexible; needles bright green, very glossy, all radially arranged and outspread, 5–7 mm long, very densely arranged, obtuse, with 1–4 intermittent stomatal lines on each side. OCC 277 (H); WDw 210 (H); WM 25E (Br), 322 (H); CCE 302. Developed before 1903 in the Van Geert Nursery, cultivated in the Kalmthout Arboretum near Antwerp, Belgium.

'Nana'. Dwarf form, globose to ovate, rarely over 1 m high, young shoots light brown to more yellowish, glabrous, rather thin and flexible, annual growth only 1.5–2.5 cm, leaf cushions very conspicuous, buds conical, only 1.5 mm long, light brown; needles all radial, only 3–5 mm long, shortest at the branch tips, less than 1 mm thick, nearly circular in cross section, terminating in an abruptly obtuse tip. WDw Pl. 15B (Br); CCE 297, 299; WM 323 (H). Originated in France before 1891. (VR)

'Nutans'. Weeping form, growth irregular and very divaricate, branches often widely spreading and nodding, of variable length; needles very dark green (= *P. orientalis nutans* Niemetz). Developed before 1905 by Niemetz in Timisoara, Romania (then Hungary); introduced by Hesse. (R)

'Pendula'. Compact, slow growing form with nodding twigs. (Hillier)

P. polita (S. & Z.) Carr. Tiger-tail Spruce. Tree, 20–25 (40) m in its habitat, stem to 1 m in diameter, bark gray, rough, exfoliating in irregular pieces, branches densely arranged, moderately long, nearly horizontal or ascending, young shoots stout, glabrous, light brown, rather stiff, buds acutely conical, 6–10 mm long, dark brown (much darker than the shoots), scarcely resinous, scales tightly appressed; needles radially arranged, very stiff, dagger-like tips, very sharp, prickly, glossy bright green, 15–25 mm long, laterally compressed, taller than wide, with 5–6 stomatal lines on either side; cones oblong-ovate, 7–10 cm long, sessile, 3–4 cm wide, brown, scales wide, rounded, limb irregular and finely dentate on the apex, leathery, seeds dark brown, 3–4 mm long. DJ 79; CCE 300, 303, 304; KIF 1: 26 (= *P. torano* Koehne). Japan, main island, on lava soil. The common name stems from the "tail-like" pendulous branches of very old trees in Japan. Fig. 124, 126 and 129. z6

P. pungens Engelm. Colorado Spruce. Tall tree, 30–40 m or more, trunk with gray-brown, thick, deeply furrowed bark, broadly conical crown, branches spreading in horizontal, sometimes rather widely spaced, plate-like whorls, young shoots light yellow-brown to orange, often also pruinose, stout, short, glabrous, buds obtuse conical, brownish-yellow, not resinous, scales loosely appressed, tips reflexed; needles radially arranged, stiff, 2–3 cm long, outspread, long acuminate and prickly, bluish-green, seldom totally green, with 4 to 5 stomatal bands on each side; cones oblong-cylindrical, 6–10 cm long, light brown, scales thin, flexible, longitudinally plaited, narrowing to the apex, rounded or truncate, undulate or toothed, seeds dark brown, 2 mm long, with 8 mm long wings. SN 54 (H); BCC Pl. 1 (H); GGy 431. Western USA; Colorado, Wyoming, Utah, Arizona, New Mexico in the mountains at 2000–3300 m, but usually not in large stands. 1862. One of the favorite ornamental conifers for its blue-white foliage forms ("blue spruce"), also grown for its tolerance to dry air. Plate 96; Fig. 125 and 128. z3

Outline of the Forms and Cultivars

● Needle color distinctly green, greenish or yellow; normal upright habit:

var. *pungens* (greenish, rarely green), 'Atroviridis' (deep green), 'Aurea' (yellow), 'Flavescens' (yellowish), 'Viridis' (green)

●● Needles lighter or darker bluish to blue-white ('Glauca' group);

* Normal upright habit, conical;

a) More or less "blue seedlings": f. glauca

b) Needles only 12 mm long: 'Microphylla'

c) Commonly grafted cultivars: 'Endtz', 'Erich Frahm', 'Hoopsii', 'Koster', 'Moerheim', 'Oldenburg', 'Spek', 'Thomsen', 'Vuyk'

d) Rarely grafted cultivars: 'Arcuata', 'Bakeri', 'Columnaris', 'Fürst (Prince) Bismarck', 'Hoto', 'Hunnewelliana', 'Lombarts', 'Mission Blue', 'Schovenhorst', 'Schwartz', 'Virgata'

** Dwarf habit;

a) flat-globose, broad: 'Glauca Globosa', 'Luusbarg', 'Pumila'

b) Broadly conical: 'Blue Trinket', 'Moll', 'Montgomery'

*** Irregular, flat, broad, low, also 2–3 m high and broad with age (often propagated from lateral shoots!): 'Compacta', 'Glauca Procumbens', 'Glauca Prostrata'

**** Weeping form: 'Glauca Pendula'

'**Arcuata**'. Normal upright habit, but much more open, branch whorls more widely spaced, branches curving upward at the tips; needles blue-green (= *P. pungens* f. *arcuata* Schwerin). Discovered in 1919 by Count Schwerin in W. Germany.

'**Argentea**' is only a collective name for forms with especially silver-white foliage and should not be used (= *P. pungens argentea* Rosenthal).

'**Atroviridis**'. Normal habit; needles deep green (= *P. pungens* f. *atroviridis* Schwer.). (EX?)

'**Aurea**' (Niemetz). Habit normal; needles attractively golden-yellow in the sun, but blue-white in the shade (= *P. pungens aurea* Niemetz). Developed in 1905 by Niemetz in Timisoara, Romania (then Hungary).

'**Bakeri**'. Tall, broadly conical; needle color somewhat darker blue than 'Moreheim', needles also longer. Selected as a seedling before 1930 in Massachusetts; distributed in 1933 by the Hiti Nurseries, R. E. Baker, of Pomfret, Connecticut, USA.

'**Blue Trinket**' (Konijn). Seedling, compact and broadly conical habit, looks almost like a compact form of 'Endtz'; needles blue-white. Selected before 1965 by L. Konijn & Co., Reeuwijk, Holland.

'**Columnaris**'. Normal upright habit, but more columnar due to the very short branches. Observed before 1909 by Schelle.

'**Compacta**'. Dwarf form, 3 m high and 4 m wide in 75 years, flat, spreading, branches horizontal; needles especially stiff and dark green, with 3–4 stomatal lines on either side (= *P. pungens compacta* Rehd.). Developed in 1863 in the Harvard Botanic Garden (not the Arnold Arboretum!), from seed collected by Dr. C. C. Parry on Pike's Peak, Colorado, USA. (VR)

'**Endtz**'. Dense conical habit, branches horizontal, with small, spur-like, erect shoots, 1-year shoots yellowish-brown, buds thick, obtuse, 10–12 mm long, tips of the scales reflexed, side buds standing ring-like around the terminal; needles blue, silvery in winter, 25–30 mm long, curving slightly sickle-shaped. KN 267 (Br); CCE 307–309 (= *P. pungens* var. *glauca endtzii*, Endtz). Introduced around 1925 by the L. J. Endtz Nursery, Boskoop, Holland.

'**Erich Frahm**' (J. Timm & Co.). Very regular conical habit; foliage an attractive blue. Selected in the J. Timm & Co. Nursery, Elmshorn, W. Germany. Introduced in 1950.

'**Flavescens**'. Normal habit; needles whitish-yellow, not really yellow, similar to *P. abies* 'Finedonensis' (= *P. pungens flavescens* Niemetz; ? *P. pungens lutea* Hess). Introduced in 1905 by Niemetz. Less attractive than 'Aurea'. Has bluish needles in the shade.

'**Fürst (Prince) Bismarck**'. Normal upright habit, conical, branches in flat, dense and regular tiers, especially on the basal portion of the plant, all branches on the apical half slightly ascending; young needles nearly white. MD 1922: 76 (H); DB 14: 49 (H). Developed by Weisse in Kamenz, E. Germany; introduced in 1887. The statement in den Ouden-Boom (p. 280), that this is a flat form without a central leader, is incorrect. (VR)

f. **glauca**. (Regel) Beissn. This name refers to those more or less bluish needled forms occurring naturally or from seed in cultivation. The selected and named clones comprise the '**Glauca**' Group.

'**Glauca Globosa**' Dwarf form, somewhat open and irregular at first, becoming flat-globose and very dense, to 1 m high and 1.5 m wide (possibly higher), annual growth 5–8 cm, twigs light yellow-brown, thin, buds acutely ovate, light brown; needles densely arranged, not completely radial, slightly sickle-shaped, white-blue, 10–12 mm long, 1 mm thick, with 3–4 stomatal lines on each side. WDw 213 (H); CCE 306; WM 326 (H) (= *P. pungens globosa* den Ouden 1949; *P. pungens glauca nana* Hesse 1961; *P. pungens* 'Glauca Globosa' Hillier 1964). Originated from seed in Anth. Kluis Nursery, Boskoop, Holland in 1937.

Introduced in 1955 by Le Feber & Co. Although the name given by den Ouden retains priority, that commonly used in the trade is given here. Plate 96.

'Glauca Pendula'. Growth curving or obliquely upward, lower branches angled downward, the upper branches usually horizontal at first, later pendulous; needles like those of the type, but silver-white, occasionally only blue-green, sickle-shaped. OCC 281 (= *P. pungens glauca pendula* Koster 1891; *P. pungens kosteriana* Henry 1912). Introduced in 1895 by Koster & Co., Boskoop, Holland. Occasionally confused with 'Koster' from the (invalid) name given by Henry (SN 55). The illustration in OCC 281 shows a plant about 4 m high, ascending nearly in an S-form, while the illustration in KN 273 (from the Arnold Arboretum) depicts a very irregularly growing large plant with a similarly crooked stem, but also with much stronger, ascending branches to the base. In any case, this form is quite variable; possibly composed of totally different clones.

'Glauca Procumbens'. Dwarf, shrubby, broadly prostrate, but very irregular, branches partly drooping, partly ascending; foliage like 'Koster'. CCE 301, 308. According to den Ouden a sport of 'Koster' discovered about 1910 in a nursery in Boskoop but propagated and introduced by H. den Ouden & Zoon, 1924. Widely distributed today. Broad growing plants without central leaders can be easily propagated from the lateral shoots of 'Koster' and the other upright growing plants.

'Glauca Prostrata'. Dwarf, completely procumbent, but as consistent as 'Glauca Procumbens'. OCC 281 (as *P. pungens* 'Glauca Procumbens'); WDw 211 (H), Pl. 15F (Br); WM 324, 325 (H). A very attractive plant stands in the Trompenburg Arboretum in Rotterdam, Holland at 2 m wide and 40 cm high.

'Hoopsii'. Normal habit, strongly upright, very dense, branches horizontal, buds densely surrounded by needles; needles very densely crowded and distinctly blue-white. SB 15: 142 (H); CCE 307; KN Pl. 6 (= *P. pungens* 'Hoopsii' Grootendorst 1958). Developed in the old Hoops Nursery, introduced by Grootendorst. This and 'Thomsen' are the best and most distinctively white-blue forms available today.

'Hoto'. Conical, rather dense, regularly branched, very fast growing, twigs light brown, terminal buds ovate, scales outspread, light brown, surrounded by a ring of somewhat twisted needles; needles 15–25 mm long, 1–1.3 mm wide, blue-gray. Origin unknown; distributed in 1972 by A. Hoogendoorn and Gebr. Van Tol, both of Boskoop, Holland. Very easily propagated. A consistent habit of growth, but not a very good blue.

'Hunnewelliana'. Dwarf form (comparable to the type of the species), but the original plant is about 8 m high and 5 m wide (in about 50 years), twigs thin, flexible, bud scales light brown, tips recurved, basal scales acuminate, keeled; needles rather thin and soft, 12–20 cm long, light sea-green (= *P. pungens* var. *hunnewelliana* Hornib. 1923). Found in a seedbed of *P. engelmannii* before 1923 in the Framingham Nursery, Massachusetts, USA. Welch was recently informed by Mr. Hunnewell that the plant, now taller, has not been propagated. It should probably no longer be considered a dwarf plant in the true sense of the word.

'Koster' (Blaauw & Co. 1901). The best known of the "blue spruce" forms, regular conical habit, branches spreading in whorls, young shoots orange-brown, buds conical, 1 cm long, 5 to 6 mm wide, wide at the base, scales tightly appressed, occasionally reflexed at the tips; needles slightly sickle-shape, curved upward from the underside of the twig, silver-blue, also in winter, 20–25 mm long. SN 45 (H); KN 269; CCE 307 (= *P. pungens glauca* 'Koster' Blaauw & Co.; *P. pungens* 'Koster' Boom 1959). A historical note, according to den Ouden-Boom: "This form was distributed shortly before 1885 by Arie Koster Mz. of Boskoop on a local basis and was developed, not as grafts of a selected individual, but rather from various good blue seedling plants. One of the buyers, J. H. Van Nes, of C. B. Van Nes & Zoon (now Blaauw & Co.) selected 10 plants, similar in form and color from Koster's inventory. These were first erroneously named *P. pungens glauca compacta* 'Koster' (1908), then changed in 1913 to *P. pungens glauca compacta*." This form is the one generally found in the trade today but by the correct name of *P. pungens* 'Koster' (1901).

'Lombarts'. Conical form, somewhat irregular, densely branched, twigs rather short, nodding, sparsely branched; needles blue-white, very densely arranged, 25–30 mm long. From P. Lombarts, Zundert, Holland.

'Luusbarg'. Very slow growing dwarf form, wider than high, about 1 m high and 2.5 m wide in 80 years, flat-globose and somewhat irregular, twigs layered in tiers; needles bluish, 15 to 20 mm long. CCE 304 (= 'Kleinood Luusbarg'). Original plant stands in the Muenchmayer Garden, Hamburg, W. Germany; planted in 1907.

'Microphylla'. Normal upright habit; needles only about 12 mm long, bluish-green (= *P. pungens microphylla* Schwerin). Developed by Count Schwerin in 1922.

'Mission Blue'. Seedling selected primarily for its rapid growth and broadly conical base (similar to 'Koster'); foliage blue-white. Introduced by the Mission Gardens, Techny, Illinois, USA.

'Moerheim'. Narrow, conical habit, dense, central leader often long, branches short, in whorls, young shoots yellowish-brown, terminal buds often 10–15 mm long, dull yellow-brown, side buds variable in size and somewhat spirally arranged under the terminal, scales distinctly reflexed at the apex; needles somewhat sickle-shaped, 25–30 mm long, blue-white pruinose, summer and winter. DB 15: 175, 19: 18 (H); CCE 308, 309 (= *P. pungens glauca* 'Moerheimii' Ruys 1912). Introduced to the trade by B. Ruys, the Moreheim Nursery, Dedemsvaart, Holland.

'Moll'. Dwarf form, similar to 'Montgomery', but somewhat slower growing, about 100 cm high in 20 years, broadly conical and very densely branched, annual growth 3–5 cm, shoots yellow-brown; needles attractively blue-white, 10–15 mm long, 1 mm thick, DB 6: 201; KN 272 (H); WM 327 (H) (= *P. pungens glauca* 'Moll' P. Moll ex Krüssm.). Developed by the Peter Moll Nursery, W. Germany. Before 1935.

'Montgomery'. Dwarf form, slow growing and very compact, broadly conical, as high as wide, annual growth about 6 cm, shoots yellow-brown, buds ovate, yellow-brown, scales reflexed; needles 18–20 mm long, gray-blue, prickly. DB 6: 329 (H); WM 328 (H) (= *P. pungens glauca* 'Montgomery' Teuscher 1949). Developed before 1934 in the Eastern Nursery and there named *Picea pungens glauca compacta globosa*; this plant was obtained by Col. R. H. Montgomery of Coscob, Conn. USA, who in turn contributed it to the New York Botanic Garden, New York, USA, where the plant grows today.

'Oldenburg' (Jeddeloh). Strong growing and very regularly conical, annual growth 10–15 cm, shoots yellow-brown, terminal about 1 cm long, ovate, scales recurved rosette-form and densely surrounded by outspread needles, the lower ones are angled forward, 20–25 mm long, steel-blue. Selected by J. D. Zu Jeddeloh; introduced into the trade under a plant patent in 1980. Especially notable is the plant's ability to quickly develop a terminal leader even on young propagules and then shoot straight upward. Promising cultivar.

'Pendula'. Normal upright habit, but the branches slant downward; needles green. SN 212 (H); CCE 309. Known well before 1920. (VR)

Fig. 131. **Picea.** A. *P. mariana,* branch and single cone; B. *P. rubens,* branch with cones;
C. *P. omorika,* branch with cones; D. *P. alcoquiana,* cone

'Pumila'. Dwarf form, globose and very compact, very slow growing; needles silvery-blue, distinctly radially arranged, especially at the branch tips, the terminal bud is totally exposed. MD 1940: Pl. 77 (H) (= *P. pungens pumila* Hahn). Introduced before 1940 by the Eisenberg Nursery near Komotau, Czechoslovakia. (VR or EX?)

'Schovenhorst'. Broadly conical habit, densely branched, similar to 'Koster' in appearance, but the branches are stiffer and more upright, the lower branches not hanging to the ground; needles a good blue, somewhat sickle-shaped. Selected in 1951 on the Schovenhorst Estate, in Putten, Gelderland, Holland and introduced in 1962 by P. Van Nes, Boskoop.

'Schwartz'. Normal habit, twigs light blue, terminal thick, ovate, yellow-brown, scales appressed, only the outermost tips very slightly spreading; needles 2–3 cm long, directed forward. American cultivar growing in the Arnold Arboretum.

'Spek'. Strong grower, conical, open, shoots stiff, light brown, buds thick, obtuse, 8–10 mm long, lateral buds irregularly arranged; needles widely spaced, somewhat sickle-shaped, recurved, waxy blue pruinose (= *P. pungens* var. *glauca spekii* Spek ex den Ouden 1933). Introduced about 1925 by the Jan Spek Nursery of Boskoop, Holland.

'Thomsen'. Strong, regularly upright, foliage nearly white-silver. DB 22: 47 (= *P. pungens glauca* 'Thomsen' Thomsen 1932). Discovered by Thomsen in a private garden in Lancaster, Penn., USA about 1928. Introduced by the Thomsen Nurseries of Mansfield, Penn., USA (this firm has been located in Skalborg, Denmark since 1934). This is, to date, the best silver-white "blue spruce", similar to 'Hoopsii', but with needles twice as thick.

'Virgata'. Upright, branches very long, horizontally outstretched spreading, with only a few lateral shoots (= *P. pungens virgata* Beissn.). Developed in the Masek Nursery of Turnau, Czechoslovakia before 1909.

'Viridis'. Like the type, but with totally green needles (= *P. pungens viridis* Regel). It is not clear whether this applies to the occasional greenish forms occurring in cultivation or to a separate pure green form. (VR)

'Vuyk'. Strong grower, conical, tall, branches in regular whorls, central leader thick and stiff, red-brown, buds thick, long acuminate, light brown, 8–10 mm long, the side buds situated somewhat under the terminal; needles more loosely arranged, nearly straight, 25 mm long, directed forward, angular to rounded in cross section, moderately silver, blue-white pruinose, more gray in winter. DB 15: 275 (Br); CCE 309 (= *P. pungens glauca vuykii* Vuyk et den Ouden). Introduced in 1912 by T. Vuyk & Zoon, Boskoop, Holland.

P. pungsaniensis Uyeki. Very similar to *P. koyamai*, but differing in the following characteristics: shoots dull yellow-brown or more greenish-brown, glabrous, widely spaced leaf cushions (close on *P. koyamai*), buds ovate, dull yellow to brown, 4–5 mm long, slightly resinous; needles on the fruiting shoots 12–23 mm long, but usually 20 mm, width 1.2 mm, usually bowed, 4 sided in cross section; cones oblong-ovate, 5.5–7 cm long, 2.5–3 cm thick, scales ovate, with an apical continuation over the bowed limb, keeled beneath, about 16 mm high, 11 mm wide, thin, rough, not glossy (glossy on *P. koyamai*), seed with 8–9 mm long wings (11–13 mm on *P. koyamai*). N. Korea; found only in 2 locations in the mountains at 1400 m thus far. Named for the 2113 m peak, P'ungsan-gun. z6

P. retroflexa M. T. Mast. Tall tree, to 50 m in its habitat, like *P. abies* in many ways, gray bark, exfoliates in thin scales, young shoots yellow, glabrous to nearly só, terminal shoot very thick and short (5 cm), leaf cushions with a square scar, buds narrowly conical, acute, about 8 mm long, scales loosely appressed, slightly resinous; needles "brush-like" in arrangement, very stiff and prickly, bluish-green or green, 12–18 (25) mm long, 4 sided in cross section, with 5–7 stomatal lines on each side; cone scales oblong-cylindrical, 10–12 cm long, seed scales leathery, apical limb round, appressed at first, later reflexed. GGy 429. China; W. Szechwan. 1911. z7

P. robertii P. Vipper. Intermediate between *P. schrenkiana* and *P. glehnii*. Further information unavailable. USSR; Tian-Shan (Central Asia).

P. rubens Sarg. American Red Spruce. Tree, to 30 m, trunk to 1.5 m in diameter or more, slender conical crown, bark red-brown, scaly and chapped, branches short, thin, outspread and persisting on the stem, shoots yellow-brown, later brown, dense, short bristly pubescent (but not glandular, like *P. mariana!*), buds acutely ovate, 7 mm long, red-brown, somewhat resinous, basal scales subulate, somewhat pubescent, the apical scales more rounded and reflexed; needles yellow-green (!!), very glossy, parted on the underside, 12–15 mm long, very densely crowded on the upper side, with a small apical tip, 4 sided in cross section, with 3–5 stomatal lines on all sides; cones oval-oblong with a stalk-like base, 2.5–4 cm long, glossy red-brown (hence the species name), scales stiff and woody, apical margin semicircular, 10–12 mm wide, quite finely irregularly dentate, somewhat resinous, green to purple-violet when young, quickly abscising when ripe, seeds 3 mm long, dark brown spotted to black, wings 10 mm long. BM 9446; OCC 285 (Br); GGy 426; BCC Pl. 22 (H); CCE 310 (= *P. rubra* Sarg.; *P. australis* Small). N. America; Nova Scotia to the Appalachian Mts. 1755. Fig. 124 and 131. z3

'Nana'. Dwarf form, broadly conical, very compact and slow growing, young shoots spreading, very short, orange-red, terminal buds 3 mm long, reddish-brown, surrounded by short needles; needles very densely arranged, radial, 4–20 mm long, bright green, tips slightly curved, short and finely acuminate, but not prickly. Originated in 1908 from seed in the Von Gimborn Arboretum, Doorn, Holland. In 1952 the plant was 1.2 m high and 1.4 m wide.

'Virgata'. Sparsely branched, branches long, thin, outspread and nearly devoid of lateral shoots, very similar in appearance to *P. abies* 'Virgata' (= *P. rubra* f. *virgata* Rehd.). Discovered as a single tree in 1893 on Mt. Hopkins, Mass., USA, and cultivated in the Arnold Arboretum. (VR)

P. × saaghyi Gayer (*P. glauca* × *P. jezoensis* (female)). Intermediate between the parents and differing in the following characteristics: Twigs glabrous, darker yellow than *P. jezoensis*, buds broad and obtusely ovate, resinous, scales acutely ovate, leaf cushions like those of *P. glauca*, but not decurrent; needles "brush-like" on the upper side of the branch at a 45° angle to the branch, as stiff as those of *P. glauca*, distinctly acuminate and prickly, only 9 mm long, distinctly keeled above, and dark green, very flat and blue-green beneath. Developed in 1917 by

Dr. I. Von Saaghy in Kámon, W. Hungary. The plant is still growing in the Kámoni Arboretum, Szombathely, Hungary.

P. schrenkiana Fisch. & C. A. Mey. Tree, to 35 m in its habitat, crown conical or more columnar, branches and twigs gray, more or less pendulous, young shoots gray-yellow, usually glabrous, occasionally with some bristles on the needle base, leaf cushions slightly swollen, buds oval, light brown, obtuse, scales tightly appressed, obtuse, basal scales keeled and acuminate; resinous; needles directed forward above, parted beneath, stiff, deep green, 18–30 mm long, 1 mm wide, sharply acuminate, straight or slightly bowed, 4 sided in cross section, with about 2–3 stomatal lines above, 3–4 less conspicuous lines beneath; cones oblong-cylindrical, 7–10 cm long, 2.5 cm thick, dark gray-brown to glossy dark brown, scales obovate, apical margin shallowly bowed, undulate, seeds 3 mm long, wings 9 mm long. BFN 233 (H); DB 22: 84 (H); DB 20: 121 (H); GGy 426; CCE 311, 312, 314 (= *P. tianshanica* Rupr.; *P. obovata* var. *schrenkiana* Mast.). Central Asia, especially in Turkestan, Tian Shan area, develops large virgin forests. 1877. Similar to *P. smithiana*, but needles deep green, twigs not pendulous. Fig. 124, 126 and 129. z6

P. sitchensis (Bong.) Carr. Sitka Spruce. Tree, to 40 m in culture, 60 m in its native habitat, crown broadly conical, with thin, horizontally spreading branches, later broad crowned, bark dark red-brown, thin exfoliating, young shoots yellow-brown, lighter than the buds, stiff, deeply furrowed, buds light brown, acutely conical, resinous; scales appressed, basal scales small; needles stiff, compressed, 15–25 mm long, radially arranged, but parted beneath on horizontal shoots, with prickly needle tips, flat in cross section, slightly keeled beneath and silvery-white from the 2 white stomatal bands, each with 6–8 lines, rounded above and glossy green with intermittent stomatal lines; cones cylindrical-oblong, 6 to 10 cm long, pale reddish or yellowish-brown, scales oblong-rhombic, thin and flexible, limb irregularly dentate, undulate, seeds brown, 2–3 mm long, wings 7–8 mm long. SN 55 (H); DJ 80; GGy 431; CCE 314, 315 (= *P. sitkaensis* Mayr.) N. America; Alaska to California. 1831. As a coastal tree this species prefers a moist to wet, sandy soil and cool, moist air. Tolerates wind. Valuable forest tree, but also very decorative in the garden. Plate 84, 97 and 98; Fig. 125, 126 and 132. z7

'Compacta'. Dwarf form, 1–2 m high, broadly conical and very dense, branches spread wide, young shoots light yellowish-brown, buds 4 mm long, brown, acute, scales appressed; needles radial, very dense on the upper side and dark green, with white or bluish stomatal bands beneath (= *P. sitchensis compacta* den Ouden). In the Trompenburg Arboretum, Rotterdam. 1949.

'Microphylla'. Dwarf form, only 25 cm high in 10 years, very narrowly conical, upright, slow growing, very openly branched, 1 year shoots very thin; needles not numerous, fine *Erica*-like, 5 to 9 mm long, with only 2(3) stomatal lines on either side (= *P. sitchensis* var. *microphylla* Hornib.). Discovered in a planting of *P. sitchensis* by Hornibrook who brought it to Blandsfort, Abbeyleix, Ireland in 1925. (EX?)

'Speciosa'. Somewhat weaker growing, branches more ascending, more densely arranged; needles shorter and stiffer, sharply acuminate, more distinctly blue-white beneath. SN 65(H) (= *P. sitchensis speciosa* Beissn.). Before 1909. (Presumably EX)

'Strypemonde'. Dwarf form, very slow growing, evenly round, globose; needles directed outward, very prickly, blue-green. Originated from a witches'-broom; original plant is in the Trompenburg Arboretum, Rotterdam, Holland.

P. smithiana (Wall.) Boiss. Himalayan Spruce. Tall tree, reaching 30–50 m in its habitat, trunk slender, 2 m or more in diameter, branches very long on older trees, young shoots weep vertically, yellowish, later more brownish, thin, glabrous, buds spindle-shaped, 8–12 mm long, red-brown, acute, resinous, basal scales bristly pubescent; needles radially arranged, light green at first, later dark green, 25–50 mm long (longest needles of all the spruces!), 1 mm thick, acuminate, but not prickly, 4 sided in cross section, but higher than wide, with 3–5 stomatal lines on each side; cones cylindrical, 12–15 cm long, asymmetrical and slightly curved, with a 10 mm long stalk, green at first, glossy brown and resinous when ripe, scales nearly circular, leathery to woody, smooth, entire, bract scales not developed, seeds 5 mm long, black-brown, with 12 mm long wings. SN 209 (H); DB 13: 258 (H); TC 18; GGy 427; CCE 312; 313 (= *P. morinda* Link). W. Himalya, Afghanistan to Nepal, in the mountains at 2100–3600 m. 1818. Cultivated only in the milder regions and protected areas. Plate 98; Fig. 124, 126 and 129. z9

P. spinulosa (Griff.) Henry. Tall tree, to 45 m in its habitat, rough bark, exfoliates in small 4 sided plates, crown openly conical, branches horizontal, twigs and young shoots long, pendulous, tail-like, glabrous and yellowish, buds ovate, 5–6 mm long, yellow-brown, nearly resin free; needles incompletely radial, flexible, straight, 25–35 mm long, slightly compressed, keeled on both sides, prickly, green above, with 2 bluish stomatal bands above, 4–8 lines in each; cones oblong, 6–10 cm long, green or gray-reddish when young, glossy yellow-brown when ripe, scales thin and flexible, apical margin circular or also truncate, finely serrate or undulate or entire, 12 to 14 mm wide, seeds 5 mm long. BM 8169; SN 239 (H); HAl 182 (H); GGy 432; CCE 317 (= *P. morindoides* Rehd.). East Himalaya; Sikkim, Bhutan, in the mountains at 2400–3000 m. Plate 98; Fig. 125, 126 and 129. z8

P. torano see **P. polita**

P. wilsonii Mast. Wilson's Spruce. Tree, to 25 m, conical crown, branches short, spreading horizontally, dense, young shoots light gray, glabrous, with only tiny leaf cushions, buds glossy dark red-brown, ovate, not resinous, scales tightly appressed, very wide at the apex; needles particularly dense on the upper side of the branch and directed forward, underside parted and at right angles to the shoot, dark green, 8–15 mm long, 1 mm thick, straight or slightly bowed, prickly, acute, 4 sided in cross section, with 1–2 stomatal lines above, 3–4 indistinct stomatal lines beneath; cones oblong-cylindrical, 4–6 cm long, abscising 1 year after ripening, light brown, scales nearly circular, entire, occasionally also finely dentate. CIS 9; CB III 66; GGy 428 (as *P. watsoniana*); BMns 106; NF 6: 16; CCE 315–317 (= *P. watsoniana* Mast.). China; NW. Hupeh and NW.

Szechwan Provinces, in the mountains from 1600–2500 m. Fig. 124, 126, 129. z6

Lit. Berg, Graf v.: Einige Spielarten der Fichte. Schrift. Naturf. Ges. Dorpat 1887 (44p., 12Pl.). ● Fukarek, P.: Die Standorte der Omorika-Fichte nach den Waldbraenden in den Jahren 1946–1947 (In Serbocroatian with German summary). Sumarskog lista 1–2, Zagreb 1951 ● Korzeniewski, L.: Variabilité de l'épicea (*Picea excelsa* Link). Monogr. Botan. I, 1–87. Warsaw 1953. ● Lacasagne, M.: Etude morphologique, anatomique et systematique de genre *Picea*. Toulouse 1934. ● Lindquist, B.: The main varieties of *Picea abies* (L.) Karst. in Europe. Act. Hort. Bergian. **14**, 1948. ● Novak, F.: Zur 50

jaehrigen Entdeckung der *Picea omorika.* Mitt. DDG 1927. ● Schroeter, C.: Über die Vielgestaltigkeit der Fichte. Zurich 1898 (130 pp., 37 illus.) ● Schroeter, C.: Übersicht über die Mutationen der Fichte nach Wuchs und Ribde. Ber. Bot. Ges. Schweiz, Zurich 1933. ● Schwerin, Graf v.: Die Formen der *Picea pungens.* Mitt. DDG 1920, 231 to 235. ● Tyszkiewicz, S.: Nowa forma szyszek swierka (*Picea excelsa*). Las Polski **14**, 1934. ● Tyszkiewicz, W.: *Wyspy swierka* (*Picea excelsa* Link) na polesiu i Wolyniu na tle podyluwialnej historii swierka we wschodniej Polsce. Lwow 1935. ● Wittrock, V. B.: De *Picea excelsa* (Lam.) Link. Praesertim de formis suecicis hujus arboris (Meddelanden om Granen). Act. Hort. Bergian. **1**, 1–94, 1914 (23 plates).

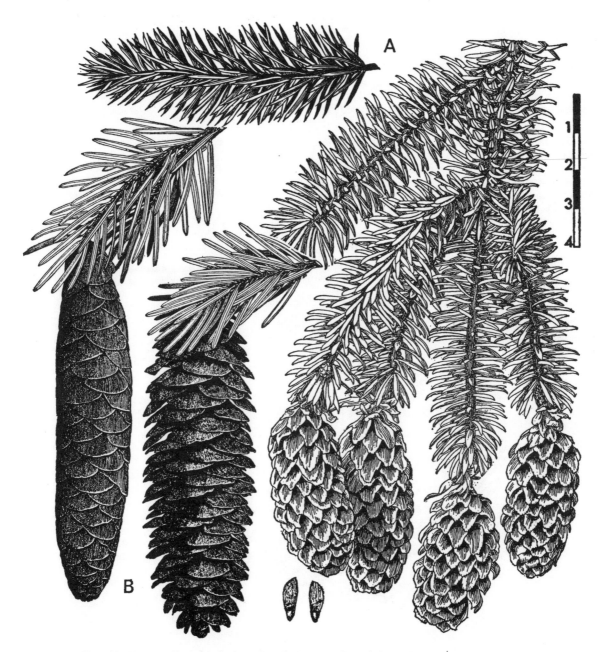

Fig. 132. **Picea.** A. *P. sitchensis,* branch with 4 cones; above left, sterile twig, 2 seeds beneath; B. *P. breweriana,* cones closed and opened (from Sudworth)

PILGERODENDRON Florin—CUPRESSACEAE

Evergreen tree or shrub, branchlets 4 sided, leaves consistently formed, opposite, 2 sided, with stomata only on the upper side, spreading to appressed imbricate; plants dioecious, male flowers in cylindrical cones, large, surrounded at the base by 2 elongated needles, with dry membranous margins; stamens opposite, nearly peltate, short stalked, erect, ovate or rhomboidal, more or less long acuminate; pollen sacs varying in number, usually 6 in the lower part of the inflorescence, distinct, dehiscing by a longitudinal crack; female inflorescence ovate or ellipsoid, surrounded at the base by 4 opposite needles; cones with 4 scales, both upper ones fertile with 2 ovules each, eventually woody-leathery, with an awl-shaped, incurved dorsal thorn, gaping open when ripe; seeds (3–)4, pale yellow-brown, obtuse triangular, with 2 uneven wings. Range map Fig. 133.

Pilgerodendron uviferum (Pilg.) Florin. Tall tree or only a shrub, crown narrowly conical, thin bark, branchlets 4 sided; leaves all alike, about 2 mm long, appressed or more or less spreading, obtuse, silver-gray from the stomata except for a green marginal line; cones on short branchlets, 8 to 12 mm long, with 4 scales, of which the basal pair are smaller, all with a stiff, central thorn. CB III 67; CCE 318 (= *Librocedrus uvifera* Pilg.; *L. tetragona* Endl.). S. America; western slopes of the Andes from S. Chile to Patagonia. Fig. 134. z9

> Differing from *Libocedrus* in the 4 sided branches with evenly formed leaves; from *Fitzroya* in the leaves being widened toward the apex. Generally only cultivated as a glass house plant since its habitat is one of the most moderate, moist climates of the world. It is difficult to understand why this plant was ever included in the genus *Libocedrus*.

Lit. Florin, R.: *Pilgerodendron,* eine neue Koniferengattung aus Sud-Chile. Svensk Bot. Tidskr. **24,** 132–135, 1930. Stockholm.

Fig. 133. Range of the genus *Pilgerodendron* (......) and *Saxegothaea* (black)

Fig. 134. *Pilgerodendron uviferum.* Branch, cone beneath (from Gard. Chron.)

PINUS L.—Pine—PINACEAE

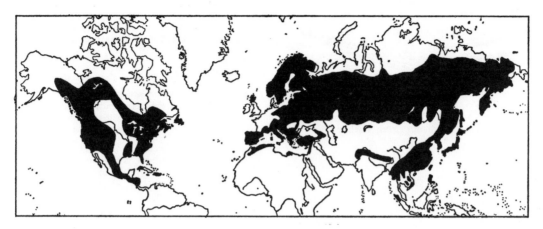

Fig. 135. Range of the genus *Pinus*

Evergreen trees, occasionally shrubs, with fissured or scaly bark; branches (at least at first) whorled; buds attractive, with numerous, imbricate scales, usually resinous, seldom resin free; leaves needle-like, in fascicles of 2–5, rarely only 1 or 6–8, triangular or semi-terete, surrounded at the base by a sheath of 8–12 scales; leaf margin usually finely dentate; stomatal lines on the dorsal side or (on the 3–5 needle species) only on the inner side; with only 1 vascular bundle (*Haploxylon* Koehne) or 2 vascular bundles (*Diploxylon* Koehne) in the center and 2 or more resin ducts; plants dioecious; male flowers axillary at the base of young long shoots, spike-form clustered, yellow, orange or red, composed of numerous, spirally arranged stamens, each with 2 pollen sacs; female flowers axillary or subterminal, solitary or several together, composed of numerous, spirally arranged seed scales, each of which has a small bract scale; cones ovate or cylindrical or globose, symmetrical or oblique, straight or curved, most pendulous or also spreading upward, ripening the 2nd or (rarely) 3rd year and then opening or remaining closed for an entire year; seed scales woody, densely imbricate, tightly appressed, the exterior of the cone usually with a characteristic, normally stout, thick scale shield (apophyse), these usually rhombic with a cross-wise keel, normally with a wart or thorn in the center (umbo); seeds 2 under each scale, normally with an adnate or easily separated wing, rarely not winged; cotyledons 4 to 15; x = 12.—Over 100 species in the Northern Hemisphere, from the polar circle to Guatemala, the West Indies, North Africa and Indonesia.

Positive identification of *Pinus* species sometimes only possible with microscopic examination of the needle cross section (oftentimes a good magnifying glass or hand lens will be sufficient) and careful study of the cones, particularly the scale ends.

The classification of the genus: A totally satisfactory division of the genus has never been achieved. The first classification of the genus, based on evolutionary characteristics, was completed by Shaw (1914). This system, with a few improve-

ments by Mirov (1967) is still in use. Although Shaw, according to Duffield (1952), overemphasized the asymmetrical, late opening cones, Shaw used many other morphological characteristics in his classification, such as the form of the cone scales, location of the resin ducts in the leaf, & form and attachment of the seed wing. Pilger, who revised the genus in Engler & Prantl's Die natuerlichen Pflanzenfamilien, retained the separation by Koehne (1893) into 2 subgenera—*Haploxylon* (needles with 1 vascular bundle) and *Diploxylon* (needles with 2 vascular bundles) and then further divided these into 11 Sections based on the number of needles on the short shoots, the location of the resin ducts in the leaf and on the morphology of the seed wings. The overemphasis on the number of needles is considered today to be a weak area in this system. Gaussen (1955) devised a totally new system of classification based on the characteristics of the pollen grains but this is, unfortunately, far too complicated for practical gardening purposes.

Because of the general disagreement among the authors as to the division of this genus it seems advisable to retain the system devised by Pilger.

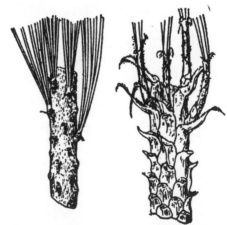

Fig. 136. **Pinus**. Left, smooth shoot without decurrent needle sheaths of *P. ayacahuite*; right, furrowed shoot from the decurrent scales of the leaf sheath on *P. jeffreyi* (from Martinez)

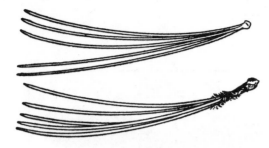

Fig. 137. *Pinus,* 5 needled leaf bundle, above without, below with leaf sheath (from Martinez)

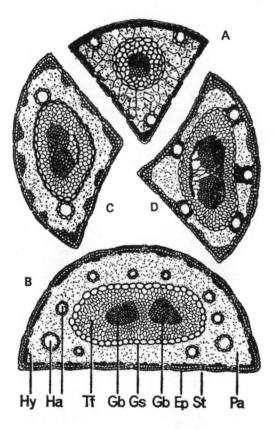

Fig. 138. **Pinus** needle cross section. A. *P. reflexa;* B. *P. remorata;* C. *P. herrerai;* D. *P. oocarpa.* Legend to the abbreviations: Hy hypoderm, Ha resin duct, Tf transfusion tissue, Gb vascular bundle, Gs vascular bundle sheath, Ep epidermis, St stoma, Pa parenchyma (from Martinez, completed)

Classification of the Genus

(From Pilger, expanded)

Subgenus Ducampopinus (A. Cheval.) de Ferré
Leaves in 2's, narrow-lanceolate, often spread apart, 1.5–4 mm wide, margin finely serrate or smooth, stomatal lines on the interior, seldom on the dorsal side; with 1 vascular bundle; cones ovate, symmetrical, scales keeled, scale ends with a thick, conical thorn; seeds with long, segmented wing:

> *P. krempfii*

Subgenus Haploxylon Koehne
Needles with 1 vascular bundle in the center; sheath totally abscising, occasionally splitting into reflexed scales at first and then abscising to a small remnant.

Section 1. *Cembra* Spach
Scale tip with an umbo, seeds thick, not winged or slightly so; leaves grouped to 5; sheath totally abscising:
> *P. albicaulis, armandii, cembra, flexilis, koraiensis, pumila*

Section 2. *Strobus* Sweet ex Spach
Cones thin scaled, long; scale tips with an umbo; seeds with a tightly adnate wing, fully covering the seed; leaves grouped in 5's; sheath totally abscising:
> *P. ayacahuite, lambertiana, monticola, morrisonicola, parviflora, peuce, strobiformis, strobus, wallichiana*

Section 3. *Paracembra* Koehne
Scale tip arched or pyramidal, thick, with the umbo, which is often thorned in the middle; leaves grouped 1–5, the sheath totally abscising, loosening by the recurved scale tips.

1. Subsection. *Cembroides* Shaw
Seeds wingless; needles grouped 1–4, occasionally 5, entire; needle sheath abscising except for a few recurved lobes:
> *P. cembroides* with its varieties, *culminicola, monophylla, nelsonii, pinceana, quadrifolia*

2. Subsection. *Gerardiana* Shaw
Seed wings very short; leaves in 3's, sheath totally abscising in the 1st or 2nd year:
> *P. bungeana, gerardiana*

3. Subsection. *Balfourianae* Shaw
Seed wings long; leaves in 5's; sheath abscising:
> *P. aristata, aristata* var. *longaeva, balfouriana*

Subgenus Diploxylon Koehne
Leaves with 3 vascular bundles in the center; leaves grouped 2–5(8); sheath tightly closed, at most somewhat shredded at the tip, rarely abscising completely; scale end arched to pyramidal, with a central umbo; wing membrane nearly always "clasping the seed like a pair of tongs," the wing easily removed (except in Section 4).

Section 4. *Sula* Mayr
Seed wing membrane adnate to the seed; leaves in 3's:
> *P. canariensis, longifolia*

Section 5. *Eupitys* Spach
Leaves in 2's (occasionally 2–3), resin ducts in the parenchyma or on the epidermis; with a persistent sheath, annual growth in 1 segment (not jointed); cones small, open; seed wings completely developed:
> *P. densiflora, heldreichii, leucodermis, luchuensis, massoniana, merkusii, mugo, nigra, pinaster, resinosa, sylvestris, tabuliformis, tuiwanensis, thunbergii, tropicalis, uncinata, yunnanensis*

Section 6. *Banksia* Mayr

Leaves in 2's, occasionally 3, with persistent sheaths; resin ducts in the parenchyma; annual growth jointed; cones usually small, sometimes oblique, often very persistent and late in opening:

P. banksiana, clausa, contorta, echinata, glabra, halepensis, muricata, pungens, virginiana

Section 7. *Pinea* Endl.

Leaves in 2's, with persistent sheaths; resin ducts at the epidermis; seeds very large, very narrowly winged; annual growth in 1 continuous shoot (not jointed):

P. pinea

Section 8. *Australes* Pilger

Leaves 2–5 (usually 3) together, with persistent sheaths, resin ducts at the vascular bundle sheath; cones usually symmetrical, abscising, opening; annual growth 1 to multisegmented:

P. caribaea, elliottii, lawsonii, occidentalis, oocarpa, palustris, pringlei

Section 9. *Khasia* Mayr

Needles in 3's, with persistent sheaths; resin ducts adjacent to the epidermis; annual growth continuous:

P. insularis, khasya

Section 10. *Pseudostrobus* Endl.

Leaves grouped 3–5, with abscising or persisting sheaths; resin ducts in the parenchyma; cones usually symmetrical, abscising, opening; annual growth usually continuous:

P. douglasiana, chihuahuana, durangensis, engelmannii, jeffreyi, leiophylla, lumholtzii, michoacana, montezumae, oaxacana, ponderosa, pseudostrobus, teocote, torreyana, washoensis

Section 11. *Taeda* Spach

Leaves in 3's, with persistent sheaths; resin ducts in the parenchyma; cones often oblique, usually opening late and very persistent; annual growth jointed:

P. attenuata, coulteri, greggii, patula, radiata, rigida, sabiniana, serotina, taeda

Pinus albicaulis Engelm. Whitebark Pine. Tree, to 10 m, rarely to 20 m, but shrubby and low at higher altitudes, bark of young trees whitish, smooth, exfoliating, branches horizontal, twigs reddish-yellow to brown or orange with smooth and scattered pubescence, buds broadly ovate, acuminate, scales loosely appressed and long acuminate; needles in 5's, persisting about 4–8 years, 4.5 to 6 cm long, stiff, but flexible, 1.5 mm thick, dark green, entire, short acuminate, outside with 2 indented stomatal lines, inside with 3–5 stomatal lines, sheath abscising in the first year; cones solitary, terminal, oval, 4–7 cm long, purple at first, later brown, with short, thick scales, not gaping open when ripe, scale apophysis with a sharp pointed umbo, seeds large, to 12 mm long, wingless. SPa 7; CCE 319. USA; British Columbia to California; Rocky Mountains, between 1350 and 3650 m. Rarely in cultivation but winter hardy. Plate 101; Fig. 139. z4

'Flinck'. Dwarf form, originated from seed of a witches'-broom. Introduced by G. Horstmann, 1983.

P. aristata Engelm. Bristlecone Pine. Tree, to 12 m, often much shorter in cultivation, occasionally procumbent, bark green and smooth on young trees, later scaly, branches in regular whorls and outspread when young,

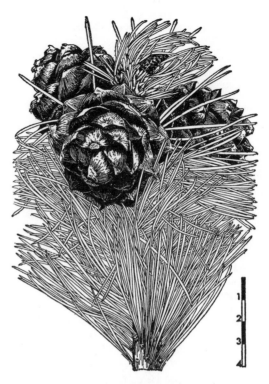

Fig. 139. *Pinus albicaulis* (from Sudworth)

tough, short, young shoots tough, light orange, glabrous to pubescent, buds acutely ovate, 8 mm long, outer scales loosely appressed; needles in 5's, persisting about 12–15 years, very densely crowded, 2–4 cm long, dark green, with scattered, white resin droplets on the needles (often mistaken for scale insects!!), without any dorsal stomatal lines, inside bluish-white, resin ducts on the epidermis, sheath torn and split in the first year, but persisting 2–4 years in rosette form at the leaf base; female flowers dark purple; cones sessile, cylindrical-ovate, 4–9 cm long, appearing after about 20 years, scale ends convex, cross keeled, umbo with a fine, about 8 mm long thorn; seed ovate, compressed, light brown with black spots, 7 mm long, with 7–10 mm long wing. SN 240; OCC 292; SPa 10; SPi 143–146; CCE 319, 320. USA, Rocky Mts. 1861. Easily distinguished from any other species by the resin droplets. Plate 85 and 86; Fig. 114. z6

'Cecilia'. Dwarf form, originated in the J. W. Spingarn Nursery, New York, USA.

var. **longaeva** (D. K. Bailey) Little. Tree with pendulous branches, becoming over 4000 years old in dry, high mountainous locations; needles persisting for 30 years, resin droplets nearly absent, with 2 resin ducts; cones with fine, short awns, these reduced or totally absent on the rounded cone base (= *P. longaeva* D. K. Bailey). Discovered in large numbers in the White Mountains of Arizona, 1954; the oldest of which were 4.5–9 m high with trunk diameters of 1.25 m at over 3000 years of age. Three specimens were established at 4600 years making these conifers older than the *Sequoiadendron*. The study was conducted by Dr. Schulmann of the University of Arizona and richly illustrated in the National Geographic Magazine, 1958. Plate 87. z5

G. Horstmann has created 2 very rare dwarf conifers propagated from witches'-brooms collected from the normal type in its native habitat. 1983.

'Sherwood Compact'. Tight conical habit, branches ascending. Very beautiful new form from the USA.

P. arizonica see: **P. ponderosa** var. **arizonica**

P. armandii Franch. Armand Pine. Medium tall tree, to 20 m, branches spreading widely and horizontally, bark thin, greenish-gray, smooth, young shoots yellow-green, glabrous, occasionally lightly glandular, buds cylindrical, obtuse with a short tip, brown, slightly resinous, bud scales long acuminate and spreading near the apex; needles loosely arranged, in 5's, persisting for 2–3 years, thin and limp, spread wide apart or somewhat pendulous, yellow-green(!) to bright green, 8–15 cm long, acute, margin dentate, without stomatal lines on the outside, inside bluish-white, resin ducts in the parenchyma, sheath abscising in the first year; cones grouped 1–3, stalked, 10–20 cm long, erect at first, pendulous in the 2nd year, oblong-conical, 4–6 cm wide, seed scales thick and woody, scale ends rounded or acutely tapered, margin occasionally curving somewhat, yellow-brown, with small, obtuse umbo, seeds red-brown, 10–12 mm long, wingless, with a scabrous margin. SN 72 (H); CIS 4; SPi 96–99; LF 29. W. and Central China. Plate 99; Fig. 147 and 160. z7

var. **amamiana** (Koidzu) Hatus. Differing from the type in the black twigs, stiffer leaves, only half as long (5–7 cm); cones ovate, much smaller than those of the type, stalk about 12 mm long, seeds likewise smaller, 12–13 mm long, wingless (= *P. amamiana* Koidzu). Japan; Yaku-shima, Tanega-shima.

var. **mastersiana** Hayata. Tree, to 20 m, trunk to 1 m in diameter, twigs spreading widely and horizontally, shoots glabrous; needles 8–15 cm long, finely serrate, bright green; cones 10–20 cm long and to 8 cm wide, scales rhombic, 3 cm long, seeds 8–12 mm long. LT 27 (C and Br). Taipei; in the mountains at 2300–3000 m.

P. attenuata Lemm. Knobcone Pine. Small tree, 9–24 m high, not very attractive, sometimes only a low shrub, bark dark brown at the base of the trunk, splitting into loose scales, upper trunk smooth and light brown, young shoots glabrous, orange-brown, buds spindle-shaped, long acuminate, 18–24 mm long, slightly resinous, scales tightly appressed; needles usually in 3's, steeply erect, persisting for 3–4 years, thin, yellowish- to bluish-green, 7–18 cm long, sharply acuminate, margin indistinctly serrate, with stomatal lines on either side, resin ducts in the parenchyma, fascicles loosely arranged, sheath about 10 mm long, persistent; cones usually grouped 2–4, 8–14 cm long, 5–6 cm wide, short stalked, distinctly curved, remaining closed for many years, scales on the sunny side of the cone very conically enlarged and angular, with thick bowed thorned umbo, the inner scales flat with shorter thorns, seeds oval, 6–7 mm long, black, wings 18–20 mm long. MP 171 (H); 8717; Gs 1934: 252 (H); SPa 22–23; SPi 317–318; CCE 320 (=*P. tuberculata* Gord.). California, coastal mountains from 800–1300 m. Relatively rare in cultivation but winter hardy. Fig. 144 and 154. z7

P. × attenuradiata Stockwell & Righter (*P. attenuata* × *P. radiata*). Intermediate between the parents in branching habit, bark color, needle strength, form and arrangement of the cones, general impression, however, resembles *P. radiata* more closely, but more winter hardy. Developed in Placerville, California, USA 1927. z6?

P. ayacahuite Ehrenb. Mexican White Pine. Tree, to 30 m, similar to *P. wallichiana* in appearance, trunk to 1 m in diameter, bark light gray, smooth on young trees, rough and scaly on older stems, young shoots light brown or gray, usually with short rusty brown pubescence, occasionally also glabrous, buds conical, 12 mm long, resinous, scales with long, distinct tips at the end; needles in 5's, usually persisting for 3 years, 7–9 cm long, thin, limply pendulous, with a silvery- or bluish-green cast due to the stomatal lines on the ventral side, without dorsal stomatal lines, margin finely dentate, resin ducts on the epidermis, needle sheath 3 cm long, abscising; cones solitary or fascicled, terminal, stalked, pendulous, curved, cylindrical, 25–30(–45) cm long, gaping open, 6–14 cm wide at the base, seed scales broadly elliptic-oblong, 5–7 cm long, channeled on the dorsal side, scale ends somewhat thickened in the middle, apex usually recurved, seeds ovate, compressed, 9 mm long, brown, darker striped, wings 25 mm long, obliquely truncate. MP 201 (H); MPi 78 and 93; SPi 103–107; CCE 321–322. Central America from Guatemala, across Mexico to the US border, in the mountains at 2400 m. 1836. Not reliably winter hardy in colder climates! Plate 99; Fig. 136. z7

var. **brachyptera** Shaw. Differing in the very short seed wing and the abnormally large seed. MP 83b, 92, 93; CCE 322. Mexico.

var. **veitchii** Shaw. Cones larger, seeds to 12 mm long, wings 12 mm long (also shorter than those of the type). MPi 81, 82, 83v, 86 (= *P. veitchii* Roezl). Mexico.

P. balfouriana Grev. & Balf. Foxtail Pine. Tree, 6–15 m in its habitat, occasionally taller, young trees narrowly conical, bark milky-white on young trees, thin and soft, dark red-brown and deeply fissured on older trees, young shoots thick, orange-brown, finely pubescent at first, buds ovate, 6 mm long, scales tightly appressed; needles in 5's, tightly crowded, 2–4 cm long, stiff, somewhat curved, entire, without dorsal stomata, silvery-white inside due to the stomatal lines, resin ducts on the epidermis, persisting 10–15 years, sheaths splitting in the first year to 5 narrow strips and reflexed rosette-like; cones terminal, short stalked, pendulous, 7–12 cm long, 3–5 cm wide, brown, scales narrow, elongated, scale ends thick, crosswise keeled, with a short thorn, seeds 7 to 8 mm long, light brown, spotted, wings tightly adnate, 13–22 mm long. MP 146 (H); DJ 83; SPa 11; SPi 157–160. California; in the mountains at 1500–2500 m. Very similar to *P. aristata*, but without the resin spots; rarely found in cultivation. Plate 86 and 99. z6?

P. banksiana Lamb. Jack Pine. Tree, to 20 m high, but usually lower or also only shrubby, bark thick, scaly, branches seldom in whorls, wavy curving(!), very irregularly arranged, annual growth usually with 2 whorls (!), young shoots flexible, green to brown, glabrous in the 2nd year, buds oval-oblong, 8 mm long, scales tightly appressed; needles in 2's, twisted and

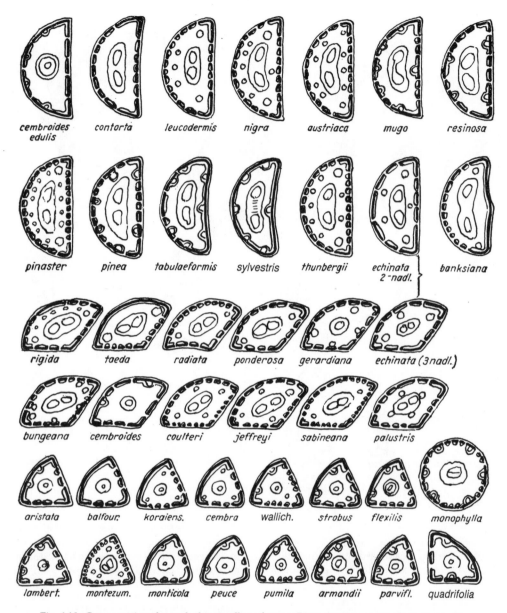

Fig. 140. Cross section through the needles of some *Pinus* species; somewhat schematic.
Both upper rows are 2 needle species, both middle rows are 3 needle species, both lower rows 5 needle
species, at right below a 1 needle and 4 needle variety (from Krüssmann, Conifers, 2nd Edition)

spreading, persisting for 2–4 years, 2–4 cm long, light green, finely and indistinctly serrate, with stomatal lines on both sides, resin ducts in the parenchyma; sheaths 3 mm long, often nearly absent on older twigs; cones usually in 2's, small, often curved finger-like, 3–5 cm long, 2 cm wide, remaining closed for many years on the tree, seeds small, 3–4 mm long, black-brown, wings 12 mm long. SN 256 (H); GTP 56; SPi 301 to 304; CCE 322–324. Colder regions of N. America and Canada to the Arctic Circle, on rock or poor sandy soil. Meritorious for its wide tolerance of soil types. Some ground hugging dwarf forms are being experimented with. Plate 99; Fig. 142, 146 and 157. z2

'Annae'. Needles partly yellowish-white (= *P. banksiana* var. *annae* Schwerin). Discovered before 1908 by Count Schwerin. (EX)

P. brutia Ten. Tree, to 20 m, with a round crown, stem and branches straight, bark silver-gray, later becoming reddish-brown and deeply fissured, not so densely branched as *P. halepensis*, shoots glabrous reddish-yellow or greenish, buds not resinous; needles in 2's, about 8–12 cm long, 1–1.5 mm wide, thick and stiff, deep green; cones horizontal to erect, 5–11 cm long, 4 cm wide, brown, somewhat glossy, scale ends convex, stalk short, not bowed, seeds 8 mm long. NSF 240; MP 253

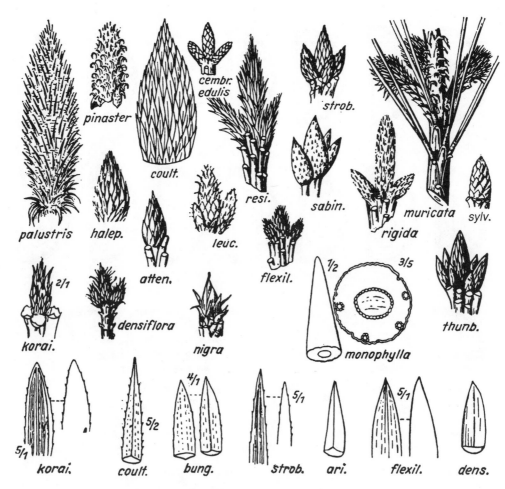

Fig. 141. Buds and needle tips of various *Pinus* species
(most from Silva Tarouca)

(H) (= *P. halepensis* var. *brutia* [Ten.] Henry; *P. pyrenaica* Lapeyr.). Asiatic Turkey, eastward to Kurdistan; Calabria, Crete, Cypress, but not in Spain and Portugal. Fig. 145 and 154. z8–9

var. **pyramidalis** Selik. Columnar habit, to 10 m, branches and twigs directed acutely upward; needles like those of the species, but shorter, 5–11 cm long, clustered at the branch tips; cones like the species in form and color, but smaller, 4–7 cm long, about 3 cm wide, without a stalk, seed 5–7 cm long. Turkey; found with the species.

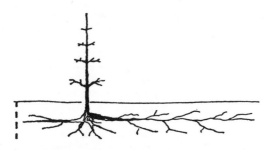

Fig. 142. *Pinus banksiana,* root system
(from Yeager)

P. bungeana Zucc. ex Endl. Lacebark Pine. Tree, 20–30 m in its habitat, often multistemmed, widely recognized for its colorful checked bark, white with red-brown and gray-green patches, exfoliating annually in thin, *Platanus*-like flakes, smooth, shoots gray-green, glabrous, glossy, buds spindle form, 12 mm long, not resinous; needles in 3's, very sparsely distributed on the twigs, persisting 3–4 years, with a turpentine scent when crushed, 5–9 cm long, 2 mm wide, finely serrate, sharply acuminate, with stomatal lines on all sides, resin ducts at the epidermis, sheath very short, abscising in the first year; cones terminal or axillary, grouped 1–2, nearly sessile, obtuse ovate, 5–6 cm long, 4–5 cm thick, scale ends wide, with a crosswise ridge and small, reflexed thorn, seeds broadly ovate, 8–10 mm long, dark marbled, with a short, easily separated wing. CIS 9; MP 273 (H); DJ 84; SPi 138–142; OCC 298 (C); CCE 322, 325; KN Plate 6. Central China, in the mountains, usually between 1400 and 2800 m; frequently planted near temples and in cemeteries. 1846. One of the more interesting but unfortunately rare pines. The bark color begins at about 10 cm diameter. Plate 86; Fig. 144 and 147. z7

P. canariensis Sweet ex K. Sprengel. Canary Island Pine. Tree, 20–30 m, narrowly conical when young, more or less oval when older with a flat peak, bark thick, reddish, flat-furrowed, branches outspread-nodding, in regular whorls, young shoots thin, yellowish, glabrous, buds large, acutely ovate, scales lanceolate, long fringes on the margin, tips distinct, very slightly resinous; needles in 3's, persisting for 2 years, densely arranged, blue-green on young plants, bright green on older trees, 20–30 cm long, 1 mm wide, acuminate, margin serrate, with stomatal lines on all sides, resin ducts in the parenchyma, sheaths about 18 mm long, persistent; cones solitary or several, terminal, pendulous on short stalks, 10–17 cm long, brown, scales thick, scale ends sharply cross keeled with a protruding tip, seeds 12 mm long, wing 3.5 cm long, dark gray. Mp 244 (H); SN 247 (H); SPi 163–165; SDK 1: 50; CCE 326. Canary Islands; only on Grand Canary and Teneriffe, in the mountains at 1100–2000 m. Subtropical Pine which does not thrive in cooler climates. Fig. 147 and 151. z9

P. caribaea Morelet. Caribbean Pine. Tree, 15–30 m in its habitat, trunk of older trees often free of branches to great heights, crown broad, round or irregular, open, bark gray to brown, furrowed, exfoliating in large, flat plates, young shoots orange-brown at first, then brown, rough and scaly, buds cylindrical, acuminate, red-brown, scales narrow, acute, white ciliate; needles usually in 3's, occasionally also 4–5 or only 2, crowded at the branch tips, abscising in the 2nd year, 15–25 cm long, dark or yellowish-green, somewhat glossy, with a horned tip, margin finely serrate, stomatal lines on all sides, resin ducts in the parenchyma, sheaths persistent, 12 mm long, light brown at first, later black-brown; cones nearly terminal, reflexed, conical, 5–10 cm long, 2.5–3 cm thick, abscising, often with a remnant remaining on the twig, scales outspread, apophysis glossy red-brown, thickened, terminating in a 1 mm long, sharp thorn, seeds triangular, narrowly ovate, 6 mm long, with 2.5 cm long, tight wings. HI 1807 (as *P. bahamensis*); MP 228 (H) (= *P. bahamensis* Griseb.). Caribbean Islands and the coast of Central America. Similar to *P. elliottii*, but the needles are predominantly 3 or 4–5 together. Economically important species. z9

P. cembra L. Swiss Stone Pine, Arolla Pine Tree, 10–20 m, occasionally somewhat higher, with a wide picturesque, often broken crown in the mountains, although in cultivation, usually acutely ovate or narrowly conical, branched from the ground up, bark gray-green and smooth at first, gray-brown and fissured with age, lateral branches short, densely twiggy, young shoots rust-yellow tomentose in the 1st year, black-gray in the 2nd year, buds ovate, 6–10 mm long, acute, resinous, scales long acuminate, tips somewhat outspread; needles in 5's, arranged in dense, brush-like clusters, persisting 3–5 years, rather stiff, straight, 5 to 8(12) cm long, obtuse acuminate, margin very finely serrate, dark green on the dorsal side and without stomata, both interior sides with blue-white stomatal bands, resin ducts in the parenchyma, sheaths abscising the 1st year; cones develop only on 60–80 year old trees, terminal, short stalked, obtuse-ovate, 6–8 cm long, 5 cm wide, violet when young, brown when ripe, not opening,

abscising with the seeds in the 3rd year, seed scales thick, broadly rhombic, to 2 cm wide, with a small, white umbo, seeds usually in 2's, red-brown, 12 mm long, 6–7 mm wide, not winged, nuts edible. SN 17(H); SPi 87–89; CCE 326–328. Middle Europe; Alps, 1300–2000 m; Carpathian Mts. at 1300–1600 m. Very important ornamental. Does well in open areas, on north slopes, and in severe climates in clay soil with sufficient moisture. Plate 100 and 109; Fig. 147 and 149. z5

'Aureovariegata.' Needles more or less yellow (= *P. cembra aureovariegata* Sénécl.; *P. cembra* var. *aurea* Fitsch.). Developed before 1869 by A. Sénéclauze. (EX?)

'Chlorocarpa' see: **P. pumila 'Chlorocarpa'**

'Compacta Glauca'. Compact conical habit, branches and twigs short and thick, ascending; needles blue-green outside, inside bluish-white, 8–9 cm long. CCE 327 (= *P. cembra compacta glauca* den Ouden). Developed before 1949 by C. Frets & Zoon in Boskoop, Holland. Plate 100. (R)

'Glauca'. No longer in cultivation.

'Globe' see: **P. pumila 'Globe'**

'Kairamo'. Needles densely crowded at all the branch tips and hanging vertically. MD 1926-I: 184(Br) (= *P. cembra* var. *sibirica* f. *kairamoi* Schwer.). Discovered before 1926 in the garden of A. O. Kairamo in Pekola, Finland.

'Monophylla'. Dwarf shrub, slow growing, the 5 needles connate for their entire length (= *P. cembra* var. *monophylla* Carr.). Observed before 1855 by Carrière. Not consistent, now and then producing normal needles on vigorous shoots. (EX?)

'Nana' see: **P. pumila 'Nana'**

'Pendula'. Branches pendulous (= *P. cembra* var. *pendula* Nels.). Known since 1866. (EX)

'Pygmaea'. Dwarf form, scarcely 40 cm high, "beehive" form in habit, branches short, very thin, outspread and drooping; needles short, unevenly long, thin, ruffled in appearance (= *P. cembra* var. *pygmaea* Hort. ex Carr. 1855). This form is surely out of existence, not identical with that often grown under this name.

var. *sibirica* see: **P. sibirica**

'Stricta'. Columnar form, branches ascending vertically, twigs tightly appressed. Gw 2: 209 (H) (= *P. cembra stricta* Carr. 1855; *P. cembra columnaris* Hellemann 1897). Discovered in cultivation by Hellemann in Moorende near Bremen, W. Germany but known earlier in France. (EX?)

'Variegata'. Needles partly yellow striped, partly yellow, or totally yellow, distributed over the entire plant (= *P. cembra variegata* R. Smith). Known in England since 1865. Occurred again in the Hans Nursery, Herrnhut, E. Germany, 1891. (EX?)

P. cembroides Zucc. Pinyon Pine, Mexican Nut Pine. Small tree, over 7 m in its habitat, with a round crown and short stem, bark of older trunks thin, scaly, branches outspread, young shoots dark orange, glabrous or pubescent, buds elliptic, 6–12 mm long, scales densely imbricate, orange-yellow, not resinous; needles grouped 1–5, persisting 3–4 years, 2.5–7 cm long, sickle-shaped, clustered on the shoot tips, apex sharply acuminate, entire, dark green, stomatal lines on all or only the interior surfaces, resin ducts at the epidermis, sheaths abscising except for some reflexed remnants at

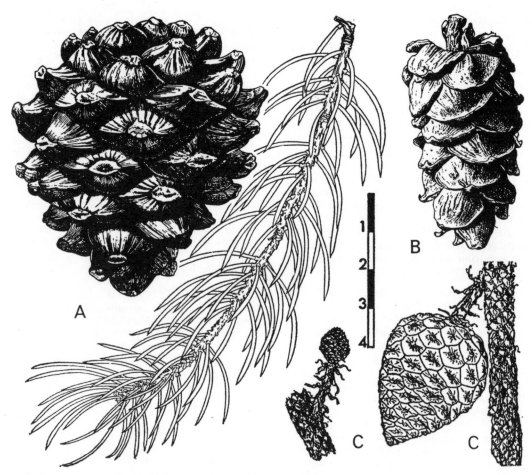

Fig. 143. **Pinus**. A. *P. monophylla*, cone and twig; B. *P. pumila*, cone;
C. *P. oocarpa*, left young, right a ripe cone (from Sudworth and Martinez)

the base; cones short stalked, globose to ovate, 3–5 cm long, 3–4 cm wide, brown, with only a few scales widely opening when ripe, scale tips rhombic, pyramidally raised, glossy brown, with a sharp cross ridge, umbo wide and compressed, seeds obovate, oblong, obtuse angular, blackish, wingless, edible. MPi 45–50; MP 55–58; DJ 86; CCE 328. Mexico, in the mountains from 1800–2650 m; New Mexico and SE. Arizona, 1450–2300 m. z7–8

'Blandsfortiana'. Dwarf form, 25 cm high in 15 years, abnormal habit, shoots densely crowded, very short, thick, but flexible, buds usually in 5's, but fused into 1; needles (1) 2–5, about 6–11 cm long, the short needles straight and reflexed, the long needles somewhat twisted, light grass green, in clusters. MD 192 (H) (= *P. cembroides blandsfortiana* Hornib.). Developed by Hornibrook before 1923. (EX?)

var. **cembroides** The type of the species, needles in 3's, occasionally 2 or 4–5, densely crowded and totally covering the shoots; cones ovate, 3–4 cm long and wide. MPi 45–50. Northern Mexico and the neighboring regions of Arizona and New Mexico. 1829. z7–8

var. **edulis** (Engelm.) Voss. Colorado Pinyon. Tree, to 15 m usually multistemmed from the ground up, irregular habit; needles usually 2 (3), about 4 cm long, stiff, dark green, sharply acuminate; cones broadly ovate, scale ends with a small, reflexed umbo, seeds

edible. QC 258; MP 152 (H); SN 263 (H); MPi 53–54; CCE 330 (= *P. edulis* Engelm.; *P. monophylla* var. *edulis* [Engelm.] Jones). Mexico, W. Texas to Wyoming, Colorado and Arizona. 1848. Plate 101; Fig. 144, 147. z7–8

var. *monophylla* see: **P. monophylla**.

var. *parryanai* see: **P. quadrifolia**.

P. chihuahuana Engelm. Tree, 15–25 m in its habitat, stem to 65 mm in diameter, bark deeply furrowed and black-brown; needles in 3's, but occasionally also 2 or 4–5 together, 6–14 cm long, rather stiff, pale green or also more bluish or yellow-green, margin finely serrate, with stomatal lines on all sides, resin ducts 3–7 in parenchyma; cones ovate, rather symmetrical, 4–6(–7) cm long, deep brown, somewhat glossy, scale ends with a short thorn, seeds 4 mm long, with 15 mm long wings. MP 206 (H) (= *P. leiophylla* var. *chihuahuana* [Engelm.] Shaw). S. Arizona and New Mexico, also south along the NW. Sierra to Mexico. z9

P. clausa (Chapm.) Vasey. Low, broad growing tree, only 5–6 m high, branches and twigs smooth, young shoots jointed, red-brown, smooth; needles in 2's, thin, 5–8 cm long, with persistent sheaths; cones oval-conical, reflexed, 5–8 cm long, in clusters, often persisting the whole year on the tree, scales concave, with short, thick, straight or bowed prickles, MP 191 (H). Alabama and Florida; only in sandy coastal areas. Very similar to *P. virginiana*, but distinguishable by the sessile, persistent cones. z7

P. contorta Dougl. ex Loud. Lodgepole Pine. Rather small, round crowned to slender conical tree, 10–25 m, often branched to the base in open areas, but tall branchless stems in dense stands, bark thin or about 2 cm thick, reddish-brown to black-brown, rather smooth to rough, small scaly; needles in 2's, dark green to yellow-green, 3–5 cm long, twisted, persisting 5–9 years, sheaths 4–6 mm long; cones ovate, usually bowed, 3–6 cm long, either springing open soon after ripening and abscising when the seeds fall out, or persisting closed for several years after which the seeds are gradually released, seed scales narrow, purple-brown with light or gray-brown apophysis with a sharp thorn, seeds 4–5 mm long, red-brown, with a 1–2 cm long wing, widest in the middle. NW. America, from S. Alaska to California, and east to the Rocky Mts. and Colorado. Fig. 154. z7

Including the following geographical varieties (a range map of the four varieties may be found in Mirov, p. 562):

var. **bolanderi** (Parl.) Lemm. Low tree, not over 11 m, crown broad, bark black-brown; needles under 5 cm long and less than 1.4 mm wide, without resin ducts; cones very asymmetrical, persistent, opening late, scale tips somewhat conical (= *P. bolanderi* Parl.). California; coastal areas near Mendocino, on acid soil. Very restricted range.

var. **contorta**. Low tree, 3 m to 11 m at most, usually lower, crown more or less round, bark to 2.5 cm thick, dark brown to gray-black, small scaly (nearly like that of *Pyrus*); needles less than 5 cm long, about 1.4–1.7 mm wide, deep green, usually with 2 resin ducts; cones very asymmetrical and curved, persistent, but usually releasing the seeds soon after ripening, scale ends somewhat conical. USA; along the coast from S. Alaska to California. Fig. 154.

'Compacta' (Jeddeloh). Dense upright habit; needles dark green.

'Frisian Gold' (Jeddeloh). Mutation of *P. contorta*, about 1962. The original tree is now about 80 cm wide and 40 cm high, eventual habit not yet known, since the oldest plants are just now 60–70 cm high and wide (presumably broadly ovate), annual shoots 8–12 cm long, terminal bud narrowly cylindrical, 10–15 mm long, 3 mm thick, resin free, black-brown, scales somewhat outspread; needles 6–7 cm long, 1 mm wide, twisted, gold-yellow, tips gold-yellow in the second year, otherwise yellow-green. KN Plate 7.

var. **latifolia** Engelm. ex S. Wats. Tall tree with a slender trunk, 20–35 m high, bark thin (scarcely over 1 cm thick), light brown or reddish-brown, crown narrowly conical; needles usually over 5 cm long, 1.3–1.7 mm wide, with 2 resin ducts; cones more or less at right angles to the twig, occasionally distinctly curved, persistent. MPi 286–290; CCE 331. The inland form with the widest range, from Canada to the north, through the Rocky Mts., and south to Colorado, east to the Black Hills. Plate 101.

var. **murrayana** (Grev. & Balf.) Engelm. A tree in its habitat, 20–25 m, occasionally higher, distinguished particularly by the only 5–6 mm thick, reddish bark, not cracked or furrowed, covered with loosely appressed scales, stem 0.6 to 1 m thick, narrowly conical crown; needles between 1.4 and 2.2 mm wide; cones symmetrical, scale ends flat, seeds released soon after the

cones are ripe and then quickly abscising. SDK 1: 60 (C) (= *P. murrayana* Balf.). This variety stretches from the Cascade Mts. and the Columbia River in the north, to the higher mountains of southern California.

P. coulteri D. Don Big-Cone Pine, Coulter's Pine. Tall tree, 25–30 m in its habitat, stem always straight, single, with thick, dark brown to black bark, crown open, pyramidal, nearly spruce-like, branches stiff, wide spreading; young shoots very thick, bluish-white pruinose, glabrous, orange-brown in the 2nd year, buds oval-oblong, long acuminate, 25–40 mm long, resinous, scales tightly appressed, fringed on the margin; needles in 3's, stiff, persisting for 2–3 years, 15–20 (30) cm long, about 2 mm wide, curved, dark blue-green, margin finely serrate, short and sharply acuminate, stomatal lines on all sides, resin ducts in the parenchyma or at the epidermis, sheaths to 4 cm long at first; cones short stalked, very large and heavy, 25–35 cm long and to 15 cm thick (opening yet wider!), yellow-brown, seed scales large and drawn out to a long, stout, hook-like curved tip, seeds oval, about 2 cm long, 2 cm wide, black, with about 3 cm long wings, edible. SN 105 (H); DJ 88; SPi 329–332; SPa 18; MPi 301–305; CCE 332. California and NW. Mexico, coastal mountains. 1832. Very beautiful tree; similar to *P. jeffreyi* (but the buds always resinous) and *P. sabiniana* (but with thicker branches and stiffer, upward directed needles). Plate 100; Fig. 146 and 161. z8

P. culmincola Andresen & Beaman. Shrub, 1–5 m, widely branched, with a dense crown; needles in 5's (occasionally 4–6), bluish-green, obtuse acuminate, sheaths about 6 mm long at first, later reflexed and like a rosette at the needle base, persistent; cones nearly globose, 3–4 cm long, with few scales, similar to those of *P. cembroides*. MP 205 (H). Mexico, Nuevo Leon, in the mountains at 3300 to 3700 m together with *P. cembroides*. z7

P. densiflora S. & Z. Japanese Red Pine. Tree, 20–30 m in its habitat, often much shorter in cultivation, crown irregular and flat spreading, somewhat resembling *P. sylvestris* in appearance, as in the reddish, thin exfoliating bark, young shoots green and pruinose, later orange-yellow and glabrous; buds oval-oblong, 12 mm long, acute, red-brown, resinous, scale ends often distinct and reflexed; needles in 2's, densely brush-like on the shoot tips, persisting for 3 years, 6–12 cm long, 1 mm wide, serrate, finely acuminate, with indistinct stomatal lines on both sides, resin ducts at the epidermis, sheaths on younger needles 15 mm long, often loosening to 2 filamentous scales; cones solitary or grouped in whorls, short stalked, directed downward, 3–5 cm long, oval to conical, opening the 2nd winter, scales thin, scale ends flat, the crosswise ridge sharp, but only slightly protuberant, umbo with a short thorn or obtuse point, seeds ovate, 6 mm long, brown, with 18 mm long wings. OCC 305; KIF 1: 28; CCE 333, 334. Japan, Korea. 1852. Plate 85 and 102; Fig. 157. z7

Of the 90 cultivars listed by Mayr in 1890, only a few are known in cultivation; den Ouden and Boom list 20 of these which are still relatively unknown.

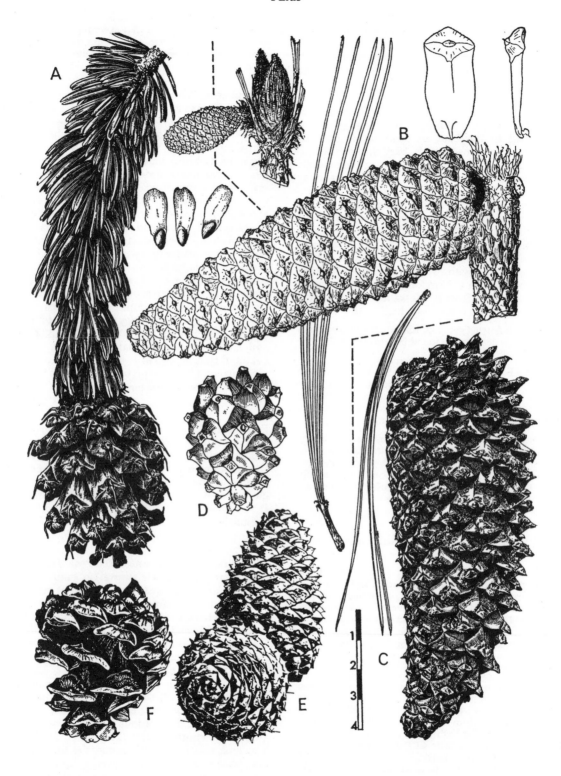

Fig. 144. **Pinus.** A. *P. aristata,* twig with cone and 3 seeds; B. *P. michoacana,* ripe cone, left young cone and bud, right above seed scales, middle a needle fascicle; C. *P. attenuata;* D. *P. cembroides* var. *edulis,* cone; E. *P. rigida,* 2 cones; F. *P. bungeana,* cone (from Sudworth, Martinez and Silva Tarouca)

'Alice Verkade'. Dwarf form, develops a very tight globe, 70 cm high and equally wide in 10 years; foliage a conspicuously fresh, light green, needles somewhat shorter than those of the type. An interesting form from the USA.

'Aurea'. Foliage light golden-yellow or with yellow spots in the normal green foliage.

'f. erecta'. Grows somewhat more erect than the normal form. According to information from Prof. Dr. S.-K. Hyun, of Seoul, National University (1980) this is a natural hybrid between *P. densiflora* and *P. thunbergii*. Its natural range is along the east coast of Korea where the parents' ranges overlap. Similar to *P. densiflora*.

'Globosa'. Hemispherical habit; needles only half as long as those of the species. Hardy.

'Oculus-draconis'. "Dragon eye Pine". Each needle with 2 yellow spots, appearing from above like 2 yellow rings on a green background. WM 339 (H); KN Plate 6.

'Pendula'. Branches pendulous, partly lying on the ground; needles to 10 cm long. WM 341 (H). 1890.

'Umbraculifera'. "Tanyosho". Shrubby, multistemmed, to 4 m high and 6 m wide, flat umbrella form, very slow growing, branches smooth, light brown, buds dark brown, without resin; needles 3–10 cm long, thin, somewhat overlapping, bright green, margin serrate. HD 134 (H); CCE 333; WM 26C (Br), 342 (H) (= *P. densiflora* var. *umbraculifera* Mayr). Common in cultivation and very attractive. Plate 86.

P. × digenea Beck (*P. uncinata* × *P. sylvestris*). Small tree, older branches with brownish-gray bark; needles 4–5 cm long, gray to dark green; cones asymmetrical, 4–5 cm long, gray-brown, scale ends pyramidal on the sunny side, all of the cone bases curved together, shaded scale ends convex or somewhat concave. On the border of N. E. Austria and Bohemia. Known since 1888. z4?

P. douglasiana Martinez. Tree, 20 m in its habitat, trunk 30–50 cm in diameter, with a dense crown, trunk with rough bark, bark of the young shoots very furrowed; needles 25–33 cm long; coarse and thick, sheaths 2–3 cm long, persistent; cones broadly ovate, somewhat asymmetrical, slightly curved, 7.5–10 cm long, usually grouped 3–5 together, stalk 12 mm long, scales with an irregular, 4 sided umbo, seeds 5 mm long, with 25 mm long wing. MPi 142–143; CCE 334. Mexico, in the mountains at 1700–2400 m. z7

P. durangensis Martinez. "Pino Real". Tree, 20–40 m in its habitat, trunk 40–70 cm in diameter, occasionally to 1.3 m, bark 15–25 mm thick, coffee-brown, crown dense and rounded, young shoots rough furrowed, dark gray with a bluish trace; needles usually in fascicles of 6, sometimes 5 or 7, occasionally also 8, finely serrate, acute, 10 to 22.5 cm long, about 1 mm thick, sheaths on young needles 16–25 mm long, but reduced to 10–16 mm long with age, cones ovate or more conical, usually 7–8 cm long, red-brown, with 6–10 cm long stalks, scales hard, 18–22 mm long, 12–14 mm wide, flattened, scale ends conically raised, seeds 5 mm long, with 12–24 mm long wings. MP 212 (H); MPi 180–184. Mexico, Durango, in the mountains at 1800–2700 m. Young trees in Mexico will grow 50–60 cm per year, even 120 cm in the first year! Very closely related to *P. montezumae*. Fig. 159. z8

P. echinata Mill. Short-leaf Pine. Tree, 15–30 m, crown conical and spruce-like, trunk with light brown bark, often with short shoots on the trunk and the larger branches, bark with many resin blisters, branches in regular whorls, thin, horizontal or often also pendulous, young shoots light green, bluish-white pruinose, later dark brown, bark exfoliating in the 3rd year, buds brown, oval-oblong, acute, 6 mm long, resinous, scales tightly appressed; needles in 2's, occasionally also 3–4 on young plants, persisting 2–5 years, dark blue-green, soft and flexible, not twisted, 7 to 12 cm long, short acuminate, margin finely serrate, with stomatal lines on both sides, sheath about 6 cm long, cones in clusters, nearly sessile, ovate to globose, obtuse, 4 to 6 cm long, to 3 cm thick, usually persistent, scale ends flat or somewhat thickened, nearly rhombic, with a sharp, but not protruding cross-ridge and a raised, incurved thorn, this often abscising before the cones are ripe, seeds small, ovate, 4–8 mm long, wing to 12 mm long. LT 28; MP 185 (H); GTP 60; SPi 260–263; CCE 335 (= *P. mitis* Michx.). SE. USA. 1739. Fig. 146 and 155. z8–9

P. elliottii Engelm. Slash Pine. Tree, 15–30 m in its habitat, stem 60–90 cm in diameter, free of branches for a considerable height, bark gray and furrowed at first, later orange-brown and exfoliating in large plates, young shoots thick, orange-brown at first, later gray-brown, rough and scaly, buds white fringed; needles grouped 2 or 3 together, densely crowded at the branch tips, usually persisting only 1 year, about 17–20(–25) cm long, stiff, dark green, somewhat glossy, finely serrate, stomatal lines on all sides, resin ducts in the parenchyma, sheath persistent, 12 mm long, light brown, later gray; cones nearly terminal, outspread or reflexed, conical to narrowly ovate, usually 7–11 cm long, 3–5 cm thick, when closed, but twice as wide when open, abscising, some scales often left on the twig, scale ends raised, terminating in a thick, gray, 1–2 mm long thorn, seeds ovate, somewhat triangular, about 6 mm long, black or gray speckled, with 15–30 mm long wings. LT 29 (= *P. taeda* var. *heterophylla* Elliott; *P. heterophylla* [Elliott] Sudw. non Koch non Presl.). SE. USA, from S. Carolina to Florida, and westward to Louisiana. Often confused with *P. caribaea*, which usually has 3 needles and is totally tropical. Plate 102. z9

var. **densa** Little & Dorman. Young plants are without a stem for a year and look like tufts of grass, old trees to 30 m with a 60 cm diameter trunk, crown broadly conical, loose, irregular and small; needles in 2's, occasionally 3. WT 6; CCE 334. S. Florida

P. engelmannii Carr. Apache Pine. Tree, 15–21 m, trunk 0.6–0.8 in diameter, bark rough, deeply furrowed; needles 30–37 cm long, grouped 3–4 together, occasionally 5, dense and very finely serrate on the margin, with 12 stomatal lines on the exterior and 6 on each of the inner surfaces, bright green or bluish or somewhat yellowish, resin ducts in the parenchyma, sheath 3 to 4 cm long, persistent, brown; cones hard and heavy, broadly ovate to oblong conical, 13–17 cm long, coffee-brown, scale ends stretched out to a thick, recurved umbo, seeds ovate, 5–7 mm long, with a 20–30 mm long, brown wing. MP 218 (H); MPi 229–234 (= *P. apacheca* Lemm.; *P. macrophylla* Engelm.; *P. ponderosa* var.

macrophylla [Engelm.] Shaw). SW. USA and Mexico. Very similar to *P. ponderosa*, but the needles are longer and grouped 3–4. z8

P. flexilis James. Limber Pine. Tree, 10–25 m, trunk 1–1.5 m in diameter, crown of young trees conical, becoming broadly rounded with age, bark dark gray on old trunks, furrowed, young shoots yellow-green, glabrous or pubescent, very flexible, buds broadly ovate, acute 9 mm long; needles in 5's, persisting about 5–6 years, densely crowded at the branch tips, directed forward, stiff, straight to somewhat bowed, 3–7.5 cm long, 1 mm wide, sharply acuminate, entire, with stomatal lines on all sides, blue-green, resin ducts at the epidermis, needle sheaths abscising; male flowers reddish, female purple; cones terminal, nearly sessile, erect at first, later pendulous, 7–15 cm long, 4–6 cm wide, light brown, glossy, seed scales thick, woody, perpendicular to the rachis when open, rounded at the apex, with an obtuse, dark umbo, seeds oval, 10–15 mm long with the rudimentary wing. SM 94 (H); BM 8467; SPa 5–6; MPi 72–77; MP 139 (H); CCE 335–337. Rocky Mts., Alberta to Colorado, USA, 1861. Quite variable species. Plate 102; Fig. 149.z2

'Firmament.'. Blue needle selection, resistant to "blister rust" which attacks the species.

'Glenmore'. Needles longer, 11.5 cm long, a good silvery-blue. Plant Patent Nr. 221 'Silver Limber Pine'. Discovered in 1944 by E. Moore in Colorado; introduced by Scott Wilmore of Wilmore Nurseries, Wheatbridge, Colorado, USA 1949.

'Nana'. Bushy dwarf form, needles only 3 cm long (= *P. flexilis nana* Noble 1951). Discovered by James R. Noble in 1947 in the Sierra Nevada around Echo Lake. In 1950 the plant was 23 cm high and 35 cm wide.

'Pendula'. Weak grower (so far as is known), stem and branches pendulous, usually trained upward at first; foliage like the type. Found in the USA.

'Tiny Temple'. Very low form, annual growth about 10 cm; needles short, 6–7 cm long, 0.7 to 1 mm wide, dark green outside, inside gray-blue. USA.

P. gerardiana Wallich ex D. Don. Tree, 10 to 20 m, crown dense and rounded, branches short and spreading horizontally, thick, bark thin, silver-gray, exfoliating plate-like (similar to *P. bungeana*), young shoots rather thick, glabrous, olive-green, later yellow-brown, buds oval-conical, acute; needles in 3's, erect-outspread, green, 6–10 cm long, finely serrate, persisting 3 years, sheaths abscising in the 2nd year; cones obtuse oval-oblong, 12–20 cm long, 7 to 11 cm wide, ripening the 2nd year, very resinous, scale ends very thick and woody, pyramidal, with a sharp cross-ridge, often reflexed, umbo triangular, short acuminate, seeds cylindrical, 20–25 mm long, 8–9 mm wide, edible ("Chilgoza"-nuts to the Indians of Afghanistan), wings very small. SPi 133–137; CCE 338. NW. Himalaya; Kashmir, Tibet, N. Afghanistan; on dry gravelly soil in the mountains. Fig. 147 and 155. z8–9

P. glabra Walter. Tree, 25–40 m, stem 40–70 cm in diameter, bark red-brown, smooth and tight, thicker on the lower trunk, more gray and thinner on the upper trunk, young shoots with scattered buds between the nodes, buds acutely ovate, brown; needles always in 2's

(!), persisting 2–3 years, thin, soft, twisted, 4–7.5 cm long, short acuminate, margin finely serrate, with stomatal lines on either side, resin ducts in the parenchyma, dark green, sheaths short; cones usually solitary, ovate, reflexed, brown-yellow, symmetrical, 4–5 cm long, short stalked, scales soft and flexible, scale ends slightly thickened, with a small, later abscising prickle, seeds triangular, rough, with a 12 mm long wing. MP 187 (H); WT 7. USA; S. Carolina, Florida, Louisiana. z9

P. greggii Engelm. ex Parl. Tree, 12–15 m, bark rough and furrowed at the base of older trunks, otherwise gray and smooth, young shoots thin, often with side shoots, buds thin, cylindrical, sharply acuminate, not resinous, scale ends distinct; needles in 3's, light green, persisting 2–3 years, 7–15 cm long, short acuminate, margin finely serrate, with thin stomatal lines on all sides, resin ducts in the parenchyma, sheath 12 mm long in the first year, only 6 mm in the 2nd; cones in clusters of 5–8 or more, oval-conical, 7–15 cm long, irregular in form, recurved, yellow-brown, persisting closed on the branch for several years, seeds ovate, 6 mm long, 20 mm long with the wing. MPi 281–285; CCE 336 (= *P. patula* var. *macrocarpa* Mast.) Mexico. Similar to *P. patula*, except for the smooth, gray upper trunk. Fig. 149. z9

P. × hakkodensis Makino (*P. parviflora* × *P. pumila*). Natural hybrid, intermediate between the parents, shrubby, low, similar to *P. pumila*, but the needles are longer, coarser and twisted. Japan, northern Honshu. Very interesting for the garden. Plate 85. z6

P. halepensis Miller. Aleppo Pine. Tree, 10–15 m, crown conical when young, but arched more umbrella-shape or globose when older, irregularly thinly branched, stem often bowed or twisted, bark smooth and silver-gray at first, eventually more red-brown and fissured, branches upright-outspreading, dense, young shoots only 2–3 mm thick, long, lightly pruinose, light gray to greenish-brown, glabrous to finely pubescent, buds ovate, 5–10 mm long, not resinous, scales with reflexed tips, "spider web"-like fringe on the margin; needles in 2's, occasionally 3, outspread, persisting for 2 years, often clustered at the branch tips, with short horn-like tips, thin 6–10 cm long, margin finely serrate, with stomatal lines on both sides, resin ducts at the epidermis or in the parenchyma, sheaths 8 mm long, persistent; cones grouped 1–3, short stalked, outspread or pendulous, normally straight, broadly conical-oblong in the 3rd year, 8–10 cm long, to 4 cm thick, red-brown to almost yellow, often persisting for several years on the branch after ripening, scale ends rhombic, smooth or with radiating rugose wrinkles, flat, umbo somewhat raised, medium size or small, gray, thornless, seed blackish, 6–7 mm long, wings 18–28 mm long, red-brown. SN 58 (H); SPi 279–283; SDK 1: 61. Mediterranean region, Asia minor, from Portugal to Afghanistan; frequently planted in this region for reforestation. 1732. Plate 108; Fig. 145 (range map), 157. z8–9

var. *brutia* see: **P. brutia**

var. **eldarica** Medwed. Differing from the type in the stiffer, thicker, 8.5–10 cm long needles, more or less appressed to the shoot; cones usually grouped 2–3 (rarely only 1), erect-

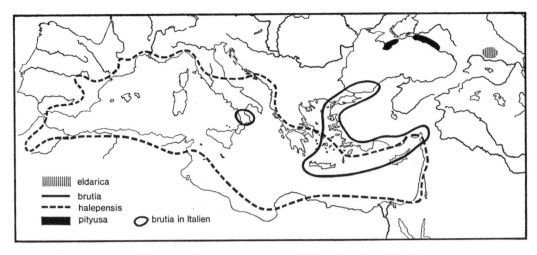

Fig. 145. Range of *Pinus halepensis,* var. *eldarica, P. brutia* and *P. pityusa*

outspread on short stalks, not pendulous, 5–6 cm long, ovate-oblong, scale ends with raised keel, slightly concave umbo, and radially arranged furrows. MP 258 (H) (= *P. eldarica* Medwed.). Transcaucasus; on the slopes of the Eilar-Ugi Mts. and on the right bank of the Jora River. z8–9

var. **halepensis.** Young shoots 2–3 mm thick, light gray, buds ovate, 5–10 mm long; needles 5–8 cm long, 0.8 mm wide, somewhat gray-green; cones stalked, as long as the needles or only slightly shorter, with a somewhat raised umbo.

var. *pityusa* see: **P. pityusa**

var. *stankewiczii* see: **P. stankewiczii**

P. heldreichii Christ. Tree, to 20 m, trunk upright or ascending, crown obtuse pyramidal, never umbrella-form, bark of older trees ash gray, splitting into angular sections 5–15 × 4–8 cm in size with furrows between, young shoots usually pruinose, very rough from the large leaf cushions after needle drop, becoming brown in the 2nd year (!!), buds oval-oblong, brown with white tips to nearly gray-white, not resinous; needles in 2's, not (!!) clustered brush-like at the branch tips like *P. leucodermis,* persisting 5–6 years, stiff, usually curved to the twig, lighter green when young than those of *P. nigra austriaca,* later glossy green, 6–9 cm long, 1.5 mm wide, prickly or obtuse, margin somewhat dentate, with stomatal lines on both sides, resin ducts in the parenchyma, sheaths 12 mm long, cones grouped 1–2, occasionally in whorls of 3, ovate, 7–8 cm long, 2.5 cm wide, yellowish-brown, scale ends flat, cross-keeled to 15 mm wide, with a short, acute, concave umbo, seeds elliptic, 6–7 mm long, with 20–30 mm long wings. BFN 110 (= *P. laricio* var. *heldreichii* [Christ] Mast.). W. Balkan Peninsula; Albania; Thessalian Olympus Mts., Greece. Growing with *Pinus nigra* and *Abies cephalonica* in its native habitat. Much rarer in cultivation than the very similar *P. leucodermis,* but equally hardy; slow growing, likes a dry, gravelly soil. Plate 103; Fig. 146 and 157. z6

P. heldreichii var. *leucodermis* (Ant.) Markgraf see: **P. leucodermis** Ant.

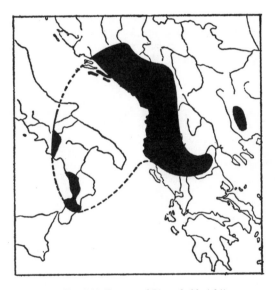

Fig. 146. Range of *Pinus heldreichii* (from Fukarek)

P. × holfordiana A. B. Jacks. (*P. ayacahuite × P. wallichiana*). Intermediate between the parents, but more similar to *P. wallichiana,* differing in the usually pubescent young shoots, the wider cones with acute scale ends (not rounded with protruding point); differing from *P. ayacahuite* in the non-reflexed tips of the seed scales and the smaller seeds with longer, more narrow wings. CBI 68 to 69; CCE 343. Developed in the Westonbirt Arboretum, England in 1906 but first described in 1933. 50-year old trees are about 24 m high and nearly 20 m wide. z7

P. × hunnewellii A. G. Johnson (? *P. parviflora × P. strobus*). Strongly growing tree, intermediate between the parents (presumably), crown open, dark brown, scaly young shoots pubescent; needles 7.5–8.5 cm long, bowed, somewhat twisted, blue-green; cones nearly sessile, stouter than those of *P. strobus*, seeds larger, 7–9 mm long, purple-brown, with a long wing (as opposed to *P. parviflora*'s short wing), but producing few cones. Discovered in 1949 in the Hunnewell Arboretum, Wellesley, Massachusetts, USA.

P. insularis Endl. Tree, 10–25 m in its habitat, annual shoots continuous (not jointed); needles in 3's, thin, flexible, 18–20 cm long; cones grouped 2–3 together, varying from narrowly cylindrical-conical to broadly ovate-conical, 5–10 cm long, scale ends thick, with a small umbo. MP 298 (H). Phillipines; develops forests in the mountains on the islands of Luzon and Mindoro (but not on Timor, as suggested by Pilger). Closely related to *P. khasya* and included here by many authors. z9

P. jeffreyi Grev. & Balf. Jeffrey's Pine. Large tree, 30–60 m or more, stem to over 1 m in diameter, bark cinnamon-brown, splitting into large plates on older trees, rounded crown, branches stout, outspreading, often somewhat pendulous, young shoots blue-white pruinose in the 1st year (!!), gray-brown in the second year, buds large, oblong-conical, red-brown, not resinous, scales with distinct tips; needles normally in 3's, clustered at the shoot tips, persisting for 2 years, 18–22 cm long, somewhat shorter on side shoots, 2 mm wide, gray-green, stiff, not glossy, sharply acuminate, margin fine and sharply serrate, with 8 to 10 stomatal lines on the dorsal side, 4–6 on the inside, resin ducts in the parenchyma, sheaths 15 mm long, cones large, short stalked, usually spreading horizontally, oval-conical, 14–20 cm long, 4–8 cm thick, light brown, scales about 4 cm long, scale ends pyramidal with a stout, sharp cross-ridge, umbo with a slender, reflexed thorn, seeds oval-oblong to nearly triangular, 10–15 mm long, with about 3 cm long wings. MPi 225 to 228; SPa 14; DJ 87; OCC 314; CCE 343, 344 (= *P. ponderosa* var. *jeffreyi* [Murray] Vasey). USA; S. Oregon to Mexico, in the mountains and on the plains. 1852. Plate 103; Fig. 136 and 156. z6

P. khasya Royle. Small to medium sized tree, 35–40 m in its Burmese habitat, trunk to 1 m in diameter, with a thick, deeply furrowed bark, young shoots slender, glabrous, light brown, buds oblong-conical, acute, scales brown, with distinct tips; needles in 3's, usually only persisting for 1 year, very thin, 12–17 cm long, green to gray-green, with fine, long tips, margin finely serrate, stomatal lines on all sides, resin ducts at the epidermis, sheath 8–18 mm long; cones solitary or in 2's, rarely in 3's, ovate, symmetrical, light brown, 5–7.5 cm long, 3 cm thick, on short, stiff stalks, scales about 2 cm long, apophysis thick and cross keeled, seeds about 8 mm long, wing rounded at the apex. MP 296 (H) (= *P. kesiya* Royal ex Gordon; *P. khasia* Engelm.; *P. khasyana* Griffith). N. Burma; Khasia Mts. to Assam and Yunnan, N. Thailand, Laos. z9

P. koraiensis L. & Z. Korean Pine. Tree, 20–30 m, similar to *P. cembra* in habit, but looser habit, bark rather smooth, gray-brown, branches strong horizontal to erect, young shoots stout, green, densely red-brown pubescent, but usually quite glabrous in the 3rd year, buds ovate-cylindrical, with short, sharp tips, 10–18 mm long, very

resinous, bud scales lanceolate, acute, the apical ones outspread, the others appressed; needles in 5's, rather loosely arranged, abscising in the 2nd year, rather stiff, 6–12 cm long, about 1 mm wide, with rather obtuse tips, margins finely and densely serrate (rough to the touch!), green on the dorsal side, other sides conspicuously blue-white with 5–7 stomatal lines, resin ducts in the parenchyma, sheaths quickly abscising; male and female flowers red or reddish; cones terminal, nearly sessile, erect, conical-cylindrical, obtuse, 9–14 cm long, 5–6 cm wide, yellow-brown, not opening, scales leathery-woody, convex on the dorsal side and with longitudinal stripes, margin sharp and somewhat undulate, tips reflexed, seeds obovate, 15–17 mm long, about 10 mm wide, gray-brown, not winged, edible. SPi 86; DJ 82; MP 267 (H); KIF 1: 32; CCE 344. Amur region, Manchuria, Korea and Japan (only Honshu Island), usually between 600 and 1000 m in altitude, but in Japan from 1200–1600 m. Very attractive pine, quite winter hardy. Plate 103; Fig. 147 and 160. z3

'**Compacta Glauca**'. Strong grower, but compact, branches short, thick, densely arranged; foliage an attractive blue-green (= *P. cembra* 'Compacta Glauca' in many nurseries). Cultivated since 1949.

'**Silveray**'.. Selection with thick, better blue needles. Originally distributed by Herm. A Hesse, Hanover, W. Germany.

'**Tortuosa**'. Needles very spirally twisted, especially on the branch tips (= *P. koraiensis tortuosa* Schelle, 1909).

'**Variegata**'. Needles either totally light yellow, yellow bordered or yellow spotted (= *P. koraiensis variegata* Nichols. 1904). Originated in 1887. (EX)

'**Winton**' (Hillier 1964). Dwarf form, habit broader than high, to 4 m wide and 2 m high (in the Hillier Arboretum); needles like the species. WM 28A (Br). 1964.

P. krempfii Lecomte. A tall tree in its habitat, bark smooth, brown, slightly furrowed; needles in 2's, 3–7 cm long and 2 to 5 mm wide, quite flat, margin finely serrate, with numerous stomatal lines on the inside, dorsal side with only a few, with 8 resin ducts, of these 2 are under the dorsal epidermis and 6 on the inside epidermis, sheath absent; cones ovate, 7–9 cm long, 3–4 cm wide, similar to those of *P. balfouriana*, scales thickened at the end and with an umbo, seeds with a 6 mm long wing. MP 542 (Br) (= *Ducampopinus krempfii* [Lecomte] Chevalier). South Vietnam, in the mountains, northeast of Dalat. The most unique of all the *Pinus* species for its up to 5 mm wide needles! Because of the abnormally wide needles many botanists have considered the possibility of a generic hybrid with *Pseudolarix* or *Keteleeria*. z9

P. lambertiana Dougl. Sugar Pine. Tree, 50–60(100, at about 500 years old) m, trunk 3–6 m in diameter, straight, often 30 m to the first branch on very tall trees, bark of younger trees smooth and light brown, thick and splitting on older specimens, branches short, in whorls, horizontal to somewhat nodding, young shoots rather stout, brown, short soft pubescent, buds ovate, only 3–8 mm long, acute, resinous, scales red-brown, tightly appressed; needles in 5's, very stiff and wide, twisted once on its axis, persisting 2–3 years, dark green, 7–10 cm long, to 2 mm wide, sharply acuminate, margin

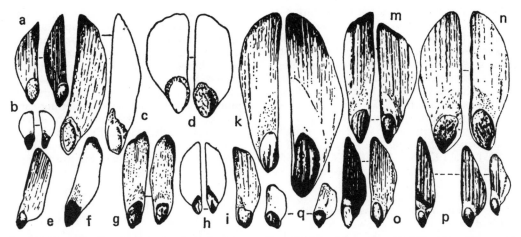

Fig. 146. **Pinus**. Seeds of a. *P. strobus*; b. *P. banksiana*; c. *P. wallichiana*; d. *P. peuce*; e. *P. rigida*; f. *P. pungens*; g. *P. radiata*;.h. *P. echinata*; i. *P. taeda*; k. *P. palustris*; l. *P. coulteri*; m. *P. pinaster*; n. *P. ponderosa*; o. *P. nigra*; p. *P. sylvestris*; q. *P. mugo* var. *mughus* (from Hickel, Graines et Plantules des Conifères)

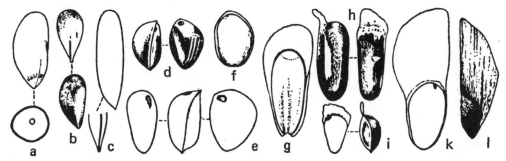

Fig. 147. **Pinus**. Seeds of a. *P. monophylla*, cross section below; b. *P. cembroides* var. *edulis*; c. *P. gerardiana*, base beneath in profile; d. *P. cembra*; e. *P. koraiensis*; f. *P. armandii*; g. *P.sabiniana*; h. *P. pinea*; i. *P. bungeana*; k. *P. lambertiana*; l. *P. canariensis* (from Hickel, Graines et Plantules des Conifères)

serrate, both inner sides with bluish-white stomatal lines, dorsal side without, resin ducts at the epidermis, sheaths about 18 mm long, abscising; cones terminal, pendulous on a 9 cm long stalk, 30–50 cm long (!!), 8–11 cm wide, light brown, abscising in the 3rd year, scales leathery, broadly cuneate, scale ends somewhat thickened, convex on the dorsal side, apex obtuse and slightly reflexed, wide spreading on open cones, seeds oval-oblong, 15 mm long, 10 mm wide, black, edible, sweet, wings 2 cm long, brown, obtuse. SN 252 (H), 253 (H); SPa 3–4; SPi 100–102; MPi 94–99; MP 141 (H). Western N. America, from the Rocky Mts. to the Pacific, and from the Columbia River to Mexico, in the mountains. 1827. The wounded bark exudes a crystal clear, slightly resinous, substance, occasionally of economic use. Plate 108; Fig. 147 and 160. z7

P. lawsonii Roezl. Tree, 20–25 m, trunk to 50 cm or more in diameter, bark dark gray and scaly, young shoots bluish pruinose; needles in 3's, but also 4–5, bluish-green, to 24 cm long, 1–1.5 mm wide, margin finely serrate, resin ducts usually 4, in the parenchyma, sheath persistent, 12–16 mm long, cones quite variable in size, scales usually asymmetrical, 5 to 7 cm long, oval-conical, scale ends slightly keeled to pyramidally raised and with a large umbo; stalk 7–12 mm long, seeds 5 mm long, with

15–18 mm long brown wings. MPi 133–137. South Mexico, in the mountains at 1200–3000 m. z9

P. leiophylla Schlechtend. & Chamisso. Tree, 15–25 m, crown irregular, bark dark brown, frequently with short shoots and clustered needles on the stem (like *P. rigida*), young shoots thin, blue-green; needles in 5's, persisting for 2 years, thin, gray-green, 10–14 cm long, margin quite finely serrate, short acuminate, stomatal lines on all sides, resin ducts usually in 2's, in the parenchyma, sheath 15–20 mm long, orange, abscising quickly; cones nearly terminal or laterally arranged, solitary or in groups, ovate, 4–6 cm long, on thin, 12–20 mm long stalks, ripening the 3rd year and frequently remaining closed on the branch for a year, scales 20 mm long, the thickened portion dark brown, scale ends more or less flat, light brown, umbo with an abscising form, seeds ovate, light brown, with a rough, speckled surface, 4 mm long, and a 12 mm long wing. MP 206 (H); MPi 104–108 (= *P. fenzlii* Ant. & Kotschy). Mexico; in the mountains at 2000–3600 m. Fig. 159. z9

P. leucodermis Ant. Bosnian Pine. Tree, to 30 m, trunk to 50 cm in diameter or more, bark more gray, leaving yellowish patches after exfoliating in irregular scales, young shoots gray-white, thick and glabrous, appearing like a snakeskin after the needles fall (persisting 5–6 years) from the very closely spaced leaf cushions, buds similar to those of *P. nigra*, but darker in color and resin free; needles in 2's, very densely arranged and brush-like clustered at the branch tips, stiff, 6–8 cm long, margins finely serrate, sharply acuminate, with stomatal lines on all sides, sheaths 10–12 mm long; cones oblong-ovate, black when young (!), 5–7.5 cm long, short stalked, dull brown, slightly glossy, scale ends of the basal scales pyramidal and with some tips, usually incurved at the base of the cone, seeds like those of *P. nigra*. NF 7: 82; BMns 190; OCC 313 (C); CCE 341, 342 (= *P. heldreichii* var. *leucodermis* [Ant.] Markgraf ex Fitsch.). Yugoslavia; Albania, Bulgaria, Greece, Italy on dry alkaline soil. Introduced in 1865 by Maly to the Vienna Botanic Garden, Austria. Very closely related to *P. heldreichii* and included here as a variety by many authors, but distinctly differing in the "snakeskin"-like shoots, needles clustered at the branch tips, and cones with different scale ends. One of Europe's most common ornamental pines. Plate 108. z6

Includes the following forms:

'Aureospicata'. Slow growing, broadly conical; needles with yellow tips (= *P. leucodermis aureospicata* Hesse). Introduced by Herm A. Hesse of Hanover, W. Germany in 1955.

'Compact Gem'. Dwarf form, compact and slow growing, 25 cm high and 30 cm wide in 10 years; foliage black-green. WM 26D (Br), 345 (H). Introduced in 1964 by Hillier under the name *P. leucodermis* 'Compacta' and 'Dwarf Form'.

'Pygmy'. Dwarf form, globose and very dense, buds 10 mm long, 5 mm wide, drawn out in a long tip, scales tightly appressed; leaf sheaths 7 mm long, white, arranged in a ring around the buds, needles dark green, 4–5 cm long, equally formed, stiff. Origin not certain.

'Satellit'. Especially narrow, conical habit; dark green. Cultivated in Holland.

'Schmidtii'. Compact habit, oval, very slow growing and densely branched; needles deep green, sharp. WM 347 (H) (= *P. leucodermis* 'Pygmy' Hillier; *P. heldreichii* var. *leucodermis* f. *Schmidtii* Pilat, 1964). Discovered in 1926 by Eugen Schmidt in the mountains near Sarajevo, Yugoslavia (then Bosnia) as a 3 m tall, over 100-year old tree. (R)

P. longaeva see: **P. aristata** var. **longaeva**

P. longifilia Roxb. = **P. roxburghii**

P. longifolia Salisb. = **P. palustris**

P. luchuensis Mayr. Luchu Pine, Okinawa Pine. Tree, to 30 m, slender stem, umbrella-shaped crown, bark thin and pure gray on young stems and the upper trunk, exfoliating in plates when older, buds reddish, resinous, scales tightly appressed; needles in 2's, 15–20 cm long, resin ducts in the parenchyma or 1 occasionally at the epidermis; cones oval-conical, about 5 cm long, scale ends glossy brown, cross keeled. LT 31; MP 284 (H). Japan; Ryukyu Islands, Okinawa (chain of islands between S. Japan and Taiwan), but many stands of this species were destroyed during World War II. z9

P. lumholtzii Robinson & Fernal. Lumholtz Pine. Tree, 15–20 m, trunk 25–40 cm in diameter, crown wide, loose and open, branches outspread, lower ones sloping dowward, young shoots somewhat pendulous, more or less

chestnut-brown, bluish pruinose; needles all hang vertically, 20–30 cm long, grouped in 3's, occasionally only 2, rarely 4, bright green or more yellow-green, margin finely serrate, with 4–9 resin ducts, most in the parenchyma, sheaths 2.5–3 cm long, abscising, chestnut-brown, the same color as the shoots and buds; cones ovate, symmetrical, 5 cm long, pendulous, on slender, more or less bowed stalks, abscising early, scale ends thickened with a raised center, brown with a darker center. MP 206 (H); MPi 116–122. Mexico; in the mountains of the West and Northwest. Very attractive pine, similar to *P. patula*, but with longer and more pendulous needles. z9

P. massoniana Lamb. Masson's Pine. Tree, 9 to 24 m, crown ovate to flattened, trunk free of branches for some height, bark gray at the base of the trunk, splitting into thick, irregular plates, but reddish on the major crown branches (similar to *P. sylvestris*) and exfoliating into thin strips, branches horizontal, young shoots brown, not pruinose, buds oblong, acute, light brown, somewhat resinous; needles in 2's, very rarely in 3's, very thin, 15–20 cm long, yellow-green to dark green, finely serrate, resin ducts marginal; cones oval-oblong, 3.5–6 cm long, abscising early, scale ends thickened, red-brown, with a cross-ridge, umbos at the cone base smooth and thornless, hooked or with a few points toward the cone apex and appressed to the next lower scale, seeds dark brown, 5 mm long, with a 12 mm long wing. LT 32; CIS 6; LF 30; SPi 176–178; MP 280 (H); CCE 341 (= *P. sinensis* Lamb.). SE. China, from Kwangsi westward through the Yangtse River Valley to Szechwan. 1829. z8–9

P. merkusii Jungh. & Vriese. Tropical tree, 18–30 m in its habitat, crown conical when young, but broad or round with age, bark of older trees gray or brown, rather thick and deeply fissured; needles in 2's, 17–25 cm long, persisting 1.5–2 years, abruptly acuminate, margin finely serrate, resin ducts marginal or in the parenchyma or intermediate, sheath 12–18 mm long; cones solitary or in groups of 2, 5–7 cm long, narrowly cylindrical, frequently curved, scales woody, oblong, scale ends rhombic, furrowed, seeds with small wings. MP 289 (H), 364 (St), 447 (H), CCE 342 (= *P. sumatrana* Jungh.). Sumatra, Indonesia, Phillipines, Thailand; develops forests in the low hills on good soil. z9

P. michoacana Martinez. Tree, 20–30 m in its habitat, with rough, red-brown, scaly bark, young shoots rough from the remnants of the leaf sheaths which persist for many years; needles in 5's, outspread and nodding, 30–35 cm long, bright green on the dorsal side, blue-green inside, margins finely serrate, with 3 resin ducts, sheaths persistent, 25–30 mm long, red-brown when young, darkening later; cones ovate or oblong-ovate, 25–30cm long, 10–12 cm thick, brown at first, later more gray, lightly resinous, usually grouped 2–3 together, persistent, on 10–15 mm long stalks, scale ends broadly conical, but flat, umbo irregularly rectangular, seeds triangular, 9–10 mm long, about 6 mm wide, black speckled, with 4–5 cm long, brown wings, only 10–12mm wide. MPi 203–218; CCE 342. Mexico. Fig. 144. z9

Martinez included 5 forms and varieties with this species which will not be covered in this work.

Plate 97

Picea sitchensis;
very old trees in their native habitat in the Hoh Valley, Olympic National Park, Washington, USA
Photo: National Park Service

Plate 98

Picea smithiana
in the Hoersholm Arboretum, Denmark

Picea sitchensis in its native habitat
Photo: U. S. Forest Service

Picea orientalis 'Aurea'
in the Dortmund Bot. Garden, W. Germany

Picea spinulosa
in Bicton Park, England

Plate 99

Pinus armandii
in Kew Gardens, London

Pinus ayacahuite
in the Dr. Folly Arboretum, Badacsonyors,
Hungary
Photo: Dr. Folly

Pinus balfouriana
in the Royal Bot. Garden, Edinburgh, Scotland

Pinus banksiana
in the Neumünster Cemetery, W. Germany

Plate 100

Pinus cembra
in Tyrol, Switzerland

Pinus sibirica
in the Leningrad Botanic Garden, USSR

Pinus cembra 'Compacta Glauca'
in the Blijdenstein Pinetum, Hilversum, Holland

Pinus coulteri
in the Hillier Arboretum, England

Plate 101

Pinus cembroides var. *edulis*
in the Royal Bot. Garden, Edinburgh, Scotland

Pinus contorta (above); *Pinus albicaulis* (below),
both in their respective habitats in Canada
Photo: Forestry Branch, Canada

Pinus monophylla
in the Royal Botanic Garden, Edinburgh, Scotland

Plate 102

Pinus densiflora in its native habitat in Japan
Photo: K. Uyehara, Tokyo

Left, *Pinus flexilis* in the Morton Arboretum, Lisle, Illinois, USA;
right, *Pinus elliottii* in its native habitat in Florida, USA
(the latter photo from the U.S. Forest Service)

Plate 103

Pinus jeffreyi
in the Angeles National Forest, California, USA
Photo: U.S. Forest Service

Pinus koraiensis
in the Amance Arboretum, France

Pinus heldreichii (left and right) and *P. peuce* (middle) in the Pirin Mts., Bulgaria
Photo: K. Browicz, Poland

Plate 104

Pinus nigra ssp. *nigra*
in the Perucica National Park, Yugoslavia

Pinus nigra ssp. *pallasiana*
near Izmir, Turkey
Photo: Nitzelius

Pinus nigra ssp. *laricio*
in the Herluftsholm Arboretum, Denmark

Pinus nigra ssp. *salzmannii*
in Les Barres Arboretum, France

Plate 105

Pinus monticola
in the Sierra National Forest, Califórnia, USA
Photo: U. S. Forest Service

Pinus roxburghii (= P. longifolia)
in the Princess Park, Pretoria, S. Africa

Pinus ponderosa in the Yosemite National Park, California, USA
Photo: U.S. Forest Service

Plate 106

Pinus peuce
on the Cakor Pass in Yugoslavia

Pinus parviflora
in Japan, Hondo, at 1200 m elevation
Photo: E. H. Wilson

Pinus pumila on the tree line in the Daisetsu volcanic chain, Hokkaido, Japan
Photo: Nitzelius, Göteborg

Plate 107

Pinus radiata, trunk at 120 cm in diameter
in Killerton Park, England

Pinus resinosa
in its native habitat in Canada

Pinus thunbergu in the Osumi Province, Japan, on Yaku-shima Island
Photo: E. H. Wilson

Plate 108

Pinus halepensis
near Dubrovnik, Yugoslavia

Pinus lambertiana
in its native habitat in the Lassen Volcanic
National Park, California, USA
Photo: Uwe Horstmann

Pinus leucodermis,
an especially old specimen
at the Decani Monastery near Pec, Yugoslavia

Pinus monophylla
in the White Mountains, California, USA
Photo: Karl Fuchs

Plate 109

Pinus cembra
at 1930 m high
in the Oetztaler Alps, Austria

Pinus pinea
in the Villa Thuret Garden in Cap d'Antibes,
southern France

Pinus nigra ssp. *nigra*
National Arboretum,
Stuttgart-Hohenheim, W. Germany

Pinus nigra ssp. *pallasiana*
in the Berggarten, Hanover, W. Germany

Plate 110

Pinus montezumae,
whose needles are grouped 3–8 (!)
and can be up to 30 cm long

Pinus palustris
is one of the most important forest trees of the
southern USA; here in a "Longleaf Pine-Turkey
Oak Forest" on the Suwannee Canal, Georgia

Pinus palustris
has adapted to withstand forest fire by spending
the first 5 years in a "grassy stage" while
developing a thick barked stem before growing
upward; the illustrated plant is 8 years old

Pinus patula
in a forest planting on Madeira Island

Plate 111

Pinus peuce in its native habitat
on the Cakor Pass, Yugoslavia

Pseudolarix amabilis with young cones
in the nursery of L. von Ehren,
Hamburg, W. Germany

Taxus baccata 'Lutea'
in the National Arboretum,
Stuttgart-Hohenheim, W. Germany

Taxus baccata 'Fastigiata'
in the park of Keir Castle, Scotland

Plate 112

Pinus sabiniana in the Sequoia National Forest, California, USA
Photo: U.S. Forest Service

P. monophylla Torr. & Frém. Single-leaf Pine. Tree, to 15 m, usually multistemmed from the ground, flat crown; needles solitary, rarely also in 2's, circular in cross section, about 5 cm long, thick, stiff, prickly, gray-green and striped, usually bowed, very sharply acuminate, sheaths abscise quickly; cones to 5 cm long and very wide, scales woody, concave, scale ends woody and much thickened, umbo obtuse and curving downward. SPa 9; OCC 303; SN 264 (H); MPi 59–62; CCE 330; KN Plate 6 (*P. cembroides* var. *monophylla* [Torr.] Voss). USA, W. Utah, N. Arizona to southern California, on the mountain slopes and plains. 1848. Plate 101, 108; Fig. 143, 147. z7–8

P. montezumae Lamb. Montezuma Pine. Tree, 20–30 m, in its habitat, bark reddish-brown, rough, irregularly furrowed, young shoots red-brown, glabrous, furrowed, with the remnants of the fallen leaf sheaths, buds acutely ovate, 20–25 mm long, resin free, scales narrow, red-brown, margins fringed; needles grouped 3–8 (!), but usually in 5's (depending on the condition of the tree), persisting for 3 years, clustered on the shoots, bluish-green, 17–30 cm long, erect or outspread, acute, margins finely serrate, with stomatal lines on all sides, resin ducts in the parenchyma, sheaths 3–5 cm long in the 1st year, persistent; cones solitary or several together, variable in form, broadly ovate to narrowly conical, lightly asymmetrical, 8.5 to 15 cm long, brown, stalked, scale ends brown, dull to slightly glossy, flat or slightly convex, with a cross-ridge and abscising thorn on the umbo, seeds ovate, 6 mm long, brownish, black speckled, with 20 mm long and 7 mm wide wings. JRHS 83: 104 (H; col.); MP 212 (H); MPi 170–179; SKD 1: 50; FS 331; CCE 345–347; KN Plate 8. Mexico; in temperate and tropical regions at altitudes of 1200–3600 m. Plate 110, 128. z9

Includes the following varieties:

var. **hartwegii** (Lindl.) Engelm. Differs principally in the smaller, somewhat resinous buds; needles stiffer (!), usually grouped 3–4, green (not blue-green!), 10–15 cm long, sheaths only 10–17 mm long, cones broadly ovate, acute, somewhat asymmetrical, 7–14 cm long, dark brown to nearly black when ripe, seeds blackish, 5 to 7 mm long, wings 12 mm long and 5 mm wide. MPi 186–189 (= *P. hartwegii* Lindl.). Central Mexico, to 3800 m in the mountains. Commonly cultivated in England and hardier than the type. Fig. 155. z9

var. **lindleyi** Loud. Needles in 5's, 27 to 35 cm long, very thin, flexible and pendulous, dark green, sheaths 25–30 mm long, persistent, chestnut-brown; cones solitary or in 2's, broadly ovate, gradually narrowing toward the apex, 12–14 cm long, with 10–12 mm long stalks, usually pendulous and curved, light brown. MPi 178–179 (C)(= *P. lindleyana* Gord.). Mexico; temperate regions. z9

f. **macrocarpa** Martinez. Differs mainly in the significantly larger, 12–20 cm cones, with very brittle scales, distinctly reflexed to the twig. MPi 176–177 (C) Mexico. z9

var. **rudis** (Endl.) Shaw. Tree, 8–25 m; needles usually in 5's, occasionally only 4, rarely 6, 10–16 cm long, occasionally to 20 cm, tough, stiff, pure green, inside bluish, occasionally somewhat yellowish-green, margins serrate, sheaths persistent, 5–25 mm long, dark brown; cones in 2's or 3–4 together, rarely solitary, broadly ovate, acute, 9–12 cm long, blue to blue-black when young, dark brown when ripe, dull or glossy, on 8–10 mm long stalks. MPi 190–193; CCE 346 (= *P. rudis* Endl.). Mexico; warm to temperate regions. z9

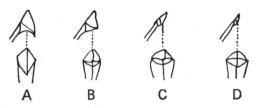

Fig. 148. **Pinus.** Apophysis of the cone scales viewed from the side and from above. A. *P. uncinata*; B. *P. uncinata* var. *rotunda*; C. *P. mugo* var. *pumilio*; D. *P. mugo* var. *mughus* (from Kirchner)

P. monticola Dougl. ex D. Don. Tree, 20–30 m or more in its habitat, crown narrowly conical, stem to 1 m in diameter, bark of older trees gray-brown, splitting into rectangular plates, young stems smooth and light brown, branches short, spreading horizontally on older trees, tips ascending, young shoots brownish, finely pubescent, buds cylindrical to globose, 12 mm long, resinous, scales appressed; needles in 5's, persisting for 3–4 years, densely arranged, stiff, 4–10 cm long, olive green, apex obtuse, margins finely and sparsely serrate, inner surfaces with about 5 stomatal lines, resin ducts at the epidermis, sheaths 18 mm long, quickly abscising; cones terminal, solitary or grouped 2 to 5, short stalked, pendulous after the first year, cylindrical, with a narrowed apex, occasionally somewhat curved, 10–25 cm long, 3–5 cm wide, green to purple when young, yellow-brown when ripe, scales leathery, scale ends thin, dorsal side convex, with a longitudinal keel and sharp margin, basal scales reflexed, umbo compressed, dark brown, seeds reddish, with black speckles, ovate, 6 mm long, with about 20 mm long wings. SPa 1–2; SPi 117–118; OCC 318; DJ 90; CCE 347, 348. Northwestern North America, from British Columbia to Central California, and eastward to Montana. 1831. Prefers a moist open site, but also thrives on a dry, sandy soil. Very susceptible to blister rust. Plate 105; Fig. 156. z7

'Ammerland' (Jeddeloh). Strong growing clone, shoots finger thick, annual growth 50 cm or more; needles an attractive blue-green, 8–12 cm long, dark green on the dorsal side, inside blue-green. Selected and propagated by Jeddeloh. Considered a substitute for *P. wallichiana* in areas in which the latter might be damaged by frost or wind. Grows equally well when grafted on *P. strobus* and *P. contorta*.

'Minima'. Dwarf form; needles shorter, blue-green. Found as a witches'-broom. (Jeddeloh). (R)

'Pendula'. Attractive form with very pendulous branches and a bowed stem. Found in a forest near Schermbeck, W. Germany. (Jeddeloh).

'Skyline'. Selection with good blue needles, otherwise like the type. USA.

P. morrisonicola Hayata. Large trees, 15–25 m, trunk to 120 cm in diameter, frequently curved, bark furrowed on older trees, young bark smooth; needles in 5's, about 8 cm long, with 2 resin ducts; cones ovate to more oblong, to 10 cm long and 4–5 cm wide, seed scales oblong-ovate, tips rounded, scale ends arched, umbo small, on the outermost tip and twisted outward, seeds ovate, about 6 mm long, wings about 14 mm long. LWT 9; LT 33

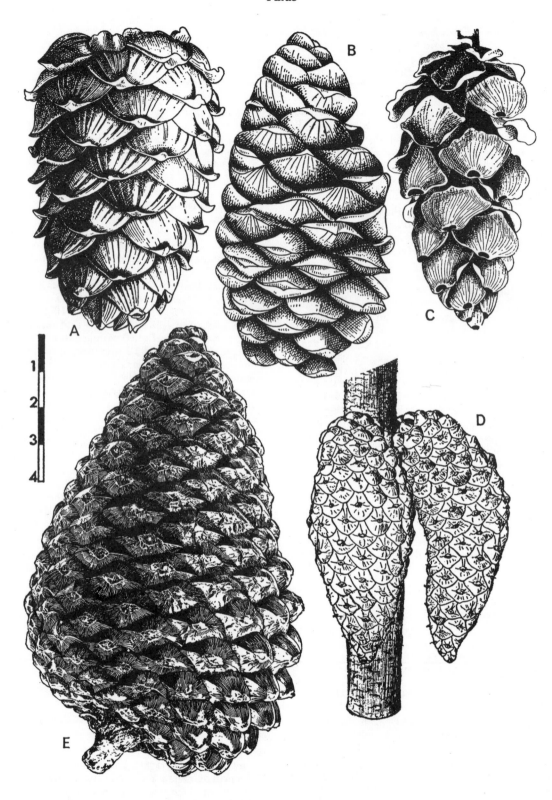

Fig. 149. **Pinus cones.**
A. *P. cembra;* B. *P. flexilis;* C. *P. parviflora;* D. *P. greggii;* E.
P. radiata

(= *P. parviflora* var. *morrisonicola* [Hayata] Wu; *P. uyematsui* Hayata; *P. formosana* Hayata). China; Taiwan; over the entire island at altitudes between 300 and 2300 m. z9

P. mugo Turra. Mugo Pine. Shrub with ascending stem or a short stem and conical crown or procumbent with many knee form, bent stems, bark gray-brown, scaly, splitting into irregular plates, but not exfoliating, young shoots light green at first, then brown to black-brown, glabrous, buds oval-oblong, 6 mm long, acuminate, very resinous, scales tightly appressed; needles in 2's, frequently sickle-shaped curved to the base, often also slightly twisted, 3–4 cm long, 1.5–2 mm wide, hornlike acuminate at the apex, margins finely serrate, with indistinct stomatal lines on both sides, resin ducts at the epidermis; cones nearly terminal, sessile to short stalked, erect or horizontal or somewhat pendulous, in groups of 1–2–3(4), ovate to more conical, 2–6 cm long, 1.5–4 cm wide, scale ends yellow-brown to dark brown, umbo lighter and flattened, surrounded by a dark ring, not reflexed and not hook-like, seeds ovate, 5 mm long, light gray-brown, with 10–15 mm long wings. BFN 425 (H); DJ 90; SPi 186–190 (= *P. montana* Mill.). Mountains of central Europe and the Balkan Peninsula, N. and Central Appenines. Fig. 157. z2

Includes a large number of cultivars and varieties:

'Allgäu'. Growth very flat with short shoots, and small needles. Discovered in Allgäu, Holland by Gebr. V. D. Nieuwendijk, Boskoop, Holland. Introduced in 1976.

"Brevifolia" see: **'Kissen'**

'Compacta'. Growth densely globose, ascending shoots, tips more or less erect; needles densely crowded, deep green, 2.5–3.5 cm long (= *P. mugo compacta* D. Hill ex Rehd.; *P. montana* f. *compacta* [Bail.] Bergm.).

'Frisia'. About 2 m high, 1.4 m wide, all branches tightly upright, very densely twiggy; needles moss-green. DB 22: 182 (H). Discovered by G. Krüssmann in the dunes near Bergen, North Holland and propagated by Jeddeloh since 1970.

'Gnom' (Den Ouden). Very dense, globose habit; about 2 m high and wide, branchlets very numerous, usually 3–5 on every spring shoot, buds oblong-conical, resinous; needles densely crowded, radially arranged, 3.5–4.5 cm long, deep green. WDw 216 (H); OCC 321; DB 18: 154 (= *P. montana mughus* 'Gnom' den Ouden 1937; *P. mugo mughus* 'Gnom' den Ouden 1949). Selected by den Ouden around 1890, but first propagated in 1920. Introduced in 1927.

'Hesse'. Dwarf form, low, very compact and cushion form, slow growing; needles 7–8 cm long, dark green, somewhat twisted. KN 302; WM 350 (H) (= *P. montana compacta* Hesse 1954; *P. montana* 'Hesse' 1955 Hesse). Not to be confused with *P. mugo* 'Compacta'!

'Humpy' (Draijer, Heemstede, Holland, 1970). Very compact habit, short branches, very slow growing, annual growth 3–4 cm, winter buds conspicuously red-brown; needles deep green, only 15 mm long. WM 351 (H).

'Kissen'. Selection of *P. mugo* var. *pumilio*, growth flat and dense, about 80 cm wide and only 30 cm high, annual growth scarcely 5 cm, buds grouped 3–5 together, 10 × 5 cm in size, obtuse, very resinous; needles dark green, only 10 mm long. WM 352 (= *P. mugo* "brevifolia" Zu Jeddeloh). Zu Jeddeloh.

'Knapenburg'. (Draijer, Heemstede, Holland 1967). Selected dwarf form, low growing, broad, irregular and dense, winter buds cylindrical, 15 × 5 mm, red-brown, thin, resinous; needles deep green, evenly 3 cm long. WM 352 (H).

'Kobold'. Dwarf form, broad globose habit, branches rather stiff and thick, buds grouped 3–5 together, widely spaced and variable in length, 5–12 mm long, thick, apex obtuse, conspicuously brown; needles densely arranged, straight, 2–3.5 cm long, 1 cm wide, sheaths rather long. OCC 322. Selected by Hugo F. Hooftman, Boskoop, Holland. Introduced in 1951.

'Kokarde'. Habit and needle size like var. *mughus*, but the needles have golden-yellow speckles, appearing like 2 yellow rings from their radial arrangement, like the Japanese 'Oculus draconis' forms. Discovered in 1952 in the Reinold Nursery, Dortmund, W. Germany. (EX)

'Mops'. Dwarf globose form, as tall as wide, slow growing and very densely branched, branches short, buds very densely arranged, variable in size, 1–2 cm long, narrow, brown, resinous; needles rather straight on the young shoots, 2–4.5 cm long, 1.5–1.8 mm wide, sheaths short, dark brown. OCC 322 (H); DB 18: 154 (= *P. montana mughus* 'Mops' Hooftman 1951). Introduced by Hugo F. Hooftman, Boskoop, Holland 1951.

var. **mughus** (Scop.) Senari. Growth usually shrubby-procumbent, branches bowed knee-like; cones symmetrical, sessile or very short stalked, horizontal or bowed downward when ripe, conical to more ovate and very regularly formed, never pruinose, yellow-brown in the fall of the first year, cinnamon-brown until fully ripe, scale ends all of equal height, quite even in size and form, sharply cross-keeled, but flatter on the lower scales, umbo in the center, usually with a prickly thorn, opening in late fall of the 2nd year (= *P. montana* var. *mughus* [Scop.] Willk.). East Alps to the Balkan Peninsula. Very common in gardens. Fig. 146, 148.

'Ophir' (Kraan). Selection of var. *mughus*, flat-globose, about 60 cm wide, 30 to 40 cm high in 6 years; needles 4–7 cm long, golden-yellow on the crown peak and the sunny side of the plant, lower portion of the plant green, occasionally somewhat twisted. Selected by K. J. Kraan, Waddinxveen, Holland.

var. **pumilio** (Haenke) Zenari. Shrubby, prostrate habit, flat-globose, occasionally to 3 m wide, branches very densely arranged, variable in length, twigs directed upward, buds very conspicuous; needles variable in length, usually short, directed upward, but spreading radially on the side shoots; cones symmetrical, nearly sessile, ovate to globose, bluish to violet in the 1st year, yellowish to dark brown when fully ripe, scale ends convex above, concave beneath, umbo below the middle, indented (= *P. montana* var. *pumilio* [Haenke] Heer). Mountains of central and eastern Europe; Alps (to 2600 m), Carpathians, Balkans. Common in cultivation. Fig. 148.

'Rigi' (Draijer). Very narrowly upright, nearly columnar. Selected and disseminated by Draijer, Heemstede, Holland.

'Slavinii'. Dwarf form, broad mat-like habit, branches more or less lying on the ground, ascending twigs, clustered; needles densely crowded, dark bluish-green. CC 14 (H); HD 199 (H); KN 303 (= *P. mugo* var. *slavinii* [Hornibr.] Bail.). Developed from Bulgarian seed by B. H. Slavin in Rochester, New York, USA before 1927.

'Variegata'. Needles yellow variegated. (VR)

'Virgata'. Branches with or without scattered side shoots, like *Picea abies* 'Virgata'. Discovered in Switzerland by C. Schroeter in 1902. (EX)

'Winter Gold' (Draijer, Heemstede, before 1967). Low, wide and open growing, about 1 m high or more, winter buds 10 × 4 mm, very resinous; needles spreading widely, twisted, 7–8 cm long, attractively golden-yellow in winter. WM 355 (H).

P. muricata D. Don. Bishop Pine. Small tree, 8–10 m, occassionally higher, crown narrow and conical when young, usually round crowned with age, trunk 60–120 cm thick, bark red-brown, splitting into thick, irregular plates, these scaly, branches irregularly spreading, young shoots green at first, then orange-brown, buds conical to cylindrical, 20–25 mm long, acute, dark red-brown, very resinous; needles in 2's, persisting about 3–4 years, 10–15 cm long, somewhat twisted, 2 mm wide, with short, horn-like tips, margin finely serrate, with stomatal lines on either side, resin ducts in the parenchyma, sheaths 8–12 mm long, persistent; cones ovate, oblique, solitary or in whorls, sessile, outspread or bowed downward, 5–9 cm long, 4–7 cm wide, glossy red-brown, often remaining closed on the branch for the entire year, seed scales on the side of the cone facing the light much more developed and with a triangular umbo, widely exserted, deep purple, with a thick, recurved thorn, seeds triangular, 6.5 mm long, rough, black, wings 20–25 mm long. MP 171 (H); MPi 293–295; SPa 24–25; SPi 315–316; BFN 382 (H). Western N. America; from California to NW. Mexico. 1848. Easily distinguished from other 2 needle pines by the persistent cones, long needles and resinous buds. Fig. 154. z8

P. × murraybanksiana Righter & Stockwell (*P. contorta* var. *latifolia* × *P. banksiana*). Intermediate between the parents, but closer to *P. contorta* var. *latifolia*, especially in habit, than in the regular and fully open cones, these however smaller, with flat scale ends and a thorn only 1 mm long or completely absent. First bred in the Eddy Arboretum, Placerville, California; repeated in 1944.

P. nelsonii Shaw. Small, bushy tree, 5 to 9 m, branches long, thin, densely crowded, bark smooth and gray, young shoots thin, bluish; needles in 3's, but so tightly bundled for much of their length as to appear nearly single, 4–9.5 cm long, margin very finely serrate; cones very divergent, grouped in 2's, cylindrical, 8.5–14 cm long, 5–6 cm thick, hanging on 3–5 cm quarter-arch curved stalks, persisting for up to 3 years, then abscising, but the stalk and some basal scales remain on the branch, scale tips orange-red, cross-keeled with an indistinct umbo, seeds large, 15 mm long, light yellow when fresh, edible when ripe, wingless. MP 204 (H); MPi 68–71. NE. Mexico, in the mountains. Easily recognized by its united needle groups and the unique cones. z9

P. nigra Arnold. Austrian Pine. Quite variable tree, 20–40(50) m, straight trunk, bark gray to dark brown, deeply fissured, crown of younger trees, especially those in cultivation, broadly conical, more umbrella-shaped with age, especially on gravelly soil in the mountains, branches of young plants in regular whorls, more irregular with age, young shoots glabrous, light brown to orange-brown, buds ovate to more cylindrical, resinous; needles in 2's, lighter or darker green, rather stiff, persisting 4(8) years, 8–12 cm long, 1–2 mm wide, straight or bowed, margins finely toothed, with 12–14 stomatal lines, with 3–17 resin ducts in the parenchyma, sheaths 10–12 mm long, persistent; cones grouped 2 to 4, sessile to nearly so, horizontally spreading, 5–8 cm long, 2–4 cm wide, yellow-brown or light brown, glossy,

opening the 3rd year, scale ends slightly or obtuse keeled, umbo dark brown, usually with a small thorn, seeds 5–7 mm long, gray, wings 4–5 mm long. BFN 396 (H); SPi 193–195. S. Europe, north to Austria and to the south Carpathian Mts. Fig.146, range map Fig. 150. z4

Outline of the Geographical Varieties
(Practical identification based on this outline will not be easy since it is partly based on anatomical characteristics (see Fukarek 1958).

★ Needles more or less wavy; 1–2(3) areas with slightly thickened hypodermal cells (= those cells under the epidermis);

    + Needles 1.2–1.9 mm thick, somewhat prickly; hypodermal cells in 1–2(3) locations:
        ssp. *laricio*

    ++ Needles 1–1.2 mm thick, not prickly; hypodermal cells in only 1 location:
        ssp. *salzmannii*

★★ Needles more or less rigid; hypodermal cells distinctly thickened in 2–5 locations.

    + Needles only 4–7 cm long:
        ssp. *dalmatica*

    ++ Needles 7–18 cm long:

        × Needles straight or curved; leaf sheaths 10–16 mm long:
            ssp. *nigra*

        ×× Needles twisted or irregularly curved; leaf sheaths (13)18–26 mm long:
            ssp. *pallasiana*

'**Aurea**'. Slow growing, in open sites branched to the ground, habit like the species; needles golden-yellow in the first year, greening in the second, partly green, partly gray-green. DB 12: 269; KN Plate 7 (= *P. nigra* var. *austriaca aurea* [Beissn.] Fitsch.). Discovered in 1909 in Hungary by Ilsemann in the Nyulas Forest of Archduke Albrecht. Distributed recently by the Kalmthout Arboretum, Belgium.

var. *austriaca* (Hoess) Loud. see: ssp. **nigra**

'**Balcanica**'. A contorted form, dwarf, cushion form; needles very densely arranged, very thin, short and straight, only 3–4 cm long, deep green (= *P. nigra* var. *balcanica* [Beissn.] Fitsch.).

'**Bujotii**'. Dwarf form, globose, shoots quite short, densely crowded; needles dark green, twisted (= *P. nigra* var. *bujoti* [Carr.] Fitsch.; *P. sylvestris bujoti* Sénécl.). Discovered in 1860 in the Bujot Nursery, Chateau Thierry, France.

var. *calabrica* (Loud.) Schneid. = ssp. **laricio** (Pour.) Maire.

var. *caramanica* (Loud.) Rehd. = ssp. **pallasiana** (Lamb.) Holmboe.

var. *cebennesis* (Godr.) Rehd. = ssp. **salzmannii** (Dunal) Franco.

'**Columnaris**'. Columnar, branches very short, curved upward (= *P. nigra* var. *columnaris* Hartmann). Found in Cyprus and distributed by Hartman before 1907.

ssp. **dalmatica** (Vis.) Franco. Small tree, crown broadly conical; needles 4–7 cm long, 1.5–1.8 mm thick, very stiff; cones only 3.5–4.5 cm long. Coast and islands of NW. Yugoslavia.

'**Géant de Suisse**' (J. P. Meylan & Cie, Switzerland, before 1981). Very straight growing tree, almost columnar, branches sharply ascending, straight growing, probably 5–8 m high and

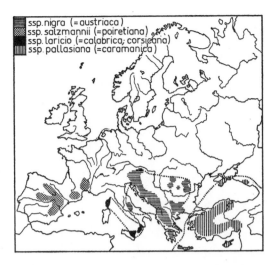

ssp. nigra (= austriaca)
ssp. salzmannii (=poiretiana)
ssp. laricio (=calabrica; corsicana)
ssp. pallasiana (=caramanica)

Fig. 150. Range of *Pinus nigra* and its subspecies

then growing a little wider; needles dark green 14–18 cm long in brush-like clusters at the end of very thick shoots, standing out on mature branches; buds acute, up to 5 cm long, light gray. Resembles *Pinus leucodermis* 'Satellit', but larger. In 1978 distributed by P. J. Kortmann, Boskoop Holland.

'Globosa'. Slow growing, branches short, terminal buds spindle-shaped, 3 cm long, light brown, slightly resinous; needles 12–16 cm long (!) and 1.5–2 mm wide, somewhat twisted. WM 356 (H). From the Arnold Arboretum.

'Hornibrookiana'. Dwarf form, broad shrubby habit, branches somewhat horizontal, thick and stiff, branchlets ascending to erect; needles densely crowded, straight, stiff, 5–6 cm long, sharply acuminate, glossy dark green. WM 27A (Br), 357 (H) (= *P. nigra hornibrookiana* Slavin). Discovered by Slavin before 1932 as a witches'-broom on a *P. nigra* ssp. *nigra* in Seneca Park, Rochester, New York, USA.

f. hornotina Beck. Form of ssp. *nigra* with cones only 6 cm long, ripening in the fall of the 1st year (instead of the 3rd year), umbo of the seed scales red-brown to black beneath. Discovered before 1890 in lower Austria.

'Jeddeloh' (Jeddeloh 1965). Compact and very dense, twigs and shoots much shorter than those of *P. nigra*; needles shorter and very prickly (*dalmatica* type?).

ssp. laricio (Poir.) Maire. Corsican or Calabrican Black Pine. Tall tree, to 40 m, crown narrowly oval-oblong, also flat on very old trees; needles 8–16 cm long, 1.2–1.9 mm thick, somewhat prickly, twisted(!); cones 6–8 cm long, yellow-brown, scale ends obtuse keeled (= *P. nigra* var. *calabrica* [Loud.] Schneid.; *P. nigra* var. *corsicana* [Loud.] Hyl.). Corsica, S. Italy (Calabria), Sicily. Plate 104.

'Monstrosa'. Dwarf form, branchlets very short and thick, sometimes also fasciated; needles densely arranged, dark green (= *P. laricio monstrosa* Carr.). Developed by Sénéclauze before 1867. (EX?)

'Moseri'. Globose form, to 2 m wide; needles bright green in summer, but golden-yellow in winter (= *P. laricio* var. *moseri* Moser). Developed before 1900 in the Nursery of Moser, Versailles, France (EX?)

'Nana'. Shrubby form, to 3 m high, erect and broad, annual growth only 4.5–5 cm long; needles like ssp. *nigra*. WM 358 (H) (= *P. laricio nana* Carr. 1855). Not a dwarf form.

ssp. **nigra.** Tall tree, crown conical, but flatter with age, especially in the mountains; needles 8–16 cm long, stiff, prickly; cones 5–9 cm long, scale ends somewhat keeled. DB 12: 12, 19: 172; OCC 331 (C) (= *P. nigra* var. *austriaca* (Hoess) Neum.; *P. austriaca* Hoess; *P. laricio* [Hoess] Loud.). From Austria to central Italy, Greece and Yugoslavia. Plate 104, 109; Fig. 157.

ssp. **pallasiana** (Lamb.) Holmb. Crimean Pine. Medium size tree, crown broadly ovate and dense; needles 12–18 cm long, 1.6–2.1 thick, cones 5 to 12 cm long. DB 15: 22; CCE 360 (= *P. nigra* var. *caramanica* [Loud.] Rehd.; *P. nigra* var. *pallasiana* Schneid.). Balkan, S. Carpathian Mts., Crimea. Plate 104, 109.

'Pendula'. Vigorous grower, broad, branches whorled, and directed downward (= *P. laricio pendula* Carr. 1855). (EX?)

'Prostrata'. Creeping form (like mugo pine), branches knee-like, bent and lying on the ground; needles normal (= *P. laricio* var. *prostrata* Beissn.). Origin unknown. (VR)

'Pumila Aurea'. Dwarf form with yellow needles (= *P. laricio* f. *pumila aurea* Beissn.). (EX)

'Pygmaea' see: **P. sylvestris 'Moseri'**

'Pyramidalis'. Narrowly conical form, ascending branches, bowed; needles to 12 cm long, bluish-green, otherwise like the species (= *P. nigra* var. *pyramidalis* Slavin). Discovered in the Durand-Eastman Park in Rochester, New York, USA about 1932. (VR)

var. **pyramidata** Acatay. Columnar habit, 20–25 m, similar to *Cupressus sempervirens* in habit, occasionally more conical, branches densely arranged, directed tightly upright, more or less parallel to the stem; needles densely packed, usually short, 5.5–12 cm long; cones about 5.5 cm long and 3 cm wide, otherwise like that of var. *pallasiana*. (MD 63: 55. Turkey.) Discovered in uniform stands in 1955 by A. Acatay in the Tavsanli region. This particularly columnar form was introduced into cultivation by Meyer, Tönisvorst, W. Germany. That in the literature as *P. nigra* 'Pyramidata', is presumably a plant selected from cultivation and not identical with the Turkish plant, which in the wild covers an area of about 250 hectares (111 acres).

ssp. **salzmannii** (Dunal) Franco. Medium size tree, 20 m at most, crown narrowly conical to cylindrical; needles 8–16 cm long, to 2 mm wide, not prickly; cones 4–6 cm long, scale ends somewhat keeled. CCE 358 (= *P. nigra* var. *cebennensis* [Godr.] Rehd.). S. France (Cevennes), Pyrenees, Central and E. Spain. Plate 104.

'Strypemonde' (Trompenburg Arboretum, Rotterdam). Originated from a witches'-broom, but rather strong growing, an 18-year old plant about 1.7 m high, gray-white basal scales recurved; needles dull dark- to more gray-green, variable in length, 5–10 cm, very stiff. WM 360 (H).

'Variegata'. Like ssp. *nigra* but with some straw-yellow needles among the normal green needles (= *P. austriaca variegata* Laws ex Gord. 1858). (VR)

'Zlatiborica'. Needles golden-yellow (= *P. laricio zlatiborica* Adamovic). Discovered by Adamovic in Zlatibor, Serbia (now Yugoslavia) before 1909. (EX?)

P. oaxacana Mirov. Tree, 20–40 m in its habitat, crown broadly ovate, open, branches spreading nearly horizontally, brown, young shoots brown with a bluish trace, nearly smooth or only slightly rough, with decurrent needle bases; needles in 5's, very rarely in 6's, about 20–35 cm long, bright green, often with a trace of yellow, finely serrate, the teeth very densely arranged, with stomatal lines on all sides, resin ducts in the

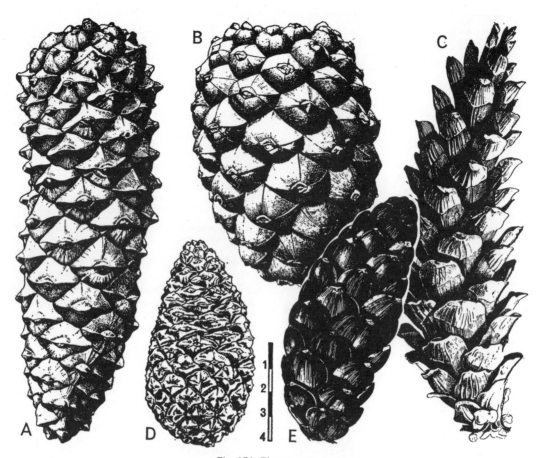

Fig. 151. **Pinus** cones.
A. *P. canariensis;* B. *P. pinea;* C. *P. strobus;* D. *P. yunnanensis;* E. *P. peuce*

parenchyma, leaf sheath about 30 mm long, brown, later gray; cones ovate or conical, somewhat asymmetrical, usually in groups of 3, occasionally 4, 10–16 cm long, the basal scales usually persisting on the branch when ripe, scales large, to 2 cm wide and 3–4 cm long, scale tips pyramidally raised and with a large, blunt thorn, seeds somewhat triangular, 7–9 mm long, with 20–35 mm long wings. MPi 163–168 (= *P. pseudostrobus* var. *oaxacana* [Mirov] Harrison). Mexico; in the States of Oaxaca, Mexico, Puebla, Guerrero, Veracruz and Chiapas; also occurs in the mountains to 3000 m. z9

P. occidentalis Swartz. Cuban Pine. Tree, 50 m or taller in its habitat, similar to *P. carribaea,* but differing in the non-segmented annual growth, pruinose when young, buds very large, scales fringed; needles fascicled 2–5, but usually in 3's, erect, 15–22 cm long, thin; cones erect when young, stalked, ripe cones ovate, symmetrical, 5–8 cm long, glossy brown, abscising early, scale ends nut-brown, glossy above, with a fine umbo, bowed to the base. GGy 329 (C) (= *P. cubensis* Griseb. non Sarg.; *P. wrightii* Engelm.). E. Cuba, Santo Domingo and Haiti at 300–3000 m. z9

P. oocarpa Scheide. Tree, 12–18 m in its habitat, trunk 40–75 cm in diameter, crown rounded and compact, young shoots bluish pruinose, buds only at the nodes;

needles in 3's or 4–5, light green, 15–30cm long, usually 22–25cm long, usually stiff and rough, occasionally thin and flexible, glossy green, resin ducts usually 5–8 in the parenchyma, sheaths 20–30 mm long, brown, with long acuminate scales; cones distinctly ovate or broadly conical, on long, usually curved stalks, 4–10 cm long, persisting, symmetrical or oblique, scale ends gray to greenish-yellow, flat or convex, seeds about 7 mm long, with 10–15 mm long wings. MP 224 (H); MPi 244–265 (= *P.oocarpoides* Lindl.). Central America; S. and W. Mexico, from Sonora to Chiapas; Guatemala, El Salvador, Honduras and Nicaragua. Fig. 138, 143 (C). z9

Martinez included 4 botanical forms which will not be considered here.

P. palustris Mill. Longleaf Pine (in USA), Pitch Pine (in Europe). Tree, 24–30 m in its habitat, trunk 60–90 cm in diameter, crown irregular in outline, bark reddish-brown, to 2 cm thick, deeply furrowed, exfoliating in thin scales, young shoots stout, orange-brown, not pruinose, roughly furrowed, buds 35–50 mm long, cylindrical, acute, not resinous, scales silver-white, fringed, reflexed at the apex, remaining an extra year at the tips of the second year shoots; needles in 3's, persisting for 2 years, very densely crowded on the shoots, thin and flexible,

20–25 cm long on older trees, to 45 cm (!!) long on young plants, clustered at the branch tips, dark green, very finely dentate, acute, with stomatal lines on all sides, sheaths 2–2.5 cm long; cones nearly terminal, spreading, cylindrical to oblong-conical, 15–20 cm long, leaving no scales on the branch after abscising, scales thin, scale ends distinctly cross-keeled, dull brown, umbo with a short, reflexed thorn, seeds about 12 mm long, with about a 3.5 cm long wing. LT 34; SN 262 (H); MP 179 (H); SDK 1: 57 (C) (= *P. australis* Michx.; *P. longifolia* Salisb. non Roxb.). SE. USA, Virginia to Florida. 1727. Economically valuable for its superior wood. Plate 110; Fig. 146, 160. z8–9

P. parviflora S. & Z. Japanese White Pine. Tree, 15–30 m in its habitat, crown conical, dense, bark gray-black, remaining smooth for some years, later exfoliating in thin scales, branches spreading widely, dense with short branchlets, young shoots greenish-brown, then light gray, usually short pubescent, buds ovate, with short tips, 5 mm long, brownish-yellow, not resinous, tips of the scales distinct; needles in 5's, persisting for 3–4 years, clustered brush-like at the branch tips, very curved and twisted, either rather stiff and conspicuously blue-white on the inside, with light, glossy young shoots or with soft, more grass-green needles and dark brown, later pubescent young shoots, 4–6 cm long, about 1 mm wide, obtuse, margins finely serrate, both inner sides with white stomatal lines, 2 resin ducts at the epidermis, needle sheaths abscising; cones solitary or in clusters, nearly sessile, spreading nearly horizontally, straight, ovate to cylindrical, 5–10 cm long, 3–4 cm wide, opening widely, persisting 6–7 years on the branch, scales less numerous, leathery-woody, brown-red, scale ends ash-gray, uneven sides, rhombic, convex and smooth on the dorsal side, tips rounded, umbo hardly protruding, seeds elliptic, blackish, 10 mm long, with short wings. DB 18: 3; SN 230 (H); OCC 33 (C); SPi 114–116. Japan; 60–2500 m. Plate 106; Fig. 149. z5

The name *P. parviflora* is retained here, but Ohwi (Flora of Japan) and other Japanese authors do not completely agree on the division of the species. Mirov handled the problem using the nomenclature "*P. parviflora*—complex" (details in Mirov, 544–545).

The Japanese authors divide the species as follows:

1. **P. pentaphylla** Mayr. (*P. parviflora* var. *pentaphylla* [Mayr] Henry). N. Japan; Hokkaido, Honshu (central and northern Honshu), and also on the Korean island of Utsurio-To; in the mountains at 60–2500 m.

   Cones smaller, scales nearly semicircular, apophysis with only a slight bulge, seed wings as long as the seed. MI 2708; GGy 354–5 to; KIF 1: 34.

2. **P. pentaphylla** var. **himekomatsu** (Miyabe & Kudo) Makino. S. Japan; the southern part of Honshu, Shikoku, Kyushu, in the mountains, at altitudes of 100–1850 m. Both forms are found together on central Honshu (= *P. himekomatsu* Miyabe & Kudo).

   Cones longer, scale ends rhombic with rounded tips and an indention (Fig. 149; as *P. parviflora*), seeds about 10 mm long. Wings much shorter than the seed. MI 2709; GGy 354–5; CCE 363. This form is identical to that generally cultivated as *P. parviflora*.

Included with *P. parviflora* (of gardens) are the following cultivars:

'**Adcock's Dwarf**'. Dwarf form, very slow growing and compact; needles only 15–25 mm long, gray-green, clustered, crowded at the branch tips. WM 29C (C), 361 (H). Developed in 1961 at the Hillier Nursery, Ampfield, England and named for the head propagator Graham Adcock.

Blue Giant'. Tree-like, fairly regular habit, to 10–15 m high; branches slanting upwards; needles curved slightly, 6–8 cm long, tightly clustered, blue-gray, silver-gray underside; cones 6–10 cm long, open, usually abundant. A vigorous selection that matures into an evenly formed tree with all the characteristics of the many cultivars of *Pinus parviflora* that are now available. It is surpassed in ornamental value by 'Tempelhof', and to a lesser extent by 'Gimborn's Ideal'. It is between these two in its vigor. Introduced by Van Vliet, 1975.

'**Brevifolia**'. Normal upright habit, narrow, sparsely branched, shoots few, short; needles rather stiff, somewhat bowed, only 2–3 cm long, 1 mm wide, blue-green outside, inside with 5–6 indistinct stomatal lines. WM 29D (Br) (= *P. parviflora brevifolia* Beissn.; = Ha-tsumari goyo). Developed before 1900 in the nursery of Barbier & Fils in Orléans, France.

'**Gimborn's Ideal**'. Large shrub, to 8 m high, branches pyramidal to columnar; needles rather fine, bluish green. Developed in the Gimborn Arboretum, Doorn, Holland; introduced through L. Konijn & Zoon, Reeuwijk.

'**Gimborn's Pyramid**'. A compact selection, broad, slow growing, more broadly oval in habit, to 3 m tall and 2 m wide, branches very densely arranged; needles especially intense blue-green in spring. OCC 332 (H); WM 29A (Br). Originated in the Gimborn Arboretum, introduced through L. Konijn & Zoon.

'**Glauca**'. Small, erect tree, 5–12 m high (perhaps higher), usually sparsely branched on young plants, outspread branches on older trees, buds 1–1.5 cm long, densely surrounded by the needles; needles stiff, bowed and twisted, 5–7 cm long, green outside, distinctly blue-white inside (= *P. parviflora* f. *glauca* Beissn.). Widely available.

'**Negishi**'. Japanese selection, final height not known, upright, open branched, ascending twigs; needles more or less twisted, 3.5–4.5 cm long, gray-green to blue-green.

'**Saentis**' (Draijer 1972). Wide growing, but compact; needles long. WM 369 (H).

'**Saphir**'. Slow and irregular growth; needles short, attractively blue. (KN Plate 8 as *P. pumila* 'Saphir.') Selected by Draijer, 1970.

'**Tempelhof**'. Selection, tree-like, with a thick trunk, fast growing. Originated in the Gimborn Arboretum, introduced by L. Konijn & Zoon.

'**Variegata**'. Needles partly yellowish-white, partly yellow speckled or bordered. Observed in Japan by Mayr before 1890.

The Hillier Nursery in England listed no less than 14 additional cultivars in 1970, most with Japanese names.

P. patula Schlechtend. & Cham. Jelecote Pine. Tree, 12–20 m or more, frequently multistemmed or forked just above the ground, bark irregularly scaly on the basal portion, upper parts paper-like exfoliating, reddish-brown, similar to *P. sylvestris*, crown broadly conical or outspread, thin branched and rather open crowned, young shoots greenish-blue, pruinose, glabrous brown in the 2nd year, buds cylindrical, long acuminate, 15–25 mm long, not resinous, scales very narrowly lanceolate, acuminate, margin fringed, distinct at the apex; needles in 3's (occasionally 4–5), persisting 3–4 years, very thin, 15–22 cm long, pendulous, acute, margins serrate, bright green, with stomatal lines on all sides, usually with 3 resin ducts in the parenchyma, sheaths about 10–15 mm long, persistent; cones laterally arranged, usually in clusters of 2–5 together, on a short, scaly stalk, oval-conical, 7–9 cm long, curved, asymmetrical at the base, light brown, glossy, late and opening irregularly, scale ends rhombic, flat or slightly convex, cross-keeled, umbo indented, with a tiny, often absent thorn, seeds triangular, gray, black speckled, 5 mm long, wings 12–18 mm long. SN 254 (H); SPi 307–310; MPi 270–280; MP 223 (H) (= *P. subpatula* Royle). Mexico; the central and eastern States, especially in Hidalgo and Veracruz, in the subtropical climates, at 1500–3000 m. Plate 110; Fig. 154. z9

P. peuce Griseb. Macedonian, Balkan Pine. Tree, 10–20 m crown slender conical, trunk often branched to the ground, bark thick, gray-brown, basal portion deeply furrowed and narrow scaly, branches short, thick and bowed upward on young trees, more or less horizontal on older trees, young shoots thick, greenish, glossy, glabrous (!), gray-brown in the second year, buds acutely ovate, 10 mm long, brown resinous; needles in 5's, persisting for 3 years, clustered brush-like at the branch tips, 7–10 cm long, straight and rather stiff, green or also gray-green, sharply acuminate, margins finely serrate, with stomatal lines on all sides, resin ducts at the epidermis, sheaths 18 mm long, abscising in the first year; cones terminal, solitary or in groups of 3–4, short stalked, outspread to pendulous, 8–15 cm long, 2–3 cm wide, cylindrical, light brown, resinous, scales abruptly thickened beneath the apex, rather distinctly longitudinally ribbed, seeds 7 mm long, ovate, wings 15 mm long. DJ 93; OCC 334–335; SPi 111–113. S. Yugoslavia, Albania, Greece; 800–2100 m. Fast growing, very winter hardy and a particularly ornamental pine. Plate 106, 111; Fig. 146, 151; range map Fig. 152. z5

'Glauca Compacta'. A blue needled, tight growing form. Selected by Jeddeloh.

P. pinaster Ait. Cluster, Maritime Pine. Tree, 20–30 m, conical crown, bark thick, red-brown, deeply split, older trees often branched only on the upper ¼, branches numerous, horizontal to drooping, young shoots reddish-brown, glabrous, the older parts rough with a furrowed effect due to remnants of the sheath scales, buds large, spindle form, 20–35 mm long, 8–12 mm wide, brown, not resinous, bud scales brown, silvery-white fringed on the margin and interwoven, tips reflexed; needles in 2's, usually persisting for 3 years, clustered at the branch tips, 10–20 cm long, stiff, glossy green, prickly acuminate, margins finely dentate, with many stomatal lines on both sides, resin ducts in the parenchyma, sheaths 20–25 mm long, blackish; cones with 15–20 mm long stalks, usually 2–4 together or also 4–7, directed obliquely downward, broadly oval-conical, asymmetrical, 9–18 cm long, 5–8 cm wide, purple when young, light brown and glossy when ripe, occasionally remaining closed for several years, scale ends rhombic, ascending pyramidally, to 15 mm wide, with a sharp

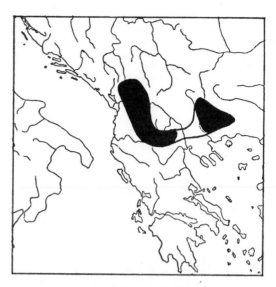

Fig. 152. Range of *Pinus peuce* (from Fukarek)

cross-keel, umbo very conspicuous, wide-compressed, acute, straight or hooked downward, seeds oval-oblong, 7–8 cm long, gray-brown, wings 2–3 cm long, obtusely truncate at the apex. DJ Pl. 33 (H); OCC 336 (C); SPi 275 to 278; CCE 367–369 (= *P. maritima* Mill.). Mediterranean region from the Atlantic to Greece, widely cultivated. Fig. 146, 155. z8

Includes a few forms:

'Aberdoniae'. Very tall tree, branches stout, spreading; needles 15–25 cm long, very distinctly channeled, deep green; cones usually solitary, cylindrical-conical, to 20 cm long, scale ends very pyramidal (= *P. pinaster hamiltonii* Parl.; *P. hamiltonii* Ten.). Discovered in the vicinity of Nice, France, about 1825; brought into cultivation by the Earl of Aberdeen. Significantly more winter hardy than the species. z7–8

'Lemoniana'. Tree, 8–10 m, broad crown, branches numerous, thick, outspread; needles glossy dark green, very stiff, long, thick, outspread, often twisted; cones solitary, terminal, rather long stalked, 6–11 cm long, glossy red-brown, scale ends with a sharp cross-keel, umbo obtuse, typically ash gray (= *P. pinaster* var. *lemoniana* [Benth.] Loud.). Developed before 1883 in England.

f. minor Loisel. Tree, 12–15 m; needles shorter, more blue-green; cones smaller, usually grouped, seldom solitary, 4–5 cm long, 3–3.5 cm wide, scale ends rhombic, raised pyramidally, distinctly cross-keeled, umbo conspicuous wide-compressed, gray. France; around Le Mans. 1812.

'Nana'. Dwarf form, hemispherical habit with a flat top, about 1 m high and wide, shoots numerous and densely arranged, thick, stiff, all ascending at acute angles, buds grouped 2–5, 1–2 cm long, red-brown; needles shorter, thick, somewhat bowed, pale green, directed forward at acute angles (= *P. pinaster* var. *nana* Nels.). Discovered as an old plant before 1939 by Hornibrook in a forest of *Pinus pinaster* around Mandelieu, Maritime Alps, France.

'Variegata'. Needles only about 5–7 cm long, straw-yellow, intermixed with green needles or entire shoot yellow variegated or only green needles (= *P. pinaster* var. *variegata* Forb.). 1839. (VR or EX?)

P. pinceana Gord. Small tree, 6–12 m, trunk often branched from the base up, bark smooth and gray, except for the base of older trunks, young shoots thin, blue pruinose, glabrous, retaining the remnants of the needle sheaths; needles in 3's, occasionally also 4 in a fascicle, about 6–8 cm long, straight, very similar to those of *P. cembroides*, but larger, bright green, blue-green due to the stomatal lines on the upper surface, the 2 resin ducts marginal, sheaths 5 mm long, abscising early; cones solitary, on 2 cm long stalks, cylindrical, 6–8 cm long, symmetrical, with a few large scales, glossy, ocher-yellow, seeds 12 mm long, wingless, edible. MPi 63 to 67 (= *P. latisquama* Engelmann p.p.). Mexico; in the dry ravines of the desert regions in the Sierra del Garambullo, in SW. Coahuila State. Probably not in cultivation. z7

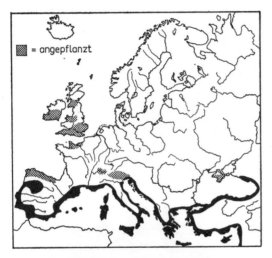

Fig. 153. Range of *Pinus pinea* in Europe [in drawing] = isolated populations

P. pinea L. Italian Stone Pine. Tree, 15–25 m, crown broadly arched, umbrella-shaped, bark of older trees reddish or more yellow-brown, deep longitudinal fissures, developing flat strips, branches more or less horizontal, shoots thin, densely foliate, gray-green, later yellow-brown, glabrous, buds acutely ovate, 6–12 mm long, resin free, scales with a long, silvery-green fringe, tips reflexed; needles in 2's, persisting 2–3 years, slightly twisted, stiff, 10–15 cm long, to 2 mm wide, yellow and sharp on the apex, margins finely dentate, dorsal side with about 12, ventral side with about 6 stomatal lines, light green (blue-green on young shoots and occasionally on individual shoots of old trees!), resin ducts at the epidermis, sheaths 10–12 mm long, light yellow-brown; cones usually solitary, terminal, occasionally grouped 2–3, inclined downward, symmetrical, ovate to nearly globose, occasionally indented at the base, 8–15 cm long, to 10 cm wide, ripening in the 3rd year, seed scales thick, slightly pyramidal, umbo black-brown beneath, scale ends of the basal scales 6 sided, the uppermost rhombic, all thick, with 5–6 radially arranged ridges, umbo large, gray-white, flat, seeds 1.5–2 cm long, 1 cm wide, dull brown, with 3–20 mm long wings, often up to 100 seeds in a cone, edible ("Pine nuts"). BFN 380 (H); DJ 94; SPi 166–169; CCE 369, 370. In the entire Mediterranean region, from the Canary Islands and Madeira to Asia Minor. Plate 109; Fig. 147, 151; range map Fig. 153. z8–9

'Correvoniana'. Dwarf form, prostrate, 20-year old plants only 30 cm wide (= *P. pinea* var. *correvoniana* Hornib.). Developed about 1910 in the Correvon Nursery near Geneva, Switzerland. (EX?)

'Fragilis'. Garden form with thin shelled seeds, cultivated for this reason (= *P. pinea fragilis* DuHamel).

P. pityusa Stev. Tree, to 25 m, broad crown, bark gray-brown; needles to 15 cm long, outspread, thicker than those of the type, about 1 mm thick; cones usually in 2's, occasionally 3–4, short stalked to nearly sessile, ovate, 6–10 cm long, 4–5 cm wide at the base, shorter than the needles, reddish-brown, scale ends nearly flat, with a low cross-keel, usually radially split, umbo wide, gray, indented. SDK 1: 61 (C) (= *P. halepensis* var. *pityusa* [Stev.] Gord.; *P. abchasica* Fisch., *P. abasica* Carr.) Western India, Caucasian coast of the Black Sea. Range map Fig. 145. z8–9

P. ponderosa Dougl. ex Laws. Ponderosa Pine. Tall tree, to 40 m in its habitat or taller, to 1.4 m in trunk diameter, bark of very old trees 8–10 cm thick, brown to nearly black, deeply fissured, exfoliating in large plates, branches short, stout, not numerous, usually in regular whorls, often pendulous with ascending tips, young shoots brownish or greenish, never pruinose (!), buds oblong-cylindrical, acute, to 2 cm long, resinous, scales red-brown, tightly appressed; needles in groups of 3, persisting for 3 years, tightly clustered at the branch tips, erect or outspread, bowed, 12–25 cm long, dark green, 1.5 mm wide, with a sharp, horned tip, margins finely serrate, with 8–12 stomatal lines on the dorsal side, 4–5 on the inner, sheaths about 22 mm long, persistent; cones terminal, solitary or also grouped 3–5, nearly sessile, horizontal or drooping slightly, symmetrical, ovate to more oblong, 8–15 cm long, 3.5–5 cm wide, light brown and glossy, often with some of the basal scales remaining on the branch after the cones abscise, seed scales about 30 mm long and 12 mm wide, scale ends flat-pyramidal or flat, with a cross-ridge and some radially arranged ridges, umbo broadly triangular, with thick, straight or somewhat curved thorn, seeds 7–10 mm long, dark brown, wing 2.5–3 cm long, dark brown, widest above the middle. SN 244 (H), 249 (H); SPa 13; SPi 229–234; MPi 219–224; CCE 371–372. Western USA, from British Columbia to California, on sandy-gravel soil. Plate 105; Fig. 146, 155. z6

var. **arizonica** (Engelm.) Shaw. Arizona Pine. Tall tree, very closely related to *P. ponderosa* and also often included within this species, but differing in the dark brown-gray to blackish, deeply furrowed bark, young shoots bluish to reddish-brown; needles grouped 3, 4 or 5 together, 10–17 cm long, sharply acuminate; cones ovate, 5 to 7.5 cm long and just as wide (when open), dull brown or more yellowish-brown, somewhat asymmetrical, sessile to short stalked, umbo with a short thorn. MP 208 (H) (= *P. arizonica* Engelm.). First discovered in Arizona, but mainly distributed in NW. Mexico, at altitudes between 2000 and 2700 m. z6

'Pendula'. Weeping form, trunk upright, branches short, horizontal at first, then distinctly pendulous. DB 19: 15 (H). Discovered in N. America before 1876. In cultivation. (VR)

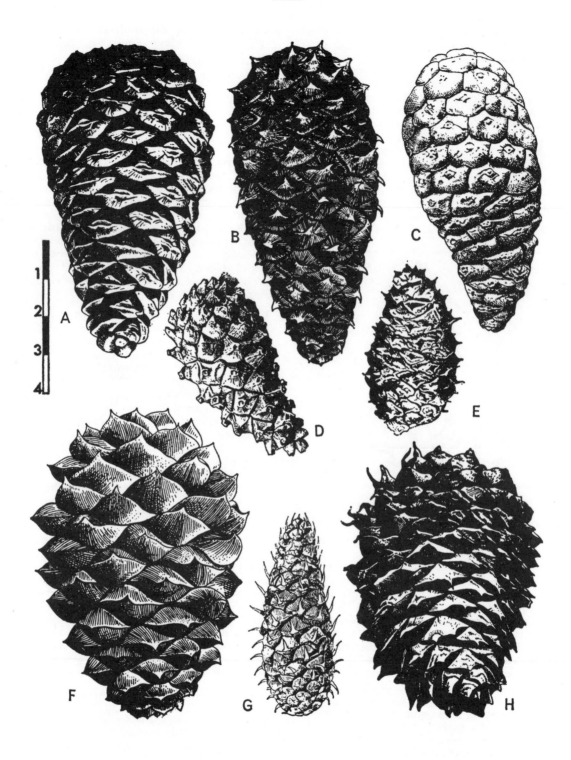

Fig. 154. **Pinus** cones. A. *P. brutia;* B. *P. attenuata;* C. *P. patula;* D. *P. sylvestris;*
E. *P. virginiana;* F. *P. muricata;* G. *P. contorta;* H. *P. pungens*

var. **scopulorum** Engelm. Grows more compactly, 25 to 30 m, bark nearly black; needles shorter, usually clustered brush-like at the ends of naked shoots, 12–16 cm long, frequently only 2 (not 3) in a sheath; cones ovate, smaller, 6–8 cm long, seed scales very thorny. SN 260; CBI 70 (= *P. scopulorum* Lemm.). USA, eastern slopes of the Rocky Mountains, together with the species, but of less value. z5–4?

P. pringlei Shaw. Tree, 15–20 m in its habitat, trunk with dark gray, scaly bark, and wide, bowed, spreading branches, irregularly arranged, developing a round crown, young shoots brown, occasionally blue-green pruinose, bark of older shoots paper thin, scaly; needles in 3's, occasionally 4 together, 12–28 cm long, but normally 20–24 cm long, about 1 mm thick, stiff, dark green, occasionally also with a bluish or yellowish trace, glossy, margins finely and densely serrate, with stomatal lines on all sides, 4–7 resin ducts in the parenchyma, sheaths 12–20 mm long, persistent, glossy brown; cones broadly ovate, 5.5–8.5 cm long, ocher-yellow, persisting for several years, on 8 to 10 cm long stalks, scale ends red-brown, thickened, seeds 5 mm long, brown, with about 17 mm long wings. MPi 266–269. SW. Mexico, subtropical regions, in the mountains at 1750–1850 m, together with *P. oocarpa* and *P. lawsonii*. Fig. 159. z9

P. pseudostrobus Lindl. Tree, 15–25 m in its habitat, branches horizontal, in whorls, crown broadly ovate and dense, bark remaining smooth for many years, becoming rough with age, young shoots thin, dark brown, very bluish pruinose, buds and needles similar to those of *P. montezumae*; needles usually in 5's, intensively green, 17–24 cm long, flexible, finely serrate, with 3 resin ducts, sheaths 12–15 mm long, brown, persistent; cones ovate or oval-conical, symmetrical or oblique, 8–10 cm long, usually in 2's, slightly curved, on 10–15 mm long stalks, persistent, often with some scales persisting with the stalk on the shoot, scales with an irregular, 4 sided apophysis, cross-ridge only slightly developed. MPi 146–168 (with its forms); MP 220 (H). Mexico; Central America, 2300–2350m, subtropical. Quite variable! Fig. 159. z9

var. **apulcensis** (Lindl.) Shaw. Tree, 15–20 m, shoots very blue pruinose; needles in 5's, rarely 6, 17–27 cm long, flexible, margin rough, sheaths 15–25 mm long; cones usually grouped 3–4 together, rarely solitary, 10–15 cm long, seed scales large, with a broad base, scale ends reflexed and with a hook-like umbo. SPi 213–214; MPi 161–162 (= *P. apulcensis* Lindl.). Mexico; Hidalgo, Pueblo, Tlaxcala, Veracruz. z9

var. **tenuifolia** (Benth.) Shaw. Tree, 15–30 m, bark remaining smooth for some years, many branches, developing a round crown, young shoots easily broken, yellow-brown, glossy needles in 5's, very thin, 20–28 cm long, pendulous, glossy, with serrate margins, sheaths 15–18 mm long; cones oblong to broadly oval, about 7.5 cm long, flattened and tapered at the base, with a 15 mm long stalk, scale ends rounded or irregularly angular at the tip, umbo nearly 4 sided, with a short, quickly abscising thorn. SPi 211–212, 215; MPi 138–141 (= *P. tenuifolia* Benth.; *P. maximinoi* H. E. Moore). Mexico and Central America, subtropical regions. z9

P. pumila (Pall.) Regel. Japanese Stone Pine, Dwarf Siberian Pine. Shrub, more or less prostrate, lacking a main stem, 50 cm to 3 m high and as wide, branches prostrate-ascending, young shoots stout, greenish in the 1st year, more gray-brown in the 2nd year, short, finely pubescent, buds cylindrical, with short tips, red-brown, about 10 mm long, very resinous, scales lanceolate, tightly appressed, the apical scales drawn out and filamentous; needles in 5's, very densely arranged, 4–7(10) cm long, more or less appressed to the branch, margins widely serrate, dark green beneath and without stomatal lines, very blue-green above due to the 5–6 conspicuous stomatal lines, 2 resin ducts at the epidermis, needle sheaths totally abscising in the 1st year; conspicuous male flowers deep red; cones grouped several together, nearly terminal, short stalked, outspread, ovate, 3.5–4.5 cm long, about 2.5 cm wide, purple-violet when young, reddish or more yellowish-brown when ripe, always closed until the seeds fill out, few scales, 15 mm wide, umbo triangular, with horizontally spreading, 2 edged tips, dark colored, seeds pear-shaped, 6–10 mm long, wingless, edible. KIF 2: 8; CCE 373 (= *P. cembra* var. *pumila* Pall.; *P. cembra nana* Hort.). E. Asia; Kamchatka, Siberia, Amur region, Sachalin, Kurile and Japan; in the coldest, most exposed areas to near the snow line. 1807. Very important garden plant. Plate 106; Fig. 143 (C). z5

Includes a few cultivars:

'**Draijers Dwarf**' (Draijer). Quite flat, compact, growing, blue. WM 365 (H).

'**Chlorocarpa.**' Cones yellow-green (*P. cembra chlorocarpa* Beissn.). Known since 1899. (VR)

'Dwarf Blue' see: **Glauca**'

'**Glauca**'. Selection, broad growing, bushy, slow, branches very stout; needles more gray-blue. Introduced in 1943 by Hugo F. Hooftman, of Boskoop, Holland.

'**Globe**'. Rather strong growing for the species, globose, very dense, to 2 m high and wide; needles 5–7 cm long, thin, attractive blue-green. WM 367 (H) (= *P. cembra*, 'Globe' den Ouden & Boom). Selected as an old plant in the Gimborn Arboretum, Doorn, Holland; introduced in 1965 by H. J. Draijer, Heemstede.

'**Jeddeloh**'. Flat, broad horizontal habit, with a depressed (nest form) center, branches brown, ascending obliquely outward, terminal bud cylindrical, 10 to 12 mm long, gray-brown, resin free, scales appressed; needles appressed to the shoot, straight, but usually curved inward in a short curl on the tips, 3–5 cm long, underside bright green, blue-white above. Selected by Jeddeloh. Very vigorous grower.

'**Jermyns**'. Dwarf form, especially slow growing, very compact and conical, quite different from the other forms in habit. Introduced by Hillier & Sons, Winchester, England in 1965.

'**Nana**'. Globose habit, 2–3 m high and as wide, branches very dense, branched to the ground; needles twisted, 5–8 cm long, in dense clusters, bright gray-green, underside pale gray-white; male flowers conspicuously wine-red; cones 4–6 cm, remaining closed, not numerous. This fairly common semi-dwarf is usually sold under the incorrect name *Pinus cembra* 'Nana'. It is obvious that it is not a form of *P. cembra*, if only because of the characteristic *pumila*-needles.

In the literature *Pinus cembra* 'Nana' is mentioned as a synonym of *P. pumila*. This clone cannot be named *P. pumila* without a problem. It seems best that *cembra* be replaced by *pumila* and that the cultivar name 'Nana'—which has been used for many years—continue to be used.

J. D. zu Jeddeloh wrote in 1969 that he has offered this form as *P. cembra* 'Compacta', but this name was never validly published. Further, by 1969 such a name was no longer acceptable as latin cultivar names were not allowed after 1959. So 'Compacta' cannot be used. Moreover, around 1960 the name 'Compacta' was used by Hillier, when it appeared that their 'Chlorocarpa' was not a true variant.

'Prostrata' (Hillier) is hardly distinguishable from 'Glauca'.

P. pungens Lamb. Table Mountain, Hickory Pine. Tree, 6–12 m, occasionally taller, with a short trunk and broad crown, only a few ascending branches, irregular, bark of older trunks, deep brown, exfoliating in irregular plates, upper trunk and the main branches exfoliating in thin scales, young shoots green at first, then glossy red-brown, glabrous, buds cylindrical, obtuse, 12–18 mm long, deep brown, resinous; needles in 2's, occasionally 3, densely crowded, persisting for 3 years, outspread, very stiff and thick, somewhat twisted, deep green, 3–8 cm long, 2 mm wide, sharp acuminate, margins serrate, stomatal lines on both sides, resin ducts in the parenchyma, sheaths 6 mm long, persistent; cones axillary, solitary or grouped 2–5 on short, thick stalks, symmetrical to somewhat oblique, ovate, 6–9 cm long, 4–6 cm wide, light brown, occasionally persisting on the branches for 15 years, scales 25 mm long and 12 mm wide, scale ends raised in pyramidal shape, with sharp cross-ridges, umbo oblong conical, with hook-like, thick thorns, seeds 5–6 mm long, brown to black, wings 20–25 mm long. OCC 344; GTP 62; SPi 298–300; CCE 374. Eastern N. America, from New Jersey to Georgia, in the mountains, dry areas in gravelly soil. 1804. Easily distinguished from the other 2 needle pines by the stiff, sharp prickly needles and the very thorny cones developed on young plants. Fig. 146, 154. z7

P. quadrifolia Parl ex Sudw. Tree, to 15 m, flat crown; needles normally in 4's, occasionally only 3 or 5, short, 3–4 cm long, blue-green, very stiff, margins smooth or sparsely serrate; cones nearly globose, 5 cm thick, scale ends very thick. MP 153 (H); SPa 8; MPi 55–58 (= *P. parryana* Engelm.; *P. cembroides* var. *parryana* [Engelm.] Voss). USA; California, dry mountain slopes. z7

P. radiata D. Don. Monterey Pine. Tree, 10–30 m in its habitat, trunk 30–60 cm in diameter, with a broad, irregular, rounded crown, bark of older trunks very thick, dark brown, deeply fissured, branches stout, spreading, young shoots yellow-brown, glabrous, buds cylindrical, 12–18 mm long, short acuminate, not resinous, bud scales chestnut-brown, loosely appressed, glossy; needles in 3's, occasionally also in 2's, very densely arranged, persisting for 3–4 years, 10–14 cm long, 1 mm wide, rather thin, with sharp tips, margins finely and densely serrate, conspicuously bright green, stomatal lines indistinct on both sides, resin ducts in the parenchyma, sheaths 8–12 mm long, persistent; cones sessile or with short stalks, solitary or grouped 3–5, outspread, very oblique and asymmetrical, oval-conical, 7–14 cm long, 5–6 cm wide, dark brown, persisting closed for many years on the tree, seed scales on the outer side of the cones very large and thick, nearly hemispherical, umbo with a fine thorn, those on the branch side of the cone much smaller, flat, all eventually nearly thornless, seeds ovate, 6 mm long, blackish, with about 25 mm long wings. SN 255 (H); SPi 319–328; SPa 10–21;

MPi 296–297; DJ 95; CCE 374; 375 (= *P. insignis* Dougl. ex Loud.). Monterey Peninsula, south of San Francisco, California, USA. 1833. Very significant forestry and garden tree in milder areas. Plate 107; Fig. 146, 149. z8–9

'Aurea'. Needles golden-yellow (= *P. radiata* var. *aurea* T. W. Adams). Originated in New Zealand.

f. **binata** Engelm. ex Brewer & Watson. Needles always in 2's. MPi 297. Guadalupe Island, California.

P. resinosa Ait. American Red Pine. Tree, 21–24 m, occasionally higher, trunk slender and of even diameter, in dense stands often unbranched to a great height and then with only a small crown, old trees in open stands however, with a broad, round crown, bark about 25 mm thick, red-brown, rather flatly furrowed, branches horizontal or nodding, young shoots stout, orange to purple-brown, not pruinose, glabrous, buds ovate to narrowly conical, long acuminate, 12 mm long, red-brown, resinous; needles in 2's, densely covering the twigs, persisting for 4 years, twisted once on the axis, appressed to the branch for 2 years, in the 3rd year outspread, dark green, flexible, 12–17 cm long, 1 mm wide, sharply acuminate, margins finely and regularly serrate, stomatal lines indistinct on both sides, resin ducts at the epidermis, needle sheaths 18–20 mm long, abscising in the 2nd year; cones terminal, grouped 1 or 2, sessile, spreading horizontally, symmetrical, oval-conical, abruptly pointed at the apex, 4–6 cm long, 3–4 cm wide, light brown, abscising in the 3rd year, some scales remaining on the branch, scale ends slightly thickened, the cross ridge indistinct, umbo very obtuse, nearly black, seeds 3 mm long, oval, light brown, wings about 18 mm long. GTP 52; SPi 170–171; CC 17 (H); CCE 376. Eastern N. America, from Newfoundland westward to Ontario, and south to Manitoba. 1736. One of the most important timber species in N. America. Plate 107; Fig. 157. z2

'Globosa'. Dwarf form, globose, densely branched, shoots very densely arranged, light yellow, buds conical; needles very densely arranged in clusters, variable in length (= *P. resinosa* var. *globosa* Rehd.). Discovered in a forest in 1921 and sent to the Arnold Arboretum.

P. × rhaetica Bruegger (*P. mugo* × *P. sylvestris*). Small tree, bark brownish-gray; needles dark-green, gray-green above, acute, 4 cm long; young cones with 3 mm long stalks, purple-brown, later directed obliquely downward, oval, acuminate, 3–3.5 cm long, asymmetrical, cinnamon-brown, dull when closed, glossy yellow-brown when open, scale ends bulging with a notably larger upper surface, umbo large and mucronulate. Discovered before 1864 in the Plaungood Forest near Samaden, Upper Engadin, Switzerland, also in other areas. Not in cultivation

P. rigida Mill. Pitch Pine. Tree, 10–15(25) m, crown irregularly open, trunk often sprouts short clusters of shoots or adventitious buds (!!), bark of older trunks black-brown and deeply fissured, thin plate-like scales on young trunks, branches stout, nearly horizontal, young shoots light green at first, then orange-brown, glabrous, furrowed, buds cylindrical to oval-oblong, sharply acuminate, 6–14 mm long, usually resinous,

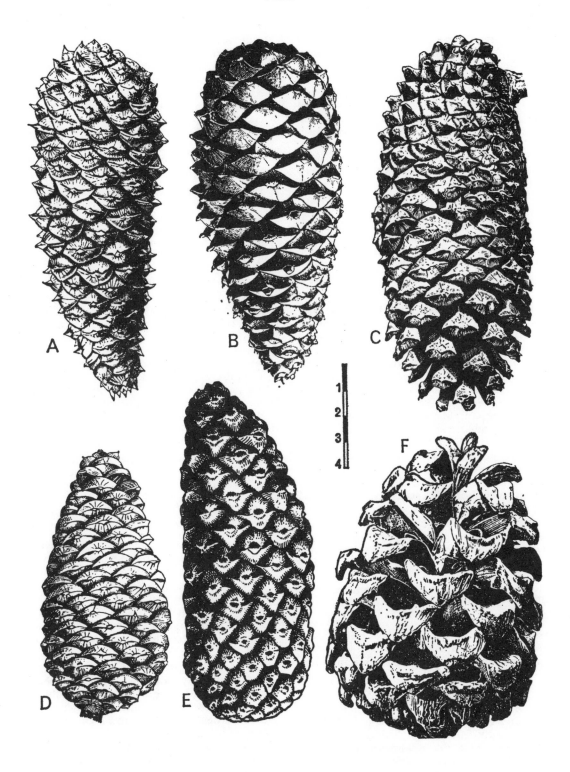

Fig. 155. **Pinus** cones. A. *P. taeda;* B. *P. pinaster;* C. *P. ponderosa;* D. *P. echinata;*
E. *P.montezumae* var. *hartwegii;* F. *P.gerardiana*

scales brown, appressed, with distinct tips; needles in 3's, stiff and outspread, persisting for 2 years, somewhat bowed and twisted, light green to yellow-green when young (!), later more dark green, 7–14 cm long, but usually 7–8 cm, long acuminate, finely dentate on the margin, flat on the dorsal side, to 2 mm wide, with many stomatal lines on either side, 9–12 mm long, red-brown, persistent; cones laterally arranged, in clusters of 2–5, on short, scaly shoots, stalk 6 mm long or also sessile, oval-conical, 7–10 cm long, somewhat curved, asymmetrical, light brown, glossy, opening late and irregularly, scale ends rhombic, flat to convex, cross-keeled, umbo flat or indented, thorn very short or totally absent, seeds triangular, gray, 4 mm long, wings 15 mm long, brownish. LT 35; MP 195 (H); GTP 54; BFN 373 (H); SN 58; OCC 346; CCE 377–378. NE. North America; Maine to Ontario and Ohio, southward to northern Georgia; on poor soil, also in swamps. 1750. Winter hardy. Plate 113; Fig. 114, 146. z4

var. *serotina* see: **P. serotina**

P. roxburghii Sarg. Long Leaved Indian Pine. Tree, to 50 m or higher, trunk 2–3 m in diameter, with a broad crown on older trees, bark of older trunks dark gray or reddish, exfoliating in large plates, deeply furrowed on young trees and exfoliating in narrow strips, young shoots gray to light brown, covered with the needle sheaths for several years, buds ovate, resin free, scales tightly appressed; needles in 3's, usually persisting for 1–3 years, totally or partly abscising in dry soil or after a long dry period and occasionally at the end of the growing season (!!), light green, thin, 20–30 cm long, eventually limply pendulous, long and finely acuminate, margins finely serrate, stomatal lines indistinct on all sides, resin ducts at the epidermis, needle sheaths 12–25 mm long; cones with short, thick stalks, oval-conical, 10–17 cm long, 6–8 cm thick at the base, scale ends thick and woody, the umbo parts thickened and reflexed, apophysis cross-keeled, apex tapered and broadly beak-form recurved, seeds 8–12 mm long, with about 25 mm long, adnate wings. HAl 112, 116, 116 (H); MP 279 (H); LT 30; SPi 160–162; SDK 1: 49 (C); CCE 378 (= *P. longifolia* Roxb. non Salisb.). Himalaya; Afghanistan to Bhutan, 450–2300 m, developing forests of solid stands. Plate 105. z9

P. rzedowskii Madrigal & Caballero (1969) from Michoacan, Mexico, can presumably be included in the Subsection *Balfourianae*, but a detailed description has not yet been made.

P. sabiniana Dougl. Digger Pine. Tree, 12–21 m, occasionally also larger, often multistemmed from the base, crown open and rounded, loosely foliate, bark gray-brown, thick, deeply fissured, exfoliating in irregular plates, thereby showing the red-brown inner bark, branches wavy and irregularly arranged, young shoots thin, blue-green, glabrous, furrowed, buds narrowly cylindrical, acute, 2–2.5 cm long, resinous, scales appressed, fringed on the margin, light brown; needles in 3's, persisting for 3 years, outspread or pendulous, light blue-green(!), 20–30 cm long, 1.5 mm wide, sharply acuminate, serrate on the margins, stomatal lines on all sides, resin ducts in the parenchyma, needles sheaths

about 25 mm long at first, light brown, silky, later reflexed; cones solitary or several laterally arranged, stalked, nodding, persisting for 3–7 years on the tree and leaving some scales on the branch when abscising, 15–25 cm long, red-brown, seed scales woody, 5 cm long, scale ends raised pyramidal form, 2 edged, tapering to a very stout umbo and terminating in a sharp, inward curving tip, basal scales lying in a deep cavity, cylindrical, 2–3 cm long, with a very thick, short membranous margin, edible. SN 252 (H); DJ 95; SPa 17, SPi 326–328; CCE 379. California; on dry hills, at 150–1500 m. Plate 112; Fig. 147, 161. z8

P. × schwerinii Fitschen (*P. wallichiana* × *P. strobus*). Tree, 10–15 m (perhaps taller), branches spreading widely, long, horizontal, tips nodding; twigs wavy, young shoots 3–4 mm thick; green, distinctly pruinose, finely short haired, buds cylindrical-conical, 6–7 mm long, resinous, scales appressed, brownish; needles 5, usually 10–11 cm long, thin, limp, pendulous, rough margined, with 3–4 blue-white stomatal lines on the ventral sides; cones nearly terminal, in groups of several together, on 2–2.5 cm long stalks, cylindrical, straight or slightly curved, 8–15 cm long, to 4.5 cm wide, brown to gray, resinous, scales only slightly convex (but not as much so as *P. wallichiana*), with a more or less distinct longitudinal bulge, scale ends faintly longitudinally striped. OCC 349 (C); DV 20: 107. Originated in 1905 in the garden of Count Schwerin, near Berlin, but first recognized in 1931. Very interesting for the garden, similar to *P. wallichiana*, but with a crown twice as wide. z7

P. serotina Michx. Small tree, bark furrowed in scales, buds very resinous; needles much longer than those of *P. rigida*, 12–20 cm long, less rough; cones nearly globose, often persisting for many years on the tree, variable in form. WT 9 (= *P. rigida* var. *serotina* [Michx.] Loud. ex Hoopes). SE. USA, from N. Carolina to Florida, on moist sites or in flat swampy areas. 1713. z8

P. sibirica Du Tour. Tree, to 33 m, narrowly conical, but often with a more ellipsoid crown as a young tree, bud scales glossy brown; needles 7 to 15 cm long, 1 mm wide; cones 6–12 cm long, 5–7.5 cm wide, more than 1.5 times longer than wide, seeds with an easily broken shell. MP 234 (H); SDK 1: 42; SN 49; CCE 237 (= *P. cembra* var. *sibirica* [Du Tour] Loud.). Siberia; often on wet bogs in its habitat. The seeds are commonly eaten in Russia. Plate 100. z3?

P. × sondereggeri H. H. Chapman (*P. palustris* × *P. taeda*). Sparsely branched tree, bark reddish-brown, young shoots light brown, buds broadly conical, light brown, scales with a white or gray ciliate limb, apices distinct; needles in 3's, with a 2 cm long sheath at first, later only 8 mm long, sharply acuminate, margins finely serrate. Natural hybrid, in the range of both of the parents, SE. USA. z9

P. stankewiczii (Sukaczev) Fomin. Needles 13–18 cm long rather stiff; cones yellow, usually solitary, rarely in 2's, oval-conical, acute, scale ends raised, rounded-rhombic, with a cross-ridge, umbo ellipsoidal, deeply indented. OCC 311; CCE 338 (= *P. halepensis* var. *stankewiczii* [Sukaczev] Fitsch.). Crimean Peninsula, southern part. z8–9

Fig. 156. **Pinus** cones. A. *P. jeffreyi*; B. *P. monticola* (from Sudworth)

P. strobiformis Engelm. "Pino Enano". Tree, to 25 m in its habitat, crown broad and round, trunk to 1 m in diameter, bark of older trunks dark brown, deeply furrowed, gray-white and smooth on young stems, branches rather thin, young shoots reddish-brown at first and finely pubescent, soon glabrous and bluish pruinose, buds brown; needles in 5's, 4–9 cm long, thin, entire or only very slightly serrate on the margin, bluish-green, sheath 1.5–2 cm long, abscising quickly; cones short stalked to nearly sessile, pendulous, cylindrical, 15–25 cm long, yellow-brown, opening when ripe, scales thick, rounded on the apex, scale ends ocher-yellow, glossy, elongated, and somewhat reflexed, umbo thornless, seeds ovate, 5–12 mm long, wingless, red-brown, black speckled. MPi 75–77; MP 202 (H) (= *P.*

reflexa Engelm.; *P. ayacahuite* var. *brachyptera* Shaw). Northern Mexico and the border states of the USA. z9

P. strobus L. Weymouth's Pine (Europe), Eastern White Pine (USA). Large tree, crown broadly conical, very old trees 25–50 m high, wide and picturesque, trunk straight, bark smooth and glossy for many years, gray-green, longitudinally furrowed when very old, dark, wrinkled, branches spreading horizontally, young shoots very thin, light greenish-brown, quite finely pubescent or also glabrous, buds oval-oblong, acute, 5–7 mm long, orange, not very resinous, scales tightly appressed, with a broad, white, membranous limb; needles in 5's, persisting for 2–3 years, straight, thin, soft, blue-green, 5–10 cm long, obtuse, margins serrate, with 2–3 stomatal lines on the ventral side, resin ducts at the epidermis; cones terminal, grouped 1–3, pendulous, on about 20–24 mm stalks, narrowly cylindrical, 8–20 cm long, to 4 cm wide, brown, ripening in the fall of the 2nd year, persisting on the tree after the seeds are released, scale ends thin, gray-yellow, slightly protruding, furrowed in the middle, with an obtuse umbo, seeds small, ovate, 5–6 mm long, brown, wings 18–20 mm long, brown. DJ 99; BFN 347; SPi 119–123. Eastern N. America, from Canada to the Alleghenies, in the plains, often on moist soil. 1705. The name Weymouth's Pine comes from Lord Weymouth who planted this tree throughout England in the 18th century. Plate 113; Fig. 146. z3

Includes the following forms:

'Alba'. Habit normal, like the type, but young needles whitish-green, upright, rather short (= *P. strobus* var. *alba* Loud.; *P. strobus nivea* R. Smith; *P. strobus* var. *argentea* Sénécl.). Cultivated in the Dortmund Bot. Garden, otherwise quite rare.

'Brevifolia'. Dwarf form, shrubby habit with a flat top, 1–2 m high and wide, usually lower; needles thinner, only 2.5–3.5 cm long. 1955.

var. **chiapensis** Martinez. Tree, 25–30 m, trunk to 1 m in diameter; needles clustered at the branch tips, 8–12 cm long, bright green underneath, glossy, blue-green above, sheaths 13–15 mm long, abscising quickly; cones on 28–35 mm bowed stalks, pendulous, cylindrical, about 14 cm long, 5 cm wide, brown, seed scales rounded at the apex, with an undulate margin. MPi 100–103. Mexico, Guatemala. z9

'Contorta'. Trunk twisted, branches ascending and twisted, also the young shoots; needles densely arranged, 5–8 cm long; cones 4–7 cm long (= *P. strobus* f. *contorta* Slavin). In Seneca Park, Rochester, New York, USA since 1932.

'Densa'. Dwarf, form, compact habit and very densely branched; needles only 4 cm long, very thin. American form.

'Fastigiata'. Columnar form, young plants, however, shrubby at first, typically narrowly upright only after a few years (= *P. strobus* var. *fastigiata* Beissn. 1884; *P. strobus* var. *pyramidalis* Schneid. 1913).

'Glauca'. Like the type, but the needles more blue-green (= *P. strobus glauca* Veillard). 1893. Occasionally found as a chance seedling.

'Gracilis Viridis'. Characterized by its delicate, thin, light green needles. OCC 350 (= *P. strobus* f. *gracilis viridis* Beissn. 1891).

'Inversa'. Branches pendulous. Developed in the USA in the garden of H. Rohrbach, Andover, Massachusetts. (1960).

'Macopin'. Originated as a witches'-broom, developing into an open, broad bush, about 1 m high and wide (or more), annual shoots dense, 7–8 cm long; needles distinctly blue-green (due to the stomata), spreading irregularly in various directions. WM 374 (H). Discovered by Gotelli, USA and named for the place of origin, Macopin, New Jersey.

'Minima'. Dwarf form, flat globose, much wider than high, twigs very thin; needles very thin, but also rather stiff, only 25 mm long, somewhat bowed, dark green (= *P. strobus* var. *minima* Hornib.). 1923. (R)

f. **monophylla** Tubeuf. Needles cling together their entire length creating the illusion of only 1 needle. 1897. (EX?)

'Nana' can only be considered a collective name; plants found under this name in nurseries are normally **'Radiata'**. Plate 113.

'Nana' (Weiss). Dwarf form, grows broadly globose, wider than high, dense, tight, and branched to the ground, very slow growing, annual growth about 5 cm. Selected in 1966 by A. &&HSM. Weiss of Seeheim, W. Germany.

'Pendula'. Tall, shrubby and multistemmed, or only single stemmed, branches spreading horizontally and widely, drooping partly to the ground. 1866.

'Prostrata'. Dwarf habit, procumbent, branches ascending from the ground up, twigs horizontal at first, spreading along the ground. DJ Pl. 34 (H); WM 377 (H); CCE 386 (= *P. strobus prostrata* Rehd.). Discovered before 1899 by A. Rehder in the Arnold Arboretum, but also found later by Beissner in a private garden in Thuringia, W. Germany. (EX?)

'Pumila'. Dwarf form, globose habit, annual growth about 5 cm, buds only 3 mm long; needles about 10 cm long, fine, silvery-green twisted and somewhat bowed (= *P. strobus pumila* Gord.). Cultivated since 1875 in England, but quite rare. Totally different from *P. strobus* 'Radiata'.

'Radiata'. Dwarf form, very compact habit, globose, to 1.5 m high and equally wide as a very old plant, twigs densely crowded, slender, slightly pubescent at the base of the needle sheaths, buds 3 mm long, scales appressed, dark brown; needles all directed upward at the branch tips, uneven in length, 7–9 cm long, sharply acuminate, green on the dorsal side, distinctly blue-green above, never pendulous (!!). OCC 351; HD 206; HiD 54; WDw 221; WM 30A (Br) (= *P. strobus* var. *radiata* Hornib.). (R)

'Umbraculifera'. Dwarf, umbrella-shaped shrub, 2–2.5 m high, much wider than high, dense, but usually not branched to the ground; needles 4–5 cm long in dense clusters, often dropping off early, especially when soil conditions are stressful, gray-green with gray-white underside. Often incorrectly labeled *P. strobus* 'Radiata'. This is understandable when the plants are young, since the differences are hardly noticeable; in maturity *P. strobus* 'Radiata' does not develop the umbrella shape. However, both are sold under the name *P. strobus* 'Nana', although this is not a published synonym of *P. strobus* 'Umbraculifera'. Welch writes in this "Manual of Dwarf Conifers" that he considers 'Umbraculifera' a dwarf form of *P. wallichina*.

'Variegata'. Needles partly yellow, partly green; but seldom consistent (= *P. strobus* var. *variegata* Nels.; *P. strobus* var. *aurea* Nels.; *P. strobus aureovariegata* Sénécl.). 1966.

P. sylvestris L. Scotch Pine. Tree, 10–30(40) m, depending on location, climate and soil, either with a straight, slender, tall branch-free trunk or much lower with a knobby, twisted, short trunk and a broad umbrella-shaped crown, bark of older trunks gray-brown, rust-red inside, split, exfoliating in irregular pieces, fox-red on young trees, thin, exfoliating, young shoots greenish, gray-brown in the 2nd year, buds oblong-ovate, 6–12 mm long, reddish-brown, normally resin free or also resinous; needles in 2's, persisting about 3 years, stiff, normally somewhat twisted, 4–7 cm long, to 2 mm wide, acute, blue or gray-green, serrate on the margins, with distinct stomatal lines above, resin ducts at the epidermis, needle sheaths 8 mm long, shorter later; cones usually solitary or grouped 2–3, with a long or short stalk, pendulous, oval-conical, 2.5–7 cm long, 2–3.5 cm wide, gray-brown, dull, scale ends on the outside of the cones more developed than those on the shady side, nearly rhombic, to 8 mm wide, flat or raised in pyramidal shape, with a slightly protruding cross-ridge, umbo small, smooth, glossy light brown (not black

Fig. 157. **Pinus** cones. A. *P. thunbergii*; B. *P. densiflora*; C. *P. resinosa*; D. *P. heldreichii*;
E. *P. nigra* ssp. *nigra*; F. *P. halepensis*; G. *P. banksiana*; H. *P. mugo*

bordered!), usually not mucronulate, seeds 3–4 mm long, oval-oblong, wings 3 times as long. BFN 415 (H); SN 18 (H); DJ 96; SPi 182–185. Europe, through Siberia to the Amur region of East Asia; mountains of the Crimean Peninsula, parts of Caucasia, Asia Minor and Iran; and in the Alps to 1800 (2100 at most) m. Fig. 146, 154; Range map Fig. 158. z2

Outline of the Varieties and Forms of *Pinus sylvestris*

1. Geographical Varieties

Gaussen 1960: 61–64 describes about 30 geographical varieties and races, most as yet not well known. Altogether, more than 150 varieties have been described. The most important of these are listed in "Flora Europa" (1964) in the following 5 groups.

Group I: var. *lapponica* Fries:
Crown narrow, much branched, bark with thin, small scales. N. Scandinavia.

Group II: var. *rigensis* (Desf.) Asch. & Graeb.; var. *septentrionalis* Schott:
Tree with a narrow, conical crown, straight trunk, thin bark. Baltic Coast.

Group III: var. *scotica* (Willd.) Schott:
Crown very long-conical, only rounded on old trees, thin bark, at least on the upper trunk. Scotland.

Group IV: var. *aquitana* Schott;
                var. *brigantiaca* Gaussen;
                var. *catalaunica* Gaussen;
                var. *hercynica* Münch;
                var. *iberica* Svob.;
                var. *pyrenaica* Svob.;
                var. *vindelica* Schott:
Conical crown, straight trunk, branches at right angles to the stem, thin bark, large scaly. Mountains of W. Europe, from central Spain to central Germany and the West Alps.

Group V: var. *batava* Schott;
                var. *borussica* Schott;
                var. *carpatica* Klika;
                var. *engadinensis* Heer;
                var. *nevadensis* Christ.;
                var. *pannonica* Schott;
                var. *rhodopaea* Svob.;
                var. *romanica* Svob.;
                var. *sarmatica* Zapal;
                var. *vocontiana* Guinier & Gaussen:
Curved trunk, crown broad rounded, branches at acute angles to the stem, bark deeply split. Lowlands and foothills of the central European mountains, eastward to Russia, south to the Northern Apennines and Sierra Nevada.
var. *armena*
f. *kakateimenos*
f. *turfosa*

2. Differing in the trunk bark

f. *annulata*   f. *kienitzii*
f. *bonapartei*   f. *seitzii*
f. *gibberosa*

3. Differing in the cones

f. *hamata*   f. *macrocarpa*

4. Differing in the flowers

f. *erythranthera*

Fig. 158. Range of *Pinus sylvestris* in Europe

5. Cultivars
a) Growth habit

Not dwarf:

columnar and conical:	'Fastigiata' 'Pyramidalis Glauca'
weeping form:	'Pendula'
whip-like form:	'Virgata'
branches twisted:	f. *anguina*, f. *tortuosa*

Dwarf forms:
'Albyns', 'Argentea Compacta', 'Beuvronensis', 'Columnaris Compacta', 'Compressa', 'Doone Valley', 'Genevensis', 'Globosa', 'Globosa Viridis', 'Hibernia', 'Nana', 'Pygmaea', 'Pyramidalis Compacta', 'Repanda', 'Repens', 'Saxatilis', 'Umbraculifera', 'Viridis Compacta', 'Watereri', 'Windsor'

b) Needle variations

Needles normal bluish-green:

shorter:	'Microphylla', f. *parvifolia*, f. *lubonii*
much wider, bluer:	f. *latifolia*, 'Glacua Draht', 'Kamon Blue'
longer:	f. *divaricata*
sickle-shaped:	f. *spiralis*
"single needled":	'Monophylla'

Needles:

silver-gray:	'Alba', f. *argentea*, 'Argentea Compacta', 'Nana', 'Pygmaea', 'Watereri'
milk-white:	'Nivea', 'Variegata'
yellow:	'Aurea' (= 'Winterfold'), 'Aureopicta', 'Beissneriana', 'Nisbet's Gem'

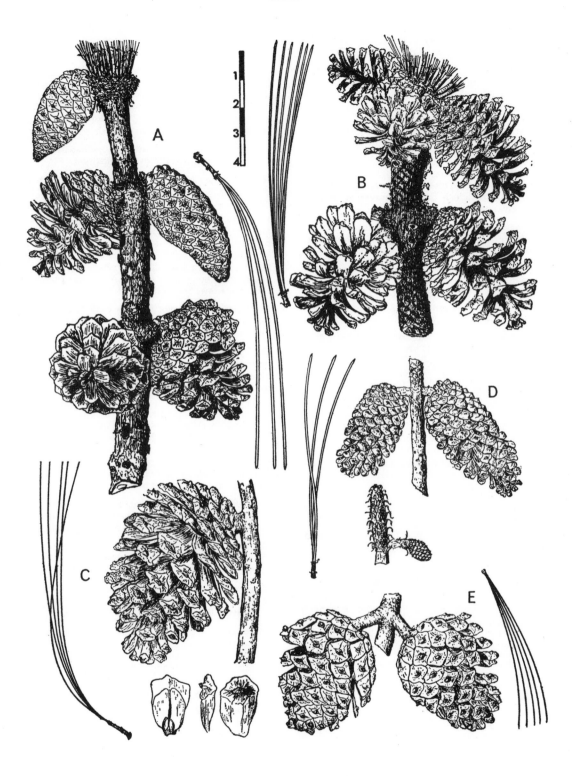

Fig. 159. **Pinus.** A. *P. pringlei,* branch with 5 cones and a needle fascicle; B. *P. durangensis,* branch with 6 cones; C. *P. pseudostrobus* with needle fasicle and 3 seed scales; D. *P. teocote,* 2 cones, terminal bud, female flower and needle fascicle; E. *P. leiophylla,* 2 cones and a needle fascicle (from Martinez)

'Alba'. Shoots light gray-brown to yellow-brown, annual growth 15–20 cm, terminal bud red-brown, spreading scale tips; needles 5–8 cm long, 1 mm wide, gray-blue. From the Bedgebury Pinetum, England.

'Albyns'. Dwarf form, lying flat on the ground, original plant only 30 cm high at 2.5 m wide, annual growth about 10 cm, branches horizontal to slightly ascending; foliage gray-green. Originated as a chance seedling about 1960 in the H. A. Albyn Nursery, Newark, Ohio, USA. Not generally cultivated in the USA, but growing in the Morton Arboretum (Illinois) and Dawes Arboretum (Ohio). (R)

f. anguina Schroed. Trunk and branches twisted back and forth, but eventually becoming a tall tree; blue-green needles; cones 4 cm long, scales conspicuously flat, very smooth at the base. 1899. Not in cultivation.

f. annulata Caspary. Shingle Pine. Differing in the form of the bark, bark scales in rings around the trunk with their bases outspread shingle-like. MD 1911: 348. Repeatedly observed in Germany and Poland. Not in cultivation.

f. argentea Stev. Tall, strong tree, bark thick, ash-gray or reddish; needles with a distinct silvery glaze, also the cones, scale ends elongated in a backward curving hook. 1839. Occurs in the wild in the Caucasus Mts.

'Argentea Compacta'. Dwarf form, conical or also more globose, 1.5–2 m high, quite densely branched; needles silver-gray. WDw 222 (H); WM 379 (H) (= *P. sylvestris argentea compacta* Ordn. 1899). Totally different from *P. sylvestris* 'Watereri'.

var. armena (K. Koch). Fitsch. Needles glossy green, distinctly acuminate, not covering the shoot; cones on thick, very short stalks when young, erect or horizontally arranged when ripe, yellow-brown, slightly glossy, apical scale ends raised, upper half of the apophysis often very bluntly keeled, basal scale ends (except on the sunny side) slightly raised or flat (= *P. armena* K. Koch). Crimea, Caucasus, Asia Minor, Iran.

'Aurea'. Compact, rounded bush, slow growing; young needles yellow-green, golden-yellow in winter (= *P. sylvestris aurea* Ottolander). Cultivated since 1876.

'Aureopicta'. Needle tips golden-yellow (= *P. sylvestris aureopicta* Sénécl.). Cultivated since 1868. (VR)

'Bakony'. Developed from a witches'-broom, blue-green. DB 18: 171. Discovered in Hungary and introduced by Barabits, Sopron.

'Beissneriana'. New growth normal green then becoming yellow and remaining so from July to winter (= *P. sylvestris* var. *beissneriana* Schwerin). Developed in the Tharandt Forest Garden, W. Germany in 1896. (EX?)

'Beuvronensis'. Dwarf form, irregular habit, about 50 cm high in 25 years, annual growth about 3.5 cm, densely branched, shoots green, glossy, smooth, buds ovate, 5–6 mm long, very resinous; needles about 1.5 cm long, blue-green, sheaths about 5 to 6 mm long. HiD 55; WDw 224 (H); WM 27B (Br), 380 (H) (= *P. sylvestris beuvronensis* Transon ex Beissn). Discovered as a witches'-broom, propagated and introduced before 1891 by Transon Frères, Orléans, France. Very attractive dwarf form.

f. bonapartei Seitz. Mussel Pine. Bark similar to that of *Picea abies*, composed of thin, concave, loose margined plates, twigs brownish, short, ascending, developing a very acute, tight crown; needles blue-green, densely arranged; cones with flat scale ends. MD 1933 Pl. 6, 1931 Pl. 38. Grows primarily in East Prussia (presently in Poland and USSR).

'Columnaris Compacta'. Columnar form, resembling a *Pinus cembra* in habit, grows to several meters high, very densely branched; needles 4–5 cm long, dark green, without a bluish tone. Rev. Hort. 1889: 393 (H) (= *P. sylvestris* var. *columnaris compacta* Croux). Discovered before 1889 by Croux in Sceaux, France. (VR)

'Compressa'. Dwarf form, columnar habit, twigs erect, tightly appressed to the stem, new shoots ascending at very acute angles, short, stiff, dark brown, annual growth 4–5 cm; needles clustered, only 1–2 cm long, occasionally twisted; cones very small. Developed in France in 1867.

f. divaricata Wahlenb. Needles longer than those of the species. Carpathian Mts. 1814. Not in cultivation.

'Doone Valley'. Dwarf form, very compact with a somewhat conical habit; needles intensely blue. WM 381 (H). English cultivar.

var. engadinensis Heer. Tree, to 15 m high or also only broad and shrubby, branched to the ground; bark thin and reddish; buds resinous; needles to 3 cm long, thick and stiff, gray-green, very densely arranged; cones oval-conical, 3.5–5 cm long, very acuminate, short stalked, yellowish, glossy, ripening late, scale ends with large, obtuse umbo, usually surrounded by a black ring. Engadine, Switzerland.

f. erythranthera Sanio. Anthers pink to carmine-brown-red. Occurs sporadically in natural stands; first observed in 1871. Not in cultivation.

'Fastigiata'. Strict, columnar habit, to 15 m high or more, branches rather stiff, tightly appressed, as are the twigs; needles blue-green; cones small, ovate. Identified in 1856 and commonly observed. Found in France, Finland, Norway and Germany.

'Genevensis'. Dwarf form, with a few, outspread branches, buds dark carmine-brown; needles in clusters at the branch tips, pale gray-blue, 18–36 mm long, very thin, differing from 'Beuvronensis' in the more compressed, less outspread, needles (= *P. sylvestris genevensis* Beissn.). Origin unknown, but presumably developed by Simon-Louis in Metz, France by whom it was introduced before 1890.

f. gibberosa Kihlmann. Knobby Pine. Stem covered with numerous knots, these can be 25–50 cm thick. Gartenflora 1905: 557 (H); MD 1911: 320. Not in cultivation.

'Glauca Compacta'. Similar to 'Watereri', but more narrowly upright; needles somewhat darker blue-green. Originally selected by Herm. A. Hesse of Weener, W. Germany.

'Glauca Draht'. Strong grower, crown broadly conical. Clone, selected for its especially intense blue needle color by the Draht Nursery in Barmstedt, Holstein, W. Germany.

'Globosa'. Low growing, compact, branches stiff, winter buds cylindrical and long acuminate, terminal buds surrounded by 3–4 smaller buds, red-brown; needles twisted, outspread, stiff, straight, only 3–4 cm long, gray-green, leaf sheaths short, black-brown. WM 382 (= *P. sylvestris globosa* Hort.; *P. sylvestris pygmaea* Beissn. 1891; *P. sylvestris pygmaea* Hornibr.).

'Globosa Viridis'. Dwarf form, rather globose or more ovate in habit, 1–1.5 m high, twigs densely crowded and outspread to the ground, shoots short; needles to 10 cm long, 2 mm wide, often twisted for half their length, rather stiff, dark green, produces new needles in late summer, these cover the winter buds. WM 27C (Br), 383 (H); CCE 383 (= *P. sylvestris globosa viridis* Beissn.). 1900.

f. hamata Stev. Cones narrowly conical, apex pointed, scale ends on the exposed side with 5 cm long hooks protruding from the otherwise flat surface, these recurved on the basal scales, partly curved toward the cone apex on the apical scales (= *P. sylvestris uncinata* Don of Forfar; *P. sylvestris* f. *reflexa* Heer). 1804. Not in cultivation.

Fig. 160. **Pinus** cones. A. *P. palustris*; B. *P. wallichiana*; C. *P. lambertiana*; D. *P. armandii*; E. *P. teocote*; F. *P. koraiensis*

The cone of *P. lambertiana* illustrated here is somewhat out of scale,
actually 30–50 cm long!

'**Hibernica**'. Dwarf form, oval, but growing about 10 cm annually on mature plants, winter buds conspicuously red; needles rather short, blue; cones produced on small plants, but abscising quickly. WM 384 (H). Found as a witches'-broom in Glendalough, County Wicklow, Ireland by J. D. Zu Jeddeloh; introduced by him in 1962.

'**Iceni**'. Strong growing 'Watereri' type, annual growth 10–15 cm, terminal bud acute-ovate, 15 mm long, brown, usually with 2 side buds; needles light blue-green, 6–8 mm long, 1.5–2 mm wide.

f. **kakateimos** Graebn. Trunk and branches procumbent, to 2 m long and 0.5 m high at most, young shoots conspicuously long and thin; needles only about 25 mm long; small cones. Found in the dunes on the east coast of Denmark, Sweden and northern Russia. 1899.

'**Kamon Blue**' (Barabits). Tree, of normal vigor, very broadly conical, densely branched; needles intensely blue, twisted (!). Selected and distributed by E. Barabits, Sopron, Hungary, about 1965.

f. **kienitzii** Seitz. Scaly Pine. Crown conical, tight, bark similar to that of *Larix decidua*, longitudinally split, with large, relatively narrow, brown, partly imbricate, very thick scales on the basal trunk, twigs short, ascending; needles densely arranged, dark green; cones with stout scale ends and a long apex. MD 1929 Pl. 13, 1933 Pl. 6. In the range of the species, especially on wet soil.

var. **lapponica** Fries. Lapland Pine. Spruce-like crown, narrow, acute, trunk predominantly straight, slow growing, branches ascending obliquely or pendulous; dense foliage, needles short, green, persisting 4–7 years; cones more yellowish, scale ends convex and hook-like, seeds small, brown, wings reddish-brown. N. and Central Scandinavia, Lapland.

f. **latifolia** Gord. Very vigorous, tall; needles much wider and longer than all of the other forms and an excellent blue-gray. In the Caucasus Mts. and in Iran.

The Hungarian cultivar 'Kamoni' should be included here.

f. **lubonii** Staszkievicz. Needles only 16–20 m long. Found before 1958 in the western Carpathian Mts.

f. **macrocarpa** Schroed. With the exception of the cones, hardly distinguishable from the normal type, cones 2–3 times larger and heavier (10 average cones weigh 180 grams verses 70 grams for the normal type), the sunny side, especially near the stalk with conspicuous hook-form, curved umbo on the scale ends. Occurs in the forests around Moscow. Observed in 1894.

'**Microphylla**'. Needles only 10–15 mm long (= *P. sylvestris* var. *microphylla* Schwerin). Developed by Count Schwerin. 1891. (EX?)

'**Monophylla**'. Much weaker grower than the species, usually an open, irregular shrub; needle pairs usually clinging together for their entire length during the first year, normally separating in the 2nd year. (= *P. sylvestris monophylla* Loud.). Before 1867.

'**Moseri**' (J. J. Moser, France, before 1890). Slow growing dwarf form, round, shrubby habit, to about 1 m high and much wider; needles 4–6 cm long, remaining on the plant 3–4 years, green, lighter than those of the species, in winter light yellow-green, twisted and variable, giving the clusters an untidy look. According to Welch there is a very old plant in the Botanical Garden of Cambridge. There is also a fairly large example in the Trompenburg Arboretum in Rotterdam. Microscopic analysis of the needle structure has established that the plant derives from *P. sylvestris* and that it is closely related to 'Globosa

Viridis', from which 'Moseri' differs by the lower growth and the yellow color of the needles in winter. The name *P. nigra* 'Pygmaea' is therefore manifestly incorrect. (= *P. nigra* 'Pygmaea' Hort.).

'**Nana**'. Dwarf form, small, bushy, only about 50 cm high, very densely branched, twigs very short, directed upward; needles widely spaced, straight, 3 cm long, blue-green. WM 385 (H) (= *P. sylvestris nana* Carr.; *P. sylvestris pygmaea* Hort. non Beissn.). 1855. "Nana" of many nurseries is actually 'Watereri'.

var. **nevadensis** Christ. Needles wide, short, stiff, conspicuously white on the top due to stomatal lines; female flowers erect, purple-red; cones short stalked to nearly sessile, spreading obliquely, reddish-gray, dull surface, scale ends on the exposed side curved to pyramidal shape. Spain; Sierra Nevada. 1863.

'**Nisbet's Gem**'. Dwarf form, needles yellow. From the collection in the RHS Gardens, Wisley.

'**Nivea**'. Needles nearly milk-white on new growth, dirty white-green in summer, otherwise developing like the normal plant. Developed in 1906 by Count Schwerin. (EX)

f. **parvifolia** Heer. Needles about 2.5 cm long (= *P. brachyphylla* Wittrock). First observed in Sweden in 1862.

'**Pendula**'. Branches distinctly pendulous, the basal branches lying on the ground (= *P. sylvestris pendula* Lawson 1852). (EX)

'**Pygmaea**'. Dwarf form, to 1 m high, globose or nearly umbrella-shaped, shoots glossy red-brown, smooth, annual growth 2.5–3 cm, buds acutely ovate, 4–5 mm long, red, scale tips distinct, resinous; needles 12–25 mm long, tough, stiff, very twisted, margins dentate, not so blue as 'Watereri', sheaths 5 mm long. WDw 233 (H); WM 386 (H) (= *P. sylvestris pygmaea* Beissn.; *P. globosa nana* Hort.). 1891. (VR)

'**Pyramidalis Compacta**'. Dwarf form, conical, narrow, compact, stem very thick, sparsely branched, these upright, shoots ascending at acute angles, appressed to the main stem (when branching from the main stem), stout, brown; needles densely crowded, 2–4 cm long, 1.5 mm wide, stout, glossy dark green, compressed, usually curved inward to the shoot, persisting about 4–5 years (= *P. sylvestris pyramidalis compacta* Hornib. 1923). Developed by Simon-Louis in Metz, France. (EX?)

'**Pyramidalis Glauca**'. Conical form, short and densely branched; needles conspicuously blue-green. 1891. (EX)

'**Rependa**'. Broad habit, quite flat and branches horizontal, shoots stout, annual growth 10–15 cm, terminal bud cylindrical, 1.5 cm long, 5 mm thick, light brown, slightly resinous; needles 5–8 cm long, gray-green.

'**Repens**'. Very weak growing nest form, developing short, horizontal side shoots after a few years; needles long, deep green. WM 387 (H). Selected by Verkade, New Jersey, USA. Blight prone. (Jeddeloh). (R)

var. **rigensis** (Desf.) Asch. & Graeb. Very strong growing, especially when young, trunk tall and straight, bark very red, few branches, twigs very thick; needles very long and wide, glossy. Western and southern Scandinavia. Although fast growing, not an important forest tree because of its inferior wood and susceptibility to wind damage.

'**Riverside Gem**'. Very dense and compact.

'**Saxatilis**'. Dwarf form, prostrate, mat form habit, without a terminal leader, twigs very densely arranged; needles 15–25 mm long. Discovered before 1867 by A. Sénéclauze. (EX?)

var. **scotica** (Willd.) Schott. Highlands Pine. Tree, vigorous, bark not as rough as the type, branches quite horizontal;

needles wider and much bluer; cones thicker and not so acute, scale ends flat at the base of the cone, apical scale ends more or less pyramidal (= *P. sylvestris* var. *rubra* [Mill.] Reichhard; *P. rubra* Mill.). Scotland.

f. **seitzii** Schwerin. Crown of older trees spreading umbrella-shaped and open, bark divided vertically and horizontally into wide, relatively thin, glossy light pink, patchwork plates, twigs more yellowish, outspread; needles light green and rather slightly prickly; cones with slightly raised scale ends. MD 1929 Pl. 13, 1936 Pl. 6, 1938 Pl. 19. On dry soil in the range of the species.

'**Sentinal**'. Slow growing, tight columnar form; needles appressed to the shoots. Can be considered an improvement on 'Fastigiata', which because of its very long annual shoots suffers under a snow load.

f. **spiralis** Carr. Strongly growing tree; needles long, bowed sickle-shaped, each in a different direction, giving the plant a ruffled appearance (= *P. sylvestris crispata* Schwerin). Observed repeatedly since 1859.

f. **tortuosa** Don of Forfar. Trunk and branches twisted; needles rather short. Observed in England and Saxony (now NW. Germany); known since 1852. Not in cultivation. (VR)

f. **turfosa** Woerl. Moor Pine. Only 1–2 m high, usually with a straight central leader, small, flat crown when older; needles only 25 mm long, bowed, often abscising in the 2nd year; cones small, numerous. NW. Germany, in the moors of the eastern sea coast, usually in sphagnum bogs; also in Denmark, Scandinavia, and N. Russia.

'**Umbraculifera**'. Broad rounded habit, low, branches few, out-spread, branchlets at nearly right angles to the branch, slightly ascending, rather thick; needles silvery-blue. 1855. (VR)

'**Variegata**'. Weak grower; needles white variegated, some also totally yellow-white or green, entire plant irregularly variegated. KN Pl. 7 (as *P. sylvestris* 'Argentea'). Often found in the wild, cultivated since 1855. (VR)

'**Virgata**'. Major branches irregularly upright and outspread, elongated, only the apical portion sparsely branched with whip- or rod-like twisted branchlets carrying few needles. Commonly found in France, Sweden, Tirol and Poland. 1882.

'**Viridis Compacta**'. Small tree, dwarf, conical, very loose, shoots yellow-green; needles very twisted, 4–8 cm long, stiff, glossy dark green on both sides, sheaths red-brown, to 2 cm long (!). 1923. (VR)

'**Watereri**'. Dwarf form, but growing 3–4 m high and nearly as wide (original tree is 7.5 m high!), annual growth about 5 cm, upright at first and broadly conical, later more globose due to the outward growing major branches, branch tips directed upward, buds acutely ovate, resinous; needles 25–40 mm long, blue-gray, narrow, stiff, twisted, sheaths persistent, white to brown, 8 mm long. WDw 226; DB 17: 325; WM 390 (H) (= *P. sylvestris watereri* Beissn. 1902; *P. sylvestris* f. *pumila* Beissn. 1891; *P. sylvestris nana* Den Ouden 1937). Discovered by Anthony Waterer in 1865 in Horsell Common, England and brought to his Knap Hill Nursery where the tree is still growing.

'**Windsor**'. Dwarf form, flat globose; needles very short, gray-green. Developed from a witches'-broom. (Hillier).

P. tabuliformis Carr. Chinese Pine. Tree, to 25 m in its habitat, but occasionally only a shrub, crown often broad and flat (but not always!!), stem short and thick, bark dark gray, fissured, young shoots light orange-yellow, pruinose at first, later light brown, glabrous, buds acute-oblong, light brown, little or no resin, scales tightly appressed, narrow, margin fringed; needles grouped 2(3), densely crowded at the branch tips, upright or outspread, 10–15 cm long, thin, often bluish-green, sharply acuminate, margins finely serrate, with stomatal lines on both sides, resin ducts usually at the epidermis, sheaths 6 mm long, persistent; cones solitary or grouped 2–3, nearly sessile, nodding, symmetrical or obliquely ovate, 4–9 cm long, light yellow-brown, dark brown when ripe, persisting for several years on the tree, scale ends nearly rhombic, compressed pyramidal, with a raised, sharp cross-ridge, umbo obtuse, apical scales only slightly mucronulate, seeds ovate, 4–5 mm long, red-brown, wings 15 mm long, brownish. CC 36 (H); SH 34 (H); SPi 201–207; LF 31–32; DJ 97; CBI 71; CIS 7 (= *P. sinensis* Mayr. non Lamb.; *P. henryi* Mast.; *P. wilsonii* Shaw). Northern and north-central China, in the mountains; also in Szechwan and N. Yunnan Provinces. 1862. Hardy. z5

var. **densata** (Mast.) Rehd. Differing in the consistently 2 needled fascicles, these 7.5–13 cm long, stiff; cones oblique, ovate, 5–6 cm long, basal seed scales with very prominent apophyses, umbo more or less curved (= *P. densata* Mast.). China; W. Szechwan Province, in the mountains.

P. taeda L. Loblolly Pine. Tree, 20–30(55) m in its habitat, trunk 0.80–1 m in diameter, young trees with gray or yellowish, smooth bark, fissured with age, crown rounded, with outspread branches, young shoots yellow-brown, glabrous, occasionally also pruinose, buds acutely conical, 6–12 mm long, light brown, not resinous, scales often fringed on the margin, tips reflexed; needles in 3's, persisting for about 3–4 years, light green, thin, but stiff, somewhat twisted, 15–25 cm long, 1.5 mm wide, long acuminate, margin finely dentate, stomatal lines on all sides, resin ducts in the parenchyma, sheaths about 25 mm long; cones laterally arranged, grouped 2–5 together, on very short, scaly shoots, sessile, symmetrical, oval-conical, 6–10 cm long, dull red-brown, scale ends light brown, somewhat compressed, pyramidal with a sharp cross-keel, umbo elongated in a stout, recurved triangular thorn, seeds rhombic, 6 to 7 mm long, brown-red, wings 2.5 cm long. SPi 264–267; CCE 386 (= *P. lutea* Walt.). USA, from southern New Jersey to Florida, east Texas, Oklahoma. 1713. Plate 113; Fig. 146, 155. z7

P. taiwanensis Hayata; Taiwan Pine. Large tree, to 35 m, trunk to 80 cm in diameter, straight, bark split into fine scales, branches spreading horizontally; needles in 2's, more or less stiff, 8–11 cm long, margins finely serrate, usually with 4 resin ducts; cones oblong-ovate, 5–7 cm long, seeds with 15–18 mm long wings. LT 36; MP 284 (H); CCE 386. China; Formosa, in the mountains, developing forests of solid stands at 750–3000 m. z9

P. teocote Cham. & Schlectend. Tree, 15–27 m, bark fissured, scaly, young shoots glabrous and pruinose, buds cylindrical-conical, about 18 mm long, resinous, scales fringed on the margin, tips distinct; needles usually in 3's, but also grouped 2–4–5, usually persisting for 3 years, spreading, stiff, 10–20 cm long, sharply acuminate, prickly, margins finely dentate, with stomatal lines on all sides, resin ducts usually 3 in the parenchyma, needle sheaths about 2.5 cm long, persistent; cones nearly terminal, occasionally lateral, solitary or in groups of 2, outspread or reflexed, oblong-ovate, about 5.5 cm long, dull brown, scales numerous, 18 mm long, 8 mm wide, scale ends flat or thickened, with cross-ridges, seeds small, with a narrow wing. MP 211 (H); MPi 123–128. Mexico; in the mountains, from 1500–3000 m. Fig. 159–160. z8–9

P. thunbergii Parl. Japanese Black Pine. Large tree, 30–40 m in its habitat, similar in appearance to *P. nigra*, crown broadly pyramidal, often also irregular, bark black-gray, fissured, branches horizontal or often somewhat pendulous, young shoots orange-yellow, gray-black in the 2nd year, glabrous, buds 12–18 mm long, ovate, acute, resin free, scales appressed, whitish, with a fringe; needles in 2's, persisting for 3 years, densely arranged, spreading, somewhat twisted, dark green, 6–12 cm long, 1.5–2 mm wide, sharply acuminate, margins finely serrate, with stomatal lines on both sides, resin ducts in the parenchyma, sheaths 12 mm long, persistent, terminating in 2 long filaments; cones terminal, either solitary or in groups of few or many (40–60 or more!!), outspread, short stalked, oval-conical, 4–6 cm long, 3–4 cm wide, brown, scale ends nearly rhombic, quite flat, compressed pyramidal, obtuse, with a low, sharp cross-ridge, umbo usually with a thorn, seeds oval-rhombic, 5 mm long, dull gray-brown, wings 15–50 mm long, light brown, dark striped, "knife-form". OCC 360; DJ 98; SPi 196 to 197; LT 8; KIF 1: 30; CCE 387, 388 (= *P. thunbergiana* Franco). Coast of Japan and S. Korea. 1852. Plate 107; Fig. 157. z5–6

Including 9 cultivars in Japan which are not included here.

P. torreyana Parry ex Carr. Torrey Pine. Small tree, 6–15 m or higher, similar to *P. sabiniana*, trunk 30–60 cm in diameter, bark irregularly and deeply furrowed, divided into wide plates, light gray, branches short and thick, young shoots light green, whitish pruinose, later reddish, buds cylindrical, long acuminate, resin free, scales fringed on the margin, needles in 5's, persisting for several years, clustered at the branch tips, very tough, dark green, 20–30 cm long, 2 mm wide, acute, apical margin finely serrate, stomatal lines on all sides, resin ducts in the parenchyma, needle sheaths about 18 mm long, persistent; cones broadly ovate, 10–15 cm long, symmetrical, stalk 3 cm long, horizontal or drooping downward, dark violet when young, glossy brown when ripe, ripening in the 3rd year, abscising the next year, scale ends distinctly thickened, umbo short and stout, occasionally elongated and incurved, seeds 20–25 mm long, ellipsoid, dull brown, speckled, edible, sweet, containing oil, wing ring-like encircling the seed. SN 242 (H); SPa 12; SPi 324–325; MP 175 (H). S. California; near San Diego and on Santa Rosa Island. 1853. Fig. 161. z8–9

P. uncinata Mill. ex Mirb. Similar to *P. mugo*, but differing in the tree-like habit, 10–20(25) m high, single stemmed; needles like those of *P. mugo*; cones very oblique, asymmetrical, 4–6 cm long, directed downward; scale ends form a 4 sided, beak-like, recurved pyramid, with a clearly exserted umbo. (Fig. 148). SN 271 (H); OCC 324 (C); CCE 189, 390 (= *P. mugo* var. *rostrata* [Ant.] Gord.; *P.*

montana var. *uncinata* [DC.] Heer; *P. mugo* var. *arborea* [Tubeuf] Hylander). Engadine Valley, Switzerland to the west Alps, Cevennes and Pyrenees at 1300–2200 m. z6

'Leuko-Like'. Dwarf form, growth upright, conical, 50 cm high in 10 years, 35 cm wide; needles dark green, 6 cm long, very closely resembling *P. leucodermis*. Discovered by G. Horstmann, Schneverdingen, W. Germany as a witches'-broom.

'Paradekissen'. Dwarf form, exceptionally flat growing, very dense, developing a mat form cushion, 10 cm high in 10 years, 30 cm wide, annual shoots 4 cm, lying nearly horizontally; needles 3 cm long. Discovered by G. Horstmann, Schneverdingen, W. Germany on an exposed, gravelly slope in Graubünden, Switzerland. The mother plant was estimated to be 400–500 years old; it was 15 cm high and 70 cm wide.

var. **rotundata** (Link) Antoine. Somewhat intermediate between *P. mugo* and *P. uncinata*, usually shrubby, but ascending to 9 m; cones conical or oval-conical, horizontally arranged or nodding, scale ends on the basal half or the exposed side elongated to a 4 sided, downward curving pyramid, upper surface of the apophysis swollen, hood-like and curved backward (= *P. rotundata* Link; *P. uliginosa* Neumann). Alps, foothills, low areas and valleys, widely distributed from 800–1200 m; also commonly found in cultivation. Fig 148.

P. virginiana Mill. Virginia, Scrub Pine. Tree, 8–15 m, occasionally taller, trunk short, 30–50 cm in diameter, often only a shrub, bark thin, brown, fissured, branches irregularly arranged, spreading, often twisted, young shoots thin, reddish, glabrous, bluish-white pruinose, buds spindle-shaped, acute, 8–12 mm long, very resinous, scales appressed; needles arranged in loose fascicles, in 2's, persisting about 3–4 years, dark green, stiff, usually twisted, 4–8 cm long, with a short prickly tip, margins serrate, stomatal lines on both sides, aromatic when crushed, resin ducts in the parenchyma; cones grouped 2–4 together, occasionally solitary, short stalked, outspread to somewhat pendulous, oblong-conical, obtuse, 4–6 cm long, symmetrical, red-brown, opening when ripe, scale ends rhombic-pyramidal, somewhat crenate on the upper margin, umbo protruding, terminating in a fine upward curving thorn, seeds ovate, 3–6 mm long, wings 9 mm long. OCC 361; GTP 58; SPi 284 to 287; CCE 377, 379 (= *P. inops* Sol.). Eastern N. America, New York to Georgia and Alabama. 1739. Fig. 154. z5

P. wallichiana A. B. Jacks. Himalayan Pine. Tree, to 50 m high in its habitat, crown pyramidal, branched to the base in open sites, bark dark ash-gray, eventually fissured and exfoliating in plates, branches spreading horizontally, the uppermost ascending, buds cylindrical-conical, 6–8 mm long, scales distinct or covered with resin; needles in 5's, persisting for 3–4 years, usually hanging limply on young shoots, thin, 12–20 cm long, acute, margins finely serrate, with white stomatal lines on the upper side, dorsal side green, resin ducts marginal, sheaths 18 mm long, abscising quickly; cones nearly terminal, solitary or grouped 2–3, erect when young, pendulous in the 2nd year, cylindrical, 15–25 cm long, 3–5 cm thick before opening, light brown when ripe, very resinous, stalks 3–5 cm long, scales keel form, longitudinally furrowed above, tips thickened, the

Fig. 161. **Pinus** cones. A. *P. torreyana;* B. *P. sabiniana;* C. *P. coulteri*
(from Sudworth). The cone of *P. coulteri* is often significantly larger and wider than that illustrated here.

basal scales often recurved, seeds ovate, wings 20–25 mm long, released soon after ripening, while the cones persist for some months longer on the tree. BFN 353 (H); DJ 99; SPi 108–110; CCE 391–393 (= *P. chylla* Lodd.; *P. excelsa* Wall.; *P. griffithii* McClelland). Himalaya, from Afghanistan to Nepal, in the mountains at 2000–4000 m. 1823. Very beautiful pine, strongly recommended for the garden. Plate 114; Fig. 146, 160. z7

'Densa'. Dense conical habit; needles shorter than those of the species.

'Glauca'. Like the type, but the needles more conspicuously blue. Occurs occasionally as a chance seedling.

'Nana'. Dwarf form, bushy-globose habit, very silvery-blue.

'Silverstar'. Globose to columnar habit, shoots and needles stiffer than those of the type, young shoots light brown, annual growth of the terminal shoot 16 cm; needles conspicuously silver-blue, 5–7 cm long. Originated in a seedbed of *P. wallichiana*. To be introduced by A. Plattner, W. Germany, shortly.

'Umbraculifera'. Dwarf form, always umbrella-form on a low stem (!!), branches densely arranged, glabrous, red-brown, buds 5 mm long; needles about 10 cm long, light green, very thin, pendulous (!!), occasionally with some needles of only half the normal length. HD 209 (H); WM 30D (Br), 393 (H) (= *P. strobus umbraculifera* Carr.). 1855. (R)

'Vernisson'. Twigs of young plants tightly upright; needles longer. More winter hardy than the species.

'Zebrina'. Strong growing, like the type, but with variegated needles, with a yellowish cross-band about 2.5 cm from the tips (appearing like a ring from above), otherwise green with yellow markings. Developed in 1874 by Croux & Fils, Sceaux, France; found in the larger collections (Arnold Arboretum, Hillier, etc.)

P. washoensis Mason & Stockwell. Medium size tree, to 18 m high in its habitat, trunk diameter to 0.90 m, with a conical crown, bark fissured, black-brown or yellow-brown, exfoliating in plates; needles in 3's, 10–15 cm long, thick, stiff, gray-green; cones 5–10 cm long, conical or ovate, nut-brown, obtuse or somewhat glossy, with some basal scales often remaining on the branch after the cones drop, cone scales with a recurved, stout thorn. Nevada (Washoe County), NE. California, USA; on gravelly slopes in the mountains at 2000–2600 m. This quite rare tree is the last to be discovered in N. America. It was found in 1938 on Mount Rose, Nevada and named in 1945 for the Washoe Indians who once used this area for a hunting ground. Hardy. z5?

P. yunnanensis Franch. Yunnan Pine. Medium size tree, 10–15 m high, usually conical, but often with a flat crown on older trees, bark usually red and thin, exfoliating on the upper trunk and major branches, irregularly furrowed and divided into thick plates on the basal trunk, the lower branches often pendulous; needles in 3's, thin and pendulous, 20–30 cm long; cones usually in groups of 3, to 9 cm long, red-brown, persisting for some time on the tree, scale ends only slightly raised, umbo indented or only slightly raised. CBI 72; CCE 393 (= *P. sinensis* var. *yunnanensis* Shaw). China; SW. Szechwan to W. Yunnan Provinces. Fig. 151. z8?

Lit Bailey, D. K.: Phytogeography and Taxonomy of *Pinus* Subsection *Balfourianae*. Ann. Miss. Bot. Gard. **57**, 219–249, 1970, pub. in 1971 (with ills. and maps). ● Bernhard, R.: Die Kiefern Kleinasiens. Mitt. Deutsch. Dendr. Ges. **43**, 29–50, 1931. ● Critchfield, W. B., & E. L. Little: Geographic Distribution of the Pines of the World. U.S.D.A. Forest Serv. Misc. Publ. **991**, 1–97, 1966. Washington (61 maps). ● Debazac, E.-F.: Note sur le comportement en France de quelques pins mexicains. Revue Forest. Franc. 1964, 929–935. ● Debazac, E.-F.: L'Aire spontanée du Pin de Salzmann en France. Revue Forest. Franc. 1963, 768–784. ● Engelmann, G.: Revision of the genus *Pinus* and description of *Pinus Elliottii*. Transact. Acad. Sci. St. Louis **4**, 161–190, 1880 (3 pl.). ● Fosberg, F. R.: *Pinus contorta* and its variations. Baileya **7**, 7–10, 1959. ● Fukarek, P.: Geschichte der Entdeckung und Erforschung der Panzerkiefer, *Pinus Heldreichii* Christ (in SerboCroatian with a German summary). Glasnika Hrvatski Zemaljski Muzeja, 1941. ● Fukarek, P.: Mitteilungen über die Verbreitung von *Pinus peuce* Griseb. (in Serbo-Croatian with a summary in German). Inst. Dendr. Phyto. Fac. Agric., Forest. Univ. Sarajevo. Sarajevo, 1951. ● Gaussen, H.: Les Gymnospermes actuelles et fossiles; genre *Pinus*. Trav. Lab. Forest. Toulouse VI, Cap. XI, 1–272. Toulouse 1960. ● Harlow, W. M.: The identification of the pines of the United States native and cultivated, by needle structure. Bull New York State Coll. Forestry **4**, 1–21, 1931. ● Jährig, M.: Beiträge zur Nadelanatomie und Taxonomie der Gattung *Pinus*. Willdenowia **3**, 329–366, 1962. ● Keng, Hsuan, & E. L. Little: Needle Characteristics of Hybrid Pines. Silvae Genetica 1961, 125–160. ● Lambert, A. B.: A description of the genus *Pinus*. London 1928 (2 vols., 189 pp., 2nd ed.). ● Little, E. L.: Key to Mexican species of Pines. Caribbean Forester **23**, No. 2, 1962 (10 pp.). ● Little, E. L., & F. I. Righter: Botanical Descriptions of forty artificial Pine Hybrids. Techn. Bull. 1345 USDA Forest Service. Washington 1965 (47 pp.). ● Look, E. E. M.: The pines of Mexico and British Honduras. Union South Africa Dept. Forestry Bull. **35**, 1–244, 1950 (ills.). ● Malejeff, W.: *Pinus pithyusa* und *P. eldarica*, zwei Relikt-Kiefern der taurisch-kaukasischen flora. Mitt. Deutsch. Dendr. Ges. **41**, 138–150, 1929. ● Martinez, M.: Los Pinos Mexicanos. Edit. 2, 1–361, 1948. Mexico City (ill.). ● Masters, M. T.: A general view of the genus *Pinus*. Jour. Linn. Soc. Bot. **35**, 560–659, 1904. ● Mirov, N. T.: The Genus *Pinus*, 1–602. New York 1967. ● Schwarz, O.: Über die Systematik und Nomenklatur der europaeischen Schwarzkiefern. Notizbl. Bot. Gart. Berlin **13**, 226–243, 1936. ● Shaw, G. R.: The Pines of Mexico. Arnold Arb. Publ. I, 1909 (29 pp.). ● Shaw, G. R.: The Genus *Pinus*. Arnold Arb. Publ. **5**, 1–96, 1914 (ill.). ● Teuscher, H.: Bestimmungstabelle für die in Deutschlands Klima kultivierbaren *Pinus*-Arten. Mitt. Deutsch. Dendrol. Ges. 1921, 68–114. ● Wu, Ch.-I: The taxonomic revision and phytogeographical study of Chinese pines (Chinese with English summary). Sinica **5**, 131–164, 1956 (ill.).

PLATYCLADUS Spach.—Cupressaceae

Many earlier botanists considered *Thuja orientalis* L. to be a separate genus, **Biota** Don ex Endlicher, 1847, based on its different cone form and branching arrangement; this notion still has some support today. In this case, however, because of the rule of priority, **Platycladus** Spach, 1842, would be used instead of *Biota*. The combination then reads: *Platycladus orientalis* (L.). Franco 1949 (= *Thuja orientalis* L. 1753; *Biota orientalis* [L.] Endlicher 1847). In this book, *Thuja orientalis* is retained.

PODOCARPUS L'Herit. ex Pers.—PODOCARPACEAE

Evergreen trees or shrubs, usually with straight, thick trunks; bark exfoliating in strips; branches usually irregularly arranged or more closely spaced and decussate, rarely whorled; leaves quite variable, close or widely spaced, usually spiraled, occasionally opposite or (nearly so) 2 ranked (like *Abies*) or densely clustered and partly overlapping, usually broad needle-like or narrow leaf-like, narrow or wide, straight or bowed sickle-shaped, to 20 cm long and 5 cm wide, partly thin and flexible, some thick and leathery tough with an involuted margin, often white striped beneath, new growth often pink or reddish; the decurrent part of the mature or fallen needles is usually slightly raised and colored the same brown as the twig bark, or with only a few occasionally remaining green; plants mono- or dioecious; male flowers solitary or clustered 2–5, axillary or many terminal in narrow, dense spikes; female flowers only 1–2, axillary or terminal, stalked or sessile, with a few, spirally arranged, adnate to the flower stalk together with the last fleshy scales; fruit usually short stalked over the receptacle, globose or ovate, drupe- or nut-like, with a more or less fleshy integument, inner seed coat woody.—About 100 species, most in the mountain forests of the warmer temperate and sub-tropical zone of the Southern Hemisphere, some species also in Japan, China, Malaya and on the Philippine Islands. Can be grown only in the mildest climates or in the conservatory. Range map Fig. 162.

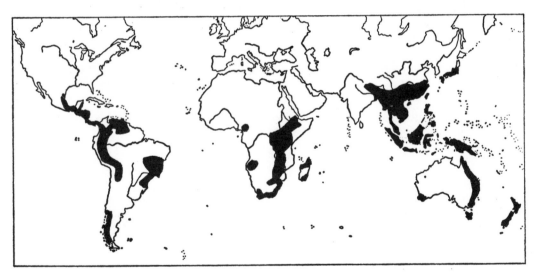

Fig. 162. Collective range of the genus *Podocarpus*

Division of the Genus (see footnote on p. 251)

● Mature foliage small, subulate or scale-like, spirally attached, stomata on both sides.

Section 1. **Dacrycarpus** Endlicher
Leaves subulate or flattened, both forms frequently occurring on the same branch; flowers terminal; carpels (megasporophyll) as long as the seed and adnate to the ovule for its entire length; seeds terminal, usually solitary, receptacle fleshy. Distributed over SE. Asia. E. India, S. Pacific and New Zealand. Including:
P. cinctus, compactus, cumingii, dacrydioides, imbricatus, papuanus, steupii, vieilaardii

Section 2. **Microcarpus** Pilg.
Leaves scale form, overlapping; carpels not adnate to the much larger ovule, female inflorescence with 1 terminal ovule, base not well developed; seed with a woody shell. 1 species in New Caledonia (*P. ustus*) with coppery-red scale leaves, parasitic on *Dacrydium*.

● ● Mature leaves large, either subulate or scale form.

+   Section 3. **Nageia** Endl.
        Leaves relatively wide, many veined, opposite or nearly so; fruit receptacle fleshy or dry. Distributed in SE. Asia, E. India, the Phillipines to New Guinea. Including:
            P. fleuryi, motleyi, nagi, wallichianus

++ Leaves narrow in relation to the length, single veined;
    × Stomata on both sides; no transfusion tissue*);

        Section 4. **Afrocarpus** Buchholz & Gray
        Leaves alternate, encircling the twig, seldom nearly opposite. Africa. Including:
            P. falcatus, gracilior, mannii

        Section 5. **Polpodiopsis** Bertrand
        Leaves opposite or decussate, but usually appearing 2 ranked. Distributed through S. America, S. Pacific, New Guinea, New Caledonia and on the Fiji Islands. Including:
            P. comptonii, minor, rospigliosii, vitiensis

×× Stomata primarily on the leaf underside;
    : Leaves without a hypodermal tissue **);

        Section 6. **Sundacarpus** Buchholz & Gray
        Leaves large, longer than 5 cm and wider than 6 cm, not appearing 2 ranked; with transfusion tissue. Distributed in E. India, Phillipines, New Guinea, Australia (Cape York Peninsula). Including:
            P. amarus

        Section 7. **Stachycarpus** Endl.
        Leaves small, shorter than 3 cm and narrower than 5 mm, often appearing 2 ranked, without transfusion tissue (some species from the Eastern Hemisphere with stomata on both sides). Distributed over Central and South America to New Zealand, Australia and New Caledonia. Including:
            P. andinus, distichus, ferrugineus, ferruginoides, harmsianus, ladei, montanus, spicatus, standleyi, utilior

    :: Leaves with hypodermis or hypodermal veins or if these are few or absent, then with a fully developed transfusion tissue; receptacle swollen, fleshy or leathery. Scattered over Central and South America, Africa, Asia, Australia and on the South Pacific Islands. Including:
            P. acutifolius, affinis, alpinus, angustifolius, annamensis, archboldii, aristolatus, brassii, brevifolius, buchii, cardenasii, coriaceus, costalis, curvifolius, decipiens, decumbens, deflexus, dispermus, drouynianus, ekmanii, elatus, elongatus, ensiculus, forrestii, gibbsii, glaucus, glomeratus, gnidioides, guatemalensis, hallii, henkelii, idenburgensis, koordersii, lambertii, latifolius, ledermannii, leonii, longifoliolatus, lucienii, macrophyllus, madagascariensis, magnifolius, matudai, milanjianus, neriifolius, nivalis, novae-caledoniae, nubigenus, oleifolius, pallidus, pendulifolius, philippinensis, pilgeri, pittieri, polystachyus, purdieanus, reichei, ridleyi, roraimae, rostratus, rumphii, rusbyi, salignus, salomoniensis, selloi, spinulosus, sprucei, steyermarkii, silvestris, tepuiensis, thevetiifolius, totara, urbanii, victorianus

*) The fine branching of the vascular bundles is absent in the leaves (needles) of conifers; there are usually 1 or 2 longitudinal veins embedded in the water conducting transfusion tissue (see Fig. 138).

**) Hypodermis is the tissue beneath the epidermis (see Fig. 138).

Podocarpus acutifolius Kirk. Upright shrub or also a small tree, to 9 m high, thin bark; needles of older plants 10–25 mm long, acuminate and prickly, 0.5–3.5 mm wide, longer on young plants, linear, green, midrib beneath indistinct; male flowers 1 to 2 cm long, grouped 1–4 together, axillary, female flowers 1–2 on a short, swollen receptacle, usually solitary, rarely in 2's, seeds narrowly ovate, 4 mm long, on an enlarged, red receptacular base. KF 39; CBI 73. New Zealand. Fig. 167. z9

P. affinis Seemann. Tree, outspread branches, shoots densely foliate; leaves spirally arranged, densely crowded, linear-elliptic, tapering to an obtuse apex, base drawn out to a short but distinct petiole, 25–50 cm long, 6–8 mm wide, erect, leathery. Fiji Islands. z9

P. alpinus R. Br. Bushy shrub, branches spreading horizontally, densely branched, 0.5–3 m high; leaves very numerous, densely crowded, indistinctly 2 ranked, linear-oblong, 6–15 mm long, obtuse, dark green above, more blue-green beneath with a conspicuous midrib; male cones 4–6 mm long, usually solitary in the leaf axils, sessile, seeds ovate, only 3 mm thick, on a fleshy, 4 mm long, bright red receptacle. CTa 1: CBI 74; DJ 100; CCE 394 (= *P. lawrencii* Hook. f.; *P. totara* var. *alpina* Carr.). SW. Australia, Tasmania, in the mountains at 1500–2000m. 1825. Plate 114; Fig. 163. z8–9

P. amarus Bl. Tall tree; leaves outspread, oblong, 5–15 cm long, 9–15 mm wide, glossy green above, lighter beneath, margin thickened and involuted, drawn out to a sharp point at the apex, the leaves on young long shoots occasionally 25 cm long; seeds globose or ellipsoid, shell reddish, blue pruinose, somewhat grooved or acuminate on the apex, 15–25 mm long when ripe, stalks 8 to 12 mm long (= *P. sprengelii* Bl.). Australia (Queensland), Java, Philippines. Fig. 169. z9

P. andinus Poepp. ex Endl. Small tree, 10 m or more, or only a shrub, *Taxus*-like in appearance (especially plants in cultivation), buds with acute, valvate (not imbricate) scales; needles spiraling but usually in a single plane and directed forward, 12–20 mm long and 2 mm wide, with a resin canal under the vascular bundle (absent on *Taxus!*), straight or sickle-shaped, bright green above, bluish-green with 2 stomatal bands beneath; plants often dioecious, rarely monoecious, male flowers in terminal and axillary clusters, cylindrical, female flowers with carpels spread apart, spike-form, 2–2.5 cm long, fruit rounded, black-blue (nearly sloe-like in appearance), without a fleshy receptacle, with a hard inner shell. DJ 101; SN 101 (H); CCE 395 (= *Prumnopitys elegans* Phil.). Chile; southern Andes, 1300 m. 1860. Plate 117; Fig. 164. z8–9

P. angustifolius Griseb. Tree-like shrub, or small tree, branches nearly in whorls; needles loosely arranged, 25–60 mm long, about 6 mm wide, linear, drawn out to a thorny tip, rather leathery; male flower cones 10–15 mm long, sessile in the leaf axils, seed 7 mm thick, with a red, fleshy receptacle. Cuba. z9

P. annamensis Gray. Tree, 5–12 m high, outer bud scales broadly triangular, acute or acuminate, keeled, to 5 mm long; needles usually straight, 3.5–10(17) cm long, 5–10(20) mm wide, obtuse or abruptly acuminate, stiff, clustered at the branch tips; male flower cones axillary, greenish-white when young, seeds with a fleshy, 8 mm long receptacle composed of 2 connate scales with distinct apices. SE. Asia; Annam, Cochin China, Burma, Hainan. z9

P. archboldii Gray. Tree, 30 m or higher, bark scaly and flat-furrowed, gray, terminal buds large, globose; leaves densely arranged, nearly sessile or short stalked, narrow-lanceolate, long acuminate, 3–8 cm long, 5–13 cm wide, margins involuted, green above, lighter and brownish beneath, midrib narrower above than beneath; male flower cones solitary, axillary, seeds nearly globose, 15 mm long, on a fleshy, 8 mm long receptacle. New Guinea and Papua Territories, in the mountain rain forests. Fig. 163. z9

P. aristulatus Parl. Tree-like shrub or small tree, branches nearly in whorls; needles more or less outspread, leathery tough, elliptic or oblanceolate, to 35 mm long and 6 mm wide, broadly acuminate with a prickly apex; male flower cones axillary and sessile, 10–12 mm long, 3 mm wide, seeds 8 to 9 mm long, 4–5 mm wide, with a fleshy receptacle (= *P. angustifolius* var. *wrightii* Pilg.). Cuba. z9

P. brassii Pilg. Shrub or small tree; needles small, stiff, leathery tough, densely crowded, elliptic-oblong to lanceolate-spathulate, 9–12 mm long, 6–7 mm wide, tapered and rounded at both ends, needles longer and more lanceolate on younger plants, glossy green above,

---

*) In 1969 D. J. De Laubenfels published a "Revision of the Malesian and Pacific Rainforest Conifers, I. Podocarpaceae, in part" in Journal of the Arnold Arboretum. He divided *Podocarpus* into 5 genera: *Podocarpus*, *Prumnopitys* and his newly created *Falcatifolium*, *Dacrycarpus* and *Decussocarpus*.

Since his work is not entirely finished, the classification of De Laubenfels will not be followed in this book. Here is, however, an outline of the new De Laubenfels classification together with synonyms:

Falcatifolium de Laubf. (1969)
    falciforme (Parl.) de Laubf.   (= *Podocarpus falciformis* Parl.)
    taxoides (Brongn. & Gris.) de Laubf.   (= *P. taxoides* Carr.)
    papuanum de Laubf. (Abb. 163)
    angustum de Laubf.

Dacrycarpus (Endl.) de Laubf. (1969)
    imbricatus (Bl.) de Laubf.   (= *P. imbricatus* Bl.)
    —var. *robustus* de Laubf.   (= *P. papuanus* Ridley,
                                 P. leptophylla* Wasscher)
    vieillardii (Parl.) de Laubf.   (= *P. vieillardii* Parl.)
    steupii (Wasscher) de Laubf.   (= *P. steupii* Wasscher)
    cumingii (Parl.) de Laubf.   (= *P. cumingii* Parl.)
    kinabaluensis (Wasscher) de Laubf.   (= *P. imbricatus* var. *kinabaluensis* Wasscher)
    cinctus (Pilg.) de Laubf.   (= *P. cinctus* Pilg.; *P. dacrydifolia* Wasscher)
    expansus de Laubf.
    compactus (Wasscher) de Laubf.   (= *P. compacta* Wasscher)
    dacrydioides (Rich.) de Laubf.   (= *P. dacrydioides* Rich.)

Decussocarpus de Laubf. (1969)
    vitiensis (Seem.) de Laubf.   (= *P. vitiensis* Seem.)
    comptonii (Buchh.) de Laubf.   (= *P. comptonii* Buchh.)
    minor (Carr.) de Laubf.   (= *P. minor* [Carr.] Parl.; *P. palustris* Buchh.)
    rospigliosii (Pilg.) de Laubf.   (= *P. rospigliosii* Pilg.)
    wallichianus (Presl) de Laubf.   (= *P. wallichianus* Presl; *P. blumei* Endl.)
    motleyi (Parl.) de Laubf   (= *P. motleyi* [Parl.] Dümmer)
    maximus de Laubf.
    fleuryi (Hickel) de Laubf.   (= *P. fleuryi* Hickel)
    nagi (Thunb.) de Laubf.   (= *P. nagi* [Thunb.] Makino
                                P. formosensis* Dümmer
                                P. nankoensis* Hayata)
    falcatus (Thunb.) de Laubf.   (= *P. falcatus* [Thunb.] R. Br.
                                P. gracillimus* Stapf)
    mannii (Hook.) de Laubf.   (= *P. mannii* Hook.
                                P. usambarensis* Pilg.
                                P. dawei* Stapf)

dull beneath, except the raised midrib and involuted margins; male flower cones solitary, stiff, cylindrical, 20–35 mm long, 4–5 mm wide, seeds broadly ellipsoid, to 10 mm long and 6 mm wide, with a receptacle composed of 2 or 3 connate, fleshy scales. CCE 394. New Guinea, high in the mountains. Fig. 163. z9

P. brevifolius (Stapf) Foxworthy. Shrub or small tree, densely foliate; needles appressed, short, thick, leathery, lanceolate, 8–30 mm long, 4–5 mm wide; male flower cones stiff, to 6 mm wide (= *P. neriifolius* var. *brevifolius* Stapf; *P. wangii* C. C. Chang). Borneo, Philippines; Hainan. z9

P. buchii Urban. Tree, to 6 m buds rather globose, scales circular, the outermost acuminate; needles dark green, densely crowded, stiff, leathery, linear-lanceolate, straight or slightly sickle-shaped, 15–27 mm long, 4–6 mm wide, with a stiff thorn at the apex, nearly sessile at the base or with a short stalk, underside with a midrib and distinct stomatal lines; seeds ellipsoid, 8 mm long, 4 mm wide, with a very fleshy, 9 mm long receptacle. Haiti, in the mountains. z9

P. cardenasii Buchholz & Gray. Tree, to 9 m high, compact crown, branches often whorled, bud scales lanceolate, long acuminate; leaves outspread, linear-lanceolate, 15–50 mm long, 2–4 mm wide, light green and bluish beneath, margins involuted, apex short acuminate thorned; male flower cones grouped 6–8, 6 mm long, on thin, 15 mm stalks, seeds globose, 5–6 mm thick, on a fleshy, 4 mm long receptacle. JA 29 Pl. 7(1). Bolivia. (Not completely known.) z9

P. cinctus Pilg. Shrub to 4 m, or a tree to 30 m, with black or brown, uneven bark; similar to *P. cumingii*, but the needles finer, thinner, not stiff, subulate, 2–5 mm long, 0.4–0.6 mm thick, involucral leaves 5 to 6 mm long, covering the young seeds, but hardly reaching to the middle of the 6–7 mm long, ripe seeds, these with a red receptacle. JA 50; 9a–b (= *P. dacrydiifolia* Wasscher; *Dacrycarpus cintus* [Pilg.] de Laubf.). Celebes to New Guinea, mountain forests, usually at 2200–3200 m. z9

P. compactus Wasscher. Shrub or a small tree, 2–15 m, bark hard, rough, warty; juvenile leaves flattened (2 sided), lanceolate, sickle-shaped, curved upward at the tips, bowed, laterally keeled, not 2 ranked (!!), 2.5 mm long, 0.6 mm thick, mature leaves not dimorphic, 2–3 mm long, compressed, slightly outspread, lanceolate, prickly; seeds globose, 7–8 mm long and nearly as wide. JA 50; 9c (= *Dacrycarpus compactus* [Wasscher] de Laubf.). New Guinea, at the tree line in the mountains, around 3200–3900 m. Fig. 163. z9

P. comptonii Buchholz. Tree, 9–12(30) m, bark brown-gray, longitudinally furrowed, very rough and exfoliating in long strips on older trunks, branches ascending to upright; needles polymorphic, either acute-triangular, 2 mm long on the stout main shoots, or ovate-elliptic, 4–6 mm long, on other main shoots and the basal branch parts, or otherwise lanceolate to elliptic, 2 ranked or decussate, 7–15 mm long, 2–5 mm wide, but also to over 25 mm long in the juvenile stage; seeds pear-shaped, about 20 mm long and 13–15 mm wide (lacking the bowed beak), with a 2–3 mm thick, blue-green shell,

becoming dark red and dry when ripe. LG 11 (= *Decussocarpus comptonii* [Buchholz] de Laubf.). New Caledonia. z9

P. coriaceus L. C. Rich. Tree, to 15 m; leaves spirally arranged, linear-lanceolate, 7 to 17 cm long, 8–18 mm wide, thick, leathery, with a long, drawn out apex, midrib very conspicuous on the underside, petiole 6 mm long; male cones axillary, to 6 cm long and 6 mm wide, seeds ovate, 9 mm long, 6 mm wide, with a thick, red, fleshy receptacle, on a 7–10 mm long stalk. LWPT 31; JA 29 Pl. 4(2) (as *P. trinitus*); CCE 400 (= *P. antillarum* R. Br.). West Indies; in mountain forests of Puerto Rico to Trinidad. z9

P. costalis Presl. Tree, densely branched; needles oblanceolate, 12–42 mm long, to 15 mm wide, thick and leathery, apex drawn out to a small point or also round, petiole short; male cones cylindrical and thick, 30 mm long, seeds ellipsoid, 9 mm long, with a fleshy, receptacle composed of 2 connate scales with 2 round tips. Philippines. Taiwan. z9

P. cumingii Parl. Tree, to 20 m or more in its habitat; similar to *P. imbricatus*, but the involucral leaves are 7–10 mm long and the ripe seeds exserted (as long as *P. imbricatus*), juvenile foliage flattened (2 sided) and 2 ranked (distichous), to 12 mm long and 1.2 mm thick, tips bowed, parallel to the shoot, but quickly becoming spirally arranged and larger, mature leaves outspread, sickle-shape, quite variable in length, the longest about 6 mm long and 0.6 mm thick; seeds globose, about 2.5 mm thick, surrounded by the 10 mm long and 0.5 mm wide involucral leaves and with a distinctly curved beak (= *Dacrycarpus cumingii* [Parl.] de Laubf.). Philippines, Sumatra. z9

P. curvifolius Carr. Large tree, with ovate-oblong, 5–12 cm long leaves, flat, leathery, apex obtuse, margin thickened, smooth and glossy above, petiole short (= *P. antarcticus* van Houtte; *P. parlatorei* Pilg.?) S. America; Andes of Chile and Patagonia. A little known species. z9

P. dacrydioides A. Rich. Tree, to 50 m or more in its habitat, trunk to 1.5 m in diameter, frequently grooved and flared at the base, shoots thin, pendulous; leaves in 2 forms: 2 ranked on young plants, 4–6 mm long, linear, flat, soft, acuminate, bronze-green, much shorter on older trees, scale-form, 2–3 mm long and spiraling in 2 rows, branches frequently with both leaf forms on a single plant; male flowers in terminal clusters, with 1 cm long cones, seeds small, solitary, broadly ovate, 4–5 mm long, black, nut-like, with a fleshy, red receptacle. KF 31–32; CBI 76; SFP 68; CCE 396. New Zealand; usually in swampy forests. An exceptionally beautiful tree but only for the very mildest regions. Plate 117; Fig. 164. z9

P. dawei Stapf see: **P. mannii**

P. decipiens Gray. Tree, very similar to *P. neriifolius*, to about 20 m high, bud scales ovate and normally with a tapered, often leaf-like apex; leaves outspread, linear-lanceolate, often slightly curved, 5.5–13 cm long, 5–18 mm wide, broad or long acuminate apex, leathery and glossy, gradually tapering to a 6–12 mm long petiole at the base, margins not involuted, midrib usually broad,

Fig. 163. **Podocarpus.** A. *P. neriifolius;* B. *P. archboldii;* C. *Falcatifolium papuanum;* D. *P. imbricatus;* E. *P. pilgeri;* F. *P. compactus;* G. *P. brassii;* H. *P. alpinus* (from Womersley); about ⅓ actual size.

but not very conspicuous; male cones nearly sessile, to 4 cm long and 5 mm wide, often in clusters, seeds nearly globose, blue-green, receptacle composed of several scales, 5 mm long. Fiji Islands. z9

P. decumbens Gray. Low, creeping shrub, only about 30–40 cm high, buds ovate, with acuminate scales, 6–10 mm long; leaves linear-lanceolate, 3–8 cm long, 4–8 mm wide, obtuse, tapering to a narrow petiole; male cones cylindrical, 15–30 mm long. LG 15. New Caledonia, only on the Montagne de Sources. Very similar to *P. gnidioides*, which occurs in the same region, but which has much smaller leaves. z9

P. deflexus Ridley. Small tree, branches spreading at right angles to the stem; leaves all distinctly drooping, very thick and stiff, 10–25 cm long, 7–12 mm wide, with a prominent midrib, widely grooved beneath; seeds elliptic-obovate, 12 mm long, 8 mm thick. Malaya. This species is often confused with *P. neriifolius*. z9

P. dispermus White. Tree, to l8 m, bark light gray-brown, somewhat scaly; leaves broadly linear to narrowly lanceolate, 10–20 cm long, acuminate, gradually tapering to a short petiole, 20–30 mm wide, dark green and glossy above, midrib conspicuous; male cones to 3 cm long, grouped 1–3 in clusters, sessile, seeds ellipsoid, 25 mm long, 15 mm wide, usually in groups of 2, on a very fleshy, scarlet-red receptacle. Australia; N. Queensland. Resembles *P. elatus*, but with broader and longer leaves and different seeds. z9

P. distichus Buchholz. Small tree, 5–7 m high, needles spirally arranged, but appearing pectinate, oblong-lanceolate to oblanceolate, 10–15 mm long, 1.5–3 mm wide, acute, oblique, tapering to the base, margins involuted, curved petiole, stomata primarily on the underside, but also with some on the upper side near the midrib, with further microscopic markings on the ventral side of the leaf; seeds 12–13 mm long. JA 29 Pl. 2(2–3), 3(2). Central New Caledonia, but rare and therefore somewhat questionable. z9

P. drouynianus F. Muell. Small shrub, *Taxus*-like, 1–2 m high, similar to *P. spinulosus*; leaves linear, to 7.5 cm long and 2.5 mm wide, nearly sessile, spirally arranged around the shoot (like *Taxus baccata* 'Fastigiata'), sharply acuminate, margin distinctly involuted, midrib very conspicuous, green above, bluish beneath; male cones 6–12 mm long, solitary or in small clusters, seeds 18 mm long, on fleshy, purple, waxy, 12–25 mm long receptacle, on a thin stalk. W. Australia, growing around springs. z9

P. ekmanii Urban. Shrub, 2–4 m high, very densely foliate, terminal buds ovate, scales keeled, the outermost scales with a tip half as long as the scale; needles linear-lanceolate, 15–25 mm long, stiff and leathery, with a thorny tip, tapering to the base and nearly sessile; seeds ovate, 6 mm long, 4 mm wide, furrowed. E. Cuba, in the mountains. z9

Fig. 164. **Podocarpus.** A. *P. dacrydioides*, with fruiting twig beneath; B. *P. andinus*; C. *P. spicatus* (twigs original, otherwise from Adams)

Plate 113

Pinus rigida
in Ocean County, New Jersey, USA
Photo: U.S. Forest Service

Pinus taeda
in the Sochi Dendrarium, USSR

Pinus strobus
in Huron National Forest, Michigan, USA
Photo: U.S. Forest Service

Pinus Strobus 'Nana'
in Knighthays Court, England

Plate 114

Pinus wallichiana
in Les Barres Arboretum, France

Podocarpus alpinus
in the Royal Botanic Garden,
Edinburgh, Scotland

Podocarpus nivalis in RHS Gardens, Wisley, England

Plate 115

Podocarpus nagi, 21 m high,
in Nara Park, Hondo, Japan
Photo: E. H. Wilson

Podocarpus hallii
in the Castlewellan Park, N. Ireland

Podocarpus macrophyllus, male flowers
Photo: Dr. Watari, Tokyo, Japan

Plate 116

Podocarpus latifolius
in Stellenbosch, South Africa

Podocarpus nubigenus
in Tremeer, Cornwall, England

Podocarpus elongatus in its habitat
in the Royal Natal National Park, South Africa

Podocarpus henkelii
in its habitat in South Africa

Plate 117

Podocarpus andinus
in Shane's Park, N. Ireland

Podocarpus salignus
in the Rowallane Park, N. Ireland

Podocarpus totara
in the Rowallane Park, N. Ireland

Podocarpus dacrydioides
in its habitat; 30m high
Photo: New Zealand Forest Service

Plate 118

Pseudolarix amabilis
in the Doorn Arboretum, Holland

Pseudotaxus chienii
Photo: R. Florin

Podocarpus macrophyllus
var. *maki*
in RHS Gardens, Wisley,
England

Pseudotsuga menziesii 'Taranto'
in the Villa Taranto Park
in Lake Maggiore, N. Italy

Sequoiadendron giganteum
'Pendulum' columnar form,
9 m high in
Les Barres Arboretum, France

Plate 119

Pseudotsuga menziesii 'Fletcheri' in RHS Gardens, Wisley, England

Saxegothaea conspicua
in its native habitat in Chile
Photo: V. Bianchi, Valparaiso

Sequoia sempervirens 'Nana Pendula'
in Kew Gardens, England

Plate 120

Pseudotsuga menziesii in its native habitat
in the Wenatchee National Forest,
Washington USA
Photo: U.S. Forest Service

Pseudotsuga menziesii f. *caesia*
in the Göteborg Bot. Garden, Sweden

Pseudotsuga menziesii 'Pendula'
in the Blijdenstein Pinetum, Holland

Pseudotsuga menziesii 'Glauca Pendula'
in Les Barres Arboretum, France

Plate 121

Taxodium distichum in its native habitat in the Santee-Cooper
swamp region, South Carolina, USA
Photo: U.S. Forest Service

Plate 122

Taxodium distichum, the more frequently found juvenile growth form at
left, occasionally mature as at right;
planted in 1830 in the Sanssouci Park, Potsdam, E. Germany

Taxodium distichum in its habitat in Wadboo Creek with the typical respiratory "knees",
in the Francis Marion National Park, South Carolina, USA
Photo: U.S. Forest Service

Plate 123

Taxus baccata 'Amersfoort' in the Blijdenstein Pinetum near Hilversum, Holland

Taxodium ascendens 'Nutans'
in the Boskoop Experiment Station, Holland

Taxus baccata anchored to a rock in the
park of Wakehurst Place, England

Plate 124

Taxus baccata, twig with fruits
Photo: C. R. Jelitto

Taxus baccata 'Standishii'
in the Blijdenstein Pinetum, Holland

Taxus baccata 'Repandens' in the Blijdenstein Pinetum

Plate 125

Taxus baccata 'Fastigiata Aurea'
in a park in Bergen, northern Holland

Taxus baccata 'Melfard'
in the Nursery of J. D. Zu Jeddeloh, W. Germany

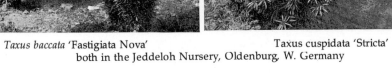

Taxus baccata 'Fastigiata Nova'
both in the Jeddeloh Nursery, Oldenburg, W. Germany

Taxus cuspidata 'Stricta'

Plate 126

Taxus cuspidata 'Nana' about 3 m high and 11 m wide;
in a private garden in Wellesley, Massachusetts, USA
Photo: R. A. Keen

Taxus cuspidata; an old, broad growing plant at the Hall Estate in Bristol, Rhode Island, USA
Photo: R. A. Keen

Plate 127

Taxus cuspidata,
very old tree on Hokkaido (Yamaba), Japan
Photo: Nitzelius

Taxus × media 'Sargentii'
in the Hillier Arboretum, England

Taxus cuspidata 'Sieboldii'
in the South Wilton Nursery, USA
Photo: R. A. Keen

Taxus cuspidata 'Hitii'
in a nursery in the USA
Photo: R. A. Keen

Plate 128

Pinus montezumae is one of the most beautiful long needled pines;
this particularly attractive specimen is in the garden of Villa Melzi on the shore of Lake Como, N. Italy

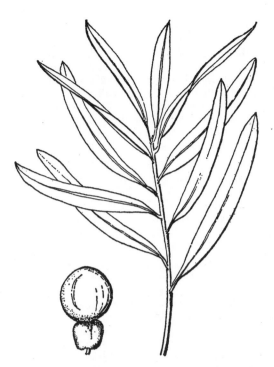

Fig. 165. *Podocarpus elatus* (from Maloney)

P. elatus R. Br. ex Mirb. Tree, to 30 m in its habitat, trunk to 1 m in diameter; leaves scattered on rather slender shoots, but variable in size and arrangement, often 5–15 cm long, occasionally to 22 cm long on young trees, 6–12 mm wide, oblong to lanceolate, midrib very conspicuous above, apex obtuse, but often with a protruding apical point, base tapered to a small petiole; male cones slender, to 5 cm long, usually grouped 2–3 together, seeds oval, 6–8 mm long, sessile on a fleshy receptacle. BAu 434; DJ 523; CCE 396 (= *P. acicularis* Van Houtte ex Gord.; *P. ensifolia* R. Br.). SE. Australia. Fig. 165. z9

P. elongatus (Ait.) L'Hér. ex Pers. Round crowned tree, to 20 m, or only a shrub, 3–6 m high, bark thin, gray or gray-green, shoots yellow-green, furrowed; leaves spiraling to nearly opposite, often clustered on the apical part of the shoot, outspread or upright, narrowly oblong-elliptic, 3–6 cm long, 4–5 mm wide, blue-green above or more gray-green, tapered to both ends, with 1 to several short stomatal lines, with numerous stomatal lines beneath; male cones solitary or grouped 2–5 together, usually sessile, seeds ellipsoid to ovate, 7 to 10 mm long, dark blue-green, on a fleshy, 9–15 mm long and 10–16 mm thick, scarlet-red receptacle. FSA 1: 37; CCE 397. S. Africa; only the western Cape Province. Plate 116. z9

P. ensiculus Melville. Tree, to 30 m, bark gray-brown, fibrous, slightly furrowed, young shoots pale green, terminal buds with ribbon-shaped outer scales, drawn out to a linear apex, the inner scales rounded and with short, sharp tips and a brown limb; leaves often pendulous, linear, 6–20 cm long, 3–10 mm wide, gradually tapering from beneath the middle of the blade to the apex, stomatal lines only on the underside; male cones solitary, axillary, 18 mm long or longer, seeds

ovate, greenish, 2.5–3.5 cm long, with a leathery receptacle, on a 6 mm long stalk. E. Africa, Tanzania; Usambara Mts. z9

P. falcatus (Thunb.) R. Br. ex Mirb. "Oteniqua Yellow Wood". Tree, 20–30 m or more, trunk about 1 m in diameter, rarely to 2 m, bark thin, brown, exfoliating in thin scales; leaves quite variable, partly spirally arranged, partly opposite or nearly so, 2–5 cm long, 2–3 mm wide, but to 12 cm long and nearly 10 mm wide on young plants, terminating abruptly in a sharp or obtuse apex, petiole short and somewhat twisted; male cones usually grouped in 3's, 6 to 8 mm long, seeds globose, 6–12 mm thick, solitary or in 2's, shell blue-green, stalk 6–12 mm long. FSA 1: 37; CCE 397 (= *P. elongata* Carr. non L'Hér.; *P. meyeriana* Endl.; *P. gracillimus* Stapf; *Decussocarpus falcatus* [Thunb.] de Laubf.). S. Africa; Cape Province, Natal, Bechuanaland, Transvaal, Portugese E. Africa. Very significant forest tree in S. Africa. z9

P. ferrugineus G. Benn ex D. Don. Tree, 15 to 25 m, trunk to 1 m in diameter, bark gray-brown to nearly black, exfoliating in thick pieces; leaves narrow-linear, acute, to 3 cm long on young plants, 1.5–2.5 cm long and 2–3 mm wide on older plants, deep green, acute, with a distinct midrib, margins somewhat involuted, 2 ranked; male cones solitary, axillary, 5–15 mm long, female flowers grouped 1–2 on a bowed, scaly, 10 mm long stalk, seeds broad-oblong, to 20 mm long, with a fleshy outer integument, purple and gray-blue pruinose, without a fleshy receptacle. KF 84; HI 542; CBI 77; SFP 60. New Zealand, frequently found in the forests of the plains. Plate 149; Fig. 167. z9

P. ferruginoides Compton. Tree, 9–15 m, vertical trunk, irregularly branched; needles spirally arranged, usually erect, leathery, about 18 mm long. JA 32 Pl. 1, Pl. 2(1); LG 12. New Caledonia, in the coniferous forests over 1000 m. Differing from the similar *P. ferrugineus* in the shorter and wider needles and the nearly globose, not pointed, seeds. z9

P. fleuryi Hickel. Tree, at least 10 m; leaves opposite, leathery, elliptic, long acuminate, 8–18 cm long, 3.5–5 cm wide, base more or less drawn out to a petiole, with stomata beneath; seeds globose, 15–18 mm thick, receptacle not fleshy. JA 50: 11 (= *Decussocarpus fleuryi* [Hickel] de Laubf.). SE. Asia; in the mountain forests from Annam to Kwangtung. Easily distinguished from *P. nagi* by the much larger leaves; from *P. wallichianus* by the stomata located only on the underside (on both sides with *P. wallichiana*). z9

P. formosensis Duemmer. Small tree, very similar to *P. nagi*, bark brownish, branches thick, gray and dark brown, shoots nearly opposite, directed upward, densely foliate; leaves decussate, narrow elliptic-lanceolate, 2.5–3.5 cm long, 7.5 cm wide, obtuse, base tapered to a broad, flat petiole, tough and stiff, smooth on both sides; male cones nearly globose, grouped 8–10 together, seeds globose, 12–14 mm thick, receptacle undeveloped, stalk thick, scarred, 7 mm long, glabrous. LT 12. China; Taiwan. Fig. 166. z9

P. forrestii Craib. & W. W. Smith. Shrub, to about 2.5 m high, very similar to *P. macrophyllus* var. *maki*, but lower growing, twigs rather stout; leaves shorter and wider, 5–8 cm long, 8–12 mm wide, oblong or more lanceolate, acute or rounded, drawn out gradually at the base to a short, winged petiole, dark green above, lighter beneath; seeds on a short, fleshy receptacle (= *P. microphyllus* Diels). W. China; Tali mountain chain. z9

P. gibbsii N. E. Gray. Tree, 10–20 m, branches upright, buds small, ovate, only 1.5 mm thick, the outer, thick scales leaf-like and to 6 mm long, with long tips; needles elliptic to lanceolate, 12–20 mm long, 4–6 mm wide, leathery tough, margin slightly involuted, midrib very conspicuous above, becoming flattened toward the apex; male cones solitary and axillary. N. Borneo, Mt. Kinabalu. Not completely known. z9

P. glaucus Foxworthy. Tree, to 15 m, branches in dense whorls; needles densely clustered, thick, erect, stiff, oblong-lanceolate, to 25 mm long, 6 mm wide, tapered to both ends, indistinct petiole; male cones solitary, cylindrical, 2.5–3 cm long, to 6 mm wide, seeds ovate, 12 mm long, sessile on a 9 mm long receptacle, composed of 2 fleshy scales. Philippines. z9

P. glomeratus D. Don. Tree, 9–12 m, bark dark brown, branches densely arranged; needles spirally arranged, 2.5–5 cm long, 3–5 mm wide, erect, leathery, linear-lanceolate, with short, sharp tips, very blue-green beneath; male cones in groups of about 6, on thin, 8–12 mm stalks, seeds 6–8 mm thick, short stalked, on a fleshy receptacle (= *P. rigida* Klotzsch). S. America; Peru, Ecuador. z9

P. gnidioides Carr. Procumbent shrub, 50 to 180 cm high, buds nearly globose, 2 mm thick; needles outspread, linear, obtuse, 12–20 mm long, 1–2 mm wide, gradually narrowing toward the base and sessile; male cones solitary on a 4 mm stalk, surrounded at the base by broad, obtuse scales, seeds ovate, 5–15 mm long, 3 mm wide, on a fleshy, bright red receptacle. LG 19 (= *P. alpina* var. *arborescens* Brongn. & Gris.; *P. alpina* var. *caespitosa* Carr.). New Caledonia. This species has not been located since its discovery and is, therefore, questionable. z9

P. gracilior Pilg. African Fern Pine. Tree, 18 m or more, stem free of branches for a considerable height, crown densely crowded with branches, young shoots long, more or less in whorls; leaves loosely scattered on young plants, to 10 cm long and 6 mm wide, densely arranged and shorter on mature trees and usually only 2–6 cm long, 3–5 mm wide, thick, tapering to a sharp tip; seeds solitary at the tips of small, foliate shoots, sessile, globose, 12–20 mm wide, thick, hard, purple, bluish pruinose, without a fleshy receptacle. CBI 78; Bai 10: 15; CCE 396 (= *Decussocarpus gracilior* [Pilg.] de Laubf.). Mountains of subtropical Africa; Ethiopia, Uganda, Kenya. z9

P. guatemalensis Standley. Tree, to 18 m, upright, with an outspread crown, bark smooth, reddish-brown, buds ovate, with broad-ovate, acute scales; leaves linear lanceolate, to 13 cm long and 12 mm wide, but smaller on fruiting twigs; male cones cylindrical, axillary, seeds ellipsoid, 8 mm long, receptacle 6 mm long, stalk 6 mm long. JA 29 Pl. 5 (1–2). Guatemala. z9

P. hallii Kirk. Tree, to 20 m, trunk to 1.2 m in diameter, very similar to *P. totara*, but more loosely branched, bark thin and papery, shoots of younger plants somewhat pendulous; leaves 25 to 40 mm long, linear-lanceolate, 4–5 mm wide, stiff, prickly, with a distinct midrib beneath; flowers like those of *P. totara*, seeds ovate, 6–7 mm long, with a short, broad beak, receptacle enlarged, red. KF 9–9A; CBI 79; CC 51 (= *P. totara* var. *hallii* [Kirk] Pilg.). New Zealand. Distinguished from *P. totara* as a young plant by the larger leaves, not so easily differentiated when older. Plate 115; Fig. 167. z9

P. harmsianus Pilg. Tree; needles *Taxus*-like, sessile, somewhat resembling those of *P. montanus*, but spirally arranged, 18–30 mm long, 2–3 mm wide, with thorny tips and a slightly raised midrib; male cones about 10 mm long, seeds 10 mm long, with a thin, fleshy outer shell. JA 29 Pl. 3 (12), Pl. 4 (21 to 23); SFV 762. S. America; Columbia, Venezuela. z9

P. henkelii Stapf (the spelling "henckelii" is incorrect!). Tree, to 35 m in its habitat, trunk to 2 m in diameter, bark usually dark gray, longitudinally split and exfoliating in long strips, young shoots light green and furrowed; leaves spirally arranged, more or less clustered on the apical part of the shoot and pendulous, deep green above and glossy, 9–12 cm long, 6.5–8 mm wide, widest in the middle and from there, gradually narrowing to the apex, also tapering to a short petiole at the base, midrib on the underside especially conspicuous, less so above, stomatal lines confined to the underside; seeds ovate-ellipsoid, 1.7–2.2 cm long, 1.4 to 1.8 cm thick, olive-green, with a hard, leathery shell, sessile on a blue-green, swollen receptacle. CBI 80; FSA 37. S. Africa; Natal and the bordering regions of the eastern Cape Province, particularly in mountain forests, less frequently found in coastal forests. Plate 116. z9

P. idenburgensis Gray. Tree, 12–30 m, with narrow shoots; leaves clustered at the branch tips, leathery, linear-lanceolate or linear-elliptic, 7–15 cm long, 10–15 mm wide, acute, with 6–10 mm stalks, midrib on top usually prominent, flat beneath; male cones 3.5 cm long, 5 mm wide, on thin, 9–12 mm stalks, seeds globose, 1 cm thick, on a very fleshy, 10 mm, receptacle, composed of 3 connate scales. New Guinea, rain forests high in the mountains. z9

P. imbricatus Bl. Tree, to 30 m in its habitat, trunk to 1 m in diameter, bark dark brown or blackish, exfoliating in small, thick, rough pieces, crown quite variable, often with long, wide arching branches, the apical shoots on young plants whip-like, to 20 cm long; leaves in 2 forms: linear on young or strong growing plants, 6–12 mm long, more or less 2 ranked, usually scale-like on older trees, 2–4 mm long (like quite small *Cryptomeria* needles), both leaf forms occasionally found on the same tree at the same time; male flower cones ovate at first and 5 mm long, but to 12 mm long when in full bloom, seeds solitary, terminal, 6 mm long, on a somewhat thickened, fleshy, red receptacle. CIS 54; JA 50: 8a (= *P. cupressina* R. Br. ex Mirb.; *P. horsfieldii* Wall.; *Dacrycarpus imbricatus* [Bl.] de Laubf.). Malaya, Indochina, China, Burma, Java, New Guinea to the Philippines, widely distributed in the monsoon region. Valuable forest tree. Fig. 163. z9

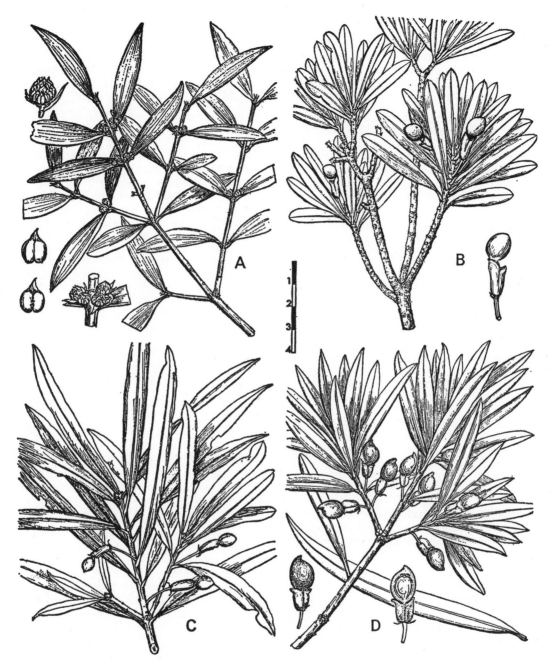

Fig. 166. **Podocarpus.** A. *P. formosensis;* B. *P. polystachyus;* C. *P. philippinensis;*
D. *P. macrophyllus* var. *nakai* (from T. S. Liu)

(Included here are *P. leptophyllus* Wasscher and *P. papuanus* Ridley, both now combined by Laubf. into *Dacrycarpus imbricatus* var. *robustus.* Illustrated in JA 50: 8c.)

var. **kinabaluensis** Wasscher. Small tree or a 2 m high shrub with 10 mm long and 1.2 mm thick needles, curved sickle-shaped with a long apex, mature foliage stout and rigid, flattened (2 sided), bowed upward, with prickly tips, quite variable in length, only 2 mm long on older trees, rectangular in cross section; ripe seeds 7 mm long, 5 mm thick, involucral leaves 5–7 mm long, not covering the ripe seeds (= *Dacrycarpus kinabaluensis* [Wasscher] de Laubf.). N. Borneo, Mt.

Kinabalu. Because of the distinctive size of the involucral leaves, this variety might belong to *P. cinctus.* z9

P. koordersii Pilg. Very similar to *P. neriifolius,* but with leaves 12–20 cm long, 10–18 mm wide, parallel margins for a large part of their length, then gradually tapering to both ends with a broad petiole, very thick and leathery, midrib thicker than *P. neriifolius;* male cones in clusters of 2–8. Java. z9

P. ladei Bailey. Upright tree, tall, with a thick trunk, bark thin, reddish-brown, rather smooth, exfoliating in paper thin scales; needles only about 12 mm long, 2–3 mm wide, usually sessile, green on both sides, upper surface with twice as many stomatal lines as the underside, obtuse; seeds ellipsoid, solitary, 12 mm thick and 18 mm long, purple with a bluish pruinose. Australia; discovered in 1905 by F. W. H. Lade near Port Douglas. Similar to *P. ferrugineus*. z9

P. lambertii Klotzsch. Large tree, with many whorled branches; needles upright, *Taxus*-like, clustered, narrow-oblong to linear-lanceolate, 25–35 mm long, 2–4 mm wide, broadly acuminate, nearly sessile; male cones numerous and in clusters of 3–6 at the ends of 5–15 mm long stalks, seeds solitary, nearly globose, on a fleshy, 4 mm long receptacle, stalk 5–8 mm long. Brazil. z9

P. latifolius (Thunb.) R. Br. ex Mirb. Tree, to 30 m or higher, trunk to 3 m in diameter, or only a shrub, to 2 m, bark dark gray, smooth on young trees, later longitudinally fissured and exfoliating in long strips, young shoots somewhat angular and furrowed; leaves spiral to nearly opposite in arrangement, often clustered on the uppermost branch tips, outspread, dark green to blue-green and glossy above, stomatal lines confined to the underside, linear-elliptic, parallel margins in the middle, quite straight or slightly sickle-shaped, 4–6 (10) cm long, 6–8 mm wide, but to 17 cm long and 15–17 mm wide on younger plants, midrib especially prominent on the underside, margins slightly involuted; seeds obovate to nearly globose, often somewhat acute, blue-green, also often dark violet, 7–11 mm thick, on a fleshy, eventually purple-red. sweet tasting (when ripe) receptacle, 8–14 mm long and wide. CBI 81; DJ 532; FSA 37 (= *P. thunbergii* Hook.). S. Africa, widely distributed. Plate 116; Fig. 169. z9

var. **latior** Pilg. is currently included with the species based on its leaf size.

P. ledermannii Pilg. Very similar to *P. neriifolius*, but with more oblong leaves, drawn out to a short point at the apex, midrib prominent; male cones usually in groups of 3. New Guinea. z9

P. leonii Carabia. Tree, to 6 m, or only a shrub, densely foliate, terminal buds with long scales; leaves narrowly elliptic, acute, 18–50 mm long, 5–10 mm wide, nearly sessile; seeds ovate, 8 mm long, 4 mm wide, on 4–5 mm long stalks. Cuba. Not well known. z9

P. leptophyllus Wasscher see: **P. imbricatus**

P. longifoliolatus Pilg. Tree, 9–12 m, stem reddish or gray, furrowed bark, buds with very long acuminate scales with a broad base, the outermost to 10 mm, leaf-like and reflexed; leaves densely arranged, leathery, erect or outspread, 5 to 10 cm long, lanceolate, gradually tapering to both ends, 6–10 mm wide, midrib on top raised or uneven, underside broader and occasionally indented; male cones solitary, 14 mm long, sessile, seeds grouped 1–3, ovate, 10 mm long, 5 mm wide, blue-green when young, on a fleshy, 8 mm long receptacle. LG 14. New Caledonia. z9

P. lucienii de Laubf. Tree, to 12 m, dioecious, bark light brown at first, then gray, longitudinally furrowed; juvenile leaves to 16 cm long and 20 mm wide, mature leaves linear-oblong, 6–11 cm long, 10–13 mm wide, obtuse to rounded, with short petiole; male cones in 3's, on 2 mm stalks, seeds ovate, about 15 mm long, 10 mm wide, on a fleshy receptacle, composed of 2 connate scales. LG 17. New Caledonia. Resembling *P. sylvestris*, but with darker bark, broader leaves, lighter and more obtuse, longer flower stalks, larger seeds. z9

P. macrophyllus (Thunb.) D. Don. Tree, 12–15 m, but frequently only a shrub from 0.5–2 m, branches horizontally arranged, thick, shoots densely crowded; leaves alternate, very dense, spirally arranged, leathery, broad-linear, 8–10 cm long and 9–10 mm wide, to 17 cm long and 12 mm wide on very vigorous plants, glossy dark green above, more yellowish green beneath, with a distinctly clear midrib, apex usually obtuse to rounded; male inflorescences cylindrical, in clusters, about 3–3.5 cm long, seeds ellipsoid, about 10 mm long, greenish, on a 12–15 mm long, thick, dark red, fleshy receptacle. LT 13; CBI 82; SN 265 (H); KIF 1: 6; CCE 398, 399 (= *P. chinensis* Wall. ex Parl.; *P. appressus* Maxim.). China; mountains in Yunnan Province at 2400 to 3000 m; Japan. 1804. Plate 115. z9

var. **angustifolius** Bl. Strong growing, to 15 m; leaves 5–12 cm long, about 9 mm wide, linear-lanceolate, long acuminate, base cuneate, new shoots yellow-green, later becoming dark green. Bai 10: 57; CCE 399. Widely cultivated in the USA, more often planted than the species.

'**Argenteus**'. Leaves white variegated.

'**Aureus**'. Leaves with broad yellow border, longer and wider than the species.

var. **chingii** Gray. Columnar habit, 7–8 m; leaves very small, only 12–30 mm long and 4 mm wide. Only known to exist in Chekiang, China.

var. **maki** Sieb. Shrub with tightly ascending branches, very densely foliate; leaves straight, linear-lanceolate, directed upward or outspread, obtuse or short acuminate, 4–7 cm long, 4–7 mm wide. Bai 1 P: 14 (= *P. maki* Sieb.). China, Formosa, Burma; cultivated in Japan. Occasionally grows narrowly columnar and very popular in this form for hedges in Japan. According to Prof. Dr. H. Kruse, Tokyo, this variety is often confused even in Japan with the very similar *Cephalotaxus harringtonia* 'Fastigiata' (see Plate 63), known in Japan as "chosenmak". Plate 118; Fig. 169.

var. **nakai** (Hayata) Li & Keng. Medium sized tree, trunk to 60 cm in diameter, bark gray and fibrous; leaves lanceolate to more linear, 6–8 cm long, 8–12 mm wide, obtuse, straight or sickle-shaped, base acute or short tapered, petiole 5 mm long; seeds obliquely ovate, 1 cm long, 8 mm wide, receptacle fleshy, nearly pear-shaped, bilabiate, 5–12 mm long, red, stalk 2–12 mm long. LT 14 (= *P. nakai* Hayata). Formosa. Fig. 166

P. madagascariensis Baker. Small tree; leaves spirally arranged, 12–15 cm long, 1–2 cm wide, lanceolate, long acuminate, with midrib conspicuous underneath, longitudinally furrowed above, thick and leathery; male cones only 12 mm long, seeds globose, pea-size, eventually black. CCE 401. Madagascar. Common forest tree. z9

P. magnifolius Buchholz & Gray. Tree, 20–25 m; leaves leathery, erect or outspread, broad lanceolate to oblanceolate, to 16 cm long and 2.5 cm wide on young plants, only 5–8 cm long and 12–13 mm wide on older trees, long acuminate, midrib distinctly indented above,

Fig. 167. **Podocarpus**. A. *P. nivalis*, twig with male inflorescences, 2 fruits left above, seeds with receptacle below right, enlarged; B. *P. totara*; C. *P. hallii*; D. *P. acutifolius*; E. *P. spinulosus*; F. *P. ferrugineus*. Particulars as explained for A.; juv. = juvenile form (from Adams; E. from Maloney)

at least at the base, raised beneath, but with a furrow on both sides, decurrent; male cones solitary, sessile, axillary. SVF 766. SE. Venezuela, Bolivia. z9

P. mannii Hook. f. Tree, 9–15 m, branches loosely arranged, short and curved upward on older trees; leaves sessile, variable in length, 10–15 cm on vigorous young plants, only about 7 cm on older trees, 8–12 mm wide, straight or slightly sickle-shaped, gradually finely acuminate; male cones axillary and sessile, solitary or in 2's, about 2.5 cm long, seeds sessile, to 2.5 cm long and 14 mm thick, not stalked, on short, foliate shoots. CCE 401 (= *Decussocarpus mannii* [Hook. f.] de Laubf.). W. Africa, Sao Thomé. Cultivated for timber in Congo and Nigeria. De Laubenfels includes *P. usambarensis* Pilg. of Uganda and *P. dawei* Stapf of Tanzania and Usambara with this species. Fig. 169. z9

P. matudai Lundell. Large tree; leaves on strong shoots to 15 cm long and 18 mm wide, on fertile shoots only 4–8.5 cm long and 10–15 mm wide; male cones 33–35 mm long, 4 mm wide, surrounded at the base by broad, keeled, acuminate scales, seeds to 1 cm long, 8 cm thick, on a thick, fleshy receptacle, composed of 2 connate scales. JA Pl. 2 (1–2). S. Mexico. z9

P. milanjianus Rendle. Tree, to 30 m, or only a shrub, bark gray-brown, exfoliating in scales, branches short; leaves dense, spirally arranged, 5–10 cm long, but 10–20 cm long on young trees, 8–12 mm wide, straight or bowed, somewhat sickle-shape with long tips on young trees, short acuminate on older trees, short stalked; male cones grouped 1–2, cylindrical, 2.5–3.5 cm long, pink-red; seeds globose, 8–12 mm thick, blue-green and pruinose, sessile on a thick, light red, bluish pruinose receptacle. CBI 83 (= *P. ulugurensis* Pilg.). Mountains in E. and SE. Africa as well as Cameroon; especially in the Milanji Mts. of E. Africa. Cultivated for timber in Kivu. z9

P. minor (Carr.) Parl. Small tree or shrub, 2–3 m high, with very rough, dark brown, somewhat scaly bark, ascending branches; leaves polymorphic: obtuse-triangular on the main shoots, 1 mm long, often abscising, or elliptic and to 4 mm long, or on short shoots, densely crowded, decussate, ascending in 4 perpendicular rows, ovate to elliptic, obtuse, 10–20 mm long and to 5 mm wide, juvenile foliage to 39 mm long, lanceolate and 2 ranked; ripe cones obliquely pear-shaped, about 20 mm long and 12 mm wide, outer shell fleshy and blue-green at first, dark red when ripe. LG 11 (= *P. palustris* Buchholz; *Decussocarpus minor* [Carr.] de Laubf.). New Caledonia, on the coast and river banks in flat and hilly sites. z9

P. montanus (Willd.) Lodd. Tree, 20–24 m, branches horizontal; needles *Taxus*-like, rather evenly 2 ranked, linear, occasionally oblique or sickle-shaped, 10–20 mm long, 2.5–3 mm wide, acute, dark green above, lighter beneath, indented above the midrib; male cones very numerous, to 25 together, each about 10 mm long, spirally arranged on a 35–50 mm long shoot, seeds about 15 mm long, ovate, violet-black. CBI 84; JA 29 Pl. 4 (24–25) (= *P. humboldtii* Hort. ex Gord.; *P. taxifolia* Kunth in Humboldt & Bonpland). Mountains of Columbia and Ecuador, at altitudes up to 2500 m. z9

P. motleyi (Parl.) Duemmer. Tree, to 40 m; foliage very similar to *P. wallichianus*, but the leaves not over 5 cm long on the average (at least 6, usually 9–14 cm long on *P. wallichianus!*), leaves opposite or nearly so, 2 ranked on an even plane, leathery tough, elliptic, apex with a protruding point, tapering to a short, thick, 2–3 mm long petiole at the base, leaf blade somewhat variable in form, usually 3–5(7.5) cm long and 15–22(28) mm wide; male flower cones solitary, axillary, sessile (!), cylindrical, 15–20 mm long, seeds globose, smooth, 13–16 mm thick, on a violet-red, swollen receptacle (= *P. beccarii* Parl.; *Decussocarpus motleyi* [Parl.] de Laubf.). Sumatra and Malaya to S. Borneo. z9

P. nagi (Thunb.) Zoll & Moritzi ex Makino. "Nagi" in Japanese. Tree, 15–20 m or more, bark smooth, reddish, branches partly opposite, partly alternate, horizontal, smooth, twigs thin, nodding; leaves opposite or nearly so, lanceolate to ovate or oblong, 3–8 cm long, 12–30 mm wide, obtuse, tapered to the base, entire, deep green and glossy above, lighter or also whitish beneath, with many parallel veins, without a midrib; male inflorescences solitary, simple or branched, about 20 mm long, on a 6 mm stalk, seeds globose, 10–15 mm thick, bluish-green, pruinose, calyx cup small, not fleshy, stalk about 10 mm long. LT 15; CBI 85; Bai 10: 16; KIF 1: 8 (= *P. nageia* R. Br.; *P. caesius* Maxim.; *P. cuspidatus* Endl.). S. Japan. Plate 115; Fig. 168. z9

Fig. 168. *Podocarpus nagi* (Original)

var. **angustifolius** Maxim. Leaves shorter and only to 12 mm wide.

var. **nankoensis** (Hayata) Masam. ex Kudo & Masam. Leaves narrower, more lanceolate, 6–9 cm long, 13–25 mm wide, sessile; male inflorescences clustered 4–5 together, 5–7 mm long; seeds globose, 10–12 mm thick, stalk scarred, 1 cm long. LT 16 (= *P. nankoensis* Hayata). China; Hainan; Formosa. z9

var. **rotundifolius** Maxim. Leaves more oval.

'Variegatus'. Leaves very attractively yellow striped, like a *Tradescantia*, shorter and more rounded than the type. Handled here as a collective name since K. Uehara (Jyumoku Daizusetsu, vol. 1, pp. 68–70) established around 30 variegated foliage forms.

P. neriifolius D. Don. Tree, to 30 m or more in its habitat, bark gray-brown, fibrous, branches horizontal and more or less in whorls; leaves alternate, narrowly lanceolate, 3.5–23 cm long, 5–25 mm wide, leathery, but flexible, glossy green above, lighter beneath, margins in large part parallel, narrower at the apex, midrib usually prominent, margins somewhat involuted, light green, short petiole; male cones usually short and sessile, grouped 1–2–4 together, 2–7.5 cm long, 2.5–3 mm wide, seeds ellipsoid to more globose, about 1 cm thick, on a fleshy, thick receptacle of 2 connate scales. BM 4655 (= *P. bracteata* Bl.; *P. discolor* Bl.; *P. discolor* Bl.; *P. leptostachya* Bl.). SE. Asia, from eastern Himalaya, Upper Burma, Malaya and the Andaman Islands, East Indies to the Fiji Islands, and north to China. Fig. 163. z9

Includes about 10 botanical forms and geographical varieties.

P. nivalis Hook. Shrub, prostrate, 1–3 m in its habitat, branches often rooting, twigs short; leaves dense and spirally arranged, stiff, leathery, margin thickened, linear-oblong, 5–15 mm long, 2–4 mm wide, obtuse; male cones axillary, 5–15 mm long and on a 3–5 mm stalk, usually grouped 1–4, female flowers solitary, on 3 mm long stalks, seeds ovate, 4–6 mm long, with a fleshy red receptacle. KF 40; HI 582; CBI 86; DJ 541; SFP 147; CCE 398, 400. New Zealand, in the mountains. One of the hardiest species, forming a good groundcover even on alkaline soil, reaching 2–3 m in width. Plate 114; Fig. 167. z7–8

var. **erectus** Cock. Upright, not prostrate, to 3 m high, with a thin stem; leaves to 25 mm long. New Zealand.

P. novae-caledoniae Viellard ex Brongn. & Gris. Shrub, to 3 m, densely branched; needles densely crowded, linear, 3.5–11 cm long, 3.5 mm wide, with a short petiole and a long or short apical tip, blue-green when young, later dark green; male cones axillary, short, slender, 8–18 mm long, seeds ellipsoid, 8 mm long, glossy, on a fleshy receptacle. LG 18; CCE 401. New Caledonia, along river banks in the hills. z9

P. nubigenus Lindl. Tree, to 20 m in its habitat; needles usually spiraled or 2 ranked, straight or sickle-shaped, 2.5–4 cm long, 3–4 mm wide, stiff and leathery, acute, bright green above, blue-green beneath; male cones short stalked, simple or branched, 3–6 mm long, seeds ovate, short stalked, on a fleshy receptacle. CBI 87; JA Pl. 8 (1–3); CCE 398, 400. S. America; in the mountains of Chile, in Patagonia and on the Island of Chiloé. Plate 116. z9

P. oleifolius D. Don. Tree, to 18 m, densely branched, bark yellowish-brown; leaves spirally arranged, 2.5–7.5 cm long, 6–12 mm wide, linear-lanceolate, acuminate, midrib narrowly channeled above, raised beneath; male flower cones solitary, sessile, about 2.5 cm long, surrounded at the base by broad, keeled scales, seeds ovate, 8 mm long, on a fleshy receptacle of 2 connate scales, sessile. JA 29 Pl. 6 (3). Mexico to Peru and Bolivia; in the mountains. z9

P. pallidus Gray. Shrub or small tree, to 6 m, branches in whorls, buds narrowly ovate; leaves especially densely crowded at the branch tips, lanceolate, light green, 2.5–10 cm long, 6–14 mm wide, somewhat involuted, long or short acuminate, petiole thick, midrib rather elevated,

narrow above, broader beneath and occasionally furrowed; male cones solitary, sessile, to 12 mm long, and 4 mm wide, seeds globose, 10–12 mm thick, on a fleshy, 10 mm long receptacle. SW. Pacific; Tonga Islands. z9

P. pendulifolius Buchholz & Gray. Small tree, to 6 m, with stout branches; leaves pendulous, lanceolate-sickle-shaped, 3–11 cm long, flat furrowed above between 2 ridges, margins thickened, but not involuted; male cones cylindrical, 20 mm long, 6 mm thick, seeds blue-green, globose. SFV 767. W. Venezuela; in mountain forests at 2000–3200 m. z9

P. philippinensis Foxworthy. Tree, 20–30 m in its habitat, bark smooth, reddish-brown, shoots cylindrical, gray; leaves linear-lanceolate, 13–17 cm long, 9–10 mm wide, apex acute, base abruptly tapered, sessile; seeds globose, 6–8(–15) mm thick, blue-green, receptacle fleshy, red when fresh, 8–10 mm long, stalk 2–3 cm long. LT 17. Philippines; Taiwan, Hengchun Peninsula. Fig. 166. z9

P. pilgeri Foxworthy. Shrub or small tree, 1.8–15 m high; leaves scattered or clustered near the branch tips, linear-lanceolate, 12–75 mm long, 4–12 mm wide, obtuse or acute, midrib conspicuous above; male cones solitary, axillary, nearly sessile, 15–50 mm long, seeds ellipsoid-globose, 8 mm long, 6 mm wide, on a fleshy receptacle composed of 2 connate scales. In the higher mountains of the Philippines and the Solomon Islands. Fig. 163. z9

P. pittieri Buchholz & Gray. Tree, to 9 m; leaves linear-lanceolate, 6–22 cm long, 7–15 mm wide, quite flat above except for the midrib near the petiole; male cones solitary, sessile, 4 cm long, with a basal scale, seeds broadly ovate, 8–12 mm long, on a thick, fleshy, 8–12 mm long receptacle and 20–25 mm long stalk. SFV 764. N. Venezuela, mountains along the north coast. z9

P. polystachyus R. Br. ex Mirb. Small tree or shrub, branches and shoots short and outspread; leaves leathery tough, narrow to linear-oblanceolate, densely clustered at the shoot tips, 5–7 cm long, 8–12 mm wide, short rounded at the apex; male flower cones grouped 3–5, seeds elliptic, dark blue when fresh, black when dry, 9–10 mm long, receptacle fleshy, cylindrical, bilabiate, 10–13 mm long. LWT 5; LT 18 (= *P. littoralis* Teysmann). Malaya, Philippines; Formosa. Fig. 166. z9

P. purdieanus Hook. Tree, to 35 m; leaves spirally arranged, lanceolate, 35–100 mm long, 6–16 mm wide, also to 12 cm long on strong young plants, and 18 mm wide, rounded or with a short apex; male cones solitary, axillary, cylindrical, 15 mm long, seeds ovate, 8 mm long, on a receptacle of 2 thick, connate scales. HIP 624 (= *P. jamaicensis* Hort.) Jamaica. z9

P. reichei Buchholz & Gray. Tree, to 20 m; leaves lanceolate, 6–15 cm long, 10–15 mm wide, midrib raised above; male cones solitary or in pairs, cylindrical, to 5 cm long, seeds broadly ovate, 12–15 mm long, 12 mm wide, on a fleshy receptacle, reddish at first, eventually dark brown. JA 29 Pl. 1 (1). Mountain forests in east-central Mexico and Costa Rica. z9

Fig. 169. **Podocarpus.** A. *P. mannii;* B. *P. amarus;* C. *P. latifolius;* D. *P. urbanii;* E. *P. salignus;*
F. *P. macrophyllus* var. *maki.* Male flowers at A. E. and F. (from Pilger)

P. roraimae Pilg. Tree, to 15 m, densely branched, outer
bud scales leaf-like; leaves ovate to oblanceolate, obtuse
acuminate, 15–30 mm long, 4–5 mm wide, leathery,
often furrowed above along the midrib; seeds oblong, 6
mm long, 4 mm wide, on a 4 mm long receptacle. On the
border region between Venezuela and Brazil; Mt.
Roraima to Mt. Duida. z9

P. rospigliosii Pilg. Tree, to about 30 m, the young
branchlets clustered nearly brush-like; needles
opposite, 2 ranked, appearing to be on an even plane,
oval-lanceolate, to 22 mm long, 10 mm wide, both sides

equal and with stomata, nearly sessile; seeds blue-black
or red, pear-shaped, 2–3 cm long, 12–18 mm thick, with a
fleshy outer shell, hard inner shell. JA 29 Pl. 5 (35–39) (=
Decussocarpus rospigliosii [Pilg.] de Laubf.). Venezuela, E.
Colombia and central Peru, in the mountains. Cultivated for timber in Venezuela. z9

P. rostratus Laurent. Small tree, to 9 m; needles *Taxus*-
like, lanceolate, 20–35 mm long, 1–2 mm wide, gradually
tapering to the apex; male cones cylindrical, about 12
mm long, 3 mm wide, solitary or grouped 2–3 together,
on a 2–5 mm long stalk. Madagascar; in the mountains.
Possibly extinct.

P. rumphii Bl. Small or medium size tree, very closely related to *P. neriifolius;* leaves thick, leathery and stiff, 6–27 cm long, parallel margins for a large part of their length, short acuminate, 10–18 mm wide; male cones solitary, seeds globose to ellipsoid, grouped 1–2 together, about 12 mm long, on a receptacle of 2–4 fleshy scales. Borneo, Moluccas and New Guinea to the Solomon Islands. z9

P. salignus D. Don. Tree, 15–20 m, branches slender, nodding, irregularly arranged; leaves narrow-lanceolate with short petiole, 5–12 cm long, 4–6 mm wide, obtuse or short acuminate, glossy light green above, with stomatal lines beneath; male cones 25–35 mm long, very narrow, in small, pendulous clusters, seeds oblong, 8 mm long, 3 mm thick, on a fleshy, dark red receptacle, long and thin stalked. CBI 75; PFG 25; DJ 547; CCE 400 (= *P. chilinus* Rich.). Chile, 1853. Plate 117; Fig 169. z9

P. salomoniensis Wasscher. Tree, to 15 m, branches outspread and somewhat pendulous, bark light brown, furrowed and fibrous; leaves outspread, 11–16 cm long, 6–8 mm wide, thick and stiff, with a prominent midrib, usually not furrowed beneath; seeds ellipsoid, 12 mm long, 8 mm wide, resting on a receptacle of 4 fleshy scales. Solomon Islands; mountain forests of San Cristoval. z9

P. selloi Kotzsch (the spelling "sellowii" is incorrect). A small tree, 6–9 m; leaves lanceolate, short acuminate, 3.5–8 cm long, 5–8 mm wide, to 15 cm long on young plants and 12–18 mm wide, leathery, short stalked; male cones 30 mm long, solitary in the leaf axils, seeds to 10 mm long, smooth, on a 5–8 mm long, fleshy receptacle, sessile and on a 6 mm long stalk. Brazil. z9

P. silvestris Buchholz. Tree, 15–18 m, twigs nearly in whorls; leaves clustered on the branch tips, linear-lanceolate, 50–80 mm (occasionally to 16 cm) long, 7–10 (15) mm wide, obtuse, tapered to the base, midrib flat or raised; male cones 8–10 mm long, 2–3 mm wide, axillary in groups of 3, sessile to short stalked, with 7 to 9 thin basal scales, seeds elongated, 12 mm long, 8 mm wide, on a fleshy, 6 mm long receptacle. LG 16. New Caledonia. z9

P. spicatus R. Br. ex Mirb. Tree, to 25 m in its habitat, trunk to 1.25 m in diameter, bark bluish-black, rough, exfoliating in thick scales, young plants with long, thin, outward bowed shoots and only a few needles; needles nearly 2 ranked, linear, straight to somewhat sickle-shaped, 10–15 mm long, 1–2 mm wide, dark green above, blue-green beneath; male flowers in 3 to 5 cm long spikes, female also in spikes with 3–10 ovules, on short axillary shoots, seeds globose, 1 cm thick, black, outer integument fleshy, receptacle not swollen. KF 4–5; CBI 88; HI 543; SFP 58. New Zealand, common in the forests on the plains. Fig. 164. z9

P. spinulosus (Smith) R. Br. Shrub, densely branched, *Taxus*-like; leaves sessile, usually spirally arranged, 18–60 mm long, occasionally also to 75 mm long, 2–4 mm wide; male cones clustered in the leaf axils, 6–8 mm long, seeds 8–12 mm long, 8 mm wide, often with a stout beak, blue-green when young, receptacle deep purple with a bluish pruinose surface, edible. BAu 444 (= *P. pungens*

Don; *P. bidwillii* Hoibrenk). Australia; New S. Wales. 1810. Fig. 167. z9

P. sprucei Parl. Tree, closely related to *P. glomeratus* and occasionally considered identical; needles however, wider, often obtuse, without a prickly leaf tip, not blue-green beneath; male cones larger and more numerous in a cluster, seeds larger, longer stalked. JA 29 Pl. 7 (2–3). Central and W. Cordillera of Ecuador and Colombia. z9

P. standleyi Buchholz & Gray. Tree, to 24 m, branches alternate and outspread; needles *Taxus*-like, nearly opposite in 2 rows, linear, occasionally somewhat sickle-shaped, acute, 12–25 mm long, 2–3 mm wide, very blue-green beneath, midrib furrowed above; male cones numerous, to 25 together, each 10–12 mm long, spirally arranged on a 20–75 mm long shoot, seeds about 10 mm long. JA 29 Pl. 4 (32–34). Costa Rica. z9

P. steupii Wasscher. Tree, to 36 m in its habitat, but usually much shorter, bark brown or gray; juvenile foliage flattened (2 sided) and 2 ranked, up to 8 mm long and 0.9 mm thick, gradually becoming shorter and no longer 2 sided with age, needle-like, 3–4 mm long, prickly, nearly square in cross section; seeds globose, 5 to 6 mm long, with a small, warty receptacle (= *Dacrycarpus steupii* [Wasscher] de Laubf.). Celebes. z9

P. steyermarkii Buchholz & Gray. Small tree, to 12 m, buds with very large, leaf-like scales; leaves lanceolate, 4–7.5 cm long, 6–11 mm wide, stiff, bowed and outspread, leathery, midrib indented above, margin involuted; seeds silver-gray, on an 8 mm long receptacle. SFV 764. Venezuela; only found in one location in the Bolivar Province. z9

P. tepuiensis Buchholz & Gray. Tree, 9–12 m; leaves broad lanceolate, acute, 15–20 mm long, to 5 mm wide; male cones solitary, sessile, to 10 mm long and 2 mm wide, seeds 7.5 mm long, 4 mm wide. SFV 772. Venezuela; Mt. Ptari-tepui, 2000 m. z9

P. thevetiifolius Zippelius. Tree, to 20 m or higher; leaves narrow-lanceolate, 2.5 to 7.5 cm long, 5–9 mm wide, thin, leathery, usually obtuse, with an indistinct midrib; seeds ellipsoid, 10 mm long, deep green. New Guinea. z9

P. totara G. Benn ex D. Don ("totara" is the Maori Indian name for the tree). Tree, to 30 m high, trunk to 2 m in diameter, bark dark brown, fibrous, thick and deeply split on old trees, outspread branches; leaves sometimes of variable density and encircling the shoot, partly also 2 ranked, dark green or also brownish, on young plants 15–30 mm long and 3–4 mm wide, on older plants to 20 mm long and 1–2 mm wide, linear-lanceolate, straight or somewhat sickle-shaped, acute and prickly, stiff, leathery, often somewhat furrrowed above, with a distinct midrib beneath, short petioled; male flowers grouped 1–3, short stalked, female grouped 1–2 on short, swollen stalks, seeds nut-like, globose, 4–5 mm long with either a dry or enlarged, red receptacle. KF 115; CC 49; CBI 89; DJ 552; SFP 60; CCE 402. New Zealand. An important forest tree in its habitat. Plate 117; Fig. 167. z9

'Aureus'. Like the type, but with more bronze-brown needles. Cultivated by Hillier. (1970).

P. urbanii Pilg. Tree, to 15 m high, *Taxus*-like; needles stiff, erect, leathery, linear-lanceolate, 18–25 mm long, 4 mm wide, but to 5 cm long and 6 mm wide on young plants; male cones cylindrical, axillary, short stalked, about 6 mm long, seeds small, 6 mm long, ovate, on a fleshy receptacle. Jamaica; Montserrat, Blue Mountains. Fig. 169. z9

P. usambarensis Pilg. see: **P. manii**

P. ustus (Viellard) Brongn. & Gris. Shrub, less than 1 m high, densely covered with coppery-red or purple, triangular scale-leaves, only 2 mm long; male flower catkins 5 mm long, cylindrical, on a 6 mm foliate stalk, seeds globose, 2.5 mm thick, purple, inside very woody, without a fleshy receptacle. ENP 13: 133; LG 10. New Caledonia. Discovered in 1862, although first established as a root parasite on *Dacrydium taxoides* in 1957 (the first gymnosperm species found to be parasitic). z9

P. utilior Pilg. Tree, to 20 m or more; needles spirally arranged, but appearing 2 ranked, on an even plane, crowded, thick, leathery, linear, 10–25 mm long, 1.5–3 mm wide, acute or obtuse, base oblique, sessile or short stalked, midrib somewhat conspicuous above; seeds globose, 8 mm wide. Peru, Bolivia. Important local timber tree. z9

P. victorianus Carabia. Stoutly branched, tree-like shrub, buds ovate, with long acuminate, upright or outspread, keeled scales; leaves limp, elliptic, 3–5 cm long, about 12 mm wide, with sharp tips, drawn out to a short petiole, midrib only raised at the base, otherwise flat; seeds 10 mm long, 5 mm wide, on a very fleshy, 15 mm long receptacle, sessile. Cuba. Not well known. z9

P. viellardii Parl. Tree, 12–15 m in its habitat, crown narrow, with a hard, dark bark; needles variable and in 2 forms: juvenile leaves 2 sided (flattened) and 2 ranked, to 10 mm long, 1 mm wide, acute and outspread, more or less parallel to the shoot, soft, gradually becoming smaller and thicker toward both ends of the shoot, mature leaves needle-like, 2 to 4 mm long, acute, not 2 ranked, rather spirally arranged and overlapping, tips incurved, blue-green, seeds ovate or globose, 5–6 mm long. LG 8; CCE 402 (= *P. taxodioides* var. *tenuifolia* Carr.; *P. tenuifolia* Carr.; *Dacrycarpus vieillardii* [Parl.] de Laubf.). New Caledonia. z9

P. vitiensis Seem. ("Dakua Salusalu" in Fiji). Tree, 18–20 m high, trunk to about 1 m in diameter, outspread crown, branches nodding; leaves opposite and clearly 2 ranked, on 15–30 cm long shoots, the individual leaves about 3 cm long, 5–6 mm wide, lanceolate, sessile, glossy green; male flowers in terminal, 25–30 mm long spikes, seeds bluish-red, pear-shaped, 20 mm long, with a sharp, protruding tip. PPF 22. Fiji Islands, New Guinea, Solomon Islands. z9

P. wallichianus Presl. Tree, to 48 m high, bark smooth, exfoliating in large, thin, irregular plates, new bark brown; leaves decussate, but appearing 2 ranked in an even plane, elliptic, acute to acuminate, 9–14 cm long, abruptly tapering to a 5–10 mm long petiole, occasionally (especially on young plants or shaded leaves) also to 23 cm long and 7 cm wide (!); male flower cones 1–2 cm long, always distinctly 2–10 mm long stalked (!), seeds globose, about 2–2.5 cm thick, on about a 7–18 mm very fleshy, eventually blackish receptacle, stalk 12–20 mm long. ENP 13: 134 (= *Decussocarpus wallichianus* [Presl] de Laubf.; *P. blumei* Endl.; *P. agathifolia* Bl.). From the East Indies to New Guinea, in the mountain rain forests, to about 1500 m. Fig. 170. z9

Lit. Buchholz, J. T., & N. E. Gray: A taxonomic revision of *Podocarpus*. I–VI. Jour. Arnold Arbor. 29, 49–76, 117–151, 1948; 32, 82–97, 1951. ● Blombery, A. M.: Australian Conifers. Australian Plants 4, 256–266, 1968. ● Gray, N. E.: A taxonomic revision of *Podocarpus*. VII–XIII Jour. Arnold Arbor. 34, 67–76, 163–175; 36, 199–206; 37, 160–172; 39, 424–477; 41, 36–39; 43, 67–79 (1953–1962). ● Gray, N. E.: The cultivated Podocarps in the United States. Baileya 10, 56–61, 1962 (with ills.). ● de Laubenfels, D. J.: A revision of the Malesian and Pacific Rainforest Conifers. I. Podocarpaceae, in part. Jour. Arnold Arbor. 50, 274 to 369, 1969. ● de Laubenfels, D. J.: Parasitic conifer found in New Caledonia. Science 130, 97, 1950. ● de Laubenfels, D. J.: Podocarpaceae. In: Flora de la Nouvelle-Calédonie et Dépendances, 15–79. Paris 1972. ● Leistner, O. A.: Podocarpaceae. Codd, De Winter, Rycroft, Flora of Southern Africa, vol. 1, 34–41, 1966 ● Pilger, R.: Podocarpaceae (in latin). In: Pflanzenfamilien, 2nd ed., 13, 211–249, 1962. ● Sharp, A. J.: La distribución del género *Podocarpus* en México. Bol. Soc. Bot. Méx. 4, 17–18, 1946. ● Wasscher. J.: The genus *Podocarpus* in the Netherlands Indies. Blumea 4, 359–481, 1941.

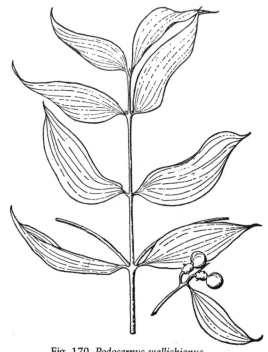

Fig. 170. *Podocarpus wallichianus*
(from Womersley)

PSEUDOLARIX Gord.—Golden Larch—PINACEAE

Deciduous, tall tree; branches horizontally whorled; twigs either as long shoots with scattered needles or as short shoots with clustered, crowded needles; leaves abscising in fall, linear, soft; plants monoecious; male flowers several, terminal on leafless shoots; female flowers solitary, globose, on short, foliate shoots; cones ovate, short stalked, erect, seed scales oval-lanceolate, outspread, leathery, woody at the base, disintegrating when ripe; seeds in 2's under each seed scale, with tough wings, nearly as long as the scale and with the seed tightly adnate, fully covering the upper side of the seed, but the largest part of the underside is distinct from the wing; cotyledons 5–6. $x = 11$.—1 species in China. Range map Fig. 100.

Pseudolarix amabilis (E. J. Nelson) Rehder. Golden Larch. Tree, 30–40 m high, trunk of older trees with a red-brown, narrowly furrowed bark, crown broadly conical, branches in whorls, horizontal, long shoots thin, glabrous pruinose, brown in the second year, terminal buds acutely ovate, scales abscising, short shoots longer than those of *Larix*, with a distinct ring form constriction at the end of each year's growth, with 15–30, umbrella-like spreading needles on the shoot tip; needles linear, soft, 3–7 cm long, 2–3 mm wide, light green, orange-yellow in fall, long acuminate, keeled beneath and with 2 distinct, gray stomatal bands, with 3 marginal resin ducts, 1 vascular bundle; cones solitary, ovate, 5–7 cm long, 4–5 cm wide, reddish-brown, ripening in the fall of the first year, bluish pruinose at first, eventually red-brown, scales small, triangular, oval-lanceolate, base cordate, emarginate on the apex, bract scales oval-lanceolate, much smaller than the seeds, seeds obovate to oval, 8 mm long, 4 to 5 mm wide, with about a 25 mm long brownish wing, obtuse on the tip. DJ 108; OCC 367; NF 2: 30; CIS 3; CCE 403, 404 (= *P. kaempferi* Gord.; *P. fortunei* Mayr; *Chrysolarix amabilis* [Nels.] H. E. Moore). E. China; Chekiang and Kiangsi. Introduced by R. Fortune into England in 1852. Quite winter hardy. Plate 111, 118; Fig. 171. z6

Includes 3 cultivars:

'Annesleyana'. Dwarf form, very broad and bushy habit, low, twigs short and spreading horizontally, branch tips pendulous; needles very densely arranged. HDw 150 (H). Presumably originated from seed, about 1860. The type of this form is in the garden of Lady Annesley in Castlewellan, County Down, N. Ireland. (VR)

'Dawsonii'. Dwarf form, conical habit, low (= *P. kaempferi* var. *dawsonii* Hornibr.). Developed from seed of a large tree in the Wellesley Pinetum by J. Dawson, then employed by the Arnold Arboretum. 1895. (VR)

'Nana'. 30–100 cm high (= *P. kaempferi* var. *nana* Beissn.). This form is grown in tubs in China and kept small by pruning. Probably not grown in the West.

Fig. 171. *Psuedolarix amabilis.*
a. Twig with 3 cones, b. male inflorescence,
c. seed scale
(from Beissner)

PSEUDOTAXUS Cheng—TAXACEAE

Monotypic genus. Evergreen shrub, very similar to *Taxus* in appearance, but differing from all the other Taxaceae in the complete absence of papillae on the underside of the leaves; otherwise recognizable by the numerous sterile scales on the male cones and many sterile scales under the ovules; aril white instead of red (= *Nothotaxus* Florin). For further characteristics, see the following species description.

Pseudotaxus chienii (Cheng) Cheng. Evergreen shrub, glabrous, not resinous, 2–4 m high, branches in whorls, twigs usually in 3 parted whorls or nearly opposite, cylindrical, longitudinally furrowed, gray to brown at first, gray to greenish or gray-yellow in the 2nd year, ringed by triangular leaves at the base; needles densely spiraled, but usually appearing 2 ranked, normally spreading at right angles, linear, straight or curved, 12–25 mm long, to 3 mm wide, base tapered to a 1–2 mm long petiole, glossy dark green above, convex, slightly concave beneath, with 2 blue-white stomatal bands, each about 1 mm wide and with 13–19 lines (others in Taxaceae yellowish-green instead of blue-white!); plants dioecious, male flowers solitary in the leaf axils, with 8 decussate, ovate to obovate, sterile scales, female flowers also in the leaf axils of the youngest shoots, on short stalks, with 14–16 scales, the ovules 2–7 mm long in the apical scales, ripe seeds 5 mm long, 4 mm wide, surrounded by the fleshy, campanulate, white aril (= *Nothotaxus chienii* [Cheng] Florin; *Taxus chienii* Cheng). Found about 1930 in the vicinity of Lungtsuan, in Maoshan, Chekiang Province, E. China. Presumably winter hardy. Plate 118; Fig. 172, 173. z6

Lit. Florin, R.: On *Nothotaxus*; a new genus of the Taxaceae from Eastern China. Acta Horti Berg. (Uppsala) 14, 385–395, 1948 (3 plates).

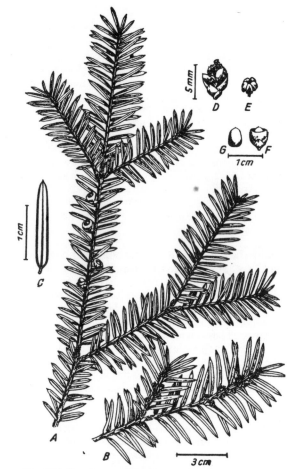

Fig. 172. *Pseudotaxus chienii.* Branch with fruit at left, with male flowers below; C. leaf; D–E. Two male flowers; F–G. fruit (from Cheng)

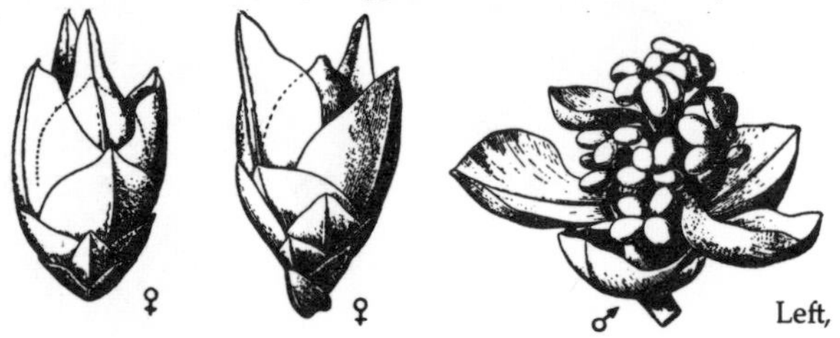

Fig. 173. *Pseudotaxus chienii.*
Left, two female flowers; right, male inflorescence (from Florin)

PSEUDOTSUGA Carr.—Douglas Fir—PINACEAE

Tall, evergreen, spruce-like trees; branches in irregular whorls; trunks of younger trees covered with many resin blisters; shoots nearly smooth, with nearly elliptical leaf scars from fallen needles; buds large, ovate to spindle-form, acute, glabrous, not resinous; leaves spirally arranged, but usually more or less 2 ranked, outspread, linear, flattened, tapered petiole-like at the base, sitting on short, oblique, leaf cushions, green and furrowed above, with 2 stomatal bands beneath, 2 marginal resin ducts and 1 vascular bundle; plants monoecious; male flowers axillary, cones composed of numerous, spirally arranged, short stalked, globose anthers; female flowers on short shoots, terminal, composed of numerous, spirally arranged, densely imbricate scales; seed scales with 2 inverted ovules at the base; bract scales with 2 incisions, 3 pointed from the awn-like, elongated midrib; cones pendulous, short stalked, oblong, ripening the first year, not disintegrating, with 2 winged seeds under each seed scale; wings large, round, partly clasping the seed; cotyledons 6–12; x = 13.—About 20 species are listed, but only about 5(6) are generally recognized. 2(3) species in N. America, the others in E. Asia. Range map Fig. 174.

Outline of the more Prominent Characteristics of the included Species

Needle tips not emarginate		Needle tips emarginate	
Cone length 10–18 cm	Cone length to 10 cm	Cone length 3–5 cm	Cone length 5–6 cm
Needles light green, usually mucronulate; rare species, only in the warmest regions: *P. macrocarpa*	Needles obtuse to acute, usually dark green or blue-green, very common: *P. menziesii*	Young shoots always glabrous, light gray-yellow; rare: *P. japonica*	Young shoots pubescent, red-brown; both very rare; a) needles 25–30 mm long; *P. sinensis* b) needles to 50 mm long: *P. wilsoniana*

Pseudotsuga japonica, (Shir.) Beissn. Japanese Douglas fir. Tree, 15–30 m high, straight trunk, bark reddish-brown, fissured, conical crown, branches spreading nearly horizontally, young shoots glabrous, gray-yellow, buds spindle-form, 10 mm long, acute, brown-red, resin free; needles parted, outspread, directed more or less forward, straight or curved, about 25 mm long, always emarginate at the apex (!), light green and glossy above, midrib furrowed, with 2 wide, white stomatal bands beneath; cones ovate, only 3–5 cm long, 2–2.5 cm thick, short stalked, brown when young with some bluish pruinose spots, red-brown when ripe, with about 15–20 scales, these shell-like, entire, 18 mm wide, wide open when ripe, bract scales somewhat longer than the seed scales, 3 lobed, the middle longest, awl-like and reflexed when ripe, the lateral lobes obtuse, margin toothed, seeds triangular, 9 mm long, 5 mm wide, glossy dark brown above, gray-white beneath, brown punctate, wings about twice as long as the seed, wide, dark brown. DJ 105; OCC 369 (C); KIF 1: 36; CCE 405. SE. Japan; Honshu (Kii and Yamato); Shikoku: in the mountains at 300–1000 m, but rare. Fig. 176. z6

P. macrocarpa (Vasey) Mayr. Tree, 12–16(25) m high, trunk diameter 60–90 cm, bark thick, dark red-brown, deeply furrowed, checkered with thick, appressed plates, branches long, spreading, young shoots dark red-brown, more gray in the 2nd year, glabrous or quite finely pubescent, buds glossy, dark brown, scales not fringed on the margin; needles parted, 25–35 mm long, usually mucronulate, indistinctly furrowed above and light green, underside with 2 white stomatal bands; cones 10–15 cm long, to 5 cm thick, on a short, thick stalk, with numerous scales, these large, stiff and thick, glabrous on the margin, bract scales erect, 3 pointed, the center point only slightly longer than the lateral ones, seeds thick, rounded, 11 mm long, light brown above, whitish beneath, wings about 10 mm long. SPa 37; DJ 110; CCE 412. S. California; from the Santa Inez Mts. to the Mexican border, from 250 to 2400 m. 1910. Range map Fig. 175, 176. z7–8

P. menziesii (Mirb.) Franco. Douglas fir. Tree, reaching 90 m or occasionally higher in its habitat, then with a trunk diameter to 4 m, bark of old trees thick and corky, deeply fissured, smooth with many resin blisters on young trees, crown of young trees conical, but broad and flat crowned with age, the lower branches then wide, drooping, branches of younger trees ascending, horizontal on older trees, young shoots finely pubescent to glabrous, yellow-green at first, eventually gray-brown, buds oval-conical, to 10 mm long, glossy

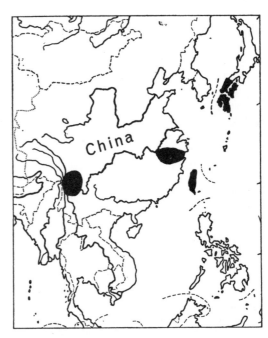

Fig. 174. Asiatic range of *Pseudotsuga*

chestnut-brown, acute, base usually somewhat resinous; needles with a slight apple scent when crushed, radially arranged, but usually parted with a broad V-form furrow, 18–30 mm long, 1–1.5 mm wide, bright green above and without stomatal lines, 2 stomatal bands beneath, each with 5–6 gray to white lines, acute or obtuse on the apex, but not emarginate; female flowers apple-green or purple; cones pendulous, on short shoots, oblong-cylindrical, to 10 cm long, 3–3.5 cm thick, seed scales circular-rhombic, leathery, entire, light brown, slightly concave, to 2 cm wide, bract scales exserted, appressed on the typical coastal form (var. *menziesii*), reflexed on the mountain form (var. *glauca*), light green at first, eventually light brown. SPa 36; DJ 11; CCE 406 (= *P. douglasii* [Lindl.] Carr.; *P. taxifolia* [Lamb.] Britt.). N. America; British Columbia to California, eastward to the Cascade Mts. of Oregon and the Sierra Nevadas in California and western Nevada, from 600–2900 m; in pure stands or mixed coniferous forest on gravelly mountain slopes. Introduced by D. Douglas into England in 1827 and named in his honor. Valuable forest tree in both the old and new worlds for its rapid growth. Plate 120; Range map Fig. 175, 176.

Including many geographical varieties and cultivars.

1. Outline of the geographical varieties

● Cones long, bract scales appressed; needles green, not pruinose:

var. *menziesii*

●● Cones short, bract scales outspread;

+ Needles green, blue pruinose:
var. *glauca* 'Blue Wonder'
++ Needles green, gray pruinose:
var. *caesia*
+++ Needles pure green, not pruinose:
f. *laeta*

2. Outline of the cultivars of var. *menziesii*

a) Normal habit, branches horizontal; needles green:
f. *brevibracteata*

Needles yellow or white variegated:
'Albospica', 'Aurea', 'Stairii', 'Variegata'

Needles crispate:
'Suringarii'

b) Habit normal; branches with only a few side shoots:
'Anguina', 'Denudata', 'Elongata'

c) Weeping forms:
'Pendula', 'Viminalis'

d) Conical habit:
'Fastigiata', 'Holmstrup', 'Marshall', 'Oudemansii', 'Pyramidata', 'Stricta'

e) Dwarf form:
'Brevifolia', 'Densa', 'Dumosa', 'Globosa', 'Leptophylla', 'Nidiformis', 'Pumila', 'Pygmaea', 'Slavinii', 'Tempelhof Compact'

Cultivars of var. *glauca*

a) Habit normal;
Needles green with bluish pruinose:
'Appressa', 'Crispa', 'Elegans Glauca', 'Moerheimii'

Needles green, white pruinose (not blue):
var. *caesia*, 'Caesia Erecta'

Needles very pruinose, nearly white:
'Argentea', 'Candida'

Needles pure green, without pruinose:
f. *laeta*

b) Weeping forms:
'Argentea Pendula', 'Glauca Pendula', 'Taranto'

c) Conical habit:
'Fretsii'

d) Dwarf forms:
'Argentea Compacta', 'Compacta Glauca', 'Fletcheri', 'Nana'

'Albospica'. Needles nearly pure white on the new growth (like white candles), becoming light green after a few weeks (= *P. menziesii albospica* [Schwer.] Krüssm.). Developed before 1920 by Ch. Van Geert in Kalmthout, near Antwerp, Belgium.

'Anguina'. So-called "Snake-form." Sparsely branched, these chaotically twisted, and with only a few secondary branches; needles green, to 5 cm long (= *P. menziesii anguina* [Dall. & Jacks.] Krüssm.). Discovered before 1923 in Endsleight, Devon, England.

'Appressa'. Branches spreading nearly horizontally; needles very white pruinose, nearly appressed on the new shoots, later spreading at acute angles, like *Picea engelmanii* (= *P. menziesii appressa* [Schwer.] Krüssm.). Cultivated before 1919 by Count Schwerin.

'Argentea'. Upright growing; needles silvery-white or bluewhite (= *P. glauca* var. *argentea* [Koster] Fitsch.). Developed about 1875 by M. Koster & Zoon, Boskoop, Holland. (EX)

'Argentea Compacta'. Dwarf form, globose habit, branched, slow growing; needles silver-gray (= *P. menziesii argentea compacta* [Beissn.] Krüssm.; *P. glauca* var. *compacta* [Beissn.] Fitsch.) Discovered in the Hans Nursery of Herrnhut, E. Germany among stock originating from Colorado. 1891. (EX?)

'Argentea Pendula'. Weeping form, needles silver-gray pruinose (= *P. glauca argentea pendula* [Beissn.] Fitsch.). Developed before 1893 in the Weise Nursery of Kamenz, E. Germany. (EX?)

'Aurea'. New growth light yellow, later becoming more whitish, very consistent (= *P. menziesii* f. *aurea* [Fluder] Krüssm.). Discovered by A. Sénéclauze in 1862. (EX?)

'Blue Wonder' (Lombarts). Conical habit, to 20 m high, twigs wide spreading; leaves directed forward on young shoots, 30–35 mm long, intensely blue-green, darker on older shoots. Selected in the nursery of P. Lombarts in Zundert, Holland in 1910; named and introduced in 1958.

f. brevibracteata (Ant.) Krüssm. Conical habit, broad, only half as tall as the species at a given age, branches stouter; needles longer and wider, light green; bract scales very short, hardly visible from the outside (= *P. douglasii brevibracteata* Ant.). Observed in 1840 in Oregon, USA and on Real de Monte, Mexico.

'Brevifolia'. Dwarf form, but becoming a small tree, normal growth habit, but very slow growing, twigs short and stout, horizontal or somewhat ascending, shoots sparse, short, red-brown, buds oval, obtuse; needles radially arranged, very densely crowded, stiff, 6–13 mm long, directed somewhat forward or also reflexed, obtuse and rounded on the apex, apple-green above, with gray-green stomatal bands. WDw 235 (Br); WM 32D (Br) (= *P. douglasii brevifolia* Mast.). Known before 1891 and still cultivated today. (VR)

f. caesia (Schwer.) Franco. An intermediate form between var. *menziesii* and var. *glauca*, twigs spreading nearly horizontally, shoots glabrous or slightly pubescent; needles pectinate-parted, gray-green, slightly scented when crushed; cones small. CCE 409 (C) (= *P. glauca* var. *caesia* [Schwer.] Fitsch.). The so-called Columbia or Fraser form of the Rocky Mts. 1907. (VR in cultivation) Plate 120.

'Caesia Erecta'. Very similar to f. *caesia*, but with erect branches (= *P. menziesii caesia erecta* [Schwer;] Krüssm.). 1922.

'Compacta Glauca'. Low growing, conical, very densely branched; needles short, sharp pointed, blue-green. CCE 410 (= *P. menziesii compacta glauca* [Ansorge] Krüssm.). Developed near Hamburg, W. Germany by Ansorge before 1902. (EX?)

'Crispa'. Needles slightly bluish, sickle-shaped crispate, especially on the new growth (= *P. menziesii crispa* [Schwer.] Krüssm.). Developed before 1919 by Count Schwerin from seed of f. *caesia*.

'Densa'. Dwarf form, to 1 m high, irregular habit, with a flattened top, branches irregularly arranged, twiggy, horizontal; needles shorter than those of the type, 13–19 mm long, bright green. BCC 21 (H); WM 32B (Br), 398 (H) (= *P. menziesii* f. *densa* [Slavin] Franco). Discovered before 1930 in the Highland Park Pinetum, Rochester, New York, USA. (VR)

'Denudata'. Central leader always stem-like and thick, side shoots few or stunted (*P. menziesii denudata* [Carr.] Krüssm.). 1867.

'Dumosa'. Dwarf form, to 2 m high, irregular habit, loose, bushy, branches intertwined, shoots irregular, nodding; needles densely crowded, twisted, thin, short, some only 4–6 cm long, some to 20 mm long at the branch tips (= *P. menziesii* f. *dumosa* [Carr.] Franco). Developed before 1866 by André Leroy of Angers, France. (VR)

'Elegans'. Normal upright habit, 5–10 m high, but irregularly branched, many branches pendulous, the others ascending, shoots very densely arranged, ascending; needles bowed irregularly, 30–50 mm long, bluish green above and with a conspicuous midrib, underside with a green midrib and indistinct stomatal bands (= *P. menziesii elegans* [Beissn.] Krüssm.; *P. douglassii* f. *densiramea* v. Dungern). Known since 1891 and of several origins. (VR)

'Elongata'. Tree branches very long, similar to 'Anguina', with sparse, short side shoots (= *P. menziesii elongata* [Schwer.] Krüssm.). Discovered on grounds of Grafen Schwerin, 1907. (EX?)

'Faberi'. Needles on the outer limbs golden-yellow. (= *P. menziesii faberi* [Schwer.] Krüssm.) Introduced 1916, by H. H. Faber, Dundee, Ill., USA.

'Fastigiata'. Conical form, growth vigorously upright, shoots ascending pyramidally, densely arranged, buds thick, conical, red; needles short, radially arranged (= *Abies douglasii fastigiata* Knight ex Gord.). Known since 1858. (R)

'Fletcheri'. Dwarf form, very slow growing, broad, flat or more globose, 1–3 m high; needles more or less radially arranged, 15–20 mm long, 1.5–2 mm wide, often twisted and bowed, green above, with midrib indented, 2 blue-green stomatal bands beneath, soft to the touch. HD 151 (H); WDw 16 (Br); CCE 407, 408; WM 399 (H) (= *P. menziesii fletcheri* [Fletcher] Krüssm.). This and 2 other dwarf forms, 'Nana' and 'Cheesemanii', developed at the same time before 1895 in the Lock King Nursery of Weybridge Kent, England. The above form was eventually introduced by the Fletcher and Son Nursery in 1915 (see also the information in Hornibrook, 226). This is one of the most common dwarf forms of *P. menziesii* in cultivation today. Plate 119.

'Fretsii'. Low tree, perhaps 5 m high or less, broadly conical, very loosely branched, branches spreading widely, central leader slow growing; needles radially arranged, 8–12 mm long, 2 mm wide, gradually becoming shorter toward the branch tips, apex rounded, dark green above, with 2 blue-green stomatal bands beneath. MD 1905: 412 (H); WDw 234 (Br); WM 32E (Br) (= *P. menziesii* 'Fretsii' [Frets] Boom; *P. fretsii* Frets, 1905). Selected by C. Frets & Zoon before 1905 from American seed. (VR)

var. glauca (Beissn.) Franco. Slow growing alpine variety, crown narrower, more conical and compact; needles shorter and thicker than those of var. *menziesii*, not always distinctly parted, often also more or less radially arranged, bluish-green above, bract scales outspread to reflexed. OCC 373 (Br); DJ 111; CCE 409 (C) (= *P. glauca* [Beissn.] Mayr). Rocky Mountains from Alberta to New Mexico. 1863. This variety includes many blue-needled cultivars; presumably of this variety since cones have not been observed.

'Glauca Pendula'. Branches drooping; needles blue-green (= *P. douglasii glauca pendula* P. Smith, 1891). Allegedly developed by Simon Louis Frères of Metz, France from seed originating from Colorado, but presumably also originating from other sources. Plate 120.

'Globosa'. Dwarf habit, regularly globose, similar to 'Pumila', but more openly branched; needles green. MD 1905: 413 (H) (= *P. menziesii globosa* [Luz] Krüssm.). Discovered in 1900 in the Carl Lutz & Son Nursery, Stuttgart, W. Germany. (EX)

'Holmstrup'. Dense, conical habit, ascending branches; needles dark green. CCE 410 (= *P. menziesii* 'Holmstrupii'). Developed in the Asger M. Jensen Nursery of Holmstrup, Denmark.

f. laeta (Schwerin) Krüssm. Normal upright habit, twigs ascending; needles pure green, not pruinose; cones short, bract scales outspread (= *P. douglasii laeta* Schwerin). The totally green needled form of var. *glauca*. (VR)

'Leptophylla'. Dwarf form, slow growing, branches ascending at acute angles, also the sparse, thin, brown shoots, thinly pubescent, buds small, conical, red; needles radially arranged, very thin, directed forward at acute angles ("heather-like"), 9 to 12 mm long, dark green and glossy, with an indented midrib above, and stomatal bands beneath (= *P. douglasii* var. *leptophylla* Hornib.). Discovered before 1923 in Blandsfort, Abbeyleix, Ireland. (EX?)

'Marshall'. Remaining low, 4–5 m high, perhaps higher, conical, very dense. Selected about 1930 at Marshall Nurseries, Arlington, Nebraska, USA.

var. menziesii. The type of the species, especially distinctive for its green, not pruinose needles, cones long, with appressed, not reflexed bract scales. Coastal regions of SW. British Columbia, NW. Washington to the central coastal region of California, and eastward to the Cascade Mts. of Oregon and to the Sierra Nevada in California and western Nevada. Named in honor of Archibald Menzies (1754 to 1842), Scottish doctor and naturalist who first discovered the tree in 1791 in Nootka Sound, Vancouver, British Columbia.

'Moerheimii'. Compact habit, but 5–10 m high, branches irregularly arranged, short, also partly bowed; needles to 4 cm long, irregularly sickle-shaped, bluish pruinose. CCE 410 (= *P. menziesii moerheimi* [Ruys] Krüssm.). Developed in 1912 by B. Ruys, Moerheim, Dedemsvaart, Holland.

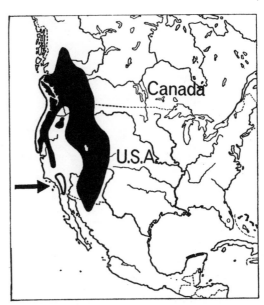

Fig. 175. Range of *Pseudotsuga menziesii* (black) and *P. macrocarpa* (arrow)

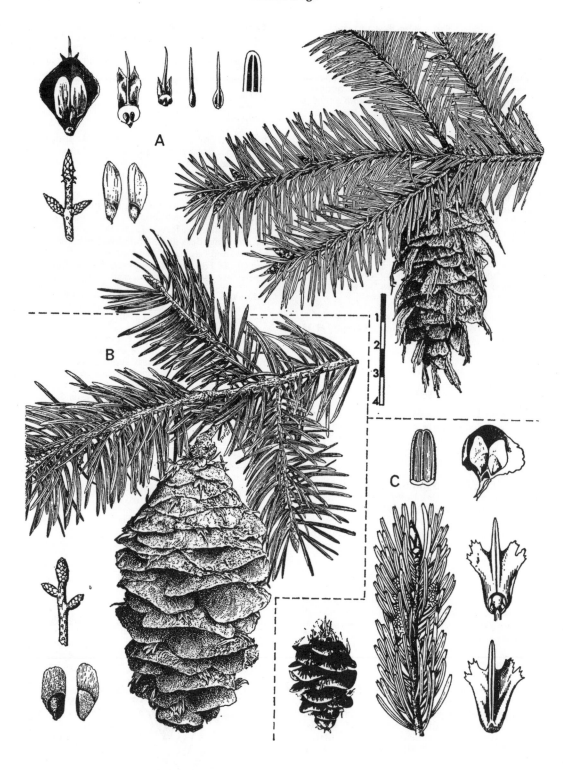

Fig. 176. A. *P. menziesii,* branch with cones, seed scale with 2 seeds at left above, next to which are 4 different bract scales and a needle apex, under these a needle-less branch tip and 2 seeds; B. *P. macrocarpa;* C. *P. japonica,* 2 bract scales at right (from Sudworth, Beissner and Silva Tarouca)

'**Nana**'. Same origin as 'Fletcheri' (which see), but somewhat stronger growing, more conical, regular growth habit as a young plant; needles more radially arranged, stiffer, very acute at the apex, bluish-green above, bluish-white beneath (= *P. glauca* var. *nana* Hornib.). Introduced by Fletcher and Son, 1915.

'**Nidiformis**' Dwarf form, broad and flat growing, very slow, 12-year old plants only 40 cm high, branches ascending outward from the middle, the middle depressed nest-like (like *Picea abies* 'Nidiformia'); needles green (= *P. douglasii* f. *nidiformis* Hahn). Developed before 1940 in the Eisenberger Nursery in Eisenberg, Mähren, Czechoslovakia.

'**Oudemansii**'. Normal habit, but lower than the type, 5–10 m high, slender, branches short, spreading nearly horizontally, shoots short, glossy brown; needles radially arranged, 15–20 mm long, 2 mm wide, dark green above, blue-green beneath. CCE 406 (= *P. douglasii* var. *oudemansii* Grootend. ex Hornib.). Developed in the Schovenhorst Pinetum, Putten, Netherlands; but brought into the trade in 1940 by H. den Ouden and Zoon.

'Pendula' is only a collective name for several different clones; many with individual names. See also the illustration at Plate 120.

'**Pumila**'. Dwarf form, densely compact, rounded, densely branched; needles light green, short, acute (= *P. douglasii pumila* Waterer 1899). Developed by Anth. Waterer, Knap Hill, Woking, England.

'**Pygmaea**'. Shoots yellowish-green; needles yellowish-green, 12–20 mm long, about 1 mm wide (= *P. douglasii* var. *pygmaea* Hornib.). This form is the most dwarf of the 3 Fletcher forms (see notes at 'Fletcheri'). (EX?)

'**Pyramidata**'. Conical habit, slow growing, low, but not dwarf; needles densely compact, short and broad, bright green. CCE 405 (= *P. douglasii* var. *pyramidata* Bail.).

'**Slavinii**'. Low, but not dwarf, dense conical form with a long peak and a broad base, branches dense, very numerous, horizontal; needles densely crowded, shorter than those of the species, 10–18 mm long, bright green. CC pl. 37 (H) (= *P. menziesii slavinii* [Slavin] Krüssm.). Discovered in Cobb's Hill Reservoir, Rochester, New York, USA before 1932.

'**Stairii**'. Normal habit; needles green, but with partly white-yellow needles on the young shoots, these greening in fall (= *P. menziesii stairii* [Gord.] Krüssm.). Discovered in the garden of the Earl of Stair, Castle Kennedy, Wigtownshire, Scotland before 1871; but like those found later, not consistent.

'**Stricta**'. Rather slow growing, twigs short, shoot tips ascending at acute angles, therefore developing a very narrow crown; needles short, green (= *P. menziesii stricta* [Carr.] Krüssm.; *P. douglasii stricta* Carr.; *P. douglasii compacta viridis* Hellemann 1902). Developed about 1862 by A. Sénéclauze; again by Hellemann in 1902. (EX?)

'**Suringarii**'. Tall tree, normal habit; needles curving hemispherically downward on all shoots (= *P. menziesii suringarii* [Schwer.] Krüssm.). Discovered by Count Schwerin in 1926 in the Park of the Oranje Nassau's Oord Sanatorium in Renkum, Holland, near Wageningen; but (EX) in 1944. Not identical with 'Crispa'!

'**Taranto**'. Very tall growing form with a straight trunk and downward curving branches; needles bluish-green. From the Taranto Botanical Gardens in Pallanza, N. Italy. Plate 118.

'**Tempelhof Compact**'. Dwarf form, very compact and globose, very densely branched; needles more or less radially arranged or parted, green, acute, 12–16 mm long. CCE 4–7; WM 32C

(Br), 401 (H). Discovered about 1960 by Van Asselt in a forest near Putten, Holland; introduced by L. Konijn. The original plant was about 60 cm high with a thick stem at about 20 years old.

'**Variegata**'. Normal growth habit; needles yellowish-brown on the branch upper side in summer (appearing chlorotic) and resembling *Picea abies* 'Finedonensis' (= *P. menziesii variegata* [McDonald] Krüssm.). Discovered in England before 1903, but without particular garden merit.

'**Viminalis**'. Tall tree, branches spreading horizontally, the shoots however, limp and vertically pendulous (= *P. menziesii viminalis* [Schwer.] Krüssm.). Discovered in 1919 by Count Schwerin in Charlottenlund Forest, near Copenhagen, Denmark.

P. sinensis Dode. Chinese Douglas-fir. Tall tree, young shoots pubescent, brown at first, later more gray and then glabrous, buds glossy, not resinous, leaf cushions very conspicuous; needles pectinately parted, straight or lightly curved, 25–35 mm long, only 15–20 mm long on the fruiting shoots, 1.5–2 mm wide, crenate at the apex, base twisted, furrowed above for the entire length, with a raised midrib beneath and 2 white stomatal bands; cones ovate, about 5 cm long, 3–4 cm wide, with about 20 soft pubescent, thick, woody scales, bract scales short, reflexed, with awl-shaped long, and 2 short side lobes, seeds with a 25 mm long wing, brown striated, wings 7–8 mm wide. LF 19; CCE 412. SW. China; Yunnan Province (Che-hai and Tungchuan; in the mountains at 2500 m, on limestone). 1912. z8–9

P. wilsoniana Hayata. Tree, 20(25) m high, closely related to *P. sinensis*, young shoots red-brown at first, later more gray, glabrous or with scattered short hairs, buds slightly resinous; needles pectinate, to 5 cm long, incised at the apex, midrib indented for the entire length above, with 2 white stomatal bands beneath; cones about 5.5 cm long and 3 cm wide, with nearly 3 cm wide scales, bract scales with reflexed tips, with long, awl-shaped middle lobes and 2 triangular, short acuminate side lobes, seed about 15 mm long with the wing, glossy dark green above, light brown speckled beneath. LWT 10; LT 39 (= *P. forrestii* Craib.). China; Yunnan and Taiwan. 1914. *P. gaussenii* and *P. salvadorii* are possibly identical to this species. Fig. 177.

Lit. Flous, F.: Révision du genre *Pseudotsuga*. Extr. Bull. Soc. Hist. Nat. Toulouse **71**, 33–164, 1936 (illus., 18 species). ● Franco, J. de A.: De Coniferarum duarum nominibus (in Latin). 1–7. Lisbon 1950 (reprinted in Bol. Soc. Broteriana ser. 2, 24, 1950). ● Franco, J. de A.: On the nomenclature of the Douglas Fir. Lisbon 1953 (6 pp.). ● Franco, J. de A.: On the legitimacy of the combination *Pseudotsuga menziesii* (Mirb.) Franco. Bol. Soc. Broteriana 1954, 115–116. ● Frothingham, E. H.: Douglas Fir: a study of the Pacific Coast and Rocky Mountain forms. W. S. Dept. Agr. Forest Serv. Circ. 150, 1–38, 1909. ● Gaussen, H.: *Pseudotsuga*. Les Gymnospermes actuelles et fossiles, XI, 535–560, 1966 (with 15 species). ● Henry, A., & M. Flood: The Douglas Firs; a botanical and silvicultural description of the various species of *Pseudotsuga*. Roy. Irish Acad. Proc. **35** (B), 67–92, 1920. ● Little, E. L. Jr.: The genus *Pseudotsuga* (Douglas-fir) in North America. Leafl. West. Bot. **6**, 181–198, 1952. ● Schwerin, F. Von: Die Douglasfichte; Benennung, Formenreichtum, Winterhärte. Mitt. DDG **32**, 53–66, 1922.

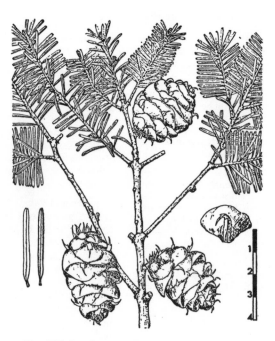

Fig. 177. *Pseudotsuga wilsoniana* (from T. S. Liu)

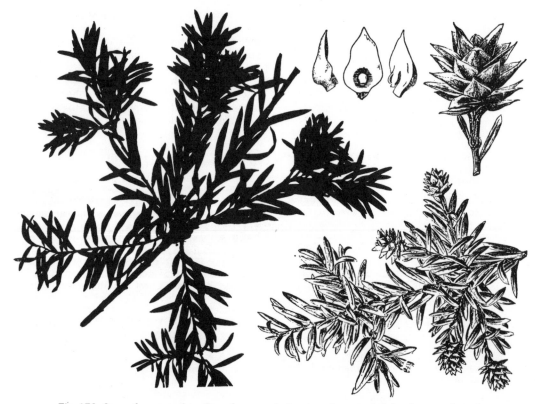

Fig. 178. *Saxegothaea conspicua.* Branch somewhat reduced; cone at right above, enlarged, details to the immediate left (left branch original, otherwise from Veitch and Pilger)

SAXEGOTHAEA Lindl.—PODOCARPACEAE

Evergreen tree, resembling *Taxus* in habit, bark gray-brown, exfoliating; branches 3–4 in whorls, spreading widely, tips nodding; buds small, globose; leaves spiraling on long shoots, indistinctly 2 ranked on the lateral shoots; plants monoecious; male flowers axillary and in small spikes, with 2 scale pairs at the base; female flowers solitary, in the leaf axils on the end of short shoots, with imbricately arranged, bluish seed scales; cones nearly globose, about 1 cm thick, composed of soft-prickly, fleshy, thickened seed scales; about 6–12 seeds in a cone, these sharply angular, hard shelled, ovate, 3 mm long, glossy brown.—1 species in Chile. Range map Fig. 133.

Saxegothaea conspicua Lindl. Small tree or shrub, similar to *Taxus*, to 24 m high in its habitat, bark exfoliating *Platanus*-like, branches with nodding tips; needles linear to linear-lanceolate, 15–25 mm long, 2–2.5 mm wide, leathery, sharp tipped, with a slightly prominent midrib above, dark green, with 2 broad bluish-white stomatal bands beneath, divided by the distinct, green midrib, base tapering abruptly to a short petiole, decurrent on the twig, fruits 12–20 mm wide, developed from the connate carpels, with few seeds. CB 3 to 73; CCE 413, 414. S. Chile; Patagonia; developing dense forests in its habitat. 1846. Named in honor of Prince Albert of Saxony-Coburg-Gotha (W. Germany), the husband of Queen Victoria of Great Britain. Plate 119, 149; Fig. 178. z8–9

SCIADOPITYS S. & Z.—Umbrella Pine— TAXODIACEAE

Evergreen tree with a narrow, conical crown, branches short, thin, spreading horizontally, in whorls when young; bark rather smooth, exfoliating in long, thin strips; buds small, red-brown, gray tomentose; young shoots glabrous, with spirally arranged scale leaves, green at first, later light brown; 2 leaf types occurring on the plant:

a) Small scale leaves, only 5 mm long, 1 mm wide, tightly appressed to the shoot, often 10–12 together

at the base of the "double-needle" whorls (easily visible in Fig. 179 to the right of "a");

b) So-called "double-needles", lengthwise connate, glossy green above, dull green beneath with 2 white stomatal bands, furrowed on both sides, 20–30 in whorls at the branch tips, abscising after 2 years.

Plants monoecious; male flowers several in dense heads at the branch tips, composed of spirally arranged

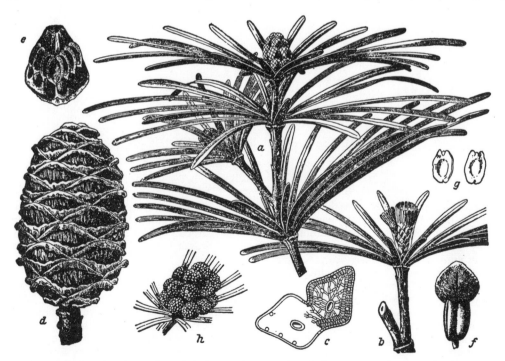

Fig. 179. *Sciadopitys verticillata*. a. branch with male flower, b. female flower, c. needle in cross section, d. cones, e. seed scales with seeds, f. stamen, g. seeds, h. male flower (from Beissner, Shirasawa)

anthers, each with 2 pollen sacs; female flowers solitary, terminal, composed of numerous spirally arranged seed scales, each with 7–9 ovules; cones oval-oblong, with thick, woody, broad rounded scales, ripening in the 2nd year; seeds ovate, compressed, with an encircling wing; 2 cotyledons; x = 10.—1 species in East Asia. Range map Fig. 96.

Sciadopitys verticillata (Thunb.) S. & Z. Tall tree, 20–30 m, to 40 m in its habitat, with a trunk diameter to 3 m, but in cultivation seldom taller than 10 m with a 0.5 m diameter trunk, crown narrowly conical, thinner with age, occasionally also with 2 stems; "double-needles" linear, obtuse emarginate, deep green above, with 2 white bands beneath, 8–12 cm long, 5–7 mm wide; cones oblong-ovate, upright, 6–10 cm long, to 5 cm thick, gray-brown, margin of the seed scales outspread or somewhat revoluted, seeds 5–9 under each fertile scale, oblong to elliptic, 8–12 mm long, with a membranous, encircling wing. KIF 1: 40; CCE 415–417 (= *Taxus verticillata* Thunb.). Japan; Honshu (Iwashiro and the west central region), Shikoku, Kyushu; in the mountains, but also frequently cultivated. 1853. Fig. 179. z6

> Two types are found in cultivation, the better one always has a straight, central leader, the other is multistemmed from the ground up, not as attractive. They both prefer a sandy, fertile, acid soil and semishade.
>
> Including the following forms:

'Aurea'. Needles golden-yellow. Japan. 1889. (VR)

'Knirps'. Dwarf form, globose, regular and very dense, 75 cm high and 80 cm wide in 17 years; needles 10–11 cm long, apices slightly lighter. Originated from seed in 1966 at the J. Hachmann nursery in Barmstedt, West Germany, propagated in 1983.

'Pendula'. Weeping branches. An old specimen stands in the Shiba Park, Tokyo, Japan.

'Pyramidalis Compacta'. Compact, broadly pyramidal. Selected by the Jeddeloh Nursery, 1958.

'Variegata'. Some of the double-needles at the branch tips yellow, others green.

SEQUOIA Endl.—Redwood—TAXODIACEAE

Monotypic genus. Tall, evergreen tree; bark 15–25 cm thick, furrowed with fibrous scales, spongy; winter buds with some imbricate scales; needles dimorphic, alternate, spirally arranged on long shoots and scale-like, appressed or somewhat outspread, with stomatal bands on the underside; needles 2 ranked on the lateral shoots, stalked, linear to linear-lanceolate, with or without some intermittent stomatal lines on the dorsal side and 2 white stomatal bands on the ventral side; plants monoecious; male flowers axillary and terminal, with numerous spirally arranged stamens; female flowers terminal, with 15–20 scales, each with 5–7 ovules in a row; cones pendulous, ovoid; scales obliquely peltate, flattened with a weak tip; seeds grouped 2–5, with 2 spongy wings near the scale margin, these somewhat narrower than the seed kernel, ripening the first year; cotyledons 2; x = 11.—1 species on the Pacific coast of North America. Range map Fig. 181.

Sequoia sempervirens (D. Don) Endl. Redwood. Evergreen tree, to 110 m in its habitat, conical; trunk to 6–8 m in diameter, straight, often branchless for half its height, bark red, deeply fissured, twigs pendulous, young shoots green and glabrous at first, later red-brown, buds with acute, leathery scales; needles spirally arranged on the terminal leader, 6 mm long, somewhat appressed to outspread, but 2 ranked on the lateral shoots, linear to more oblong, often sickle-shaped, 6–20 mm long, dark to bluish-green above, furrowed, with 2 white stomatal bands beneath; cones pendulous, on short shoots, 2–2.5 cm long, black-brown, ripening the first year, seeds red-brown (= *Taxodium sempervirens* D. Don in Lambert). N. America, Pacific coast, from SW. Oregon to S. California, on the seaward side of the coastal mountains at 500–1000 m. The age of some of the larger trees is estimated to be 800–2200 years. This species is faster growing than *Sequoiadendron giganteum*. Fig. 180. z8

Includes some cultivars:

'Adpressa'. Dwarf form, broadly conical, with numerous branches, densely twiggy, buds and shoot tips white; needles very densely arranged, oblong-oval, 6–8 mm long, abruptly truncated. WDw Pl. 16K (Br), 282 (H); WM 33B (Br), 402 (H) (= *S. sempervirens adpressa* Carr.; *S. sempervirens albospica* Veitch). Developed before 1867 by André Leroy in Angers, France. More sensitive in cultivation than the species; very attractive dwarf conifer. z9

'Filifera Elegans'. Major branches spreading horizontally, twigs and branch tips nodding slightly and drawn out to a filamentous tip; needles gradually becoming smaller toward the branch tips and eventually only scale-form on the whip-like shoots. Developed before 1904 in the Fratelli Rovelli Nursery in Pallanza, N. Italy. z9

'Glauca'. Shoots more slender than those of the species; leaves about 12 mm long, distinctly blue-green. OCC 381 (= *S. sempervirens* f. *glauca* [R. Sm.] Rehd.). 1874. z8–9

'Nana Pendula'. Dwarf weeping form, branches outspread and nodding, also spreading across the ground on older specimens. WDw 238 (H); WM 403 (H). Known since 1923; discovered in the rock garden in Curragh Grange, County Kildare, Ireland. According to Welch, possibly propagated from a side shoot of 'Pendula'; totally different from 'Prostrata'. Plate 119.

'Pendula'. Weeping form, trunk vertical, branches arching widely, shoots nodding gracefully; needles 2 ranked, normal, like those of the species. TC 159; SN 267 (H). Originated from seed in 1899 by Rovelli in Italy.

'Prostrata'. Dwarf form, shoots lying carpet-like on the ground; needles 2 ranked, elliptic, acute, much wider than those of the type, distinctly blue-green or gray-green. OCC 381 (Br, as 'Nana Pendula'); WDw 237 (H); WM 33A (Br), 404 (H) (= *S. sempervirens prostrata* Gilmour; *S. sempervirens nana pendula* ex JRHS 1951, non Hornib.; *S. sempervirens* 'Cantab' Hort.). Originated as a bud mutation before 1953 in the Cambridge Bot. Garden, England.

'Variegata'. Like the type, strong growing, densely branched, but often with very short shoots; needles blue-green, frequently yellowish or yellow variegated. Discovered before 1890 by Carrière in the Croux nursery in Sceaux, near Paris, France.

Lit. Podhorsky, J.: Die Sequoien Kaliforniens; ihre Bedeutung in ihre Heimat und fuer Mitteleuropa. Mitt. DDG 1940, 1–29 (with 4 plates). ● Stanford, E. F.: Redwoods away. 8th Annual Fac. Res. Lecture, College of the Pacific, Stockton, Calif., 1958, 1–28. ● Martin, E. J.: Die Sequoien und ihre Anzucht. Mitt. DDG 1958, 1–62.

Fig. 180. *Sequoia sempervirens.*
Branch original; other details from Beissner

SEQUOIADENDRON Buchholz—Giant Sequoia—TAXODIACEAE

Tall, evergreen tree, bark spongy, deeply fissured, to 50 cm thick on large trunks; winter buds naked; needles spirally arranged, appressed to slightly spreading, awl-shaped-lanceolate, acute, thick, with stomata on both sides; male flowers sessile, terminal on short shoots and appearing in large numbers, with ovate, toothed anther scales; female flowers with about 30 scales, terminating in a cylindrical thorn, with 3–12 or more erect ovules in 2 rows; cones ellipsoid, ripening the 2nd year, very woody, persisting for many years on the tree; scales cuneate, the apophysis crosswise rhombic, to 2 cm wide, slightly cross keeled and rugose, with a depression and a small prickle in the center; seeds with 2 thin wings, these wider than the seed kernel; cotyledons usually 4(3–5); x = 11.—1 species in California. Range map Fig. 181.

Sequoiadendron giganteum (Lindl.) Buchh. Giant Sequoia. Tree, 80–100 m or higher in its habitat, trunk columnar, free of branches to 50 m high in its habitat, with a 10–12 m diameter at breast height, bark soft, spongy, exfoliating in fine scales, fissured, light red-brown, crown pyramidal, branches arising from all sides of the trunk, most directed somewhat downward, but with ascending tips, shoots blue-green at first, later red-brown; needles spiraling in 3 longitudinal rows, scale-like to lanceolate or subulate, sharply acuminate, more

or less appressed to the shoot, 3–6 mm long, also to 12 mm long on vigorous shoots, with stomata on both sides, persisting about 4 years; cones terminal on short shoots, solitary or grouped, ellipsoid, 5–8 cm long, 3 to 5 cm thick, red-brown, erect in the first year, pendulous in the 2nd year, seeds light yellow, 3–6 mm long, flat (= *Wellingtonia gigantea* Lindl.; *Sequoia gigantea* [Lindl.] Decne.; *Sequoia wellingtonia* Seem.). California; western slopes of the Sierra Nevada, from Placer County to Tulare County, at 1500–2500 m together with other conifers. Plate 130, Fig. 182. z7

It is not known for certain who first introduced this tree into European cultivation. An Englishman, John Bidwell, discovered the plant in 1841 on a trip from Sutter's Fort to the Sacramento River, but it was not studied or described at that time. Bidwell's find was confirmed in 1852 by a hunter, A. T. Dowd, while following a wounded bear in the Calaveras region. Dowd informed William Lobb, a plant collector in the employ of James Veitch & Son Nursery of Exeter, England. Lobb sent large quantities of seed to his employer in England in 1853, from which many trees were grown. But it appears that some months before, a Scottish plant collector, John D. Matthew was collecting seed in the Calaveras region which reached Scotland before that collected by Lobb. So it is generally presumed that the old specimens in Scotland were grown from seed sent by Matthew and those in England from

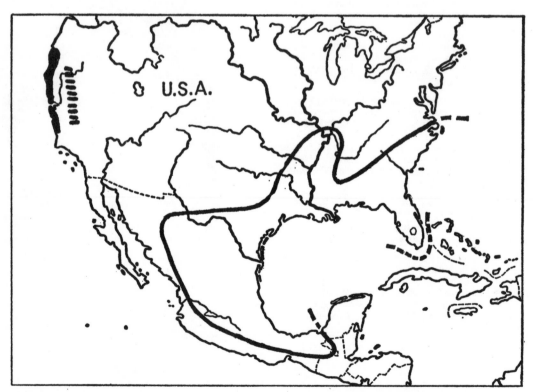

Fig. 181. Range of the genus *Sequoia* (black), *Sequoiadendron* (dashes) and *Taxodium* (below heavy line)

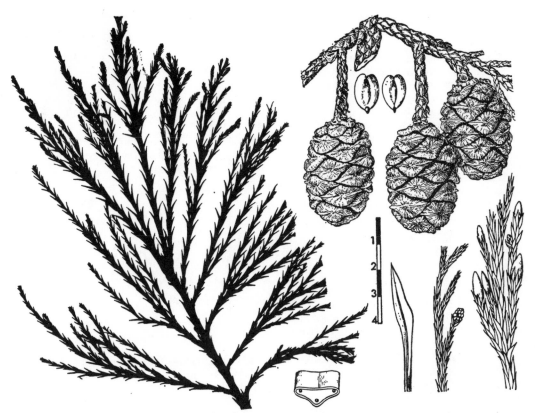

Fig. 182. *Sequoiadendron giganteum.* Branch, cones; at right below are male and female flowers and an individual leaf (branch original, others from Sudworth and Pardé)

Lobb. Any alleged earlier introductions are probably *Sequoia sempervirens* which was discovered in 1795 and more easily obtainable.

Studies have shown most of the California Giant Sequoias to be between 400 and 1500 years old, but it is recognized that some of the larger trees are from 3000–3500 years old. They are no longer considered the oldest trees in the world since the discovery of the ancient *Pinus aristata* var. *longaeva* in Arizona (see *P. aristata* var. *longaeva*).

The tallest tree in Calaveras National Forest measured 135 m, the second highest 114 m; neither are alive today. The Giant Sequoias are not the tallest trees in the world, being surpassed by the Australian *Eucalyptus amygdalina* at 155 m. There are, however, a number of trees in California today at heights from 80 to 100 m.

The "General Sherman" tree, generally considered the largest tree on earth, is 83 m high, 11 m in diameter at the base, over 8 m in diameter at 3 m high and about 3500 years old (see also *Taxodium mucronatum!*). The "General Grant" tree in General Grant National Park is 89 m high and 12 m in diameter at the base.

Includes a number of cultivars:

'Argenteum'. Needles with a peculiar white shimmer (= *Sequoia gigantea* var. *argentea* Beissn.; 1891). Presumably (EX)

'Aurea'. Shoots and needles yellow. Developed in the Lough Nurseries of Cork, Ireland. 1856.

'Compactum'. Slender growing, narrow, pyramidal, to 20 m high, twigs short, outspread; needles very appressed, conspicuously bluish on the young shoots (= *Sequoia gigantea glauca pyramidalis compacta* Beissn. 1891). Developed in the Delaunay Nursery at Angers, France.

'Glaucum'. Exactly like the type, but with distinctly blue-green needles.

'Pendulum'. Trunk at first (not always!) narrowly columnar, then the peak nods but continues to ascend, commonly also chaotically branched, twigs often short or long and weeping mane-like, occasionally developing a grotesque shape (Plate 118, 151). Commonly grown in France; not to be grafted on *Sequoia sempervirens* because of its susceptibility to frost damage.

'Pygmaeum'. Dense, bushy dwarf form, scarcely over 2 m high and wide, perhaps higher, generally without a dominant central leader. WDw 239; Gard. Chron. 1960: 524 (H); WM 33 C (Br), 405 (H). Developed in France before 1891. Cultivated in the Kalmthout Arboretum, Belgium.

Lit. See also those listed at *Sequoia*. ● Buchholz, J. T.: The generic segregation of the Sequoias. Amer. J. Bot. **26**, 535–538, 1939 (the *Sequoiadendron* genus is described here). ● Feucht, O.: Hundert-jährige Wellingtonien in Württemberg. Kosmos 1965, 184–187 (with ill.). ● Hadfield, M.: The Story of the Wellingtonia, Gard. Chron. 2/27/1965, 210–211. ● Kammeyer, H. F.: Mammutbäume. Wittemberg 1960 (100 pp. with a large bibliography).

TAIWANIA Hayata—TAXODIACEAE

Tall, evergreen, densely foliate trees; leaves needle- to scale-like, very similar to *Cryptomeria*; male flowers grouped 5–7, densely clustered on the ends of short branchlets; stamens 15, filaments thread-like; female flowers terminal, small, scales without a clear distinction between seed and bract scales, densely spiraled, leathery, somewhat woody when ripe, obcordate or conical, flat, the apical and basal seed scales sterile, the middle ones 12–20, each with 2 (3 on *Cryptomeria!!*) inverted ovules; seeds oblong, with a rather wide encircling wing, the wings emarginate above and below; cotyledons 2; x = 11.—2 species in China; Yunnan and Taiwan. Range map Fig. 183.

Taiwania cryptomerioides Hayata. Tree, to over 50 m in its habitat, trunk to 2 m in diameter and free of branches to 15 m on tall trees, conical crown, outspread branches, shoots densely foliate; needles scale-like on older trees, 5–6 mm long, triangular, with a short, somewhat incurved apex, furrowed on the sides, stomata on all sides, both sides keeled, tightly appressed for nearly the entire length of the shoot, needles of younger plants narrow-linear to sickle-shaped, laterally compressed, keeled above and beneath, to 17 mm long, with a broad, decurrent base, conspicuously blue-green (!); cones terminal, nearly globose or ovate, 8–12 mm long, similar to *Tsuga* cones, scales rounded with a short prickly tip, seeds 1–2 under each seed scale, 4–6 mm long with the wing. NF 2: 98; LF 34; SN 295 (H); LWT 13. Taiwan; Mt. Morrison, 1800–2400 m; discovered there in 1904 by Konishi. Plate 149; Fig. 184. z9

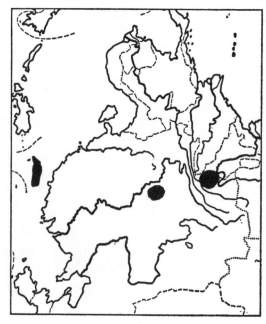

Fig. 183. Range of the genus *Taiwania*

T. flousiana Gaussen. Differing from the above species in the 4–5 mm long scale-leaves, to 14 mm long, very densely clustered on young plants; cones oblong, 14–20 mm long, gray-violet, seeds 6–7 mm long, with light brown wings. GGy 264 (Br, C). China; Upper Burma; Yung-Tschang-Salween and the Salween-Kien-Chang mountain range. Presumably all plants found on the Chinese mainland belong to this species. Since the differences are very slight between the 2 species, many authors include this one with *T. cryptomerioides*. Cultivated by Hillier in Winchester, England for several years. Fig. 184. z9

Lit. Hayata, B.: On *Taiwania,* a new genus of Coniferae from the Island of Formosa. Jour. Linn. Soc. 37, 330–331, 1906 (pl. 16). ● Sorger, O.: Die systematische Stellung von *Taiwania cryptomerioides* Hayata. Oesterr. Bot. Z. **74**, 81–102, 1925.

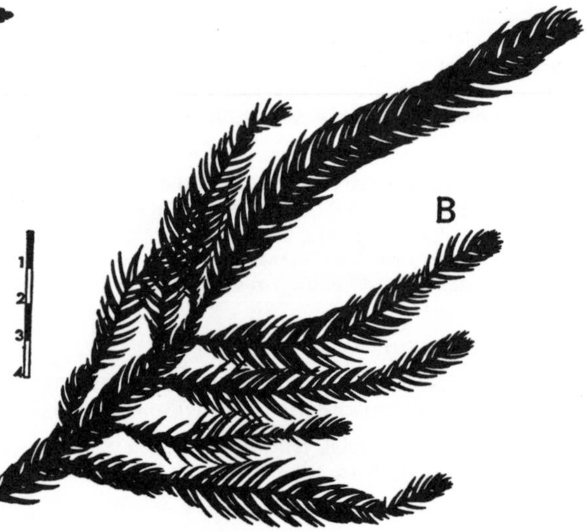

Fig. 184. **Taiwania.** A. *T. cryptomerioides;* above, a twig with cones, B. *T. flousiana* (Original; upper ill. from Hayata)

TAXODIUM Rich.—Swamp, Bald Cypress—TAXODIACEAE

Deciduous or semi-evergreen, tall tree; bark furrowed and scaly, light brown; branches directed upward, or horizontal; twigs developed in 2 forms, some at the shoot tips and with buds (these persistent), others at the shoot base, without buds (these abscising with the leaves); buds globose, scaly; leaves alternate, needle-like, flat, thin, with 2 stomatal bands beneath, outspread in 2 rows on the abscising twigs, radially arranged on the persistent shoots; plants monoecious, male flowers in 7–15 cm long, branched stands at the ends of the previous year's shoots; female flowers nearly globose, irregularly distributed along the shoot; cones short stalked, globose-ovate, woody, opening when ripe; cone scales abruptly widened from a thin stalk to irregularly 4 sided; seeds 2 under each scale, rather large, irregularly 3 sided and 3 winged, shell thickened; cotyledons 5–9; x = 11.—3 species in the southern USA and Mexico, commonly in swamps or very wet sites, and then with the typical respiratory knees. Range map Fig. 181.

Prominent characteristics of the Species

Branch arrangement	Needles	Occurrence in cultivation
irregular, usually stiff, erect	*T. ascendens* appressed, subulate, 5–10 mm long	relatively rare
more or less horizontal	*T. distichum* 2 ranked, linear, 7–17 mm long	common
long pendulous, thin	*T. mucronatum* semi-evergreen, abscising in the 2nd year	not as hardy!

Taxodium ascendens Brongn. Deciduous tree, to 25 m high, branches irregularly arranged, outspread, trunk usually gradually thickened toward the base, bark thick, furrowed, light brown, twigs short, erect; needles appressed to the shoot, subulate, 5–10 mm long, curved, light green, attractive red-brown in fall; flowers and cones very similar to those of *T. distichum*. WT 12 (= *T. distichum* var. *imbricarium* Croom; *T. distichum* var. *nutans* [Ait.] Sweet). Southeast USA, from Virginia to Florida and Alabama. Although many botanists consider this plant a variety of *T. distichum* rather than an individual species, the old classification is retained here. Fig. 185. z7

'**Nutans**'. Tree, 12–15 m high, columnar, trunk very wide at the base, branches very short, horizontal, but partly upright, paralleling the stem, branchlets densely crowded, erect at first, later nodding, light green. CCE 426, 427. Good winter hardiness. Plate 123.

T. distichum (L.) Rich. Swamp, Bald Cypress. Tree, 30–50 m high, crown of younger trees regularly conical, very old trees occasionally broad and with or without a central stem, this often free of branches to a great height, bark thin, smooth, red-brown; older trees, especially when in or near water, with knee-shaped hollow outgrowths from the roots around the base of the tree (presumably respiratory organs, but possibly also for stability in the swampy soil); shoots green at first, later red-brown; needles 2 ranked on the 5–10 cm long short shoots, linear, 10–17 mm long, light green, red-brown in fall; needles scale-like on the persistent shoots and spirally arranged; cones nearly sessile, oval, 2–3 cm long, scales with a rough plate (apophysis) and usually with a small thorn; seeds 6 mm long, with a thick, warty, horn-like shell. CBI 3: 76 (Br and C), Southeast N. America, in swamps and along river banks. Plate 121, 122, 131; Fig. 185.

Of the cultivars selected over the last century, only the following are still in general cultivation.

var. *nutans* (Ait.) Sweet. See *T. ascendens*.

'**Pendens**'. Tree, conical habit, branches nearly horizontal, with nodding tips, shoots all distinctly nodding. OCC 389 (= *T. distichum nutans* Carr. [1855] non Sweet; *T. distichum* f. *pendens* Rehd.)

T. mucronatum Ten. Mexican Swamp Cypress. Semi-evergreen to evergreen tree, similar to *T. distichum*, but the branches slightly bowed, twigs thin, long arching; short shoots abscising with the needles in the 2nd fall season; male flowers and cones larger. OCC 391; MD 1920: Pl. 30. Mexico; in the temperate highlands, 1400–2300 m, often along rivers and mountain streams. z9

Near Santa Maria del Tule, in southwestern Mexico, not far from Oaxaca, there is a giant specimen of this species, about 40 m high with a crown circumference of about 60–62 m. Some fantastic figures have been published about this tree, even in text books, giving the age at from 2000 to 10,000 years! More precise investigations have proven these reports to be greatly exaggerated. Because of the tree's irregular form, is is probable that this is actually a group of several united individuals. The age is now thought to be hardly more than 1000 years, possibly less. A detailed report of this tree with a bibliographical outline of other literature on the subject may be found in J. Kluger: Die Lebensdauer der Mexikanischen Sumpfzypresse, Mitt. Dt. Dendr. Ges. 1939: 64–72.

Fig. 185. *Taxodium distichum.* a. Branch with cones; b. staminate inflorescence; c. stamen; d. pistillate inflorescence; e. seed scale; f. seed, g–h. in cross section. i. *Taxodium ascendens,* twig segment (from Beissner and Silva Tarouca)

TAXUS L.—Yew—TAXACEAE

Tree or shrub with reddish-brown bark, exfoliating on older stems; shoots usually long, spreading, buds small, scaly; needles persisting about 8 years, appearing more or less 2 ranked or radially arranged on erect shoots, with the stalk-like tapered base decurrent on the twig, dark green above, vaulted and glossy, with a slightly revolute margin beneath, midrib distinct, otherwise yellowish-green with indistinct stomatal lines, horn-like acuminate; plants usually dioecious, rarely monoecious, axillary; male flowers solitary in the leaf axils, stamens 6–14; female flower shoots nodding downward, covered with tiny scales, in the axils of the uppermost scales are solitary flowers surrounded by 3 scale pairs; seeds ovate, distinctly compressed, usually 2 sided, surrounded by a campanulate, fleshy, red aril; x = 12.—Depending upon the interpretation, either a group of 7–8 species or only 1 large species with a number of subspecies differing by geographical origin. Range map Fig. 186.

The needles contain the poisonous alkaloid, taxin, which deadly in small amounts for horses; only the sweet, slimy, red aril is not poisonous, the enclosed seed also contains the poison.

Outline of the Species

Species	Needle length (mm)	Needle		Bud scales arrangement	
		distinctly horizontally parted	keeled, acute	not horizontally parted	not keeled, obtuse
T. baccata	10–30	×	—	×	×
T. celebica	20–40	×	—	—	×
T. floridana	20–25	×	—	—	×
T. brevifolia	10–16	×	—	×	—
T. canadensis	12–20	—	×	×	—
T. wallichiana	25–30	—	×	×	—
T. globosa	20–35				
T. cuspidata	15–25	—	×	×	—

Taxus baccata L. English Yew. Tree, 12 to 25 m high, crown ovate or more globose, shoots long, outspread or also ascending, bark red-brown, buds with tightly appressed scales, rounded at the tips, young shoots green; needles 2 ranked on spreading shoots, more or less radially arranged on erect shoots, 1–3 cm long, linear, gradually short acuminate, base abruptly tapered to a short petiole; seeds 2 sided, occasionally also 4 sided, 6 mm long, olive-brown with a fleshy, red aril. Europe, N. Africa, Asia Minor, Caucasus (see range map, Fig. 186). Cultivated for centuries. Includes many cultivars which are not always easy to distinguish. Plate 123, 124; Fig. 187. z6

Outline of the Cultivars of *Taxus baccata*

A. Habit columnar or conical, of normal vigor (no dwarf forms); needles radially arranged

  ● Needles green
  Columnar forms:
      'Cappenberg', 'Columnaris', 'Davisii', Fastigiata', 'Fastigiata Nova', Fastigiata Robusta', 'Fastigiata Variegata', 'Fastigiata Viridus', 'Flushing', 'Melfard'

  Intermediate forms:
      'Hessei', 'Imperialis', 'Intermedia', 'Neidpathensis', 'Overeynderi', 'Thomsen's Dwarf', 'Erecta', 'Barmstedter Typen', 'Schwarzgrün'

  Conical forms:
      'Cheshuntensis', 'Handsworthiana', 'Raket'

  ●● Needles yellow or yellow variegated:
      'Beteramsii', 'Fastigiata Aurea', 'Fastigiata Aureomarginata', 'Fastigiata Aureovariegata', 'Standishii', 'Erecta Aurea', 'Erecta Aureovariegata', 'Wiesmoor Gold'

B. Habit spreading, normal, dwarf forms upright; needles radially arranged or parted

  I. Branches more or less nodding or curved upward at the apex:

'Contorta', 'Dovastoniana', 'Dovastonii Aurea', 'Expansa', 'Fisheri', 'Glauca', 'Gracilis Pendula', 'Horizontalis', 'Horizontalis Elegantissima', 'Jacksonii', 'Nissens Corona', 'Nissens Kadett', 'Nissens Page', 'Nissens Präsident', 'Nissens Regent', 'Pendula Graciosa', 'Spieckermann'

  II. Branches neither nodding nor curved upward at the apex:

    1. Growth rate normal; no dwarf forms;

  ★ Needles to 1 cm long:
      'Adpressa', 'Adpressa Aurea', 'Adpressa Erecta', 'Adpress Pyramidalis', 'Adpressa Variegata', 'Amersfoort' (needles radial!), 'Backhousii'

  ★★ Needles over 1 cm long;

  ● green:
      'Linearis', 'Lutea' (seeds yellow)

  ●● yellow, yellow variegated or white variegated:
      'Albovariegata', 'Argentea Minor', 'Aurea', 'Aureovariegata', 'Barronii', 'Elegantissima', 'Ingeborg Nellemann', 'Pumila Aurea', 'Semperaurea', 'Summergold', 'Washingtonii'

    2. Dwarf forms

  flat, broad:
      'Buxtoniensis', 'Cavendishii', 'Procumbens', 'Prostrata', 'Pseudoprocumbens', 'Repandens'

  conical:
      'Compressa', 'Paulina', 'Pygmaea'

  irregular:
      'Decora', 'Elvastonensis', 'Epacrioides', 'Ericoides', 'Knirps', 'Nana', 'Nutans'

  globose:
      'Compacta'

'Adpressa'. Only females, quite deviant, small leaved form, broad shrubby and growth irregular, to 6 m high and wide, shoots ascending; needles oblong-ovate, rounded at the apex, with short, prominent tips, 5–9 mm long, 2–3 mm wide, dark green above, somewhat bluish-green beneath; female flower branchlets somewhat longer than those of the type, with numerous scales; aril often shorter than the seed, these usually 3–4 angled above. SN 285 (H); CCE 434 (= *T. baccata adpressa* Carr.; *T. baccata tardiva* Wells). Originated from seed about 1838 in the F. F. Dickson Nursery, Chester, England; but also occasionally found in the wild. Fig. 188.

'Adpressa Aurea'. Female plants, very similar to 'Adpressa', but only half as high and wide; needles golden-yellow at the branch tips, other needles only yellow variegated. GC 1954 II: 84 (H); CCE 434 (= *T. baccata adpressa aurea* Beissn. 1897). Developed in the Handsworth Nursery in Sheffield, England, 1885; introduced by the Standish Nurseries, Ascot.

'Adpressa Erecta'. Female, upright shrub, broad conical habit, 3–5 m high, ascending shoots, lateral shoots outspread; needles very regularly arranged; 15 mm long, 3 mm wide, obtuse acuminate, deep green above, light green beneath (= *T. baccata adpressa erecta* [Nels.] Nich.; *T. baccata adpressa stricta* Carr.). Developed before 1867 in the Standish Nursery, Ascot, England.

'Adpressa Pyramidalis'. Very similar to 'Adpressa Erecta', but the twigs more tightly upright; needles only 1 mm wide (3 mm on 'Adpressa Erecta'!). Originated from seed before 1949 by C. Frets & Zoon in Boskoop, Holland.

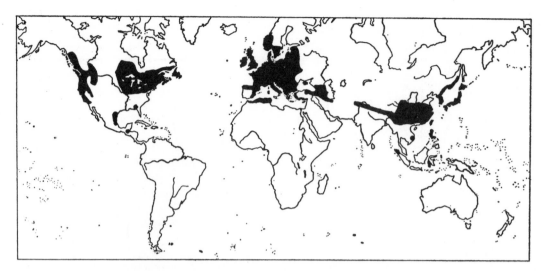

Fig. 186. Range of the genus *Taxus*

'**Adpressa Variegata**'. Open branched, apical shoots ascending; needles yellow variegated, often also yellowish-white, but lighter than 'Adpressa Aurea' and with green midstripes. WDw 240, Pl. 20E (Br); WM 35C (Br) (= *T. baccata adpressa variegata* [Nels.] Beissn.; *T. baccata adpressa aureovariegata* Beissn.). Either developed in Glasnevin (Dublin, Ireland) before 1866 or only disseminated from there.

'**Albovariegata**'. Leaves with white variegated markings, in summer and winter, peculiarly crispate. Developed in the L. Späth Nursery, Berlin before 1883. (EX?)

'**Amersfoort**'. Small shrub, slow growing, conical, loosely branched, branches rather stiff and outspread, shoots densely arranged, short, brown; needles short, oval-oblong, 5–7 mm long, 3–4 mm wide, somewhat reflexed, radially arranged, dark green above, lighter beneath. OCC 393; WM 34A (Br) (= *T. podocarpoides* Hort.). Developed in France, but discovered by the D. B. B. van den Hoorn Nursery of Boskoop and planted at the Amersfoort Hospital in Holland. At first considered a *Podocarpus* because of its great dissimilarity to other *Taxus* forms, but later this was cleared up by a closer anatomical inspection. Plate 123.

'**Argentea Minor**'. Dwarf form, very slow growing, annual growth only about 2 cm, shoots nodding; needles with a distinct silvery-white shimmer (= *T. baccata* 'Dwarf White' Boom & den Ouden). In the Bedgebury Pinetum, England.

'**Aurea**'. Female, slow growing, bushier, more compact shrub, to 4 m high with age, only pyramidal when sheared, shoots yellow when young; needles densely arranged, rather narrow, golden-yellow or only yellow striped, but totally green in the second year. CCE 434 (= *T. baccata variegata aurea* Carr. 1855). (EX?)

'**Aureovariegata**'. Growth more like the species, broad and open, 3–5 m high, but becoming much wider; needles yellow variegated. 1865.

'**Backhousii**'. English cultivar, shoots very densely arranged, short, very densely foliate; needles outspread, 10–12 mm long, 2–2.5 mm wide, rather obtuse, dark green and dull above, dull light green beneath. Introduced into the trade years ago by Backhouse & Son of York, England.

'**Barmstedter Types**'. A clone selected and vegetatively propagated at the Barmstedter Nursery, in Holstein,

W. Germany.

Type I : Broad, bushy habit;
Type II : Loose, upright habit, needles blue-green;
Type III: Broad growing, shoots nodding.

'**Barronii**'. Yellow needled cultivar, similar to 'Aurea', but with a regular, conical habit and yellow shoots and needles. Introduced in 1868 by Wm. Barron, Elvaston Castle, Derbyshire, England; developed from seed of *T. baccata* 'Aurea'. Occasionally confused with 'Elvastonensis', which see.

'**Beteramsii**'. Columnar form, strong growing, shoots erect, young shoots yellowish-white at first, but later greening; needles larger than those of the type, deep green. Developed by the Jac. Beterams Nursery, Geldern, W. Germany; introduced in 1927.

'**Buxtonensis**'. Dwarf form, flat and broad growing, habit similar to that of 'Repandens', but the needles sickle-shaped, erect and directed forward, about 20–25 mm long, 2 mm wide, deep green above, light green beneath (= *T. baccata buxtonensis* Gibbs; 1926). Origin unknown. A 70-year old specimen in the Kalmthout Arboretum, Belgium is only 50 cm high and 4–5 m wide.

'**Cappenberg**'. Columnar form, but compact and very slow growing, twigs very short; needles only about 9–15 mm long, deep green. Discovered in 1954 by G. Bootsman in the Blijdenstein Pinetum, Hilversum, Holland; introduced by L. Konijn & Co.

'**Cavendishii**'. Dwarf form, prostrate, very slow growing, to 40 cm high, but to 2 m wide or more, branches spreading across the ground, shoot tips pointing to the ground, shoots penniformly arranged; needles outspread, directed upward and forward, flat, slightly sickle-shaped, dark bluish-green above with a distinct midrib, yellow-green beneath, 20–30 mm long, 2–2.5 mm wide, semi-radially arranged. WDw 245, Pl. 20C (Br). Origin unknown, but cultivated before 1932 in England and much valued. Differing from the similar 'Repandens' in the longer, darker and bowed needles. Plate 132.

'**Cheshuntensis**'. Transition form between the species and 'Fastigiata', very fast growing, broadly conical, branches ascending, gracefully branched; needles very densely arranged, smaller than those of the type, becoming smaller

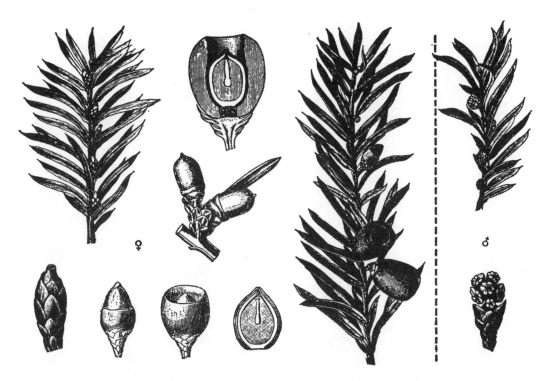

Fig. 187. *Taxus baccata*. Branch with female flowers and seeds, the aril is depicted in the
various stages of development; male flower at right (from Beissner and Pilger)

toward the branch tips, glossy green above, dark blue-green
beneath (= *T. baccata cheshuntensis* Paul). Developed by Paul in
Cheshunt, England around 1857 from seed of *Taxus baccata*
'Fastigiata'. Fig. 188.

'Columnaris'. Narrow columnar form, very slow growing,
shoots very short, very densely arranged on the central leader;
needles small, green with a yellow margin. Cultivated in France
in 1867. (VR).

'Compacta'. Dwarf form, globose habit, to about 1.3 m high and
wide, branches spreading regularly, twigs numerous, 4–6 cm
long; needles radially arranged, 5–10 mm long, 1–1.5 mm wide,
somewhat sickle-shaped, glossy dark green above, somewhat
lighter beneath with a darker middle line. WM 34C (Br) (= *T.
baccata compacta* Beissn.). Introduced in 1910 by H. den Ouden
& Zoon, Boskoop. The descriptions of this plant by Beissner
and den Ouden & Boom are not consistent, since Beissner
described, at the time, a 45 cm tall young plant, his description
is no longer valid. Plate 132; Fig. 191.

'Compressa'. Dwarf form, narrowly conical, densely compact,
twigs upright, numerous, stiff, thin; needles turning to all sides,
short, light green (= *T. baccata compressa* Carr. 1867). (VR)

'Contorta'. Twigs twisted, shoots and needles crispate,
arranged in all directions (= *T. baccata* var. *contorta* Gibb.).
Developed in the Arnold Arboretum. (VR)

'Davisii'. Very narrowly conical, branches and twigs upright;
needles dense radially arranged, thin, usually 20 mm long and
2 mm wide, dark blue-green above. SN 300 (H) (= *T. baccata
davisii* Hesse 1913). (VR)

'Decora'. Dwarf form, upright growing with a flat top, twigs
short, nodding, very densely arranged; needles about 30 mm
long, 3–4 mm wide, all bowed upward, very glossy. WDw 242;
KN Pl. 8. Very attractive cultivar. Cultivated in England but
totally different from the plant described under this name in

1939 by Hornibrook which is presumably no longer in
existence.

'Dovastoniana'. Male (but with female branches occurring
occasionally on the plant), tree or shrub form, 3–5 m high,
branches spreading horizontally and very long, the shoot tips
hanging at nearly right angles, bark dark brown; needles very
dark green, nearly black-green, 20–35 mm long, to 3 mm wide.
SM 238 (H); CCE 438, 439 (= *T. baccata* var. *dovastoniana*
Leighton 1841; *T. baccata dovastoniana* Lindl. & Gord. 1850).
Developed in 1777 by John Dovaston in Westfelton near
Shrewsbury, England. The original plant still exists. Germina-
tion of the occasional seed results in plants of the species.
Greatly valued cultivar.

'Dovastonii Aurea'. Grows exactly like the green form, but
much slower, and with golden-yellow shoots; needles usually
yellow-green with a yellow margin, yellow-green beneath.
CCE 439 (= *T. dovastonii aurea* Sénécl. 1868). Developed by
Sénéclauze.

'Elegantissima'. Only female plants, strong grower, branches
spreading widely, the middle branches horizontal, dense,
stout, twigs pale yellow; needles 1–1.5 cm long, yellow striped
at first; later more white variegated, but becoming green in the
shade; fruits abundantly. Developed in the Handsworth
Nursery before 1852. Fig. 188.

'Elvastonensis'. Shrubby habit, conical, very slow growing,
young shoots orange; needles golden-yellow, but orange in
winter, older trees gradually becoming green (= *T. baccata
elvastonensis* Barron 1868). Originated as an orange-yellow
mutation on a normal *Taxus baccata* in Elvaston Castle,
Derbyshire, England; before 1868.

'Epacrioides'. Dwarf form, compact habit, bushy, densely
branched, scarcely over 1 m high, branches short, secondary
branches densely arranged; needles turning to all sides, short,

Fig. 188. *Taxus baccata* forms. A. 'Adpressa'; B. "Repens Aurea"; C. 'Elegantissima';
D. 'Cheshuntensis' (Original)

13–17 mm long and sharply acuminate, light green, 2 ranked on older shoots. WM 34F (Br). Cultivated in England before 1866. (VR or EX) z7?

'Erecta'. Only the male known, strong grower, broadly bushy, but upright, wider than high (can grow to 8 m high), twigs fine, ascending; needles more gray-green, very short and narrow. CCE 437 (= *T. baccata* var. *erecta* Loud. 1838). Originated from seed of *T. baccata* 'Fastigiata'. Seldom cultivated today.

'Erecta Aurea'. Like 'Erecta', but the needles are totally golden-yellow and without green stripes (= *T. baccata erecta aurea* Barron 1880; *T. baccata brilliantissima* Hort.). It is questionable whether the plant illustrated on Plate 132 from the Bedgebury Pinetum is correctly labeled. (VR)

'Erecta Aureovariegata'. Like 'Erecta', but needles green, margin yellow, evenly pale yellow beneath, later becoming green-yellow inside the plant, very densely arranged, thin, flat, curved upward, 20–25 mm long, 2 mm wide. 1874 (R)

'Ericoides'. Dwarf shrub, to 1 m high, very slow growing, shoots very thin and short, erect and outspread, buds considerably larger; needles small, "heather-like", outspread (= *T. baccata ericoides* Carr. 1855). Fig. 190. (VR) z7?

'Expansa'. Wide prostrate form, bushy, often asymmetrical, ascending branches; needles 25 to 30 mm long, often sickle-shaped, deep green, parted (= *T. baccata procumbens* Kent 1900, non Lodd. 1838). Unknown outside of cultivation.

'Fastigiata'. Columnar Yew. Female, broad columnar, 4–7 m high, occasionally nearly as wide as high when very old, then with many equally long apical shoots, plants in cultivation 2–3 m high and usually narrowly columnar or spindle-form,

branches numerous, stiffly erect, short and densely branched; needles outspread on all sides, 20–30 mm long, curved downward, black-green; aril oblong. CCE 436 (= *T. baccata* var. *fastigiata* [Lindl.] Loud.; *T. fastigiata* Lindl.; *T. baccata stricta* Laws.; *T. baccata* var. *hibernica* Hook. ex Loud.). Two specimens were discovered about 1780 by Willis (a farmer) in the mountains above his farm not far from Florence Court, County Fermanagh, Ireland. One plant was transplanted to his garden where it lived until 1865; the other was given to his landlord in Mount Florence. Cuttings were obtained by London's largest nursery of the period, Lee & Kennedy, by whom it was distributed. The plant doesn't come true from seed. Male plants were unknown until one was found in 1927 in Sussex, England. Plate 111; Fig. 189.

Here is an outline of the 'Fastigiata' group:

Needles green:
    'Fastigiata', 'Fastigiata Nova', 'Fastigiata Robusta', 'Fastigiata Viridis', 'Cappenberg', 'Cheshuntensis', 'Hessei', 'Melfard', 'Neidpathensis'

Needles pure yellow:
    'Fastigiata Aurea', 'Standishii'

Needles yellow variegated:
    'Fastigiata Aureovariegata', 'Fastigiata Variegata'

'Fastigiata Aurea'. Similar to the normal 'Fastigiata', but with the young shoots and needles golden-yellow. 1868. Plate 125.

'Fastigiata Aureomarginata'. Like 'Fastigiata', but the needles of the young shoots golden-yellow bordered, gradually

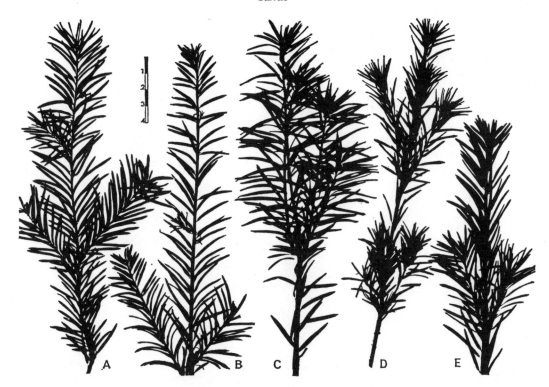

Fig. 189. *Taxus baccata* forms. A. 'Repandens'; B. 'Washingtonii'; C. 'Fastigiata';
D. 'Melfard', E. 'Fastigiata Robusta' (Original)

becoming light green (= *T. baccata fastigiata aureomarginata* Fisher ex Veitch 1881; *T. hibernica grandis* Fisher & Son & Sibray 1891; *T. baccata fastigiata grandis* Dall. & Jacks. 1923). Developed about 1880 by Fisher & Son & Sibray in the Handsworth Nursery in Sheffield, England.

'Fastigiata Aureovariegata'. Like 'Fastigiata', but the needles yellow variegated, not pure golden-yellow. Introduced in 1860 by Fisher & Holmes. Apparently no longer in existence.

'Fastigiata Nova'. Like 'Fastigiata', but more slender, fast growing and stouter; needles finer, deep green, but less bluish-green. Developed before 1903 in the Forstecker Nursery in Kiel, W. Germany. Particularly winter hardy. Plate 125.

'Fastigiata Robusta'. Like 'Fastigiata', but more narrowly columnar, coarser, needles longer, lighter green and more outspread. OC 398 (H); CCE 437, 438. Discovered before 1940 by the H. Zulauf Nursery in Schinznach, Aargau, Switzerland in a garden and introduced in 1949. Especially tolerant of frost and winter sun. Fig. 189.

'Fastigiata Variegata'. Like 'Standishii', but needles at first whitish, later either green or deep green. (= *T. baccata argenteo-variegata* Veitch 1881). (EX?)

'Fastigiata Viridis'. Strong columnar form; needles very densely arranged, flat, thin, 25 mm long, soft to the touch, glossy light green above, pale green beneath. Originated from seed of 'Fastigiata' about 1928 by K. Wezelenburg in Hazerswoude, Holland.

'Fisheri'. Broad growing, without a central leader, main branches horizontal, shoots and needles partly yellow, partly green. Presumably developed by Fisher & Holmes before 1865. (EX?)

'Flushing'. (J. Vermeulen & Son, USA; also known in Holland as 'Parade'). Columnar form, somewhat intermediate between *T. baccata* 'Fastigiata' and *T. media* 'Hicksii', but with better winter hardiness than the former, deep green and fruiting.

'Glauca'. Strong growing, open, branches spreading; needles 15–25 mm long, curved upward, dark, dull blue-green above, lighter blue-green beneath (= *T. baccata glauca* Carr. 1855; *T. baccata nigra* Paul 1861; *T. baccata* 'Blue John' Hort. angl. 1891). (VR)

'Gracilis Pendula'. Rather strong growing, with a distinctly erect terminal shoot and whorled, gracefully nodding twigs; needles bluish-green, very densely arranged, rather broad, sickle-shaped. WM 35A (Br), 413 (H). 1880.

'Handsworthiana'. Quite narrow conical habit, but compact, very densely branched, shoots short, erect; needles 15–18 mm long, 3 mm wide, curving downward, deep green above, lighter beneath (= *T. baccata handsworthiana* Fisher & Son & Sibray, Handsworth Nurseries, Sheffield 1880). (VR)

'Hessei'. Upright, very densely branched; needles conspicuously long and wide, 30–35 mm long, 3.5–4 mm wide (nearly like a *Cephalotaxus*!), partly sickle-shaped, deep green above, with a distinct midrib, lighter green beneath. CCE 435. Introduced in 1932 by Herman A. Hesse.

'Horizontalis'. Very broad, without a central leader, branches distinctly spreading, the uppermost branches curved upward; needles often somewhat sickle-shaped, to 25 mm long and 4 mm wide. CCE 436 (= *T. horizontalis* Pépin). Developed before 1850 by the Bertin Nursery of Versailles, France. (R)

'Horizontalis Elegantissima'. Similar to 'Horizontalis', but the needles yellow variegated. 1914.

'Imperialis'. Upright habit, branches ascending, densely branched, but not as stiff as those of 'Fastigiata'; needles outspread, radial, 25–30 mm long, to 3 mm wide, thin, slightly sickle-shaped, glossy dark green. 1855.

Fig. 190. *Taxus baccata* forms. A. 'Nissens Kadett', B. 'Ericoides'; C. 'Neidpathensis';
D. 'Overeynderi' (Original)

'Ingeborg Nellemann'. Broad, compact growth, to hemispherical, 1 m high and 1.3 m wide in 10 years, tips nodding; young shoots intensely golden-yellow for some time, older needles consistently with a golden-yellow margin, especially in the sun. Meritorious newcomer, the most attractive yellow form to date. Selected in the Thomsen Nursery, Skalborg, Denmark.

'Intermedia'. Broad, strong grower, branches thick, upright, short branched; needles radially arranged, rather widely spaced, straight, stiff, thickish, 15–25 mm long, 2–3 mm wide, tapering toward the apex with a reddish tip. Originated as a seedling of 'Fastigiata' by Briot in the Trianon Garden, Versailles, France, 1867.

'Jacksonii'. Broad, branches spreading gracefully and nodding like 'Dovastoniana', but not as regular; needles sickle-shaped, incurved and covering the apical part of the shoot, light green (= *T. baccata* f. *pendula* [Nelson] Pilg.). Developed by Wm. Paul in Cheshunt, England and introduced in 1861.

'Knirps'. Dwarf form, very slow growing, broad and irregular, only 30–50 cm high in 20 years, shoots deep brown; needles dark green, 8 to 25 mm long, 2–3 mm wide, more or less radially arranged. Developed before 1935 by Peter Moll in Heisterbacherrott, W. Germany. Plate 132.

'Linearis'. Wide growing, branches long, shoots outspread; needles long and narrow, often light yellow-green. Discovered in the wild by Rosenthal in the Tatra Mts., Czechoslovakia; distributed by Späth. Plate 132.

'Lutea'. Shrub, 3–5 m high, upright; needles deep green; fruits light yellow (instead of red) (= *T. baccata lutea* Endl. 1847; *T. baccata* var. *xanthocarpa* Ktze. 1864; *T. baccata* f. *luteobaccata* Pilg. 1903). Discovered about 1817 in the garden of the Bishop of Kildare in Glasnevin, Dublin, Ireland but remaining unnoticed until 1833. Observed again in 1833 in the garden of Clonarf Castle and distributed from there. Plate 111.

'Melfard'. Columnar form of the 'Fastigiata' type, but more compact, needles also smaller, dark green (= *T. baccata* 'Melfardii'). Developed in Denmark. Quite winter hardy. Plate 125; Fig. 189.

'Nana'. Dwarf form, growth low and wide, not over 60 cm high; needles small, deep green. WM 436 (H) (= *T. baccata* Nana Carr. non Paul, non Gord.; *T. baccata foxii* Knight.). 1855. (VR)

'Neidpathensis'. Male, stiffly columnar to nearly conical, opening up at the peak, otherwise resembling 'Cheshuntensis', but stiffer (= *T. baccata neidpathensis* Paul 1861). Discovered at the Neidpath Castle, Tweeddale, Scotland. Fig. 190.

'Nissens Corona'. Growth regular and strong, about 10 m wide and 1.8 m high in 30 years; needles light green (= *Taxus* 'Aprather Type 1' Nissen). Selected about 1937 by J. Nissen, Wuppertal-Aprath, W. Germany. Plate 134.

'Nissens Kadett'. Growth more loosely upright, without a central leader, branches ascending, about 4–5 m high and 1.8 m wide in 30 years; needles dark green, fine (= *T. baccata* 'Aprather Type 2' Nissen). Selected by Nissen in 1934. Plate 134; Fig. 190.

Plate 129

Larix decidua, 600–800 year old trees in the Stafelwald, 1980 m, at Saas Fee, Switzerland

Plate 130

Sequoiadendron giganteum
in the Yosemite National Park,
Mariposa Grove, California, USA
Photo: Karl Fuchs

Tsuga mertensiana,
14 m high, in the Loek garden, Elbchaussee,
Hamburg, W. Germany

Sequoiadendron giganteum, the famous 80-year old allée in Benmore, Scotland

Plate 131

Taxodium distichum,
about 40 m high and 700 years old,
in the Corkscrew Swamp Sanctuary, Florida, USA

Taxodium distichum
in the old Hamburg Botanic Garden, W. Germany

Taxodium distichum
in the Okefenokee Swamp, Georgia, USA

pygmaea Beissn.). Developed by Dervaes, Wetteren, Belgium; distributed about 1910 by den Ouden.

'Raket'. Broadly conical habit, very densely branched; needles 15–20 mm long, 2–2.5 mm wide, dark green above, lighter beneath. CCE 438. Selected as a seedling before 1967 by Haalboom, Holland. Received a merit award in 1967 in Boskoop. Especially well suited for hedges because of its narrow habit.

'Repandens'. Female dwarf form, procumbent and wide spreading, seldom higher than 40–50 cm, with a width of 2–5 m, occasionally also 5–6 m wide, major branches horizontal, lateral shoots drooping, rather stiff; needles about 20–30 mm long to 3 mm wide, sickle-shaped, directed forward and upward, glossy dark green above with a conspicuous midrib, flat beneath, dull green. WDw Pl. 20B (Br); CCE 439. Distributed in 1887 by Parsons, USA. One of the more common forms available today. Plate 124; Fig. 189.

"Repandens Aurea" and "Repens Aurea" are 2 names for the same plant. WM 414 (H). Both names are listed here only for the record; it is presumed that they are nothing more than a propagated lateral shoot of 'Dovastonii Aurea'. Both of these names are, in any case, incorrect. Fig. 188.

'Schwarzgrün'. Growth regular, broad bushy-upright; needles especially dark green. Selected by Hinrich Kordes Nursery, Bilsen, Holstein, W. Germany. Good frost hardiness. Recommended for hedges.

'Semperaurea'. Shrubby habit, broadly upright, with a slanted peak, to 2 m high and wide, branches outspread, shoots numerous, very short, yellowish-brown; needles 10–20 mm long, gradually becoming shorter toward the branch tips, somewhat sickle-shaped, some bowed upward, some downward, always golden-yellow above, light yellow-green beneath or only yellow margined. WDw 247 (H); WM 415 (H); CCE 440 (= *T. baccata semperaurea* Dall. 1908). Very popular form, since it retains the golden-yellow needle form during the entire year.

'Standishii'. Columnar form, but very compact and slow growing, shoots upright; needles usually 25 mm long on the terminal leader, 3.5–4 mm wide, golden-yellow, with a distinctly raised midrib, also yellow beneath. CCE 438 (= *T. baccata fastigiata standishii* Dall. 1908). The best of the yellow needled columnar forms. Plate 124.

'Spieckermann'. Growth wider than high, without a central leader.

'Summergold'. Seedling selection, broad and flat growing, shoots somewhat obliquely ascending; needles sickle-shaped, 20–30 mm long, 2–3 mm wide, margin a wide yellow band, usually totally yellow in summer, very constant in full sun, not susceptible to sunscald. Originated in the J. V. Ravensberg Nursery, Hazerswoude, Holland, before 1967.

'Thomsen's Dwarf'. Broad, open columnar form, growth rate weaker than that of 'Overeynderi'; needles deep dark green. Very winter hardy. Little used. A good hedging plant which needs little shearing.

'Washingtonii'. European plants female, but predominantly male in the USA! Compact habit, loose, 1.5–2 m high, very wide, branches outspread, tips nodding, twigs variable in length, yellow-green; needles sickle-shaped, directed upward, greenish-yellow with a narrow, yellow margin in summer, more bronze-yellow in winter, however the yellow color generally not very intense. CCE 440 (= *T. baccata* var. *washingtonii* [R. Smith] Beissn.). Cultivated since 1874 and rather common. Fig. 189.

'Wiesmoor Gold'. Weak to medium grower, irregularly columnar, habit similar to that of 'Hicksii'; needles yellow in summer, golden-yellow in winter. Doesn't suffer from sunscald. Developed in the Martin Zimmer Nursery, Wiesmoor, Holland (1968).

T. brevifolia Nutt. Pacific Yew. Small tree, 5–10 (rarely to 15) m, crown broadly conical, irregular, trunk to 1.2 m in diameter, bark thin, smooth, red-brown, branches thin, delicate, spreading, usually horizontal and somewhat pendulous, shoots yellowish-green, bud scales keeled, acute, loose, yellowish; needles narrow-linear, distincly 2 ranked and horizontal, 10–16 (to 20 in cultivation) mm long, dark yellowish-green above, lighter beneath, to 1.5 mm wide, abruptly tapered and sharply acuminate, petiole yellowish; seeds ovate, about 5 mm long, 2–4 sided, aril bright red. SPa 76; CCE 441 (= *T. baccata* var. *brevifolia* [Nutt.] Koehne; *T. lindleyana* Laws.; *T. boursteri* Carr.). N. America; British Columbia to California and Montana, in shady areas and in ravines in the mountain forests. Quite hardy but not often seen in cultivation. Plate 133; Fig. 192. z4

Fig. 192. *Taxus brevifolia*
(from Sudworth, completed)

T. canadensis Marsh. Canadian Yew. Shrub, 1–1.8 m high, occasionally 3–4 m wide, branches outspread, procumbent, stiff, abundantly branched, often also creeping and rooting, twigs short, densely foliate, buds yellowish-brown, scales ovate, obtuse, keeled; needles very densely arranged, 2 ranked, narrowly linear, apex short-rounded and short-acute, 10–20 mm long, 0.5–2 mm wide, dark green above to more yellowish-green, red-brown in winter (!), with 2 blue-green stomatal bands beneath, these about as wide at the green margin, midrib conspicuous and raised on both sides; seeds depressed, wider than high, aril bright red. BB 135; CCE 441, 442 (= *T. baccata* var. *canadensis* Gray; *T. procumbens* Lodd.). Atlantic N. America, from Newfoundland to Virginia, Iowa and Manitoba; in moist forests as understory thickets. Extraordinarily winter hardy, but not very attractive, otherwise requiring much moisture and shade; quite rare in cultivation. z2

'Aurea'. Dwarf form, conical habit, densely branched, upright; needles small, densely arranged, yellow variegated (= *T. canadensis aurea* Sénécl.). Developed by Sénéclauze in France before 1868; presumably by pollinating *T. canadensis* from *T. baccata* 'Aurea'.

'Pyramidalis'. Dwarf form, narrowly upright, branches ascending with nodding tips, new growth yellow-green, becoming light green over the summer, brown in winter; needles to 18 mm long at the branch base, 2.5 mm wide, gradually becoming shorter toward the shoot tip (= *T. canadensis pyramidalis* Rinz; *T. canadensis* var. *stricta* Bail.). N. America, found in the northern part of the species range. Cultivated since 1857.

T. celebica (Warburg) Li. Large shrub or tree, to 15 m high, normally broad and bushy in cultivation, trunk of trees to 1 m in diameter, bark reddish, shoots short, thin, outspread; needles slightly sickle-shaped, linear-lanceolate, 12–27 mm long, to 4 cm long in cultivation, 2–2.5 mm wide, relatively wide in relation to the length, abruptly acuminate, base usally oblique and decurrent, dark green above, light green beneath with 2 broad brownish-yellow stomatal bands, densely covered with papillae on the stomatal bands; seeds flat-ovate, about 6-7 mm long, 3–4 mm wide, often also triangular, aril reddish. LWT 2 (Br); CIS 54; SN 35 (H); LT 11; CCE 442; 446 (= *T. chinensis* Rehd. pp.; *T. mairei* [Lemée & Lévl.] Hu ex Liu; *T. speciosa* Florin). Central and W. China. According to present opinion, this is the plant cultivated in British gardens under the name *T. chinensis*. However, it is not yet certain whether the segregated stands in SW. China, Taiwan, Philippines and the Celebes can collectively be included here. Plate 133; Fig. 193, 196. z6?

T. chinensis see: **T. celebica**

T. cuspidata S. & Z. Tree, to 20 m high or more in its habitat, often shrubby in cultivation, branches horizontal or ascending, bark reddish-brown, annual growth reddish, bud scales usually ovate, the basal ones more triangular and keeled; needles irregularly 2 ranked, linear, abruptly acuminate with a small mucronulate tip, 15–25 mm long, to 3 mm wide, base abruptly tapered to a distinct, yellowish petiole, deep green above, with 2 yellowish stomatal bands beneath; seeds ovate, compressed, slightly 3–4 angular, aril red. KIF 1: 2; CCE 443, 444 (= *T. baccata cuspidata* Carr.). Japan; on Hondo at 1000–2000 m; on Shikoku at 1400–2400 m. Valued for its winter hardiness and deep green foliage; more commonly grown in the USA than *T. baccata* for these reasons. Plate 126, 127; Fig. 194. z4

Includes a number of cultivars:

'Aurescens'. Low growing, compact, only 30 cm high and 90 cm wide in 20 years; young needles yellow, later greening. WM 416 (H); CCE 443, 446 (= *T. tardiva aurea* Hort.). Already in cultivation in 1923 on the Hall Estate in Bristol, Rhode Island, USA.

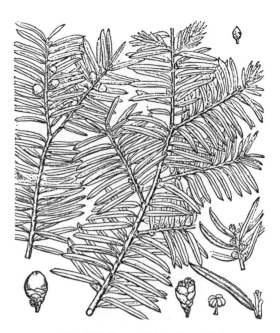

Fig. 193. *Taxus celebica* (from Liu)

'Capitata'. American trade name for a tightly upright growing plant with a dominant central leader, strong growing, later becoming tree-like. Male and female plants.

'Columnaris'. Broadly columnar form, older plants wider at the peak than at the base, then sparsely branched at the base, medium strong grower; needles deep green (= *T. cuspidata pyramidalis* Hort.; *T. cuspidata Parsonii* Hort.). Developed in the USA before 1940.

'Densa'. Female form, very slow growing, broad and very flat, but to 1.2 m high and 6 m wide in 50 years, very short erect shoots with deep green needles (= *T. cuspidata* var. *densa* Rehd.). Introduced by Parsons from Japan before 1917. Fig. 195.

'Expansa'. Vase-form habit, also with a constricted midsection, 3 m high and wide in 20 years. Not a clone! American trade name for low, broad growing seedling plants or also those propagated from side shoots. See also 'Capitata'.

Fig. 194. *Taxus cuspidata* (from Shirasawa)

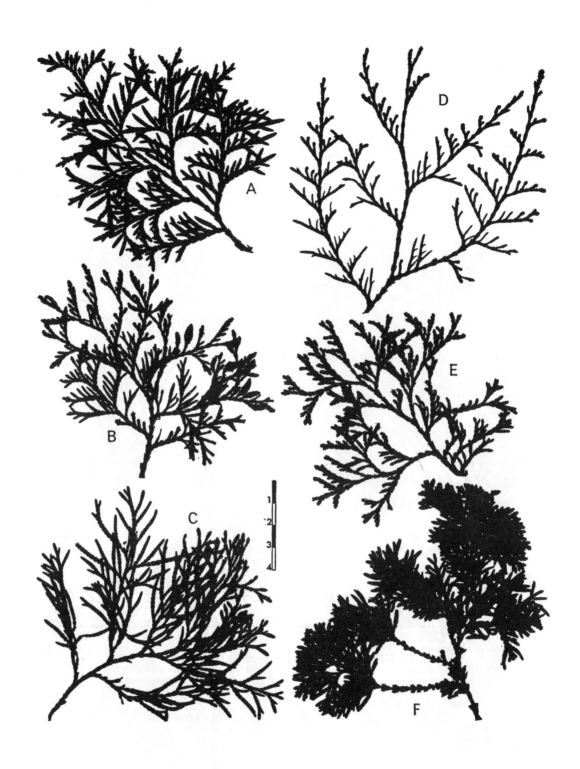

Fig. 203. Forms of *Thuja occidentalis*. A. 'Malonyana'; B. 'Fastigiata'; C. 'Smaragd';
D. 'Buchananii'; E. 'Recurva Nana'; F. 'Spiralis' (Original)

'Indomitable'. Mutation of 'Elegantissima', strong growing, twigs outspread; foliage deep green, but partly also reddish-brown in winter. Developed about 1960 by L. Konijn & Co. in Reeuwijk, Holland. Noted for its extraordinary winter hardiness. Fig. 212.

'Little Champion'. Dwarf form, strong growing when young to a height of 50 cm, then slower growing, globose, branching open, upright and outspread; needles green, but somewhat brownish in winter. CCE 458; WM 428 (H). Discovered as a seedling about 1935 in the McConnell Nursery of Port Burwell, Ontario, Canada; introduced in 1956. Plate 137.

'Little Gem'. Dwarf form, slow growing, broader than high, to 2 m wide and 1 m high, twigs spreading partly horizontally, thin, branchlets more or less crispate, dark green, glandular on both sides, to 3 mm wide, very flat, some vertical, some horizontally arranged. WDw 261 (H); KN 386 (Br); WM 37B (Br), 429 (H). Introduced under this name by Späth in 1891; origin unknown. Remains a meritorious form, although restricted to large gardens because of its wide habit.

'Lombarts' Dwarf'. Dwarf form, densely globose, slow growing, branches and branchlets erect, tips nodding; needles green. Introduced to the trade in 1942 by the Pierre Lombarts Nursery of Zundert, Holland.

'Lombarts' Wintergreen'. Conical habit, the foliage is green on both sides of the branchlets, color remains constant in winter. Developed in 1950 in the nursery of Pierre Lombarts of Zundert, Holland.

'Lutea'. Slender conical form, to 10 m high, branches and foliage golden-yellow, more green-yellow beneath. BFN 481 (H); KEv 217; CCE 459 (= *T. occidentalis lutea* Veitch; *T. occidentalis aurea* Hort.; *T. occidentalis* 'George Peabody' Hort. Americ.). Developed before 1873 in Geneva, New York, USA and still one of the best yellow forms.

'Lutea Nana'. Conical form, upright, to 2 m high, very dense, could be a dwarf form of 'Lutea', foliage somewhat resembles 'Ellwangeriana Aurea', but with larger scale leaves, these to 2 mm wide, otherwise never producing needle leaves, a very attractive golden-yellow in winter, but more greenish-yellow in summer. WM 430 (H) (= *T. occidentalis lutea nana* Veitch 1881).

'Malonyana'. Quite narrow, acute columnar form, 10–15 m high, densely branched, twigs short, brown, branchlets densely crowded, flat; leaves glossy green, distinctly glandular. SN 305 (H); Gs 1921: 183 (H); CCE 459 (= *T. occidentalis* var. *pyramidalis* f. *malonyana* Schnd.). Originated before 1913 in the garden of Counts Ambrozy-Migazzi in Malonya, Hungary (Mlynany, Czechoslovakia today). Quite meritorious. Plate 139; Fig. 203.

'Mastersii'. Compact conical form, branches short, stiff, shoots flat and arranged in a vertical plane; leaves dense, glossy, deep green with a brownish trace, more bluish-green beneath, distinctly glandular (= *T. occidentalis* f. *mastersii* Rehd. 1939; *T. occidentalis plicata* Mast. 1897). More commonly cultivated in the USA. Not a consistent form since many seedlings display a transition to 'Wareana'.

'Mecki'. (Kordes 1965). Globose habit, very compact, slow growing, bright green, very robust. Selected by Hinrich Kordes of Bilsen, Holstein, W. Germany.

'Meinekes Zwerg'. Dwarf globose form, about 60 cm high and wide in 15 years, dark green, young branch tips cream-white. Discovered in 1956, but first introduced in 1973 by K. Meineke, W. Germany. (R)

'Minima'. Dwarf form, similar to 'Hetz Midget', ball form habit, light green in summer, bronze-brown in winter. American

cultivar. Not *T. occidentalis minima* Hornib.

'Nigra'. Compact upright; foliage very dark green, also in winter. OCC 425 (H). From the USA; 1933 or before.

'Ohlendorffii'. Dwarf form, uneven and shrubby growing, to about 1 m high, with 2 forms of shoots: branches long, only slightly branched at the apex, upright, needles scale-like, tightly appressed, small, keeled or plaited, nearly square in cross section; the other form with needle leaves, decussate, subulate, about 12 mm long, reddish-brown. HD 247 (H); BCC 47–48 (Br); WDw 262 (H); CCE 458, 461; WM 431 (H) (= *T. occidentalis* Ohlendorffii Beissn. 1887; *T. occidentalis spaethii* P. Smith 1890). Developed before 1887 by J. H. Ohlendorff & Sons Nursery of Hamburg, W. Germany. Plate 136; Fig. 205.

'Parson's Compacta' see: **'Compacta'**

'Pendula'. Weeping form to 5 m high, irregular habit, upright, but with the stem and branches flexuose, directed downward, twigs pendulous; needles blue-green, more gray-green in winter. Developed before 1862 in the Standish Nursery of Bagshot, England. (R)

'Pumila'. Dwarf form, but to 2 m high with age, globose-ovate habit, twigs and branchlets spreading horizontally, the branchlets slightly twisted and not touching, flat, to 2 mm wide, deep green above, lighter beneath, color somewhat similar to 'Little Gem', but narrower and more delicate. WDw 255–256 and Pl. 17K (Br); WLM 432 (H). Occasionally confused with 'Little Gem' in the literature.

'Pygmaea'. Dwarf form, very irregular habit, twigs short, crowded and twisted; leaves very densely arranged, short, exceptionally thick, overlapping, both sides with distinct oil glands and glossy, light green at the branch tips in summer, in winter quite dark blue-green. WMw 264 (H); WM 36E (Br), 433 (H).

Fig. 204. *Thuja occidentalis* 'Recurva Nana' (Original)

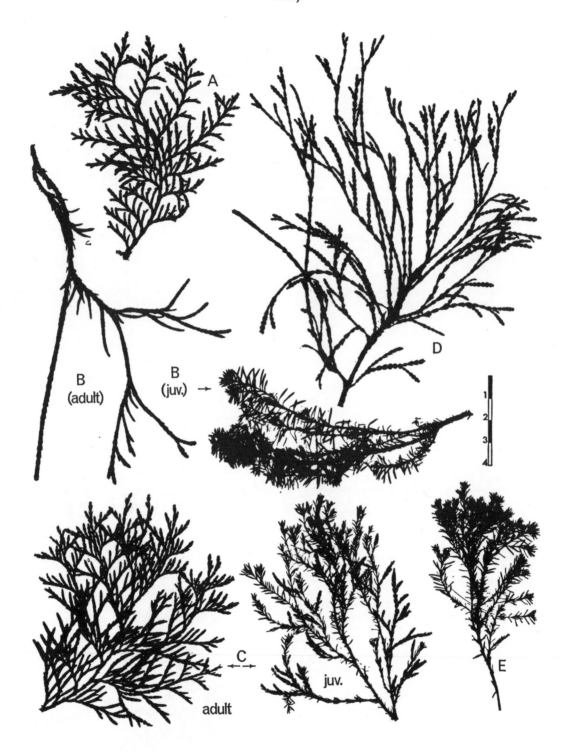

Fig. 205. Forms of *Thuja occidentalis*. A. 'Gracilis'; B. 'Ohlendorffii';
C. 'Ellwangeriana Aurea'; D. 'Filiformis'; E. 'Rheingold' (Original)

'**Pyramidalis**'. Probably = 'Fastigiata'.

'**Pyramidalis Compacta**'. Growth dense, conical, tall, about 10 m high or more, branches ascending, often with strong side shoots, therefore creating 2 peaks, shoots erect, compressed, short; needles larger, flatter, wider and more acute than the otherwise similar 'Columna', but not so glossy and lighter green, KN 378 (as 'Columna'); CCE 461. Known since 1904. Very widely distributed form.

'**Recurva Nana**'. Dwarf form, regular habit, globose, often becoming conical with age, to 2 m high, branches upright to outspread, branch tips drooping, branchlets twisted, partly bowed or twisted at the apex, somewhat brown in winter. TC 108; WDw 251 (Br); WM 38D (Br), 434 (H) (= *T. occidentalis recurva nana* Carr. 1867). Often confused with 'Dumosa', which is however, easily distinguished by the widely exserted thin shoots in spring. Plate 137; Fig. 203.

'**Recurvata**'. Compact conical habit, branches dense, twigs partly drooping, tips partly contorted and twisted. 1891 (VR or EX?) Fig. 206.

'**Rheingold**'. Plants cultivated under this name are nothing more than the propagated "ericoid" young shoots of *T. occidentalis* 'Ellwangeriana Aurea', also the shoots with needle-leaves; plants so propagated retain the golden-yellow to orange-yellow color for a long time, pure coppery-yellow in winter, older plants more often developing scale-form leaves, hence reverting back to the original *T. occidentalis* 'Ellwangeriana Aurea'. TC 108; OCC 427; CCE 459; WM 38B (Br). Developed about 1900 by Rud. Vollert, Lübeck, W. Germany; first named in 1904. Plate 133; Fig. 205.

'**Riversii**'. Broadly conical form, to 5 m high, shoots yellow-brown; needles yellow in summer, yellowish-green in winter. Before 1891.

'**Rosenthalii**'. Exceptionally slow growing columnar form, only 2–3 m high in 50 years, very densely branched, twigs short, stiff, branchlets crowded, more or less in a vertical plane; needles glossy dark green. Introduced before 1884. Still widely cultivated.

'**Semperaurea**'. Conical form, 5–10 m high, dense and widely branched, branches outspread; needles glossy green, with golden-yellow tips, yellowish-brown in winter. CCE 460 (= *T. occidentalis* var. *semperaurea* Rehd.; *T. occidentalis aureospicata* Beissn. 1893).

'**Skogholm**' (Skogholmens Nursery, Sweden). Columnar, dense, vigorous, resembling 'Rosenthalii', but the needles brighter green and apparently never with brown (dead) needles inside the plant.

'**Smaragd**'. Compact conical form, loosely branched, twigs more or less in a vertical plane, branchlets sparsely arranged, glossy bright green in summer and winter. CCE 461, 462. Selected by D. T. Poulsen, Kvistgaard, Denmark; introduced in 1950. Fig. 203.

'**Sphaerica**'. Dwarf globose form, but to about 1 m high in time, then more ovate, twigs very densely arranged and quite fine, finely crispate on the tips, branchlets only about 1 mm (!) wide or even narrower. WDw Pl. 18A (Br); WM 36F (Br) (= *T. occidentalis* var. *sphaerica* Hornib.). Known since 1874. (VR)

'**Spiralis**'. Slender conical form, 10–15 m high, branches very short, twigs conspicuously spirally arranged and somewhat twisted, branchlets somewhat fern-like; needles blue-green. CCE 458. Cultivated since 1920; origin unknown. Fig. 203.

'**Sunkist**'. Conical habit, fast growing and dense; foliage golden-yellow. CCE 462. Developed before 1960 by Gebr. Boer in Boskoop, Holland. Considered an improvement on *T. occidentalis* 'Lutea'.

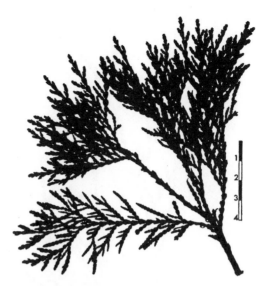

Fig. 206. *Thuja occidentalis* 'Recurvata' (Original)

'**Techny**'. Compact conical form with a broad base; foliage deep green, also remaining unchanged in very cold winters. Discovered in the Mission Gardens, Techny, Illinois, USA.

'**Thujopsoides**'. Open growing, twigs widely spaced, vigorous, branchlets heavy, broad, thick sectioned, nodding; bearing conspicuously large cones (= *T. occidentalis thujopsoides* Beissn.). Developed before 1894 by Schneiders in Duisburg, W. Germany.

'**Tiny Tim**'. Dwarf form, very slow growing, about 40 cm wide and 30 cm high in 8 to 10 years, globose, very finely branched, somewhat brown in winter. Developed in the Little Tree Farm Ltd. of London, Ontario, Canada.

'**Umbraculifera**'. Dwarf form, regularly hemispherical to flat-globose and eventually to 80 cm high and 1.5 m wide, branches more or less erect, also the twigs, very densely arranged, often somewhat twisted; leaves very thin, about 2 mm wide or less, conspicuously blue-green (thereby easily distinguished from all other dwarf forms!). KN 388 (H); WDw Pl. 18 (Br); OCC 429 (H); WM 435 (H) (= *T. occidentalis umbraculifera* Beissn.). Developed before 1890 by Chr. Neder in Frankfurt, W. Germany.

'**Van der Bom**'. Dwarf form, globose only when young, later more ovate; needles deep green (= *T. occidentalis* 'Van der Bom' den Ouden 1949; *T. occidentalis* 'Compacta' Van der Bom Hort.).

'**Vervaeneana**'. Slender conical form, 12–15 m high, branches thin, branchlets numerous, densely crowded, outspread, fine; foliage partly dappled, some lighter dark green, some light or dark yellow, more bronze-brown in winter. CCE 463 (= *T. occidentalis vervaeneana* van Geert 1862). Developed before 1862 by Verbaene in Ledeberg near Ghent, Belgium.

'**Wagneri**'. Narrow, dense conical form, delicate, branches tightly upright, outermost tips nodding slightly; foliage fine, green. BFN 132 (H) (= *T. occidentalis wagneri* Froebel 1895; *T. occidentalis wagneriana* Froebel 1896; *T. occidentalis versmanii* Cordes 1896). Selected before 1890 by Karl Wagner in Leizig-Gohlis (near Leipzig), E. Germany from seed of *T. occidentalis* 'Wareana'.

'**Wansdyke Silver**'. Low conical form, to 1.5 m high, very dense and narrow, very slow growing; foliage white variegated, remaining constant throughout the entire year. WDw 266 (H); WM 436 (H). Origin unknown. Discovered and named by H. J. Welch in 1961.

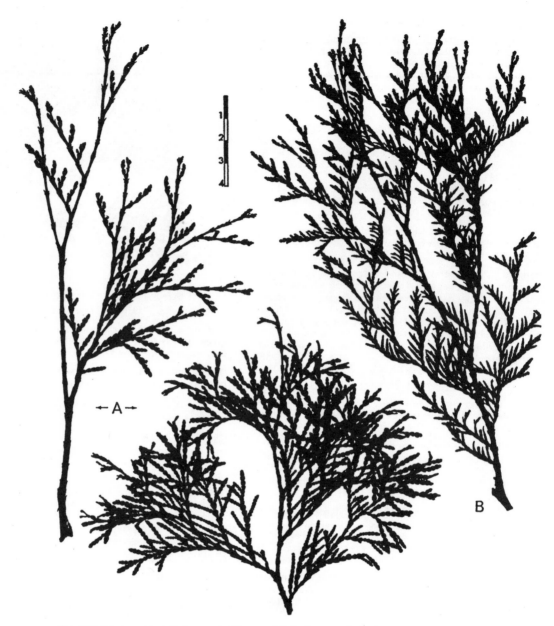

Fig. 207. *Thuja occidentalis* forms. A. 'Dumosa' (left, tip growth during summer; below, standard side branch); B. 'Hoveyi' (Original)

'Wareana'. Dense columnar form, to 7 m high, branches outspread, twigs broadly fan-shaped, branchlets thickish, short compressed, often vertically arranged, similar to *T. occidentalis* 'Mastersii', but usually much more robust and with larger needles, these bright green, without a brown tone. KEv 217 (= *T. occidentalis wareana* [Booth] Gord. 1862; *T. wareana* Booth 1839; *T. occidentalis robusta* Carr. 1855). There are 2 versions to the origin of this cultivar: the English literature (Bean and others) cites the breeder Th. Ware in Coventry; den Ouden-Boom say that Th. Ware never had a nursery in Coventry (rather in Feltham) and the breeder was G. Weare, whose father owned a nursery and was the mayor or Coventry from 1825–1827. Greatly valued form; habit not consistent as it is often grown from seed. Fig. 202.

'Wareana Lutescens'. Like 'Wareana', but more compact and lower; needles light yellow. TC 109; CCE 460. Developed before 1891 in the Herm. A. Hesse Nursery. Occasionally found in cultivation.

'Waxen'. Delicate form, open with nodding branch tips; foliage greenish-yellow, but only in summer. Introduced by Späth in 1891, but originally from the Arnold Arboretum, USA.

'Woodwardii'. Dwarf form, globose more broadly rounded with age (2.5 m high and 5 m wide at 70 years old in the Arnold Arboretum; but still displaying good form), twigs more vertically arranged, flat branchlets pure green, coarse, to 3 mm wide, both sides somewhat equally colored, remains green in winter or only browning somewhat at the tips. WDw 276 (H), Pl. 18F (Br); BCC Pl. 21 (H); OCC 431 (H); CCE 459; WM 37C (Br), 437 (H) (= *T. occidentalis* Späth 1891). Origin unknown. Plate 137; Fig. 202.

T. orientalis L. Oriental Arborvitae. Small tree, 5–12 m high, often multistemmed from the base and much branched, bark thin, exfoliating in fibers, crown broadly conical or also ovate or irregular, ascending branches, twigs spreading flat in a vertical plane, both sides evenly bright green or yellow-green; leaves tightly appressed, with a slightly resinous scent when crushed; cones erect on short shoots, 10–15 mm long, oblong, blue-green pruinose before ripening, usually with 6 scales, these with a large, horn-like, recurved extension of the apex, the apical pair of scales sterile, 2 seeds under each scale, ovate, not winged, 3 mm thick (= *Biota orientalis* L.; *Platycladus orientalis* [L.] Franco.). China, Japan, Manchuria, Korea. 1752. To 15 m high in England, trunk diameter then 75 cm. Plate 141; Range map Fig. 201; Fig. 200. z7 (some cultivars are more tender!)

Includes a number of cultivars, but many fewer than those of *T. occidentalis.*

Outline of the Cultivars

Forms with needle-leaves (juvenile forms):
  'Juniperoides', 'Rosedale', 'Rosedalis', 'Sanderi'
Forms with needle and scale-leaves:
  'Meldensis', 'Minima'
Forms with filamentous branching:
  'Filifera'. 'Filiformis Erecta', 'Flagelliformis', 'Intermedia', 'Tetragona'
Forms with normal green scale-leaves:
  'Blue Cone', 'Compacta Nana', 'Densa Glauca', 'Dwarf Greenspike', 'Nepalensis', 'Sieboldii', 'Stricta'
Forms with yellow scale-leaves;
  tall growing (over 1.5 m):
    'Aurea', 'Beverleyensis', 'Blijdenstein', 'Conspicua', 'Elegantissima', 'Golden Surprise', 'Magnifica', 'Pyramidalis Aurea', 'Semperaurea'
  dwarf forms:
    'Aurea Nana', 'Bonita', 'Hillieri', 'Westmont'

'Athrotaxoides. Dwarf form, more open habit, globose, irregular, 2 m high with age, 3 m wide, densely branched, branchlets thickish, 4 sided, contorted, twisted, forked antler-like at the apex. WDw 268; Rev. Hort. 1861: 229; CCE 468; WM 39D (Br), 438 (H) (= *T. orientalis athrotaxoides* [Carr.] Nichols.; *T. defresneana* Hort.). Found among seedling of *T. orientalis* 'Sieboldii' before 1861 in the Jardin des Plantes, Paris. The largest plant stands in the National Botanic Garden, Glasnevin, Dublin, Ireland (2 × 3 m). Plate 139; Fig. 208. (VR)

"Aurea" should only be used as a collective name since the various golden-yellow forms with distinctive growth habits have particular names. See the outline above.

'Aurea Nana'. Dwarf form, globose to ovate, not over 60 cm high, very densely branched, twigs all vertical and nearly parallel in arrangement; foliage quite light yellow-green, later somewhat more light green, brownish yellow in winter. WDw 269 (H); WM 39E (Br), 438 (H); CCE 463 (= *T. orientalis aurea nana* [Sénécl.] Rehd.). Plate 148.

The following names are often given for 'Aurea Nana': 'Aurea Densa', 'Aurea Compacta', 'Aurea Globosa', 'Millard's Gold' and 'Minima Aurea'. See also 'Semperaurea'.

'Berckmans Golden Biota' developed by P. J. Berckmans in Augusta, Georgia, USA before 1902; is correctly *T. orientalis* **'Conspicua',** but often grown in American nurseries as 'Aurea Nana'.

'Beverleyensis'. Tall columnar form or conical; foliage golden-yellow at first on the young shoots, needles not so tightly appressed as those of the other forms (= *T. orientalis* var. *beverleyensis* Rehd.; *T. orientalis* 'Beverley Hill' Wyman). Widely disseminated; especially in California where the form originated in 1917.

'Blijdenstein'. Broadly ovate, to 2 m high and 1 m wide, very slow growing and exceptionally densely branched, shoots very flat; needles appressed, but distinct at the apex, light yellowish green, more silvery green on the new spring growth. CCE 468. Originated before 1949 in the Blijdenstein Pinetum at Hilversum, Holland. Plate 138.

'Blue Cone'. Conical habit, upright, branchlets flat, vertical, with a distinct blue-green tone. USA (Monrovia Nurseries).

'Bonita'. Dwarf form, broadly conical, slow growing; foliage golden yellow at first, later becoming light green (= *T. orientalis bonita* Slavin 1932). Very popular form in the USA.

'Compacta' = **'Sieboldii';** which see. Plate 138.

'Compacta Nana'. Dwarf form, ovate to conical, very dense and slow growing, all twigs in a vertical plane; foliage exceptionally blue-green, with violet tips in winter, the basal twigs having some needle-leaves in 3's and totally distinct, while the transition leaves have only distinct tips (= *T. orientalis compacta nana* Hornib.; *Biota orientalis nana compacta* Henk & Hochst. 1865). Plate 140. (VR)

'Conspicua'. Low conical form or more columnar, to 1.5 m high, densely branched, twigs vertically arranged; foliage light green, becoming more light yellow toward the branch tips (= *T. orientalis aurea conspicua* Rehd.). This is the plant developed by Berckmans in the USA before 1902; see 'Berckmans Golden Biota'. Plate 138; Fig. 209.

'Densa Glauca'. Dwarf form, globose, densely branched, similar to 'Sieboldii', but with conspicuously blue-green foliage. Developed before 1891 by G. Jackman & Son of Woking, England.

'Dwarf Greenspike'. Dwarf form, compact, conical, to 1.5 m high; juvenile form, all leaves needle-like in appearance, but soft to the touch, arranged in 4 rows, 4–5 mm long, green. Discovered as a mutation on a *T. orientalis* at the Oklahoma State University Experiment Station, USA, 1940.

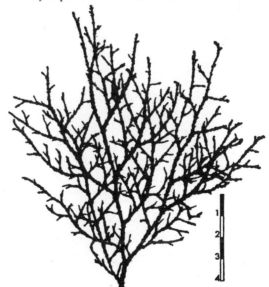

Fig. 208. *Thuja orientalis* 'Athrotaxiodes' (Original)

'Elegantissima'. Broadly columnar, to 5 m high, branches upright, stiff, branchlets fan-like; leaves golden-yellow in spring, later greenish yellow, brown in winter. WDw 271 (H); CCE 467 (= *T. orientalis elegantissima* [Gord.] de Vos 1867). Fig. 209.

'Elegans Aurea Nana' is presumably nothing more than 'Aurea Nana'. Plate 148.

'Filifera'. Growth broadly bushy, to 3 m high and wide, an unclear form; the plant growing in Les Barres Arboretum, France is labeled *T. orientalis* 'Filifera'; in Silva-Tarouca-Schneider, Freiland-Nadelgehoelze, 2nd ed., a quite similar plant is illustrated on p. 291 as *T. orientalis* 'Filiformis' (from the Allard Arboretum, France). Both plants are however, presumably *T. orientalis* 'Flagelliformis'.

'Filiformis Erecta'. Dwarf form, globose-ovate at first, tightly upright, later conical, all twigs filamentous and in very dense upright fascicles; lateral and facial leaves similar, yellowish green in summer, more brownish in winter. WDw 270 (H), Pl. 19a (Br); WM 39F (Br), 440 (H); CCE 462 (= *Biota orientalis filiformis erecta* Sénécl.; *T. orientalis* var. *filiformis stricta* [Beissn.] Rehd. 1902). Developed from seed of 'Flagelliformis' in Belgium before 1900.

'Flagelliformis'. Strong growing, upright, branchlets filamentous, similar to 'Filiformis Erecta', but the shoots more widely spaced, much less dense; needle color bright yellow-green. CBI 3: 77; WDw Pl. 19B (Br); CCE 464; WM 40A (Br) (= *T. orientalis flagelliformis* Jacques). Frequently planted near temples in Japan. Occasionally found in seedbeds of *T. orientalis*. Plate 140. z8–9.

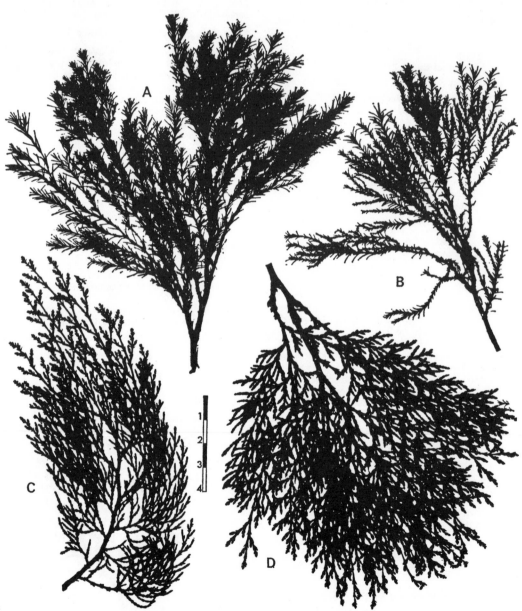

Fig. 209. *Thuja orientalis* forms. A. 'Rosedale'; B. 'Meldensis'; C. 'Conspicua'; D. 'Elegantissima' (Original)

'Golden Surprise' (Konijn 1977). Broadly conical habit, dense, apex rather acute; foliage an attractive yellow, later brownish yellow-green, an intense orange-brown in winter.

'Hillieri'. Dwarf form, compact, ovate, very slow growing, twigs directed tightly upright; needles light yellow at first, soon becoming green. KN 394 (H) (= *T. orientalis hillieri* 1930).

'Intermedia'. An intermediate form between *T. orientalis* and 'Flagelliformis', similar in appearance to 'Flagelliformis', but with the twigs not so pendulous, the needles longer, and not so tightly appressed (= *T. orientalis intermedia* Mast. 1903). Described by Carrière in 1855 as *Biota pendula intermedia*; also similar to *T. orientalis* 'Filifera'.

'Juniperoides'. Juvenile form, dwarf, scarcely higher than 1 m, broadly rounded, apex round, branches and twigs very densely arranged, shoots very numerous; needles all subulate, decussate, stiff, the distinct portion about 8 mm long, light gray-green in summer, conspicuously gray-purple in winter, concave above with white-gray channels. WDw 272, Pl. 19F (Br); WM 39C (Br), 441 (H) (= *T. orientalis* f. *juniperoides* [Carr.] A. & Gr. 1897; *Retinospora juniperoides* Carr. 1867; *T. orientalis* var. *decussata* [Hemsl.] Mast. 1892). Cultivated in England since about 1850; origin unknown. Plate 140; Fig. 210. z8.

orientalis var. *decussata* [Hemsl.] Mast. 1892). Cultivated in England since about 1850; origin unknown. Plate 140; Fig. 210. z8.

'Magnifica'. Narrowly conical habit, 2–3 m high, very densely and regularly branched, like 'Elegantissima', but the young shoots remain yellow longer, later similarly yellow-green, brownish in winter. CCE 468, 469. Origin unknown.

'Meldensis'. Juvenile form, globose to more broadly columnar, multistemmed, scarcely 1 m high, tight; leaves all needle-like, about 5 mm long, stiff, dull green, occasionally purple-brown in winter, rough to the touch, scale-like leaves occasionally present; sets fruit, the seed of which produces the normal *T. orientalis*. WDw 273 (H), Pl.19F (Br); CCE 463; WM 39A (Br), 442 (H) (= *T. meldensis* Quet.; *T. orientalis meldensis* [Quet.] Mast. 1892). Developed before 1852 by Cauchois in Meaux, near Paris (meldensis = from Meaux). Plate 140; Fig. 209.

'Minima'. Very dwarf form, globose habit, very dense, twigs erect; leaves partly short needle-like and outspread, partly also distinctly scale-like, light yellow-green in spring, dark green in fall, dirty brown in winter (appearing nearly dead!). WDw 274 (H), Pl. 19E (Br); WM 39G (Br), 443 (H) (= *T. orientalis* var. *minima glauca* [Beissn.] Hornib.). Cultivated since before 1891, but origin unknown. Since 'Minima' and 'Minima Glauca' are not different in color, and the latter is not bluish, they should be considered identical.

'Nepalensis'. Ascending habit, branches widely spaced, slender, outspread, finely branched, bright green, growth habit less attractive and not as regular as the other forms (= *Biota orientalis* var. *nepalensis* Endl. 1847; *T. orientalis gracilis* [Carr.] Jaeg. 1865. Discovered in Nepal.

'Pyramidalis Aurea'. Tall growing form, narrowly conical when young, but rather broad at the base on older plants, about a third as wide as high, very densely branched, young shoots a persistent golden-yellow, later more greenish-yellow, not turning brown in winter. KN Plate 8. Distributed from Italy around 1960.

'Rosedale'. Juvenile form, quite dwarf, somewhat similar to 'Minima' but the leaves smaller and more needle-like, bright green. WM 39B (Br) (= *T. orientalis* var. *Rosedale* Mast. 1901). Developed before 1900 in the Rosedale Nursery in Washington County, Texas, USA. First named 'Rosedale Hybrid'. Fig. 209. (VR)

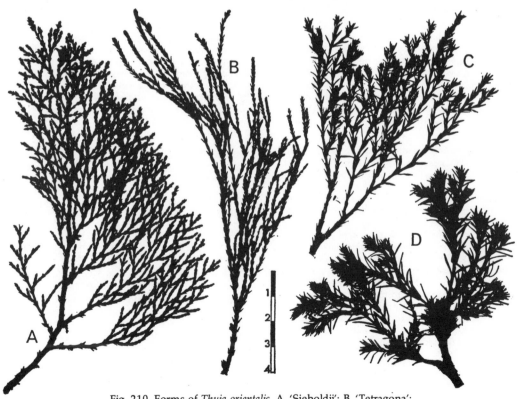

Fig. 210. Forms of *Thuja orientalis*. A. 'Sieboldii'; B. 'Tetragona'; C. 'Rosedalis'; D. 'Juniperoides' (Original)

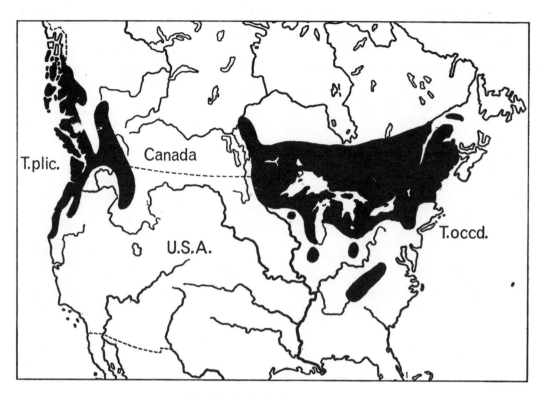

Fig. 211. *Thuja*; American range

'Rosedalis'. Dwarf form with needle-like leaves, bushy, ovate, very dense, branches and twigs very thin, similar to 'Juniperoides', but finer and limper, nearly heather-like, annual shoots 3–9 cm long; new growth golden-yellow, later gradually becoming light green, purple-blue in winter, needles very soft to the touch(!). WDw 275 (H), Pl. 19G (Br); WM 443 (H) (= 'Rosedalis Compacta'). Origin unknown, but distributed before 1923 by L. Chenault of Orléans, France. One of the most popular juvenile forms. Fig. 210.

'Sanderi'. Dwarf form, slow growing, broadly conical or also more or less globose, branches spreading horizontally or erect, unevenly thick; leaves all needle-like and decussate, linear, thickish, about 5 mm long, obtuse at the apex, concave above with a green midline, convex beneath with decurrent grooves, bluish green in summer, purple-violet in winter, very stiff to the touch. WDw 81 (H); WM 445 (H) (= *Chamaecyparis obtusa ericoides* Beissn.; *Chamaecyparis obtusa* f. *sanderi* [Sander ex Mast.] Rehd.; *Juniperus sanderi* Sander; *Shishindenia ericoides* Makino). Introduced in 1894 by L. Boehmer from Yokohama, Japan. It was unclear as to which species this cultivar belonged for some years. In the meantime, Makino had assigned it a provisional genus. A British investigation of the resin properties showed an exceptionally close relationship with the juvenile forms of *Thuja orientalis* and a considerable difference from all the other species. The same conclusion was reached in tests by the Forestry Experiment Station of Asakawa, Japan in 1964. z8

'Semperaurea'. To 3 m high, ovate, dense, branches and twigs tightly upright; leaves always golden-yellow at the branch tips, the others only yellow-green (= *T. orientalis semperaurea* T. Moore 1871; *Biota orientalis* f. *semperaurescens* K. Koch 1873). Developed before 1871 by V. Lemoine in Nancy, France.

'Sieboldii'. Dwarf form, broadly rounded, nearly beehive-like in appearance, densely branched from the ground up, branches numerous, twigs and branchlets very fine and densely clustered, erect, yellow-green on new growth, but soon becoming totally green. KEv 219; CCE 467; WM 40C (Br) (= *T. orientalis* var. *sieboldii* [Endl.] Laws.; *T. orientalis* var. *nana* [Carr.] Schneid.). Very widely disseminated cultivar in Japan. Very winter hardy. Plate 138 (as 'Compacta'); Fig. 210.

'Stricta'. Tall columnar form or also a small tree, all branches and twigs narrowly upright; needles light green; cones smaller than those of the species and the scales with a large bowed thorn. CCE 467 (= *T. orientalis* var. *stricta* Loud. 1838; *T. orientalis* var. *pyramidalis* [Ten.] Laws. 1851; *T. orientalis* var. *tatarica* Loud. 1838).

'Tetragona'. Dwarf form, similar to 'Filiformis Erecta', but more regular in habit, shoots more or less quadrangular (= *Biota orientalis* f. *filiformis tetragona* Beissn. 1891). Plate 138; Fig. 210.

'Westmont' (Moore). Broadly ovate habit, peak rounded, slow growing, 70 cm high and 50 cm wide in 10 years, branchlets partly upright, partly irregularly arranged, deep green with golden-yellow tips, color persisting until fall. US Plant Pat. 2685; Monrovia Nurseries, California. 1966.

T. plicata J. Donn ex D. Don. Western Red Cedar. A 30–60 m tree in its habitat, trunk diameter 60 cm to 2.5 m, occasionally over 4.5 m, widely flared at the base, bark red-brown, splitting into thick strips, crown acutely

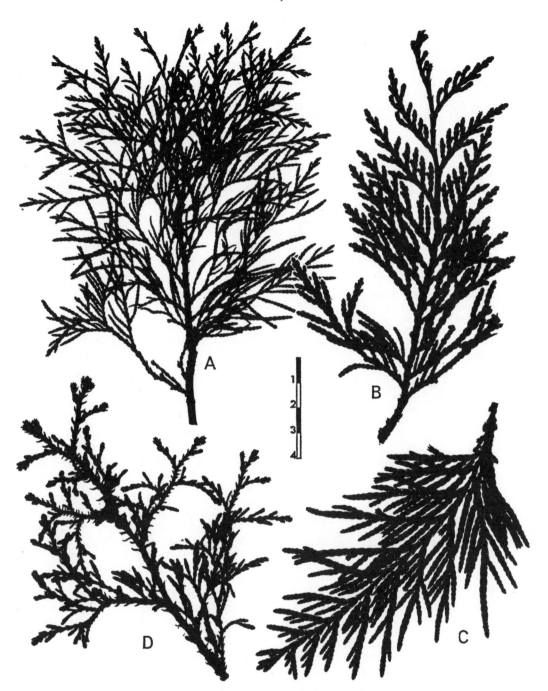

Fig. 212. Cultivars of *Thuja*. A. *T. plicata* 'Gracilis Aurea'; B. *T. occidentalis* 'Indomitable';
C. *T. plicata* 'Aurea'; D. *T. plicata* 'Hillieri (Original)

conical, branches scattered, outspread to nodding, branchlets distinctly 2 ranked and densely alternating, 2 mm wide, compressed, glossy green above, bluish pruinose beneath; leaves decussate on the stout terminal shoots, ovate and long acuminate, usually with distinct glands, smaller on the lateral shoots, more obtuse and often without glands, very aromatic when crushed; cones on short shoots, erect, oblong-ovate, 12 mm long, green in summer, brown in winter, ripening the first year, with about 10 scales, the central pairs fertile, seeds with encircling wings, emarginate at the apex. CCE 470–472 (= *T. gigantea* Nutt.; *T. lobbii* Hort. ex Gord.). N. America, west coast, to the Rocky Mts., Alaska to California, at altitudes of 1200–1500 m, near water. Plate 135, 141; Range map Fig. 211, 200. z7

T. plicata is an imposing, vigorous tree which can be justifiably used as a specimen as well as a hedging plant. Likes moisture. Specimens planted about 1860 are now 40 m high. A good forestry tree. Grows faster than spruce, especially on marsh lands where spruce won't grow.

> The very light wood of Western Red Cedar is very tough and decay resistant. It is, therefore, much used in the production of shingles, windows, doors and greenhouses. The Indians of the Pacific Northwest carved their totem poles from this wood, and their special war canoes were hollowed out of the larger trunks (hence the common name "canoe cedar").

> Includes a few cultivars.

'Atrovirens'. Grows like the species, but the leaves are especially deep dark green. CCE 473 (= *T. plicata atrovirens* [R. Smith] Sudw. 1897). Good winter hardiness.

'Aurea'. Needles yellowish, but with many patches of yellow foliage irregularly scattered over the tree (= *T. plicata* var. *aurea* [Sénécl.] Dall. & Jacks.; *T. lobbii aurea* Sénécl.). From New Zealand; cultivated by Hillier. Fig. 212.

'Aurescens'. Tall, like the species, but the tips of the young shoots greenish-yellow.

'Cuprea'. Dwarf form, growth dense and slow, conical form, to 1 m high, twigs short and closely spaced, tips outspread, the spreading, nodding shoots evenly copper- or bronze-yellow, more green in summer. Developed in the Red Lodge Nursery around 1930 from seed of *T. plicata* 'Aurea' by W. H. Rogers & Son, Southampton, England.

'Dura'. Growth normally upright, narrowly conical, rather slow growing, twigs dense, ascending, shoot tips slightly brownish, branchlets long, deep green; needles narrower than those of the type. KN 397 (Br). Selected by Timm & Co., Elmshorn, W. Germany, 1907; introduced to the trade in 1948.

'Euchlora'. Narrowly conical, tall, twigs stout, loosely arranged, branchlets numerous, long, with conspicuously little further branching, thin, soft, bright green. KN 397 (Br). Discovered in a private garden in Upper Bavaria (at 1200 m) and propagated by Timm & Co., 1955. Very winter hardy.

'Excelsa'. Open columnar form, tall, branches spreading nearly horizontally, twigs loosely arranged, sparsely branched toward the base, shoot tips ascending, branchlets tough, substantially larger than those of the type, glossy dark green. KN 397 (Br). Discovered in 1926 in a cemetery in Berlin, W. Germany and propagated by Timm & Co.; introduced into the trade (without a name) in 1941, named in 1947. Very winter hardy.

'Fastigiata'. Columnar form, narrowly ascending habit, like a pyramidal poplar, branches shorter, more densely arranged, somewhat finer than the species. TC 112 (= *T. gigantea fastigiata* [Carr.] Schneid.; *T. plicata* var. *pyramidalis* Bean 1914; *T. gigantea columnaris* Carr. 1867).

'Gracilis'. Growth upright at first, later broad and loosely conical, slow growing, twigs finer and lighter than those of the species; needles very small, green (= *T. lobbii gracilis* de Vos 1887).

'Gracilis Aurea'. Similar to 'Gracilis', but growth much slower, texture more delicate; needles yellow especially on the tips. WM 41D (Br); CCE 471, 473. Cultivated by Hillier. Fig. 212.

'Green Survival'. Strong grower, broadly conical, upright; foliage bright green summer and winter. Originated as unnamed seedling in the Darthuizer Nursery of Leersum, Holland; introduced in France in 1971.

'Hillieri'. Dwarf form, but 2–3 m high and wide in time, irregular and very dense, branches short, thick, partly brown, partly green, branchlets very densely clustered at the branch tips and very irregular, stiff, spreading in all directions; needles loosely appressed, small, blue-green, bronze-brown in winter. KN 310 (Br); CCE 474; WM 41E (Br), 446 (H) (= *T. plicata* var. *hillieri* Hornib.). Cultivated by Hillier in Winchester, England since about 1900. Plate 141; Fig. 212.

'Rogersii'. Dwarf form, globose, dense, to 1 m high in 25 years, somewhat narrower than high, becoming more conical as an old plant, when the terminal shoot is somewhat elongated; foliage very small, golden-yellow, but more bronze-yellow in winter, dark green inside the plant. TC 112; HD 272; OCC 441; CCE 474; WM 41A (Br), 447 (H) (= *T. plicata* Rogersii Aurea Hornib. 1929). Origin the same as that of *T. plicata* 'Cuprea', which see. Plate 141.

'Stoneham Gold'. Dwarf form, much stronger growing than 'Rogersii', to 2 m high, but after many years, more compact, upright, bushy, twigs broad, flattened, the 2.5 cm long, prominent branch tips are an attractive golden-yellow or bronze-yellow. WDw 278 (H); CCE 471; WM 41C (Br), 448 (H). Developed by W. H. Rogers & Son, Southampton, England; named in 1948.

'Zebrina'. Tall growing conical form, 12–15 m high, twigs outspread, tips nodding slightly on older plants; foliage "zebra-like" yellowish striped, later more whitish striped. CCE 473 (= *T. plicata* var. *aureovariegata* [Beissn.] Boom 1942; *T. gigantea albo-maculata* Beissn. 1902). Because of the variable color, often assigned different names; not unusual in cultivation.

T. standishii (Gord.) Carr. Japanese Arborvitae. Tree, to 30 m high in its habitat, crown broadly conical, bark reddish-brown, thin, exfoliating in narrow, paper thin strips, branches irregularly distributed, spreading horizontally or somewhat ascending, branchlets somewhat thickish, compressed, green above, with triangular, whitish spots beneath; needles somewhat unpleasantly scented like spruce resin when crushed, facial leaves obtuse, with linear oil glands, lateral leaves with short, incurved tips; cones ovate, light brown, with 8 to 10 scales, seeds small, narrow, winged, not emarginate on the apex, with 3 seeds under each scale. OCC 442 (Br); KIF 1:48; CCE 475, 476 (= *T. japonica* Maxim.; *Thujopis standishii* Gord.). Central Japan, in the mountains, 900–1800 m. R. Fortune sent seed of this species from Japan to the Standish Nursery in Bagshot, England in 1860. Young plants are occasionally damaged by a late frost. Range map Fig. 201; Fig. 200. z7

T. sutchuensis Franch. Small tree or shrub, branchlets flat, directed upward; lateral leaves with obtuse tips, dorsally convex, without glands, facial leaves furrowed; cones leathery, on short branchlets, with 8 scales, these overlapping, without a hook-like extension on the apex, only slightly thickened; seeds winged. OCC 443 (Br). China; NE. Szechwan. Not yet found in cultivation. z6

Lit. Penzes, A.: *Biota* tanulmanyok (Studies on *Biota*) (Hungarian with an English summary). Pub. Fac. Garden & Viticulture Univ. Agr. Sci. Budapest 1953, 93–98 (1 plate).

THUJOPSIS S. & Z.—False or Hiba Arborvitae—CUPRESSACEAE

Monotypic genus. Evergreen tree, often only a shrub in cultivation; outspread branches, branchlets very broad and flat; leaves scale-like, thick; plants monoecious, male flowers terminal on lateral shoots, solitary, cylindrical, with 12–20 opposite stamens; female flowers solitary, terminal, with about 8–10 decussate, thick, fleshy scales, the uppermost and basal ones sterile; cones globose, nearly upright, scales thickened, leathery-woody, hard, recurved at the apex; seeds narrow, 2 winged, with 4–5 seeds under each scale; cotyledons 2. Japan. Range map Fig. 201.

Thujopsis dolabrata (L. f) Sieb & Zucc. Hiba. Tree, to 30 m in its habitat, trunk thin, twigs irregularly whorled or scattered, wide spreading or nodding, branchlets all flat and in a single plane, 5–6 mm wide, horizontally arranged; leaves glossy and dark green above, 4–6 mm long, with distinct white markings beneath, lateral leaves with somewhat incurved tips; cones broadly ovate, 12–15 mm long, with 6–10 scales, these much thickened at the apex, terminating in an obtuse, triangular tip, seeds oblong or circular, compressed, both sides narrowly winged. KIF 1: 50; CCE 477, 478. Japan; in moist forests. Plate 144; Fig. 213. z7

Includes the following cultivars:

'Altissima'. Luxuriant grower, columnar, particularly fast growing, twigs short, nodding. Originated from seed before 1902 at the Ansorge Nursery, Hamburg, W. Germany. (EX?)

'Cristata'. Compact conical form, twigs tough, broadly fan-shaped, ascending, shoot tips somewhat fasciated-crispate, but not contorted. Originated from seed before 1902 at the Ansorge Nursery of Hamburg, W. Germany.

var. dolabrata. The type of the species, lateral leaves with incurved tips; cones broadly ovate, 15 mm long, scales thickened at the apex, with a triangular prominence, with a thick cross-keel on the dorsal side (= *T. dolabrata* var. *australis* Henry). Exported from Japan in 1853. Commonly found in cultivation.

'Gracilis'. Delicately branched; leaves smaller (= *Libocedrus dolabrata gracilis* Nelson 1866). (R)

var. hondai Makino. Tree, to 30 m high, twigs somewhat more densely arranged than those of the type; leaves smaller and more crowded, lateral leaves obtuse, not incurved at the apex; cones more globose, scales not thickened, with a very short, incurved projection, seed wings broader than those of the type. KIF 1: 50 (= *T. hondai* [Makino] Henry). N. Japan, in dense stands. Quite unusual in cultivation.

'Nana'. Dwarf form, dense, bushy, without a central leader, twigs finer than those of the type, with only 1.5–2 mm long leaves, bright green summer and winter. CC 18; WM 40D (Br), 449 (H) (= *T. dolabrata laetevirens* [Lindl.] Henk. & Hochst.). Exported from Japan to England in 1861 by J. G. Veitch. Fig. 213.

'Robusta'. Rapidly growing form, branches conspicuously thick, terminal leader vigorous, with only a few lateral shoots. Described by Beissner in 1891. (EX?)

'Variegata'. Twigs white variegated, but not very decorative and not consistent. CCE 467. Brought from Japan to Holland in 1859 by Von Siebold. Not uncommonly found today, must always be propagated from the white variegated shoots.

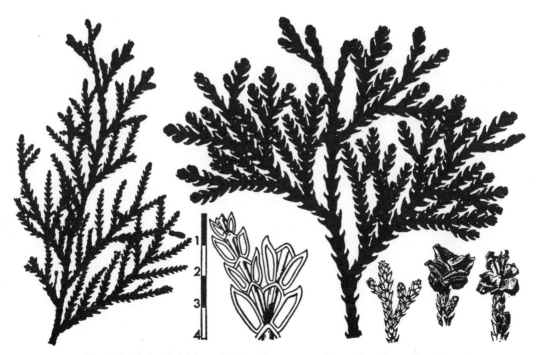

Fig. 213. *Thujopsis dolabrata.* Twig, solitary cones, leaves from beneath, enlarged; shoot at left from *T. dolabrata* 'Nana' (Original)

TORREYA Arn.—Nutmeg—TAXACEAE

An evergreen tree in its habitat (often only shrubby in cultivation) with fissured bark and whorled branches; twigs nearly opposite; buds with a few, decussate, abscising scales; needles distinctly 2 ranked, persisting for 3–4 years, linear, stiff, prickly, upper side slightly convex and glossy, underside with 2, often only slightly conspicuous stomatal bands; plants dioecious, rarely monoecious; male flowers ovate or elliptic, about 8 mm long, stalked, composed of 6–8 whorls of 4 stamens each, axillary; female flowers sessile, in pairs, in the leaf axils, but only one becoming fully developed; seeds ovate, to 5 cm long, with 4 scales at the base, with a thin woody shell, surrounded by a thick, fleshy aril, ripening the second year; x = 11.—6 species in N. America and E. Asia. Range map Fig. 214.

Torreya californica Torr. Tree, 15–20(30) m high, crown regularly conical, but eventually more rounded, bark gray-brown, narrow-longitudinally fissured, branches spreading and somewhat nodding, twigs light green the first year, later more olive, red-brown the 2nd year, buds ovate, scales very stiff, triangular-round, acute; needles nearly 2 ranked, 30–60 mm long, 3–3.5 mm wide, outspread, stiff, flattened above, dark green, linear to narrowly linear, long and gradually acuminate, tips prickly, with 2 narrow, indented, bluish stomatal bands; seeds 3–3.5 cm long, ovate or more oblong, light green, purple spotted when ripe, pulp thin and woody, seed coat furrowed. SN 310 (H); SPa 75; CBI 3:60; BM 4780; CCE 478–480 (= *T. myristica* Hook. f.). California; valleys and river banks. 1851. All parts of the plant aromatic when crushed. Plate 142; Fig. 215. z8

T. californica × T. nucifera. This hybrid is still unnamed; first observed in the Allard Arboretum in Angers, France, where it stands today as a tall tree. Cultivated by Hillier.

T. fargesii Franch. As yet an incompletely known species, similar to *T. grandis*, but differing in the very conspicuously parted, outspread needles tapering very gradually from the rounded base, these 15–22 mm long, 2–3 mm wide, rather long and stiff, prickly tipped, with 2 narrow, indented, dark red-brown stripes beneath; seeds ovate-globose, 16 mm long. CCE 483. China; Szechwan, Hupeh Provinces, at 1400 m in the mountains. Included with *T. grandis* by Rehder.

T. grandis Fort. Tree, to 25 m in its habitat, but occasionally more shrubby, crown loosely open, umbrella-shaped or broad, bark gray-green or gray-brown, young shoots yellow-green at first, yellow-brown in the 2nd year; needles linear to linear-lanceolate, straight or slightly sickle-shaped, 12–25(30) mm long, yellowish-green and glossy above, stiff, with short, sharp, but hardly prickly tips, with 2 whitish, indented, but inconspicuous stomatal bands, without a sharp scent from crushed needles; fruits oblong-elliptic, 2–3 cm long, nut red-brown, irregular and quite flat furrowed. DJ 124; LF 5–6; CBI 3: 61; CCE 481 (= *T. nucifera* var. *grandis* Pilg.). SE. and Central China; Chekiang, Fokien, Hupeh, Szechwan. Introduced into England by R. Fortune in 1855. Plate 142. z8

var. **dickii** Hu. Tree, to 20 m high, round crowned, bark gray and furrowed; leaves light green, densely arranged, wider, shorter; seeds obovoid, blue-green, with a short, prickly tip. China; Chekiang Province.

var. **merrillii** Hu. Differing from the type in the coarser branching; needles larger, darker in color, more obtuse, but with a prominent, short tip; fruits ellipsoid. China; Chekiang Province.

var. **sargentii** Hu & Chun. Tree, to 12 m, bark dark gray, flat furrowed, twigs outspread, thin, smooth; needles brownish-green, oblong-lanceolate, obtuse acuminate; seeds small, with 4 scales at the base. China; Anhwei Province.

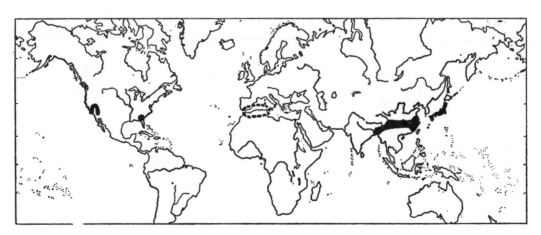

Fig. 214. Range of the genus *Torreya* (black) and *Tetraclinis* (——)

Distinguishing Characteristics of the Branches of *Torreya*

	Color of the 2nd year shoots	Needle length in mm	Scent of the crushed needles	Stomatal bands
T. californica	red-brown	30–60	very aromatic	deeply indented, hardly visible
T. fargesii	yellow-brown	15–22	?	deeply indented, red-brown
T. grandis	yellow-brown	15–25(30)	nearly lacking a scent	deeply indented, white
T. jackii	red-brown	60–80	very aromatic	—
T. nucifera	red-brown	15–25(30)	sharply aromatic	very conspicuous
T. taxifolia	yellow-brown	25–35	foul smelling	slightly indented

T. jackii Chun. Tree, 7–10 m high, but often only a stoutly branched shrub, ascending branches, shoots broadly spreading or somewhat pendulous, greenish-brown when young, later red-brown and glossy; needles sickle-shaped, gradually tapering to a thorny tip, 60–80 mm long, to 5 mm wide, scented like sandalwood when crushed; fruits obovoid, 2.5 cm long, sessile, blue-green. LF 7; CIS 14. China. 1924. Resembling *T. californica*, but the needles are longer, fruits obovoid. z9

T. nucifera (L.) Sieb. &. Zucc. Kaya. Small tree, 5–24 m in its habitat, often shrubby in cultivation, crown dense, ovate to conical, branches widely spaced, numerous, stiff, shoots opposite, green at first, becoming red-brown the 2nd year, spreading on an even plane, buds ovate, with stiff, keeled, flossy scales; needles spirally arranged, but spreading on an even plane, linear to broadly linear, 15–25 mm long, rarely to 30 mm long, 3 mm wide, somewhat sickle-shaped, glossy dark green above, with 2 bluish, narrow, indented stomatal bands beneath, tips thorny, crushed needles very aromatic, as are the 2.5–3 cm long, ellipsoid, sessile, green fruits, these with a reddish trace, edible. CEI 3: 62; SN 130 (H); CCE 482, 484. Japan; on Hondo to 1000 m, on Shikoku to 1400 m. Plate 142, 143, 149; Fig. 216. z7

'Prostrata'. Dwarf form, strong grower, becoming 6–8 m wide and 1 m high in about 50 years, twigs spreading horizontally. WDw 280; WM 42A (Br), 451 (H) (= *T. nucifera* var. *prostrata* Hornib.). Originated in the Glasnevin Botanic Garden, Dublin, Ireland, presumably around 1900 or earlier. Still in cultivation.

var. **radicans** Nakai. Stem absent, branches bushy, ascending, branched from the base, prostrate and rooting along the branches, young shoots bright red the 2nd year (= *T. fruticosa* Nakai). Japan; Honshu; in the mountains.

var. **igaensis** (Doi & Morikawa) Ohwi. Needles only 10–18 mm long, terminating abruptly in a thorny tip; seeds 20 mm long. Japan; Honshu, Iga Province. (R)

var. **macrosperma** (Miyoshi) Koidz. Seeds 3.5–4 cm long. Japan; Honshu, Iga and Omi Provinces.

T. taxifolia Arnott. Small tree, to 12 m high, conical crown, bark thin, shallowly furrowed, branches spreading and somewhat pendulous, shoots green, stiff, gray-brown the 2nd year; needles narrowly linear-lanceolate, somewhat sickle-shaped, stiff, 25–35 mm long, 3 mm wide, spirally arranged, but spreading on an even plane, glossy green above and prickly tipped, with 2 gray stomatal bands beneath, twigs and needles with a strong and pungent odor, particularly when crushed; seeds 25–30 mm long, 20–25 mm wide, deep green when ripe with purple stripe and whitish pruinose. KTF 2; ST 90; CBI 3:63; WT 14; CCE 482, 484. Florida; eastern bank of the Apalachicola River and in Georgia. (VR) Fig. 217. z8

'Argentea'. Young shoots partly white or yellowish white, irregularly distributed over the plant. OCC 447 (Br) (= *T. "tenuifolia argentea"* Rovelli).

An 8 m tall specimen stands in the Allard Arboretum in Angers,

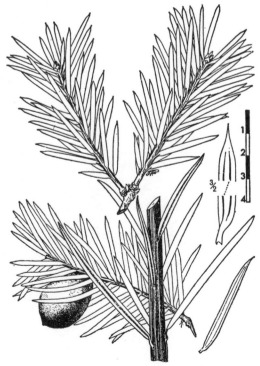

Fig. 215. *Torreya californica* (from Sudworth)

France; another grows in the Kalmthout Arboretum, Belgium.

Lit. Hu, H.-H.: Synoptical Study of Chinese Torreyas; with supplemental notes on the distribution and habitat by R. C.

Ching. Contrib. Biol. Lab. Sci. Soc. China **3**, 1–37, 1927. ● Morikawa, K.: *Torreya igalensis*, a new species of the genus *Torreya*, and *Torreya macrosperma*. Bot. Mag. Tokyo **42**, 533–536, 1928.

Fig. 216. *Torreya nucifera* (Original)

Fig. 217. *Torreya taxifolia*
(from Sargent and Beissner)

TSUGA Carr.—Hemlock—PINACEAE

Evergreen, usually a tall tree, twigs very thin, usually with pendulous tips, buds very small; needles usually parted, needle-like to narrowly linear, flat and furrowed above or convex and without furrows, often emarginate at the apex, tapering to a short leaf petiole at the base which protrudes only moderately from the twig, the decurrent portion slightly segmented from the petiole and remaining as an obliquely protruding leaf cushion; plants monoecious; male flowers on the previous year's shoots, axillary, small, nearly globose or cylindrical, with a densely scaly, short stalk; female flower terminal on the previous year's wood, solitary, very small, erect, bract scales only slightly shorter than the rounded seed scales at flowering time, later only a half or a third as long; cones small, pendulous or nodding, ripening the first year, but persisting on the tree to the 2nd year; seeds very small, winged and with resin blisters; cotyledons 2; x = 12.—10–18 species depending on the botanical interpretation, in temperate N. America and E. Asia, from Himalaya to Japan; most are winter hardy. Range map Fig. 218.

Outline of the Genus

Section I. **Micropeuce** (Spach) Schneid.
Needles flat, longitudinally furrowed above, stomata only beneath, usually distinctly 2 ranked; pollen without wings; cones 35 mm long at the most. Including:
T. blaringhemii, calcarea, canadensis, caroliniana, chinensis, diversifolia, dumosa, formosana, forrestii, heterophylla, patens, sieboldii, tschekiangensis, yunnanensis

Section II. **Hesperopeuce** Engelm.
Needles thick, convex on both sides, also with stomatal bands above. Including:
T. crassifolia, longibracteata, mertensiana, × jeffreyi

Tsuga blaringhemii Flous. Incompletely known as yet, but closely related to T. diversifolia, differing in the deep brown, densely pubescent shoots, buds oval, 3 mm long, 2 mm wide, not so numerous as those of T. diversifolia, scales elongated, numerous, finely dentate on the margin, inner scales slightly keeled; needles straight or slightly sickle-shaped, entire, furrowed above, 15–19

Outline of the more prominent characteristics

Tusga species	Juvenile shoots			Needles						Cones		
	not pubescent	short pubescent	long pubescent	Length in mm	Margin			Apex		Length in mm	smooth	dentate
					acute	round	crenate	sessile	stalked			
formosana	×			15–25	×			×	×	15–25	×	
sieboldii	×			6–22	×				×	6–22		×
chinensis		×		10–18	×	×			×	15–25		×
longibracteata		×		11–22	×		×			20–30		×
crassifolia		×		12–25	×			×		35–60	×	
blaringhemii		×		15–19	×				×	20		×
forrestii		×		10–25	×				×	25–30		×
tschekiangensis		×		6–12	×				×	20	×	
diversifolia		×		5–15	×				×	18–20	×	
dumosa		×		15–30	×	×				18–25	×	
yunnanensis		×		10–18	×	×				12–23	×	
caroliniana		×		15–20	×			×	(×)	20–35	×	
patens		×		7–21	×				×	25	×	
calcarea		×		6–20	×				×	15–20		
canadensis			×	10–18	×			×		15–20		×
heterophylla			×	5–20	×			×		20–25	×	
× jeffreyi			×	10–15	×			×		10–20	×	
mertensiana			×	10–20	×			×		50–80	×	

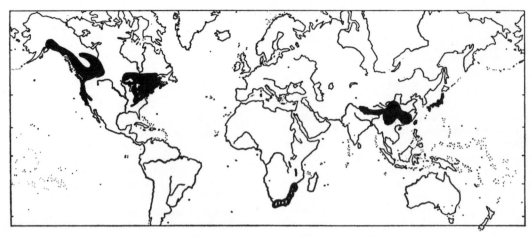

Fig. 218. Range of *Tsuga* (black) and *Widdringtonia* (|||)

mm long, the shortest only 4 mm long, width 1.8–2.5 mm, with 2 stomatal bands beneath, each with 6–12 lines, apex emarginate; cones globose, 20 mm long and wide, scales nearly quadrangular, with 2 small auricles at the base, seeds with 10 mm long wings, seed kernel alone is 4 mm. FTs 45. Japan; Central Hondo. z7

T. calcarea Downie. Closely related to *T. chinensis*, but the young shoots are light reddish-brown, densely short haired; needles straight or slightly sickle-shaped, 6–20 mm long, 2 mm wide, crenate at the apex, the longer needles often dentate on the margin, bright green above, with 2 whitish stomatal bands beneath, with 6–9 lines; cones globose, 15–20 mm high, scales small, nearly pentagonal, seeds 15 mm long, of which the actual kernel is 5 mm. FTs 55 (= *T. wardii* Downie). China; Yunnan. z7

T. canadenisis (L.). Carr. Canadian Hemlock. Tree, 25–30 m high, trunk diameter 1–2 m, trunk slender, often forked, bark eventually brownish, deeply furrowed, crown broadly pyramidal, more or less rounded at the apex, central leader short nodding, young shoots yellow to gray-brown, rather evenly long haired, buds light brown, acutely ovate; needles nearly regularly 2 ranked, 10–18 mm long, to 1.5 mm wide, gradually tapering from the base to the tip, apex rounded, glossy furrowed above, with 2 white stomatal bands beneath, each with 5–6 lines, the green margin usually broader than the white bands; cones short stalked, ovate, obtuse, 15–20 mm long, persisting after the seeds fall, scales leathery, rounded, light brown, margin indistinctly dentate, bract scales small, hidden, seeds small, light brown. CCE 486. N. America; from Hudson Bay to the Carolinas and Alabama. 1736. Needs a moist, airy site, won't tolerate hot dry locations. Plate 146, 147; Fig. 219. z5

Outline of the forms of *Tsuga canadensis* described:

( ) parentheses indicate collective names

1. Grows with normal vigor:
   'Atrovirens', 'Densifolia', 'Geneva', 'Kingsville'

   Needles green, but differing from the type:
   'Angustifolia', ('Latifolia'), ('Macrophylla'), ('Microphylla')

   Needles variegated;
   yellow: 'Aurea'
   white: 'Albospica', 'Dwarf Whitetip'

   Weeping forms:
   'Gable Weeping', 'Kelsey's Weeping', ('Pendula')

2. Low or dwarf habit;

   Procumbent:
   'Abbott Weeping', 'Cole', 'Prostrata'

   Flat spreading:
   'Armistice', 'Curtis Spreader', 'Gracilis', 'Gracilis Oldenburg', ('Nana')

   Flat with an indented middle:
   'Beaujean', 'Bennett', 'Fantana', 'Jeddeloh'

   Globose or hemispherical:
   'Brandley', 'Cinnamomea', ('Globosa'), 'Globosa Erecta', 'Harmon', 'Horsford', 'Milfordensis', 'Minima', 'Minuta', 'Pygmaea', 'Rugg's Washington Dwarf', 'Von Helms Dwarf', 'Warners Globe'

   Conical forms:
   'Boulevard', 'Bradshaw', 'Compacta', 'Curtis Ideal', 'Fremdii', 'Hicks', 'Jenkinsii', 'Meyers', 'Pumila', 'Stockmans Dwarf', 'Stranger', 'Vermeulen's Pyramid'

   Irregularly bushy forms:
   'Bristol', 'Callicoon', 'Dawsoniana', 'Elm City', 'Greenwood Lake', 'Hussii', 'Jervis', 'Mansfield', 'Moll', 'Parvifolia', 'Sparsifolia', 'Taxifolia'

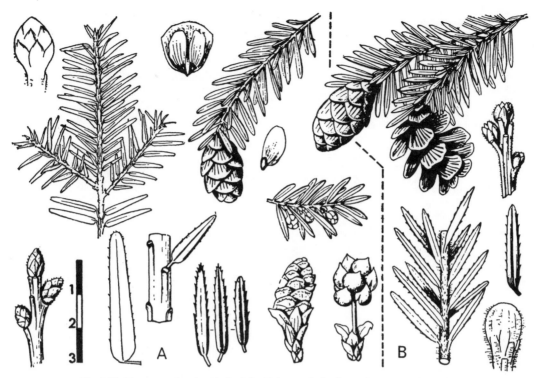

Fig. 219. *Tsuga canadensis* at left, right *T. heterophylla* (from Sargent and Fitschen)

'Abbott Weeping'. Dwarf form, nearly procumbent, only 20 × 10 cm in ultimate size; needles especially deep green (= *T. canadensis* 'Abbott's Dwarf').

'Albospica'. Compact conical form, slow growing, branch tips white or white variegated, especially in summer. CCE 487 (= *T. canadensis* var. *argenteovariegata* Fitsch.). Cultivated since 1866.

> Including some forms ('Hood's Variety', 'Labar') cultivated by Hillier, England.

'Angustifolia'. Small, irregular, bushy tree, branchlets clustered, shoots heavier than those of the type, densely pubescent; needles very small, about 10 times longer than wide, deep green. Developed before 1939 in the nursery of G. L. Ehrle, Clifton, New Jersey, USA.

'Armistice'. Dwarf form, flat topped bush, branches spreading horizontally; needles deep green and glossy. CCE 487; WM 43E (Br).

'Atrovirens'. Scarcely differing from 'Macrophylla'. Developed in Europe before 1897. Also see 'Hicks'.

'Aurea'. Compact habit, conical, slow growing, but becoming tall in time, branch tips and needles golden-yellow at first, gradually becoming green in the 2nd year. OCC 454 (H) (= *T. canadensis* 'Everitt's Golden'). Known since 1866, but often chlorotic in appearance. (R)

'Beaujean'. Dwarf form, similar to 'Nana', but the branches directed symmetrically upward and sideways, creating a conical form with an indented center, lateral shoots much shorter than the terminal shoots, more pubescent and darker redbrown; needles only 3–9 mm long (= *T. canadensis* 'Saratoga Broom' Swartley 1945). Discovered by A. C. Beaujean, Yonkers Nursery, New York, as a witches'-broom in a forest near Saratoga, New York, USA. 1926.

'Bennett'. Dwarf form, broader than high, very compact, annual growth only about 15 cm, somewhat resembling *Picea abies* 'Nidiformis' in habit, twigs spreading horizontally, shoots slender, summer shoots distinctly regular and spreading nearly fan-like; needles only to 10 mm long, but usually much shorter, densely arranged, light green. CCE 488 (= *T. canadensis* 'Bennett's Minima'). Developed about 1920 in the nursery of M. Bennett, Highlands, New Jersey, USA.

'Boulevard'. Compact conical form, branches irregular in length; needles densely arranged, long, deep green. Selected in 1930 by the Boulevard Nursery, Newport, Rhode Island, USA. (EX?)

'Bradshaw'. Compact conical form, branches outspread tips rather steeply ascending and very dense, lateral shoots more horizontal. OCC 450 (H); CCE 488. Selected in 1936 by H. Horman, Kingsville Nurseries, Kingsville, Md., USA.

'Brandley'. Dwarf globose form at first, but later to 1 m high or more, branch tips nodding; needles broad and long, deep green. Selected around 1918 by the J. Bradley Nursery in Walpole, Massachusetts, USA.

'Bristol'. Low compact, very broad, bushy form, upright, multi-stemmed, branches spreading horizontally, twigs filamentous; needles very obtuse. OCC 451 (H). Selected in the Bristol Nurseries, Bristol, Connecticut, USA. (EX?)

'Broughton'. Dwarf form, conical-irregular, slow growing; needles rather long, densely arranged. CCE 488. Before 1945 in the Leslie M. Broughton Nursery in Madison, Ohio, USA.

'Callicoon'. Medium strong grower, habit similar to that of *Juniperus chinensis* 'Pfitzeriana', about twice as wide as high, branches drooping, tips nodding. OCC 452 (H); WM 453 (H). Selected in the Curtis Nurseries, Callicoon, New York, USA 1942.

'Cinnamomea'. Dwarf form, very slow growing, flat-globose, young shoots elongated, densely red-brown pubescent; needles acute near the branch tips, older needles more obtuse and spathulate. Selected in 1929 by L. Abbott of Athens, Vermont, USA.

'Cole'. Dwarf form, completely procumbent, major branches totally appressed to the ground, about 1 m wide in 20 years, then only 15 cm high. CCE 486; WM 42D (Br), 454 (H) (= *T. canadensis* 'Cole's Prostrata'). Collected by H. R. Cole in 1929 at the foot of Mount Madison in New Hampshire. One of the best conifers for the rock garden. Plate 153.

'Compacta'. Very old plants grow to about 3 m high and wide, regularly conical, very densely branched; deep green and coarsely foliate, nearly *Taxus*-like in appearance. BCC Pl. 32 (H); American Nurseryman of 7/17/1961: 11 (H); CCE 487. Although this name has been in use since 1869, it should probably be considered a collective name.

'Curtis Ideal'. Dwarf form, quite broadly conical to globose, all shoots very densely arranged, tips nodding; needles irregularly arranged, not distinctly 2 ranked, loosely appressed to the shoots, to 15 mm long and 2 mm wide, but much smaller on the terminal shoots, widely spaced, light green. OCC 453 (H); WM 455 (H). Developed before 1945 in the Curtis Nurseries, Callicoon, New York, USA.

'Curtis Spreader'. Dwarf form, branches spreading horizontally, 150–180 cm wide, but only half as high, supposedly growing to 2 m high in time. Americ. Nurseryman from 7/15/1961: 11 (H). Distributed by the Curtis Nurseries, USA, before 1961.

'Dawsonia'. Compact grower, bushy, multistemmed, stems erect at first, then outspread, but rather regular, shoots slender; needles broad, very obtuse at the apex. Selected by S. Dawson in the Hunnewell Arboretum, Wellesley, Massachusetts, USA, 1927.

'Densifolia'. Tree, slower growing than the type and without the delicate habit; needles very densely crowded, but of normal length. Known since 1939 but also a collective name for a number of variations.

'Dwarf Whitetip'. Dwarf form, broadly conical, graceful, branches and twigs densely arranged; needles white in late spring and early summer, but gradually becoming green during the course of the summer. OCC 453 (H); WM 456 (H). Original plant is in the Morris Arboretum, Philadelphia, USA, but the origin is uncertain, possibly the Arnold Arboretum. 1890.

'Elm City'. Irregular form, erect and outspread, multistemmed, branches nodding, the basal ones more horizontal. Selected in the Elm City Nursery, Elm City, Connecticut, USA; 1932.

'Fantana'. Dwarf form, similar to 'Bennett', usually somewhat broader than high; foliage color not as good as 'Bennett'. CCE 490. Selected in 1913 from plants imported from France and propagated by P. T. Avogardo in Bellmore, Long Island, New York, USA.

'Fremdii'. Low form, broadly conical, somewhat irregular, branches densely arranged, ascending, shoots crowded; needles not conspicuously 2 ranked, densely arranged, relatively wide, dark green. OCC 455 (H); CCE 490. Selected in 1887 by Charles Fremd in Rye, New York; later introduced by P. Koster of Boskoop, Holland.

'Gable'. Several types ("2", and "5", etc.), selected by Joseph B. Gable, Stewartstown, Pa., USA. (VR)

'Gable Weeping'. Especially attractive, broadly pendulous form. WM 458 (H). Fig. 220.

'Geneva'. Low form, very slow growing, reaching about 5m high in 70 years, globose to more bushy, but with a terminal leader, branches erect, twigs very densely arranged; needles deep green. The mother plant came from the garden of the Trinity Church Home in Geneva, New York, USA.

'Globosa'. Can actually only be considered a collective name, since there are a large number of globose clones.

'Globosa Erecta'. Dwarf form, globose or ovate, erect, with many, thin, erect branches, lateral shoots more or less horizontally spreading. OCC 456 (H) (= *T. canadensis globularis erecta* Kunkler).

'Gracilis'. Dwarf form, low growing, flat-globose, branches all nodding, sparsely branched, WDw 283 (H); CCE 486 (= *T. canadensis* 'Nana Gracilis' and 'Gracilis Nana'; DB 1970: 29). Very unclear form, since it is no longer discernible if the plant introduced under this name by Waterer & Godefroy in Knap Hill, England, 1862 is identical with that described and illustrated by Welch; the latter is considered valid in this text.

'Gracilis Oldenburg'. (A new name for 'Gracilis' cultivated in the nurseries around Oldenburg, W. Germany; although those by this name in England are slightly different in appearance.) Dwarf form, slow growing, about 25 cm high and 40–50 cm wide in 10 years (about 2 m high in 75 years), hemispherical, with a nest form depression in the center at first, branch tips nodding, shoots very short; needles only 6–10 mm long, deep green. DB 1967: 27 (as *T. canadensis* 'Gracilis'). Origin of this form unknown, but first distributed by Heinrich Bruns Nursery, Westerstede, Oldenburg, W. Germany.

'Greenwood Lake'. Dwarf form, very slow upright grower, irregular and open, branches very compressed, twigs densely crowded, variable in length; needles partly 2 ranked, outspread, but more or less radially arranged at the branch tips, 6 mm long, 1.25 mm wide, rounded at the apex. CCE 490. Discoverd before 1939 near Greenwood Lake, New Jersey, USA; introduced by George L. Ehrle, Clifton, New Jersey. One of the most beautiful, meritorious *Tsuga*-cultivars of all. Retains a bright color in winter and is absolutely frost hardy.

'Harmon'. Compact dwarf form, ellipsoid, very dense, to 1.5 m high and about 1 m wide, very regular habit, terminal shoots only slightly longer than the side shoots. OCC 457 (H). Discovered before 1945 in Stroudsbury, Pennsylvania, USA. Cultivated in the Hemlock Arboretum, Far Country, Pa.

'Hicks'. Conical form, slow growing, very similar to 'Macrophylla', but the branches spreading widely (erect on 'Macrophylla'!); needles very densely arranged, longer than those of 'Macrophylla' and always with a yellowish tone (= *T. canadensis atrovirens* Hort. American. non Beissn.). Allegedly exported from France and introduced by Hicks; name changed in the USA and usually found as 'Atrovirens' in collections.

'Horsford Dwarf'. Dwarf form, very compressed and irregular, flat-globose, shoots and branches somewhat drooping; needles very short, obtuse, densely crowded. WDw 284 (H); WM 459 (H). Origin unknown.

'Hussii'. Dwarf form, very slow growing, annual growth 12–25 mm, erect, picturesque, irregular, branches very thick, erect, twigs very short, irregularly branched, normally without a terminal bud, shoots and buds densely crowded; needles layered, short, only 3–10 mm long deep green above, bluish-white beneath. WM 43F (Br); CCE 489. Discovered by J. F. Huss, Horticulturist at Hartford, Connecticut, USA around 1900. Very popular form today for its interesting growth habit.

'Jeddeloh'. Dwarf, hemispherical, with a peculiarly spiraling branch arrangement (when viewed from above) and nearly funnelform depression in the center; needles tough, 8–16 mm

Plate 145

Tsuga chinensis
in the RHS Gardens, Wisley, England

Tsuga diversifolia
in the Gimborn Pinetum, Holland

Tsuga sieboldii
Photo: Günter Kordes

Tsuga canadensis 'Microphylla'
in the Charlottenlund Bot. Garden, Denmark

Plate 146

Tsuga heterophylla in Benmore, Scotland
Photo: H.-D. Warda

Tsuga heterophylla 'Conica'
in the Gimborn Pinetum, Holland (Original plant)

Tsuga heterophylla, branch with cones

Tsuga canadensis, branch with cones

Plate 147

Tsuga canadensis
in its native habitat in North Carolina, USA
Photo: U.S. Forest Service

Tsuga diversifolia
in its habitat in Japan
Photo: E. H. Wilson, Arnold Arboretum

Tsuga canadensis 'Pendula' in the Herm. A. Hesse Nursery, W. Germany
Photo: H.-D. Warda

Plate 148

Thuja koraiensis has a silvery-white underside,
Hamburg Botanical Garden, W. Germany

Thuja occidentalis 'Ericoides'
in the Royal Botanic Garden, Edinburgh, Scotland

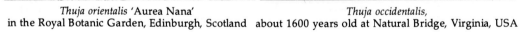

Thuja orientalis 'Aurea Nana'
in the Royal Botanic Garden, Edinburgh, Scotland

Thuja occidentalis,
about 1600 years old at Natural Bridge, Virginia, USA

Plate 149

Podocarpus ferrugineus
in the Hamburg Bot. Garden, W. Germany

Saxegothaea conspicua
in the Hamburg Bot. Garden

Taiwania cryptomerioides
in the Hamburg Bot. Garden

Torreya nucifera; the oil-containing, edible "fruits" of
the Japanese Nutmeg are up to 3.5 cm long and 1.6 cm
wide

Plate 150

The garden at Mainau Island, Southern W. Germany is especially rich in large, old and rare conifers; depicted here is a very impressive conifer group of *Calocedrus, Metasequoia, Cedrus atlantica* and *Cedrus atlantica* 'Glauca'

Plate 151

Sequoiadendron giganteum 'Pendulum';
this curiously formed specimen grows in the Lausanne Botanic Garden, Switzerland
Photo: Krüssmann

Plate 152

Tsuga canadensis 'Jeddeloh'
in the Jeddeloh Nursery, W. Germany

Tsuga canadensis 'Rugg's Washington Dwarf'
in RHS Gardens, Wisley, England

Tsuga diversifolia in Baekkeskov Park, Denmark

Plate 153

Widdringtonia cupressoides, a typical grouping on a sandstone outcropping where it cannot be reached by forest
fire, in the Cedarberg Mts. of Cape Province, South Africa
Photo: U. of S. Af. Forest Dept.

Tsuga canadensis 'Cole' is a very densely procumbent dwarf form
quite suitable for the rock garden
Photo: Günter Kordes

Plate 154

Widdringtonia cupressoides in its native habitat in the Drakensberg Mts.,
Giants Castle Game Reserve, Natal Province, South Africa
Photo: H. Friede, Johannesburg

Plate 155

Widdringtonia cupressoides, young trees
in the National Botanic Garden,
Kirstenbosch, South Africa

Widdringtonia cupressoides, young trees with many
cones in the National Botanic Garden, Kirstenbosch,
South Africa

Widdringtonia cedarbergensis in the Brummeria
National Botanic Garden, Pretoria, South Africa

Widdringtonia schwarzii in the National Bot. Garden,
Kirstenbosch, South Africa

Plate 156

Royal Botanic Garden, Edinburgh, Scotland;
rock garden with many dwarf conifers

Dortmund Botanic Garden, W. Germany;
part of the dwarf conifer collection

Plate 157

Conifer collection at the Arnold Arboretum, Massachusetts, USA
Photo: Arnold Arboretum

Dwarf conifer collection in the Arnold Arboretum
Photo: Arnold Arboretum

Plate 158

View in the Pygmy Pinetum at Devizes, Wiltsire, England
Photo: H. J. Welch

Sochi Dendrarium on the Black Sea, USSR;
a view from the highest point in the garden over the extensive conifer collection

Plate 159

The Blijdenstein Pinetum near Hilversum, Holland
Photo: H. J. Welch

A view ot the Gotelli conifer collection in the U.S. National Arboretum in Washington D.C., USA
Photo: H.-D. Warda

Plate 160

The National Pinetum in Bedgebury, Kent in southern England is one of the most complete conifer collections in Europe; above is a view of the collection of *Chamaecyparis lawsoniana* cultivars. Photo: Krüssmann

long, 1–2 mm wide, bright green above, lighter and with gray-white stomatal bands beneath. CCE 489; WM 43H (Br), 461 (H). Discovered about 1950 by J. D. zu Jeddeloh in a cemetery. The most widely distributed dwarf form of *Tsuga canadensis* in Germany. Plate 152.

'Jenkinsii'. Conical habit, branches nodding gracefully, irregularly arranged; needles short, 3 to 8 mm long, very similar to 'Microphylla'. Discovered in the Towson Nursery at Towson, Maryland, USA in 1931 (some sources cite the origin as Chestnut Hill, Philadelphia, Pa.).

'Jervis'. Dwarf form, compressed habit, exceptionally slow growing, one of the smallest forms, branches irregularly arranged; needles very small, about 7 mm long, 1.5 mm wide, densely crowded and irregularly arranged. CCE 491; WM 43C (Br).

'Kelsey's Weeping'. Very asymmetrical form, with some stout branches spreading and ascending in various directions, the secondary branches spreading horizontally, younger shoots hanging more or less vertically, long, shoots very flexible; needles about 10 mm long, 2 mm wide. OCC 457 (H). Discovered in 1929 in the H. P. Kelsey Nursery of East Boxford, Massachusetts, USA.

'Kingsville'. Coarsely branched form with very short branches. Discovered in 1936 in the nursery of H. J. Hohman, Kingsville, Maryland, USA.

'Latifolia'. Branches long, outspread and regularly distributed, partly horizontal, nodding at the tips; needles very densely arranged, not 2 ranked, flat, ovate-elliptic, straight or slightly curved, 2–3 mm wide, incised at the apex, margin slightly involute (= *T. canadensis latifolia* Sénéclauze 1868). Selected by Sénéclauze, of France before 1867.

'Macrophylla'. Only a collective name today for several shrubby clones, low forms with dense foliage and needles about 10–15 mm long (larger than those of the type), about 2 mm wide and truncate at the apex. OCC 458 (= *T. canadensis* var. *macrophylla* [Beissn.] Fitsch.). Known since 1891.

'Mansfield'. Narrowly upright form, branches dense, and much divided from the base, increasingly so with age. Discovered in the wild before 1945 as a collection of individuals by Dr. Raymond Wallace of the Univ. of Connecticut, Storrs (near Mansfield), Conn., USA.

'Meyers'. Compact conical form, branches distinctly stouter than normal and with more axillary buds on the shoots, these well developed; needles rather broad, deep green. Discovered in the E. W. Meyers Nursery in Hatboro, Pennsylvania, USA in 1941. Considered particularly tolerant to wind.

'Microphylla'. Very delicate habit, twigs fine and light; needles very fine, only 5–7 mm long, stomatal bands blue-green. CCE 489, 491 (= *T. canadensis microphylla* [Lindl.] Sénécl. 1868). Can only be considered a collective name today since several clones possess identical qualities. Plate 145.

Fig. 220. *Tsuga canadensis* forms. A-B. 'Pendula' forms in European gardens; C. 'Sargentii' (Brookline type); D. 'Gable Weeping' (original drawing)

'Milfordensis'. Dwarf form, more or less globose, branches crowded, twigs slender; needles not quite 2 ranked, rather short, about 3–9 mm long (= *T. canadensis microphylla* var. *milfordensis* [Young ex Gord.] Nichols. 1887). The original plant, selected before 1887 by Young in Milford, England, has been lost; Swartley selected a new plant in 1934 with about the same characteristics and gave it the same name.

'Minima'. Dwarf form, very slow growing, loose globose, branches ascending, tips nodding, shoots very short; needles only 5–8 mm long, often shorter on many shoots. OCC 459 (H); CCE 498; WM 43B (Br), 462 (H). Introduced by Herm. A. Hesse, Weener, W. Germany; 1891.

'Minuta'. Dwarf, probably the most dwarf of all known forms, presumably not over 45 cm high, somewhat irregular, as broad as high, shoots very densely arranged, annual growth only about 1 cm; needles 6–10 mm long, 1–1.5 mm wide, dark green above, with 2 white stomatal bands beneath. OCC 460 (H); Amer. Nurseryman from 7/15/1961: 11 (H); WM 43D (Br) (= *T. canadensis* var. *minuta* Abbott ex Teuscher 1935). This plant (which comes true from seed!!) was discovered in 1927 by F. L. Abbott of Saxton's River, Vermont, USA. There are several different opinions as to the discovery of the plant; see Teuscher in New Flora and Silva 1935: 274; Den Ouden-Boom, Manual p. 460; Brooklyn Bot. Gard. Report, Autumn 1949: 141.

'Moll'. Shrubby, compact habit, to 3 m high, about as wide as high, irregular, branches loosely arranged, densely foliate. KN 406 (H). Selected before 1935 by P. Moll, Heisterbacherott, W. Germany; but first named in 1955. (VR)

'Nana'. Dwarf form, to only 1 m high, branches procumbent, horizontal and long, twigs short and sparse; needles like those of the type. CCE 493 (= *T. canadensis* var. *nana* Carr. 1855). There is enough uncertainty about this form that it should probably be considered a collective name. A 30-year old plant growing at Hillier's in England was 2.5 m high and 3.5 m wide. The illustration in KN 411 is nearly the same as that in WDw 283 (the latter is cited as 'Gracilis').

'Nana Gracilis' in the Germany nurseries should be considered **'Gracilis Oldenburg'**. See the notes at *T. canadensis* 'Gracilis'.

'Parvifolia'. Dwarf form, bushy, multistemmed, branches spreading gracefully, thus usually indented in the center, branchlets very thin, much thinner than those of the type; needles 2 ranked, 3–8 mm long, relatively wide, obtuse, medium green. CCE 492. Originated before 1881 in England and repeatedly found in seedbeds.

'Pendula'. This name should be considered a collective name. In Europe, both types at Fig. 220 A-B are called 'Pendula'; 'Sargentii', in the USA (Fig. 220 C) is only one of 4 types originally given this name. Welch gave this type (C of Fig. 220) the name 'Brookline'. A totally different type is 'Gable Weeping' (D of Fig. 220). Plate 147.

'Prostrata'. Dwarf form, very slow growing, branches horizontal, tightly appressed to the ground, twigs very short, center of the plant usually somewhat glaborous; needles normal, persisting for only 2 years. First discovered by W. J. Bean in the Renton Garden, Perth, Scotland, before 1930; later discovered again by H. R. Cole of Haverhill, Massachusetts, USA, at the base of Mount Madison, New Hampshire, USA; 1931.

'Pumila'. Dwarf form, growth broadly conical, with a central leader, about as wide as high, annual growth only 2–3 cm, branch tips nodding gracefully; needles layered, broader than those of the type. Selected by Ordnung at Eisenberg Nurseries, before 1909.

'Pygmaea'. Very similar to 'Minuta', according to Welch possibly smaller and with shorter needles. Cultivated by Hillier.

'Rugg's Washington Dwarf'. Dwarf form, densely globose to cushion-form habit, shoots compressed; foliage bronze-yellow, especially in spring. WM 43A (Br); CCE 493. One of the best cultivars. Plate 152.

'Sargentii'. See 'Pendula'. WM 464 (H).

'Sparsifolia'. Dwarf form, compact, twigs ascending, total plant appearing nearly like a *Juniperus*; needles irregularly arranged around the shoot, never 2 ranked. Known since 1891.

'Stockman's Dwarf'. Dwarf form, growth very slow, conical; needles short, thick, densly crowded. Americ. Nurseryman from 8/15/1961: 10 (H). Selection of Stockman's Nursery, Greenlaw, N.Y., USA, before 1961.

'Stranger.' Low form, very compact, about 4 m, then as wide as high, similar to 'Fremdii', but with thicker shoots, these more densely pubescent, needles likewise thicker and shorter. CCE 493 (= *T. canadensis* var. *strangeri* Swartley). Originated in the Cherry Hill Nursery of West Newbury, Massachusetts, USA; 1939.

'Taxifolia'. Loose shrubby habit, slow growing, tips of the young shoots attractively pendulous, with *Taxus*-like foliage; needles densely clustered at the branch tips, very irregularly arranged, 4–20 mm long, to 2.5 mm wide, partly narrowed and twisted at the apex, tips obtuse or acute, very soft to the touch. OCC 463 (H) (= *T. canadensis* var. *taxifolia* Swartley 1938). Discovered about 1928 by F. L. Abbott near Athens, Vermont, USA.

'Vermeulen's Pyramid'. Low form, slender conical, very fast growing, branches very densely arranged and ascending; needles very densely arranged. Americ. Nurseryman of 8/15/1961: 10 (H). Discovered in the wild in 1915 by W. C. Horsfold in Vermont, USA; introduced by Vermeulen 1942.

'Von Helms Dwarf'. Dwarf form, to about 1 m high; needles very densely arranged, not 2 ranked. Selected in 1942 in the William Von Helms Nursery, Monsey, New York.

'Warner's Globe'. Dwarf form, globose; even as a small plant; foliage light green. WM 467 (H).

T. caroliniana Engelm. Carolina Hemlock. Tree, to 15 m, occasionally higher, crown conical, dense, branches outspread, young shoots glossy gray or light yellow-brown, short haired (occasionally only in the furrows), buds rounded-ovate; needles linear, 15–20 mm long, 1.5–2 mm wide, entire(!!) or very rarely slightly dentate on the apical half, rounded apex or nearly truncate, rarely slightly emarginate, with 2 white stomatal bands beneath; cones sessile, oblong-cylindrical, 20–35 mm long, seed scales finely haired, the basal ones nearly circular, the middle and apical ones more ovate and longer than wide, seeds 4 mm long with 13–14 mm long wings. BCC Pl. 31 (H); CBI. 1: 65; OCC 464 (H); FTs 67; CCE 494, 499. N. America; in the mountains from SW. Virginia to N. Georgia. 1886. Fig. 211. z6

'Arnold Pyramid'. Conical form, 8–10 m high, peak rounded. Originated in 1938 from seed in the Kelsey Nursery of East Boxford, Mass. USA and named by the Arnold Arboretum.

'Compacta'. Dwarf form, low, broader than high and very densely branched, twigs horizontal. This form is apparently not consistent; D. Wyman reported in Arnoldia in 1955 that the plant eventually develops into a normal *T. caroliniana*.

T. chinensis (Franch.) Pritz. Chinese Hemlock. Tree, 20–25(40) m high, young shoots yellowish, later more gray-yellow, pubescent in the furrows, buds rounded or

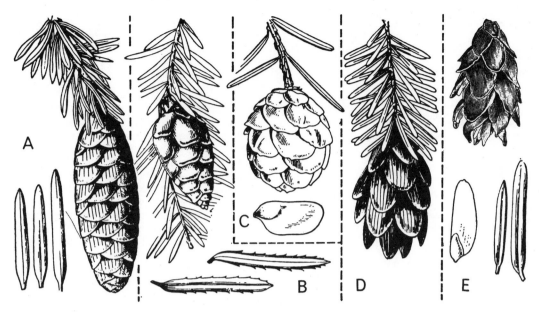

Fig. 221. *Tsuga*. A. *T. mertensiana*; B. *T. dumosa*; C. *T. yunnanensis*; D. *T. caroliniana*
(from Sargent and Gard. Chronicle)

short-cylindrical, quite obtuse at the apex; needles linear, 10–18 mm long, 1.5–2.5 mm wide, entire, with a few teeth at the apex and crenate, dark green and glossy, with pale green stomatal bands beneath, eventually quite indistinct; cones stalked, ovate, 15–25 mm long, seed scales rounded, yellowish-brown, glossy, somewhat striped. LF 22; BM 9193; NF 2: 101; FTs 73; CBI 4: 74; CCE 495, 496 (= *T. dumosa* var. *chinensis* Franch.). W. China; Szechwan. 1900. Plate 145. z6

T. crassifolia Flous. Tree, similar to *T. blaringhemii* in habit and size, young shoots short pubescent, light orange, eventually silver-gray, buds conical, 5 mm long, 2 mm thick, scales very narrow, distinctly pubescent; needles more or less bowed, entire, 12–25 mm long, 1–1.3 mm wide, obtuse, tapering distinctly to a 2 mm long stalk, convex above, shallowly keeled beneath and with 2 stomatal bands of 4–6 lines each; cones oval-oblong, 3.5–6 cm long, 2–2.5 cm wide, violet when young, light brown when ripe, scales oval and auriculate, seeds 4 mm long, with 3–4 large glands and a 7 mm long wing. USA; California and Nevada. z6

T. diversifolia (Maxim.) Mast. North Japanese Hemlock. A tree in its habitat, to 25 m, but often only a shrub in cultivation, crown narrowly conical, young shoots short pubescent, yellow or red-brown, buds dark brown to nearly carmine, the terminal bud pear-shaped, thickened at the apical end, very truncate at the apex; needles very densely arranged, linear-oblong, usually slightly broader at the apex, 5–15 mm long, to 2.4 mm wide, dark green above and very glossy, furrowed, with 2 chalk-white stomatal bands beneath, each with 8–10 lines; cones nearly sessile, ovate, 2 cm long, scales oval, slightly emarginate, glossy, seeds short winged. CBI 1: 66; FTs 81; DJ 535; KIF 1: 38; CCE 496, 497 (= *T. sieboldii nana* Carr.). Japan. 1861. The most frost hardy and wind tolerant species; tolerates semishade. Cultivated in the Moscow Botanic Garden. Plate 145, 147, 152; Fig. 223. z5

'**Nana**'. Dwarf form. Like the species, tolerant of extremely cold or warm sites. Selection of the Jeddeloh Nursery, W. Germany (1970).

T. dumosa (D. Don) Eichler. Himalayan Hemlock. Tree, to 40 m in its habitat, branches outspread, twigs nodding, often only a shrub in cultivation (where present and hardy!), young shoots light brown, short pubescent, buds globose, pubescent; needles densely arranged, nearly 2 ranked, 15–30 mm long, gradually tapering from the base to the apex, margins dentate, apex acute and reflexed, nearly silver-white beneath, margins scarcely green; cones sessile, ovate, 18–25 mm long, scales circular, striped. H. Al. 180 (H); CBI 1: 63; FTs 51 (= *T. brunoniana* [Wall.] Carr.). Himalaya, Nepal, in the mountains at 2500–3500 m. Plate 144; Fig. 211. z9

T. formosana Hayata. A tree in its habitat, to 50 m, trunk to 2 m in diameter, bark gray, furrowed, young shoots light yellowish, later gray-yellow, pubescent in the furrows, buds ovate to nearly globose, acute or obtuse; needles linear, 15–25 mm long, 2–3 mm wide, entire, apexes rounded or emarginate; cones ovate, 15–25 mm long scales nearly circular, glossy yellowish-brown, margin irregularly finely serrate, seeds with 7 mm long wings. LWT 11; LT 40; FTs 87 (= *T. chinensis* var. *formosana* [Hayata] Li & Keng). China, in the southwest, east and center, also in Taiwan. 1905. Fig. 222. z9

T. forrestii Downie. Resembling *T. chinensis*, but differing as follows: young shoots brown to reddish-brown, short pubescent; needles 10–25 mm long, 2 mm wide, apex crenate, otherwise entire, greenish beneath, stomatal bands very pale; cones short stalked, ovate to more oblong, 25–30 mm long, seed scales nearly circular, somewhat wider than long, 12 mm long,

Fig. 222. *Tsuga formosana* (from Liu)

yellowish to light yellow-brown, the basal, covered portion densely pubescent, seeds 3 mm long, wings 7 mm long. FTs 91. China; Yunnan. z8–9

T. heterophylla (Raf.) Sarg. Western American Hemlock. Tall tree, 30–60 m high, trunk diameter 1.2 m to occasionally 2 m, bark rather thick, red-brown, crown narrowly conical, peak with a very long, nearly flagellate terminal shoot with very short, lateral branches spreading nearly horizontally, tips nodding, young twigs yellow-brown at first, later dark brown, long shaggy and persistently pubescent, buds ovate to globose, small, pubescent, needles usually loosely arranged, linear, 5–20 mm long, margins finely dentate, apex obtuse-rounded and never emarginate, glossy dark green and furrowed above, with 2 white stomatal bands beneath, each with 7–8 lines, the green margin quite narrow; cones sessile, oblong, 20–25 mm long, scales obovate, longer than wide, entire, seeds 2–3 mm long, wings 4–6 mm long. SPa 34; CBI 1: 67; FTs 97; CCE 498–500. Western North America from Alaska to California, in the coastal region. A very fast growing, attractive tree, hardy but only for regions with high soil and air moisture; out of the wind. Plate 146; Fig. 219. z6

'Argenteovariegata'. Shoots slightly white pulverulent when young. SN 317 (H). 1909. (VR)

'Conica'. Dwarf form, to 3 m high (possibly higher), broadly ovate, very densely branched, twigs ascending, tips nodding; needles nearly like the type. OCC 468 (H); KN 412 (H). Originated from seed around 1920 in the Von Gimborn Pinetum at Doorn, Holland. Very attractive form. Plate 146.

'Dumosa'. Bushy dwarf form, 60 cm high in 10 years, branches outspread, stiff, shoots short, stiff; likewise the young shoots; needles 12–15 mm long, around 2 mm wide, deep green. Discovered in 1934 in the Bijvoet Nursery in Oosterbeck, Holland

T. × jeffreyi (Henry) Henry (*T. heterophylla* × *T. mertensiana*). Small tree, very densely branched, branches ascending-outspread, buds acutely ovate; needles outspread to all sides, like *T. mertensiana*, but smaller and distinctly greenish, margins finely dentate on the apical half, flat above, distinctly furrowed to the middle, apex with short stomatal lines, 2 stomatal bands beneath for the entire length. CBI 4: 75; FTs 107 (= *T. pattoniana* var. *jeffreyi* Henry). Occurs naturally in the vicinity of the parents. Plate 144. (R) z6

T. longibracteata Cheng. Tree, to 10 m high, young shoots yellowish-brown, later gray, glabrous or scattered pubescent, buds acutely ovate, 2–4 mm long, about 2 mm wide, scales ovate, tightly appressed, glossy brown, margin somewhat fimbriate; needles linear, 11 to 22 mm long, 1–2 mm wide, entire, acute, light green beneath, with stomatal lines on both sides, petiole 1.5 mm long, twisted; cones short stalked, ovate to somewhat more oblong, 20–30 mm long, to 20 mm thick, scales usually nearly rhombic, 10–15 mm long, 10–13 mm wide, auriculate, lightly pubescent and striped, bract scales nearly spathulate, about 8 mm long, narrow at the base, apex broad and acute, seeds 4 mm long, ings 6 mm long. FTs 111. China; Kweichow Province. z6

T. mertensiana (Bong) Carr. Mountain, Black Hemlock. Tree, 10–30 m high, occasionally taller in its habitat, crown narrowly conical, branches and twigs thin and nodding, young shoots red-brown, pubescent in the first 2 years, buds acutely ovate; needles all radially arranged around the shoot (!); linear, 10–20 mm long, 1–1.2 mm wide, obtuse, convex above and also often keeled, nearly round in cross section, entire, with stomatal lines on both sides, gray-green to silver-white; cones sessile, oblong to cylindrical, somewhat narrowed at both ends, 5–8 cm long, blue-purple when young, scales thin, wider than long, pubescent, irregularly toothed on the margin, seeds 5 mm long, wings 9 mm long. FTs 103; SPa 35; BFN 82; CCE 500–502 (= *T. pattoniana* [Jeffr.] Engelm.; *T. hookeriana* Carr.). Western N. America, from southern Alaska to northern Montana, Idaho and California in the mountains and sporadically along the coast. 1854. Easily distinguished from all the other species by the radially arranged, blue-green to nearly silver-blue needles. Plate 130; Fig. 221. z5

'Argentea'. Needles more silvery, otherwise like the species. SN 319 (H) (= *T. mertensiana* var. *argentea* [Beissn.] Sudw.). Known since 1891.

'Blue Star'. Conspicuously blue needled form. CCE 504. Selected by L. Konijn, Reeuwijk, Holland; before 1965.

'Glauca'. Selection with conspicuously blue-green needles, very slow growing.

'Glauca Fastigiata'

T. patens Downie. Similar to *T. chinensis* but differing as follows: young twigs yellow-brown, short haired, buds globose, large, glabrous; needles 7–21 mm long, 2–2.5 mm wide, the longer ones dentate on the apical third, occasionally somewhat whitish beneath, crenate at the apex; cones ovate, 25 mm long, seed scales like those of *T. chinensis*, but opening wide when ripe (!), developing nearly a right angle with the axis, seed 3 mm long, wing 5 mm. FTs 115. China; W. Hupeh. Found by E. H. Wilson in 1907. z6

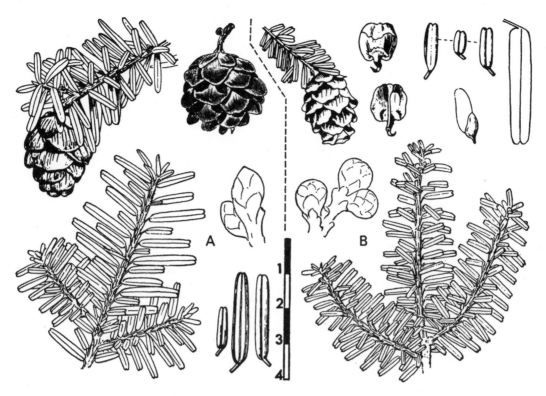

Fig. 223. Left *Tsuga sieboldii, T. diversifolia* at right
(from Clinton-Baker, Fitschen, Shirasawa)

T. sieboldii Carr. Southern Japanese Hemlock. Tree, to 30 m high, crown conical to ovate, often only a shrub or small tree in cultivation, branches spreading horizontally, branch tips nodding, young twigs light brown, glabrous, buds ovate, obtuse acuminate, yellow-brown or reddish-yellow; needles not distinctly 2 ranked, rather loosely arranged, linear, evenly wide, 6–22 mm long, 3 mm wide, emarginate, entire, with 2 slightly conspicuous stomatal bands beneath; cones stalked, oval, 20–25 mm long, seed scales rather circular, glossy brown, seeds 4 mm long, wings 4 mm long, whitish. SN 104 (H); CBI 1: 68 (H); FTs 121; KIF 1: 38 (= *T. aragi* Koehne). S. Japan; moist mountain forests. 1850. Quite hardy but particular as   to growing sites. Frequently confused with *T. diversifolia*, but easily distinguished by the pubescent young shoots and white undersides of the needles. Plate 145; Fig. 223. z6

T. tschekiangensis Flous. Not completely known, closely related to *T. chinensis*, but differing as follows: young shoots red-brown, short pubescent, buds ovate or more cylindrical, 2.5–3.5 mm long, 2 mm wide, scales not as numerous; needles linear, straight, entire, furrowed for the entire length above, 6–12 mm long, 2 mm wide, glossy dark green above, with 2 stomatal bands beneath, each with 5–6 lines, crenate on the apex; cones oval, 2 cm long and about as wide, seed scales circular, base cuneate with 2 small auricles, finely striped, seeds 3.5

mm long, wings about 6 mm. FTs 125. China; S. Chekiang Province.

T. yunnanensis (Franch.) Pritz. Tree, to 30 m, branches outspread, young shoots yellow-brown or reddish-gray, hispid, buds ovate, very obtuse, short haired, lateral buds globose; needles linear, 10–18 mm long, 1.5 mm wide, finely dentate, apex not emarginate, with 2 white stomatal bands beneath; cones ovate, 12–23 mm long, with only a few scales, these nearly circular, apical margins slightly reflexed, dull (!), with fine longitudinal stripes, thin, seeds 4 mm, wings 4 mm long. CBI 4: 76; FTs 131 (= *T. dura* Downie; *T. intermedia* Hand.-Mazz.). W. China, Yunnan; N. Burma. 1906. Growing in the Arboretum at Les Barres, France. Fig. 221. (VR) z6?

Lit. Cheng, W.-C.: A new *Tsuga* from southwestern China. Contrib. Biol. Lab. Sci. Soc. China **7**, 1–3, 1932. ● Downie, D. G.: Chinese Species of *Tsuga*. Notes Bot. Gard. Edinburgh **14**, 13–19, 1923. ● Fitschen, J.: Die Gattung *Tsuga*. Mitt. Deutsch. Dendrol. Ges. 1929, 1–12. ● Flous, F.: Révision du genre *Tsuga*. Extr. Bull. Soc. Hist. Nat. Toulouse **71**, 315–340, 1936. ● Corley, R. S.: Varieties of *Tsuga canadensis*. Gard. Chron. 1963 (II), 396–397. ● Wyman, D.: Widely recognized as most graceful of Conifers, Hemlock Species few. Am. Nurseryman from 12/1/1960, 12–13, 48–49. ● Lewis, Cl. E.: Landscaping with Hemlocks; parts 1–3. Am. Nurseryman, June-Aug. 1961. ● Fordham, A. J.: Four Fathers of the Sargent Hemlock. Am. Nurseryman of 12/15/ 1962, **9**, 80–81.

WIDDRINGTONIA Endl.—CUPRESSACEAE

Evergreen trees or shrubs, similar to *Callitris* in appearance, but differing in the smaller, paired leaves and the (normally) 4 scaled cones; leaves in 2 types; juvenile foliage needle-like and spirally arranged, linear, long, flat and acute; scale-like and appressed on older plants (except on long shoots), opposite or alternate, but never in whorls of 3 or 4, occasionally intermediate on long shoots, but these also occasionally with juvenile leaves, scale leaves and transition forms; monoecious; male flowers small, 4 mm long, terminally arranged on short shoots, sessile; female flowers axillary, short stalked or sessile, on elongated shoots, solitary or in clusters; scales normally 4, of equal size and whorled, occasionally with 5 or 6 scales, corky-leathery, with several ovules at the base of each scale; ripe cones oval to nearly globose, 1.3–2.5 cm thick, opening at the apex, with 4 very thick, woody valves, exterior smooth warty, often with a thick prominence on the tip of each scale; seeds ovate or triangular; cotyledons 3, green, needle form.—3 species in S. and SE. Africa. Range map Fig. 218.

Widdringtonia cedarbergensis Marsh. Tree, normally 5–7 m high, occasionally to 20 m, then with a trunk diameter of 2 m, crown conical when young, spreading widely with age, bark of young trees reddish-gray, thin, fibrous, exfoliating in scales; needles in 2 types: juvenile leaves on seedlings and young plants outspread, needle-like, 1–2 cm long, 1–2 mm wide, mature leaves scale-like, appressed, ovate, 2–4 mm long, usually distinctly decussate, semicircular in cross section, adnate at the base, the distinct portion of the leaf often much shorter than the adnate part; cones nearly globose, about 2.5 cm wide, usually composed of 4 (seldom 5–6) woody valves, these rough, with regularly distributed papillae on the valve margins, seeds ovate, indistinctly winged, triangular; cotyledons to 35 mm long and 5 mm wide. FSA 11; CCE 504. S. Africa, Cape Province, Cedarberg Mts., in rocky areas between 1000 and 1600 m. Plate 155; Fig. 224.

W. cupressoides (L.) Endl. Shrub or tree, to 9 m high, to 50 m high in the tropics and then with a trunk diameter of 2 m, crown conical when young, but spreading widely with age, bark of young trees reddish-gray, thin, fibrous, scaly exfoliating; needles in 2 types: juvenile leaves on seedlings and young plants needle-like, 1–2 cm long, 1–2 mm wide, mature leaves scale-like, appressed, narrow-oblong, often not exactly opposite, nearly triangular in cross section, adnate at the base, the distinct and appressed portions often equally long; cones usually composed of 4 woody valves, these smooth or rugose, but not papillate on the valve margin, or if resinous, then irregular, seeds ovate, distinctly winged, somewhat flattened, outline with the wing oblong-obovate, wings truncate at the apex; cotyledons 20–25 mm long, 2 mm wide. CBI 4: 77; FSA 11; CCE 504 (= *W. whytei* Rendle; *W. dracomontana* Stapf.; *W. nodiflora* [L.] Powrie). S. Africa; Transvaal, Natal, Cape Province. Since there are really no significant characteristics distinguishing the 3 "species" *W. cupressoides*, *W. whytei* and *W. dracomontana*, the latter 2 should be considered synonyms of the former. Plate 153–155; Fig. 224, 225 (as *W. whytei*). z6

W. schwarzii (Marloth) Mast. Tree, usually 17 to 26 m high, by exception to 40 m high and then with a trunk diameter of 5 m, crown conical, usually not spreading with age (!), bark of younger trees reddish-gray, thin, fibrous, exfoliating in scales; needles in 2 types: juvenile foliage on seedlings and young plants needle form, outspread, 1–2 cm long and to 2 mm wide, mature leaves scale form, appressed, ovate, usually distinctly decussate, semicircular in cross section, adnate at the base, the distinct portion often much shorter than the adnate portion; ripe cones usually 4 valvate, the valves rough from the regularly arranged papillae on the valve margin, seeds ovate, distinctly winged, somewhat flattened, having an oblong-obovate outline with the wing, wings truncate at the apex; cotyledons 20–25 mm long, 2 mm wide. FSA 11. S. Africa, Cape Province; Willowmore District, in the mountains. Plate 155; Fig. 224. z6

Lit. Masters, M.T.: Notes on the genus *Widdringtonia*. Jour. Linn. Soc. **37**, 267–274, 1905 ● Marsh, J. A.: *Widdringtonia*. In: Codd/de Winter/Rycroft, Flora of Southern Africa, vol. 1, 44–48, 1966.

Key to the species

	mature needles (cross section)	juvenile leaves		valves of the cones	seeds
		length (m)	width (m)		
W. cupressoides		20–25	2	smooth to rugose	ovate, distinctly winged
W. cedarbergensis		35	5	regularly papillate	indistinctly winged
W. schwarzii		20–25	2	regularly papillate	flattened, distinctly winged

Fig. 224. **Widddringtonia.** A. *W. cedarbergensis;* B. *W. whytei;* C. *W. schwarzii*
(from J. A. Marsh, Bailey, Sinn; C. Original)

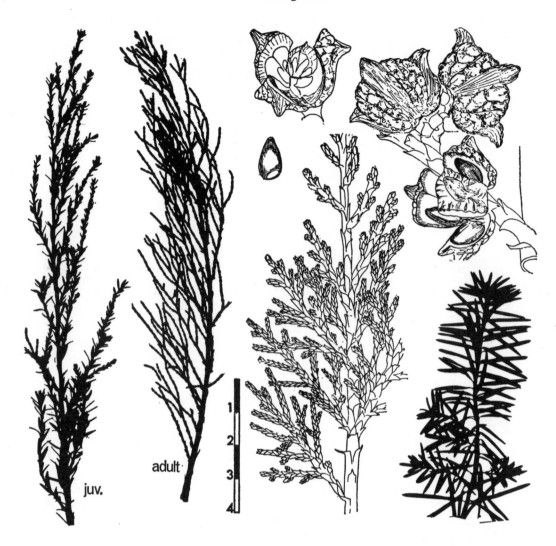

Fig. 225. *Widdringtonia cupressoides.*
The black twig is original, a young seedling plant is far right

Alphabetical Reference to the Botanical Terminology

To facilitate the use of this book by readers of all language groups, the most frequently used botanical terms have been arranged in alphabetical order. The word is then followed by the scientific (generally Latin, but occasionally Greek) word and then by the equivalent terms in German, French and Dutch.

English	Latin	German	French	Dutch
abscising	caducus	hinfällig	caduc	afvallend
achene	achenium	Nüsschen	achaine, akène	nootje
acrodrome	acrodromus	spitzläufig (Nerven)	acrodrome	acrodroom
acuminate	acuminatus	lang zugespitzt	terminé en queue	lang toegespitst
acute	acutus	spitz	aigu	spits
adult leaves	folia adulta	Altersblätter	feuilles adultes	ouderdomsbladeren
albumen	albúmen	Eiweiss	albumen	eiwit
alternate	alternans	wechselständig	alterne	afwisselend
alternate (of leaves)	alternifolius	—(von Blättern)	à feuilles alternes	afwisselend
angiosperms	angiospermae	Bedecktsamer	angiospermes	bedektzadigen
angle of nerves		Nervenwinkel	aisselle des nerves	nerfaksel
anther	anthera	Staubbeutel	anthère	helmknop
apex, top	apex	Blattspitze	pointe	top
apiculate	apiculatus	fein zugespitzt	apiculé	puntig
applanate	applanatus	abgeflacht	aplati	afgeplat
appressed	adpressus	angedrückt	appressé	aangedrukt
arrow-headed	sagittatus	pfeilförmig	sagitté	pijlvormig
ascending	ascendens	aufsteigend	ascendent	opstijgend
auriculate (eared)	auriculatus	geöhrt	muni d'oreillettes	geoord
awn	arista	Granne	arête	baard (van gras)
awned	aristatus	grannig	aristé	met baard (van gras)
axillary	axillaris	achselständig, seitenständig	axillaire	okselstandig
bark	cortex	Rinde, Borke	écorce	bast
bearded	barbatus	Achselbart	barbé	okselbaard
berry	bacca	Beere	baie	bes
biennial	biennis	zweijährig	bisannuel	tweejarig
bilabiate	bilambatus	zweilippig	bilabié	tweelippig
blade	lamina	Blattspreite	limbe	bladschijf
blunt	obtusus	stumpf	obtusé	stomp
boat-shaped	navicularis	kahnförmig	naviculaire	bootvormig
brachidodrome	brachidodromus	schlingenläufig (Nerven)	brachidodrome	brachidodroom
bract	bractea	Hochblatt	bractée	schutblad
branch	ramus	Ast	branche	tak
branchlet	ramellus	Zweiglein	petite branche	twijgje
bristle	seta	Borste	soie	borstel
bristle-pointed	setosus	borstig	seteux	borstelig
bud	gemma	Knospe	bourgeon	knop
bullate	bullatus	aufgetrieben, blasig	boursoufflé, bullé	opgeblazen
calyx	calyx	Kelch	calice	kelk
campanulate (bell-shaped)	campanulatus	glockig	campanulé	klokvormig
camptodrome	camptodromus	bogenläufig (Nerven)	camptodrome	camptodroom
capitula (head)	capitulum	Köpfchen	capitule	hoofdje

English	Latin	German	French	Dutch
capsule	capsula	Kapsel	capsule	doos
carpel	carpellum	Fruchtblatt	carpelle	vruchtblad
catkin	amentum	Kätzchen	chaton	katje
channeled	canaliculatus	rinnenförmig	canaliculé	gootvormig
ciliate	ciliatus	gewimpert	cilié	gewimperd
cirrhous	cirrhus	Wickelranke	vrille	rank
clavate	clavatus	keulenförmig	claviforme	knodsvormig
claw	unguis	Nagel	onglet	nagel
clawed	unguiculatus	genagelt	onguicule	genageld
climbing	scandens	kletternd, klimmend	grimpant	klimmend
clustered	fasciculatus	büschelig	fasciculaire	gebundeld
coarse	grossus	grob	grossier	grof
compound	compositus	zusammengesetzt	composé	samengesteld
compressed	compressus	zusammengedrängt	comprimé	samengedrukt
concave	concavus	vertieft	concave	uitgehold
conduplicate	conduplicatus	zusammengefaltet	condupliqué	samengevouwen
connate	connatus	verwachsen	conné	vergroeid
connective	connectivum	Mittelband	connectif	konnektief
convex	convexus	gewölbt	convexe	gewelfd
convolute	convolutus	übergerollt	convoluté	opgerold
cordate	cordatus, cordiformis	herzförmig	cordé, cordiforme	hartvormig
corky	suberosus	korkig	subéreux, liégeux	kurkachtig
corolla	corolla	Blumenkrone	corolle	bloemkroon
corymb	corymbus	Doldentraube	corymbe	schermtros
cotyledon	cotyledon	Keimblatt	cotyledon	kiemblad
craspedrome	craspedromus	randläufig (Nerven)	craspedrome	craspedroom
creeping	repens, reptans	kriechend	rampant	kruipend
crenate	crenatus	gekerbt	crénelé	gekarteld
crescent-shaped	lunatus	mondförmig	luniforme	halvemaanvormig
crispate	crispus	gekraust	crispé, ondulé	gekroesd
cross-section	sectio transversa	Querschnitt	section transversale	dwarse doorsnede
cross-wise	decussatus	kreuzständig	décussé	kruisgewijs
crown	corona, cacumen	Krone	couronne	kroon
cuneate (wedge-shaped)	cuneatus	keilförmig	en forme de coin	wigvormig
cupulate (cup-shaped)	cupulaeformis	becherförmig	cupuliforme	bekervormig
cupule	cupula	Fruchtbecher	cupule	vruchtbeker
cuspidate	cuspidatus	feinspitz	cuspidé	fijn toegespitst
cyme	cyma	Scheinquirl, Trugdolde	cime, cyme	bijscherm, tuil
deciduous	deciduus	abfallend	caduc	afvallend
decumbent	decumbens	liegend	décombant	liggend
decurrent	decurrens	herablaufend	decurrent	aflopend
decussate (deeply cut)	incisus	eingeschnitten	incisé	ingesneden
deflexed	declinatus	niedergebogen	déliné	neergebogen
delicate	gracilis	zierlich	gracieux	sierlijk
dentate	dentatus	gezähnt	denté	getand
digitate	digitatus	gefingert	digité	vingervormig
dioecious	dioecus, dioicus	zweihäusig	dioique	tweehuizig
distichous (2 ranked)	distichus	zweizeilig	distique	tweerijig
double	bi-, plenus (of flowers)	doppelt, gefüllt	double	dubbel-, gevuld

English	Latin	German	French	Dutch
downy	pubescens	weichhaarig	pubescent	zachtharig
drooping	cernuus	übergebogen	penché	overgebogen
drupe	drupa	Steinfrucht	drupe	steenvrucht
dull	opacus	matt	mat	mate, dof
elliptic	ovalis	oval	elliptique	ovaal, elliptisch
elliptical	ellipticus	elliptisch	elliptique	elliptisch
emarginate	emarginatus	ausgerandet	émarginé	uitgerand
enclosed/covered	vestitus	bedeckt	couvert	bedekt
entire	integer, -rimus	ganzrandig	entier	gaafrandig
epigynous	epigynus	unterständig	épigyne	onderstandig
equitant	amplex	umfassend	amplexe	omvattend
evergreen	sempervirens	immergrun	toujours vert	groenblijvend
exserted	exsertus	vorragend	saillant	eruit stekend
falcate	falcatus	sichelförmig	en forme de faux	sikkelvormig
fascicle	fasciculus	Büschel	fascicule	bundel
fastigiate	fastigiatus	fastigiat	fastigié	fastigiaat
female flower (pistillate)	flos femineus	Stempelblüte	fleur féminin	stamperbloem
filament	filamentum	Faden	filet	helmdraad
fissured	fissura	rissig	fissurer	spleet, scheur
flagellate (whip-formed)	flagellaris	peitschenartig	flagellaire	zweepvormig
flat, plain	planus	eben, flach	plat	vlak, glad, ondiep
flexuose	flexuosus	hin und hergebogen	flexueux	zigzag gebogen
floccose	floccosus	flockig-filzig	floconneux	vlokkig, viltig
follicle	folliculus	Balgfrucht	follicule	
fragrant	odoratus	duftend	odorant	geurend
fringed	fimbriatus	gefranst	fimbrié	met franjes
fruit	fructus	Frucht	fruit	vrucht
funnelform	infundibuliformis	trichterförmig	infundibulé	trechtervormig
furrowed	sulcatus	gefurcht	silloné	gegroefd
gaping	ringens	rachenblütig	fleur en gueule	mondvormig
geniculate	geniculatus	geknickt	genouillé	geknikt
genus	genus	Gattung	genre	geslacht
glabrous	glaber	kahl	glabre	kaal
gland	glans	Drüse	gland	klier
glandulary-hairy	glanduloso-pubescens	drüsenhaarig	glanduleux-pubescent	klierachtig behaard
glaucous	glaucus	bereift	pruineaux	berijpt
globose	globosus	kugelig	globeux	bolvormig
glossy	lucidus, nitidus	glänzend	brillant, luisant	glanzend
gymnosperms	gymnospermae	Nacktsamer	gymnospermes	naaktzadigen
habit	habitus	Habitus, Gestalt	forme	habitus
hair-covering	indumentum	Behaarung	pubescence	beharing
hairy	pilosus	behaart	pileux	behaard
hastate	hastatus	spiessförmig	hasté	spiesformig
herbaceous	herbaceus	krautartig, krautig	herbacé	kruidachtig
hermaphrodite	hermaphroditus	zwittrig	hermaphrodite	hermafrodiet
hilum	hilum	Nabel	hile	navel
hirsute	hirsutus	rauhhaarig	hirsute	ruwharig
hispid	hispidus	steifhaarig	hispide	stijfharig
husk	siliqua	Schote	silique	hauw
hypanthium	hypanthium	Blütenboden	hypanthium	bloembodem
hypogynous	hypogynus	oberständig	hypogyne	bovenstandig

English	Latin	German	French	Dutch
imbricate	imbricatus	dachziegelig	imbriqué	dakpansgewijze
incised	incisus	eingeschnitten	incisé	ingesneden
inflorescence	inflorescentia	Blütenstand	inflorescence	bloeiwijze
involucre	involucrum	Hüllkelch	involucre	omwindsel
involute (rolled inward)	involutus	eingerollt	enroulé	ingerold
irregular	irregularis	unregelmässig	irregulier	onregelmatig
jointed	articulatus	gegliedert	articulé	geleed
juvenile leaves	folia juvenilia	Jugendblätter	feuilles juveniles	jeugdbladeren
keeled	carinatus	gekielt	caréné	gekield
kernel, stone	nucleus	Kern	noyeau	kern
kidney-shaped	reniformis	nierenförmig	en forme de rein	niervormig
lanceolate	lanceatus, lanceolatus	lanzenförmig, lanzettlich	lancéolé	lancetvormig
large, broad	latus	breit	large	breed
latex	latex	Milchsaft	laiteux	melksap
leaf	folium	Blatt	feuille	blad
leaf base	basis	Blattgrund	base de feuille	bladvoet
leaf cushion	pulvinus	Blattkissen, Blattpolster	coussinet foliaire	bladkussen
leaf margin	margo	Blattrand	contour de feuille	bladrand
leaf scar	cicatricula	Blattnarbe	cicatrice foliaire	bladmerk
leaflet	foliolum	Blättchen	foliole	blaadje
leathery	coriaceus	lederartig	coriace	leerachtig
leprous	lepidisotus	schülferschuppig	lepidote	schubbig
ligulate	ligula	Zungenblüte	ligule	tongetje
limb	limbus	Saum	limbe	zoom, rand
linear	linearis	linealisch	linéaire	lijnvormig
lobe, loculicidal	loba	Lappen	lobe	lob
lobed	lobatus	gelappt	lobé	gelobd
locule (chamber of ovary)	loculum	Fach	loge	hok
long shoot		Langtrieb	rameau longue	langlot
male flower (staminate)	flos masculus	Staubblüte	fleur mêle	meeldraadbloem
mane-like	jubatus	mähnenartig	criniforme	manenvormig
mealy	farinosus	mehlig	farineux	melig
monoecious	monoecus	einhäusig	monoique	eenhuizig
mucronate	mucronatus	stachelspitz	mucroné	gepunt
mucronulate	mucronulatus	stachelspitzig	mucronulé	fijn gepunt
naked	nudis	nackt	nu	naakt
narrow	angustus	schmal	étroit	smal
needle-form	acerosus	nadelförmig	acéré	naaldvormig
nodding	nutans	überhängend	incliné	overhangend
not shining	opacus	glanzlos	opaque	mat, dof
nut	nux	Nuss	noix	noot
obcordate	obcordatus	obcordat, verkehrt herzförmig	obcordate	omgekeerd hartvormig
oblanceolate	oblanceolatus	oblanzettlich	oblancéolé	omgekeerd lancetvormig
oblate	oblatus	oblat	oblate	oblaat
oblique	obliquus	schief	oblique	scheef
oblong	oblongus	länglich	oblong	langwerpig
obovate	obovatus	obovat, verkehrt eiförmig	obovate	omgekeerd eirond, eivormig

English	Latin	German	French	Dutch
obvolute	obvolutus	halbumfassend	obvoluté	halfomvattend
opposite (of foliage)	oppositus, oppositifolius	gegenständig (bei Blättern)	opposé	tegenoverstaand
orbiculate	orbicularis	kreisrund	corbiculaire	cirkelrond
outspread	patulus	abstehend	étendre	afstaan
ovary	ovarium	Fruchtknoten	ovaire	vruchtbeginsel
ovate	ovatus, ovulum	eiförmig, eirund	ovate	eirond, eivormig
ovule	ovulum	samenanlage	ovule	eitje
palmate	palmatus	handförmig, handteilig	palmé	handdelig, handvormig
panicle	panicula	Rispe	panicule	pluim
papilionaceus (butterfly-like)	papilionaceus	schmetterlingsförmig	papilionacé	vlinderbloemig
papilla	papilla	warze	papille	wratachtig
pappus	pappus	Haarkelch	aigrette	zaadpluis
pectinate	pectinatus	kammförmig	pectiné	kamvormig
pedate	pedatus	fussförmig	pedatiforme	voetvormig
pedicel	pediculus	stielchen	pedicelle	steeltje
peduncle	pedunculus	Blütenstiel	pedoncule	bloemsteel
pedunculate	pedunculatus	gestielt (Blüte)	pédonculé	gesteeld
peltate	peltatus	schildförmig	pelté	schildvormig
pendulous (weeping)	pendulus	hängend	pendant	hangend
penniform	pinnatiformis	fiederförmig	penniforme	veervormig
perfoliate	perfoliatus	durchwachsen	perfolié	doorgroeid
perianth	perianthemum	Blütenhülle, Perigon	périanthe	bloembekleedsel
perigynous	perigynus	mittelständig	périgyne	halfonderstandig
petal	petalum	Blütenblatt	pétale	kroonblad
petiole	petiolus	Blattstiel	pétiole	bladsteel
petioled	petiolatus	gestielt (Blatt)	petiolé	gesteeld
phylloclades	phyllocladium			
phyllode	phyllodium	Phyllodium	foliace	phyllodium
phyllotaxis	Phyllotaxis	Blattstellung	phyllotaxis	bladstand
pinnately cleft	pinnatifidus	fiederspaltig	pennatifide	veerspletig
pinnately partite	pinnatipartitus	fiederteilig	pennatipartite	veerdelig
pinnatisect	pinnatisectus	fiederschnittig	pinnatiséqué	veervormig ingesneden
pistil	pistillum	Stempel	pistil	stamper
pistillate (see: female flower)				
pith	medulla	Mark	moelle	merg
plaited	plicatus	gefaltet	plié	gevouwen
pod	legumen	Hülse	gousse	peul
poisonous	venenatus	giftig	vénéneux	vergiftig
pollen	pollen	Blütenstaub	pollen	stuifmeel
polygamous	polygamus	vielehig	polygame	polygaam
prickle	acus	Stachel	aiguillon	stekel
prickly	aculeatus	stachelig	muni d'aiguillons	stekelig
procumbent	procumbens	niederliegend	tracant	neerliggend
prostrate	prostratus	niedergestreckt	couché	neerliggend
pruinose	pruinosus	bereift	pruineux	berijpt
pubescent	pubescens	feinhaarig	pubescent	fijn behaard
pulverulent	pulverulentus	bepudert, bestäubt	pulverulent	bepoederd, bestoven
punctate (dotted)	punctatus	punktiert	ponctué	gestippeld

English	Latin	German	French	Dutch
pungent	pungens	stechend	piquant	stekend
quadrangular	quadrangulatus	vierkantig	à quatre angles	vierhoekig
raceme	racemus	traube	grappe	tros
racemose	racemosus	traubig	en grappe	trosvormig
radiate	radiatus	strahlig	radiaire	radiaal
receptacle	receptaculum	Blütenboden	receptacle	bloembodem
reflexed	reflexus	zurückgebogen	re1flechi	teruggeslagen
regular	regularis	regelmässig	régulaire	regelmatig
resinous	resinosus	harzig	résineux	harsachtig
reticulate	reticulatus	netznervig	reticulé	netvormig
retuse	retusus	eingedrückt	émoussé	ingedrukt
revolute	revolutus	zurückgerollt	revoluté	teruggerold
rhizome	rhizoma	Wurzelstock	rhizome	wortelstok
rhombic	rhombicus	rautenförmig (=rhombisch)	rhombique	ruitvormig
rooting	radicans	wurzelnd	radicant	wortelend
rotate (wheel-shaped)	rotatus	radförmig	rotacé	radvormig
rough	asper	rauh	rude	ruw
rounded	rotundatus	abgerundet	arrondi	afgerond
roundish	suborbiculatus	rundlich	arrondi	afgerond
rugose	rugosus	runzelig	rugueux	gerimpeld
runner	sobol, stolon	Ausläufer, Sprössling	drageon, stolon	uitloper, wortelspruit
salver-shaped	hypocraterimorphus	stieltellerförmig	hypocratériforme	schenkbladvormig
samara	samara	Flügelfrucht	samare	gevleugeld nootje
scabrous	scaber	scharf	scabre	ruw
scaly	squama	Schuppe	squameux	schub
scattered	sparsifolius	zerstreut (Blättern)	espacé	verspreid
schizocarp	schizocarpium	Spaltfrucht	schizocarpe	splitvrucht
scion	vimen, virga	Rute	verger, scion	twijg, roede
seed	semen	Samen	graine, semence	zaad
semidouble	semiplenus	halbgefüllt	demi-double	half gevuld
semi-terete	semiteres	halbrund	demi-cylindrique	halfrond
sepals	sepala	Kelchblätter	sépales	kelkbladen
serrate	serratus	gesägt	serré	gezaagd
serrulate	serrulatus	feingesägt	serrulé	fijn gezaagd
sessile	sessilis	sitzend	sessile	zittend
shaggy	villosus	zottig behaart	poilu	donzig
shell	epicarpium	Schale	écorce	schil van vrucht opeen gehoopt
shoot	ramulus	Trieb	pousse	scheut
short branch		Kurztrieb	rameau court	kortlot
shrub	frutex	Strauch	arbuste, arbrisseau	struik, heester
silky	sericeus	seidenhaarig	soyeux	zijdeachtig
simple	simplex	einfach	simple	enkelvoudig
sinuate	sinuatus	gebuchtet	sinué	bochtig
slightly drooping	cernuus	nickend	penché	knikkend
smooth	laevis	glatt	lisse	glad
solitary	solitaris	einzelstehend	solitaire	alleenstaand
spathulate	spathuliformis	spatelförmig	spatulé	spatelvormig
species	species (sp)	Art	espèce	soort
spike	spica	Ähre	épi	aar
spindle, rachis	rhachis, rachis	Spindel	fuseau	spil

English	Latin	German	French	Dutch
spiral	spiralis	schraubig	spiralé	spiraalvormig
spur	crus	Sporn	éperon	spoor
stamen	stamen	Staubblatt	1etamine	meeldraad
staminate (see: male flower)				
standard		Hochstamm	haute-tige	hoogstam
stellate	stellatus	sternhaarig	étoilé	sterharig
stem	culmus	Halm (Gramineae)	tige	halm
stem-clasping	amplexicaulis	stengelumfassend	amplexicaule	stengelomvattend
sticky	glutinosus, viscosus	klebrig	poisseux, visqueux	kleverig
stigma	stigma	Narbe	stigmate	stempel
stipule	stipula	Nebenblatt	stipule	steunblad
straggly	divaricatus	sparrig	divariqué	uitgespreid
strap-form	loratus	riemenförmig	loriculé	riemvormig
strap-shaped	loratus	bandförmig	loriculé	bandvormig
striated	striatus	gestreift	strié	gestreept
strict	strictus	straff	raide	opgaand
strigose	strigosus	striegelhaarig	à poils rudes	scherpharig
subspecies	subspecies (ssp)	Unterart	sous-espèce	ondersoort
subulate (awl-shaped)	subulatus	pfriemförmig	subulé	priemvormig
syncarp	syncarpium	Sammelfrucht	syncarpe	vruchten
tapering	attenuatus	verschmälert	attenue	versmald
terete	teres	stielrund	cylindrique	rolrond
terminal	terminalis	endständig	terminal	eindstandig
terminal bud		Endknospe	bourgeon terminal	eindknop
ternate	ternatus	dreizählig	terné	drietallig
tessellate	tessellatus	würfelnervig	tessellé	schaakbord-vormig
thorn	spina	Dorn	épine	doorn
thorny	spinosus	dornig	épineux	gedoornd
throat	faux	Schlund	gorge	keel
tomentose	tomentosus	filzig	tomenteux	viltig
tooth	dens	Zahn	dent	tand
toothed	dentatus	gezähnt	denté	getand
translucent	pellucidus	durchscheinend	pellucide	doorschijnend
triangular	triangularis, triangulatus	dreieckig, dreikantig	à trois angles, triangulaire	driehoekig, driekantig
trichoma	trichoma	Haare	trichome	beharing
trifoliate	trifoliatus	dreiblättrig	trifoliolé	driebladig
trioecious	trioecus	triözisch	trioique	driehuizig
truncate	truncatus	abgestutzt	tronqué	afgestompt
truncated	truncatus	gestutzt	tronqué	afgestompt
tube	tubus	Röhre	tube	buis
tubercled	tuberculatus	höckerig	tuberculeux	bultig
twig (secondary branches)	ramulus	Zweig	branche	twijg
twining	volubilis	windend	volubile	windend
twisted	tortus, tortuosus	gedreht	tortueux	gedraaid
two-edged	anceps	zweischneidig	à deux faces	tweezijdig
umbel	umbella	Dolde	ombelle	scherm
underside		Unterseite	face de dessous	onderzijde
undulate	undulatus	gewellt	ondulà	gegolfd
unisexual	unisexualis	eingeschlechtig	unisexuel	eenslachtig
upper side		Oberseite, oben	face de dessus	bovenzijde, boven

English	Latin	German	French	Dutch
upright	erectus	aufrecht	dréssé	oprecht
urceolate	urceolatus	krugförmig	urcéiforme	kruikvormig
v-valved	valvatus, -valvis	klappig	-valve	klepvormig
variety	varietas (var.)	Varietät	variété	varieeteit
velvety	holosericeus	samthaarig	velute	fluweelhaarig
viscid	viscidus	schmierig	viscide	kleverig
warty	verrucosus	warzig	verruqueux	wrattig
whorled	verticillatus	quirlig	verticillé	kransstandig
winged	alatus	geflügelt	ailé	gevleugeld
wintergreen	semipersistens	wintergrün	semi-persistant	wintergroen
woolly	lanatus, lanuginosus	wollhaarig, wollig	laineux, lanugineux	wollig, 'zachtharig

Outline of the Botanical Terms and their Meaning

This outline contains only those terms present in the descriptions of the conifers (including the Taxaceae and *Ginkgo*); they are arranged under the following headings: Habit, Stem, Leaves, Flowers, Cones, Seed, "Fruits", Seedlings and Other Technical Terms. The terms will be found under the most appropriate heading.

1. HABIT

Habit:	General impression of the tree or shrub.
conical = pyramidal:	Shaped like a cone, also narrowing from a circular base to a pointed top; the longitudinal section forms a triangle.
fastigiate:	Narrow, nearly columnar crown, all branches more or less parallel, usually developing a peak from many, nearly equally long branches, peak rounded.
columnar:	All branches and twigs either densely appressed to the stem or all erect, very short and nearly of equal length; apex acute.
umbrella-shaped:	A crown, in which the basal and middle branchlets die out leaving a distinctly umbrella-shaped crown (*Pinus pinea, Araucaria araucana, Pinus nigra*)
ovate:	A regular crown in which the diameter is widest below the middle.
globose:	About as high as wide.
flat-globose:	Wider than high.
divaricate:	Branches spreading in various directions.
pendulous:	General term for more or less downward growing branches or other parts.
shrubby:	When a main stem is absent.

1a) Stem, branch, crown and base

stem:	Is the elongated main axis, the side axes are the branches, these further divided are the twigs, the youngest of which are the new shoots.
on trees:	Erect, woody, normally single stemmed, occasionally multistemmed (*Thuja, Chamaecyparis*).
on shrubs:	The whole range from erect to prostrate, single to multistemmed.
crown:	The upper, branched portion of a tree.
basal roots:	Those supporting roots found at the base of the trunk (the actual roots are not described in this book).
knees (pneumatophores):	Root structures occurring on *Taxodium*, developing all around the base of the tree, especially when growing in standing water, and becoming up to 1 m high.

1b) Direction of Growth

erect:	growing vertically upward.
tightly, narrowly upright:	all branches conspicuously vertical.
straight:	growing straight as opposed to bowed.
drooping:	erect growing, tips bowed to horizontal.
nodding:	erect growing, tips bowed toward the ground.
deflexed:	erect at first, then bending in a wide arch toward the ground.
pendulous:	either the stem is vertical and the branches hang down or the stem grows obliquely upward and its branches hang like a mane (in many cases the branches are pendulous as a result of poor mechanical structure).
ascending:	growing horizontally at first, then inclined upward.
procumbent:	branches lying flat on the ground, not inclined upward.
or prostrate:	for example, some cultivars of *Picea abies* with branches growing densely over one another.
decumbent:	branches lying on the ground their entire length with only the tips inclined upward, not developing roots.

creeping:	branches lying on the ground, forming roots.
tortuous, twisted:	stem and branches more or less chaotically twisted.

1c) Covering of the stem and branches

smooth:	without depressions.
glabrous:	hairless and also not resinous.
resinous:	either with a resinous coating or with resinous lumps on the stem (such as *Abies, Pseudotsuga*).
striated:	with fine longitudinal lines.
pruinose:	with a fine waxy coating (as on many *Pinus* species, *Juniperus*, etc.)
epidermis periderm bark	a covering tissue, sooner or later dying but replaced by a secondary membranous tissue, and eventually becoming either:

very tough, deeply furrowed:	*Pinus, Pseudotsuga;*
corky:	*Abies lasiocarpa* var. *arizonica;*
striated, shredding:	*Cryptomeria;*
spongy and very thick:	*Sequoiadendron;*
plate-like:	*Pinus nigra, P. leucodermis;*
checked:	*Pinus contorta;*
peeling:	*Abies squamata.*
bark color:	usually brown, gray or blackish tones (except: *Pinus bungeana,* silver-white with red-brown and gray-green patches).

1d) Arrangement of the branches

alternate:	the branches arising singly at various levels along the stem.
opposite:	2 branches standing at equal height opposed to one another.
whorled:	multiple branches arising radially from one point on the stem.
plate-like:	when a whorl is very much branched and flat (as some cultivars of *Picea pungens* var. *glauca*).
spiral:	branches arising in a spiral fashion around the stem, normally in several rows.

1e) Characteristics of the branches and twigs

Long and short shoots:	(i.e. on *Larix* and *Cedrus*) Normal annual growth results in long shoots, while short shoots are the short side sprouts in the leaf axils of the long shoots which bear the needle fascicles.
persistent:	are those branches on old conifers (as opposed to *Taxodium, Metasequoia* and *Glyptostrobus,* whose young twigs abscise in the fall).
elastic:	Branches are tough or brittle, rigid or flexible, firm or slack. Elastic branches may be bent into a circle without breaking (even older branches of *Pinus flexilis* are very elastic).
fasciated:	an abnormal flattening or cockscomb-like apex of the branches (i.e. *Cryptomeria* whose such branches die out each year but always resprout).
witches'-broom:	a very dense cluster of sprouts, often nest-like in appearance and often caused by a fungus or insect. Many dwarf conifers originated as such witches'-brooms (*Pinus, Abies, Picea, Chamaecyparis, Thuja,* etc.).
flat spray:	more or less arranged in a horizontal or (on *Thuja orientalis*) vertical plane (also many *Chamaecyparis* forms).
branched to one side:	characteristic of *Chamaecyparis* and *Thuja.*
two ranked:	arranged in two opposing rows along an axis (*Taxodium, Taxus, Metasequoia,* many *Abies,* etc.).
finely branched:	characteristic of *Callitris.*
segmented:	apparently separated by distinct nodes.
filamentous:	twigs or branchlets very thin and often pendulous.

Fig. 226. Properties of the branches and buds: Smooth and furrowed branches of *Abies squamata* (far left) and *A. homolepis* (next right); needle-free branch tip with terminal buds of *Picea* and *Abies* (from left, *Picea mariana, P. wilsonii; Abies procera, A. bracteata*)

shell-like:	as, for example, *Chamaecyparis obtusa* 'Nana Gracilis'.
contorted, monstrosus:	diverging greatly from normal growth habit, often grotesquely deformed.
crispate:	irregularly divided and twisted.
furrowed:	young branches of many *Abies* species have grooves, they are also often pubescent in the grooves. Fig. 226.
pruinose:	with a thin waxy coating (*Pinus jeffreyi, Glyptostrobus*).

1f) **Buds** (especially important in the identification of *Abies, Picea* and *Pinus*)

bud form:	round, ovate, conical, acute, cylindrical, spindle form.
size:	from very small (on *Tsuga*) to very large (on *Pinus*).
terminal buds:	present and conspicuous on many conifers; often wreathed by needles.
axillary buds:	usually several beside or somewhat beneath the terminal bud.
bud scales:	very important characteristic for identification; either loosely covering or tightly appressed, resinous or not so, quite straight or reflexed or revolute at the apex; color also variable.
limb of the scales:	entire or fringed, ciliate or interwoven.

2. **LEAVES** (Needles)
2a) **Needle arrangement** (*Phyllotaxis*, Fig. 227)

opposite:	*Calocedrus, Metasequoia, Cupressaceae*
decussate:	*Podocarpus wallichianus*
whorled:	*Juniperus*

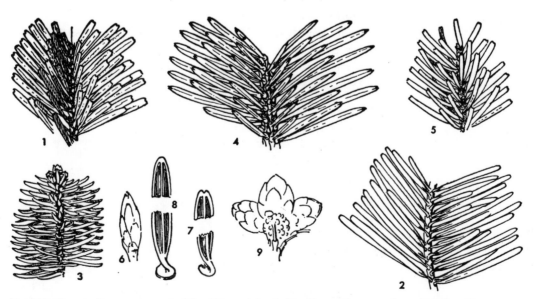

Fig. 227. The needle arrangement of the *Abies* species. 1. Needles on the upper branch surface, the narrow furrow between the needles distinct; 2. Needles flat outspread; 3. Needles radiating in all directions; 4. Branches spruce-like furrowed; 5. Needles not parted; 6. Buds of *A. bracteata* (from Beisner); 7. Emarginate needle; 8. Needle with rounded apex; 9. Terminal bud of *A. nordmanniana*

Fig. 228. Branch section of *Chamaecyparis nootkatensis* (left) and *Thuja occidentalis;*
F = Flat leaves, K = Keeled leaves

alternate:	*Pinaceae*
two ranked:	*Taxus, Pseudotsuga, Abies grandis*
spiraled:	*Araucaria, Sequoia, Cryptomeria*
densely packed or more widely spaced:	*Abies, Picea*
bottle brush form or parted or V-furrowed:	*Abies*
radially arranged:	*Picea*
fascicled 1, 2, 3, 4 or 5 together:	*Pinus*
clustered brush-like:	on the short shoots of *Larix, Cedrus, Pseudolarix*
scattered:	long shoots of *Larix, Cedrus, Taxodium, Metasequoia.*
clustered:	short shoots of *Larix, Cedrus, Cathaya*
imbricate:	as with many *Juniperus, Araucaria,* etc.
lateral and facial leaves:	each 2 ranked on the *Cupressaceae;* see Fig. 228.

2b) Properties of the leaves

thin and soft:	*Metasequoia, Larix, Taxodium, Pseudolarix*
tough:	*Araucaria, Abies, Agathis*
leathery:	*Agathis, Phyllocladus, Taxus*
stiff:	*Abies, Juniperus*
rigid:	*Juniperus*

2c) Life of the leaves

deciduous:	*Larix, Taxodium* (except *Taxodium mucronatum*), *Metasequoia, Glyptostrobus, Ginkgo*
evergreen:	all the other genera

The persistence of the leaves is quite variable, from 4–5 years on *Abies* and *Picea* to 10 or 15 years on *Auracaria.*

2d) Form of the leaves (needles)

linear:	on *Taxus, Abies, Picea, Larix*
lanceolate:	on *Cryptomeria, Sequoia, Abies*
oblong:	on *Agathis, Podocarpus*
fan-shaped:	on *Ginkgo*
scale-like:	on the *Cupressaceae*
keeled:	on the *Cupressaceae*
needle-like:	on the *Pinaceae*
dagger-form:	on the *Abies*
awl-shaped, subulate:	on *Abies, Picea, Juniperus,* etc.

2e) Special forms

doubled:	two needles fused together on one side of the branch (*Sciadopitys*).
phylloclades:	leaf-like; often diamond-rectangular, flat sprouts, arranged in the axils of tiny scale leaves (as on *Phyllocladus*).

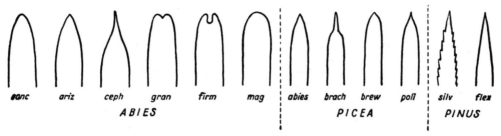

Fig. 229. A few of the commonly found needle tips on *Abies*, *Picea* and *Pinus*.
The abbreviations refer to: *Abies concolor, arizonica, cephalonica, grandis, firma, magnifica;*
Picea abies, brachytyla, breweriana, polita; Pinus sylvestris, flexilis.

spathaceous:	arrangement of the leaves on the *Ephedra* species.
	Also notable is the dimorphism of many conifer leaves; such as
scale and needle leaves:	on *Juniperus*
double-needle and triangular scale needles:	on *Sciadopitys*
	This dimorphism can either be permanent, as with the mentioned genera, or occurring only in certain developmental stages, i.e. juvenile forms with needle leaves, and mature forms with scale leaves such as on *Chamaecyparis*, *Thuja*, *Widdringtonia*. Between the juvenile and mature forms there exists a transition stage in which both leaf forms are present, for example, *Chamaecyparis pisifera* 'Intermedia', *Dacrydium.*
primary needles:	needles of the juvenile form; quite different in size and form from the mature needles. Especially conspicuous on *Pinus canariensis*, all *Squarrosa* forms.
juvenile:	juvenile form.
intermediate:	transition form.
mature:	mature form.

2f) Leaf apex

acute:	generally the opposite of obtuse.
obtuse:	general term for blunt.
acuminate:	apical portion generally tapering to the tip.
mucronate:	with a distinct, more or less protruding apical spur.
rounded:	with a hemispherical apex.
truncate:	squared off.
emarginate:	see Fig. 229, *Abies grandis.*
incised:	see Fig. 229, *Abies firma.*
two tipped, bifid:	with two distinct tips.

2g) Leaf margin

smooth, entire:	without incisions or appendages.
sharp:	like a knife edge.
more or less finely dentate:	*Tsuga*
microscopically finely serrate:	*Pinus*
margins longitudinally involute:	*Abies recurvata,* and others.

2h) Leaf base

distinct:	*Abies, Picea, Pseudotsuga*
adnate:	*Araucaria*
broadly decurrent:	*Sequoia, Cryptomeria*
cuneate or round:	*Abies, Cephalotaxus, Keteleeria, Taxus*

distinctly petioled:	*Tsuga, Pseudotsuga, Taxus, Cephalotaxus*
base widened shield-like:	*Abies*
with a sheath:	*Pinus,* of varying length, persistent or abscising.

2i) Attachment of the leaves [see also 2h)]
the leaf base is

petioled:	see 2h);
sessile:	blade is attached to the branch without a petiole;
distinct:	as in *Pinus, Picea, Abies;*
adnate, appressed:	*Cryptomeria, Sequoiadendron;*
outspread:	*Picea, Abies,* etc.
leaf cushion:	Point of attachment of the leaf to the twig. *Abies* needles leave only a flat round scar, the branch surface remains smooth. On *Picea* the needle sits on a raised, petiole-like cushion. When the needle abscises this raised spot remains on the twig. Form and size of these "bumps" is often characteristic for a species.

2j) Color of the leaves

light green, yellow green:	*Larix, Chamaecyparis obtusa* forms, *Podocarpus* species, *Phyllocladus.*
blue-green:	on many *Picea, Abies, Pseudotsuga, Taiwania.*
dark green:	on *Taxus, Cephalotaxus.*
black-green:	on *Abies balsamea* var. *hudsonia, Pinus nigra* ssp. *nigra.*
white variegated:	on many *Chamaecyparis* forms, *Thuja, Cryptomeria, Juniperus.*
yellow variegated or golden-yellow:	(especially on the new growth) as above.
banded:	on *Pinus* species, when viewed from above appearing as rings. Usually called "Oculus-draconis" in the case of Japanese cultivars.
turning purple:	*Juniperus horizontalis,* especially in winter.
brown:	winter color of many cultivars of *Thuja occidentalis, Cryptomeria japonica* 'Elegans' and *Microbiota.*
violet:	winter color of *Cryptomeria japonica* and *C. japonica* 'Elegans'.
orange to bronze:	winter color of many other yellow needled forms.
	The new growth on many *Abies* and *Picea* forms is more white or yellow but turns green over a period of time (*Albospica* forms).

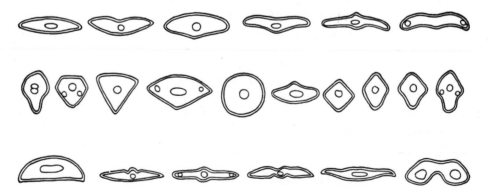

Fig. 230. Schematic leaf blade cross sections (from left to right).
Upper row: *Abies concolor, A. nordmanniana, A. pinsapo, A. arizonica, Taxus baccata, Abies amabilis;* Center row: *Cryptomeria japonia, Cedrus libani, Pinus cembra, Pinus ponderosa, Pinus monophylla, Picea omorika, P. asperata, P. polita, P. abies, P. smithiana;* Lower row: *Pinus sylvestris, Cephalotaxus fortunei, Larix gmelinii* var. *japonica, Tsuga canadensis, Cunninghamia lanceolata, Sciadopitys verticillata.*

2k) Epidermis of the leaves

glossy or dull, with or without openings (stomata); these appear on many conifers as white, bluish or green (yellowish on *Taxus*) stomatal bands on the leaf underside, on both sides of the midrib, visible with a hand lens as lines or rows of fine dots. On many *Abies* species they appear to be short lines on the upper surface at the leaf apex, rarely running to the base. Number of the lines rather consistent for each species.

2l) Blade cross section

flat or even:	*Tsuga, Pseudotsuga,* many *Abies, Taxus, Larix* and others.
furrowed:	the furrows are present on the upper side of the needle, many genera, the others are smooth.
keeled:	with an elevated midrib, either, above or beneath or on both sides, as in *Picea.*
triangular:	on 3 and 5 needle *Pinus* species.
rectangular:	many *Picea.*
semicircular:	on the 2 needle *Pinus* species.
circular:	only *Pinus monophylla.*
parenchyma:	green tissue.
vascular bundles:	conductive tissue which carries water and secreted substances.
xylem:	woody portion of the vascular bundles, contained within the woody part of the stem.
phloem:	vascular tissue (sieve tubes) under the bark of the stem.
bicollateral:	two sided (vascular bundle with two sided sieve tubes)
resin blisters:	present in many conifers in the wood and bark.
resin ducts:	resin develops in special glands and is secreted through resin ducts whose number is quite variable (in *Pinus* from 2 to 12); located either in the epidermis, center of the parenchyma or occasionally in the vascular bundle walls (see Fig. 138 under *Pinus*).

2m) Leaf scars

Like the broadleaves, the conifers have a characteristic small scar which is left on the branch after leaf fall. It is:

circular:	on *Abies.*
rectangular:	on *Picea.*
on a leaf cushion (see 2i):	on *Picea, Tsuga.*
oval:	on *Pseudotsuga.*

3. FLOWERS

unisexual:	either male or female.
plants are monoecious:	when flowers of both sexes appear on the same plant (most conifers).
plants are dioecious:	when male and female flowers are found on separate plants (as with all the *Taxaceae, Ginkgo,* most species of *Ephedra* and *Podocarpus*).
flowers solitary:	only on the *Taxales.*
flowers in inflorescences:	characteristic of the other conifers.
staminate flowers (male):	in small strobili, usually solitarily arranged or in loose formations.
pistillate flowers (female):	usually in more or less abundantly flowered strobili, composed of spiraled, opposite or whorled bract scales (= subtending leaves) along an axis which contains the seed scales. These normally have several ovules, always 2 in the *Pinaceae, Araucaria* 1, *Sequoia* with 2–5, 7–9 on *Sciadopitys,* many on *Cupressus,* etc.
seed scales:	the much reduced female conifer flower, is fused to the so-called seed scale which is in turn adnate to the bract scale.

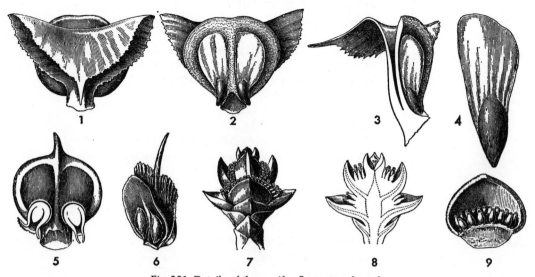

Fig. 231. Details of the conifer flowers and seed
1 bract scale (foreground) and seed scale (background) of *Abies alba*, from outside; 2 the same as 1, from the inside, with both seeds; 3 like 1, in cross section; 4 winged seed of *Abies alba*; 5 ovules of *Pinus sylvestris*; 6 ovules of *Larix decidua*, with bract scale in the background; 7–9 female inflorescence of *Cupressus sempervirens*, 8 in longitudinal section, 9 ovules (from Kerner, altered)

bract scale (= a modified bract):	part of the pistillate conifer flower, usually adnate to the seed scale; occasionally longer than the seed scale (on *Abies, Pseudotsuga* and others).
ligulate scales:	narrow or wide form of the bract scale on *Araucaria*.
dorsiventral:	two sided (with dorsal and ventral sides).
pollination:	completed by the wind, occasionally by insects, i.e. on *Welwitschia* and *Ephedra*. Pollen grains of *Abies, Picea, Pinus* and others are provided with wings to help keep them airborne during pollination.
fertilization:	follows pollination after varying lengths of time (up to 1 year on *Pinus* and *Juniperus*, other conifers only 1–2 months). For further information as to the very complicated fertilization process, please refer to a botany text; particularly for the fertilization by spermatozoids of *Ginkgo biloba*.
cilia:	appendages on spermatozoids of *Ginkgo*.

4. CONES

cones:	originating from the female inflorescence. Arranged either erect along the branch (*Abies, Cedrus*) or later pendulous (*Picea, Pinus*, etc.) Seed scales are arranged spirally around an axis and enlarged after fertilization to form cones. The bract scales (= modified bracts) are usually small and nearly hidden behind the seed scales (*Pinus, Tsuga*, etc.), on other genera these are exserted (*Abies, Pseudotsuga*), on *Abies bracteata* even drawn out awn-like.
"berry" cone:	(on *Juniperus*) composed of a 3 parted whorl of scales, of which the uppermost becomes fleshy after pollination and gives rise to a fleshy, globose "mock berry".
fruit cone:	with a woody or berry-like fleshy hull (on *Ephedra*).
cone scales:	are characteristic in form and size for each species, woody to leathery.
scale shields, apophysis:	found on the outer end of the cone scales of *Pinus*, usually with a prominent, often thorny outgrowth in the middle (the umbo). On many *Pinus* species the tip of the cone scale is curved hook-like.
cone ripening:	upon ripening the cone scales split open allowing the winged seeds to fall out (*Picea, Larix, Pseudotsuga*), or they completely disintegrate leaving only the rachis on the branch (*Abies, Cedrus, Pseudolarix*). The empty cones either abscise quickly (*Picea*) or persist for many years on the branch (many *Pinus* species, *Cupressus, Widdringtonia, Callitris*).

5. SEEDS

usually have a hard or leathery shell, are oval to oblong, often also compressed, frequently winged. Seeds of *Picea, Abies* and *Pinus* (not all winged) have 1 large wing; *Calocedrus* has 1 large and 1 small wing; *Chamaecyparis* and *Thuja* have an encircling wing. Many species are not winged (*Juniperus, Pinus cembra*).

"fruits": present on the Taxaceae, Podocarpaceae, Cephalotaxaceae and *Ginkgo.* On *Taxus, Torreya* and *Austrotaxus* the seed is surrounded by a fleshy seed coat (aril), the Podocarpaceae seeds are often fully enclosed when ripe by a one sided, fleshy seed hull (perisperm); globose cones with fleshy scales on *Saxegothaea.*

6. SEEDLINGS, COTYLEDONS

cotyledons: variable in number for each genus and species; usually 2 for the Cupressaceae and Taxaceae, usually 3–4 on the Pinaceae, but up to 15–18 on *Pinus sabiniana.*

location: normally above ground, but also underground on *Araucaria.*

size: on many species larger than the true leaves which follow (*Pinus, Abies, Larix*); quite variable on many *Pinus* (*Pinus armandii, P. canariensis, P. pinea*), to 5 cm long and very thick, only about 1 cm long and thin on *P. contorta.*

form: usually linear and flat, three sided on many *Pinus* species, usually entire, but distinctly toothed on *Pinus strobus;* apexes usually acute, but obtuse or incised on *Abies.*

life span: abscising in the first year on most species, on *Taxus* in the 3rd year, the 4th year on *Abies.*

hypocotyl: seedling stem; the part between the roots and the cotyledons.

7. OTHER TECHNICAL TERMS

cultivar: international term (abbreviated cv. or denoted by single quotes) for a cultivated plant notable for a particular quality and held constant by vegetative, or occasionally sexual propagation.

clone: a collection of individuals, originating from a single plant and maintained through vegetative propagation (cuttings, division, grafting, etc.).

chromosome: component of the cell nucleus bearing genetic material.

mutation: hereditary alteration; caused by a change in germ or somatic cells (bud mutation).

monotypic: only one species within the genus.

endemic: being limited to a particular region, or native to a given area.

Key to the Coniferous Genera

(with the kind consent of Prof. F. H. Meyer, 1983)

1. Leaves all needle-like 2
— Leaves scale-like or at least
partly scale-like 24
2. All needles abscising in autumn,
more or less thin and soft 3
— Needles evergreen, more or less hard 6
3. Needles partly clustered on knobby short shoots,
partly solitary on long shoots 4
— Needles not clustered; part of the shoot
abscising in fall 5
4. Needles about 1.5 mm wide; bud scales long
acuminate; cones disintegrate when ripe . . . . **Pseudolarix**
— Needles 0.5–1 mm wide; scales rounded on the bud
apex; cones do not disintegrate when ripe,
persisting for some time on the twig . . . . **Larix**
5. Needles and buds opposite . . . . **Metasequoia**
— Needles and buds alternate . . . . **Taxodium**
6. Needles in clusters (2–8 or 10–40 needles
per cluster) or needles solitary and clustered 7
— Needles always solitary 9
7. 2–8 . . e . . er cluster . . . . **Pinus**
— 10–40 Needles per cluster 8
8. Needles 5–50 mm long, with needles
solitary and clustered . . . . **Cedrus**
— Needles 8–15 cm long, in umbrella-like
whorls at the branch tips . . . . **Sciadopitys**
9. Needles opposite or in whorls of 3 10
— Needles spirally arranged, some parted,
appearing to be in 2 rows 12
10. Needles with distinct white stripes
(stomatal bands) on the upper side (that nearest
the shoot) . . . . **Juniperus**
— Needles without distinct white stripes above 11
11. Needles with whitish stripes beneath. Juvenile
form of . . . . **Chamaecyparis**
— Needles green on both sides. Juvenile form of . . . . **Thuja**
12. Needles ovate-triangular, 2.5–5 cm long, 1–2 cm wide
at the base, glossy dark green on both sides,
stiff and prickly, arranged in a tight spiral
around the stem and covering the latter . . . . **Araucaria**
— Needles otherwise 13
13. Bark of the annual growth yellowish,
brownish or reddish; needles distinctly
separated from the shoot 14
— Bark of the annual growth greenish; needles
less distinctly separated from the shoot 17
14. Needles attached directly to the branch
epidermis with a plate-like flared base,
shoot therefore smooth after leaf abscission . . . . **Abies**
— Needles sessile on a branch "hump" (leaf cushion),
shoot therefore distinctly rough after
leaf abscission 15

15. Needles not tapered stalk-like at the base, with nearly the total width sessile on the branch "hump" (leaf cushion) .... **Picea**
— Needles distinctly tapered to a small petiole at the base 16
16. Petiole appressed to the shoot, needles 1–2.5 cm long; buds small, rounded .... **Tsuga**
— Petiole at an oblique angle from the shoot, needles 2–3.5 cm long; buds spindle form, acuminate, to 10 mm long, glossy red-brown .... **Pseudotsuga**
17. Needles stalked 18
— Needles not stalked, not visibly separated from the shoot 21
18. Needle undersides with slightly conspicuous stomatal lines, needles, therefore, only slightly lighter green beneath than above 19
— Needle undersides with conspicuously blue to gray-white stomatal lines 20
19. Needle upper surface with a raised midrib .... **Taxus**
— Needle upper side with indented midrib .... **Podocarpus (nivalis)**
20. Stomatal bands broader than the green marginal stripes and the midstripes .... **Cephalotaxus**
— Stomatal bands narrower than the green stripes .... **Torreya**
21. Points of needle attachment spiraled, but the needles appearing 2 ranked (distichous) in arrangement on the side shoots 22
— Needles not appearing 2 ranked 23
22. Needles 3–7cm long, gradually tapered to a very prickly, sharp apex .... **Cunninghamia**
— Needles 6–20 mm long .... **Sequoia**
23. Needles spirally arranged around the shoot in 5 longitudinal rows, 6–20 mm long, usually sickle-shaped, apices incurved, therefore not prickly, cones 1–3 cm long .... **Cryptomeria**
— Needles spirally arranged around the shoot in 3 longitudinal rows, 3–8 mm long, not curved, sharply acuminate, prickly, cones 5–8 cm long .... **Sequoiadendron**
24. Twigs rounded or 4 sided, scale leaves even on all sides 25
— Twigs flattened, facial scale leaves therefore totally different in form (flat) than the lateral scale leaves (keeled) 26
25. Woody globose cones with 6–12 peltate cone scales; leaves all scale-like .... **Cupressus**
— Fleshy globose fruit (berry-like), developed from 3 or 6 connate fleshy scales; leaves either all scale-like or partly scale-like and partly needle-like .... **Juniperus**
26. Younger shoots 4–8 mm wide, glossy green above, underside with conspicuous white stomatal bands .... **Thujopsis**
— Younger shoots narrower than 4 mm 27

27. Tips of the lateral and facial scale-leaves
at an even height, margins of the lateral
scale leaves not touching...**Calocedrus**
— Tips of the facial scale leaves exserted
past the lateral ones, margins of the
lateral scale leaves touching on the
basal portion...28
28. Young shoots only slightly flattened,
nearly 4-sided 29
— Young shoots distinctly flattened...30
29. Scales truncate at the apex, facial
scales usually keeled like the
lateral scales; hybrid...× **Cupressocyparis**
— Facial and lateral scales with long
drawn out tips; broad growing,
procumbent, 20–40 cm, 1 m high at most................................**Microbiota**
30. Terminal shoot usually "whip-like"
nodding; cones globose, the peltate
scales touching only at the margins................................**Chamaecyparis**
— Terminal shoot steeply erect; cones
oblong to ovate, their flat scales
overlapping (imbricate) ....**Thuja**

List of the Genera, Species and Forms
(including Cultivars)

Genus	Page	Species Described	Forms and Cultivars
Abies	27	52	170
Acmopyle	47	3	—
Actinostrobus	48	3	—
Agathis	48	14	—
Amentotaxus	50	4	—
Araucaria	51	15	32
Athrotaxis	56	3	—
Austrocedrus	57	1	—
Austrotaxus	57	1	—
Callitris	58	14	3
Calocedrus	60	3	6
Cathaya	62	1	—
Cedrus	63	4	67
Cephalotaxus	66	8	15
Chamaecyparis	69	7	390
Cryptomeria	93	1	46
Cunninghamia	99	3	2
×Cupressocyparis	101	(4)	6
Cupressus	103	15	50
Dacrydium	111	14	1
Diselma	114	1	—
Ephedra	115	26	11
Fitzroya	119	1	—
Fokienia	120	1	—
Ginkgo	121	1	12
Glyptostrobus	123	1	—
Juniperus	123	58	287
Keteleeria	153	7	1
Larix	157	15	37
Libocedrus	164	5	—
Metasequoia	167	1	5
Microbiota	168	1	—
Microcachrys	168	1	—
Microstrobos	169	2	—
Neocallitropsis	170	1	—
Papuacedrus	171	3	—
Phyllocladus	173	5	—
Picea	175	44	242
Pilgerodendron	206	1	—
Pinus	207	101	234
(Platycladus)	249		
Podocarpus	249	102	14
Pseudolarix	265	1	3
Pseudotaxus	266	1	—
Pseudotsuga	266	5	50
Saxegothaea	273	1	—
Sciadopitys	273	1	5
Sequoia	274	1	7
Sequoiadendron	276	1	6
Taiwania	278	2	—
Taxodium	279	3	2
Taxus	280	8	142
Tetraclinis	294	1	—
Thuja	295	6	138
Thujopsis	311	1	7
Torreya	312	6	9
Tsuga	315	18	75
Widdringtonia	324	3	—
		607	2075

Index to Invalid Plant Names

Index to Common Names

This list is alphabetically arranged according to the name most commonly found in the trade literature. In the case of double names, i.e. Mugo Pine or Balsam Fir, the plant will be found under the generic name, in this case, Pine or Fir. "Red cedar" (not a true cedar) and "Umbrella Pine" (not a true pine) among others, will be found alphabetically under "red" and "umbrella". The numbers found after the genus and species names indicate the page on which the plant is described.

Index to the More Prominent Conifer Collections

EUROPE

Austria

- Frohnleiten
  Alpengarten; only dwarf conifers.

- Vienna-Mariabrunn
  Arboretum of the Federal Forestry Research Institute.

- Vienna-Schönbrunn
  Castle Park; old conifers.

Belgium

- Kalmthout, near Antwerp
  The arboretum of the De Belder brothers, with many old and rare conifers, also cultivars.

- Tervueren, near Brussels
  The arboretum of du Domaine; plants geographically arranged; a very extensive collection; of particular interest to foresters.

Czechoslovakia

- Lednice (Eisgrub)
  Horticultural School; old conifers.

- Mlynany (earlier Malonya)
  Arboretum of the Slovakian Academy of Science; many conifers.

- Pruhonice (near Prague)
  Botanic Garden; an expansive area, many conifers.

- Zehusice
  Federal Conifer Nursery; a large variety.

Many old parks over the entire country with old conifers.

Denmark

- Charlottenlund
  Forest Botanic Garden; very rich collection, with many conifers.

- Gisselfeld
  Castle Park, one of the most beautiful and comprehensive parks in the country, with many conifers.

- Herluftsholm
  Pinetum; very extensive, forestry species.

- Hesede
  "Planteskole", deciduous plants and conifers, also cultivars.

- Hoersholm
  Forest Botanic Garden; largest and most prominent collection in the country, one of the best in Europe.

- Copenhagen
  Botanic Garden; many conifers and cultivars.

- Kvistgard
  Arboretum of the D. T. Poulsen Nursery; many coniferous hybrids, many species.

East Germany

- Berlin-Baumschulenweg
  Arboretum of the Museum of Natural Science at the Humboldt University (previously the Späth Arboretum).

  Eberswalde-Finow
  Forest botanic garden; Institute of Forestry; 26 ha. (58½ acres)

  Tharandt
  Forest Botanic Garden of the Dresden Technical University.

Finland

  Koria
  Mustila Arboretum; very strong on conifers.

France

Indeed there are many old parks with notable old coniferous plants, but collections of forestry or horticultural significance are only found in the following locations:

- Amance (near Nancy)
  Arboretum of the National School of Forestry, 13 kilometers east of Nancy; with 140 conifer species of forest importance, mostly divided into plots.

- Angers
  La Mauléverie (founded by Gaston Allard); very extensive collection with many very old conifers.

- Harcourt
  Arboretum de l'Académie d'Agriculture de France; 5 ha. (11¼ acres), many old conifers.

- Lyon
  Botanic Garden of the Ville de Lyon au Parc de la Tête d'Or; a good conifer collection.

  Montoire (Loir-et-Cher)
  Arboretum de la Fosse; private; admission only for professionals, by appointment.

- Nogent-sur-Vernission
  Arboretum de Domaine; the French National Arboretum, with a very extensive collection of conifers and other hardy landscape plants.

  Versailles
  Arboretum de Chèvreloup, between Les Trianons and Rocquencourt, part of the Domaine National de Versailles, 205 ha. (461¼ acres); of which 25 ha. (56¼ acre) is designated

the "zone horticole" (cultivars).

Villeneuve-sur-Allier
Arboretum de Balaine; private; one of the largest and most significant arboreta in the world.

Great Britain

Of the many gardens containing large and interesting conifer collections, only the most important will be mentioned here; many photos in this book were taken in these gardens.

- Ardingly (S. England)
  Wakehurst Place, a branch of the Royal Botanic Gardens, Kew (Kew Gardens); many beautiful conifers, very old *Taxus*.

- Bedgebury (S. England)
  National Pinetum; extraordinarily extensive, forest plants as well as cultivars. Plate 160.

- Benmore (Scotland)
  Belongs to the Royal Botanic Garden, Edinburgh; many large, old conifers.

- Caerhays (N. Ireland)
  Very spacious; large, ancient conifers.

- Castlewellan (N. Ireland)
  One of the most beautiful conifer collections in the country, near Belfast.

- Dawyck (Scotland)
  Very old conifers, the oldest *Pseudotsuga* in Europe and many others.

- Devizes (W. England)
  "Pygmy Pinetum", collection of Dwarf conifers, the best in the country; founded by H. J. Welch. Plate 158.

- Edinburgh (Scotland)
  Royal Botanic Garden; one of the most beautiful botanic gardens in all of Europe, with many conifers and dwarf conifers. Plate 156.

- Nymans (S. England)
  Georgeous, old park, outstanding dendrological garden.

- Richmond (near London)
  Royal Botanic Gardens, Kew (Kew Gardens), the largest and most prominent botanic garden of Europe; many conifers, also tropical and subtropical species in the conservatory.

- Wisley (southwest of London)
  Royal Horticultural Society Gardens with its pinetum and rock garden; primarily cultivated species and forms.

Hungary

- Badacsonyörs
  Arboretum of Dr. Folly; primarily conifers.

- Sopron
  Forest Botanic Garden; extensive.

- Szarvas
  Arboretum; very large, many conifers.

- Szeleste
  Arboretum; about 100 species of conifers.

- Szombathely
  Kamoni Arboretum; very extensive collection.

Ireland

- Birr (west of Dublin)
  Birr Castle; a very abundant collection, many rare species, assembled by the Earl of Rosse.

- Cork
  Fota Estate; University of Cork, 25 ha. (56¼ acres); many old conifers; closed to the public.

- Dublin
  Glasnevin, National Botanic Garden; many conifers, particularly very old dwarf conifers.

- Malahide (north of Dublin)
  Park of Malahide Castle; specializing in New Zealand and Australian conifers (an extensive arboretum).

Italy

- Madre Island, Bella Island (Lake Maggiore)
  Many old, attractive conifers.

- Pallanza (Lake Maggiore)
  Villa Taranto Botanic Gardens; an extensive collection including conifers.

Netherlands

- Boskoop
  Rijkstuinbouwschool; a good collection of horticulturally important conifers.

- Doorn
  Arboretum von Gimborn, part of the University of Utrecht; very extensive.

- Hilversum
  Blijdenstein Pinetum; very extensive. Plate 159.

- Oldenzaal (near Enschede)
  Port Bulten Pinetum; extensive.

- Putten (Gelderland)
  Schovenhorst Pinetum; conifers of forest significance arranged in plots.

- Reeuwijk (near Boskoop)
  Konijn Nursery; the largest cultivar collection, primarily dwarf conifers.

- Rotterdam
  Trompenburg Arboretum; many conifers.

- Wageningen
  Arboretum of the Agriculture College; pinetum also grows cultivars.

Poland

Kornik near Poznon
Arboretum; most extensive collection in the country, grows cultivars.

Warsaw
University Botanic Garden.

Portugal

- Coimbra
University Botanic Garden; subtropical conifers.

- Lisbon
University Botanic Garden; extensive collection.

- Porto
Botanic Garden.

Romania

- Cluj (Klausenburg)
Botanic Garden; very extensive.

Dofte ana (Bakau region)
Dendrological Garden.

Tincabesti (near Bucharest)
Dendrological Garden.

Soviet Union

- Batumi
Botanic Garden; abundant collection.

- Kiev (Ukraine)
Central Botanic Garden; the largest plant collection in the country.

- Leningrad
Botanic Garden (Komarov); many old conifers.

- Moscow
Central Botanic Garden; many conifers.

- Nikita, Jalta (Crimea)
Botanic Garden; many conifers, also subtropical plants.

- Sochi (Black Sea Coast)
Dendrarium; the largest conifer collection in the country. Plate 158.

- Suchumi (Black Sea Coast)
Botanic Garden; only small, but rich in species, also conifers.

- Tbilisi (Caucasus)
Botanic Garden; many old conifers.

Spain

- Blanes (Costa Brava)
Marimurtra Garden; few conifers.

- Barcelona
Botanic Garden; Montjuich.

- Costa del Sol
Conifers in private gardens.

- Madrid
Botanic Garden; few conifers.

- Valencia
Botanic Garden; extensive.

Sweden

- Bastad (north of Hälsingborg)
Norvikken Garden; many old conifers, very large specimens.

- Bjuv (near Malmö)
Flinck Arboretum; the largest private collection in the country; many conifers.

- Göteborg
Botanic Garden; abundant conifer collection, especially Asiatic conifers.

Hamsö Island, Härnösand (Norrland)
Drafle Arboretum.

- Stockholm
Bergianska Trädgarden; also conifers.

Switzerland

- Brissago (Island)
Botanic Garden of Canton Tessin.

- Geneva
Botanic Garden and many private gardens with beautiful conifers.

- Grüningen (near Zurich)
Botanic garden and arboretum (belongs to the Zurich Botanic Garden); 5 ha. (11¼ acres).

- Lucerne
Private gardens; especially Villa Fiora in St. Niklausen.

- Lugano
Public and private gardens.

- St. Gallen
Botanic Garden; very extensive.

- Zurich
Botanic Garden; very abundant collection.

West Germany

There are no pure pineta; but particularly good conifer collections may be found in the following botanic gardens: Dortmund, Elmshorn, Grafath (near Munich), Hamburg, Hanover-Münden, Cologne, Preetz and Schmalenbeck.

- Badenweiler
City park with many old conifers.

- Berlin-Dahlem
Botanic garden; many conifers, also subtropical species under glass.

- Bonn
Botanic garden; with many subtropical species.

- Darmstadt
  Botanic Garden.

- Dortmund
  Botanic Garden (Romberg Park); very extensive collection, also many dwarf conifers and cultivars. Plate 156.

- Dyck (Castle), near Neuss
  Various old conifers.

- Elmshorn
  Thiensen Arboretum, Ellerhoop.

- Essen
  Botanic Garden; cultivars.

  Göttingen
  Forestry Botanic Garden and arboretum at the University (under development).

  Grafrath, near Munich
  Arboretum of the Munich Forestry Research Institute (contains only those species of importance in forestry).

- Hamburg
  Institute for General Botany and Botanic Garden; an extensive collection, with many subtropical species under glass. Plate 44.

  Arboretum of the Federal Research Institute for Forestry, Hamburg 80 (Lohbrügge); many conifer species!

- Hanover-Herrenhausen
  Alpine garden; many conifers.

- Hanover-Münden
  Forest Botanic Garden; many conifers, also rare species.

- Heltorf (near Dusseldorf)
  The garden of Count Spee; many very old and large conifers.

- Mainau
  Many large conifers. Well known for its *Metasequoia* allée! Plate 150.

- Munich-Nymphenburg
  Botanic Garden; extensive.

- Oldenburg
  Botanic Garden; many cultivars from the Oldenburg nurseries.—To study the genus *Pinus* one should visit the nursery of J. D. Zu Jeddeloh (near Oldenburg) which has a vast assortment of cultivars.

- Preetz (south of Kiel)
  Lehmkuhlen Arboretum (private); a very abundant, old collection, but somewhat neglected.

- Schmalenbeck, near Ahrensburg
  Tannenhöft Arboretum of the Federal Research Institute for Forestry, Division of Forest Genetics and Cultivation; many conifers, numerous cultivars.

- Schneverdingen
  Dwarf conifer collection of Günter Horstmann; very good collection.

- Stuttgart-Hohenheim
  National Arboretum.

- Weener-Ems
  Stock block of the Herman A. Hesse Nursery; very comprehensive.

- Weinheim
  Forest of exotics of Count von Berkheim; 32 ha. (72 acres), species of forestry importance, also *Sequoiadendron*.

Yugoslavia

- Dubrovnik
  Arboretum Trsteno, not far from Dubrovnik.

  Opeka, p. Vinica pri Varazdinu
  Conifer collection in the public gardens.

  Radomlje pri Ljublijana
  Arboretum Volcji Potok, still young.

  Zagreb
  Sumski vrt (Dendrological Garden of the University Forestry Department).

NON-EUROPEAN GARDENS

In these gardens one can see large collections of conifers.

Canada

- Montreal
  Botanical Gardens; very extensive.

- Ottawa
  Dominion Arboretum and Botanic Garden.

Chile

Vinha del Mar
National Botanic Garden, Casilla 683; 400 ha. (900 acres).

Japan

- Hachioji Shi, Tokyo
  Asakawa Experiment Forest and Arboretum; has the largest conifer collection of forestry significance in the country (50 kilometers west of Tokyo).

South Africa

- Kirstenbosch
  National Botanic Gardens of South Africa, Kirstenbosch, Newlands, Cape Province.

- Paarl (near Cape Town)
  Arboretum; the largest arboretum in the country, very extensive, but still under development.

- Pretoria
  Arboretum of the Horticultural Research Station; extensive, many subtropical species.

United States

California
San Francisco, Staybing Arboretum and Golden Gate Park.

- Illinois
  Lisle, Morton Arboretum; very extensive.

Massachusetts
Jamaica Plain, Arnold Arboretum, one of the most significant arboreta in the entire world; a very large collection. Plate 157.

- New York
  New York City, Bronx Park Botanical Garden; very abundant collection.

  Rochester, Highland Park and others.

- Washington, D.C.
  U.S. National Arboretum; many conifers; also a large dwarf conifer collection established by Gotelli (earlier in South Orange, New Jersey). Plate 159.